INTRODUCTION TO
Local Government Finance

FIFTH EDITION 2023

Edited by
Connor H. Crews

The School of Government at the University of North Carolina at Chapel Hill works to improve the lives of North Carolinians by engaging in practical scholarship that helps public officials and citizens understand and improve state and local government. Established in 1931 as the Institute of Government, the School provides educational, advisory, and research services for state and local governments. The School of Government is also home to a nationally ranked Master of Public Administration program, the North Carolina Judicial College, and specialized centers focused on community and economic development, information technology, and environmental finance.

As the largest university-based local government training, advisory, and research organization in the United States, the School of Government offers up to 200 courses, webinars, and specialized conferences for more than 12,000 public officials each year. In addition, faculty members annually publish approximately 50 books, manuals, reports, articles, bulletins, and other print and online content related to state and local government. The School also produces the *Daily Bulletin Online* each day the General Assembly is in session, reporting on activities for members of the legislature and others who need to follow the course of legislation.

Operating support for the School of Government's programs and activities comes from many sources, including state appropriations, local government membership dues, private contributions, publication sales, course fees, and service contracts.

Visit sog.unc.edu or call 919.966.5381 for more information on the School's courses, publications, programs, and services.

Aimee N. Wall, Dean
Jeffrey B. Welty, Senior Associate Dean for Faculty Affairs
Anita R. Brown-Graham, Associate Dean for Strategic Initiatives
Willow S. Jacobson, Associate Dean for Graduate Studies
Kara A. Millonzi, Associate Dean for Research and Innovation
Lauren G. Partin, Senior Associate Dean For Administration
Sonja Matanovic, Associate Dean for Strategic Communications
Jen Willis, Associate Dean For Advancement and Partnerships

FACULTY

Whitney Afonso
Gregory S. Allison
Lydian Altman
Rebecca Badgett
Maureen Berner
Frayda S. Bluestein
Kirk Boone
Mark F. Botts
Brittany LaDawn Bromell
Peg Carlson
Melanie Y. Crenshaw
Connor Crews
Crista M. Cuccaro
Leisha DeHart-Davis
Shea Riggsbee Denning
Sara DePasquale
Kimalee Cottrell Dickerson
Phil Dixon, Jr.

Jacquelyn Greene
Timothy Heinle
Margaret F. Henderson
Cheryl Daniels Howell
Joseph Hyde
James L. Joyce
Robert P. Joyce
Diane M. Juffras
Kimberly Kluth
Kirsten Leloudis
Adam Lovelady
James M. Markham
Christopher B. McLaughlin
Jill D. Moore
Jonathan Q. Morgan
Ricardo S. Morse
C. Tyler Mulligan
Kimberly L. Nelson

Kristi A. Nickodem
Obed Pasha
William C. Rivenbark
John Rubin
Jessica Smith
Meredith Smith
Michael Smith
Carl W. Stenberg III
John B. Stephens
Charles Szypszak
Shannon H. Tufts
Emily Turner
Amy Wade
Richard B. Whisnant
Teshanee T. Williams
Kristina M. Wilson

© 2023
School of Government
The University of North Carolina at Chapel Hill

Cover photo of Wilmington, NC City Hall building by pabrady63 - stock.adobe.com

Printed in the United States of America
27 26 25 24 23   1 2 3 4 5
ISBN 978-1-64238-079-8

Summary Contents

III. FINANCIAL MANAGEMENT

IV. SELECT EXPENDITURE CATEGORIES

Contents

Chapter 5

Property Tax Policy and Administration

Chapter 6

Revenue Forecasting

Chapter 7
Financing Capital Projects

III. FINANCIAL MANAGEMENT

Chapter 8

Managing and Disbursing Public Funds

Chapter 9

Internal Control in Financial Management

Chapter 10

Accounting, Financial Reporting, and the Annual Audit

Chapter 11

Procurement, Contracting, and Disposal of Property

Chapter 12

Ethics and Conflicts of Interest

IV. SELECT EXPENDITURE CATEGORIES

Chapter 13

Financing Public Enterprises

Chapter 14

Financing Public Schools

Chapter 15

Financing and Public-Private Partnerships for Community Economic Development

Preface

Finance—the acquisition, management, and expenditure of money and other financial resources—is critical to local government operations. How a local government approaches finance significantly affects how its officials and employees perform their duties and how it can serve its constituents. But North Carolina's local governments do not operate with complete independence or at the sole discretion of their officials or employees. Instead, our state's local governments derive all of their powers from the North Carolina General Assembly—and the General Assembly, through a variety of laws, has delineated the manner in which local governments may acquire, manage, and expend public funds.

Now in its fifth edition, this book introduces readers to these key legal rules affecting local government finance and basic principles of revenue forecasting, budgeting, governmental accounting, and financial management. It continues to serve as the textbook for Introduction to Local Government Finance, the foundational course of the UNC School of Government's local government finance curriculum. Intended for local government officials and employees who manage, supervise, or oversee any aspect of local government finance, the course is particularly recommended for new finance officers and other finance personnel, managers, budget officers, purchasers, tax collectors and other tax office personnel as well as local government attorneys. The course provides a survey of the statutory, strategic, and practical limits of local government finance and financial management. Areas of instruction include the basic legal authority and limitations relating to local government revenues, budgeting processes, cash management, purchasing and contracting, expenditure control, conflicts of interest, fund accounting, and financial reporting. It also covers special public records laws relating to local government finance records and information.

Like the School of Government's course, this book is a collaborative effort among School faculty members that specialize in local government finance. Unless otherwise specified in a given chapter, it reflects statutory provisions and case law through July 1, 2023. It is divided into four sections:

- **Section I ("Legal Framework")** discusses the public purpose clause of the North Carolina Constitution and provides a brief overview of the Local Government Budget and Fiscal Control Act (LGBFCA), which comprises the set of state statutes that govern budgeting, accounting, and financial management of public funds by North Carolina's local governments.
- **Section II ("Budgeting and Revenues")** surveys sources of revenue available to local governments and discusses the processes by which local governments budget for operating and capital expenditures.

- **Section III ("Financial Management")** describes several processes and requirements of the LGBFCA that affect local government finance operations, namely, cash management and investments, expenditure control, and governmental accounting and financial reporting. Section III also contains a new chapter—Internal Control in Financial Management—that describes certain statutory internal controls mandated by the LGBFCA and other general principles of internal control. It lastly covers state and selected federal laws and regulations that govern local government procurement and regulate conflicts of interest.
- **Section IV ("Select Expenditure Categories")** highlights the financing authority for selected major functions of North Carolina's local governments—public enterprises, public schools, and community and economic development.

The authors are grateful to Melissa Twomey for her careful review and editing of each chapter of this Fifth Edition; Kevin Justice for his coordination of efforts among editors, authors, and designers; and Kit Sweeney for her thoughtful and careful design. Special thanks is also owed to Kara Millonzi, the editor of the first four editions of this book, for her efforts to create the book and ensure its timely updates over the last decade.

This text has benefited from continued interactions between School of Government faculty and local government officials and employees from across North Carolina since the publication of the Fourth Edition. In the coming years, local government officials, employees, and all readers are encouraged to contact the author of each chapter with questions or suggestions for improvement.

Connor H. Crews
Assistant Professor of Public Law and Government
July 2023

I. LEGAL FRAMEWORK

Chapter 1

The Public Purpose Requirement

by Kara A. Millonzi

Introduction

The North Carolina Constitution is the foundation of our state's government. Among other things, it establishes the state legislature (General Assembly) and authorizes it to create, and define the powers of, local government entities. Specifically, Section 1 of Article VII states as follows:

> The General Assembly shall provide for the organization and government and the fixing of boundaries of counties, cities and towns, and other governmental subdivisions, and, except as otherwise prohibited by this Constitution, may give such powers and duties to counties, cities and towns, and other governmental subdivisions as it may deem advisable.[1]

The constitution also sets certain limitations on the legislature's authority. Some of those limitations provide protections for citizens against government intrusion and coercion. Others guarantee rights to citizens. And some limitations prohibit certain government actions or impose process requirements as a condition of certain government undertakings. Among these limitations are several that relate directly or indirectly to local government finance. They include

- uniformity of property tax rate (art. V, § 2(2));
- prohibition against contracting away taxing authority (art. V, § 2(1));
- authorization for special taxing districts (art. V, § 2(4));
- limitations on property-tax exclusions and exemptions (art. V, § 2(2));
- requirement to distribute clear proceeds of certain fines, penalties, and forfeitures to public schools (art. IX, § 7);
- public-school funding mandate (art. IX, § 2; art. 1, § 15);

This chapter reflects the law as of June 1, 2023.

1. N.C. CONST. art. VII, § 1.

- limitations on authorizing debt financing (art. V, § 4(1));
- requirement for voter approval to pledge full faith and credit as security for debt (art. 5, § 4(2));
- prohibition against loaning or aiding government credit without general law authority and voter approval (art. V, § 4(3));
- authorization for project-development financing (art. V, § 14);
- prohibition against expending public funds except by authority of law (art. V, § 7(2));
- authorization for government entities to contract with private entities to accomplish public purposes (art. V, § 2(7));
- prohibition against exclusive privileges or emoluments (art. I, § 32).

Some of these provisions apply directly to local governments. The rest are limitations on the legislature's grants of authority to local governments. Regardless, local officials always must interpret their statutory grants of authority in a manner that is consistent with constitutional requirements. It is thus important for local government officials to have a general understanding of the relevant constitutional provisions.

Most of the constitutional provisions related to local government finance are discussed in other chapters in this text. This chapter introduces the fundamental constitutional limitation on local government finance—the public purpose clause.

Defining Public Purpose

Section 2(1) of Article V of the North Carolina Constitution provides that the "power of taxation shall be exercised in a just and equitable manner, for public purposes only, and shall never be surrendered, suspended, or contracted away."

Known as the public purpose clause, this provision requires that all public funds, no matter their source, be expended for the benefit of the citizens of a unit generally and not solely for the benefit of particular persons or interests. According to the North Carolina Supreme Court, "[a]lthough the constitutional language speaks to the 'power of taxation,' the limitation has not been confined to government use of tax revenues."[2] The public purpose clause is better understood as a limitation on government expenditures. In other words, a government entity may not make an expenditure of public funds that does not serve a public purpose.

The constitution does not define the phrase "public purpose." We must discern its meaning through (ever-evolving) legislative enactments and judicial interpretations. "The initial responsibility for determining what is and what is not a public purpose rests with the legislature. . . ."[3] North Carolina courts have been deferential to legislative declarations that an authorized undertaking serves a public purpose but have not considered them to be determinative. The state supreme court has set forth two guiding principles to analyze whether a government activity

---

2. Madison Cablevision v. City of Morganton, 325 N.C. 634, 643 (1989); *see also* Dennis v. Raleigh, 253 N.C. 400 (1960) (applying public purpose analysis to nontax revenues); Greensboro v. Smith, 241 N.C. 363 (1955) (same).

3. Mitchell v. N.C. Indus. Dev. Fin. Auth., 273 N.C. 137, 144 (1968).

satisfies the constitutional requirement. First, the activity must "involve[] a reasonable connection with the convenience and necessity" of the particular unit of government. Second, the "activity [must] benefit[] the public generally, as opposed to special interests or persons. . . ."[4]

A close review of the case law reveals that there are actually three parts to the inquiry. For one, the expenditure has to be for an appropriate government activity. For another, the expenditure has to provide a primary benefit to the government's citizens/constituents. Finally, the expenditure also has to benefit the public generally, not just a few private individuals or entities.

Appropriate Government Activity

When we think of appropriate government activities, certain functions usually come to mind— police and fire protection, street construction and maintenance, public health programs, utilities, parks and recreation. North Carolina courts routinely have held that these, and similar traditional government functions, serve a public purpose. But to constitute an appropriate government activity for a particular local government, the local government must have statutory authority to engage in the activity. This authority is granted by the General Assembly through general laws, local acts, and charter provisions. If a local government does not have statutory authority for a particular purpose, that purpose is not an appropriate government activity for that local unit. According to the North Carolina Supreme Court,

> "Public Purpose" as we conceive the term to imply, when used in connection with the expenditure of municipal funds from the public treasury, refers to such public purpose within the frame of governmental and proprietary power given to the particular [government entity], to be exercised for the benefit, welfare and protection of its inhabitants and others coming within the municipal care.[5]

Thus, in analyzing public purpose, a threshold question is whether or not there is statutory authority for the proposed expenditure. As a practical matter, for most undertakings this is the only inquiry that counts. If there is clear statutory authority to engage in an activity and a public official acts within that authority, it is likely that the activity constitutes a public purpose. As noted above, courts are deferential to the legislature's determination that an undertaking satisfies the public purpose clause. Most of the authority granted to counties is found in Chapter 153A of the North Carolina General Statutes (hereinafter G.S.), although there are various additional provisions sprinkled throughout several other chapters. Similarly, G.S. Chapter 160A prescribes most, but not all, authority applicable to municipalities. Public authorities must look to their various enabling statutes to determine the contours of their powers and authorities.

There are some activities, however, that the General Assembly may not grant authority to local governments to undertake. These activities are not appropriate for government action and should instead be reserved for the private sector. Determining this division between public and private is often difficult, though. As the state supreme court repeatedly has explained,

> [a] slide-rule definition to determine public purpose for all time cannot be formulated; the concept expands with the population, economy, scientific knowledge, and changing conditions. As people are brought closer together in congested areas, the

---

4. *Madison Cablevision*, 325 N.C. at 646.
5. Morgan v. Town of Spindale, 254 N.C. 304, 305–06 (1961) (citation omitted).

public welfare requires governmental operation of facilities which were once considered exclusively private enterprises, and necessitates the expenditures of tax funds for purposes which, in an earlier day, were not classified as public.[6]

The courts, thus, have sometimes held that "new" activities that are perceived as outgrowths of more-traditional government functions serve a public purpose. "Whether an activity is within the appropriate scope of governmental involvement and is reasonably related to communal needs may be evaluated by determining how similar the activity is to others which this Court has held to be within the permissible realm of governmental action."[7] In *Martin v. North Carolina Housing Corp.*,[8] the state supreme court held that government funding of low-income residential housing served a public purpose. In so holding, the court tied the government's concern for safe and sanitary housing for its citizens to its traditional role of combating slum conditions. Similarly, in *Madison Cablevision, Inc. v. City of Morganton*,[9] the court held that the municipal provision of cable television services served a public purpose because such services were a natural outgrowth of the types of communications facilities that local governments had been operating for many years, including auditoriums, libraries, fairs, public radio stations, and public television stations. In *Maready v. City of Winston-Salem*,[10] the court acknowledged that the "importance of contemporary circumstances in assessing the public purpose of governmental endeavors highlights the essential fluidity of the concept."[11] In that case, the court upheld a variety of economic-development incentive payments against a public purpose challenge.[12]

In a few cases, the courts have found that an activity is neither a traditional government activity nor an outgrowth of a traditional government activity and, consequently, that the activity does not serve a public purpose. In *Nash v. Tarboro*,[13] the court held that it was not a public purpose for a town to issue general obligation bonds in order to construct and operate a hotel, finding that, at least at the time, owning and operating a hotel was purely a private business with no connection to traditional government activities. (Although the case has not been overturned, it is possible that a court would not rule the same way today, reflecting the fact that what constitutes a public purpose evolves over time.)

And, occasionally, courts have determined that activities that appear to be natural extensions of traditional government activities, nonetheless, do not satisfy the public purpose clause. In *Foster v. North Carolina Medical Care Commission*,[14] the court held that the expenditure of public funds to finance the construction of a hospital facility that was to be privately operated, managed, and controlled did not serve a public purpose even though the "primary purpose" of a "privately owned hospital is the same as that of a publicly owned hospital."[15] In 1971,

---

6. Martin v. N.C. Hous. Corp., 277 N.C. 29, 43 (1970) (internal quotation marks, citations omitted).

7. Maready v. City of Winston-Salem, 342 N.C. 708, 722 (1996).

8. 277 N.C. 29.

9. 325 N.C. 634.

10. 342 N.C. 708.

11. 342 N.C. at 721.

12. For more on the *Maready* case, see Chapter 15, "Financing and Public-Private Partnerships for Community Economic Development."

13. 227 N.C. 283 (1947).

14. 283 N.C. 110 (1973).

15. 283 N.C. at 125.

the legislature had enacted the North Carolina Medical Care Commission Hospital Facilities Finance Act, which established a commission and authorized it to issue revenue bonds to finance the construction of public and private hospital facilities. The Council of State had allotted $15,000 to the commission from the state's contingency fund to implement the revenue bond program. It was this allocation that the court found violated the public purpose clause. The state's authority to expend tax funds to construct and operate a public hospital did not extend to expending funds to subsidize a privately owned hospital, even if both were providing the same type of public benefits. According to the court, "[m]any objects may be public in the general sense that their attainment will confer a public benefit or promote the public convenience but not be public in the sense that the taxing power of the State may be used to accomplish them."[16] Thus, a court must look not only at the ends sought, but also at the means used to accomplish a public purpose.

Note, however, that the constitution was amended after *Foster* to specifically authorize the state legislature to enact laws to allow a government entity to "contract with and appropriate money to any person, association, or corporation for the accomplishment of public purposes only."[17] The legislature subsequently provided broad authority for general-purpose local governments—counties and municipalities[18]—to contract with a private entity to perform any activity in which the local unit has statutory authority to engage.[19] This authority allows a local government to contract with a private entity to act as an agent of the government in performing the specific function. The local government must undertake certain oversight functions to ensure that the private entity carries out the public purpose.[20] This issue is further explored in the last section of this chapter, addressing funding for nonprofits and other private entities.

Benefits the Government's Citizens or Constituents

In addition to being for an appropriate government activity, an expenditure of public funds must benefit the citizens or constituents of the government entity that is engaging in the activity. That is, the primary benefit from an expenditure of public funds must be the citizens or constituents of the jurisdiction making the expenditure. The benefit to the unit's citizens or constituents is a far more important concern than the location of the activity.

Courts have upheld expenditures of public funds on activities or projects located outside the jurisdiction of a unit so long as the primary benefit was for the unit's citizens or constituents. In *Martin County v. Wachovia Bank & Trust Co.*,[21] the state supreme court held that Martin County did not violate the public purpose clause by paying the majority of the costs of building a bridge between it and Bertie County, even though most of the structure was located in Bertie County. In so holding, the court focused on the benefit of the bridge project to Martin County citizens. Furthermore, it is okay if the benefit extends beyond a unit's citizens or constituents.[22]

---

16. 283 N.C. at 126 (citations omitted).

17. N.C. Const. art. 5, § (2)(7); *see* Hughey v. Cloninger, 297 N.C. 86 (1979).

18. As used in this book, the term "municipality" is synonymous with "city," "town," and "village."

19. *See* G.S. 153A-449 (counties); 160A-20.1 (municipalities).

20. *See* Dennis v. Raleigh, 253 N.C. 400 (1960). For more information on contracting with private entities to perform government functions, see Kara Millonzi, "Local Government Appropriations/Grants to Private Entities," *Coates' Canons: NC Local Government Law* blog (June 17, 2010).

21. 178 N.C. 26 (1919).

22. *See* Jamison v. Charlotte, 239 N.C. 682 (1954).

As long as the local benefit accompanies the broader benefit, the activity may serve a public purpose. In *Briggs v. City of Raleigh*,[23] the supreme court rejected a challenge to a legislative grant of authority to the municipality to issue general obligation bonds, upon voter approval, to provide $75,000 of funding to the state fair. The state fair was located just outside the city limits. Nonetheless, it was a public purpose for the municipality to support the state fair to retain it within its vicinity. Although the fair promoted the general welfare of the citizens of the state and not just the citizens of Raleigh, its location provided a unique benefit to them. Note that in both these cases the local units had statutory authority to make the extraterritorial expenditures. As discussed below, statutory authority is necessary to satisfy the public purpose clause.

Private Benefit Ancillary to Public Benefit

There is another element to the benefit inquiry. An expenditure of public funds must "primarily benefit the public and not a private party."[24] That does not mean, however, that private individuals or entities cannot gain from a government undertaking.

In fact, private individuals and entities benefit from most, if not all, government activities. When fire personnel suppress a fire and save a residential structure, it benefits the owners/occupants of that structure. When a municipality runs recreational summer camps, it benefits the participants in those camps. When a county builds a new school building, it benefits the students who are educated there. When a water and sewer authority expands its water line to a new subdivision, it benefits the property owners/occupants in that area. Given this reality, it is not surprising that the state supreme court has held that the "fact that a private individual benefits from a particular [government] transaction is insufficient to make out a claim under [the public purpose clause]."[25] The court has further opined, "[i]t is not necessary, in order that a use may be regarded as public, that it should be for the use and benefit of every citizen in the community. It may be for the inhabitants of a restricted locality, but the use and benefit must be in common, and not for particular persons, interests, or estates."[26]

The public purpose clause requires that the general benefit from the government expenditure outweigh private, individual gain. In other words, "the ultimate net gain or advantage must be the public's as contradistinguished from that of an individual or private entity."[27] If an expenditure "will promote the welfare of a state or a local government and its citizens, it is for a public purpose."[28] In *Bridges v. Charlotte*,[29] the supreme court held that it was a public purpose for Charlotte to contribute to a retirement system for its public employees. Obviously, the individual employees were direct beneficiaries of the contributions. The court, however, based its holding on the fact that the employees were serving a public purpose by working for the government entity. The retirement payments were merely an incentive to attract and retain employees.

Courts often resort to balancing public and private benefits, invalidating an expenditure only if the private benefit is found to be predominant. Unfortunately, as several courts have

---

23. 195 N.C. 223 (1928); *see also Jamison*, 239 N.C. at 682.
24. Maready v. City of Winston Salem, 342 N.C. 708, 724 (1996).
25. Peacock v. Shinn, 139 N.C. App. 487, 494 (2000).
26. *Briggs*, 195 N.C. at 227.
27. Martin v. N.C. Housing Corp., 277 N.C. 29, 43 (1970).
28. *Maready*, 342 N.C. at 724.
29. 221 N.C. 472 (1942).

noted, "[o]ften public and private interests are so co-mingled that it is difficult to determine which predominates."[30]

This issue comes up most often in the context of expenditures for community and economic-development programs, with the outcome of the analysis largely depending on how the benefits are characterized. In *Mitchell v. North Carolina Industrial Development Financing Authority*,[31] for example, the supreme court determined it was not a public purpose to use state funds to acquire sites and construct and equip facilities for private industrial development. Significantly, the court considered the "benefits" to simply constitute a windfall available to only a few private companies at the expense of other companies and of the public generally. It thus found that the expenditure of public funds for this purpose did not serve a public purpose. Contrast that with the court's later decision in *Maready v. City of Winston-Salem*,[32] upholding a lower court ruling that economic-development incentive grants to private businesses did not violate the public purpose clause. In this case, the court took a much broader view of these "benefits," stating that the ultimate goal of providing such incentives to one or more private entities was to improve the community at large—through, among other things, increased tax revenues and job opportunities. The *Maready* court held that a public purpose exists if the "public advantages are not indirect, remote, or incidental; rather they are directly aimed at furthering the general economic welfare of the people of the communities affected."[33] The case appears to reflect the court's recognition of the "trend toward broadening the scope of what constitutes a valid public purpose that permits the expenditure of public revenues" in modern society.[34] Of course, there is a great deal of subjectivity in this analysis, which is why the courts appear to be fairly deferential to the legislature's determination that a particular activity benefits the public.

That does not mean there are no limits to what constitutes a public purpose. As Tyler Mulligan discusses in Chapter 15, "Financing and Public-Private Partnerships for Community Economic Development," it probably is a mistake to assume that all economic-development incentive agreements will pass constitutional muster. Several state court of appeals opinions appear to interpret the *Maready* holding somewhat narrowly.[35] This is still an evolving area of the law, and local units should proceed cautiously.[36]

Does a local government entity have to document the benefit to its citizens before undertaking a particular activity? For most activities the answer is "no." For some expenditures, however, the authorizing legislation requires a unit's governing board to make specific findings as to the need or potential benefit of the undertaking. And in limited circumstances, a board must first consider citizen input or receive citizen approval before proceeding.

The courts also generally have not required a unit to engage in a formal benefit analysis (beyond what is required by the enabling statute). There are a few exceptions. As noted by Tyler

---

30. *Martin*, 277 N.C. at 45.

31. 273 N.C. 137 (1973).

32. 342 N.C. 708.

33. 342 N.C. at 725.

34. 342 N.C. at 722.

35. *See, e.g.*, Haugh v. Cnty. of Durham, 208 N.C. App. 304 (2010); Blinson v. State, 186 N.C. App. 328 (2007); Peacock v. Shinn, 139 N.C. App. 487 (2000).

36. Another grey area involves government expenditures on private distributed-generation energy systems. *See* Kara A. Millonzi, "Addressing Climate Change Locally: North Carolina Local Government Financing Programs for Private Energy Efficiency Projects," *Local Finance Bulletin* No. 41 (Feb. 2010).

Mulligan in the above-referenced chapter, the court seems to require that a unit make findings and abide by procedural formalities, some of which are not statutorily mandated, before it engages in certain economic-development activities. These are aimed at ensuring the necessity of the economic-development incentive, providing for sufficient public input, and confirming adequate public benefit from the expenditure.[37]

The supreme court also has held that before purchasing or constructing an off-street parking facility, a local government must adopt a resolution finding that local conditions of traffic, congestion, and the like necessitate the facility. Furthermore, a public hearing must be held before the resolution is adopted.[38] (In recent years, off-street parking has become a common municipal undertaking. It is not clear that a court would continue to impose these special procedural requirements.)

Applying Framework to Proposed Government Activity

There is substantial case law related to the public purpose clause. The cases cited above, however, are representative of the current framework North Carolina courts use to analyze this issue. Local officials may adapt this framework to provide prospective guidance about whether a proposed activity serves a public purpose. A unit must first determine if there is statutory authority for the undertaking. Statutory authority is necessary but not always sufficient. A local government should also ensure that both the means used and the ends sought constitute a traditional government activity or a natural extension or outgrowth of a traditional government activity. Furthermore, the activity must benefit the citizens of the unit making the expenditure generally. That does not mean it has to benefit all citizens equally. It also does not mean that the proposed expenditure of public funds cannot significantly and directly benefit specific individuals or entities. But the overall purpose of the activity must be to benefit the unit and its citizens, and, ultimately, this broader public benefit should predominate over the benefit to any single individual or entity. Figure 1.1 provides a flowchart process for local government officials to use when analyzing whether or not a proposed expenditure serves a public purpose.

Funding Nonprofits and Other Private Entities

How does this framework apply to funding requests from nonprofits and other private entities? Such requests are common and can range from a simple contribution to a community festival to subsidizing the capital and/or operating budget of the private entity. As stated above, both counties and municipalities have constitutional and statutory authority to contract with private entities. There is an important limitation on this authority, though. The appropriations

---

37. *See Maready*, 342 N.C. 708. For more information on the additional requirements, see C. Tyler Mulligan, "Economic Development Incentives and North Carolina Local Governments: A Framework for Analysis," 91 *North Carolina Law Review* (2021) 2013.

38. *See* G.S. Horton v. Redevelopment Comm'n, 262 N.C. 306 (1964); Henderson v. New Bern, 241 N.C. 52 (1954).

Figure 1.1 Does the Proposed Expenditure Serve a Public Purpose?

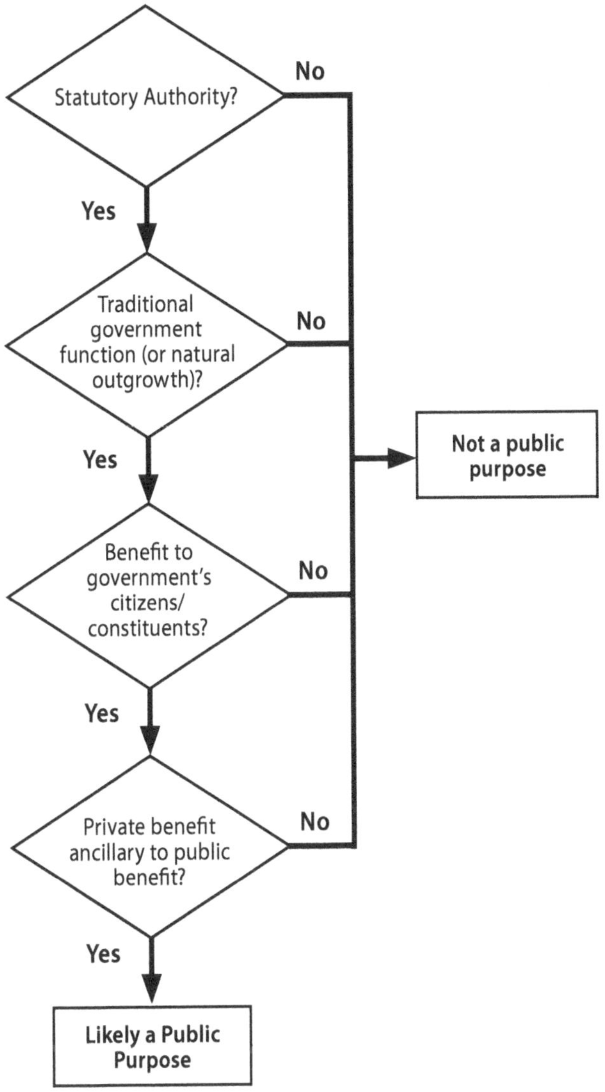

ultimately must be used to "carry out any public purpose that the [local governments are] authorized by law to engage in."[39]

Thus, the statutory authorization incorporates the constitutional public purpose requirement. It also places a further limitation on the appropriation of public funds to private entities—the private entity that receives the public funds is limited to expending those funds only on projects, services, or activities that the local government could have supported directly. In other words, if a municipality or county has statutory authority to finance a particular program, service, or activity, then it may give public moneys to a private entity to fund that program, service, or activity. But a municipality or county may not grant public moneys to any private entity, including nonprofit agencies or other community or civic organizations, if the moneys ultimately will

39. Millonzi, note 20 above, quoting G.S. 160A-20.1 (municipalities) and 153A-449 (counties).

be spent on a program, service, or activity that the government could not fund directly. This authority allows local governments to contract with private entities to operate government programs or provide government services. It also allows local governments to support private entities, at least to the extent that those private entities seek to provide programs, services, or activities that a local unit is authorized to provide directly.

For example, a local unit may appropriate funds to a community group, nonprofit, or even a religious organization to fund a community festival that is open to all citizens of the unit because the local unit has statutory authority to undertake the activity itself.[40] However, with few exceptions,[41] a local unit may not appropriate funds to that same organization to finance capital projects or to fund the organization's general operating expenses, because the unit does not have authority to spend moneys directly on this type of project. Perhaps a more common example arises when a local unit is asked to become a dues-paying member of a civic or community organization, such as a chamber of commerce or rotary club. The local government must be very careful to ensure that its dues are expended only for purposes that the government could have funded directly. The local government should ask the organization to make a request for funds for a specific project, service, or activity and then execute a contract with the organization for this purpose.

When a local government contracts with a private entity, it must ensure that public funds are expended for the statutorily authorized purpose. At a minimum, a local government must require a recipient organization to provide some sort of performance accounting. The North Carolina Supreme Court has provided some guidance to local governments on this issue, sanctioning a particular oversight method in *Dennis v. Raleigh*.[42] That case involved a challenge to an appropriation of funds by the City of Raleigh to a local chamber of commerce to be spent on advertising the city. The chamber of commerce engaged in a variety of activities, some of which were unlikely to be considered public purposes. Thus, the city sought to ensure that the public funds it appropriated to the chamber of commerce were spent appropriately. The city put in place three separate "controls." First, the appropriation to the chamber of commerce was specific—it stated that the moneys were to be used "exclusively for . . . advertising the advantages of the City of Raleigh in an effort to secure the location of new industry."[43] Second, the city council reserved the right to approve each specific piece of advertising. Third, the chamber of commerce had to account for the funds at the end of the fiscal year. On the basis of the control exercised by the city over the expenditure of the public funds, the court upheld the appropriation.

The first and third "controls" placed on the chamber of commerce by the City of Raleigh in *Dennis* likely are particularly instructive. These controls parallel the appropriation and annual

---

40. *See* G.S. 160A-353.

41. The General Assembly has given local governments broader authority to fund the capital and/or operating costs of certain private entities. *See, e.g.,* G.S. 160A-487 (cities and counties may fund certain capital and operating expenses of rescue squads); 153A-233 (a county may provide general financial assistance to a nonprofit fire department serving the county); 160A-488 (cities and counties may contract with any private entity to establish and support museums, art galleries, arts centers, arts facilities, and arts programs); 160A-493 (cities may support private animal shelters).

42. 253 N.C. 400 (1960).

43. 253 N.C. at 405.

audit requirements placed by the Local Government Budget and Fiscal Control Act (LGBFCA)[44] on moneys spent directly by a municipality or county. At a minimum, a local government should provide clear guidelines and directives to a private entity as to how and for what purposes public moneys may be spent, and the unit should require some sort of accounting from the private entity that it fully performed its contract obligations. Additionally, a local unit may require a private entity to provide a financial accounting. The accounting does not have to rise to the level of an official audit, though G.S. 159-40 authorizes local governments to require any nonprofit agency receiving $1,000 or more in any fiscal year (with certain exceptions) to have an audit performed for the fiscal year in which the funds are received and to file a copy of that report with the local government. And state law requires any nonprofit corporation that receives more than $5,000 of public funds within a fiscal year, in the form of grants, loans, or in-kind contributions, to provide certain financial information upon written request from any member of the public.[45]

---

44. The LGBFCA is set out in Article 3 of G.S. Chapter 159. It is presented also in the appendix to this book.

45. G.S. 55A-16-24. The required information includes the following:

(1) The nonprofit's latest financial statements. The financial statements must include a balance sheet as of the end of the fiscal year and a statement of operations for that year. They also must contain "details about the amount of public funds received and how those funds were used." G.S. 55A-16-24(a).

(2) The nonprofit's most recently filed Internal Revenue Service (IRS) Form 990, Form 990-EZ, or a copy of its Form 990-N submittal confirmation. A nonprofit may redact information not required for public disclosure pursuant to 26 U.S.C. § 6104(d)(3). Alternatively, a nonprofit may satisfy this requirement if it posts this information on its website or if another entity posts the information as part of a database of similar documents. The information must be accessible by the general public without charge. Also, if another entity maintains the information, the nonprofit must include a link to the other entity's website on its own website. G.S. 55A-16-24(a).

Chapter 2

The Local Government Budget and Fiscal Control Act

by Kara A. Millonzi

Introduction

The authority to raise money and to expend it for particular purposes varies among the different types of local entities. Almost all local entities are subject to a uniform set of rules governing fiscal management, though. Most of these rules are contained in a series of statutory provisions known as the Local Government Budget and Fiscal Control Act (LGBFCA). The act comprises Article 3 of Chapter 159 of the North Carolina General Statutes (hereinafter G.S.). It prescribes for North Carolina local governments and public authorities "a uniform system of budget adoption and administration and fiscal control," detailing the proper procedures for budgeting, managing, disbursing, and accounting for public funds.[1]

This chapter reflects the law as of June 1, 2023.
   1. G.S. 159-7(c).

The LGBFCA covers five main topic areas related to fiscal management. The following statutory provisions, listed by topic area, are included within the act:

Finance Personnel and Local Government Commission

G.S. 159-9	Budget officer.
G.S. 159-24	Finance officer.
G.S. 159-25	Duties of finance officer and internal control procedures subject to Commission regulation.
G.S. 159-26	Accounting system (including Commission regulations).
G.S. 159-29	Fidelity bonds.
G.S. 159-35	Secretary of Commission to notify units of debt service obligations.
G.S. 159-36	Failure of local government to levy debt service taxes or provide for payment of debt.
G.S. 159-181	Enforcement of chapter.
G.S. 159-182	Offending officers and employees removed from office.

Budgeting Public Funds

G.S. 159-8	Annual balanced budget ordinance.
G.S. 159-10	Budget requests.
G.S. 159-11	Preparation and submission of budget and budget message.
G.S. 159-12	Filing and publication of the budget; budget hearings.
G.S. 159-13	The budget ordinance; form, adoption, limitations, tax levy, filing.
G.S. 159-13.1	Financial plan for intragovernmental service funds.
G.S. 159-13.2	Project ordinances.
G.S. 159-14	Trust and agency funds; budgets of special districts.
G.S. 159-15	Amendments to the budget ordinance.
G.S. 159-16	Interim budget.
G.S. 159-17	Ordinance procedures not applicable to budget or project ordinance adoption.
G.S. 159-17.1	Vending facilities.
G.S. 159-35	Secretary of Local Government Commission to notify units of debt service obligations.
G.S. 159-36	Failure of local government to levy debt service taxes or provide for payment of debt.

Managing Public Funds

G.S. 159-27	Distribution of tax collections among funds according to levy.
G.S. 159-27.1	Use of revenue bond project reimbursements; restrictions.
G.S. 159-30	Investment of idle funds.
G.S. 159-31	Selection of depository; deposits to be secured.
G.S. 159-32	Daily deposits.

Dispersing Public Funds

G.S. 159-25	Dual signatures on checks.
G.S. 159-28	Budgetary accounting for appropriations.
G.S. 159-28.1	Facsimile signatures.
G.S. 159-32.1	Electronic payment.

Accounting for Public Funds

G.S. 159-18	Capital reserve funds.
G.S. 159-19	Amendments.

G.S. 159-20	Funding capital reserve funds.
G.S. 159-21	Investment.
G.S. 159-22	Withdrawals.
G.S. 159-26	Accounting system.
G.S. 159-33	Semiannual reports on status of deposits and investments.
G.S. 159-33.1	Semiannual reports of financial information.
G.S. 159-33.2	Interim event reporting.
G.S. 159-34	Annual independent audit; rules and regulations.
G.S. 159-37	Reports on status of sinking funds.
G.S. 159-40	Special regulations pertaining to nonprofit corporations receiving public funds.

This chapter focuses on the first category; it discusses which local entities are subject to the LGBFCA and introduces the various actors involved in ensuring compliance with the act's provisions. Other chapters in this textbook flesh out the requirements of the LGBFCA in the remaining topic areas: budgeting public funds,[2] managing public funds,[3] disbursing public funds,[4] and accounting for public funds.[5]

Entities Subject to the LGBFCA

Before delving into the requirements of the Local Government Budget and Fiscal Control Act (LGBFCA), it is important first to determine if a particular local entity is covered by the act. There are two types of entities that are subject to the act—"units of local government" and "public authorities."[6] Most local entities can be characterized as one of these two types. Almost all of the act's requirements and limitations apply equally to both, but occasionally units of local government are treated differently from public authorities. It is therefore important to know if a local entity is a unit of local government or a public authority to determine if the entity is subject to the LGBFCA and, if so, to determine which of the act's provisions apply.

Unit of Local Government

A unit of local government is defined as "a municipal corporation that is not subject to the State Budget Act and that has the power to levy taxes . . . and all boards, agencies, commissions, authorities, and institutions thereof that are not municipal corporations."[7] There are three important components to this definition. First, the entity must be a municipal corporation. A municipal corporation is a public agency with corporate status. If the enabling legislation for a

---

2. *See* Chapter 3, "Budgeting for Operating and Capital Expenditures," and Chapter 7, "Financing Capital Projects."

3. *See* Chapter 10, "Accounting, Financial Reporting, and the Annual Audit."

4. *See* Chapter 8, "Managing and Disbursing Public Funds," and Chapter 11, "Procurement, Contracting, and Disposal of Property."

5. *See* Chapter 10, "Accounting, Financial Reporting, and the Annual Audit."

6. G.S. 159-7.

7. G.S. 159-7(b)(15).

local entity specifically states that it is a municipal corporation or otherwise indicates that the entity is a "body corporate and politic" or a "public corporation," then the entity is a municipal corporation.[8] Second, the entity may not be part of the state's budgeting system. G.S. Chapter 143C, known as the State Budget Act, governs the budgeting and expenditure of state money by state agencies. Although local entities are subject to several provisions of the State Budget Act with respect to the receipt of state funds, they are not required to comply with the actual budgeting requirements of the act.[9] Third, the local entity must have the power to levy taxes. Based on this definition, the following local entities constitute units of local government:

- counties (G.S. Chapter 153A);
- municipalities (cities, towns, villages)[10] (G.S. Chapter 160A);
- consolidated municipal-county governments (G.S. Chapter 160B);
- sanitary districts (G.S. Chapter 130A, Article 2, Part 2);
- county water and sewer districts[11] (G.S. Chapter 162A, Article 6);
- metropolitan sewerage districts (G.S. Chapter 162A, Article 5);
- metropolitan water districts (G.S. Chapter 162A, Article 4);
- mosquito control districts (G.S. Chapter 130A, Article 12, Part 2);
- special airport districts (G.S. Chapter 63, Article 8);
- regional public transportation authorities (G.S. Chapter 160A, Article 26).

For purposes of the LGBFCA, a unit of local government also includes all boards, agencies, commissions, authorities, and institutions that are established or created by the unit's governing board or that are not themselves municipal corporations. Governing boards often appoint citizen advisory boards for the administration of libraries and parks and recreation. Counties and municipalities also are served by functional boards and commissions in the areas of health, social services, elections, and planning. If these entities are not municipal corporations (and many are not) then their fiscal affairs are the responsibility of the county, municipality, or other unit of government with which they are associated.[12]

---

8. *See generally* Carolina-Va. Coastal Highway v. Coastal Tpk. Auth., 237 N.C. 52, 61 (1953) ("[A] corporation formed for purely governmental purposes is a municipal corporation."); Wells v. Hous. Auth. of City of Wilmington, 213 N.C. 744, ___, 197 S.E. 693, 697 (1938) ("[W]hen applied to corporations the words 'political,' 'municipal,' and 'public' are used interchangeably.").

9. Note that before Fiscal Year 2007–2008, the terms "unit of local government" and "public authority" in G.S. 159-7 were defined as not being subject to the provisions in G.S. Chapter 143, Article 1, and G.S. Chapter 143, Article 1, did not define the entities subject to its provisions to include units of local government and public authorities. However, G.S. Chapter 143 was repealed as of July 1, 2007, and replaced with G.S. Chapter 143C. Somewhat confusingly, G.S. Chapter 143C does include units of local government and public authorities in its definition of entities subject to its provisions. This appears to be a drafting oversight. It is commonly understood that units of local government and public authorities are subject to the budgeting requirements of the LGBFCA and not the State Budget Act.

10. In North Carolina, unless a statute specifically provides otherwise, there is no legal difference among a city, town, or village. As used in this book, the term "municipality" is synonymous with "city," "town," and "village."

11. G.S. 162A-89 specifies that a county's governing board also serves as the governing board of the county water and sewer districts within its jurisdiction.

12. There are some boards and commissions established by local act that are invested with corporate status.

Occasionally, the LGBFCA refers to a "special district." A special district is a unit of local government created for the "performance of limited governmental functions or for the operation of a particular utility or public service enterprises."[13] Any local entity that meets the definition of a unit of local government set forth above that is not a county, municipality, or consolidated municipal-county government is a special district for purposes of the LGBFCA (see the last seven items in the above list).

Public Authority

A local entity also is subject to the LGBFCA if it is a *public authority*. This is an umbrella term that covers a variety of special-purpose local government entities. G.S. 159-7(b)(10) defines two different categories of public authorities. The first has three distinguishing characteristics, two of which are analogous to a unit of local government. First, the local entity is a municipal corporation, and second, it is not part of the state's budgeting system. The third and differentiating characteristic, however, is that the entity does not have the power to levy taxes. Under this definition, the following local entities are public authorities:

- housing authorities[14] (G.S. Chapter 157, Article 1);
- redevelopment commissions[15] (G.S. Chapter 160A, Article 22);
- water and sewer authorities (G.S. Chapter 162A, Article 1);
- soil and water conservation districts[16] (G.S. Chapter 139, Article 1);
- parking authorities (G.S. Chapter 160A, Article 24);
- public transportation authorities (G.S. Chapter 160A, Article 25);
- tourism development authorities (local act[17]);
- regional transportation authorities (G.S. Chapter 160A, Article 27);
- regional natural gas districts (G.S. Chapter 160A, Article 28);
- single- and multi-county public health authorities (G.S. Chapter 130A, Article 2, Part 1B).

The second type of public authority has five distinguishing characteristics. First, it is *not* a municipal corporation. Second, it is not part of the state's budgeting system. Third, it has no power to levy taxes. Fourth, it operates on an area, regional, or multi-unit basis. Fifth, it is not part of the budgeting and accounting system of a unit of local government. The last two

---

13. G.S. 159-7(b)(13).

14. A county's or municipality's governing board may adopt a resolution assuming responsibility for the fiscal affairs of a housing authority. If a unit adopts such a resolution, the housing authority is not a public authority for purposes of G.S. 159-7(b); rather, it is a department or agency of the county or municipality. G.S. 157-4.2.

15. A county's or municipality's governing board may adopt a resolution assuming responsibility for the fiscal affairs of a redevelopment commission. If a unit adopts such a resolution, the redevelopment commission is not a public authority for purposes of G.S. 159-7(b); rather, it is a department or agency of the county or municipality. G.S. 160A-505.1.

16. Several soil and water conservation districts are treated as departments of the counties in which they are located. Although technically still public authorities and thus independently subject to the LGBFCA, these districts often rely on county governments to manage most if not all of their fiscal affairs.

17. Many local governments are authorized to levy occupancy taxes pursuant to local act. The local acts establishing this authority often require a local unit to establish a tourism development authority (TDA) to manage the expenditure of occupancy tax proceeds. TDAs typically are municipal corporations that are not subject to the state's budgeting system and not authorized to levy taxes.

characteristics are particularly important. As mentioned above, there are many local entities that are not municipal corporations, are not part of the state budgeting system, and lack the power to levy taxes. In fact, most of the boards, agencies, commissions, authorities, and institutions of a unit of local government satisfy these criteria. Very few are not part of the budgeting and accounting system of a unit of local government, though. Local entities that satisfy this second definition of public authority include the following:

- councils of government (G.S. Chapter 160A, Article 20, Part 2);
- regional planning commissions (G.S. Chapter 153A, Article 19);
- regional economic-development commissions (G.S. Chapter 158, Article 2);
- regional planning and economic-development commissions (G.S. Chapter 153A, Article 19);
- single- and multi-county area mental health, developmental disabilities, and substance abuse authorities (G.S. Chapter 122C, Article 4, Part 2);
- district health boards (G.S. Chapter 130A, Article 2, Part 1);
- regional libraries (G.S. Chapter 153A, Article 14; G.S. Chapter 160A, Article 20).

Sometimes a public authority that is independently subject to the LGBFCA chooses to contract with another local entity to perform many or even all its duties under the act. For example, many tourism development authorities (TDAs) contract with the county or municipality with which they are associated to manage, disperse, and properly account for their funds. And, though technically independent public authorities, several soil and water conservation districts rely on the county governments with which they are associated to adopt their budgets and perform some or all other financial management duties. In these cases, the governing board of the public authority still is responsible for ensuring full compliance with the LGBFCA.

There are a few special-purpose local governments that are not public authorities, including local school administrative units and Alcoholic Beverage Control (ABC) boards. These entities are subject to separate budgeting and fiscal control provisions, although many of the requirements are parallel to those in the LGBFCA.[18]

Private Entities Not Subject to LGBFCA

If an entity is not a unit of local government or a public authority, or a department, agency, board, commission, or institution of one of these entities, it is not subject to the LGBFCA. This may seem obvious, but some private entities, such as nonprofits, are closely aligned with, and even created by, government entities.[19]

A nonprofit may receive most, if not all, of its funding from the government.[20] It may be treated as a component unit of a local government under applicable accounting rules. And, at

---

18. Local school administrative units are governed by the School Fiscal Control Act, located in G.S. Chapter 115C, Article 31. The budgeting and fiscal management requirements for ABC Boards are found in G.S. 18B-702.

19. G.S. 159-42.1 explicitly authorizes a public authority to create a nonprofit corporation. Many counties and municipalities also have established nonprofit corporations, pursuant to their general administrative authority, to aid in fundraising or other support efforts. A local government or public authority must notify the state Local Government Commission if it creates a nonprofit. G.S. 159-7(e).

20. For more information on providing funding to nonprofits, see Chapter 1, "The Public Purpose Requirement."

times, it may even effectively be controlled by a local entity through board appointments or budget-approval requirements. Because of its close ties to a public agency, a nonprofit may be treated as a public agency for some purposes. For example, a nonprofit agency that has close enough ties to a government entity may be subject to public records laws and open meetings laws that typically apply only to public agencies.[21] Such a nonprofit likely would not be subject to the LGBFCA, though, because it does not satisfy the definition of a covered entity.

A local government or public authority may, however, require a nonprofit or other private organization to comply with some or all of the LGBFCA's provisions as a condition of contracting with the local entity and receiving public funds.[22] In fact, the LGBFCA specifies that if a county or municipality appropriates $1,000 or more to a nonprofit corporation in any fiscal year, the local unit may require that the nonprofit have an independent audit performed for the fiscal year in which the funds were received and provide a copy of that audit to the local government.[23] The statute exempts certain entities from this requirement—most significantly, nonprofits that "provide hospital services or operate as a volunteer fire department, rescue squad, [or] ambulance squad. . . . "[24] While a local entity may require these exempt nonprofits to provide an accounting of how any public funds were expended during a fiscal year, the entity is prohibited from requiring that exempt nonprofits undergo independent audits. A local entity also is free to require any nonprofits (including those exempt from the independent audit requirement) or other private entities to comply with any of the other LGBFCA provisions as a condition of doing business with the government or receiving public funds.

State law also requires a nonprofit that receives more than $5,000 of public funds (from a local government, the state, or the federal government) within a fiscal year, in grants, loans, or in-kind contributions, to provide the following information upon written request from any member of the public:

1. The nonprofit's latest financial statements. The financial statements must include a balance sheet as of the end of the fiscal year and a statement of operations for that year. They also must contain "details about the amount of public funds received and how those funds were used."[25]

2. The nonprofit's most recently filed Internal Revenue Service (IRS) Form 990, Form 990-EZ, or a copy of its Form 990-N submittal confirmation. A nonprofit may redact information not required for public disclosure pursuant to 26 U.S.C. § 6104(d)(3). Alternatively, a nonprofit may satisfy this requirement if it posts this information on its website or if another entity posts the information as part of a database of similar

---

21. For more information on when a private entity may be treated as a public agency for certain purposes, see Frayda Bluestein, "When Do Government Transparency Laws Apply to Private Entities?," *Coates' Canons: NC Local Government Law* blog (June 1, 2011).

22. As discussed in Chapter 1, "The Public Purpose Requirement," a local unit must require a nonprofit to provide some accounting of its contract performance. The provisions mentioned in this chapter are optional additional contracting terms.

23. G.S. 159-40.

24. G.S. 159-40. The statute also exempts nonprofits that operate as junior colleges, colleges, or universities duly accredited by the southern regional accrediting association, as well as those that provide sheltered workshops, adult development activity programs, private residential facilities for the intellectually or developmentally disabled, and developmental day care centers.

25. G.S. 55A-16-24(a).

documents. The information must be accessible by the general public without charge. Also, if another entity maintains the information, the nonprofit must include a link to the other entity's website on its own website.[26]

The act exempts a few entities from disclosing this information because they already are required to report it to a state agency: (1) nonprofits required to report to the N.C. Medical Care Commission, (2) nonprofits required to report to the state Local Government Commission, and (3) certain private colleges required to report to the state. These entities must provide information on their public websites about how to access the information, though.

Ensuring Compliance with the LGBFCA

For those local entities that are subject to the Local Government Budget and Fiscal Control Act (LGBFCA), who within the entity is responsible for ensuring compliance with the act's provisions? A local entity's governing board ultimately is responsible for directing and overseeing the financial management of the entity and for ensuring the integrity of the unit's fiscal internal controls. The LGBFCA assigns some functions to specific finance personnel, though. In addition, the state Local Government Commission (LGC) is legally responsible for monitoring and ensuring the fiscal health of all local entities subject to the LGBFCA.

Governing Board

A local entity's governing board is responsible for the entity's financial management.[27] In this vein, the board's most important job is to set the tone at the top. In other words, the board must establish an expectation that all officials and employees will comply with financial policies and other internal controls. To hold others accountable, board members need to abide by strict internal controls and statutory compliance. The board also needs to develop sufficient knowledge and understanding of the unit's finances. Board members, however, do not generally perform specific financial management tasks. These are assigned or delegated to staff members. There are certain, non-delegable duties that the LGBFCA assigns specifically to the governing board:

- The governing board must adopt (and make any amendments to) the entity's annual budget ordinance.[28] If a unit adopts or amends one or more project ordinances, these actions also must be taken by the governing board.[29]
- The board must select the entity's official depositories (bank accounts).[30]

---

26. G.S. 55A-16-24.

27. *See generally* G.S. 153A-12 (counties); 160A-12 (municipalities).

28. G.S. 159-13, -15. The board may delegate to the entity's budget officer the authority to move moneys within a fund in the annual budget ordinance. The budget officer must report any such changes to the board at its next meeting.

29. G.S. 159-13.2. There is no authority to delegate any movement of moneys within a project ordinance to the entity's budget officer.

30. G.S. 159-31.

- The board also must select the entity's auditor, execute the audit contract, receive the yearly audit report, and respond in writing to the LGC about any material deficiencies or financial performance indicators of concern.[31]
- Finally, the board must designate one or more individuals to serve certain statutory roles related to financial management—specifically, the budget officer,[32] tax collector,[33] deputy finance officers,[34] and, in some cases, the finance officer.[35] If the budget officer, tax collector, or finance officer is fired, resigns, or is otherwise unable to carry out the position's assigned duties, the governing board must ensure that a successor is appointed as soon as possible. As discussed below, there are several statutory duties that may be carried out only by individuals officially appointed to one of these positions.

Budget Officer

The LGBFCA requires each local government and public authority to appoint a budget officer.[36]

Duties of Budget Officer

The budget officer has two main duties: (1) to prepare the entity's annual budget for submittal to the governing board and (2) to execute the local entity's annual budget ordinance and any project ordinances. These are fairly substantial duties. The individual who serves in this role often is a conduit between the unit's or authority's departments and staff members and its governing board. The budget officer provides a technical review of departmental requests and estimates to ensure accuracy and completeness. More important, he or she is in a position to critically evaluate departmental needs and recommend funding levels for various services and projects that are consistent with the unit's overall priorities and goals.

Who Can Serve as Budget Officer?

The budget officer is appointed by, and serves at the pleasure of, the entity's governing board. The board's appointment discretion is limited by statute, though.[37] Who can or must serve as the budget officer differs both by type of local entity and by type of governance structure, as illustrated in Table 2.1.

Delegating Budget Officer Duties in Units with Manager Form of Government

In some units in which the manager is the statutory budget officer, a budget director, who reports to the manager (or occasionally to the finance officer), actually performs most of the duties of the budget officer. The manager remains legally responsible for the budget officer's statutory duties, though, and should establish policies and procedures to ensure proper oversight.

---

31. G.S. 159-34.
32. G.S. 159-9.
33. G.S. 105-349.
34. G.S. 159-28.
35. G.S. 159-24. Under a council-manager form of government, the finance officer typically is appointed by, and serves at the pleasure of, the local unit's manager. G.S. 153A-82 (counties); 160A-148 (municipalities).
36. G.S. 159-9.
37. G.S. 159-9.

Table 2.1 Budget Officer Eligibility

Type of Local Entity	Form of Government	Eligible to Serve as Budget Officer
County	Council-Manager	The manager serves as the budget officer.
County	Mayor-Council	The governing board may confer the duties of the budget officer on the county finance officer or on any other county officer or employee except the sheriff and, in most counties, the register of deeds.
		In counties with populations less than or equal to 7,500, the register of deeds may serve in this capacity.
Municipality	Council-Manager	The manager serves as the budget officer.
Municipality	Mayor-Council	The governing board may confer the duties of the budget officer on any municipal officer or employee, including the mayor if he or she consents.
Special District		The governing board may impose the duties of the budget officer on its chairperson, on any other member of the governing board, or on any other officer or employee.
Public Authority		The governing board may impose the duties of the budget officer on its chairperson, on any other member of the governing board, or on any other officer or employee.

Questions sometimes arise, particularly in smaller units, as to whether a governing board member may serve as a budget officer in a jurisdiction with a manager form of government. For municipalities with the manager form of government, the mayor or another council member may not serve as the manager and thus may not serve as the budget officer.[38] For counties with the manager form of government, the board may confer the duties of county manager and, therefore, county budget officer, on its chairperson or on another member of the board of commissioners. A board member may receive reasonable compensation for serving in this capacity.[39]

Finance Officer

The LGBFCA also requires the governing board of each local government and public authority to designate a finance officer.[40]

---

38. G.S. 160A-151. The mayor and members of the council also are ineligible to serve as manager or budget officer on an acting or interim basis. *Id.*

39. G.S. 153A-81.

40. "Each local government and public authority shall, at all times, have a finance officer appointed by the local government, public authority, or designated official to hold office at the pleasure of the appointing board or official." G.S. 159-24.

Duties of Finance Officer

Sometimes referred to as accountant, treasurer, finance director, or chief financial officer, the individual in this position is legally responsible for performing the following duties:

- establishing and maintaining the unit's accounting system;
- controlling expenditures and disbursing moneys;
- preparing and presenting financial reports;
- managing the receipt and deposit of moneys, including routinely auditing accounts of other officials and employees;
- managing the unit's debt service obligations;
- supervising investments.[41]

The finance officer is not limited to executing just these statutory duties. At the behest of the governing board, he or she may perform or supervise other functions for the unit. It is not uncommon, for example, for a finance officer to be involved with budgeting, purchasing and contracting, utilities, information technology, risk management, and even general administration of the unit.

Who Can Serve as Finance Officer?

The duties of the finance officer "may be imposed on the budget officer or any other officer or employee on whom the duties of budget officer may be imposed."[42] However, the Machinery Act,[43] which governs the assessment and collection of property taxes, forbids conferring the duties of tax collector and finance officer on the same person except with the written permission of the secretary of the LGC.[44] For municipalities, any other person or official who may serve as budget officer also may serve as finance officer, and the two positions may be combined. For counties, the sheriff may not be appointed finance officer, and in counties with a population greater than 7,500, the register of deeds may not be appointed finance officer. Otherwise, any other person or official who may serve as budget officer also may serve as finance officer, and the two positions may be combined.

Who Appoints the Finance Officer?

Who appoints a finance officer varies by jurisdiction. For a county or municipality without the manager form of government, as well as for special districts and public authorities, the governing board normally makes the appointment. For a county or municipality with the manager form of government, the manager is empowered to designate the finance officer.[45] The finance officer serves at the pleasure of whomever makes the appointment.

---

41. G.S. 159-25. Note that the position of finance officer may by referred to by any "reasonably descriptive title." G.S. 159-24.

42. G.S. 159-24.

43. Subchapter II of G.S. Chapter 105.

44. G.S. 105-349(e).

45. *See* G.S. 153A-82 (counties); 160A-148 (municipalities). Occasionally, a municipal charter will specify that the finance officer be appointed by the board. In those cases, the charter provisions control.

Special Eligibility Requirements for Finance Officer

The individual serving as finance officer need not be a certified public accountant (CPA) or hold any specific degrees or certifications, but he or she should be well versed in the legal and financial rules, regulations, and best practices governing public finance. There are two threshold legal requirements that must be satisfied before the finance officer may assume the duties of the position: (1) the individual must be bonded and (2) the individual must take the oath of office.[46]

Bonding Requirement

Effective January 1, 2023, the General Assembly made changes to the finance officer bonding requirement. The finance officer must "give a true accounting and faithful performance bond with sufficient sureties" in an amount to be set by the governing board.[47] At a minimum, the amount of the bond must be the greater of the following: (1) $50,000 or (2) an amount equal to 10 percent of the local unit's annually budgeted funds, up to a maximum coverage of $1,000,000.[48] A finance officer "is bound to perform the duties of his office faithfully, and to use reasonable skill and diligence, and to act primarily for the benefit of the public."[49] A true accounting and faithful performance bond typically insures for loss sustained by the failure of an employee to properly account for all moneys and property received by virtue of his or her position or the failure to otherwise faithfully perform his or her other duties. The bond inures to the benefit of the unit, and it typically covers acts or omissions due to the finance officer's negligence, carelessness, or incompetence.[50] The bond does not protect the bonded finance officer. In fact, if a bonding company makes good any loss to the protected unit, the right to recover the loss directly from the defaulting employee succeeds to the unit. The unit's governing board pays the premium for the bond.

Position bond not allowed. May a unit procure a bond for the position of finance officer (sometimes referred to as a position bond) that would offer coverage no matter who occupies the position at any given time? The answer is no. The statute states that a "person who is unable to secure the bond required by this section cannot assume the duties for which a bond is required under this section."[51] The purpose of the bonding requirement is to protect the unit from actions or inactions of the specific employee. In order to be fully protected, a unit needs to ensure that the individual who serves as finance officer actually is covered by the bond. If a unit procures a position bond, that bond may not cover certain individuals—for example, persons with criminal records or those who have committed other dishonest acts. Some units run background checks on potential employees. Others do not; thus, a unit may not realize that a particular employee does not qualify for bond coverage until it seeks to apply for the bond. Once hired, the finance

---

46. The LGC may impose additional minimum qualifications for finance officers. *See* G.S. 159-24(c).

47. G.S. 159-29. Note that G.S. Chapter 58, Article 72 imposes some additional process requirements for accepting and registering a county finance officer's official bond.

48. For more information on the bonding requirement, see Connor Crews, "Impending Changes to Bonding Requirements for Finance Officers: Prepare Now for January 1, 2023, and Beyond," *Local Finance Bulletin* No. 62 (Nov. 23, 2022).

49. Avery Cnty. v. Braswell, 215 N.C. 270, 275 (1939).

50. *Braswell*, 215 N.C. at 275 ("Where a public officer is required to give a bond for the faithful performance of the duties pertaining to his office, the engagement of the surety executing the bond rests on the same legal obligation as is imposed by law upon the officer himself.").

51. G.S. 159-29(b).

officer also must remain bondable during his or her full tenure. The bonds normally are continuous, renewed each year by payment of an annual premium.

Bonding requirement when individual serves as finance officer for more than one unit. How is the bonding requirement satisfied if an individual serves as the finance officer for more than one unit or public authority? For example, what is the bonding requirement for an individual who serves as the finance officer for a county (a unit of local government for purposes of the LGBFCA) and also as the finance officer for the local tourism development authority (a public authority for purposes of the LGBFCA)?[52] An individual who serves as a finance officer for more than one unit of government or public authority must satisfy the bonding requirement for each separate unit. The provisions of the LGBFCA apply to each "unit of local government" and "public authority" in the state.[53] As reflected in the different definitions, a unit of local government is a separate and distinct legal entity from a public authority. Each of these entities is independently required to comply with the provisions of the act. The act requires each unit of local government and each public authority to appoint a finance officer to perform certain duties for that unit. And the finance officer for each unit of local government and each public authority must be bonded.[54] It may be possible to include coverage for multiple units in the same bond, but the bond must clearly delineate the different beneficiaries as if there were separate bonds. The bond also must provide at least $50,000 in coverage for each unit.

Oath of Office

Article VI, Section 7, of the North Carolina Constitution requires that elected and appointed public officers take an oath of office.[55] The position of finance officer likely qualifies as "public officer" and is thus subject to the oath requirement. The text of the oath is as follows:

> I, [finance officer's name], do solemnly swear (or affirm) that I will support and maintain the Constitution and laws of the United States, and the Constitution and laws of North Carolina not inconsistent therewith, and that I will faithfully discharge the duties of my office as finance officer, so help me God.

A finance officer must take the oath before assuming the duties of the office. The oath typically is administered by the mayor, chairman of the board, or clerk to the board, though it also may be administered by a few other officials.[56] For counties and municipalities, the oath must then be filed with the clerk to the board.

---

52. A tourism development authority is a public authority that is created by local act of the General Assembly to promote travel, tourism, and general development of a unit or region.

53. G.S. 159-7.

54. For more information on the bonding requirement when a finance officer serves multiple units, see Kara Millonzi, "Finance Officer Fidelity Bonds: When Are Multiple Bonds Required?," *Coates' Canons: NC Local Government Law* blog (Jan. 12, 2012).

55. *See also* G.S. 153A-26 (counties); 160A-61 (municipalities).

56. See G.S. 11-7.1 for a list of officials authorized to administer the oath.

Delegating Finance Officer Duties

The finance officer has many responsibilities. Even in a small unit, these could prove difficult for a single person to handle. In many units, the finance officer delegates the performance of some of his or her duties to other employees or officials.[57] For example, one or more staff members might be assigned to track accounts payable/receivable, run payroll, make deposits, monitor investments, prepare reports, and even affix the finance officer's signature to certain documents. The finance officer remains legally obligated to perform these functions, and he or she may be held legally liable for failing to comply with certain LGBFCA provisions. It is imperative, then, that a finance officer establish policies and procedures that allow for sufficient oversight.

Deputy Finance Officers

A unit's governing board may assign certain finance officer functions to one or more other employees or officials by designating them deputy finance officers.

Duties of Deputy Finance Officers

Deputy finance officers legally may perform duties mandated by the LGBFCA related to the obligation and disbursement of public funds.[58] The governing board must adopt a resolution or ordinance to make the deputy finance officer appointments. It may not delegate this task to the manager or finance officer. Once the appointment is made, a deputy finance officer legally is obligated to perform assigned functions in accordance with the LGBFCA. Like the finance officer, a deputy finance officer may be held legally liable for failing to comply with applicable law. A deputy finance officer may perform duties beyond obligating and disbursing public funds; however, the legal liability for these duties remains with the unit's finance officer.

Who May Serve as Deputy Finance Officer?

Generally, any employee or official of a unit may serve as a deputy finance officer.[59] The governing boards in larger units often designate one or more department heads as deputy finance officers in order to allow for more flexibility in ordering goods, entering into contracts, and disbursing funds at the department level.

Bonding Requirements for Deputy Finance Officers (and Other Officials and Employees)

Each officer or employee of a unit who handles or has in his or her possession more than $100 or who has access to any of the unit's inventories must "give a faithful performance bond with sufficient sureties payable to the local government or public authority."[60] This requirement applies to deputy finance officers. In fact, it applies to most, if not all, employees and officials of a unit. There is no statutorily prescribed amount for the bond; it is to be set by the governing board. The unit may pay the premium on the bond each year, though it is not required to do so. The bond must be filed with the clerk to the board.

---

57. Note that duties related to accounting or treasury management may not be delegated to the unit's tax collector without prior approval of the LGC. *See* G.S. 105-349.

58. *See* G.S. 159-28. The duties are discussed in detail in Chapter 8, "Managing and Disbursing Public Funds."

59. Note that duties related to accounting or treasury management may not be delegated to a unit's tax collector without prior approval of the LGC. *See* G.S. 105-349.

60. G.S. 159-29.

Instead of requiring individual bonds for each deputy finance officer (and for each employee and official), a unit may adopt a system of blanket faithful performance bonding.[61] Most units utilize this option and cover all of their employees and officials, up to a specified amount, with one bond.

Note that a blanket bond does not satisfy the individual bond requirement for the finance officer,[62] tax collector,[63] sheriff,[64] or register of deeds.[65] These employees may also be covered by a blanket bond, however, if the blanket bond protects against risks not protected against by the employees' individual bonds.

Tax Collector

In addition to the budget officer and the finance officer, the governing board of each local government and special district must appoint a tax collector, for a term to be determined by the appointing body, to collect the taxes it levies.[66] A public authority needs to appoint a tax collector only if it levies taxes. The position of tax collector is not mandated by the LGBFCA but rather by the Machinery Act,[67] which governs the procedures for assessing and collecting taxes.[68] The specific duties performed by a tax collector, and the eligibility requirements for this position, are discussed in Chapter 5, "Property Tax Policy and Administration."

Local Government Commission (LGC)

The LGC is a nine-member state body situated in the Department of State Treasurer.[69] The commission approves most local government borrowing transactions and issues bonds on behalf of local units. It also monitors the fiscal health of local units in the state. The General Assembly has empowered the commission to "issue rules and regulations having the force of law governing procedures for the receipt, deposit, investment, transfer, and disbursement of money and other assets [by local units]. . . . "[70] The commission also may "inquire into and investigate the internal control procedures of a local government or public authority, may require any modifications in internal control procedures which, in the opinion of the Commission, are necessary or desirable to prevent embezzlements or mishandling of public moneys, and may adopt rules establishing minimum qualifications for finance officers."[71]

State law allows the LGC to take more drastic action if a unit willfully or negligently fails to take corrective action or otherwise comply with the LGBFCA's provisions in response to the commission's notices or warnings. Specifically, G.S. 159-181(c) allows the commission

---

61. G.S. 159-29(c).
62. G.S. 159-29.
63. G.S. 105-349.
64. G.S. 162-8.
65. G.S. 161-4.
66. G.S. 105-349.
67. Subchapter II of G.S. Chapter 105.
68. Note that the provisions governing the office of tax collector outlined below are those authorized under general law. Several jurisdictions have local acts that create the office of tax collector. Units should look to those local acts to determine eligibility, duties, appointment, and removal requirements for the office of tax collector.
69. G.S. Chapter 159, Article 2.
70. G.S. 159-25(c).
71. G.S. 159-25(c).

to "impound the books and records [of the unit] and assume full control of all its financial affairs. . . . " The commission becomes "vested with all the powers of the governing board as to the levy of taxes, expenditure of money, adoption of budgets, and all other financial powers conferred upon the governing board by law."[72] The commission may assume full control of a unit's water or sewer system and assume all powers of the governing board as to the operation of the public enterprise if the system, for three consecutive fiscal years, experiences negative working capital, has a quick ratio of less than 1.0, or experiences a net loss of revenue.[73]

To aid the LGC in its oversight role, commission staff members review the yearly financial audits of each local government and public authority in the state. Staff members often work with local officials to remedy any financial issues or potential financial issues. The commission issues warning letters to the governing boards of local units, identifying any problems and often demanding that a unit take remedial actions within a specified period of time.[74] If the LGC issues a warning letter to a local unit, the LGC also may mandate that the unit's finance officer and/or one or more of its deputy finance officers participate in training sponsored by the LGC.[75] The LGC also may require a unit to contract with outside entities if the local government or public authority has received a unit letter from the commission due to a deficiency in complying with the LGBFCA or if the unit has an internal control finding in the most recently completed financial audit.[76]

In recent years, the LGC has established a more robust support process for units that are in financial distress or are demonstrating other financial indicators of concern. The LGC may place a unit on its Unit Assistance List (UAL) if, based on audited financial statements and associated data submitted to the LGC as required under G.S. 159-34(a), it identifies concerns related to the unit's general fund, water/sewer quick ratio, income, cash flow, or internal controls. A unit also may be placed on the UAL if it fails to submit its annual audit to the LGC in a timely manner. Placement on the UAL triggers additional assistance for the unit. It also imposes additional statutory obligations and limitations on the unit, including the following:

- City and county managers of units on the UAL must complete a minimum of six clock hours of education, including fiscal management and the requirements of the LGBFCA.[77] (This is in addition to training requirements that may be imposed on finance staff.[78])
- Units on the UAL must obtain LGC approval of contracts relating to the lease, acquisition, or construction of capital assets with terms that exceed three years and

---

72. G.S. 159-181(c).

73. *See* S.L. 2013-150 (S.B. 207). "Working capital" is defined as "current assets, such as cash, inventory, and accounts receivable, less current liabilities. . . . " *Id.* A quick ratio of less than 1.0 "means that the ratio of liquid assets, cash and receivables, to current liabilities is less than 1.0." *Id.*

74. As discussed in Chapter 10, "Accounting, Financial Reporting, and the Annual Audit," the LGC requires a local governing board to respond in writing to any "significant deficiencies [or] material weaknesses" identified in the annual audit or to "other findings or if the auditor determined that Financial Performance Indicators of Concern were identified based on information presented in the audited financial statements. . . ." Title 20, Chapter 03, Section .0508 of the N.C. Administrative Code. The governing body must submit to the LGC a "Response to the Auditor's Findings, Recommendations, and Fiscal Matters," signed by a majority of the governing board members, within 60 days of the auditor's presentation. *Id.*

75. *See* G.S. 159-25(d), (f).

76. G.S. 159-25(d).

77. *See* G.S. 153A-82 (counties); 160A-148 (municipalities).

78. G.S. 159-25.

$50,000 (and meet the other criteria set out in G.S. 159-148, as applicable) and must obtain LGC approval for installment financings or other agreements involving the lease of, or the lease of with the option to purchase, motor vehicles where the contract amount equals or exceeds $50,000.[79]

Conclusion

Each local government and public authority in the state is subject to the provisions of the Local Government Budget and Fiscal Control Act (LGBFCA). These provisions establish a unified budgeting process and set certain mandated internal controls to ensure proper handling of public moneys. The LGBFCA also prescribes procedures for disbursing public funds and accounting for all of a unit's financial transactions. A unit's governing board is ultimately responsible for ensuring compliance with the act's requirements, though specific duties are assigned to several different officers or employees of the unit. The state's Local Government Commission aids a unit's governing board by identifying legal and financial management problems and by providing technical assistance to the unit to remedy these problems.

---

79. G.S. 159-148.

II. BUDGETING AND REVENUES

Chapter 3

Budgeting for Operating and Capital Expenditures

by Kara A. Millonzi and William C. Rivenbark

Introduction

North Carolina counties, municipalities, and public authorities (collectively, local units) are required to budget and spend money in accordance with the Local Government Budget and Fiscal Control Act (LGBFCA), codified as Article 3 of Chapter 159 of the North Carolina General Statutes (hereinafter G.S.).[1] In fact, a local unit may not expend any funds, regardless of their source, unless the money has been properly budgeted through the annual budget ordinance, a project ordinance, or a financial plan adopted by the unit's governing board.[2] On the expenditure side, a local unit may spend public funds only for purposes specifically authorized by the state legislature, through general laws, charter provisions, or other local acts. Revenues and expenditures for the provision of general government services are authorized in the annual budget ordinance.[3] Revenues and expenditures for an internal service fund are authorized in the annual budget ordinance or in a financial plan.[4] Revenues and expenditures for capital projects or for projects financed with grant proceeds are authorized in the annual budget ordinance or in a project ordinance.[5]

This chapter describes the legal requirements for budgeting for operating and capital expenditures. It also presents common budget tools and techniques for both the annual (operating) and capital budgeting processes. The chapter is divided into three sections. The first discusses how to prepare, adopt, and amend a unit's annual budget ordinance and presents various tools available to assist local officials during the budgeting process. The second briefly details the requirements for adopting and implementing a financial plan. Finally, the third section focuses on the adoption of a project ordinance for capital projects and expenditures. It also discusses common strategies for capital planning.

This chapter reflects the law as of June 1, 2023.

1. For a description of the types and functions of public authorities, see Chapter 2, "The Local Government Budget and Fiscal Control Act." As used in this book, the term "municipality" is synonymous with "city," "town," and "village."

2. There is an exception to this inclusiveness requirement. The LGBFCA permits the revenues of certain local government trust and custodial funds to be spent or disbursed without being budgeted. G.S. 159-13(a)(3). For example, many counties and municipalities set aside and manage moneys in a pension trust fund to finance special separation allowances for law enforcement officers. The employees and retirees for whom the local government is managing these moneys have ownership rights. Although a county or municipality must budget its initial contributions on behalf of employees into the pension trust fund, once the moneys are in the fund, earnings on the assets, payments to retirees, and other receipts and disbursements of the funds should not be included in the local government's budget. Municipalities sometimes maintain perpetual trust funds for the care and maintenance of individual plots in the unit's cemetery.

Another example is when a county or municipality collects certain revenue for another governmental unit and records this revenue in a custodial fund. Although the moneys are held temporarily by the county or the municipality, they belong to the other unit. The collections, therefore, are not revenues of the county or municipality collecting them and should not be included in its budget.

3. G.S. 159-13.

4. G.S. 159-13.1.

5. G.S. 159-13.2.

Annual Budget Ordinance

The annual budget ordinance is the legal document that recognizes revenues, authorizes expenditures, and levies taxes for a local unit for a single fiscal year. (Each unit's fiscal year runs from July 1 through June 30.)[6] The budget ordinance must be adopted by the unit's governing board. At its core, it reflects the governing board's policy preferences and provides a roadmap for implementing the board's vision for the unit. The Local Government Budget and Fiscal Control Act (LGBFCA), however, requires the board to include certain items in the budget ordinance and to follow a detailed procedure for adopting the budget ordinance.

Substantive Budget Ordinance Requirements and Restrictions

The LGBFCA imposes certain substantive requirements and limitations on the budget ordinance.

Balanced Budget

Perhaps the most important statutory requirement is that the budget ordinance be balanced. A budget ordinance is balanced when "the sum of estimated net revenues and appropriated fund balances is equal to appropriations."[7] The law requires an exact balance; it permits neither a deficit nor a surplus. Furthermore, each of the accounting funds that make up the annual budget ordinance (e.g., general fund, enterprise fund, etc.) also must be balanced.[8]

Estimated net revenues is the first variable in the balanced-budget equation; it comprises the revenues a unit expects to actually receive during the fiscal year, including amounts to be realized from collections of taxes or fees levied in prior fiscal years. (Typically, debt proceeds are not considered a form of revenue, but for budgetary purposes debt proceeds that are or will become available during the fiscal year are included in estimated net revenues.) The LGBFCA requires that a unit make reasonable estimates as to the amount of revenue it expects to receive.[9] A unit should have some demonstrable basis for its estimates, such as historical trends or other comparable data. The law places a specific limitation on property tax estimates. The estimated percentage of property tax collection budgeted for the coming fiscal year cannot exceed the percentage of collection realized in cash as of June 30 during the fiscal year preceding the budget year.[10]

Revenues must be budgeted by "major source."[11] This includes, at a minimum, property taxes, sales and use taxes, licenses and permits, intergovernmental revenues, charges for services, specific grant programs, and other taxes and revenues. A unit is free to group revenues in more-detailed categories.

---

6. G.S. 159-8(b). The Local Government Commission (LGC) may authorize a public authority (as defined in G.S. 159-7) to have a different fiscal year if it facilitates the authority's operations.

7. G.S. 159-8(a).

8. For a description of the purpose and function of accounting funds, see Chapter 10, "Accounting, Financial Reporting, and the Annual Audit."

9. G.S. 159-13(b)(7).

10. G.S. 159-13(b)(6). The statute provides for a different calculation when budgeting for property taxes on registered motor vehicles. The percentage of collection is based on the nine-month levy ending March 31 of the fiscal year preceding the budget year, and the collections realized in cash with respect to this levy are based on the twelve-month period ending June 30 of the fiscal year preceding the budget year.

11. G.S. 159-13(a).

The second variable in the balanced-budget equation is *appropriated fund balance.* Appropriated fund balance is best understood as the amount of cash reserves needed to fill the gap between estimated revenues and appropriations. Only a portion of a local unit's fund balance is available for appropriation each year. The LGBFCA defines the fund balance available for appropriation as "the sum of cash and investments minus the sum of liabilities, encumbrances, and deferred revenues arising from cash receipts, as those figures stand at the close of the fiscal year next preceding the budget year."[12] Legally available fund balance is different from fund balance for financial reporting purposes as presented on the balance sheet of a local government's annual financial report. It includes only cash and investments, not receivables or other current assets. Legally available fund balance results when any of the following occurs: unbudgeted fund balance carries forward from prior years, actual revenues exceed estimated revenues in the current fiscal year, actual expenditures are less than appropriations in the current fiscal year, or actual revenues exceed actual expenditures in the current fiscal year. A portion of this fund balance usually is legally restricted to certain expenditures. A governing board may appropriate restricted fund balance only for those specified purposes.

The calculation for determining the amount of legally available fund balance that may be appropriated to cover new expenditures starts with an estimate of cash and investments at the end of the current year and subtracts from them estimated liabilities, encumbrances, and deferred revenues from cash receipts at the end of the current year. All these figures are estimates because the calculation is being made for budget purposes before the end of the current year. If the estimate of available fund balance is for the general fund, typical liabilities are payroll owed for a payroll period that will carry forward from the current year into the budget year and accounts payable representing unpaid vendor accounts for goods and services provided to the local government toward the end of the current year. Encumbrances arise from purchase orders and other unfulfilled contractual obligations for goods and services that are outstanding at the end of a fiscal year. They reduce legally available fund balance because cash and investments will be needed to pay for the goods and services on order. (Note that the board is required to appropriate this portion of the fund balance to cover the encumbered amounts that will be paid out in the next fiscal year.) Deferred revenue from a cash receipt is revenue that is received in cash in the current year, even though it is not owed to the local government until the coming budget year. Such prepaid revenues are primarily property taxes. They should be included among revenues for the coming year's budget rather than carried forward as available fund balance from the current to the coming year.

A unit's governing board is not required to appropriate all the resulting fund balance, only that which is required, when added to estimated net revenues, to equal the budgeted appropriations for the fiscal year. The remaining moneys serve as cash reserves of the unit, to be used to aid in cash flow during the fiscal year. A unit also may use unappropriated fund balance to save money to meet emergency or unforeseen needs and to be able to take advantage of unexpected opportunities requiring the expenditure of money. And some units accumulate fund balance as a savings account for anticipated future capital projects, which also helps them maintain or improve their respective credit ratings.

---

12. G.S. 159-13(b)(16).

The third variable in the balanced-budget equation is *appropriations for expenditures*. An appropriation is a legal authorization to make an expenditure. But it is not an actual expenditure. An appropriation is a necessary predicate to incurring obligations (through contracts and agreements) and making expenditures. Only a governing board may authorize appropriations. The LGBFCA allows a governing board to make appropriations in the budget ordinance by department, function, or project.[13] For example, a board may appropriate total sums to the finance department, public works department, law enforcement department, planning and zoning department, and so on. Each department then has flexibility to fund its operational and capital expenditures from its budget allocation. The term "function" has two possible meanings for budgeting purposes. It allows a local government to group together multiple departments, such as law enforcement and fire under a broader budgeting category of "public safety." Alternatively, it allows a board to appropriate moneys for major expenditure categories within each department, such as salaries/benefits, utilities, supplies, insurance, capital, and the like. In this case, the budget officer/manager, department heads, and other staff may not exceed the amounts budgeted for each function category. The same is true if a board appropriates by project. A governing board may not make appropriations by line item or by an individual object of expenditure in the budget ordinance itself. The budget ordinance is a summary document that, for ease of exposition, aggregates expenditures. Many governing boards require submittal of more-detailed, line-item budgets by each department to justify the expenditures being requested. A board may require the manager or head of each department to follow the more-detailed budgets ("working budgets") during the fiscal year. The budget ordinance represents the legal appropriations of the unit, though.[14]

Required Budget Ordinance Appropriations

In addition to the balanced-budget requirement, the LGBFCA directs a governing board to include certain appropriations in its budget ordinance.[15] These requirements apply to the initial adoption of the budget ordinance as well as to any subsequent amendments.

Debt service. A governing board must appropriate the full amount estimated by the local government's finance officer to be required for debt service during the fiscal year.[16] During the spring, the LGC notifies each finance officer of that local government's debt-service obligation on existing debt for the coming year. If a county or municipality does not appropriate enough money for the payment of principal and interest on its debt, the LGC may order the unit to make the necessary appropriation; if the unit ignores this order, the LGC may itself levy the local tax for debt-service purposes.[17]

---

13. G.S. 159-13(a).

14. This distinction is significant. For example, the statute governing disbursements of public funds requires that before an obligation may be incurred by a unit, the finance officer or a deputy finance officer must verify that there is an appropriation authorizing that particular expenditure. G.S. 159-28(a). The statute refers to an appropriation in the budget ordinance, not in more-detailed, working budgets.

15. Note that the budget ordinance requirements discussed in this chapter generally are limited to those imposed by the LGBFCA. Units must be mindful that other statutory provisions may place additional requirements or restrictions on the budget ordinance.

16. G.S. 159-13(b)(1).

17. G.S. 159-36. Note that the LGC may not require a unit to make appropriations for repayment of installment-financing debt incurred under G.S. 160A-20 because of the requirement of a

Continuing contracts. A governing board must make appropriations to cover any obligations that will come due during the fiscal year under a continuing contract, unless the contract terms expressly authorize the board to refuse to do so in any given budget year.[18] Continuing contracts are those that extend for more than one fiscal year.

Fund deficits. A governing board must make appropriations to cover any deficits within a fund. A deficit occurs if the amount actually encumbered exceeds appropriations within the fund. If a unit follows the provisions on expenditure control in the LGBFCA, a deficit should not occur. However, should a deficit occur, a governing board must appropriate sufficient moneys in the next fiscal year's budget to eliminate that deficit.

Property taxes. If a local unit levies property taxes (which it is not required to do), the governing board must do so in the budget ordinance.[19] The property tax levy is stated in terms of rate of cents per $100 of taxable value.[20]

Encumbered fund balance. If a local unit incurs obligations in the prior year that have not/will not be paid during the prior fiscal year, the unit must appropriate sufficient amounts to cover those expenditures in the new fiscal year. Once the fiscal year expires, there is no budget authority to disburse funds under the prior year's budget. The moneys must be included in the new budget ordinance before they can be disbursed. This often occurs when a unit orders goods or enters into service contracts toward the end of the fiscal year.

Limits on Appropriations

Other LGBFCA provisions place upper or lower limits on certain appropriations in the budget ordinance. The statute also specifies the types of funds that may (and sometimes must) be used.

Contingency appropriations. In each fund a governing board may include a contingency appropriation, that is, an appropriation that is not designated to a specific department, function, or project. The contingency appropriation may not exceed 5 percent of the total of all other appropriations in the fund, though.[21] The governing board may delegate authority to the unit's budget officer to assign contingency appropriations to specific departments, functions, or projects during the fiscal year.[22]

Tax levy limits. If a unit levies property taxes, the proceeds must be used only for statutorily authorized purposes. A governing board may not include an appropriation of property tax revenue that is not authorized by law. In addition, there is a $1.50 per $100 property valuation aggregate property-tax rate cap.[23] Furthermore, the estimated percentage of collection of

---

non-appropriation clause. The provision also does not apply to contractual obligations undertaken by a local government in a debt instrument issued pursuant to G.S. Chapter 159G unless the debt instrument is secured by a pledge of the full faith and credit of the unit.

18. G.S. 159-13(b)(15).

19. G.S. 159-13(a).

20. The property tax levy process is described in greater detail in Chapter 4, "Revenue Sources," and Chapter 5, "Property Tax Policy and Administration."

21. G.S. 159-13(b)(3).

22. *See* G.S. 159-15.

23. G.S. 159-13(b)(4). Note that G.S. 160A-209 and 153A-149 authorize a municipality and a county, respectively, to seek voter approval to levy property taxes for purposes not authorized under general law. If a unit receives voter approval to expend property tax proceeds for another purpose, the total of all appropriations for that purpose may not exceed the total of all other unrestricted revenues and property taxes levied for the specific purpose. G.S. 159-13(b)(5). Voters also vote on levying tax rates for one or more purposes such that the combined total rate exceeds the $1.50 per $100 valuation cap.

property taxes used in the rate calculation may not exceed the percentage of the levy actually realized in cash as of June 30 during the prior fiscal year.[24]

Required funds. Each unit must maintain funds applicable to it according to generally acceptable accounting principles.[25]

Limits on Interfund Transfers

The annual budget ordinance sometimes includes appropriations to transfer money from one fund to another. The LGBFCA generally permits appropriations for interfund transfers, but it sets some restrictions on them, each designed to maintain the basic integrity of a fund in light of the purposes for which the fund was established. In addition, the LGBFCA prohibits certain interfund transfers of moneys that are earmarked for a specific service.

Each of the limitations on interfund transfers discussed below is subject to the modification that any fund may be charged for general administrative and overhead costs properly allocated to its activities as well as for the costs of levying and collecting its revenues.[26]

Voted Property Tax Funds

Proceeds from a voted property tax may be used only for the purpose approved by the voters. Such proceeds must be budgeted and accounted for in a special revenue fund[27] and generally may not be transferred to another fund,[28] except to a capital reserve fund[29] (if appropriate).

Custodial Funds for Special Districts

A special district is a unit of local government, other than a county or municipality, "created for the performance of limited governmental functions or for the operation of a particular utility or public service enterprises."[30] Some units collect moneys on behalf of a special district. These moneys must be budgeted and accounted for in a custodial fund and are not part of the local unit's annual budget ordinance.[31]

Enterprise Funds

A governing board may transfer moneys from an enterprise fund to another fund only if other appropriations in the enterprise fund are sufficient to meet operating expenses, capital outlays, and debt service for the enterprise.[32] This limitation reflects the policy that enterprise revenues must first meet the expenditures and the obligations related to the enterprise. (Note that other

---

24. For more information on calculating the property tax rate(s), see Chapter 5, "Property Tax Policy and Administration."

25. G.S. 159-26.

26. G.S. 159-13(b).

27. G.S. 159-26(b)(2).

28. G.S. 159-13(b)(10).

29. A unit may establish and maintain a capital reserve fund to save moneys over time to fund certain designated capital expenditures. G.S. 159-18. For more information on capital reserve funds, see Chapter 7, "Financing Capital Projects."

30. G.S. 159-7(b)(13).

31. G.S. 159-14(b).

32. G.S. 159-13(b)(14). Note that "[a] county may, upon a finding that a fund balance in a utility or public service enterprise fund used for operation of a landfill exceeds the requirements for funding the operation of that fund, including closure and post-closure expenditures, transfer excess funds accruing due to imposition of a surcharge imposed on another local government located within the State for use of the disposal facility, as authorized by G.S. 153A-292(b), to support the other services supported by the county's general fund." *Id.*

statutory provisions further restrict or prohibit a unit from transferring moneys associated with certain public enterprises.)

Although transferring money from an enterprise fund to another fund is legally allowed, it may result in negative consequences. It may, for example, negatively impact a local unit's credit rating or disqualify the unit from certain state loan and grant programs.[33]

Reappraisal Reserve Fund

A reappraisal reserve fund is established to accumulate money to finance a county's next real property revaluation, which must occur at least once every eight years. Appropriations to a reappraisal reserve fund may not be used for any other purpose.[34]

Service District Funds

A service district is a special taxing district of a county or municipality. Although a service district is not a separate local government unit, both the proceeds of a service district tax and other revenues appropriated to the district belong to the district. Therefore, no appropriation may be made to transfer moneys from a service district fund except for the purposes for which the district was established.[35]

Optional Budget Ordinance Provisions

The annual budget ordinance must contain revenue estimates, appropriations for expenditures, and, if applicable, the property tax levy. The ordinance must show revenues and expenditures by fund and demonstrate a balance in each fund. A governing board, however, is free to include other sections or provisions in the ordinance. For example, it might include instructions on its administration. If a fund contains earmarked revenues and general revenues or supports a function for which property taxes may not be used, the ordinance might specify the use of the earmarked funds or direct which non–property tax revenues are to support the function in question. The ordinance also may authorize and limit certain transfers among departmental or functional appropriations within the same fund and set rates or fees for public enterprises or other governmental services.

Adoption of Annual Budget Ordinance

In addition to imposing certain substantive requirements related to the annual budget ordinance, the LGBFCA also prescribes a detailed process for adopting the ordinance.

Role of Budget Officer

Before discussing the specifics of the budget process, it is important to understand the role of the budget officer. The governing board of each unit must appoint a budget officer.[36] In a county or municipality having the manager form of government, the manager is the statutory budget officer. Counties that do not have the manager form of government may impose the duties

---

33. *See* G.S. 159G-37; *see also* Kara Millonzi, "Transferring Money from an Enterprise Fund: Authority, Limitations, and Consequences," *Coates' Canons: NC Local Government Law* blog (June 5, 2015).

34. G.S. 159-13(b)(17).

35. G.S. 159-13(b)(18). This restriction also applies to any other revenues that the local unit has appropriated to the service district.

36. G.S. 159-9.

of budget officer on the finance officer or on any other county officer or employee except the sheriff or, in counties with a population greater than 7,500, the register of deeds. Municipalities not having the manager form of government may impose the duties of budget officer on any municipal officer or employee, including the mayor if he or she consents. A public authority or special district may impose the duties on the chairperson of its governing board, on any member of that board, or on any other officer or employee.

The LGBFCA assigns to the budget officer the responsibility of preparing and submitting a proposed budget to the governing board each year. Having one official who is responsible for budget preparation focuses responsibility for timely preparation of the budget, permits a technical review of departmental estimates to ensure completeness and accuracy, and allows for administrative analysis of departmental priorities in the context of a local unit's overall priorities. In many units, the statutory budget officer often delegates many of the duties associated with budget preparation to another official or employee, for example, the finance officer or a separate budget director or administrator. This is strictly an administrative arrangement, with the official or employee performing these duties under the direction of the statutory budget officer. Under the law, the budget officer retains full responsibility for budget preparation.

Once the budget ordinance is adopted, the budget officer is charged with overseeing its enactment. As discussed below, the governing board also may authorize the budget officer to make certain limited modifications to the budget ordinance during the fiscal year.

Budgeting Process

Before the budgeting process begins, the budget officer, often with guidance from the governing board, establishes an administrative calendar for budget preparations and prescribes forms and procedures for departments to use in formulating requests. Budget officers often include fiscal or program policies to guide departmental officials in formulating their budget requests. The LGBFCA specifies certain target dates for the key stages in the budgeting process, which should be incorporated into the budget officer's plan.

A budget officer's calendar often includes other steps that, though not statutorily required, are integral to an effective budgeting process. For example, many units kick off the annual budget process with one or more budget retreats or workshops for governing board members, department heads, and others. This allows governing board members to set policy for the coming year and provide directives to the budget officer and department heads about budget requests at the outset of the budget process.

Sometimes a budget officer will need to include other boards, organizations, or citizens in the budgeting process. Counties must provide funding for several functions that are (or may be) governed by other boards, such as public schools, community colleges, elections, social services, mental health, and public health. These boards have their own processes for formulating proposed budgets and requesting funds from the county. In addition, both counties and municipalities routinely receive requests from nonprofits, other private organizations, or citizens for appropriations to support certain community activities and projects. (A county or municipality generally does not have authority to make grants to private entities (including nonprofits). The county or municipality may, however, enter into a contract with a private entity and pay it to perform a function on behalf of the local government.[37]) The budget officer often serves as the liaison between these other boards, private entities, and citizen groups and the governing board. The budget officer should work with the governing board to establish an organized process for the board to receive and evaluate these various requests.

Budget Calendar

By April 30: Departmental Requests Must Be Submitted to the Budget Officer

The LGBFCA directs that each department head submit to the budget officer the revenue estimates and budget requests for his or her department for the budget year. Each department, or the unit's finance officer, also must submit information about current-year revenues and expenditures. The budget officer should specify the format for, and detail of, these submissions.[38]

By June 1: Proposed Budget Must Be Presented to the Governing Board

The budget officer must compile each department head's revenue estimates and budget requests and submit a proposed budget for consideration by the governing board.[39] Generally the proposed budget must comply with all the substantive requirements previously discussed. A governing board, however, may request that the budget officer submit a budget containing recommended appropriations that are greater than estimated revenues.[40] This affords the board a ready opportunity to discuss different expenditure options.

When the budget officer submits the proposed budget to the governing board, he or she must include a budget message.[41] The message should contain a summary explanation of the unit's goals for the budget year. It also should detail important activities funded in the budget and point out any changes from the previous fiscal year in program goals, appropriation levels, and fiscal policy.

If a revaluation of real taxable property in the unit occurs in the year preceding the budget year, the budget officer must include in the proposed budget a statement of the revenue-neutral tax rate, "the rate that is estimated to produce revenue for the next fiscal year equal to the revenue that would have been produced for the next fiscal year by the current tax rate if no reappraisal had occurred."[42] While the LGBFCA is silent on where the revenue-neutral tax rate must be included in the proposed budget, an appropriate place would be the budget message.[43] The rate is calculated as follows:

1. Determine a rate that would produce revenues equal to those produced for the current fiscal year.
2. Increase the rate by a growth factor equal to the average annual percentage increase in the tax base due to improvements since the last general reappraisal.
3. Adjust the rate to account for any annexation, de-annexation, merger, or similar events.

---

37. G.S. 153A-449 (counties); 160A-20.1 (municipalities).
38. G.S. 159-10.
39. G.S. 159-11(a).
40. G.S. 159-11(c).
41. G.S. 159-11(b).
42. G.S. 159-11(e).
43. *See* Shea Riggsbee Denning and William C. Rivenbark, "Statement of Revenue-Neutral Tax Rate and Provision for Mid-Year Property Tax Rate Change," *Local Finance Bulletin* No. 32 (Nov. 2004).

After Proposed Budget Presented to Governing Board but before Its Adoption: Notice and Public Hearing

When the budget officer submits the proposed budget to the governing board, a copy must be filed in the office of the clerk to the board, where it remains for public inspection until the governing board adopts the budget ordinance.[44] The clerk must publish a statement that the proposed budget has been submitted to the governing board and is available for public inspection.[45] The LGBFCA does not specify where or when the statement must be published. The clerk should follow the general provisions for legal advertising in Article 50 of G.S. Chapter 1. The clerk also must make a copy of the proposed budget available to all news media in the county. It may be helpful, though it is not legally mandated, for a unit to also post the proposed budget on its website.

The governing board is required to wait at least ten days after the budget officer submits the proposed budget before adopting the budget ordinance. This is true even if the board makes no changes to the proposed budget.[46] This interim period affords citizens time to review the proposed budget and to voice their opinions or objections to governing board members.

The governing board also must hold at least one public hearing on the proposed budget before adopting the budget ordinance. During the public hearing any person who wishes to be heard on the budget must be allowed time to speak. The board should set the time and place for the public hearing when it receives the proposed budget, if not before. This information should be included in the notice published by the clerk. Sometimes a board holds a series of budget review meetings and briefings on each of the major budget categories. These do not satisfy the statutory requirement. The law requires that at least one public hearing be held on the entire budget. The statute requires no specific minimum number of days between the date on which the notice appears and the date on which the hearing is held; however, the notice should be timely enough to allow for full public participation at the hearing.

By July 1: Governing Board Must Adopt Budget Ordinance

After the governing board receives the proposed budget from the budget officer, it is free to make changes to the budget before adopting the budget ordinance. In fact, based on citizen input, as well as that from other boards and department heads, the governing board often makes adjustments to the proposed budget before finalizing and adopting the budget ordinance. Questions often arise when a board makes changes to the proposed budget about whether and to what extent it must make the changes known to the public before adopting the budget ordinance. The statute requires only that the budget officer's proposed budget be made available for public inspection and that one public hearing be held after the proposed budget is submitted to the board. A unit is under no legal obligation to formally solicit public input of modifications to the proposed budget before its adoption.

---

44. G.S. 159-12(a).

45. G.S. 159-12(a). The notice also must specify the date and time of the public hearing to be held on the budget.

46. G.S. 159-13. The ten-day period begins to run the day after the notice is published. Weekend days and legal holidays count toward the total number of days. However, the ten-day period may not end on a Saturday, Sunday, or legal holiday. It must instead end on the next weekday that is not a legal holiday. *See* Rule 6, N.C. Rules of Civil Procedure, G.S. 1A-1.

The LGBFCA allows a budget ordinance to be adopted at any regular or special meeting, at which a quorum is present, by a simple majority of those present and voting.[47] The board must provide sufficient notice of the regular or special meeting, according to the provisions in the applicable open meetings law.[48] The budget ordinance is entered in the board's minutes, and within five days of its adoption, copies are to be filed with the budget officer, the finance officer, and the clerk to the board.[49]

Once the board adopts the budget ordinance, it may not repeal it. Any modifications are made pursuant to G.S. 159-15 (discussed below). This is true even if the board adopts the budget ordinance before July 1.[50]

Interim Appropriations

Missing the April 30 or June 1 deadline does not invalidate the budgetary process or budget ordinance. There are some consequences to missing the July 1 deadline, though. After June 30, a unit has no authority to make expenditures (including payment of staff salaries) under the prior year's budget. If a board does not adopt the budget ordinance by July 1 and needs to make expenditures, it must adopt an interim budget, making "interim appropriations for the purpose of paying salaries, debt-service payments, and the usual ordinary expenses" of the unit until the budget ordinance is adopted.[51] This is a stopgap measure. An interim budget should not include appropriations for salary and wage increases, capital items, and program or service expansion. It may not levy property taxes, nor should it change or increase other tax or user fee rates. The purpose of an interim budget is to temporarily keep operations going at current levels. An interim budget need not include revenues to balance the appropriations. All expenditures made under an interim budget are charged against the comparable appropriations in the annual budget ordinance once it is adopted. In other words, the interim expenditures eventually are funded with revenues included in the budget ordinance.

LGC Action for Failure to Adopt a Budget Ordinance

At some point, if a local unit's governing board refuses or is unable to adopt its budget ordinance, the LGC may take action. State law empowers the LGC to "assume full control" of a unit's financial affairs if the unit "persists, after notice and warning from the [LGC], in willfully or negligently failing or refusing to comply with the provisions" of the LGBFCA.[52] If the LGC takes this action, it becomes vested "with all of the powers of the governing board as to the levy of taxes, expenditure of money, adoption of budgets, and all other financial powers

---

47. G.S. 159-17. Adoption of the budget ordinance is not subject to the normal ordinance-adoption requirements of G.S. 153A-45 for counties and 160A-75 for municipalities.

48. *See* G.S. 143-318.12. However, G.S. 159-17 specifies that "no provision of law concerning the call of special meetings applies during [the period beginning with the submission of the proposed budget and ending with the adoption of the budget ordinance] so long as (i) each member of the board has actual notice of each special meeting called for the purpose of considering the budget, and (ii) no business other than consideration of the budget is taken up."

49. G.S. 159-13(d).

50. *See* Kara Millonzi, "Amending a Newly Adopted Budget Ordinance before July 1," *Coates' Canons: NC Local Government Law* blog (June 13, 2011).

51. G.S. 159-16.

52. G.S. 159-181(c).

conferred upon the governing board by law."[53] LGC takeover will only occur in extreme cases, though. Most of the time, a unit's governing board is left to work out any differences and adopt its budget ordinance.

Budgetary Accounting

The LGBFCA requires local units to maintain an accounting system with applicable funds as defined by generally accepted accounting principles (GAAP).[54] Local units enter their adopted budgets into their accounting systems at the beginning of the fiscal year; this allows them to accurately track the difference between an appropriation and the accumulated expenditures and encumbrances applied against that appropriation. Budgetary accounting is considered a best practice for several reasons. It provides the foundation for budget-to-actual variance reports, providing critical information to departments for remaining within their budgets and to elected officials who possess the ultimate fiduciary responsibility of the organization. It also provides the information needed for managing budget amendments and for complying with the pre-audit requirement.[55] Finally, it provides the needed information for following GAAP when local units issue their annual financial statements.

Amending the Budget Ordinance

The adopted budget ordinance encompasses a unit's legal authority to make all expenditures during the fiscal year. Before a unit may incur an obligation (order goods, enter into service contracts, or otherwise incur obligations of the unit), the finance officer or a deputy finance officer must ensure that there is an appropriation authorizing the expenditure and that sufficient moneys remain in the appropriation to cover the expenditure.[56] Events during a fiscal year may cause greater or less spending than anticipated for some activities, or needs may arise for which there is no appropriation or for which the existing one is exhausted. To address these situations the local unit may need to amend the budget ordinance.

The budget ordinance may be amended at any time after its adoption.[57] A governing board may modify appropriations for expenditures, recognize additional revenue, and/or appropriate fund balance to cover new expenditures. As amended, however, the budget ordinance must continue to be balanced and comply with the other substantive requirements previously discussed. Although not legally required to do so, a governing board also may amend the budget ordinance to reflect changes in revenue estimates during the fiscal year.

A budget ordinance may be amended by action of a simple majority of governing board members so long as a quorum is present. There are no notice or public hearing requirements. Alternatively, a governing board may delegate to the budget officer the authority to make certain changes to the budget. This authority is limited to (1) transfers of moneys from one appropriation to another within the same fund or (2) allocation of contingency appropriations to certain

---

53. G.S. 159-181.
54. G.S. 159-26.
55. See G.S. 159-15 for budget amendments. See G.S. 159-28 for the pre-audit requirement.
56. *See* G.S. 159-28(a).
57. G.S. 159-15. Sometimes a board adopts the budget ordinance before July 1. The budget ordinance is not effective until July 1; however, it may be amended at any time after its adoption subject to the limitations set forth in G.S. 159-15.

expenditures within the same fund. All other changes to the budget ordinance, including any revenue changes, must be made by the governing board.

Changing the Property Tax Levy

Local government units are limited in their ability to legally change the property tax levy or otherwise alter a property taxpayer's liability once the budget ordinance has been adopted. The property tax levy includes the general property tax rate plus any special taxing district rates. A board may alter the property tax levy only if (1) it is ordered to do so by a court, (2) it is ordered to do so by the LGC, or (3) the unit receives revenues that are substantially more or less than the amount anticipated when the budget ordinance was adopted.[58] A board may change the tax levy under the third exception only if it does so between July 1 and December 31.

Common Budgeting Tools and Techniques

Local units may adopt any budgeting process that facilitates effective decision making for adopting a balanced budget ordinance so long as it complies with the legal requirements of the LGBFCA. Local units, historically, have approached the budget process as a financial exercise, focusing primarily on the financial inputs and outputs of the organization. Today, however, local units often take a broader perspective of the budgeting process and include information derived from their strategic plans and performance-measurement systems to help guide budgetary decision making. The goal, as articulated by the reinventing government movement of the early 1990s, is for local units to make decisions that enable them to steer the boat rather than just row it.[59]

Line-Item Budgeting

Line-item budgeting places the focus of decision making on revenue estimates by each revenue category and on appropriations by each expenditure account. This form of budgeting is often criticized for its incremental approach to decision making, resulting in an adopted budget for the forthcoming fiscal year that merely reflects the current year's budget with slight adjustments, the assumption being that the group of services contained in the current year's budget should continue for the following fiscal year. While line-item budgeting is often criticized for this reason, it nonetheless provides the foundation of budgetary accounting. Local units prepare line-item budgets to accurately appropriate the necessary resources for each expenditure account contained in the categories of personnel, operations, and capital outlay; to record the line-item budgets in the local unit's financial management system to track budget-to-actual variances over the course of the fiscal year; and ultimately to document budgetary compliance as required by the LGBFCA.[60]

---

58. G.S. 159-15. This limitation applies once the budget ordinance is adopted, even if that occurs before July 1.

59. David Osborne and Ted Gaebler, *Reinventing Government* (New York: Penguin, 1992).

60. G.S. 159-26(a).

Strategic Budgeting

A management tool that local units often use to embrace long-term decision making is the creation and adoption of a strategic plan. As previously mentioned, local units often begin their budgetary processes with budget retreats or workshops for elective officials. At these events, officials tend to focus on how the forthcoming budget will help advance the long-term goals contained in their local unit's strategic plan. For example, a local unit may want the annual budget process to focus on infrastructure because economic development is a long-term, community goal. Broadening the budget process to include the organization's strategic plan enables the local unit's leadership to shift the focus from individual line-item accounts to long-term strategic goals that impact the direction of the community.

Performance Budgeting

Another common management tool used by local units to track service efficiency and effectiveness is performance measurement, wherein individual programs adopt mission statements, goals, objectives, and performance measures to demonstrate the outputs, efficiencies, and outcomes of service delivery. For example, a major output for public safety is the number of service calls. A major outcome is the timeliness of these service calls as tracked by response time. An advantage of performance budgeting, or the incorporation of performance-measurement information in the budget, is that it enables the local government unit to make resource-allocation decisions based on efficiency and effectiveness measures.[61] Returning to the public safety example, performance budgeting represents the process of deciding whether or not to add an additional officer based on the objective of responding to 95 percent of service calls within four minutes rather than solely on the local unit's ability to afford an additional position.

Zero-Based Budgeting

A technique that is commonly cited for its advantage of eliminating or reducing incremental budget decisions is zero-based budgeting. This budgeting technique, in theory, requires that every line item be reviewed and justified from a base budget of zero rather than from the current year budget. Zero-based budgeting, in practice, requires each department to submit three budget packages for review: its current-year budget, a reduced budget, and an expansion budget.[62] Departments are ranked based on the priorities of the organization and, based on that ranking, assigned one of the three budget packages, thereby reducing the probability that all departmental budgets reflect current year budgets with slight adjustments. However, reviews on the effectiveness of zero-based budgeting for eliminating or reducing incremental decision making have been mixed.

---

61. Janet M. Kelly and William C. Rivenbark, *Performance Budgeting for State and Local Government*, 2nd ed. (Armonk, N.Y.: M. E. Sharpe, 2011).

62. Robert L. Bland, *A Budgeting Guide for Local Government*, 2nd ed. (Washington, D.C.: International City/County Management Association, 2007).

Balanced Scorecard

The balanced scorecard is designed specifically to help local units translate their visions and missions into tangible objectives and outcomes.[63] Originally designed for the private sector, the balanced scorecard was adopted in the public sector as part of administrative reform and is now used as a management tool that helps local units broaden their budgeting processes during the preparation, implementation, and evaluation stages. The balanced scorecard requires a local unit to track the collection of metrics within the four quadrants of citizens, operations, financial resources, and employees, thereby providing local units with a broader, more balanced context in which to make budgetary decisions.

Financial Plans for Internal Service Funds

An internal service fund may be established to account for a service provided by one department or program to other departments in the same local unit and, in some cases, to other local governments. A service often accounted for in an internal service fund is fleet maintenance. If a local unit uses an internal service fund, the fund's revenues and expenditures may be included either in the annual budget ordinance or in a separate financial plan adopted specifically for the fund.[64]

Adopting a Financial Plan

The governing board must approve any financial plan adopted for an internal service fund, with such approval occurring at the same time the board enacts the annual budget ordinance.[65] The financial plan also must follow the same July 1 to June 30 fiscal year as the budget ordinance. An approved financial plan is entered into the board's minutes, and within five days after its approval, copies of the plan must be filed with the finance officer, the budget officer, and the clerk to the board.

Balanced Financial Plan Requirement

A financial plan must be balanced. This is accomplished when estimated expenditures equal estimated revenues of a fund.[66]

Internal service fund revenues are principally charges to county, municipality, or authority departments that use the services of an internal service fund. These charges are financed by appropriated expenditures of the using departments in the annual budget ordinance. Internal service fund revenues or other resources also may include an appropriated subsidy or transfer unrelated to specific internal service fund services, which would come from the general fund or some other fund to be shown as a transfer in, rather than as revenue for the internal service fund.

---

63. William C. Rivenbark and Eric J. Peterson, "A Balanced Approach to Implementing the Balanced Scorecard," *Popular Government* 74, no. 1 (Sept. 1, 2008): 31–37.

64. G.S. 159-8(a), -13.1.

65. At the same time he or she submits the proposed budget to the governing board, the budget officer must also submit a proposed financial plan for each intragovernmental service fund that will be in operation during the budget year.

66. G.S. 159-13.1.

Expenditures from an internal service fund are typically for items necessary to provide fund services, including salaries and wages; other operating outlays; lease, rental, or debt service payments; and depreciation charges on equipment or facilities used by the fund.

In adopting the annual financial plan for an internal service fund, a governing board must decide what to do with any available balance or reserves remaining from any previous year's financial plan. The law permits fund balance or reserves to be used to help finance fund operations in the next year or, if the balance is substantial, to fund long-term capital needs of the fund. Alternatively, fund balance may be allowed to continue accumulating for the purpose of financing major capital needs of the fund in the future, or it may be transferred to the general fund or another fund in the budget ordinance or to a project/grant ordinance for an appropriate use. A unit should avoid amassing in its financial plans large fund balances that are unrelated to the specific needs of the internal service fund.

Amending a Financial Plan

A financial plan may be modified during the fiscal year, but any change must be approved by the governing board.[67] Any amendments to a financial plan must be reflected in the board's minutes, with copies filed with the finance officer, the budget officer, and the clerk to the board.

Capital Budgeting

In North Carolina, local units may budget revenues and expenditures for the construction or acquisition of capital assets (capital projects) or for projects that are financed in whole or in part by federal or state grants (grant projects) either in the annual budget ordinance or in one or more project ordinances. A project ordinance appropriates revenues and expenditures for however long it takes to complete the capital or grant project rather than for a single fiscal year.[68]

Capital Projects

The Local Government Budget and Fiscal Control Act (LGBFCA) defines a capital project as a project that (1) is financed at least in part by bonds, notes, or debt instruments or (2) involves the construction or acquisition of a capital asset. Although a capital-project ordinance may be used to recognize revenues and appropriate expenditures for any capital project or asset, it typically is used for capital improvements or acquisitions that are large relative to the annual resources of the unit, that take more than one year to build or acquire, or that recur irregularly. Expenditures for capital assets that are not expensive relative to a unit's annual budget or that happen annually usually can be handled effectively in the budget ordinance.

---

67. G.S. 159-13.1(d).
68. G.S. 159-13.2.

Grant Projects

A grant-project ordinance may be used to budget revenues and expenditures for operating or capital purposes in a project financed wholly or partly by a grant or settlement funds from the federal government, the state government, or a private entity. This budgeting vehicle is most appropriate for multi-year grants, but it can be used even for single-year grants and may provide better documentation for grant compliance than the annual budget ordinance. A grant-project ordinance should not be used to appropriate state-shared taxes provided to a unit on a continuing basis, though. Such revenue or aid, even if earmarked for a specific purpose, should be budgeted in the annual budget ordinance.

Creating a Project Ordinance

A governing board may adopt a project ordinance at any regular or special meeting by a simple majority of board members so long as a quorum is present. This can be done at any time during the year. The ordinance must (1) clearly identify the project and authorize its undertaking, (2) identify the revenues that will finance the project, and (3) make the appropriations necessary to complete the project.[69]

Each project ordinance must be entered in the board's minutes, and within five days after its adoption copies of the ordinance must be filed with the finance officer, the budget officer, and the clerk to the board.

The budget officer also must provide certain information about project ordinances in the proposed annual budget submitted to the governing board each year. Specifically, the budget officer must include information on any project ordinances that the unit anticipates adopting during the budget year. The proposed budget also should include details about previously adopted project ordinances that likely will have appropriations available for expenditure during the budget year.[70] This is purely informational. The board need take no action to reauthorize a project ordinance once it is adopted.

Balanced Project-Ordinance Requirement

The LGBFCA requires a capital or grant project ordinance to be balanced for the life of the project. A project ordinance is balanced when "revenues estimated to be available for the project equal appropriations for the project."[71]

Estimated revenues for a project ordinance may include bond or other debt proceeds,[72] federal or state grants, revenues from special assessments or user fees, other special revenues, and annually recurring revenues. If property tax revenue is used to finance a project ordinance it must be levied initially in the annual budget ordinance and then transferred to the project ordinance. Other annually recurring revenues may be budgeted in the annual budget ordinance and transferred to a project ordinance or appropriated directly in a project ordinance.

---

69. A local unit should adopt a separate project ordinance for each capital project or each grant.

70. G.S. 159-13.2(f).

71. G.S. 159-13.2(c).

72. As with the annual budget ordinance, debt proceeds are treated as revenues for budgeting purposes. A local unit may include debt proceeds that it reasonably expects to receive to fund a project. If a bond issuance requires voter approval and/or LGC approval, it likely is not reasonable to include the debt proceeds in the revenue estimate until the local unit has obtained those approvals.

Appropriations for expenditures in a capital project ordinance may be general or detailed. A project ordinance may make a single, lump-sum appropriation for the project authorized by the ordinance, or it may make appropriations by line item, function, or other appropriate categories within the project. Appropriations in a grant-project ordinance should be specific enough to align with applicable grant-compliance requirements. For federal grants, that likely requires appropriations to occur at the cost-item level for each project.

The key characteristic of a project ordinance is that it has a project life, which means that the balancing requirement for such an ordinance is not bound by or related to any fiscal year or period. Estimated revenues and appropriations in a project ordinance must be balanced for the life of the project but do not have to be balanced for any fiscal year or period that the ordinance should happen to span.

Amending a Project Ordinance

A project ordinance may be amended at any time after its adoption but only by the governing board.[73] If expenditures for a project exceed the ordinance's appropriation, in total or for any expenditure category for which an appropriation was made, an amendment to the ordinance is necessary to increase the appropriation and identify additional revenues to keep the project ordinance balanced. A board also may amend a project ordinance to change the nature or scope of the project(s) being funded.

Closing Out a Project Ordinance

Unlike the annual budget ordinance, a project ordinance does not have an end date. It remains in effect until the project is finished or abandoned. There are no formal procedures for closing out a project ordinance when a project is done. Projects sometimes are completed with appropriated revenues remaining unspent. Practically speaking, such excess revenues are equivalent to a project fund balance. The remaining moneys should be transferred to another appropriate project, fund, or purpose at the project's completion. Annual revenues budgeted in a project ordinance that remain after a project is finished may be transferred back to the general fund or to another fund included in the annual budget ordinance. Bond proceeds remaining after a project is finished should be transferred to the appropriate fund for other projects authorized by the bond order or to pay debt service on the bonds. Note that any earmarked revenues in a project ordinance retain the earmark when transferred to another project or fund.

Justification for Capital Budget

The National Advisory Council on State and Local Government Budgeting encourages the adoption of a comprehensive policy for successfully implementing and managing the various aspects of capital budgeting.[74] A common question in local government is why local officials need to manage two budgeting processes, one for the operating budget and another for the capital budget. There are several reasons for implementing and managing a separate capital budgeting process.[75]

---

73. G.S. 159-13(e).

74. National Advisory Council on State and Local Government Budgeting, *Recommended Budget Practices* (Chicago: Government Finance Officers Association, 2003).

75. Bland, note 62 above.

The first reason involves the lasting impact of decisions. For example, a decision to expand bus routes during the current operating budget process can be changed during the operating budget process for the following fiscal year. A decision to expand a police station, however, is more permanent in nature, requiring a level of review beyond incremental adjustments to the operating budget.

A second reason, which builds on the first, is that debt financing is often used to acquire capital assets. The issuing of debt has a long-term impact on a county or municipality because the law requires that debt-service payments be appropriated as part of the budget ordinance.[76] The processes and procedures for capital budgeting can provide a more structured review for a critical decision, such as issuing debt, where additional debt-service payments may impact the organization's financial condition and possibly reduce future operating budget flexibility.

A third reason for implementing and managing a separate capital budgeting process can be traced back to state law. The budget ordinance adopted by counties and municipalities in North Carolina covers a single fiscal year beginning July 1 and ending June 30.[77] The acquisition of major capital assets or the completion of infrastructure projects often extends over multiple fiscal years from approval to completion. State law allows local units to adopt their capital budgets with a capital-project ordinance, which authorizes all appropriations necessary for project completion and prevents project proceeds from having to be re-adopted in subsequent fiscal years.

A final reason is the variation in assets and costs as compared to the operating budget, wherein decisions are often incremental from one fiscal year to the next. In any given fiscal year during the capital budgeting process, local officials may be faced with using cash reserves for anything from purchasing a new fire truck for $750,000 to issuing $20 million of debt for infrastructure improvements. Capital budgeting allows for the use of specific techniques for evaluating and prioritizing capital requests in terms of organizational need, capacity for acquisition, and community impact.

Capitalization and Capital Budget Thresholds

An important policy decision for local units is establishing a capitalization threshold, which dictates how the costs associated with the acquisition of capital assets are reported in the annual financial statements as required by G.S. 159-25(a)(1). The Government Finance Officers Association (GFOA) defines *capital assets* as tangible items (e.g., land, buildings, building improvements, vehicles, equipment, and infrastructure) or intangible items (e.g., easements and technology) with useful lives that extend beyond a single reporting period.[78] The GFOA recommends that local governments adopt a capitalization threshold of no less than $5,000 for any individual item, which means that capital assets costing $5,000 or less are reported as expenditures or expenses in the period in which they are acquired. Capital assets costing more than $5,000 are reported on the balance sheet and depreciated based on their estimated useful lives.

It is a professional practice for counties and municipalities to establish a financial threshold to determine what capital requests are considered part of the operating budget process and what

---

76. G.S. 159-13(b)(1).
77. G.S. 159-8(b).
78. GFOA, "Establishing Appropriate Capitalization Thresholds for Capital Assets," approved by the GFOA executive board on February 24, 2006.

capital requests are considered part of the capital budget process—referred to as the *capital budget threshold*. This threshold is often based on the size of the local government. For example, a smaller local government with a population of approximately 20,000 might establish a capital budget threshold of $50,000, meaning that capital assets costing $50,000 or less would be part of the operating budget process and capital assets costing more than $50,000 would be part of the capital budget process. An additional criterion often used in determining this threshold is the estimated useful life of the capital asset; this is because capital assets with longer estimated useful lives are more appropriate for the capital budget than for the operating budget. A reason for applying this additional criterion is that debt is often used to finance capital assets, and debt payments should never exceed the estimated useful life of the asset.[79]

Common Capital Budgeting Tools and Techniques

As with the annual budgeting process, a local unit may adopt any capital budgeting process that facilitates effective decision making so long as it complies with the legal requirements of the LGBFCA. An essential component of any well-designed capital budgeting process is planning. Many units have adopted a formalized capital improvement program (CIP) to facilitate the planning process. And, increasingly, units are relying on more sophisticated analysis relating to the financial condition of the unit to make accurate budget forecasts.

Capital Improvement Program

A CIP is a forecast of capital assets and funding sources over a selected period of time. While local officials often refer to the capital budget and CIP as one and the same, they are separate management tools. The capital budget covers one fiscal year and is adopted by ordinance.[80] The CIP, which commonly contains five years of proposed capital assets and funding sources beyond the capital budget, is approved as a long-term plan that local officials update on an annual basis.

There are numerous reasons why local officials prepare and approve a CIP in conjunction with their capital budget. It provides a schedule for the replacement and rehabilitation of existing capital assets, which is fundamental to all capital improvement programs. It allows time for project design and for exploring financing options, both of which are critical to evaluating the merits of a capital asset from a cost-benefit perspective. It also is the primary vehicle for providing the necessary infrastructure to support economic and community development in a coordinated manner, which is fundamental to land use and master plans. As well, a CIP has the potential to help a local government maintain or improve its credit rating due to the premium that bond-rating agencies place on planning.

Table 3.1 provides an example of a capital budget for a local government. The capital budget of $900,000 is adopted by ordinance for fiscal year 2022, appropriating the necessary financing sources to fund the capital assets aggregated by functional area. The major capital project for fiscal year 2022 is the expansion of the public safety building, which is funded by $100,000 from annual operating revenue and $400,000 from general obligation (GO) bonds. The $200,000 of

---

79. Justin Marlow, William C. Rivenbark, and A. John Vogt, *Capital Budgeting and Finance*, 2nd ed. (ICMA Press, 2009).

80. The phrase "capital budget" refers to appropriations for capital outlay in a single fiscal period. A government board may make these appropriations in the annual budget ordinance or in a capital-/ grant-project ordinance.

Table 3.1   Capital Budget and Capital Improvement Program (CIP)

Item	Capital Budget FY 2022	CIP FY 2023	FY 2024	FY 2025	FY 2026	FY 2027
Capital Assets by Function						
Public safety	500,000	50,000	50,000	50,000	50,000	50,000
Environmental services			250,000			250,000
Streets and transportation	200,000			400,000		
Parks and recreation			100,000			
Water and sewer	200,000	50,000			200,000	
Total	**900,000**	**100,000**	**400,000**	**450,000**	**250,000**	**300,000**
Financing Sources						
Operating revenue	100,000	50,000	50,000	50,000	50,000	50,000
Capital reserve fund		50,000	250,000			250,000
Grants			100,000			
General obligation bonds	600,000			400,000		
Revenue bonds	200,000				200,000	
Total	**900,000**	**100,000**	**400,000**	**450,000**	**250,000**	**300,000**

asphalt maintenance (streets and transportation) is funded from the remaining GO bonds, and revenue bonds will be used to fund an expansion of the water and sewer system.

Table 3.1 also provides an example of a five-year CIP for the local government, beginning with fiscal year 2023. While the CIP represents a plan and is updated on an annual basis as new requests are considered, it gives local officials time to prepare for future events. In fiscal year 2024, for example, $100,000 is allocated for a new park, giving local officials the time required to negotiate with multiple landowners to secure the necessary property. And in fiscal year 2025, $400,000 is allocated for general obligation (GO) bonds, giving local officials time to prepare for a bond referendum. These two examples highlight another critical reason why local officials prepare CIPs: doing so allows them to anticipate how the funding of capital assets will impact future operating budgets. Once the park is functional, adequate proceeds must be appropriated in the annual operating budget for additional park maintenance. The operating budget also must appropriate the debt-service payments for the issuance of the GO bonds as required by G.S. 159-13(b)(1). Preparing CIPs enables departments to consider the impact of proposed capital assets on their operating budgets when evaluating and submitting capital improvement requests.

Financial Condition and Forecasting

The CIP is a management tool that facilitates long-term planning for the acquisition of capital assets in local government. There are two additional management tools that support the capital budgeting process from a financial perspective, financial condition analysis and financial forecasting. This is critical given the ways in which the acquisition of capital assets can impact an organization's current financial condition and future operating budget flexibility.

Financial Condition Analysis

The first of these additional management tools, financial condition analysis, allows local officials to move beyond reporting on the financial position of the organization with an unmodified audit opinion of its annual financial statements to analyzing and interpreting the financial statements in order to determine and report on the financial condition of the organization. The reason financial condition analysis is so important to capital budgeting and finance is that acquiring and financing capital assets has the potential to drastically change the financial condition of a county or municipality; therefore, it is imperative to monitor these changes on an annual basis for the financial sustainability of the local government.

Fortunately, local officials have access to two Web-based dashboards that provide key financial ratios for analyzing the financial condition of any county or municipality in North Carolina. The Local Government Commission (LGC) benchmarking tool, which is located on the North Carolina Department of State Treasurer's website (www.nctreasurer.com), provides selected financial ratios for a local unit's governmental activities, general fund, water and sewer fund, and electric fund. The tool calculates the ratios over a five-year period and benchmarks them against other local governments. The North Carolina water and wastewater rates dashboard, which is located on the Environmental Finance Center's website at the School of Government (www.efc.sog.unc.edu), provides selected operations, debt service, and liquidity financial ratios for water and wastewater activities.

While the details of financial condition analysis are beyond the scope of this chapter, two financial ratios associated with the general fund and two financial ratios associated with an enterprise fund are discussed below to highlight the critical connection between acquiring financial capital assets and the financial condition of a local government.[81]

General Fund Financial Ratios

A financial ratio from the general fund's statement of revenues, expenditures, and changes in fund balance is the *debt service ratio*, which is calculated by dividing principal and interest by total expenditures. This ratio provides feedback on the percentage of annual expenditures being committed to annual debt service, which impacts service flexibility. The International City/County Management Association (ICMA) cautions local governments not to exceed 10 percent;[82] however, counties in North Carolina often exceed this percentage because of school financing. This ratio plays an important role when local officials are making the decision to issue additional debt for capital assets. Another financial ratio from the general fund's balance sheet is *fund balance as percentage of expenditures*. This ratio provides feedback on the solvency of the general fund, which is extremely important to monitor as cash reserves often are used to finance capital assets.

81. For more information on financial condition analysis, see William C. Rivenbark, Dale J. Roenigk, and Gregory S. Allison, "Communicating Financial Condition to Elected Officials in North Carolina," *Popular Government* 75, no. 1 (Fall 2009): 4–13.

82. International City/County Management Association, *Evaluating Financial Condition*, 4th ed. (Washington, D.C.: International City/County Management Association, 2003).

Enterprise Fund Financial Ratios

Two critical ratios calculated from the financial statements of an enterprise fund are the *debt coverage ratio* and the *capital-assets-condition ratio*. The enterprise fund's debt-coverage-service ratio is calculated by dividing net income of the enterprise by annual debt service—for example, a ratio of 1.25 means that net income exceeded debt service by 25 percent. This ratio is an important indicator of the financial condition of an enterprise fund. It is also important to creditors and bond-rating agencies, particularly when local officials seek to issue revenue bonds. The capital-assets-condition ratio provides feedback on the accumulated depreciation of the capital assets assigned to an enterprise fund (the ratio is 1.0 minus accumulated depreciation divided by capital assets being depreciated). A high ratio suggests that a county or municipality is investing in its capital assets; a low ratio, that a local unit needs to review its annual investment in capital assets.

Financial Forecasting

Financial condition analysis provides extremely important information about capital budgeting and finance; however, financial ratios are typically calculated from audited financial statements (historical data). The second management tool, which is more aligned with the CIP, is financial forecasting—a projection of revenues and expenditures (expenses) over a selected period of time to show the future operating results of a fund on the basis of an agreed-upon set of assumptions.[83] Research has shown that a five-year model is standard in local government, which reconciles with the typical CIP.[84] The implementation of a capital budget and CIP, as previously discussed, addresses the operating results of the respective funds based on additional debt-service payments, changes in positions and operating expenses, and additional revenue. Financial forecasting provides local officials with a methodology to estimate how the acquisition of capital assets contained in the CIP will affect the relationship between the inflow and outflow of resources in a fund over the selected forecast period.

Table 3.2 presents an example of a five-year financial forecast for a local government's general fund. The forecast of all revenues and expenditures is based on a 2 percent growth rate, except for property taxes and debt service. The forecast for property taxes is based on a 3 percent growth rate, and the forecast for debt service is based on amortization schedules. The current fiscal year (CFY) balance, as noted, is an estimate based on nine months of annualized data; however, the estimate shows that revenues are expected to exceed expenditures by $5,449 for the CFY, increasing fund balance by that amount. The forecast shows that estimated revenues are expected to exceed estimated expenditures for the following two fiscal years, increasing fund balance to $134,947 at the end of fiscal year 2024. The forecast then shows that estimated expenditures are expected to exceed estimated revenues for the remaining three fiscal years, reducing fund balance to $79,935 at the end of fiscal year 2027. The reason for the reverse in trend is that the local government expects to double its debt-service payment from $50,000 to $100,000 in fiscal year 2025 due to the implementation of its CIP.

83. Larry Schroeder, "Local Government Multiyear Budgetary Forecasting: Some Administrative and Political Issues," *Public Administration Review* 42, no. 2 (1982): 121–27.

84. William C. Rivenbark, "Financial Forecasting for North Carolina Local Governments," *Popular Government* 73, no. 1 (Fall 2007): 6–13.

Table 3.2   Five-Year Financial Forecast for General Fund

Item	CFY* FY 2022	Forecast FY 2023	FY 2024	FY 2025	FY 2026	FY 2027
Fund balance, beginning	$100,000	$105,449	$117,006	$134,947	$109,551	$91,112
Revenues						
Property taxes	500,140	515,144	530,598	546,516	562,911	579,799
Local option sales taxes	101,985	104,024	106,105	108,227	110,391	112,600
Permits and fees	52,444	53,492	54,562	55,653	56,767	57,902
Intergovernmental	50,000	51,000	52,020	53,060	54,121	55,204
Sanitation fees	74,785	76,280	77,806	79,362	80,949	82,568
Total	779,354	799,940	821,091	842,818	865,139	888,073
Expenditures						
Administration	100,691	102,705	104,759	106,854	108,991	111,171
Public safety	246,123	251,045	256,066	261,188	266,411	271,740
Environmental services	182,654	186,307	190,033	193,834	197,711	201,665
Transportation	98,585	100,557	102,568	104,619	106,712	108,846
Parks and recreation	95,852	97,769	99,724	101,719	103,753	105,828
Debt service	50,000	50,000	50,000	100,000	100,000	100,000
Total	773,905	788,383	803,150	868,214	883,578	899,250
Difference	5,449	11,557	17,941	(25,396)	(18,439)	(11,177)
Fund balance, ending	$105,449	$117,006	$134,947	$109,551	$91,112	$79,935

*Current fiscal year (CFY) balance is an estimate based on nine months of annualized data.

The five-year financial forecast shown in Table 3.2 gives local officials time to begin discussing how the county or municipality can afford the additional debt-service payment schedule for fiscal year 2025. Changes can be made to operating revenues and expenditures, for example, or to the capital budget and CIP to reduce the impact of taking on more debt. Local officials need information on the different ways in which counties and municipalities in North Carolina can use pay-as-you-go strategies to acquire capital assets and on how they can issue and structure debt to accommodate the needs of the organization and community.

Summary

Local units in North Carolina are required to budget and spend money in accordance with the Local Government Budget and Fiscal Control Act (LGBFCA), which provides a comprehensive legal framework for preparing, adopting, and amending the units' annual budget ordinance, financial plans, and project ordinances. Most of this chapter, as a result, focused on interpreting the numerous statutes in the LGBFCA, including the definition of a balanced budget ordinance, the limits on appropriations and interfund transfers, the adoption and amending of the budget ordinance, and the use of financial plans and project ordinances. After a brief overview of budgetary accounting, the chapter presented management tools and processes used by local government to make budgetary decisions within the broader context of the organization.

Chapter 4

Revenue Sources

by Connor H. Crews

Introduction

The governing board of a unit of local government must identify and obtain sufficient revenue to cover the costs of the services it provides. Although the services that a given North Carolina county or municipality chooses to offer can vary between jurisdictions, all county and municipal officials must understand how to legally finance the services in which their unit engages.

North Carolina law requires counties and municipalities[1] to provide for and fund, in whole or in part, certain activities. Although municipalities must provide only one service—building code enforcement—counties must fund a wide variety of services, including public education, social service programs, mental health programs, emergency medical services (EMS), courts, jail facilities, and building code enforcement. Counties and municipalities also have legal authority to provide a range of other services that include, among other things, zoning and land use planning, water and sewer utility services, recreation and cultural activities, and economic development. With a few notable exceptions, counties and municipalities legally may provide, and fund, most of the same discretionary services.

North Carolina's counties and municipalities may only impose taxes and fees when the General Assembly gives them such authority. At present, the major sources of revenue available to counties and municipalities are (1) locally imposed taxes; (2) locally imposed user fees, assessments, and charges; and (3) taxes and charges imposed by the state but shared in part with each type of local government.

A local government's choice of revenue mechanism has legal implications, including whom and what the unit can legally tax or charge, and what procedures the unit must follow to impose the tax or fee. For example, if a county or municipality chooses to fund its services through the imposition of a property (*ad valorem*) tax, then property owned by government and nonprofit organizations (e.g., religious organizations, state agencies, public and private educational institutions, and federal facilities) in the jurisdiction will be exempt from taxation. In addition, North Carolina law may restrict the rate of tax that a unit charges and, under certain circumstances, require a unit to obtain voter approval to levy a tax. Conversely, a unit employing a user fee to fund a service, in part or in whole, typically only requires that those availing themselves of the service pay. In such a case, a unit's rate structure must be reasonable and bear some relationship to the service provided to each user.

Appendix 4.1, "Local Revenue Authority and Limitations," outlines the major revenue sources available to North Carolina's counties and municipalities. It specifies (1) whether the source of revenue is available to counties, municipalities, or both types of units; (2) whether the General Assembly has authorized the imposition of the tax, fee, charge, or assessment through general law or local act; and (3) any restrictions on the use of proceeds. The remainder of this chapter describes each revenue source in more detail.

---

1. As used in this book, the term "municipality" is synonymous with "city," "town," and "village."

Local Taxes

Taxes are compulsory charges that governments levy upon individuals, entities (e.g., corporations), or property.[2] In general, the amount or character of a tax need not bear any relationship to the benefit that a taxing government provides to a taxpayer.[3]

A unit of local government may levy a tax only with legislative authorization—via general law or local act—from the General Assembly. The legislature has authorized counties and municipalities to levy a range of taxes. The majority of county and municipal revenues in North Carolina consist of two types of taxes: property (*ad valorem*) taxes and local sales and use taxes. Both counties and municipalities may levy property taxes; only counties may levy local sales and use taxes, but by law, municipalities are entitled to a share of the proceeds of most of these taxes. This section details property taxes, local sales and use taxes, and other taxes that North Carolina's local governments may levy.

The Property (*Ad Valorem*) Tax

The property tax is levied against real and personal property within the jurisdiction of a unit of local government. It attaches to property—not just to the property owner. The following sections describe the property tax in more detail.

Property Tax Base

A "tax base" consists of assets that a governmental entity may tax. The tax base for local property taxation in North Carolina consists of real property (e.g., land, buildings, and other improvements to land); personal property (e.g., business equipment and automobiles); and the property of public service companies (e.g., electric power companies, telephone companies, railroads, airlines, and certain other companies) that is not exempt or excluded from taxation.[4]

Certain types of property are exempt from taxation. For example, the North Carolina Constitution exempts government-owned property from taxation.[5] In addition, the General Assembly may, on a generally applicable statewide basis, exempt certain property from taxation or classify property to exclude it from taxation, reduce its valuation, or subject it to a reduced tax rate.[6] A local government may not exempt, classify, or otherwise give a tax preference to property within its jurisdiction.

---

2. *See generally* Barnhill Sanitation Serv., Inc. v. Gaston Cnty., 87 N.C. App. 532, 541 (1987) (noting that a "tax" within the meaning of the North Carolina Constitution is a "charge levied and collected as a contribution to the maintenance of the general government, and . . . is imposed upon the citizens in common at regularly recurring periods for the purpose of providing a continuous revenue").

3. *But see* N.C. CONST. art. V, § 2(1) (requiring that "[t]he power of taxation . . . be exercised in a just and equitable manner"); IMT, Inc. v. City of Lumberton, 366 N.C. 456 (2013) (holding that a municipality's 59,500 percent increase in privilege license tax upon for-profit businesses operating sweepstakes violated Article V, § 2(1) of the North Carolina Constitution).

4. Chapter 5, "Property Tax Policy and Administration," discusses the administration of the property tax in much greater detail.

5. *See* N.C. CONST. art. V, §§ 2(2), (3).

6. *See* N.C. CONST. art. V, §§ 2(2), (3); Chapter 105, Sections 275 through 282.1 of the North Carolina General Statutes (hereinafter G.S.).

Tax Rate Limitations and Voter Approval

North Carolina law does not require a county or municipality to always levy a property tax. Instead, the governing board of each municipality and county must determine whether to levy a property tax each year and, if it chooses to levy a property tax, the applicable rate or rates of taxation.

A governing board may adopt a single tax rate and use the revenue generated from the tax to fund a variety of services. Alternatively, a board may adopt a series of tax rates and earmark the proceeds for specific services.[7] A governing board also may adopt a combination of these two methods. For example, a county's governing board might establish a combined rate of property tax for most of its programs and services but a separate rate for public schools, libraries, or fire services.

Property taxes are subject to statutory rate limitations and, in a few cases, must be approved by the voters. In particular, the North Carolina Constitution prohibits the General Assembly from authorizing any "unit of local government to levy taxes on property except for purposes authorized by general law uniformly applicable throughout the State, *unless the tax is approved by a majority of the qualified voters of the unit who vote thereon.*"[8] In other words, a local government must obtain voter approval to levy a property tax unless the General Assembly has authorized all units across the state to levy property taxes for a particular purpose.

The General Assembly has enacted two statutes that list the purposes for and rates at which counties and municipalities may levy property taxes without voter approval: Chapter 153A, Section 149 of the North Carolina General Statutes (hereinafter G.S.) for counties, and G.S. 160A-209 for municipalities.

Under these statutes, a unit's combined rates of property tax generally may not exceed $1.50 per $100.00 of assessed valuation.[9] Counties and municipalities may levy some property taxes without limitation on the rate or amount.[10] For example, a municipality may levy taxes without any rate restriction to fund debt service on its general obligation debt.[11] Counties may levy property taxes without any rate restriction to finance many of the services that they legally must provide: court operations and facilities, schools, social services, courts, jails, and elections.[12]

A county or municipality may seek voter approval to use property tax proceeds to fund an activity not specified in G.S. 153A-149 or 160A-209 but which the respective unit has statutory authority to undertake.[13] It also may seek voter approval to increase a county's or municipality's overall property tax rate cap above $1.50 per $100.00 of assessed valuation.[14]

---

7. The governing board of a unit of local government has no legal obligation to spend the tax proceeds according to designations in the budget ordinance or on a taxpayer's tax bill. *See* Long v. Comm'rs of Richmond Cnty., 76 N.C. 273, 280 (1877).

8. N.C. CONST. art. V, § 2(5) (emphasis added).

9. *See* G.S. 153A-149(c) (counties); 160A-209(c) (municipalities).

10. *See* G.S. 153A-149(b) (counties); 160A-209(b) (municipalities).

11. *See, e.g.,* G.S. 160A-209(b)(1).

12. G.S. 153A-149(b)(1)–(2), (4)–(5), (7)–(8).

13. *See* G.S. 153A-149(d); 160A-209(e).

14. *See* G.S. 153A-149(e); 160A-209(f). In Fiscal Year 2022–2023, the highest rate of county property tax was $.9900 per $100.00 of assessed valuation (Scotland County), while the highest rate of municipal property tax was $.9270 per $100.00 of assessed valuation (Enfield). *See* N.C. Department of Revenue, *Fiscal Year 2022-2023 County and Municipal Property Tax Rates and Year of Most Recent Reappraisal*

Tax Levy Formula

Governing boards of counties and municipalities must adopt a balanced budget for each fiscal year, whereby the sum of estimated net revenues and appropriated fund balance is equal to the appropriations in each fund.[15] If a unit's estimated revenues from sources other than the property tax *plus* appropriated fund balance will not equal the appropriations in each fund, a county or municipality must levy a property tax at a rate sufficient to balance the budget.[16]

To determine its annual property tax rate, a local government can follow the steps below. Following Steps 1 through 3 will yield the variables needed to perform the calculation set forth in Step 4.

Step 1: Determine the unit's total estimated appropriations (i.e., expenditures) and the amount of money that revenue sources other than the property tax are expected to yield. The difference between the unit's total estimated expenditures and revenues is the amount necessary to balance the unit's budget. This total is the "Estimated Required Property Tax Revenue."

Step 2: Determine the percentage of property taxes collected in the prior fiscal year, expressed as a decimal (e.g., 0.95). This total is the "Last Fiscal Year Collection Percentage."[17]

Step 3: Determine the total value of taxable property in the jurisdiction. This total is the "Total Taxable Valuation of Property."

Step 4: Using the figures from Steps 1 through 3, perform the calculation below. The resulting figure is the rate of property tax per $100.00 assessed valuation.

$$\left(\frac{\left(\dfrac{\textit{Estimated Required Property Tax Revenue}}{\textit{Last Fiscal Year Collection Percentage}} \right)}{\textit{Total Taxable Valuation of Property}} \right) * (\$100.00) = \textit{Rate of Property Tax}$$

To illustrate, assume that (1) a unit must obtain $10,000,000.00 in property taxes to balance its budget; (2) its rate of property taxes collected in the prior fiscal year was 95 percent (or 0.95); (3) the unit's taxable valuation of property is $1.5 billion. Using these figures in the formula above yields a tax rate of $.7017 per $100.00 of assessed valuation.

The governing board of a county or municipality sets its rates of property tax when it adopts its annual budget ordinance—and with very limited exceptions, the governing board may not

---

(last visited Feb. 28, 2023). Therefore, a referendum to raise the rate of property tax above $1.50 per $100.00 of assessed valuation is unlikely to occur.

15. G.S. 159-13(c).

16. *See* G.S. 159-13(c).

17. Because some individuals and entities fail to pay property taxes when due, local governments never collect the full property tax levy (i.e., the total dollar value of the tax enacted). Instead, North Carolina's local governments collect on average between 96 and 99 percent of their levy. See, e.g., the following memoranda from the N.C. Department of State Treasurer, State and Local Government Finance Division and the Local Government Commission (LGC): LGC Memo #2022-03, *Management of Cash and Taxes and Fund Balance Available — Counties — for the Fiscal Year Ended June 30, 2020* (Aug. 11, 2021), 2; LGC Memo #2022-04, *Management of Cash and Taxes and Fund Balance Available —Municipalities— for the Fiscal Year Ended June 30, 2020* (Aug. 17, 2021), 2–3. When setting the rate of property tax, North Carolina law prohibits a county or municipality from using a percentage of property taxes collected that exceeds the percentage of the levy actually realized in cash as of June 30 during the preceding fiscal year. *See* G.S. 159-13(b)(6).

Table 4.1. Primary Purposes for Which Counties and Municipalities May Create Service Districts

Authorized County Service Districts[a]	Authorized Municipal Service Districts[b]
• Beach erosion and flood and hurricane protection works • Fire protection • Recreation • Sewage collection and disposal • Solid waste collection and disposal • Water supply and distribution • Ambulance and rescue services • Watershed improvement, drainage, and water resources development • Cemeteries	• Beach erosion and flood and hurricane protection works • Downtown revitalization projects • Urban area revitalization projects • Transit-oriented development projects • Drainage projects • Sewage collection and disposal systems • Off-street parking facilities • Watershed improvement, drainage, and water resources development projects

a. G.S. 153A-301(a)(1)–(11). Counties may create service districts for a few other specified purposes.
b. G.S. 160A-536(a)(1)–(6). Municipalities may create service districts for a few other specified purposes.

change a rate of property tax after adopting a budget.[18] Property taxes are due on September 1, but taxpayers may delay payment until January 5 without incurring a penalty.[19] As a result, local governments typically do not receive the bulk of property taxes owed until the middle of their fiscal year and must rely on fund balances and other revenue sources to finance expenditures during the first part of the fiscal year.

Uniformity of Taxation and Special Taxing Districts

Although the North Carolina Constitution requires that a local government's rates of property tax be uniform throughout each jurisdiction,[20] it also authorizes the General Assembly to permit counties and municipalities to (1) delineate one or more geographic areas within the unit as special taxing districts and (2) levy taxes within those districts to finance or provide services or facilities to a greater extent than those financed or provided in other parts of the jurisdiction.[21] The General Assembly has exercised that authority in several cases described below.

Special Taxing Districts

Service Districts

The General Assembly has authorized counties and municipalities to create "service districts."[22] Service districts are geographic areas within which a county or municipality may levy additional property taxes to provide services or capital projects in the district. Counties and municipalities may establish service districts for the respective purposes listed in Table 4.1.

---

18. *See* G.S. 159-15. The governing board may not amend the rate of property tax unless (1) ordered to do so by a court of competent jurisdiction or by a state agency with authority to compel property taxes or (2) the local government receives revenues that are "substantially more or less than the amount anticipated." *Id.*

19. *See* G.S. 105-360(a).

20. *See* N.C. Const. art. V, § 2(2).

21. N.C. Const. art. V, § 2(4).

22. G.S. Ch. 153A, Art. 16 (counties); Ch. 160A, Art. 23 (municipalities).

Counties most often use service districts to finance the operational and capital expenses of fire and rescue services.[23] Municipalities most often use service districts to finance projects and programs in their central business districts.[24]

— Process for Establishing a Service District

Counties and municipalities follow different statutory procedures to establish service districts. Those procedures are detailed in tables 4.2 and 4.3.

The governing board may initiate the process of creating a service district upon its own accord—it need not receive a petition from property owners.[25] Nor must a county or municipality obtain voter approval via referendum to create a service district. A county service district may not include land within the corporate limits of a city or sanitary district unless the governing body of the city or sanitary district agrees, by resolution, to such inclusion.[26]

— Taxing Authority in a Service District

Under North Carolina law, a service district is not a unit of government. It is instead a geographic designation: a portion of a county's or municipality's territory in which the county or municipality, respectively, may levy an extra property tax to provide specific services or capital projects benefitting property within that district.

— District Tax Rate

The governing board of a unit that has created a service district may, but is not required to, levy an additional tax upon all taxable properties within the district. A unit that chooses to levy a service-district tax typically sets the district tax rate each year in its annual budget ordinance. The rate of service-district tax, when combined with the unit's generally applicable rate of property tax, may not exceed $1.50 per $100.00 of assessed valuation of property in the district unless a majority of voters residing within the district approve such a rate.[27]

Statutory exemptions and exclusions to the property (*ad valorem*) tax also apply to service-district taxes.[28] If real or personal property is exempt from property tax, it also is exempt from service-district tax.

A unit must use all proceeds of service-district taxes to provide services or undertake capital projects in the district,[29] but it also may use other unrestricted revenues to provide

---

23. For more information on taxing districts for fire services, see Kara A. Millonzi, "County Funding for Fire Services in North Carolina," *Local Finance Bulletin* No. 43 (May 2011).

24. For more information on taxing districts for downtown revitalization, see Kara Millonzi, "A Guide to Business Improvement Districts in North Carolina," *Coates' Canons: NC Local Government Law* blog (April 1, 2010).

25. *But see* G.S. 160A-537(a1) (permitting owners of property to petition the governing board of a municipality to create a service district).

26. *See* G.S. 153A-302(a1).

27. *See* G.S. 153A-307; 160A-542(c). In 2015, the legislature placed an additional limitation on a municipality's rate-setting process, requiring a municipal governing board to set the rate of service-district tax "so that there is no accumulation of excess funds beyond that necessary to meet current needs, fund long-range plans and goals, and maintain a reasonable fund balance." *See* G.S. 160A-542(d); S.L. 2015-241, § 15.16B.(b). No comparable restriction applies to rates of county service-district taxes.

28. *See* G.S. 105-274(a).

29. *See* G.S. 153A-307; 160A-542(a).

Table 4.2. Required Procedures for Establishing a County Service District

Step	Required Action
1[a]	The governing board must consider • resident or seasonal population and population density of proposed district, • appraised value of property subject to taxation, • present tax rates of the county and any cities or special districts in which the district or any portion thereof is located, • the ability of the proposed district to sustain the additional taxes necessary to provide the services planned for the district, and • any other matters that county commissioners believe might have a bearing on whether the district should be established.
2[b]	The governing board must find that • there is a demonstrable need for providing one or more authorized services in the district, • it is impossible or impracticable to provide those services on a countywide basis, • it is economically feasible to provide the proposed services in the district without unreasonable or burdensome annual tax levies, and • there is a demonstrable demand for the proposed services by persons residing in the district.
3[c]	Staff must prepare a report containing • a map of the proposed district, showing its proposed boundaries; • a statement showing that the proposed district meets the standards set out in Step 1; and • a plan for providing one or more of the authorized services.
4[d]	Staff must make the report available in the office of the clerk to the governing board for at least four weeks prior to the public hearing on the proposed service district.
5[e]	Staff must prepare notice of public hearing. The notice must include • the date and hour of the hearing, • the place of the hearing, • the subject of the hearing, • a map of the proposed district, and • a statement that the report described in Step 3 is available for public inspection in the office of the clerk to the governing board.
6[f]	Staff must mail notice to all owners of property in the proposed service district, as reflected in the county tax records on January 1 of the preceding year, at least four weeks prior to the date of the hearing.
7[g]	Staff must certify in writing to the governing board that the mailing required by Step 6 has been completed.
8[h]	Staff must publish notice of public hearing at least one week prior to the date of the public hearing on the proposed service district.
9	The governing board must hold a public hearing on the proposed district.
10[i]	The governing board adopts a resolution establishing the district. The district may take effect at the beginning of a future fiscal year.

a. G.S. 153A-302(a).

b. G.S. 153A-302(a1).

c. G.S. 153A-302(b).

d. G.S. 153A-302(b).

e. G.S. 153A-302(c).

f. G.S. 153A-302(c). A county need not mail notice to all property owners if (1) the board proposes to create a service district and (2) the board publishes a notice of proposal to establish the district once per week for four successive weeks before the date of the public hearing on the proposed district. *See* G.S. 153A-302(e) (countywide law enforcement district); 153A-302(f) (countywide districts for counties in which only one incorporated municipality is located within the county but whose land area is located primarily in another county and consists of less than 100 acres in such a county).

g. G.S. 153A-302(c).

h. G.S. 153A-302(c).

i. G.S. 153A-302(d).

Table 4.3. Required Procedures for Establishing a Municipal Service District

Step	Required Action	
1	**Board-Initiated Process**[a] The governing board must find that a proposed district is in need of one or more authorized services, facilities, or functions. **OR**	**Citizen-Initiated Process**[b] A majority of the owners of real property within a municipality must submit a petition to the governing board establishing that the area is in need of one or more authorized services, facilities, or functions. The petition must contain • the names, addresses, and signatures of the real property owners within the proposed district; • the proposed district boundaries; and • the authorized services, facilities, or functions that would serve as the basis for establishing the proposed district.
2[c]	Staff must prepare a report containing • a map of the proposed service district, showing its proposed boundaries; • a statement showing that the proposed district meets the standards set out in Step 1; and • a plan for providing one or more of the authorized services.	
3[d]	Staff must make the report available in the office of the clerk to the governing board for at least four weeks prior to public hearing on the proposed service district.	
4[e]	Staff must prepare notice of public hearing. The notice must include • the date and hour of the hearing, • the place of the hearing, • the subject of the hearing, • a map of the proposed district, and • a statement that the report described in Step 3 is available for public inspection in the office of the clerk to the governing board.	
5[f]	Staff must mail notice to all owners of property in the proposed service district, as reflected in the county tax records on January 1 of the preceding year, at least four weeks prior to the date of the hearing.	
6[g]	Staff must certify in writing to the governing board that the mailing required by Step 5 has been completed.	
7[h]	Staff must publish notice of public hearing at least one week prior to the date of the public hearing on the proposed service district.	
8[i]	The governing board must hold a public hearing on the proposed district.	
9[j]	At the public hearing or no later than five days after the date of the public hearing, an owner of a tract or parcel of land located within the proposed service district may submit a written request to the governing board asking that the owner's tract or parcel be excluded from the proposed district. The request must specify • the tract or parcel for which exclusion is requested; • the particular reason(s) why the tract or parcel is not in need of the services, facilities, or functions of the proposed district to a demonstrably greater extent than the remainder of the tracts and parcels in the municipality; and • any other additional information the owner deems relevant.	
10[k]	If the governing board finds that a tract or parcel for which exclusion is requested is not in need of the services, facilities, or functions of the proposed service district, the board may, but is not required to, exclude the tract or parcel from the proposed district.	
11[l]	At a meeting of the governing board, a majority of voting members present must vote to adopt an ordinance establishing the service district. The district may take effect at the beginning of a future fiscal year unless the adopting ordinance states that general obligation bonds or special obligation bonds are anticipated to be authorized for the project. In that case, the governing board may make the ordinance effective immediately or as otherwise specified in the ordinance—but the municipality may not levy an *ad valorem* tax for a partial fiscal year.	
12[m]	At a second meeting of the governing board, a majority of voting members present must vote to adopt an ordinance establishing the service district.	

a. G.S. 160A-537(a).

b. G.S. 160A-537(a1). The governing board may, but is not required to, establish a policy to hear all petitions at regular intervals, but no less than once per year. *Id.*

c. G.S. 160A-537(b).

d. G.S. 160A-537(b).

e. G.S. 160A-537(c).

f. G.S. 160A-537(c).

g. G.S. 160A-537(c).

h. G.S. 160A-537(c).

i. G.S. 160A-537(c).

j. G.S. 160A-537(c1).

k. G.S. 160A-537(c1).

l. G.S. 160A-537(d).

m. G.S. 160A-537(f).

services or undertake capital projects within the district. A unit may not appropriate proceeds of service-district taxes for other purposes unrelated to the district.[30]

— PROVIDING SERVICES AND PROJECTS IN A SERVICE DISTRICT

A municipality may "provide services, facilities, functions, or promotional and developmental activities in a service district with its own forces, through a contract with another governmental agency, or by any combination thereof."[31] If a county or municipality levies a service-district tax, it must "provide, maintain, or let contracts for" the services involved within a reasonable time not exceeding one year.[32] In addition, a contract between a municipality and a third-party service provider must

(1) specify the purposes for which municipal funds will be used;
(2) require an appropriate accounting of moneys paid out under the contract at the end of a fiscal year (or another appropriate period of time); and
(3) if the contract is between a municipality and a private agency, require the private entity to provide certain information about subcontractors, including "the name, location, purpose, and amount paid to any person or persons with whom the private agency contracted to perform or complete any purpose for which [municipal] moneys were used for that service district."[33]

A municipality that contracts with a private third-party service provider in certain historic district overlay service districts and in service districts created for downtown revitalization or urban area revitalization also must (1) require the private provider to report annually to the municipality; (2) specify, by contract, the scope of services to be provided; and (3) limit any contract to a term of five years or less.[34] Such a municipality also must (1) solicit public input from district residents prior to entering into a contract; (2) use a bid process to select the private provider; and (3) hold a public hearing on the proposed contract, with notice of the hearing published in a newspaper of general circulation for at least two successive weeks prior to the hearing.[35]

---

30. *See* G.S. 159-13(b)(18) (prohibiting appropriations from a service-district fund to any other fund except (1) to the appropriate debt-service fund or (2) to an appropriate account in a capital reserve fund unless the district has been abolished).

31. G.S. 160A-536(d). While an exact copy of this authorizing authority does not appear in G.S. Chapter 153A, Article 16, counties likely have comparable authority under their general authority to "contract with and appropriate money to any person, association, or corporation, in order to carry out any public purpose that the county is authorized by law to engage in." G.S. 153A-449(a).

32. G.S. 153A-305(a); 160A-540(a).

33. G.S. 160A-536(d). A county should, but is not statutorily required to, include similar provisions in its contracts with service providers in county service districts.

34. *See* G.S. 160A-536(d1). For more information, see Kara Millonzi, "2015 Changes to Municipal Service District (MSD) Authority," *Coates' Canons: NC Local Government Law* blog (Oct. 19, 2015).

35. *See* G.S. 160A-536(d1). Comparable requirements do not apply to any county service district.

— Borrowing Money to Fund Capital Projects in a Service District
In general, a county or municipality may borrow money to fund capital projects located in a service district to the same extent, and in the same manner, as it funds similar projects outside of a service district. For more detailed information on this topic, see Chapter 7, "Financing Capital Projects."

Other Special Taxing Districts
Counties also may establish special taxing districts for rural fire-protection services,[36] public schools,[37] and water and sewer services.[38] These districts provide counties with additional mechanisms to fund capital and operating expenses for the statutorily specified purposes. For a county to levy a tax for rural fire protection or public schools, a majority of qualified county voters voting in a referendum must approve the tax.[39]

Local Sales and Use Taxes

North Carolina sales and use taxes are comprised of two components: (1) a tax on the retail sale of certain "items" (including tangible personal property, certain digital property, and some services)[40] and (2) a complementary "use" tax on (a) tangible personal property purchased, leased, or rented for storage or use in North Carolina; (b) certain digital property purchased for storage or use in the state; or (c) services sourced to North Carolina.[41] Where a retailer fails to collect sales tax upon a taxable sale, the individual or entity that uses the item sold must pay use tax at an equivalent rate of tax.[42]

The State of North Carolina levies statewide sales and use taxes upon certain items—generally at a rate of 4.75 percent—but certain types of local governments also may levy "local" sales and use taxes that apply apart from this statewide rate. This section describes (1) which local governments may impose "local" sales and use taxes, (2) how local sales and use taxes are collected, and (3) how the proceeds of local sales and use taxes are allocated among each county and distributed for use.

Authority to Impose Local Sales and Use Taxes

Only counties—not municipalities within those counties—may levy local sales and use taxes. As of July 1, 2023, Chapter 105 of the General Statutes provides that authority to counties in four separate articles: Article 39 (authorizing the imposition of a 1-cent tax); Article 40 (authorizing the imposition of a 0.5-cent tax); Article 42 (authorizing the imposition of a 0.5-cent tax); and Article 46 (authorizing the imposition of a 0.25-cent tax). As of December 31, 2022, all counties

---

36. G.S. Ch. 69, Art. 3A.
37. G.S. Ch. 115C, Art. 36.
38. G.S. Ch. 162, Art. 6.
39. *See* G.S. 69-25.1–.25.4 (rural fire-protection services); 115C-508(b) (public schools).
40. *See* G.S. 105-164.4(a).
41. G.S. 105-164.6(a).
42. *See* G.S. 105-164.6(b).

levy Article 39, 40, and 42 taxes, but only 47 counties levy Article 46 taxes.[43] Counties may levy Article 46 taxes only with voter approval.[44]

Each Article sets out the sales and uses to which its sales and use taxes apply. The tax bases for local sales and use taxes and statewide sales and use taxes are not identical.[45] For example, sales of non-prepared food (i.e., groceries) are not subject to statewide sales and use tax but are subject to Article 39, 40, and 42 taxes.[46]

Collection of Local Sales and Use Taxes

Retailers must collect local sales taxes in connection with each taxable sale and remit the proceeds to the North Carolina Department of Revenue (NCDOR).[47] If a retailer fails to collect sales tax, the purchaser or user of an item must remit use tax—at a rate equivalent to the rate of applicable sales tax—to NCDOR.[48] Counties and municipalities have no legal obligation or authority to collect local sales or use taxes from public or private organizations with such liabilities.

Allocation of Local Sales and Use Taxes

Once NCDOR collects local sales and use taxes, it allocates the revenues of each local sales and use tax according to restrictions contained in each local sales and use tax Article.

NCDOR allocates the revenues of Article 39 and 42 taxes to counties on a point-of-origin basis, meaning generally that NCDOR sources proceeds of each tax to the county in which the purchased goods are delivered.[49] NCDOR allocates the revenues of Article 40 taxes among counties on a *per capita* basis, meaning that the allocation is based solely upon the relative population of each county—not upon the amount of taxable transactions occurring in each jurisdiction.[50] NCDOR allocates the revenues of Article 46 taxes to the counties in which the purchased goods are delivered.[51]

By statute, NCDOR makes further adjustments to these initial allocations. For example, NCDOR adjusts each county's initial *per capita* allocation of Article 40 taxes by multiplying that allocation by an "adjustment factor" for each county specified in the General Statutes.[52] This

---

43. *See* Ronald G. Penny, N.C. Department of Revenue, *Memorandum to Finance Directors of Counties and Municipalities, Local Government Sales and Use Tax Distribution* (Feb. 10, 2023).

44. *See* G.S. 105-537.

45. Each Article sets forth the sales and uses to which the particular local sales and use tax applies. *See* G.S. 105-467, -468, -468.1 (Article 39); 105-483 (Article 40); 105-498 (Article 42); 105-538 (Article 46).

46. *See* G.S. 105-467(a)(5) (imposing Article 39 tax upon the sales price of food exempt from state sales and use tax pursuant to G.S. 105-164.13B); 105-483 (imposing same rule upon Article 40 tax); 105-498 (imposing same rule upon Article 42 tax).

47. *See* G.S. 105-471 (Article 39); 105-483 (Article 40); 105-498 (Article 42); 105-538 (Article 46).

48. *See* G.S. 105-471 (Article 39); 105-483 (Article 40); 105-498 (Article 42); 105-538 (Article 46).

49. *See* G.S. 105-472(a) (Article 39); 105-501(a) (Article 42). This allocation method results in higher relative allocations of sales taxes to counties with higher levels of commercial activity. To learn more about how North Carolina law "sources" a taxable sale or use to a particular jurisdiction for the purposes of sales and use tax, see Connor Crews, "Location, Location, Location: Sourcing Principles for North Carolina Sales and Use Taxes," *Coates' Canons: NC Local Government Law* blog (Oct. 20, 2022). Proceeds of Article 39, 40, and 42 taxes levied on food undergo an alternate allocation. *See* G.S. 105-469(a).

50. *See* G.S. 105-486(a). This allocation results in higher relative allocations of sales taxes to counties with larger populations.

51. *See* G.S. 105-538.

52. *See* G.S. 105-486(b).

adjustment causes some counties to receive more and some counties to receive less in Article 40 taxes than they would receive under a pure *per capita* allocation.

The statutes also direct NCDOR to further adjust the allocations of Article 39, 40, and 42 taxes. In particular, it must place a portion of each of these taxes into a separate "statewide pool" created under Article 44 of G.S. Chapter 105.[53] Beginning in Fiscal Year 2016–2017, the General Statutes directed NCDOR to place a total of $84,800,000.00, deducted and divided proportionally from Article 39, 40, and 42 taxes otherwise allocated to each county, into this Article 44 "statewide pool."[54] In each fiscal year following Fiscal Year 2016–2017, NCDOR has adjusted and will continue to adjust this total amount based upon the annual percentage change in Article 39, 40, and 42 collections. NCDOR allocates the "statewide pool" to each county based upon an "allocation percentage," which results in seventy-nine generally more rural counties receiving an allocation and twenty-one generally more urban counties not receiving an allocation from the statewide pool.[55]

Distribution of Local Sales and Use Tax Proceeds

On a monthly basis, NCDOR distributes the allocated proceeds of local sales and use taxes under Articles 39, 40, 42, and 46, as well as the Article 44 statewide pool.[56]

Distributions of Article 39, 40, 42 Taxes and Article 44 Statewide Pool Moneys

Although NCDOR allocates all the proceeds of Article 39, 40, and 42 taxes and Article 44 statewide pool moneys to counties, it ultimately does not distribute all of these proceeds to counties. Instead, the General Statutes direct NCDOR to distribute a portion of the proceeds of these taxes to municipalities.

North Carolina law entitles the governing board of each county to annually choose one of two methods that NCDOR must follow to distribute the allocated proceeds of Article 39, 40, and 42 taxes and Article 44 statewide pool moneys to counties and municipalities located within their county: (1) the *per capita* method, under which NCDOR divides and distributes the proceeds of taxes allocated to each county between the county and each municipality located in the county based upon their relative populations, or (2) the *ad valorem* method, under which NCDOR divides and distributes the proceeds of taxes allocated to each county based upon the relative property tax levies of the county and each municipality located in the county.[57]

---

53. *See* G.S. 105-524(b).

54. *See* G.S. 105-524(b). The General Assembly projected that this amount would approximate the increase in local sales and use tax proceeds attributable to the expansion of the sales and use tax base to include certain repair, maintenance, and installation services to tangible personal property and motor vehicles.

55. *See* G.S. 105-524(c).

56. *See* G.S. 105-469 (Article 39 taxes on food); 105-472(a) (Article 39 taxes on non-food); 105-486(c) (Article 40); 105-501(a) (Article 42); 105-524 (Article 44 statewide pool); 105-538 (Art. 46). The Department of Revenue prepares monthly distribution reports, which are accessible online. *See* N.C. Department of Revenue, *Local Government Distributions* (last visited March 1, 2023).

57. *See* G.S. 105-472(b). The *ad valorem* method includes *ad valorem* taxes levied by a county or municipality on behalf of a taxing district (e.g., a service district or fire district) and collected by the county or municipality. *See* G.S. 105-472(b)(2). For more information on the *per capita* and *ad valorem* calculations, see Kara Millonzi, "Local Sales and Use Tax Distributions: Where Does the Money Go?," *Coates' Canons: NC Local Government Law* blog (Jan. 30, 2012). North Carolina law entitles counties—and counties

Boards of county commissioners must make this choice each April. After August 2021, any change in a method is effective as of the fiscal year following the succeeding fiscal year after the change occurs.[58] For example, a county's election to change distribution methods in April 2023 would become effective as of July 1, 2024.

Distributions of Article 46 Taxes

NCDOR distributes the allocated proceeds of Article 46 taxes only to counties.[59] Counties that levy Article 46 taxes are neither required nor authorized to share the proceeds of those taxes with their municipalities or other taxing units in the county.

Use of Local Sales and Use Tax Proceeds

Municipalities that receive distributions of Article 39, 40, and 42 tax proceeds or Article 44 statewide pool proceeds may use these moneys for any public purposes for which they have legal authority to expend funds.

Counties must reserve a portion of local sales tax proceeds that they receive for specific purposes. In particular, a county must reserve 60 percent of Article 42 tax proceeds and 30 percent of Article 40 tax proceeds for public school capital outlay or debt service incurred for public school construction projects.[60] A county also must use any proceeds of a distribution of Article 44 statewide pool proceeds for "economic development, public education, and community college" purposes.[61] Counties may use all other proceeds of Article 39, 40, and 42 taxes for any public purpose for which counties are authorized to engage.

"Hold Harmless" Payments and State Contributions

Medicaid Hold Harmless

In 2007 and 2008, the General Assembly adopted legislation that (1) limited and amended county and municipal authority to impose local sales and use taxes and (2) directed that the state assume responsibility for Medicaid expenses previously covered by county governments.[62] Under this legislation, counties must hold municipalities incorporated before October 1, 2008, harmless for the revenue that such a municipality would have received from a formerly authorized 0.50 percent local sales and use tax under Article 44 of G.S. Chapter 105 that was distributed on a point-of-origin basis.[63] In other words, each of these municipalities must continue to receive the equivalent amount of revenue were that tax still in effect.

---

alone—to elect the *per capita* method or *ad valorem* method. For more information, see Connor Crews, "N.C. Court of Appeals Addresses a Dispute Over Local Sales and Use Tax Distributions: Town of Boone v. Watauga County," *Coates' Canons: NC Local Government Law* blog (Nov. 22, 2022).

58. *See* S.L. 2021-124, § 1 (revising G.S. 105-472(b)).

59. *See* G.S. 105-538.

60. *See* G.S. 105-502(a) (Article 42); 105-487(a) (Article 40). If the amount allocated to a county under Article 40 is higher than the amount allocated to the county under Article 42, the county also must use 60 percent of the difference between those two amounts for public school capital outlay purposes. *See* G.S. 105-502(a).

61. G.S. 105-524(d).

62. *See* S.L. 2007-323, § 31; S.L. 2007-345, § 14; S.L. 2008-134, §§ 13–15. For more information on this legislation, see Kara A. Millonzi and William C. Rivenbark, "Phased Implementation of the 2007 and 2008 Medicaid Funding Reform Legislation in North Carolina," *Local Finance Bulletin* No. 38 (Sept. 2008).

63. *See* G.S. 105-522(b).

The General Statutes calculate that sum by adding (1) the proceeds of Article 40 sales and use tax allocated to a municipality (the "base hold harmless amount") to (2) 50 percent of the base hold-harmless amount *less* 25 percent of Article 39 sales and use tax proceeds allocated to a municipality.[64] The "base hold-harmless amount" accounts for the loss of Article 44 tax revenue, while the latter figure accounts for a change in distribution method in half of Article 42 sales and use tax proceeds from *per capita* to point-of-origin. NCDOR adds this total hold-harmless payment to the distributions of other local sales and use taxes that municipalities receive and derives the revenue to make this distribution from each county's allocation of Article 39 sales and use tax proceeds.[65]

Since Fiscal Year 2017–2018, the General Assembly has guaranteed to counties that if (1) the sum of the annual amount a county would have received from formerly-imposed Article 44 sales and use taxes (the "repealed sales tax amount")[66] *plus* the amount the county is required to pay to its municipalities to hold them harmless for the repeal of Article 44 sales and use taxes *exceeds* (2) the amount that the state assumed for the county's proportionate share of Medicaid costs, then the state shall pay that difference to a county.[67] NCDOR estimates all of these figures for a fiscal year and sends to eligible counties 90 percent of its estimated payment for that fiscal year with other sales tax distributions in March.[68] NCDOR then determines the actual estimated payment for the fiscal year by August 15 of the next fiscal year and remits the remaining balance to eligible counties.[69]

Transportation Sales and Use Taxes

Under Article 43 of G.S. Chapter 105, counties and certain transportation authorities also may levy an additional type of local sales tax—a transportation sales and use tax—to fund public transportation systems. Mecklenburg County; a regional transportation authority encompassing Wake, Durham, and/or Orange County; and a regional transportation authority encompassing Forsyth and/or Guilford Counties each may adopt a 0.5-cent sales and use tax.[70] All other counties may levy a 0.25-cent transportation sales and use tax.

---

64. *See* G.S. 105-522(a)(2). The amounts used in making this calculation do not reflect the reallocations under G.S. 105-524. *See* G.S. 105-522(a)(2).

65. *See* G.S. 105-522(b).

66. A county's "repealed sales tax amount" is equal to the sum of (1) the proceeds of Article 40 sales and use taxes allocated to a county and (2) 50 percent of Article 40 taxes allocated to a county *less* 25 percent of Article 39 sales and use tax proceeds allocated to a county. *See* G.S. 105-523(b)(3).

67. *See* G.S. 105-523(c). Prior to Fiscal Year 2014–2015, the General Assembly guaranteed that all counties would receive a net benefit of at least $500,000.00, but the General Assembly incrementally phased out that guarantee beginning in Fiscal Year 2014–2015. *See* S.L. 2014-100, §§ 37.2.(a), (b), (c), (d).

68. *See* G.S. 105-523(d).

69. *See* G.S. 105-523(d).

70. *See* G.S. Chapter 105, Article 43, Part 2 (Mecklenburg), Parts 3 and 4 (regional transportation authority encompassing Wake, Durham, and/or Orange County), Parts 3 and 5 (regional transportation authority encompassing Forsyth and/or Guilford County). As of March 1, 2023, the regional transportation authority that encompasses Wake, Durham, and/or Orange County is the Regional Triangle Regional Public Transportation Authority d/b/a GoTriangle. The regional transportation authority that encompasses Forsyth and/or Guilford County is the Piedmont Authority for Regional Transportation.

Governing boards of these units of local government may levy a transportation sales and use tax only after voters approve such a levy by referendum.[71] The proceeds of transportation sales and use taxes are allocated either to (1) one or more special districts that a regional transportation authority creates[72] or (2) on a *per capita* basis among the county and other units of local government in the county that operate public transportation systems.[73] In each case, counties, municipalities, and regional transportation authorities may only use the proceeds of transportation sales and use taxes for financing, constructing, operating, and maintaining public transportation systems.[74]

Other Local Taxes

The General Statutes authorize counties and municipalities to levy several other types of taxes, including a rental car gross receipts tax, an animal tax, a heavy equipment rental tax, and motor vehicle license taxes. The General Assembly also has authorized, via separate local acts, certain counties and municipalities to levy a variety of taxes, including occupancy taxes, prepared food and beverage taxes, deed transfer taxes, and motor vehicle taxes. This section details taxes authorized by general law and local act. Although these local taxes make up a relatively insignificant proportion of the total revenues that North Carolina's local governments receive, they produce, at a minimum, hundreds of thousands of dollars for many counties and municipalities—and even more for some of the state's largest local governments.

Taxes Authorized by General Law

Except for county motor vehicle license taxes and a portion of municipal motor vehicle license taxes, counties and municipalities may use the revenues from the taxes described in this section for any public purpose for which they may spend funds under general law.

Rental Car Gross Receipts Tax

Counties and municipalities may, but are not required to, levy a gross receipts tax on the "short-term lease or rental" of vehicles at retail.[75] The maximum rate of such tax, where levied, is 1.5 percent of the gross receipts derived from the short-term lease or rental of vehicles.[76]

---

71. *See* G.S. 105-507.1 (Mecklenburg); 105-509 (Wake, Durham, and Orange); 105-510 (Forsyth and Guilford); 105-511.2 (all other counties). At present, a transportation sales and use tax is in effect in the counties of Mecklenburg, Wake, Durham, and Orange.

72. *See* G.S. 105-508.2.

73. *See* G.S. 105-511.4.

74. *See* G.S. 105-507.3(b); 105-508.2(b); 105-511.4(b).

75. G.S. 153A-156 (counties); 160A-215.1 (municipalities). Neither a county nor a municipality may levy property (*ad valorem*) taxes on a "vehicle offered at retail for short-term lease or rental [that] is owned or leased by an entity engaged in the business of leasing or renting vehicles to the general public for short-term lease or rental." G.S. 105-275(42); *see also* S.L. 2000-2, § 1 (excluding such vehicles from *ad valorem* tax). The rental car gross receipts tax serves "[a]s a substitute for and in replacement of the *ad valorem* tax" that counties and municipalities levied upon these vehicles prior to 2001. G.S. 153A-156(a); 160A-215.1(a).

76. *See* G.S. 153A-156(a); 160A-215.1(a).

Animal Tax

Counties and municipalities may levy taxes on the privilege of keeping an animal.[77] A local government may decide which domestic animals it may tax and the rates of tax it will charge. Rates often vary based upon the type of animal and whether the animal has been spayed or neutered. Units often charge higher rates to animals that have not been spayed or neutered. A unit of local government may use the proceeds of these taxes for any authorized public purpose.[78]

Short-Term Heavy Equipment Rentals Tax

Counties and municipalities may levy a tax on the gross receipts of individuals or entities whose principal business is the "short-term lease or rental" of "heavy equipment" at retail.[79] "Heavy equipment" includes "[e]arthmoving, construction, or industrial equipment that is mobile" and that is either (1) "a self-propelled vehicle that is not designed to be driven on a highway" or (2) "industrial lift equipment, including material handling equipment, industrial electrical generation equipment, or a similar piece of industrial equipment."[80]

A county may, by resolution, impose a tax at a rate of 1.2 percent of gross receipts derived from the short-term lease or rental of heavy equipment if the place of business from which the equipment is delivered is located in the county.[81] A municipality may, by ordinance, impose a tax at a rate of 0.8 percent of gross receipts derived from the short-term lease or rental of heavy equipment if the place of business from which the equipment is delivered is located in the municipality.[82] Where imposed, these taxes are payable quarterly to the respective unit and due by the last day of the month following the end of each calendar quarter.[83]

---

77. G.S. 153A-153 (counties); 160A-212 (municipalities). The county statute authorizes an "annual license tax on the privilege of keeping dogs and other pets within the county," while the municipal statute authorizes "an annual license tax on the privilege of keeping any domestic animal, including dogs and cats, within the [municipality]." It is likely that this difference was intended to prohibit counties from levying a privilege tax on livestock. *See* David M. Lawrence, *Local Government Finance in North Carolina* (UNC Institute of Government, 1977), 42.

78. Prior to February 1, 1974, G.S. 67-13 required some counties to use the proceeds of animal taxes to compensate individuals injured by dogs. *See* S.L. 1973-822, § 6(b). After that date, counties are neither required nor authorized to use animal taxes for such a purpose. *See* Lawrence, note 77 above, at 42.

79. G.S. 153A-156.1 (counties); 160A-215.2 (municipalities). Since July 1, 2009, North Carolina law has prohibited counties and municipalities from applying property (*ad valorem*) taxes to heavy equipment offered at retail for short-term lease or rental. *See* G.S. 105-275(42a); *see also* S.L. 2008-144, § 1 (enacting G.S. 105-275(42a)). The General Assembly authorized counties and municipalities to levy a short-tern heavy equipment rentals tax when it prohibited the imposition of property taxes to such heavy equipment. *See* S.L. 2008-144, §§ 2–3.

80. *See* G.S. 153A-156.1(a)(1); 160A-215.2(a)(1). The term also includes an attachment for heavy equipment, regardless of the attachment's weight.

81. G.S. 153A-156.1(b).

82. G.S. 160A-215.2(b).

83. *See* G.S. 153A-156.1(c); 160A-215.2(c).

Motor Vehicle License Taxes

Municipalities may levy an annual motor vehicle license tax of up to $30.00 upon individuals or entities for the privilege of keeping a vehicle within the municipality.[84] A municipality is bound by the following restrictions when using the proceeds of these taxes:

(1) the municipality may use up to $5.00 of the proceeds for any lawful purpose;
(2) if it operates a "public transportation system" (as defined in G.S. 105-550),[85] it may use up to $5.00 of the proceeds for financing, constructing, operating, and maintaining such local public transportation system; and
(3) the municipality may use the remainder of the tax for "maintaining, repairing, reconstructing, widening, or improving public streets in the [municipality] that do not form a part of the State highway system."[86]

The General Assembly has authorized some municipalities, via local act, to levy motor vehicle license taxes to be used in amounts and for purposes other than those identified above.[87]

A county may levy an annual vehicle registration tax of up to $7.00 for each vehicle located within the county if it—or a municipality within the county—operates a "public transportation system."[88] A levying county must distribute the proceeds of these taxes to municipalities operating a "public transportation system," if any, on a *per capita* basis.[89] The county and any recipient municipalities must use the proceeds of such taxes to finance, construct, operate, or maintain a public transportation system.[90]

Municipalities may levy an annual tax of up to $15.00 on each vehicle operated as a taxicab within the municipality—and may use the proceeds of such taxes for any public purpose.[91] Municipalities and counties have no legal authority, however, to extend this tax to vehicles used by drivers for a transportation-network company (TNC) (e.g., Uber or Lyft).[92]

---

84. G.S. 20-97(b1).

85. *See* G.S. 105-550(5).

86. G.S. 20-97(b1).

87. *See, e.g.*, S.L. 2008-16, § 2.(b) (authorizing the Town of Chapel Hill to use up to $15.00 in motor vehicle license taxes for any lawful purpose and any levy in excess of $15.00 for public transportation purposes).

88. G.S. 105-570(a). A "public transportation system" has the meaning set forth in G.S. 105-506.1. *See* G.S. 105-570(d).

89. *See* G.S. 105-570(c).

90. *See* G.S. 105-570(d). Operation can include (1) contracting with another unit, via interlocal agreement, to provide public transportation or (2) contracting with a private entity for the operation of a public transportation system. *See* G.S. 105-570(e).

91. *See* G.S. 20-97(d).

92. For more information about the regulation of TNC services in North Carolina, see Connor Crews, "Can North Carolina's Local Governments Tax or Charge Fees to Online Ride-Sharing Services?," *Coates' Canons: NC Local Government Law* blog (Oct. 10, 2022).

Privilege License Taxes

For fiscal years beginning on or after July 1, 2015, neither a municipality nor a county may assess or collect a privilege license tax.[93] Prior to that date, the General Assembly authorized municipalities and counties—albeit in differing forms—to levy taxes upon the privilege of carrying on a business or engaging in certain types of occupations, trades, employment, or activities.[94]

Malt Beverage and Wine License Taxes

When it prohibited the county and municipal imposition of privilege license taxes, the General Assembly did not revoke the authority of counties and municipalities to charge similar license taxes applicable to the retail sale or wholesale of malt beverages (i.e., beer) and wine.

Entities and individuals that sell beer and wine at retail must obtain certain permits from the North Carolina Alcoholic Beverage Control (ABC) Commission.[95] These permit holders must obtain a malt beverage or wine license from the county and municipality, if any, in which the selling establishment is located.[96] The corresponding tax for each type of license ranges from $5.00 to $25.00.[97]

A municipality may also require a business "located inside the city" that acts as a wholesaler of beer or wine to obtain a license to engage in such activity and pay a corresponding tax.[98] Such a tax may not exceed $37.50. The General Assembly has not granted comparable authority to counties.

A county or municipality may use the proceeds of malt beverage and wine license taxes or wholesaler license taxes for any lawful purpose.

Business Registration Fees

Municipalities and counties may "by ordinance . . . regulate and license occupations, businesses, trades, professions, and forms of amusement or entertainment and prohibit those that may be inimical to the public health, welfare, safety, order, or convenience."[99] With two exceptions, each entity likely has legal authority to require businesses with a physical location within their jurisdiction to (1) register with the respective municipality or county and (2) charge a reasonable

---

93. *See* S.L. 2014-3, § 12.3.(a) (repealing G.S. 160A-211, which previously authorized municipalities to collect a privilege license tax); § 12.3.(b) (repealing, among other statutes, G.S. 153A-152, which previously authorized counties to collect a privilege license tax). For more information about this repeal, see Christopher McLaughlin, "The Axe Finally Falls on Local Privilege License Taxes," *Coates' Canons: NC Local Government Law* blog (May 30, 2014).

94. *See* G.S. 153A-152 (repealed); 160A-211 (repealed).

95. For more information, see N.C. Alcoholic Beverage Control Commission, *Retail Permit Types*, abc.nc.gov (last visited Feb. 20, 2023).

96. *See* G.S. 105-113.77 (municipalities); 105-113.78 (counties). Only the Town of Cary may decline to require a person who receives a covered ABC permit to obtain such a license. *See* G.S. 105-113.71(c) (enacted by S.L. 2021-150, § 4.2). For more information about these taxes, see Christopher McLaughlin, "Local Beer and Wine Privilege License Taxes," *Coates' Canons: NC Local Government Law* blog (Jan. 30, 2017).

97. *See* G.S. 105-113.77 (municipalities); 105-113.78 (counties).

98. G.S. 105-113.79.

99. G.S. 153A-134(a) (counties); 160A-194(a) (municipalities).

fee to businesses in connection with such registration.[100] The charging unit of local government must use the proceeds of these fees to operate the business-registration program.

Taxes Permitted by Local Act

Occupancy Taxes

As of November 2022, the General Assembly has granted authority to units of local government in more than seventy counties, via local act, to levy occupancy taxes.[101] With some exceptions, these taxes generally apply to the short-term use or rental of an "accommodation"—"a hotel room, a motel room, a residence, a cottage, or a similar lodging facility for occupancy by an individual."[102] Counties levy most of these taxes, and many of the local acts authorizing such taxes require a county to distribute a portion of these taxes to municipalities.[103] Many of the local acts also restrict the use of proceeds to particular purposes—most commonly, to purposes related to travel or tourism—but some permit the use of the proceeds for any public purpose.[104]

Prepared Food and Beverage Taxes

The General Assembly has authorized several counties and municipalities to levy taxes on the retail sale of prepared food and beverages.[105] The local acts authorizing the imposition of such a tax typically restrict the amount of the tax and the purposes for which the collecting unit of local government may spend the tax proceeds.[106] Where a unit of local government has levied taxes upon the sale of prepared food and beverages, state and local option sales taxes may also apply.

---

100. Counties and municipalities may not "examine or license a person holding a license issued by [a state occupational licensing board]." G.S. 153A-134(b); 160A-194(b). They also may not regulate or license a "TNC service" (i.e., an online ride-sharing service like Uber or Lyft) regulated under Article 10A of G.S. Chapter 20. *See* G.S. 153A-134(c); 160A-194(c). Therefore, counties and municipalities likely lack authority to charge a business-registration fee to these entities. For more discussion on this issue, see Trey Allen, "Business Registration Programs: 10 Questions and Answers," *Coates' Canons: NC Local Government Law* blog (Aug. 28, 2015).

101. *See* N.C. General Assembly, *Occupancy Tax Overview Updated as of November 2022* (last visited Feb. 20, 2023), 1–80 (hereinafter Occupancy Tax Overview).

102. Local occupancy taxes generally apply to the rental of an "accommodation" that is subject to North Carolina state sales tax. *See* G.S. 105-164.4(a)(3) (applying the general rate of state sales tax to gross receipts derived from the rental of an "accommodation"); 105-164.3(1) (defining "accommodation"). For more detail on the types of accommodations to which local occupancy taxes apply, see Rebecca L. Badgett & Christopher B. McLaughlin, *Regulation and Taxation of Short-Term Rentals* (UNC School of Government, 2019), 51–57.

103. *See generally* Occupancy Tax Overview, note 101 above.

104. *See* Occupancy Tax Overview.

105. As of July 1, 2023, the General Assembly has given such authorization to (1) the counties of Cumberland (S.L. 1993-413), Dare (S.L. 1991-177), Durham (S.L. 2008-116), Mecklenburg (S.L. 1989-821), and Wake (S.L. 1991-594; S.L. 1995-458) and (2) the municipalities of Charlotte (S.L. 1989-821), Hillsborough (S.L. 1993-449), and Monroe (S.L. 2005-261). The General Assembly made some of these authorizations contingent upon voter approval (and some measures failed to receive voter approval). For more information, see Connor Crews, "A Lesser-Known Local Government Revenue Source in North Carolina: 'Meals' Taxes," *Coates' Canons: NC Local Government Law* blog (March 27, 2023).

106. For example, the General Assembly limited Dare County's tax on prepared food and beverages to 1 percent of the retail sales price of such items and required that the proceeds be spent primarily to promote tourism in the county. *See* S.L. 1991-177, §§ 3, 7.

Real Estate Transfer Taxes

The General Assembly has authorized seven coastal counties to assess an excise tax of 1 percent upon certain conveyances of real property in each county.[107] The local acts authorizing the imposition of such taxes typically restrict the purposes for which the collecting county may spend the tax proceeds.[108]

Local Fees, Charges, and Assessments

Local governments do not rely solely upon the proceeds of taxes to fund the services that they provide. Units of local government have access to a variety of other revenue sources other than taxes, and most fall into the following six categories: (1) general user fees and charges, (2) regulatory fees, (3) public enterprise fees and charges, (4) franchise fees, (5) statutory fees, and (6) special assessments.

General User Fees and Charges

Many units of local government now rely upon mechanisms for targeted revenue generations like user fees and charges, which are paid only by the citizens or property owners that benefit most directly from a service that unit provides. These types of fees and charges are typically an appropriate funding source for services that have specific, identifiable beneficiaries rather than the public at large.[109]

A unit of local government typically accounts for revenue generated from general user fees and charges in its general fund, and, unless state law restricts the expenditure of these fees and charges, a unit may use these fees for any lawful purpose. The General Assembly may grant express legal authority in the General Statutes or in a local act to a unit of local government to assess a user charge or fee; a unit of local government also may assess a user charge or fee where legal authority to assess a user charge or fee can reasonably be implied from the legislature's authorization for a unit of local government to conduct an activity or provide a service.

Units of local government commonly fund a variety of services at least in part through general user fees and charges, including recreation and cultural activities, art galleries and museums, auditoriums, coliseums, convention centers, emergency medical services, on- and off-street parking, cemeteries, certain public health services, and certain mental health services.

---

107. These counties include Camden (S.L. 1985-954), Chowan (S.L. 1985-881), Currituck (S.L. 1985-670), Dare (S.L. 1985-525), Pasquotank (S.L. 1989-393), Perquimans (same), and Washington (same).

108. For example, the General Assembly required the proceeds of taxes collected by the counties of Pasquotank, Perquimans, and Washington to be used for public school capital expenditures. *See* S.L. 1989-393, § 1(e).

109. Harry Kitchen, Melville McMillan, and Anwar Shah, *Local Public Finance and Economics: An International Perspective* (2019), 365.

Regulatory Fees

A regulatory fee is a charge assessed to cover the cost of performing a regulatory program or service that a local government may or must provide. In some cases, the General Statutes expressly authorize a county or municipality to charge a fee for the performance of a regulatory activity. For example, a municipality may "regulate all vehicles operated for hire" in its jurisdiction and require all "drivers and operators of taxicabs" to obtain a license or permit from the city at a cost not to exceed $15.00.[110] In other cases, though, the General Statutes authorize a county or municipality to perform a regulatory function but do not contain explicit authority to impose a fee or charge upon a person or entity that the local government is regulating. For example, municipalities have express statutory authority to adopt an ordinance that "regulate[s], restrict[s] or prohibit[s] . . . the business activities of itinerant merchants, salesmen, promoters, drummers, peddlers, flea market vendors and hawkers" and requires that these individuals receive a municipal permit to engage in these business activities.[111] That statutory authority does not, however, expressly authorize municipalities to charge a fee for the issuance of such a permit. In that case, do municipalities have implied legal authority to impose such a fee?[112]

In a 1994 ruling—*Homebuilders Association of Charlotte, Inc. v. City of Charlotte*—the North Carolina Supreme Court held that the legal authority of a local government to charge a fee may be implied from express statutory authority to engage in a regulatory activity.[113] But the court also held that such regulatory fees charged must be "reasonable"—in other words, not exceeding the direct and indirect costs of performing the regulatory activity—and used for the sole purpose of defraying the cost of regulation.[114] The state supreme court has issued a number of subsequent decisions that apply and interpret the 1994 *Homebuilders* ruling,[115] and a local government should work closely with its legal counsel prior to relying upon implied authority to impose a fee or charge.

At present, county boards of commissioners have express authority to set fees and charges for services or duties that county officers or employees may or must perform.[116] Although no analogous statute applies to municipalities, a municipality may have implied authority to impose

---

110. *See* G.S. 160A-304(a).

111. G.S. 160A-178.

112. For a discussion of this issue, see Trey Allen, "Legal Authority for Peddler Permit Fees," *Coates' Canons: NC Local Government Law* blog (Sept. 22, 2014).

113. *See* Homebuilders Ass'n of Charlotte, Inc. v. City of Charlotte, 336 N.C. 37 (1994). In *Homebuilders*, the court relied heavily upon G.S. 160A-4, which provides that grants of power to municipalities "shall be construed to include any additional and supplementary powers that are reasonably necessary or expedient to carry them into execution and effect." Applying that rule of construction to the City of Charlotte's express statutory authority to regulate zoning, the subdivision of land, streets, and erosion and sedimentation control, the court held that the City of Charlotte possessed implied authority to establish and collect reasonable fees for the purpose of defraying the cost of, among other things, the performance of driveway, drainage, erosion control and other plan and zoning reviews; building permit inspections; and the issuance of land use permits.

114. *See Homebuilders*, 336 N.C. at 46–47.

115. *See, e.g.,* Lanvale Props., LLC v. Cnty. of Cabarrus, 366 N.C. 142 (2012) (holding that a county did not have legal authority under its general zoning authority to require a developer to pay an "adequate public facilities fee" to be used for school construction).

116. *See* G.S. 153A-102.

a reasonable fee or charge for performance of a regulatory function and use the proceeds of that fee to defray the cost of the function.

Local governments continue to commonly assess regulatory fees to cover the costs of performing certain regulatory activities like issuing building permits, evaluating environmental impacts, reviewing development plans, and enforcing other local ordinances. Prior to the General Assembly's 2020 comprehensive revision and restatement of North Carolina's land use and planning laws in G.S. Chapter 160D, counties and municipalities had express statutory authority to "fix reasonable fees for issuance of permits, inspections, and other services of an inspections department" and to use any such fees collected "for support of the administration and activities of the inspection department and for no other purpose."[117] Now, this statutory authority permits counties and municipalities to "fix reasonable fees for support, administration, and implementation of programs authorized by . . . Chapter [160D], and [to use] such fees . . . for no other purposes."[118] Chapter 160D authorizes counties and municipalities to engage in a range of regulatory programs, including, among other things, issuing building permits, performing inspections of structures, and approving plats for the subdivision of land.[119]

Typically, a unit of local government adopts a schedule of fees on an annual basis. Although the General Statutes do not prescribe formal procedural requirements to adopt or amend fees or a fee schedule, the General Statutes impose certain procedural requirements upon the imposition or increase of fees or charges applicable solely to the development of subdivisions.[120]

Public Enterprise Fees and Charges

Counties and municipalities have legal authority to operate a range of public enterprises.[121] Public enterprises are activities of a commercial nature that the private sector could provide but that the public sector has chosen to provide. The most common public enterprises that North Carolina's counties and municipalities operate are water supply and distribution systems, sewage collection and treatment, and solid waste collection and disposal utilities. But counties and municipalities also may legally operate other types of public enterprises, including airports, public transportation, off-street parking facilities, and stormwater systems, and municipalities

---

117. G.S. 153A-354 and 160A-414. Each of these statutes was repealed as of June 19, 2020. *See* S.L. 2019-111, §§ 2.2, 2.3, 3.2, *as amended by* S.L. 2020-25, §§ 51.(a)–(b). For a discussion of fees authorized by these now-repealed statutes, see Adam Lovelady, "Administering Development Regulations and Accounting for Permitting Fees," *Coates' Canons: NC Local Government Law* blog (Sept. 4, 2018).

118. G.S. 160D-402(d).

119. *See* G.S. 160D-1110 (building permits); 160D-1104 (duties and responsibilities of inspections department); Ch. 160D, Art. 8 (subdivision of land). The authority to charge fees in G.S. 160D-402(d) should be read to extend only to these and similar *regulatory* functions authorized by Chapter 160D. For example, even though Chapter 160D now contains the statutory authority for counties and municipalities to engage in community development programs (see G.S. 160D-1311), it is unlikely that the General Assembly intended G.S. 160D-402(d) to authorize the use of regulatory fees for non-regulatory purposes like community development.

120. *See* G.S. 160D-805(a). For information on similar requirements that applied prior to the adoption of Chapter 160D, see Kara Millonzi, "(Electronic) Notice of Subdivision Construction Development Fees Revisited," *Coates' Canons: NC Local Government Law* blog (Aug. 19, 2010).

121. *See* G.S. 153A-274 (counties); 160A-311 (municipalities).

have additional authority to operate public enterprises for electric power generation and distribution, gas production and distribution, and cable television.[122]

A unit of local government that provides public enterprises may assess a variety of fees and charges to cover the capital and operating expenses necessary to operate those public enterprises. Many of these public enterprises are self-supporting, meaning that the revenue the enterprise generates through fees and charges is sufficient to cover the cost of providing services. Chapter 13, "Financing Public Enterprises," outlines the legal authority of counties and municipalities to impose fees and charges for public enterprise activities.

Franchise Fees

A franchise is a legal privilege to engage in a type of business in the boundaries of a particular jurisdiction. With authorization from the General Assembly, North Carolina's counties and municipalities may grant franchises to private entities to engage in a variety of activities. However, authority to grant a franchise does not necessarily include authority to charge a franchise fees. Counties have authority to grant franchises and charge licensing fees for solid waste collection and disposal.[123] Municipalities can grant franchises for a much wider range of purposes, including airports, ambulance companies, off-street parking, and solid waste collection and disposal.[124] Municipalities also may grant franchises and charge franchise fees for taxicabs.[125]

Statutory Fees

The General Statutes establish a variety of fees that units of local government—and, in particular, specific offices within units of local government—must or may charge. This section details a number of statutory fees collected or received by units of local government.

Fees of Public Officers

Sheriff

A county sheriff may collect a variety of fees. Among others, a county sheriff is entitled to collect fees from a convicted defendant for arresting that defendant or serving that individual with criminal process,[126] fees for providing pretrial release services to such a defendant,[127] and fees for lawfully confining an individual in jail prior to trial.[128] A county sheriff also may collect fees for the service of civil process[129] and the sale of real or personal property to satisfy a judgment.[130]

---

122. *See* G.S. 153A-274 and 160A-311.

123. *See* G.S. 153A-136.

124. *See* G.S. 160A-319 (permitting grants of franchises for telephone systems and any of the enterprises listed in G.S. 160A-311).

125. *See* G.S. 160A-304; 20-97. This authority does not permit a municipality to grant a franchise to a transportation-network company (e.g., an online ride-sharing service like Uber or Lyft). *See* G.S. 160A-304(c).

126. *See* G.S. 7A-304(a)(1). If a municipality employs the law enforcement officer that made the arrest, this fee shall be paid to the municipality. *See id.*

127. *See* G.S. 7A-304(a)(5).

128. *See* G.S. 7A-313.

129. *See* G.S. 7A-311(a)(1).

130. *See* G.S. 7A-311(a)(3).

Register of Deeds

Registers of deeds collect fees in connection with the wide variety of services that they perform.[131] Although fees for recording deeds and other legal instruments affecting titles to real property make up the bulk of the fees that registers of deeds collect, other major sources of revenue include fees for issuing marriage licenses. In many counties, the register of deeds collects fee revenue that exceeds the costs of operating its office.

On a monthly basis, each county must deposit with the North Carolina Department of State Treasurer an amount equal to 1.5 percent of the fees collected by registers of deeds under G.S. 161-10.[132] Counties must remit portions of other fees collected under G.S. 161-10 to a variety of other state-level entities for specific purposes.[133]

Court Facilities and Related Fees

The state assesses fees against criminal defendants and civil litigants to help offset the cost of operating state courts. These fees include a variety of "facilities" fees: (1) a fee assessed to a convicted criminal defendant to be remitted to the unit of local government (most commonly, a county) that provides the judicial facility in which judgment is rendered;[134] (2) a fee assessed in civil actions to be remitted to the unit of local government (most commonly, a county) that provides the judicial facility in which judgment is rendered;[135] (3) a fee assessed for special proceedings in superior court, to be remitted to the county;[136] and (4) a fee assessed for the use of a courtroom and related judicial facilities in, among other things, the administration of the estates of decedents, minors, incompetents, and missing persons, to be remitted to the county.[137] The proceeds of all these fees must be used by the recipient for "providing, maintaining, and constructing adequate and related judicial facilities."[138]

Special Assessments

A special assessment is a charge levied against real property to pay for public improvements that benefit that property. It is neither a user charge nor a tax but shares characteristics of each. Like a user charge, a special assessment is levied in some proportion to the benefit that the assessed

---

131. *See* G.S. 161-10(a). Registers of deeds charge fees for services ranging from the issuance of marriage licenses to the recording of documents affecting titles to real property.

132. *See* G.S. 161-50.2(a). Such fees are credited to a supplemental pension fund for registers of deeds that the State Treasurer maintains.

133. *See* G.S. 161-11.1 (portion of marriage license fees to be remitted to N.C. Department of Health and Human Services for deposit in Children's Trust Fund), -11.2 (portion of marriage license fees to be forwarded to N.C. Department of Administration for deposit in Domestic Violence Center Fund), -11.3 (portion of fees collected pursuant to G.S. 161-10 shall be expended for computer imaging and technology needs for preservation of public records), -11.5 (portion of fees collected pursuant to G.S. 161-10 shall be remitted to State Treasurer for deposit in Flood Plain Mapping Fund, General Fund, or Archives and Records Management Fund of Department of Natural and Cultural Resources).

134. *See* G.S. 7A-304(a)(2).

135. *See* G.S. 7A-305(a)(1).

136. *See* G.S. 7A-306(a)(1).

137. *See* G.S. 7A-307(a)(1).

138. *See* G.S. 7A-304(a)(1).

property receives. But like a property tax, it is levied against property rather than individuals and creates a lien on each parcel of real property assessed.[139]

Counties and municipalities in North Carolina may use special assessments to fund certain capital improvement projects.[140] Chapter 7, "Financing Capital Projects," discusses special assessments in detail.

State Revenues Shared with Local Governments

The State of North Carolina generates certain revenues that it shares with units of local government. State officials, rather than local officials, bear the political burden of imposing these revenues, but local governing boards largely lack control over their imposition or distribution. The General Assembly may at any time reduce or eliminate the sources of revenue that it shares with units of local government.

The state currently shares a variety of tax and fee revenues with counties: video programming services taxes, malt beverage and wine taxes, solid waste tipping taxes, real estate transfer taxes, disposal taxes, and a 911 charge upon voice communication services. With the exception of real estate transfer taxes and disposal taxes, the state also shares a portion of each of those revenues with municipalities. Municipalities also receive a portion of state-levied electric franchise taxes, telecommunications taxes, piped natural gas taxes, and motor fuels taxes. This section explains each of these state revenue sources in more detail.

Video Programming Services Taxes

The General Assembly has levied a statewide sales tax—at the "combined general rate"[141] of 7.0 percent—upon sales of video programming services (including direct-to-home satellite services).[142] The North Carolina Department of Revenue (NCDOR) collects these taxes and, on a quarterly basis and within seventy-five calendar days of the end of each calendar quarter, distributes a portion of the proceeds of these taxes—along with a portion of the proceeds of

---

139. The lien may be foreclosed in the same manner as property tax liens. For more information on enforcing property tax liens, see Chapter 5, "Property Tax Policy and Administration."

140. *See* G.S. Ch. 153A, Arts. 9, 9A (counties); G.S. Ch. 160A, Arts. 10, 10A (municipalities).

141. The "combined general rate" includes the state's general rate of state sales and use tax (4.75 percent), plus the combined maximum rates of local option sales taxes that may be levied in all 100 counties (i.e., those under Articles 39 (1 percent), 40 (0.5 percent), 42 (0.5 percent), and 46 (0.25 percent) of G.S. Chapter 105). *See* G.S. 105-164.3(37).

142. *See* G.S. 105-164.4(a)(6). "Video programming" services include "[p]rogramming provided by, or generally considered comparable to programming provided by, a television broadcast station, regardless of the method of delivery." G.S. 105-164.3(277). Prior to January 1, 2007, North Carolina law authorized counties and municipalities to award franchises for cable service and to levy an annual franchise tax upon companies to which a county or municipality awarded a franchise. *See* G.S. 153A-137, -154 (each repealed by S.L. 2006-151); 160A-214 (repealed by S.L. 2006-151). The General Assembly revoked that authority as of January 1, 2007, and in doing so gave the State of North Carolina exclusive authority to award franchises for cable service and levy sales tax upon video programming services. *See* S.L. 2006-151. As part of the repeal, the General Assembly mandated that the NCDOR distribute a portion of the proceeds of the tax to counties and municipalities. *See* G.S. 105-164.44I (enacted by S.L. 2006-151, § 8).

state sales taxes levied upon telecommunication services—to counties and municipalities.[143] In particular, NCDOR must distribute: (1) 7.7 percent of the net proceeds of taxes collected during the quarter upon telecommunications services, (2) 23.6 percent of the net proceeds of taxes collected during the quarter on video programming services other than direct-to-home satellite services, and (3) 37.1 percent of the net proceeds of taxes collected during the quarter on direct-to-home satellite services.[144] The following sections explain how NCDOR distributes these proceeds.

Distribution of Supplemental "PEG Channel" Support

First, NCDOR distributes a portion of the proceeds of these taxes to municipalities and counties that operate "qualifying PEG channels." A "qualifying PEG" channel is a public, educational, or governmental access channel provided to a county or city that operates for at least ninety days during a fiscal year and that (1) delivers at least eight hours of scheduled programming a day, (2) delivers at least six hours and forty-five minutes of scheduled non-character-generated programming a day, and (3) does not repeat more than 15 percent of the programming content on any other PEG channel provided to the same county or municipality.[145]

By July 15 of each fiscal year, counties and municipalities that operate qualifying PEG channels must certify to NCDOR all of the qualifying PEG channels provided for its use during the preceding fiscal year.[146] Based upon these certifications, NCDOR determines a share to be distributed to each certifying county and municipality on a quarterly basis. The General Statutes direct NCDOR to divide $4,000,000.00 in the proceeds of the taxes identified above, *plus* any funds returned to NCDOR due to a county or municipality's improper certification of a PEG channel, among each certifying county and municipality in proportion to the total number of qualifying PEG channels statewide.[147] The formula is set forth below.

$$(\$4,000,000.00 + \textit{Any Returned Funds}) * \left(\frac{\textit{Jurisdiction's Number of Qualifying PEG Channels}}{\textit{Total Statewide Number of Qualifying PEG Channels}} * (0.25) \right)$$

= Municipality or County's Quarterly Distribution of Supplemental PEG Channel Support

A county or municipality that receives a distribution of supplemental PEG channel support payments must use such moneys for the operation and support of each qualifying PEG channel and must distribute the funds to a PEG channel operator within thirty days of receipt.[148]

---

143. G.S. 105-164.44I(a). For more information about state sales taxes levied upon telecommunications services, see "Telecommunications Taxes," below.

144. G.S. 105-164.4I(a).

145. *See* G.S. 105-164.44J(a)(4).

146. *See* G.S. 105-164.44J(b). For an example of the certification form, see N.C. Department of Revenue, *TR-PEG Cable PEG Channel Certification*, ncdor.gov (last visited Feb. 23, 2023). If a county or municipality improperly certifies a PEG channel, it must submit a revised certification to NCDOR and return to NCDOR all funds improperly received as a result of such error. *See* G.S. 105-164.44J(d).

147. *See* G.S. 105-164.44I(b). A certifying unit may not receive PEG channel support for more than three qualifying PEG channels. *See id.*

148. *See* G.S. 105-164.44J(c).

Remaining Proportionate Share

NCDOR then distributes the net proceeds of the taxes remaining after the distribution of supplemental PEG channel support funds. It determines the amount of this distribution according to each municipality and county's "proportionate share."[149] A unit's proportionate share is the ratio of its "base amount" to the sum of the "base amount" for all municipalities and counties. A "base amount" is (1) for any unit that imposed a cable franchise tax before July 1, 2006—the amount of cable franchise tax and subscriber fee revenue that the county imposed from July 1, 2006, through December 31, 2006, or (2) for any unit that did not impose a cable franchise tax before July 1, 2006—the unit's most recent annual population estimate *times* $2.00.[150] For fiscal years following the 2007 fiscal year, NCDOR further adjusts the "proportionate share" of each county and municipality to account for its growth or decline in population in the preceding fiscal year.[151]

Restrictions on Use of Proceeds

A county or municipality that imposed subscriber fees between July 1, 2006, and December 31, 2006, must use a portion of these funds to provide for the operation and support of PEG channels.[152] In addition, a county or municipality that used a portion of its franchise tax revenue in fiscal year 2005–2006 for the operation and support of PEG channels or for a publicly owned and operated television station must use funds distributed to it to continue the same level of support for such channels and public stations. A county or municipality, after reserving funds for these purposes, may use remaining funds for any public purpose.

Malt Beverage and Wine Taxes

The State of North Carolina levies several taxes on the sale of alcoholic beverages, including excise taxes on malt beverages (i.e., beer) and wine.[153] The state distributes a portion of these excise taxes to municipalities and counties: 20.47 percent of the net amount of taxes collected on the sale of malt beverages; 49.44 percent of the net amount of taxes collected on the sale of unfortified wine; and 18 percent of the net amount of taxes collected on the sale of fortified wine.[154]

A municipality or county may receive a share of this distribution only if beer or wine legally may be sold within its boundaries.[155] North Carolina permits the sale of beer and wine throughout the state but permits counties to hold an election in which voters may prohibit "on-premises" or "off-premises" sales of malt beverages and unfortified wine.[156] A municipality located within

---

149. G.S. 105-164.44I(c).

150. G.S. 105-164.44I(c).

151. *See* G.S. 105-164.44I(d).

152. *See* G.S. 105-164.44I(e). Such a county or municipality must use the proportionate share of funds used for this purpose in fiscal year 2006–2007, which was equal to two times the amount of subscriber fee revenue that a unit imposed between July 1, 2006, and December 31, 2006. *See id.*

153. *See* G.S. 105-113.80 (excise taxes on malt beverages, wine, and liquor), -113.81 (exemptions to excise taxes). These taxes are payable to the North Carolina Department of Revenue (NCDOR) by the resident wholesaler or importer who first handles the beverages in the state. *See* G.S. 105-113.83(b).

154. *See* G.S. 105-113.82(a).

155. *See* G.S. 105-113.82(a1). To be eligible to receive a distribution, a municipality incorporated on or after January 1, 2000, must satisfy certain additional requirements. *See* G.S. 105-113.82(h).

156. *See* G.S. 18B-600(b) (permitting elections); 18B-602 (prescribing forms of ballot).

a county in which such sales have been prohibited by election may hold a subsequent election to permit the sale of malt beverages and unfortified wine.[157] A municipality or county that only permits the sale of one type of beverage may only share in the proceeds of excise taxes levied upon the type of beverage that may be sold.[158]

The North Carolina Department of Revenue (NCDOR) distributes the proceeds of these excise taxes to eligible counties and municipalities based upon the ratio of the recipient unit's population to the population of all eligible counties and municipalities.[159] NCDOR must distribute the revenue within sixty days of March 31 and typically makes the distribution on an annual basis.[160] Counties and municipalities that receive a distribution may spend the proceeds for any authorized public purpose.

Solid Waste Disposal Taxes

The State of North Carolina imposes an excise tax throughout the state—at a rate of $2.00 per ton—upon the (1) disposal of municipal solid waste and construction and demolition debris in any landfill for which the North Carolina Department of Environmental Quality (NCDEQ) has granted a permit and (2) transfer of municipal solid waste and construction and demolition debris to a transfer station to which NCDEQ has granted a permit.[161] Either the owner or operator of each landfill and transfer station must collect the tax and remit the tax to NCDOR.[162]

After retaining a portion of the proceeds of these taxes as compensation for its cost of collection, NCDOR distributes 18.75 percent of the proceeds of these taxes to eligible counties and 18.75 percent of the proceeds of these taxes to eligible municipalities.[163] To be eligible to receive a distribution, a county or municipality must provide, or contract and pay for, solid waste management programs or services.[164] NCDOR then makes distributions to eligible counties and municipalities based upon their relative populations.[165] Recipient counties and municipalities may only use the proceeds of this distribution to fund solid waste management programs and services.[166]

---

157. *See* G.S. 18B-600(c), (c1).

158. *See* G.S. 105-113.82(a1). Notwithstanding that restriction, in a county in which Alcoholic Beverage Control (ABC) stores have been established by petition, NCDOR shall distribute revenues as though the retail sale of a beverage is permitted in the entire county. *See* G.S. 105-113.82(d).

159. *See* G.S. 105-113.82(a1).

160. *See* G.S. 105-113.82(c). For example, NCDOR scheduled the 2023 distribution of alcoholic beverage tax for May 26, 2023. *See* N.C. Department of Revenue, *Local Government Distribution Schedule for Fiscal Year 2022-2023*, ncdor.gov (last visited Feb. 23, 2023).

161. *See* G.S. 105-187.61(a). "Municipal solid waste" includes "any solid waste resulting from the operation of residential, commercial, industrial, governmental, or institutional establishments that would normally be collected, processed, and disposed of through a public or private solid waste management service." G.S. 130A-290(a)(18a).

162. *See* G.S. 105-187.61(b).

163. *See* G.S. 105-187.63(2).

164. G.S. 105-187.63(2).

165. For the purposes of this calculation, a county's population does not include the population of a municipality located in a county. *See* G.S. 105-187.63(2).

166. *See* G.S. 105-187.63(2).

Real Estate Transfer Tax

The State of North Carolina imposes an excise tax upon legal instruments recorded with registers of deeds that convey an interest in real property.[167] The tax is levied at a rate of $1.00 per $500.00 of the consideration paid for the interest.[168] For example, if an individual sells an acre of land for $100,000.00, the excise tax upon the deed that conveys the property would total $200.00.

The register of deeds for the county in which the real property is located collects any tax due and remits the proceeds to such county's finance officer.[169] After retaining up to 2 percent of the proceeds as compensation for the cost of collecting the excise tax, the finance officer must credit one-half of the proceeds to the county's general fund and remit the other one-half to NCDOR.[170] The county may use its portion of the excise tax for any authorized public purpose.

Scrap Tire Disposal Tax

The state imposes and collects a tax upon the sale of new automobile tires sold by a retailer, or sold by a retailer wholesale merchant to a wholesale merchant or retailer, for placement on a vehicle offered for sale, lease, or rental by the retailer or wholesale merchant.[171] After retaining a portion of the proceeds of these taxes as compensation for its cost of collection, NCDOR distributes 70 percent of the proceeds of these taxes to counties on a *per capita* basis.[172] A county may use the proceeds of these taxes only for the disposal of scrap tires or the abatement of a tire collection site that constitutes a nuisance.[173]

White Goods Disposal Tax

The state imposes and collects a tax upon the retail sale of "white goods."[174] After retaining a portion of the proceeds of these taxes as compensation for its cost of collection, NCDOR distributes 70 percent of the proceeds of these taxes to counties on a *per capita* basis.[175] A county may use the proceeds of these taxes only for the management of discarded white goods.[176]

---

167. *See* G.S. 105-228.30(a). Several types of instruments are exempt from excise tax, including deeds in which a unit of government conveys an interest in real property. *See* G.S. 105-228.28, -228.29.

168. The General Assembly has authorized the imposition of a separate, additional tax upon the transfer of deeds in the counties of Camden, Chowan, Currituck, Dare, Pasquotank, Perquimans, and Washington. *See* note 107 above and accompanying text.

169. *See* G.S. 105-228.30(a).

170. *See* G.S. 105-228.30(b).

171. *See* G.S. 105-187.16(a).

172. *See* G.S. 105-187.19(b).

173. *See* G.S. 105-187.19(c); 130A-309.54; 130A-309.60. If the county has an agreement with another unit of local government under which the other unit provides for the county's disposal of solid waste, the county must transfer the proceeds of the tax—to be used for the same purposes—to that other unit. *See* G.S. 105-187.19(c).

174. *See* G.S. 105-187.21. "White goods" include "refrigerators, ranges, water heaters, freezers, unit air conditioners, washing machines, dishwashers, clothes dryers, and other similar domestic and commercial large appliances." *See* G.S. 105-187.20(2); 130A-290(a)(44).

175. *See* G.S. 105-187.24. Some counties may not be eligible to receive a distribution. *See* G.S. 130A-309.87(a).

176. *See* G.S. 105-187.24; 130A-309.82.

911 Service Charge

Since 2008, the North Carolina 911 Board—now contained within the State Department of Information Technology—has overseen a consolidated, statewide plan to administer 911 systems and communications between public safety answering points (PSAPs) that call and dispatch public safety agencies for response to a 911 call.[177]

The state levies a monthly 911 service charge on each (1) active voice communications service connection that provides access to the 911 system and (2) retail purchase of prepaid wireless telecommunications services.[178] The 911 Board maintains revenues derived from these service charges in a state-level 911 Fund, from which it makes certain distributions to, among other entities, "primary PSAPs"—entities that serve as the first point of reception for a 911 call.[179]

The 911 Board must make monthly distributions to eligible primary PSAPs from the 911 Fund based upon a funding formula.[180] To receive a distribution from the 911 Fund, a local government must (1) serve as a primary PSAP, (2) provide "enhanced 911 service,"[181] and (3) have received distributions from the 911 Board in the 2008–2009 fiscal year.[182] It also must comply with a host of other requirements.[183]

A primary PSAP may use the 911 charge proceeds only for certain expenditures specified by statute. In particular, it may use distributions provided after July 1, 2021, to pay for

(1) the lease, purchase, or maintenance of (a) emergency telephone equipment, including necessary computer hardware and software; (b) telecommunicator failure; (c) dispatch equipment located exclusively within a building where a PSAP or back-up PSAP is located (but excluding the costs of base-station transmitters, towers, microwave links, and antennae used to dispatch emergency-call information from the PSAP or back-up PSAP); or (d) emergency medical, fire, and law enforcement pre-arrival instruction software;

(2) costs incurred by a city or county that operates a PSAP to comply with the terms of certain intergovernmental support agreements with a military installation;

(3) expenditures for in-state training of 911 personnel regarding the maintenance and operation of the 911 system; and

(4) charges associated with a service supplier's 911 service and other service supplier recurring charges (but excluding service supplier 911 service and other recurring charges supplanted by the state ESInet costs paid by the 911 Board).[184]

---

177. *See* S.L. 2007-383 (establishing the 911 Board).

178. *See* G.S. 143B-1403(a), (b).

179. *See* G.S. 143B-1400(23) (defining "primary PSAP"); 143B-1404(a) (creating the 911 Fund); 143B-1406 (authorizing distributions to primary PSAPs).

180. G.S. 143B-1406(a)(3) contains factors that the 911 Board must consider in creating the formula.

181. *See* G.S. 143B-1400(14) (defining "enhanced 911 service").

182. *See* G.S. 143B-1406(a). Local governments are not authorized to levy any charges for 911 services. *See* G.S. 143B-1403(f).

183. *See* G.S. 143B-1406(f).

184. G.S. 143B-1406(d).

The 911 Board must notify each primary PSAP of its estimated distribution by December 31 of each year and determine actual annual distributions by June 1.[185] The PSAP must deposit any funds received into a special revenue fund designated as the Emergency Telephone System Fund.[186]

A PSAP may carry forward distributions for eligible expenditures for capital outlay, capital improvements, or equipment replacement.[187] If the amount carried forward exceeds 20 percent of the average yearly amount distributed to the PSAP in the prior two years, the 911 Board may reduce the PSAP's distribution.[188]

Electricity Taxes

The General Assembly has levied a statewide sales tax—at the "combined general rate"[189] of 7.0 percent—upon sales of electricity.[190] The North Carolina Department of Revenue (NCDOR) collects these taxes and, on a quarterly basis and within seventy-five calendar days of the end of each calendar quarter, distributes a portion of the proceeds of these taxes to municipalities.[191] In particular, NCDOR must distribute 44 percent of the net proceeds of taxes collected on electricity *less* NCDOR's costs of administering such distribution.[192]

NCDOR calculates one portion of a municipality's distribution according to its "quarterly franchise tax share" and the other portion based upon its "ad valorem share."[193] A municipality's "quarterly franchise tax share" is equal to the total amount of franchise taxes on electricity that it received in the same related quarter in fiscal year 2013–2014.[194] A municipality's ad valorem share is its "proportionate share" of the amount remaining for distribution after determining each municipality's quarterly franchise tax share.[195] A municipality's "proportionate share" is the ratio of ad valorem (property) taxes levied in that municipality to all property taxes levied by municipalities across the state.[196] Any municipality that receives a distribution of electricity taxes may spend these revenues for any authorized public purpose.

---

185. G.S. 143B-1406(a)(1).

186. G.S. 143B-1406(e).

187. *See* G.S. 143B-1406(c).

188. *See* G.S. 143B-1406(c).

189. For the definition of "combined general rate," see note 141 above.

190. *See* G.S. 105-164.4(a)(9). Prior to July 1, 2014, the State of North Carolina levied a franchise tax upon electric utilities and shared a portion of the tax proceeds with municipalities. *See* G.S. 105-116, -116.1 (each repealed by S.L. 2013-316, § 4.1.(a)). As part of the repeal, the General Assembly applied a sales tax to the sale of electricity and mandated that the North Carolina Department of Revenue (NCDOR) distribute a portion of the proceeds of the new tax to municipalities. *See* G.S. 105-164.44K (enacted by S.L. 2013-316, § 4.3.(a)).

191. G.S. 105-164.44K(a).

192. *See* G.S. 105-164.44K(a).

193. *See* G.S. 105-164.44K(a).

194. *See* G.S. 105-164.44K(b). If the total amount available to be distributed is not sufficient to provide each municipality with its FY 2013–2014 franchise tax amount for the equivalent quarter, then each municipality's allocation will be reduced by an equal percentage. *See* G.S. 105-164.44K(a).

195. *See* G.S. 105-164.44K(c).

196. *See* G.S. 105-164.44K(c). In making this calculation, ad valorem taxes that a municipality collects on behalf of a taxing district are disregarded.

Telecommunications Taxes

The state has levied a statewide sales tax—at the "combined general rate"[197] of 7.0 percent—upon sales of telecommunications services and ancillary services.[198] The North Carolina Department of Revenue (NCDOR) collects these taxes and, on a quarterly basis and within seventy-five calendar days of the end of each calendar quarter, distributes a portion of the proceeds of these taxes to municipalities.[199] In particular, NCDOR must distribute 18.7 percent of the net proceeds of these taxes *less* $2,620,948.00.[200]

The General Assembly enacted a sales tax upon telecommunications services in 2001 to replace a previously applicable gross receipts tax upon telecommunications services.[201] A municipality incorporated prior to January 1, 2001, receives a distribution of these taxes based upon its "proportionate share" of the taxes to be distributed to all municipalities incorporated before that date. A municipality's "proportionate share" is equal to the same percentage share of telephone gross receipts taxes that it received in the same related quarter in which those prior taxes were still in effect.[202] A municipality incorporated on or after January 1, 2001, receives a *per capita* share of the amount to be distributed to all municipalities incorporated on or after this date that is based upon the ratio of its population to the population of all municipalities incorporated on or after this date.[203] Any municipality that receives a distribution of telecommunications taxes may spend these revenues for any authorized public purpose.

Piped Natural Gas Taxes

The state has levied a statewide sales tax—at the "combined general rate"[204] of 7.0 percent—upon sales of piped natural gas.[205] NCDOR collects these taxes and, on a quarterly basis and within seventy-five calendar days of the end of each calendar quarter, distributes a portion of the proceeds of these taxes to municipalities.[206] In particular, NCDOR must distribute 20 percent of the net proceeds of these taxes *less* the cost of administering the distribution.[207]

NCDOR calculates one portion of a municipality's distribution according to its "quarterly excise tax share" and the other portion based upon its "ad valorem share."[208] A municipality's

---

197. For the definition of "combined general rate," see note 141 above.

198. G.S. 105-164.4(a)(4c). Telecommunications services include, among other things, "[t]he electronic transmission, conveyance, or routing of voice, data, audio, video, or any other information or signals to a point, or between or among points." G.S. 105-164.3(269). Ancillary services include "[a] service associated with or incidental to the provision of a telecommunications service," including "detailed communications billing, directory assistance, vertical service [e.g., call forwarding, caller ID, three-way calling, and conference bridging], and voice mail service." G.S. 105-164.3(19).

199. G.S. 105-164.44F(a).

200. G.S. 105-164.44F(a)(1). 7.7 percent of the net proceeds of taxes collected upon telecommunications services and ancillary services are included in NCDOR's distribution of video programming services taxes. *See* "Video Programming Services Taxes," above.

201. *See* S.L. 2001-430, § 10. *See also* G.S. 105-116.1 (repealed July 1, 2014).

202. *See* G.S. 105-164.44F(c).

203. *See* G.S. 105-164.44F(b). Certain additional requirements apply to municipalities incorporated on or after January 1, 2000. *See* G.S. 105-164.44F(e).

204. For the definition of "combined general rate," see note 141 above.

205. G.S. 105-164.4(a)(9).

206. G.S. 105-164.44L(a).

207. G.S. 105-164.44L(a).

208. G.S. 105-164.44L(a).

"quarterly excise tax share" is equal to the amount of excise taxes on natural gas that it received in the same related quarter in fiscal year 2013–2014.[209] A municipality's ad valorem share is its "proportionate share" of the amount remaining for distribution after determining each municipality's quarterly excise tax share.[210] A municipality's "proportionate share" is the ratio of ad valorem (property) taxes levied in that municipality to all property taxes levied by municipalities across the state.[211] Municipalities that operated a piped natural gas distribution system as of July 1, 1998, receive an additional distribution.[212] Any municipality that receives a distribution of piped natural gas taxes may spend these revenues for any authorized public purpose.

"Powell Bill" Funds (Motor Fuels Tax)

The State of North Carolina levies an excise tax, pursuant to a statutory formula, upon certain types of "motor fuel," including gasoline.[213] In 1951, the North Carolina General Assembly adopted legislation mandating that the state distribute a portion of the proceeds of motor fuel taxes to municipalities to be used for "maintaining, repairing, constructing, reconstructing or widening" any municipally-maintained street.[214] The initial, principal sponsor of that legislation in the North Carolina State Senate was Senator Junius K. Powell, and, for that reason, these distributions often are called "Powell Bill" funds.

In 2015, the General Assembly modified the longstanding tie between the state's motor fuels tax and the amount of street aid distributed to municipalities.[215] Now, the General Statutes do not automatically appropriate a certain percentage of the state's motor fuel tax revenues to municipalities as street aid. Instead, the General Assembly must appropriate moneys on an annual basis to the North Carolina Department of Transportation (NCDOT) for that purpose.[216]

Even though the funding scheme for municipal street aid has changed, the use of the term "Powell Bill funds" is still widespread. NCDOT distributes yearly appropriations of Powell Bill funds made by the General Assembly according to a two-part formula: three-quarters of the proceeds are distributed among municipalities on a *per capita* basis, and one-quarter of the proceeds are distributed according to the proportion of miles of public, non-state streets in a given municipality when compared to the miles of such public, non-state streets in all municipalities eligible to receive Powell Bill funds.[217]

---

209. *See* G.S. 105-164.44L(b). Taxes in this fiscal year were distributed pursuant to G.S. 105-187.44, which the General Assembly repealed effective July 1, 2014. *See* S.L. 2013-316, § 4.1(d).

210. *See* G.S. 105-164.44L(c).

211. *See* G.S. 105-164.44L(c). In making this calculation, ad valorem taxes that a municipality collects on behalf of a taxing district are disregarded.

212. G.S. 105-164.44L(b1). These municipalities include Bessemer City, Greenville, Kings Mountain, Lexington, Monroe, Rocky Mount, Shelby, and Wilson. *See id.*

213. *See* G.S. 105-449.81 (imposing the tax); 105-449.80 (establishing the rate of tax). "Motor fuel" includes "gasoline, diesel fuel, and blended fuel." G.S. 105-449.60(31).

214. *See* S.L. 1951, ch. 260, §§ 2, 3.

215. *See* S.L. 2015-241, § 29.17.D.(a). Prior to 2015, G.S. 136-41.1(a) contained an automatic, annual appropriation of 10.4 percent of the net amount of motor fuels taxes for distribution to municipalities. *See id.*

216. *See* G.S. 136-41.1(a).

217. G.S. 136-41.1(a). A non-state street is "any public road maintained by a municipality and open to use by the general public, and having an average width of not less than 16 feet." For the 2021–2023 fiscal biennium, the General Assembly mandated that (1) eligible municipalities with a population of 400,000

To receive Powell Bill funds, a municipality incorporated after January 1, 1945, must have (1) held the most recent election to elect municipal officials required under its charter or the general law, (2) levied a property tax for the current fiscal year of at least $0.05 per $100.00 in assessed valuation and collected at least 50 percent of the total property tax levy for the previous fiscal year, (3) adopted a budget ordinance in substantial compliance with general law requirements, and (4) appropriated funds for at least two of eight services specified by statute.[218] A municipality incorporated after January 1, 2000, must appropriate funds for at least four of those same eight services specified by statute in order to receive Powell Bill funds.[219] A municipality incorporated before January 1, 1945, must only demonstrate that it has conducted an election of municipal officers within the preceding four-year period and that it currently imposes a property tax or provides other funds for the general operating expenses of the municipality.[220]

NCDOT distributes Powell Bill funds to eligible municipalities twice per year—half on or before October 1 and half on or before January 1.[221]

Permissible Uses of Powell Bill Funds

A municipality that receives Powell Bill funds has three options when expending these moneys.[222]

1. The municipality may accept all or a portion of the funds allocated to the municipality for use as authorized by G.S. 136-41.3(a).

    G.S. 136-41.3(a) requires a recipient municipality to use such funds *"primarily for the resurfacing of streets within the corporate limits of the municipality[,] . . . but [it] may also [use such moneys] . . . for the purposes of maintaining, repairing, constructing, reconstructing or widening of any street or public thoroughfares including bridges, drainage, curb and gutter, and other necessary appurtenances within the corporate limits of the municipality."*[223] Other permissible expenditures include the purchase and maintenance of traffic-control devices and signs, a

---

or more receive the same amount of Powell Bill funds allocated for the 2020–2021 fiscal year and (2) eligible municipalities with a population of 400,000 or less receive an appropriation based upon the formula contained in G.S. 136-41.1. The legislature appropriated $154.875 million in Powell Bill funds in both fiscal year 2021–2022 and fiscal year 2022–2023. *See* S.L. 2021-180, § 3.1.

218. *See* G.S. 136-41.2. These services include police protection, fire protection, solid waste collection or disposal, water distribution, street maintenance, street construction or right-of-way acquisition, street lighting, and zoning. *See* G.S. 136-41.2(c).

219. *See* G.S. 136-41.2(c).

220. *See* G.S. 136-41.2A.

221. *See* G.S. 136-41.1(a). A municipality that fails to meet certain filing deadlines is ineligible to receive Powell Bill distributions for the fiscal year in which it failed to meet the deadline. *See* G.S. 136-41.3(b1).

222. *See* G.S. 136-41.4(a).

223. G.S. 136-41.3(a) (emphasis added). The General Assembly revised G.S. 136-41.3(a) to require municipalities to use such funds "primarily" for resurfacing—but neither the revised statute nor the Session Law making the change define what "primarily" means. *See* S.L. 2015-241, § 28.17D.(b). This provision likely requires a municipality to satisfy its yearly street resurfacing needs before using the funds for other permissible expenditures. A municipality may not use any Powell Bill funds to construct a sidewalk "into which is built a mailbox, utility pole, fire hydrant, or other similar obstruction that would impede the clear passage of pedestrians on the sidewalk." *Id.*

municipality's proportionate share of special assessments for street improvements, and debt service on bonds issued exclusively for streets and sidewalks.[224]

2. The municipality may use some or all the funds allocated to the municipality to match federal funds administered by NCDOT for independent bicycle and pedestrian improvement projects within the municipality's limits or within the area of any metropolitan planning organization or rural transportation planning organization.[225]

3. The municipality may elect to have some or all of its allocation reprogrammed for any Transportation Improvement Project currently on the approved project list within the municipality's limits or within the area of any metropolitan planning organization or rural transportation organization.[226]

Generally, a municipality may not accumulate an amount greater than the sum of the past ten distributions (five years' worth).[227] NCDOT must annually report to a legislative committee of the General Assembly on the use that each municipality makes of its Powell Bill funds during the preceding fiscal year.[228]

Other Local Revenues

Counties and municipalities receive a variety of other revenues, including the proceeds of Alcoholic Beverage Control (ABC) store profits, investment earnings, federal, state, and private grants, fines and penalties, and other miscellaneous revenue sources.

Alcoholic Beverage Control (ABC) Store Profits

Counties and municipalities—through local ABC boards—may operate ABC stores.[229] After distributing a portion of its gross receipts for particular purposes specified by statute and retaining a portion of gross receipts as working capital to operate its ABC system, an ABC board generally may distribute its net profits to the county or municipality for which the ABC board was established.[230] Although the general law permits remaining funds to be spent for any authorized public purpose, a local act applicable to a particular ABC board may require that all or some of the net profits be spent for a particular purpose.[231]

---

224. *See* N.C. Department of Transportation, *Powell Bill Expenditure Guidance*, connect.ncdot.gov (last visited Feb. 27, 2023).

225. *See* G.S. 136-41.4(a)(2).

226. *See* G.S. 136-41.4(a)(3).

227. *See* G.S. 136-41.3(b1). A "small municipality"—which NCDOT defines as a municipality with a population of less than 5,000 people—may apply to NCDOT to accumulate up to the sum of the past twenty distributions. *See id*; *see also* N.C. Department of Transportation, *NCDOT Powell Bill Program Administration NCDOT Policy F.28.0100*, connect.ncdot.gov (last revised April 28, 2022), 2–3.

228. *See* G.S. 136-41.3(b).

229. *See* G.S. 18B-600 (permitting, among other things, municipalities and counties to approve the operation of ABC stores). As of March 1, 2023, 174 active local ABC systems operated in North Carolina. *See* N.C. Alcoholic Beverage Commission, *North Carolina ABC Board List*, abc.nc.gov (last visited Feb. 27, 2023).

230. *See generally* G.S. 18B-805.

231. *See* G.S. 18B-805(e) (noting that, "unless some other distribution or some other schedule is provided for by law," the net profits of an ABC board should be remitted on a quarterly basis to the general fund of the municipality or county for which the board is established).

Investment Earnings

Counties and municipalities may invest the cash balances of any fund.[232] North Carolina law prescribes the types of investments that counties and municipalities may make, and in doing so, it generally seeks to minimize investment risk and maximize liquidity.[233] Counties and municipalities most commonly invest in certificates of deposit in banks and savings and loan associations; obligations of the U.S. government (colloquially referred to as "treasuries"); obligations of certain agencies established by federal law (colloquially referred to as "agencies") that mature no later than eighteen months from the date of purchase; and the North Carolina Capital Management Trust, a mutual fund for local government investment. The interest earned on investments must be credited proportionately to the funds from which the invested moneys were drawn.[234] The amount of investment income that a unit earns fluctuates each year because of changes in short-term interest rates.

Grants

Counties and municipalities may, and commonly do, receive grants from the federal or state government, or from the private sector (e.g., a nonprofit organization).[235] Local governments vary as to how frequently they seek or receive grants and as to the purposes for which they obtain grants. Many use grant revenue to fund educational programs and activities, housing projects, economic development activities, energy programs, police programs, or infrastructure projects. Receiving a grant from the federal government, in particular, may trigger a host of compliance obligations.

Fines and Penalties

Local governments sometimes impose penalties for ordinance violations or for delinquent payments for government services. Some counties and municipalities also collect fines and penalties imposed by statute (e.g., penalties for failing to timely list property taxes or failing to pay property taxes). Although the primary purpose of these penalties and fines is to punish violators and deter future violations, the revenue generated from penalties and fines also may serve to compensate a local government for enforcement or collection costs. In many instances, however, the North Carolina Constitution prohibits a unit of local government from retaining the proceeds of fines and penalties that it collects.

The North Carolina Constitution requires that "the clear proceeds of all penalties and forfeitures and of all fines collected in the several counties for any breach of the penal laws of the

---

232. *See* G.S. 159-30(a).

233. *See generally* G.S. 159-30. For more detail on the types of investments that G.S. 159-30 permits, see the heading "Investments" within Chapter 8, "Managing and Disbursing Public Funds."

234. *See* G.S. 159-30(e).

235. *See* G.S. 160A-17.1(a) (authorizing counties and municipalities "to make contracts for and to accept grants-in-aid . . . from the federal and State governments"); G.S. 153A-11; 160A-11 (generally authorizing municipalities to contract for and accept property). In the wake of the COVID-19 pandemic, counties and municipalities accepted substantial amounts of federal aid. Every municipality and county in North Carolina was entitled to receive distributions of federal financial assistance from the Coronavirus Local Fiscal Recovery Fund created under the American Rescue Plan Act of 2021. *See* American Rescue Plan Act of 2021, Pub. L. No. 117-2 § 603, 135 Stat. 4, 228 (2021) (ARPA). Many of these units also received indirect allocations of federal aid under ARPA through the General Assembly's disbursal of moneys received under the Coronavirus State Fiscal Recovery Fund created under the ARPA. *See* ARPA, § 602.

State" be used for maintaining the public school system.[236] Although the text of this provision applies only to breaches of North Carolina's "penal laws," North Carolina courts have held that this provision restricts the use of locally collected penalties and fines because they actually are assessed for *either* (1) a violation of the state's penal (i.e., criminal) law or (2) a violation of a state statute or state regulatory scheme where the penalty or fine is intended to punish the violator.

For example, a county or municipality may specify in a county or municipal ordinance that the violation of such an ordinance (1) constitutes a criminal offense and (2) results in the imposition of a fine.[237] The "clear proceeds" of any fine attached to the criminal violation of a county or municipal ordinance must be distributed to the public schools. As an alternative to criminalizing the violation of a county or municipal ordinance, a local government that does not specify that the violation of a county or municipal ordinance constitutes a criminal offense may instead choose to attach *civil* penalties to such a violation. Typically, a local government may retain the proceeds of any such civil penalties.[238]

When a local government collects a civil penalty or fine imposed under state law and that penalty is intended to punish the violator, then the clear proceeds of any such penalty or fine collected must be remitted to the local school administrative unit in the county in which the penalty was assessed. For example, these penalties include, among other things, those imposed for (1) the late listing of or failure to list property for ad valorem property taxation,[239] (2) the submission of a worthless check for payment of ad valorem property taxation,[240] (3) the failure to file or failure to pay occupancy taxes,[241] (4) the failure to file or failure to pay prepared food or meal taxes,[242] and (5) the failure to file or failure to pay motor vehicle and heavy equipment rental gross receipts taxes.[243]

Lastly, if the violation of a county or municipal ordinance constitutes a separate violation of state "penal" law, the clear proceeds of any civil penalty that the local government imposes

---

236. *See* N.C. Const. art. IX, § 7. The North Carolina Supreme Court has held that the term "clear proceeds" includes the gross proceeds of a penalty or fine *less* reasonable costs of collection (but not including the administrative costs of enforcing an ordinance). *See* Cauble v. City of Asheville, 314 N.C. 598, 604–5 (1985). When enacting a statutory provision that requires other governmental entities to remit the "clear proceeds" of fines and penalties to the state's public schools, the General Assembly has permitted a collecting unit to retain up to 10 percent of a penalty or fine to the extent that such amount reflects the actual costs of collection. *See* G.S. 115C-437. For more information on this topic, see Kara Millonzi, "Locally-Collected Penalties & Fines: What Monies Belong to the Public Schools?," *Coates' Canons: NC Local Government Law* blog (Nov. 17, 2011); Kara Millonzi, "Locally-Collected Fines & Penalties: Calculating and Distributing Clear Proceeds," *Coates' Canons: NC Local Government Law* blog (Dec. 8, 2011).

237. Effective December 1, 2021, a violation of a county or municipal ordinance is a criminal offense under North Carolina law *only if* the county or municipality so specifies in the ordinance. *See* G.S. 153A-123(b); 160A-175(b) (each enacted by S.L. 2021-138). Prior to the adoption of S.L. 2021-138, violations of county and municipal ordinances constituted criminal misdemeanors under North Carolina law by default. Counties and municipalities may not impose criminal penalties for certain types of ordinance violations. *See* G.S. 153A-123(b1); 160A-175(b1). For more information regarding S.L. 2021-138, see Jeff Welty, "North Carolina's Decriminalization of Most Local Ordinance Violations," *North Carolina Criminal Law: A UNC School of Government Blog* (March 23, 2022).

238. *But see* Fearrington v. City of Greenville, 282 N.C. App. 218 (2022).

239. G.S. 105-312.

240. G.S. 105-357(b)(2).

241. G.S. 153A-155(e); 160A-215(e); 105-236.

242. G.S. 153A-154.1(c); 160A-214.1(c); 105-236.

243. G.S. 153A-156(f); 153A-156.1(d); 160A-215.1(f); 160A-215.2(d); 105-236.

for such a violation must be distributed to the public schools. For example, counties may adopt ordinances and collect a civil penalty to enforce a separate state statute that criminalizes passing a stopped school bus.[244] The clear proceeds of any such civil penalty collected by a local government for this purpose must be remitted to the public schools.[245]

Minor Revenue Sources

Units of local government receive a variety of additional, minor revenues. For example, many units receive payments from other local governments to provide joint or contractual programs. Many units of local government also receive funds from the management of their property, such as the leasing of government-owned building space or land or the sale of surplus equipment or real property.[246]

In addition, counties and municipalities receive refunds of the state and local sales and use taxes they pay.[247] Many units receive periodic donations of money or property from individuals or entities to fund one or more services or activities.[248] Occasionally, a local government receives a bid-bond forfeiture from a prospective vendor or contractor.[249] Finally, in limited cases, local governments receive payments from federal or state government entities because such entities are exempt from property taxation. These payments often are referred to as payments in lieu of taxation (PILOTs).

---

244. *See* G.S. 153A-246(b) (permitting civil enforcement); 20-217 (setting forth the offense).

245. In addition to the penalties and fines that must be distributed to the public schools by operation of Article IX, Section 7 of the North Carolina Constitution and G.S. 115C-437, the General Assembly also may direct local governments to distribute certain revenues to local school administrative units that are not covered by the constitutional provision. For example, G.S. Chapter 15, Article 2 prescribes procedures for disposing of personal property that is seized by, is confiscated by, or in any way comes into the possession of a local police department or a local sheriff's department. A unit is authorized to sell this property at auction after complying with certain notice and waiting period requirements. The net proceeds (after deduction of certain costs and expenses) must be distributed to the local school administrative unit(s) in the county in which the sale is made. This statutory mandate goes beyond what would be required under Article IX, Section 7. For more information on which fines and penalties must be distributed to the public schools and how, see Kara Millonzi, "*Richmond County Board of Education v. Cowell*: Clear Proceeds of Improper Equipment Offense Surcharge Belongs to Public Schools," *Coates' Canons: NC Local Government Law* blog (Sept. 17, 2015); Shea Denning, "Parking Enforcement: Civil Penalties, Infractions and Wheel Locks," *Coates' Canons: NC Local Government Law* blog (Dec. 13, 2010).

246. For additional information on this topic, see Chapter 11, "Procurement, Contracting, and Disposal of Property."

247. *See* G.S. 105-164.14(c) (setting forth the refund for state sales and use tax); *see also* G.S. 105-467(b) (Article 39) ("The State refund provisions contained in G.S. 105-164.14 and G.S. 105-164.14A apply to the local sales and use tax authorized to be levied and imposed under this Article."); 105-483 (Article 40); 105-498 (Article 42); 105-507.2, -509.1, -510.1, -511.3 (Article 43); 105-538 (Article 46) (collectively applying the refund provisions of G.S. 105-164.14(c) to the refund of each locally imposed sales and use tax).

248. For more information on this topic, see Kara Millonzi, "Donations to Local Governments," *Coates' Canons: NC Local Government Law* blog (Nov. 30, 2016).

249. *See* G.S. 143-129(b) (permitting a local government to retain a bidder's deposit of, among other things, a bid bond in the amount of 5 percent of a bid amount if the bidder fails to execute a contract).

Appendix 4.1 Local Revenue Authority and Limitations

Revenue Source (by Category)	Available to Counties, Cities, or Both?[a]	Restriction on Use of Proceeds?
Local Taxes		
Property Tax	Both	Proceeds may be expended only for purposes specified in G.S. 153A-149 (counties) or 160A-209 (cities) unless voters approve otherwise in referendum.
Local Sales and Use Tax	County only (but certain proceeds must be shared with cities)	A portion of a county's distribution must be used for public school capital outlay. A separate portion must be used for public schools, community colleges, or economic development. The remaining funds may be expended for any public purpose in which the unit is authorized to engage. A municipality may expend its share for any public purpose in which the unit is authorized to engage.
Transportation Sales and Use Tax	County only (but in some cases proceeds must be shared with cities)	Proceeds must be expended to finance, construct, operate, and maintain local public transportation systems.
Rental Car Gross Receipts Tax	Both	Proceeds may be expended for any public purpose in which the unit is authorized to engage.
Short-Term Heavy Equipment Rentals Tax	Both	Proceeds may be expended for any public purpose in which the unit is authorized to engage.
Motor Vehicle License Taxes	Both	Counties must expend proceeds to fund the construction, operation, and maintenance of one or more public transportation systems. Cities may expend proceeds for any public purpose in which the unit is authorized to engage.
Occupancy and Meal Taxes	Authorized by local act only	Local act typically restricts use of proceeds to particular purpose(s).
Local Fees, Charges, and Assessments		
General User Fees and Charges	Both	Proceeds may be expended for any public purpose in which the unit is authorized to engage.
Regulatory Fees	Both	Proceeds must be used to fund direct and indirect costs of performing regulatory activity.
Public Enterprise Fees and Charges	Both	Some proceeds are restricted to use only for the particular public enterprise activity.
Franchise Fees	Both (but county authority very limited)	Proceeds may be expended for any public purpose in which the unit is authorized to engage.
Special Assessments	Both	Proceeds may be expended for any public purpose in which the unit is authorized to engage.
Statutory Fees	Both (mainly county)	Most of the proceeds are restricted to use only for a particular purpose.

(continued)

Appendix 4.1 Local Revenue Authority and Limitations *(continued)*

Revenue Source (by Category)	Available to Counties, Cities, or Both?[a]	Restriction on Use of Proceeds?
State-Shared Revenue		
Video Programming Services Taxes	Both	Some proceeds must be used to support local public, educational, or governmental access channels. The remaining proceeds may be used for any public purpose in which the unit is authorized to engage.
Beer and Wine Taxes	Both	Proceeds may be expended for any public purpose in which the unit is authorized to engage.
Real Estate Transfer Taxes	County only	Proceeds may be expended for any public purpose in which the unit is authorized to engage.
Disposal Taxes	County only	Proceeds must be used to manage the disposal of tires or white goods.
911 Charge	Both	Proceeds restricted to certain, specified expenditures related to the operation of a 911 system.
Electric Taxes	City only	Proceeds may be expended for any public purpose in which the unit is authorized to engage.
Telecommunications Tax	City only	Proceeds may be expended for any public purpose in which the unit is authorized to engage.
Piped Natural Gas Taxes	City only	Proceeds may be expended for any public purpose in which the unit is authorized to engage.
Motor Fuels Tax (Powell Bill Funds)	City only	Proceeds must be used primarily for the resurfacing of municipal streets.
Other Local Revenues		
Alcohol Beverage Control Store Profits	Both	Some of the proceeds are earmarked for alcohol and substance abuse research and education programs. Under general law, the remaining funds may be expended for any public purpose in which the unit is authorized to engage. Local acts of the General Assembly frequently earmark all or some portion of a system's profits for a particular purpose.
Investment Earnings	Both	Proceeds may be expended for any public purpose in which the unit is authorized to engage.
Grants	Both	Proceeds typically are restricted to a particular purpose.
Fines and Penalties	Both	The clear proceeds of some locally collected fines and penalties must be distributed to the public schools. Other fine and penalty revenue typically may be expended for any public purpose in which the unit is authorized to engage.

a. Note that there may be certain eligibility requirements to qualify for a particular revenue stream or employ a particular revenue-raising mechanism.

Chapter 5

Property Tax Policy and Administration

by Christopher B. McLaughlin

Introduction

The goal of this chapter is to educate North Carolina local government officials about the basic structure and operation of our state's property tax system. It should give local officials the information they need to know what local governments must do, what they may do, and, perhaps most importantly, what they cannot do with property taxes. For more details on the topics discussed below, please see Christopher B. McLaughlin, *Fundamentals of Property Tax Collection Law in North Carolina* (UNC School of Government, 2011).

Non-Legal Considerations

This chapter focuses mainly on the legal issues surrounding property taxes. But local governments also face a number of important non-legal decisions concerning property tax policy and practice.

The most basic of these decisions is whether the local government wishes to levy a property tax. Although property taxes are optional, all 100 counties and nearly all the state's 500-plus municipalities levy this type of tax.

Taxpayers may wonder why local governments tax at all in light of the substantial federal and state taxes already affecting their incomes and activities. The simple answer to this question is that without property tax revenues, local governments would be forced to drastically cut services. Property taxes are the *single largest source* of unrestricted revenues for both counties and municipalities in North Carolina. Revenue from these taxes supports the wide variety of services provided by local governments.

The property tax is popular among local governments because it is one of the few sources of revenue under their complete control. Most other taxes are levied at rates set by state statutes or produce revenue that must be shared with the state or with other local governments. Not so for property tax rates and revenues, which are controlled entirely by local governments and subject only to a rather generous statutory maximum rate.

Property tax rates vary across the state from just a few pennies to more than $1 per $100 of property value. The legal parameters concerning the tax rate calculation are discussed in "The Property Tax Rate" section, below. But for the most part, the tax rate decision rests on a policy question beyond the scope of this book: What level of services should the local government provide and how should those services be funded?

Other non-legal decisions include how to organize the tax office, whether a municipality should collect its own taxes or contract with the county for such services, what types of enforced collection actions the collector will be authorized to pursue, and when countywide reappraisals of real property should occur. This chapter discusses the relevant statutory constraints and identifies best practices, but it does not attempt to suggest the correct answers to these questions. As with most issues involving local government, there is no one-size-fits-all approach to property taxes.

The Big Picture

As noted above, property taxes represent the single largest source of unrestricted revenue for both counties and municipalities. For fiscal year 2020–2021, property taxes represented 49 percent of county revenues and 25 percent of municipal revenues. Figures 5.1 and 5.2 illustrate the relative importance of property taxes as compared to other revenue sources. Note that both figures exclude debt proceeds, which must be paid back in the future using other revenue sources and therefore are not truly revenue sources.[1]

---

1. Searchable statistics are available on the N.C. Department of State Treasurer's website at https://logos.nctreasurer.com/Reporting/Report/External?applicationCode=AFIR. The statistics available as of March 2023 appear to dramatically underreport property tax revenues for fiscal year 2021–2022, so this chapter is relying on the statistics from fiscal year 2020–2021.

Figure 5.1 2020–2021 County Revenues: $16.5 Billion Total

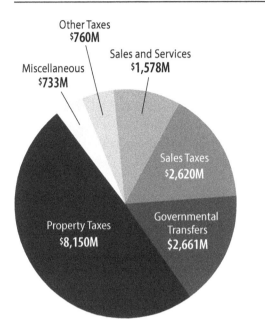

Other Taxes $760M

Sales and Services $1,578M

Miscellaneous $733M

Sales Taxes $2,620M

Property Taxes $8,150M

Governmental Transfers $2,661M

Figure 5.2 2020–2021 City Revenues: $12.9 Billion Total

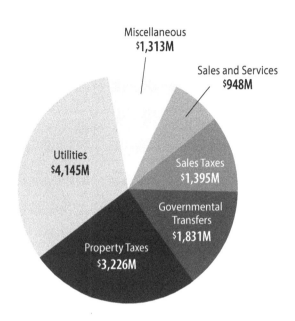

Miscellaneous $1,313M

Sales and Services $948M

Utilities $4,145M

Sales Taxes $1,395M

Governmental Transfers $1,831M

Property Taxes $3,226M

Although utility fees represent a larger percentage of municipal revenues than do property taxes, those funds are not *unrestricted* revenues because generally they must be used to cover the cost of providing those utilities. Were utility fees and charges excluded from the calculation, property taxes would represent more than 36 percent of municipal revenues.

The Governing Law and the Cast of Characters

Article V (finance), Section 2 (state and local taxation) of the North Carolina Constitution sets the basic ground rules for property taxes. Chapter 105, Subchapter II of the North Carolina General Statutes (hereinafter G.S.), commonly known as the Machinery Act, provides the details.

Actors at both the state and local levels play major roles in the property tax process. Table 5.1 identifies the principal characters at both levels of government.

As mentioned above, the property tax process is governed by statutes enacted by the *General Assembly* as part of the Machinery Act. The state *Local Government Division of the N.C. Department of Revenue (NCDOR)* is charged with ensuring that local governments adhere to

Table 5.1   Property Tax Cast of Characters

State Level	Local Level
• General Assembly	• Governing Board
• Department of Revenue, Local Government Division	• Assessor (County)
• Property Tax Commission	• Tax Collector
• Court of Appeals	• Board of Equalization and Review (County)
• Supreme Court	

Why Is It Called the "Machinery Act," and Where Can I Find It?

G.S. 105-271 and -272 state that the collection of property tax statutes in Subchapter II of Chapter 105 can be referred to as the Machinery Act because "[t]he purpose of this Subchapter is to provide the *machinery* for the listing, appraisal, and assessment of property and the levy and collection of taxes on property by counties and municipalities" (emphasis added).

   The North Carolina Department of Revenue usually produces a hard copy of the Machinery Act every two years to capture the most recent changes to its many sections. However, because the Machinery Act is amended almost every legislative session and the hard copy is produced only every other year, the best source for the most up-to-date Machinery Act provisions is the searchable General Statutes page on the General Assembly's website, www.ncga.state.nc.us/gascripts/statutes/Statutes.asp.

---

the Machinery Act's requirements. This division also provides education, training, and guidance to local government tax officials and assesses and allocates public-service-company property to the counties so that it can be subject to local property taxes.

   Note that NCDOR's Local Government Division is distinct from the Local Government Commission (LGC), which operates out of the N.C. Department of the State Treasurer. The LGC monitors the fiscal and accounting practices of the state's local governments but does not play a direct role in property tax administration.

   County *boards of equalization and review*, the state *Property Tax Commission*, the state *court of appeals*, and the state *supreme court* are all involved with the resolution of appeals concerning property tax values and property tax exemptions and exclusions.

   An *assessor* is responsible for listing and assessing all taxable property in a county for property taxes. In other words, he or she must determine the what, the where, the who, and the how much for all property that will be taxed for the coming fiscal year. A *tax collector* must collect the taxes levied on that property, if necessary by use of the enforced collection remedies available under the Machinery Act and other statutes. In many counties, the county commissioners have chosen to appoint a single individual as both assessor and tax collector under the title of "tax administrator."

   The role of the *local government governing board* in the property tax process is summarized in Table 5.2. Table 5.3 lists the important dates in the property tax calendar. More details on all these issues are provided in subsequent sections of this chapter.

Real Property versus Personal Property

Collection remedies under the Machinery Act differ depending on whether the property being taxed is real or personal. Real property is essentially land, buildings, and things that are permanently affixed to those buildings—think of light fixtures or kitchen cabinets. Personal property is everything else: vehicles, boats, planes, business equipment, and so forth. With very few exceptions, personal property is taxable only if it is tangible. Intangible personal property—such as cash, stocks, bank deposits, patents, and franchise rights—is not taxable.

Table 5.2 Rights and Duties of Local Government Governing Boards

Board of County Commissioners	Town/City Council
• Adopts property tax rate annually	• Adopts property tax rate annually
• Appoints assessor and tax collector	• Appoints tax collector or contracts with county for tax collection
• Reviews performance of assessor and tax collector	• Reviews performance of tax collector
• Accepts settlement of prior year's taxes from tax collector and charges tax collector with responsibility for current year's taxes	• Accepts settlement of prior year's taxes from tax collector and charges tax collector with responsibility for current year's taxes
• Decides when to conduct countywide reappraisals of real property (at least every eight years)	• Rules on taxpayer requests for refunds and releases
• Appoints Board of Equalization and Review (the county commissioners may serve as this board)	
• Rules on taxpayer requests for refunds and releases	

Table 5.3 Important Dates on the Property Tax Calendar

January 1	• Listing date (ownership, situs, value, and taxability determined) • Tax liens attach to real property
July 1	• Fiscal year begins • Deadline for adoption of new budget and tax rate
September 1	• Discounts end (if offered) • Taxes due
January 6 (following year)	• Taxes become delinquent, interest accrues, and enforced collections may begin
June 30 (following year)	• Fiscal year ends, annual collection rate is determined

Why Cars Are Different

Cars, trucks, vans, motorcycles, and trailers with valid registrations and license plates are called "registered motor vehicles" (RMVs) by the Machinery Act. Although they are considered personal property under the Machinery Act, RMVs are subject to very different tax rules than those applied to other types of personal property.

In a nutshell, the taxation of RMVs is tied to the registration and renewal process. Registration of most motor vehicles is staggered throughout the year so that different due dates and delinquency dates apply for different RMV taxpayers. Under the "Tag & Tax Together" program which debuted in 2013, owners pay property taxes on their vehicles at the time they obtain their initial registrations or renew their registrations for those vehicles with the N.C. Division of Motor Vehicles (DMV). If the owner refuses to pay the taxes, the DMV will refuse to register the motor vehicle. Under this new system, local governments no longer have any collection authority or responsibility for the property taxes they levy on registered motor vehicles. See the section titled "Registered Motor Vehicles," below, for more details on RMV taxes.

Table 5.4A County and Municipal Property Tax Rates, 2022–2023

	Lowest Rate	Highest Rate	Median Rate
Counties	.320 (Watauga)	.990 (Scotland)	.66
Municipalities	.013 (Wesley Chapel)	.920 (Enfield)	.47

Source: North Carolina Department of Revenue.

Table 5.4B County Tax Bases, 2021

Smallest	$433 Million	Tyrrell County (population 3,254)
Largest	$190 Billion	Mecklenburg County (population 1,122,000)
Median	$16 Billion	
Average	$13 Billion	

Source: North Carolina Department of State Treasurer.

The Property Tax Rate

Although local governments are not required to levy property taxes, nearly all do. The rates at which they levy those taxes vary greatly, as Table 5.4A indicates. Traditionally, the lowest rates were found in counties located along the coast and in the mountains in counties with lots of expensive vacation homes.

Property tax rates for a particular local government are generally capped at $1.50, but that cap is subject to many exceptions. For example, there is no statutory limit on the rate for property taxes used to fund schools or jails. And for uses that are subject to the statutory cap, a local government may obtain voter approval to exceed the $1.50 maximum tax rate.[2]

The $1.50 cap applies to individual taxing jurisdictions, not to individual taxpayers. A taxpayer who lives in a municipality could very well wind up paying a total property tax rate greater than $1.50 because that taxpayer's property is subject to both county and municipal taxes. As a result, a municipality need not worry about the county's property tax when setting its own rate, or vice versa.

The amount of revenue that each county can generate from its property tax depends on that county's tax base, of course. As Table 5.4B demonstrates, county tax bases vary widely. A 1¢ increase in Tyrrell County's property tax would produce an additional $43,300 in tax revenue. In Mecklenburg County, that same 1¢ property tax rate increase would generate $19,000,000.

Tax Rate Uniformity and Tax Districts

Article V, Section 2(2) of the North Carolina Constitution requires that all property within a specific taxing jurisdiction must be subject to the same tax rate. This uniformity requirement prohibits local governments from adopting different tax rates for different property or for

---

2. G.S. 153A-149 (counties); 160A-209 (municipalities).

> ### How Do I Use the Tax Rate to Calculate a Tax Bill?
>
> Tax rates are expressed as "$ of tax per $100 dollars of taxable value." For example, if a home is valued for tax purposes at $200,000 and the county tax rate is $.25, the county property taxes on that home will be $500. First divide the taxable value by 100 ($200,000 / 100 = $2,000), then multiply the result by the tax rate ($2,000 × .25 = $500).

different areas of that jurisdiction. For example, a county could not adopt one tax rate for real property and a different tax rate for motor vehicles. Nor could a county choose to adopt one tax rate for its incorporated areas and a different tax rate for its unincorporated areas.

The only exception to the uniformity requirement is the constitutional provision that permits special tax districts. Often called service districts, these tax districts are authorized by Article V, Section 2(4) of the North Carolina Constitution to fund additional services in their geographic areas.[3] Multiple tax districts are permitted in the same local government, so long as each tax district is created for a permissible purpose. The uniformity requirement applies to these special districts in that the additional tax rate levied in a particular district must be uniformly applied to all property sited in that district.

Counties most often use special tax districts to fund fire protection in unincorporated areas, but they can also use them to fund such services as trash collection, sewer and water systems, and beach erosion control. Municipalities can use special tax districts to fund many of those same services, but they more often create districts for downtown revitalization projects. This category is broadly defined to cover a variety of expenditures, including new parking facilities, improved lighting, additional police protection, and tourism promotion within the downtown core.

Another type of special tax district is a special supplemental school district.[4] The supplemental school district tax must be approved by voters before it can be levied and must be used only to fund the public schools in that district. Once adopted, a supplemental school tax applies to all property within that particular school district.

The taxes levied in a special tax district count toward the $1.50 cap on general property tax rates. This means that the total of regular property taxes and special district taxes levied by a local government on a particular piece of property cannot exceed $1.50 for certain uses unless the local government obtains voter approval to exceed that cap.

Use-Specific Taxes

A local government may adopt a single property tax rate to satisfy all its budgetary needs, or it may adopt multiple tax rates with the revenue from each earmarked for a specific use. For example, instead of funding police and fire protection services out of its general property tax revenue, a municipality could choose to adopt two property tax rates: one for general fund revenue and one to fund police and fire services.

---

3. For more information regarding service districts, see Chapter 4, "Revenue Sources."
4. G.S. Ch. 115C, Art. 36.

There is no limit on the number of different use-specific property tax rates that may be adopted by a local government, so long as each such tax applies uniformly to all taxable property within the jurisdiction. Use-specific taxes may be adopted as part of a local government's annual budget and do not require voter approval.

A key difference between use-specific property taxes and special tax district taxes is that use-specific taxes must apply to the entire jurisdiction. Special tax district taxes may be levied on portions of a jurisdiction to fund specific services in that district.

The North Carolina Supreme Court has ruled that spending decisions by local governments are not bound by use-specific property taxes.[5] A local government may change its spending for a particular use regardless of what it promised to spend on that use in its budget through a use-specific tax rate.

For example, assume that a county adopts a $.50 general tax rate, a $.12 tax rate for law enforcement, and a $.02 tax rate for libraries. Based on its budgeted tax base, the $.12 tax would raise $1,200,000 for county law enforcement and the $.02 tax would raise $200,000 for county libraries. Despite the adoption of these use-specific taxes, the county could choose to spend more or less than these amounts on law enforcement and libraries in the coming fiscal year. Voters may not take kindly to such variations from the budget, but they are legal.

Setting the Tax Rate

Property taxes are levied on a fiscal year basis despite the fact that many of the important dates on the property tax schedule seem to be configured around the calendar year. A local government that levies property taxes must set its property tax rate(s) in its annual budget, which should be adopted by July 1, the beginning of the fiscal year.[6]

Until a budget is adopted, there can be no property tax levy. Although interim budgets are permitted, they authorize only continued spending by local governments and not the levy of taxes. A delay in the adoption of the budget can delay property tax collections and do serious harm to a local government's revenues.

The property tax rate should be based on the amount of revenue the local government needs to balance its budget after all other revenue sources are accounted for, given the expected tax base for the coming year. Obviously, this amount will be driven by important decisions regarding what services the local government can and should provide.

When balancing the budget with property taxes, a local government must be realistic about how much of its tax levy it will actually collect. While property tax collection percentages are generally very good—99 percent on average—no local government collects every penny of its property taxes.[7] For budget purposes, state law prohibits local governments from assuming a higher collection rate for the coming year than it experienced in the current year.

---

5. Long v. Comm'rs of Richmond Cnty., 76 N.C. 273, 280 (1877).

6. See the Local Government Budget and Fiscal Control Act, G.S. Chapter 159, Article 3.

7. See, e.g., the following memoranda from the N.C. Department of State Treasurer, State and Local Government Finance Division and the Local Government Commission (LGC): LGC Memo #2022-03, *Management of Cash and Taxes and Fund Balance Available — Counties — for the Fiscal Year Ended June 30, 2020* (Aug. 11, 2021), 2; LGC Memo #2022-04, *Management of Cash and Taxes and Fund Balance Available —Municipalities— for the Fiscal Year Ended June 30, 2020* (Aug. 17, 2021), 2–3.

Calculating the Tax Rate

Assume Carolina County needs to generate $50,000,000 in property tax revenue to balance its budget for the coming fiscal year. The basic property tax calculation is as follows:

(Tax Base / 100) × Tax Rate = Tax Revenue.

First, the county should get from the tax collector the estimated property tax collection percentage for the current fiscal year. This percentage will be an estimate because the current fiscal year will not have ended at the time Carolina County creates the budget for the next fiscal year.

Assume the estimated collection percentage for the current fiscal year is 97 percent. The county should divide the revenue target by this percentage to account for the fact that not every penny of the property tax levy will be collected.

$50,000,000 / .97 = $51,550,000.

The result is the adjusted revenue target for the next fiscal year. In other words, if the county wishes to produce $50,000,000 in property tax revenue next year, it must levy $51,550,000 in property taxes.

Second, the county should get from the assessor the estimated tax base for the next fiscal year. It will be an estimate because subsequent tax appeals, discoveries, and motor vehicle registrations will affect the final figure.

Assume that the estimated tax base is $10,000,000,000. The county should divide the estimated tax base by 100 to reflect the fact that the tax rate is "per $100 in value."

$10,000,000,000 / $100 = $100,000,000.

Finally, the county should divide the adjusted revenue target by the result above to determine the rate.

$51,550,000 / $100,000,000 = $.516.

Carolina County must levy a property tax of $.516, or 51.6¢ per $100 of value, to meet its budgetary needs for the coming fiscal year.

When budgeting, many local governments start with a tax rate target rather than a revenue target. Regardless of the approach used, the local government must account for the current year's tax collection percentage when budgeting for next year.

For example, assume that Carolina County wishes to keep its tax rate at $.51 per $100 of value for the coming year. If next year's tax base is estimated to be $10,000,000,000, a tax rate of $.51 would produce tax revenue of $51,000,000. However, this estimated revenue must be reduced by this year's collection percentage:

$51,000,000 × .97 = $49,470,000.

As a result, if Carolina County plans to keep its tax rate at $.51 for the coming year, it should budget for no more than $49,470,000 in property tax revenue.

Changing the Tax Rate

Once the total tax rate is set in the budget, the governing board is generally prohibited from changing it. Absent an order from a judge or from the Local Government Commission, the only justification for adjusting a tax rate after adoption of the budget is when the local government receives revenues that are substantially different from what was expected. And even then, the change must occur before January 1 following the start of the fiscal year. For example, if a governing board wished to change its 2023–2024 tax rate due to a substantial change in revenues, it would need to act before January 1, 2024.[8]

What type of events could justify a change in the total tax rate under this standard? The relevant statutes do not provide additional details, but presumably changes could occur after a misfortune such as a bankruptcy filing by a large industrial taxpayer that would prevent collection of a substantial portion of the local government's property tax levy or the elimination of an important revenue source due to new legislation enacted by the General Assembly. Good news—such as the creation of a major new revenue source for the local government—could also justify a mid-year change in the tax rate, but such occurrences are rare.

As mentioned above, local governments may adopt multiple tax rates for different uses. These use-specific rates may be changed during a fiscal year without regard for statutory restrictions so long as the total tax rate levied by the local government does not change.

Consider again the example in which a county adopts a general tax rate of $.50, a law enforcement tax of $.12, and a library tax of $.02, for a total combined rate of $.64. The county would be free to alter any or all of its three different tax rates so long as the total combined rate still equaled $.64.

The Revenue-Neutral Tax Rate

To help taxpayers compare tax rates before and after countywide reappraisals of real property, local governments are required to calculate and publish revenue-neutral tax rates (RNTRs) following their reappraisals.[9]

The RNTR would produce the same amount of revenue using the new tax base as was produced in the present year from the existing tax rate and tax base. In other words, if a new tax rate adopted by a governing board is higher than the RNTR, then the local government has increased its total property tax levy, and if the new rate is lower than the RNTR, the local government has decreased its total property tax levy.

In normal economic times, tax bases increase after reappraisals. When the tax base increases, the tax rate can be lowered without decreasing tax revenue. Therefore, the RNTR is normally lower than the existing tax rate. However, when market prices drop, as they have done of late in many areas of the state, a local government's tax base can decrease after a reappraisal. In these circumstances, the government board that wishes to keep revenues constant must raise the tax rate. As a result, the RNTR will be higher than the existing tax rate.

Local governments are not required to adopt the RNTR, but they must publish it as part of their annual budget process. Even if the RNTR is adopted, individual taxpayers may see their tax bills increase or decrease because their individual property appreciated or depreciated more than did the tax base in the aggregate. Much confusion surrounds the RNTR, in large part because, despite its name, it does not guarantee that taxpayers' bills will remain constant.

For example, assume that Carolina County's tax base increased by 10 percent following its 2023 reappraisal. The RNTR is calculated to be $.50 per $100 of value, a bit lower than the county's 2022–2023 tax rate of $.55 per $100 of value. The county commissioners decide to

---

8. G.S. 159-15.
9. G.S. 159-11(e).

adopt the RNTR as the tax rate for 2023–2024 and proudly announce that they have avoided a tax increase. However, when the 2023 tax bills are mailed in August, Tommy TarHeel is furious because his new tax bill is higher than last year's tax bill.

How can this be? The likely answer is that Tommy's real property appreciated more than 10 percent, which was the average increase in value for all real property in the county. Assume that Tommy's real property tax appraisal increased from $100,000 to $150,000 as a result of the 2023 reappraisal. For 2022–2023, Tommy's tax bill was $550 ($100,000/100 × $.55). For 2023–2024, his tax bill is $750 ($150,000/100 x $.50). The drop in the tax rate was not enough to offset the increase in Tommy's tax appraisal, meaning that Tommy's tax bill increased by $200 despite the county's adoption of the RNTR.

By adopting the RNTR, a local government may keep its aggregate property tax revenue constant. But individual taxpayers' bills are not guaranteed to remain constant because individual properties are likely to have appreciated or depreciated differently from the countywide tax base.

Listing and Assessing

The process of determining what taxable property exists in a jurisdiction, who owns it, and how much it is worth is known as listing and assessing property for taxation. The county assessor oversees this process, which is closely regulated by the Machinery Act and is intended to be (mostly) uniform from county to county. The only property over which the assessor does not have listing and assessing authority is public-service-company property, described in more detail below.

As a general rule, local government governing boards do not get involved with assigning tax values to individual properties. That process is accomplished by the assessor and his or her staff, ideally free from political pressures.

However, local government governing boards—especially boards of county commissioners—do retain some discretion as to how and when the process unfolds. These discretionary duties include

- appointing the assessor and setting his/her term of office,
- approving the budget for the assessor's office,
- deciding when to hold countywide reappraisals of real property,
- ruling on taxpayer appeals of tax values and tax exemptions while sitting as the board of equalization and review (or appointing a separate board of equalization and review), and
- waiving or refusing to waive discovery bills.

One property tax issue over which local governments have no authority is the creation of property tax exemptions. The North Carolina Constitution grants this authority exclusively to the General Assembly.[10] As a result, property tax exemptions are products of state statutes,

---

10. N.C. Const., art. V, § 2(2).

not local ordinances. Counties and municipalities may not create their own exemptions from property taxes. Nor may they decide to ignore exemptions mandated by the Machinery Act.

This section briefly describes the listing and assessing process and the appropriate role for governing boards in that process. Readers who seek more details should take a look at *A Guide to the Listing, Assessment, and Taxation of Property in North Carolina*, a comprehensive guide to the process written by my School of Government colleague Shea Riggsbee Denning.

Appointing the Assessor

The assessor, appointed by the board of county commissioners, is responsible for listing and assessing all taxable property in the county. This process includes determining the *situs*—a fancy word for taxable location—of that property, determining who owns that property, deciding whether that property and its owner are eligible for an exemption or exclusion from tax, and, perhaps most controversially, assigning a value for tax purposes to that property.

The Machinery Act creates some minimum qualifications for assessors, but for the most part the board of county commissioners retains great discretion as to who should serve in this role. Candidates must be at least twenty-one years of age, must hold a high school diploma or equivalent, and must be certified by the N.C. Department of Revenue within two years of taking office. Certification involves passing four assessment courses and a comprehensive exam. The assessor must be appointed for a fixed term set by the county commissioners that can vary from two to four years. Once the assessor's term length is set by the commissioners, it cannot be changed until after the term ends or after the assessor is removed from office.[11]

Unlike most employees in most counties, assessors are not at-will employees and cannot be removed from office at the discretion of the commissioners. An assessor may be removed from office before his or her term ends only for "good cause," a term not defined by the Machinery Act. However, similar good cause provisions covering appointed officials elsewhere in the General Statutes suggest that adequate grounds for removal include inefficiency, misconduct in office, and commission of a felony or other crime involving moral turpitude. In other words, the conduct that justifies the removal must either be directly tied to the assessor's job performance or be so serious as to call into question the assessor's fitness for office. For example, the failure to pay property taxes in a timely fashion likely would justify the firing of an assessor, but a conviction for driving under the influence might not.

If the county commissioners wish to remove the assessor from office, they must first provide the assessor with written notice of that intent and the opportunity to be heard at a public session of the board. For obvious reasons, the county attorney should be intimately involved with this process.

The Machinery Act does not create term limits for assessors. A board can repeatedly reappoint a particular assessor for as long as it wishes.

---

11. G.S. 105-294.

Why Are There No Municipal Assessors?

More than five hundred North Carolina municipalities levy property taxes, but not a single one lists and assesses its own property for tax purposes. The Machinery Act requires municipalities to rely on the county assessor to answer the what, where, who, and how much questions related to property taxes, with one exception. Any municipality that sits in more than one county is authorized to appoint its own assessor to list and assess all of its property for taxation. Plenty of municipalities qualify for this exception, but none takes advantage of it. The reasons behind those decisions likely vary from town to town, but the expense involved is almost certainly a driving factor. Why pay for a service that the municipality can get for free from the county? Taxpayer confusion may be another consideration. If a municipality were to appoint its own assessor, taxpayers residing in that jurisdiction could wind up with two different tax values placed on their homes, cars, and other taxable property—one assigned by the county and one assigned by the municipality. More than a few taxpayers would question this result.

What, Where, Who, and How Much?

The what, where, who, and how much decisions concerning property taxes on *personal* property are made as of the annual listing day, which is the January 1 before the fiscal year begins.[12] For taxes on *real* property, the how much decisions (appraisals) are made as of January 1 of the reappraisal year, but ownership and taxability decisions are made as of January 1 each year, just as they are for personal property. In other words, a snapshot is taken every January 1, and the results of that snapshot control property taxes for the coming fiscal year.

For example, if Tom Taxpayer buys a new boat on February 1, 2023, he will not be required to list that boat for 2023–2024 property taxes because he did not own the boat on January 1. If Tina Taxpayer owns a house in Carolina County on January 1, 2023, that house is taxable by the county for the 2023–2024 fiscal year even if it burns to the ground the very next day. If Tim Taxpayer owns a vacant lot in Carolina County on January 1, 2023, and breaks ground on a new house on that lot on January 2, the new house will not be taxable by the county for 2023–2024 because it did not exist on January 1, the listing day. The house first will be listed and taxed as of January 1, *2024*, meaning it first will be taxed by the county in the 2024–2025 fiscal year. Construction that is partially complete as of January 1 should be assessed a percentage of its estimated value once complete.

Situs

The situs (taxable location) of real property should be easily determined and immutable except when municipalities change their boundaries through annexation or de-annexation or, less often, when two counties adjust their borders. But the situs of personal property—cars, boats, and planes especially—can present a major challenge. That movable property is not in a jurisdiction on January 1 does not necessarily mean that the jurisdiction cannot tax that property for the coming year.

With respect to personal property, situs means property that is more or less permanently located in a jurisdiction. For example, if a private jet is flown all over the country throughout the year but always returns to a hangar in Carolina County, Carolina County should be able to tax that plane even if it is not in the county on January 1.

---

12. G.S. 105-285.

Figure 5.3   Revaluation Cycles across North Carolina

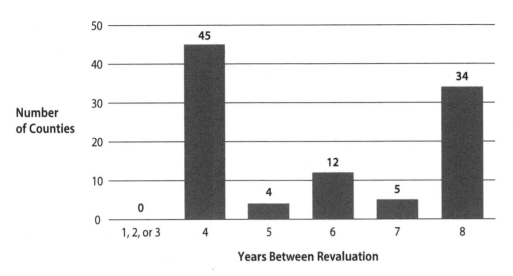

Source: North Carolina Department of Revenue, 2023.

Appraisal of Personal Property

The Machinery Act requires that all property be assessed for tax purposes at its "true value," defined to be the property's market value were it sold in an arms-length transaction between two willing, able, and informed parties under no compulsion to buy or sell the property.[13]

As mentioned above, all taxable personal property—in other words, all taxable property that is not land or buildings—is appraised annually as of January 1. Generally tax appraisals for cars, boats, planes, factory equipment, and other personal property decrease from year to year because that property depreciates and loses value over time.

Appraisal of Real Property

The most time-consuming and controversial part of the property tax process is the countywide reappraisal of real property, during which all land and buildings are assigned new tax values. Just as is true for personal property, real property must be valued at its true market value that would be obtained in an arms-length transaction. Because foreclosure sales are involuntary sales, they are generally not considered when calculating appraisals.

Reappraisals—or "revals" as they commonly are called—must occur at least every eight years. Within this eight-year limitation, a county can choose whatever reappraisal cycle it prefers. A county is also free to change its reappraisal cycle in between reappraisals, so long as it stays within the eight-year limitation.[14]

In an ideal world, every county would reappraise all of its real property every year so that its tax values would be pegged to true market value as closely as possible. But annual reappraisal of the many thousands of real estate parcels in each county is simply not practical from either an expense or a workload perspective. As Figure 5.3 demonstrates, just under half of the state's

13. G.S. 105-284.
14. G.S. 105-286.

100 counties are on four-year cycles and about one-third of them are on eight-year cycles. This is a substantial change from a decade ago, when more than two-thirds of the state's counties were on eight-year cycles.

Depending on the size of its assessor's office, a county can either conduct a reappraisal using only in-house staff or hire external consultants to do some or all of the required appraisal work. The process involves what is known as a mass appraisal, meaning not every parcel of real property is inspected by appraisers. Usually a small representative sample of a county's real property will be individually appraised. The rest of the county's real property will be assigned tax values based on an analysis of market prices and physical characteristics at the neighborhood level.

Changes to Real Property Tax Values in Non-Reappraisal Years

In between reappraisals, real property tax values generally should change only due to physical or zoning changes to the property. Changes in general economic conditions or in the local real estate market should not be reflected in tax values until the next reappraisal.[15]

For example, assume that Billy BlueDevil owns Parcel A that was appraised at $300,000 in Carolina County's 2020 reappraisal. The county's next reappraisal is not scheduled until 2024. Billy sells Parcel A to Tommy TarHeel in late 2022 for $400,000 in an arms-length, non-foreclosure transaction. Although the true market value of Parcel A may be $400,000 as of January 1, 2023, the tax value of Parcel A should not change until the next reappraisal in 2024. The tax value of Parcel A must remain its true market value as of January 1, 2020. The same would be true if Billy's house sold in 2022 for less than its 2020 tax value.

Now assume that instead of selling Parcel A, Billy increases the size of his house on that lot by 2,000 square feet in 2022. This physical change to Parcel A should be reflected in the 2023 tax value of Parcel A. The tax value of Billy's house would also need to be changed prior to the next reappraisal if it burned down or were rezoned to make it more or less valuable for future development or use.

Public-Service-Company Property

Only one type of property is assessed at the state level: real and personal property owned by electricity providers, gas companies, railroads, telephone service providers, and other public-service companies.[16]

Each year these companies are required to list their taxable property with the N.C. Department of Revenue (NCDOR), which then assigns a tax value to that property and allocates that value to local governments for taxation. For real property, such as a power plant, the allocation is based on location. For movable personal property, such as buses and trains, the allocation is based on the miles driven in a jurisdiction, the miles of track in a jurisdiction, or a similar formula. If a local government's sales assessment ratio falls below 90 percent in certain years, that local government can lose a percentage of its public-service-company property value.[17] (See the next section for more on sales assessment ratios.)

---

15. G.S. 105-287.
16. G.S. Ch. 105, Art. 23.
17. G.S. 105-284.

Once public-service-company property value has been allocated to a local government, it may tax that property just as it taxes all other property in its jurisdiction. Unlike regular property tax appeals, appeals of public-service-company property tax values go directly to the state Property Tax Commission and are not handled at the county level.

Sales Assessment Ratios

Each year, NCDOR studies a sample of real estate sales from each county and compares the sales prices to the property tax appraisals of the sold properties. Foreclosures and other transactions that were not arms-length transactions are excluded from these studies. A ratio is created for each property by dividing the tax appraisal by the sales price. The median of all of the ratios is that county's sales assessment ratio.

This ratio is a rough measure of how closely the county's tax values reflect actual market values. Ideally the ratio would be 100 percent, meaning that, on average, tax appraisals are pegged right at market values. If the ratio is below 100 percent, then, on average, tax appraisals fall below market values. If the ratio is greater than 100 percent, then, on average, tax appraisals fall above market values.

In healthy economic times, sales assessment ratios decrease in the years following appraisals because tax values remain basically constant while market values slowly but steadily increase. When a county conducts its reappraisal, its sales assessment ratio will jump back up close to 100 percent. Only a handful of counties will have ratios over 100 percent, usually those few in which reappraisals have just been conducted and their tax values have been pegged slightly above the market. In weaker economic times, when real property prices are falling or are flat, more counties will have ratios under 100 percent.

The most recent sales assessment ratio from NCDOR reflects the strong real estate market experienced by most of the state in the past few years.[18] Only three counties have sales assessment ratios above 100 percent, with the average ratio at 83.4 percent.[19]

Why the Sales Assessment Ratio Matters

County leaders can use the sales assessment ratio to evaluate the effectiveness of their reappraisals. The ratio can also help predict how the county's tax base will change in the next reappraisal: if a county's sales assessment ratio is well above 100 percent, county leaders should be prepared for a drop in the tax base after the next reappraisal.

There are statutory reasons to pay attention to the sales assessment ratio as well. It is the basis for two Machinery Act provisions intended to promote more frequent appraisals of real property.

The first provision deals with public-service-company property. If a county's sales assessment ratio falls below 90 percent in the fourth or seventh year after a reappraisal, then that county's assessed value of public-service-company property will be reduced. The reduction will roughly equate to the actual sales assessment ratio: if the county's ratio is 85 percent, the county will be allocated and will be able to tax only 85 percent of the full assessed value of the public-service-company property it would otherwise have been allocated.[20]

---

18. N.C. Department of Revenue, Property Tax Division, *Sales Assessment Ratio Studies as of January 1, 2022* (Sept. 2022).

19. *Sales Assessment Ratio Studies as of January 1, 2022.*

20. G.S. 105-284(b).

Figure 5.4   Value of Property Covered by the Four Major Exemptions, 2021–2022

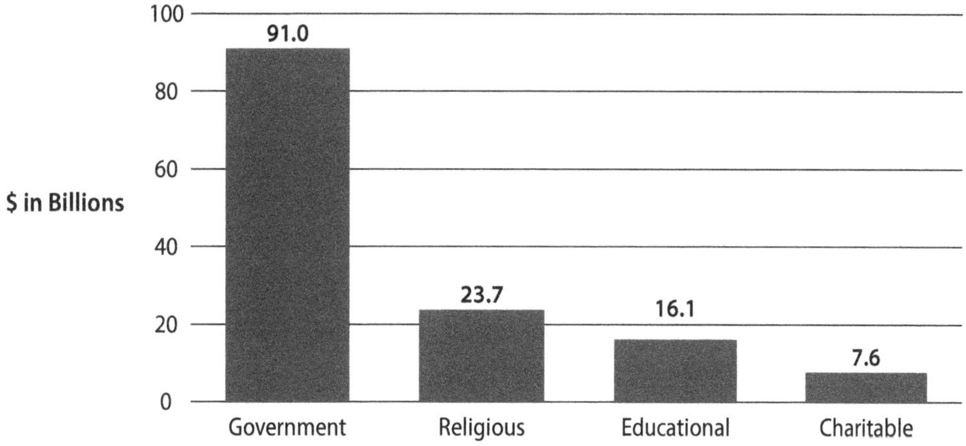

Source: North Carolina Department of Revenue.

The second provision involves mandatory reappraisals for counties with populations greater than 75,000. If such a county's sales assessment ratio is below 85 percent or above 115 percent, then the county must conduct a reappraisal within three years.[21] Thanks to the very strong real estate market across the state, in 2022, NCDOR reported that twenty-eight counties triggered mandatory reappraisals.[22] That total is almost twice as many as had done so cumulatively in the previous fifteen years.

Property Tax Exemptions and Exclusions

Only the General Assembly has the authority to create exemptions from local property taxes. Local governments may not carve out their own exemptions, nor may they choose not to administer the exemptions created by the General Assembly. Although the Machinery Act uses two terms—exemption and exclusion—to describe statutes that partially or completely remove property from taxation, for the purposes of this section those terms are interchangeable.

The single largest property tax exclusion category is present-use-value property.[23] This exclusion, which applied to nearly $34 billion of property in 2021–2022, reduces the taxable value of land that is used for agricultural, forestry, or wildlife conservation purposes. Under this program, land owners are allowed to pay taxes on the value of their property at its value for its current use, as opposed to its actual market value for development or any other use. The taxes on the difference between the land's present-use value and its market value are deferred, with the most recent three years of deferred taxes due and payable when the property is sold or is no longer used for agricultural, forestry, or wildlife conservation purposes. The next most-common exemptions are those for government, religious, charitable, and educational property. As Figure 5.4 illustrates, the largest of these four exemptions is the one for property

---

21. G.S. 105-286(a)(2).

22. Email to author from John Simpson, Director, Local Government Division, N.C. Department of Revenue (March 6, 2023).

23. G.S. 105-277.2 through -277.6.

owned by a government—federal, state, or local.[24] Local governments have no authority to tax property owned by another branch of government, regardless of how that property is being used.

Three property tax exclusions are aimed specifically at elderly and disabled homeowners. The most popular of the three is the homestead exclusion, which reduces the taxable value of a residence by the greater of $25,000 or 50 percent.[25] To be eligible, a homeowner must be 65 or older or totally disabled and must satisfy an income requirement, which was $33,800 or less for 2023.[26] For example, if Tina Taxpayer is eligible for the elderly and disabled exclusion and her home is assessed at $200,000, she will pay taxes only on $100,000 of that value. Roughly $6.7 billion of residential property benefited from this exclusion in 2021–2022.

The other two exclusions are the disabled veterans exclusion (G.S. 105-277.1C), which allows qualified taxpayers to reduce the taxable value of their homes by $45,000, and the circuit-breaker deferred tax program (G.S. 105-277.1B), which permits senior homeowners to cap their current taxes at either 4 or 5 percent of their income. The circuit-breaker program is similar to the present-use value program in that three years of deferred circuit-breaker taxes are due when the taxpayer sells the home or stops using it as his or her primary residence. These two exclusions are much smaller than the homestead exclusion, especially the circuit breaker. In 2020–2021, the disabled veterans exclusion applied to $1.9 billion of property while the circuit breaker applied to less than $1 million.[27]

Exemption and Exclusion Applications

The default rule is that a property owner must file an annual application to receive any exemption or exclusion.[28]

Many exemptions require only a single application, including those for present-use value, educational, religious, and charitable property.[29] Additional filings by the taxpayer are required only if an exempt taxpayer acquires additional property, makes physical changes to the exempt property, or changes its use of the exempt property.

A handful of exemptions, most importantly the one for government property, apply automatically without the need for an application from the property owner.[30]

Applications for most exemptions and exclusions are due by the end of the listing period, which is January 31 unless the county commissioners decide to extend it. Applications for the three residential property relief programs—the elderly and disabled exclusion, the circuit-breaker exclusion, and the disabled veterans exclusion—are due on June 1.

Despite these deadlines, the Machinery Act permits governing boards to accept applications through December 31 for "good cause shown."[31] Because this term is not defined by the Machinery Act, governing boards have a good amount of discretion when deciding which late applications to consider. The only limitation courts have placed on this discretion is that local

---

24. G.S. 105-278.1.

25. G.S. 105-277.1.

26. *See* N.C. Department of Revenue Form AV-9 (2023), Application for Property Tax Relief.

27. Email to author from George Hermane, Local Government Division, N.C. Department of Revenue (Dec. 7, 2022).

28. G.S. 105-282.1(a).

29. G.S. 105-282.1(a)(2).

30. G.S. 105-282.1(a)(1).

31. G.S. 105-282.1(a1).

Table 5.5　The Property Tax Appeal Process

1. Informal appeal to the assessor
2. County Board of Equalization and Review
3. State Property Tax Commission (taxpayer only)
4. N.C. Court of Appeals
5. N.C. Supreme Court (maybe)

governments should not base their decisions solely on the amount of property taxes related to a particular application.

An assessor makes the initial determination on all exemption and exclusion applications. North Carolina courts have made clear that all exemptions and exclusions must be strictly construed in favor of taxation.[32] In other words, assessors should begin with a presumption in favor of taxability. The burden of proof is on the taxpayer to prove that an exemption or exclusion is deserved.[33] If the taxpayer disagrees with the assessor's decision concerning an exemption or exclusion, the taxpayer may pursue an appeal to the county board of equalization and review and beyond, as described below.

Taxpayer Appeals

County commissioners play significant roles in resolving taxpayer appeals concerning their tax values and their eligibility for exemptions or exclusions, primarily through the appointment of the county board of equalization and review (BOER). The commissioners themselves may sit as the BOER or, as is most common, they may appoint other individuals to serve in that capacity.

Confusingly, the Machinery Act does not create a fixed deadline for taxpayers to submit appeals to the BOER. Instead, the appeal deadline is tied to the date that the BOER adjourns, which can vary from county to county and from year to year.[34]

In non-reappraisal years, the BOER must adjourn by July 1. In reappraisal years, it must do so by December 1. But in practice, most counties adjourn their BOERs on the same day as or shortly after the BOER's first meeting, which must occur between the first Monday in April and the first Monday in May. Once it adjourns, the BOER may still meet to hear appeals that were submitted before adjournment but cannot accept any new appeals.

Table 5.5 lists the five stages of a property tax appeal. Not surprisingly, most appeals occur in reappraisal years when every parcel of real property receives a new tax value. Historically, about 10 percent of real property owners contest their values after a reappraisal. The assessor usually resolves 90 percent of those initial inquiries informally.

Those appeals that are not resolved to the satisfaction of the taxpayer move to the BOER for formal hearings. The BOER's decision is binding on the county, meaning that if the taxpayer prevails, the county has no right of appeal. However, if the county prevails, the taxpayer has the right to appeal to the North Carolina Property Tax Commission, a five-member panel that hears cases in Raleigh. The party that loses before the Property Tax Commission can appeal

---

32. *In re* R.J. Reynolds Tobacco Co., 52 N.C. App. 299 (1981).
33. *In re* Martin, 286 N.C. 209 (1974).
34. G.S. 105-322(g)(2)(a).

Table 5.6   Bill for 2023 Discovery of $200,000 House

Year	Assessed Value	Tax Rate	Tax	Penalty	Totals
2023	$200,000	.51	$1,020	$102 (10%)	$1,122
2022	$200,000	.51	$1,020	$204 (20%)	$1,224
2021	$200,000	.50	$1,000	$300 (30%)	$1,300
2020	$200,000	.52	$1,040	$416 (40%)	$1,456
2019	$200,000	.52	$1,040	$520 (50%)	$1,560
2018	$200,000	.50	$1,000	$600 (60%)	$1,600
Totals			**$6,120**	**$2,142**	**$8,262**

the case to the North Carolina Court of Appeals, which often is the final stop for property tax appeals. A losing party has the right to continue its appeal to the North Carolina Supreme Court only if at least one judge from the court of appeals voted in its favor. The supreme court may also exercise its discretion to hear the appeal of a unanimous decision from the court of appeals, but that rarely occurs.

Discoveries

A "discovery" occurs when an assessor learns of taxable property that has not been listed for property taxes. The term also applies when the value or volume of property was substantially understated or when a property has received an exemption or exclusion for which it did not qualify.[35]

After a discovery is made, the assessor must correct the listing and assessment of the property and then bill the corrected taxes for the current year plus the five previous years. If the discovery involves personal property or buildings, discovery penalties of 10 percent per listing period apply to the discovery bill. Penalties do not apply to the failure to list land.[36]

For example, assume that Billy BlueDevil builds a house on his vacant lot in 2016 but fails to list the building for taxation with the county. The county finally learns of the house's existence in 2023. Under the discovery provisions, the county is entitled to list, assess, and bill that property for the current year (2023) plus the five previous years (2018–2022). Although the house should have been listed and taxed in 2017, the Machinery Act does not permit the county to extend its discovery bill back past 2018.

The discovery bill must be based on the assessed value and the tax rate in effect for each year the property was not listed. Table 5.6 shows how Billy BlueDevil's discovery bill would be calculated, assuming that the house would have been assessed at $200,000 as of January 1, 2018, and that the county had not conducted a reappraisal since that date. The penalties are calculated at 10 percent per missed listing period for each tax year: for example, the 2018 penalty is 60 percent because Billy missed six listing periods (2018–2023).

35. See the definition of the term "discover property" in G.S. 105-273(6b).
36. G.S. 105-312.

Waiving Discovery Bills

Local governing boards possess unusually broad authority over discovery bills. The Machinery Act permits discovery bills to be waived by a governing board at its unfettered discretion.[37] The governing board may agree to waive the entire bill or just a portion of it. It could waive all penalties, the tax and penalties from certain years, or any combination thereof.

In comparison, regular tax bills, penalties, and interest generally cannot be waived by governing boards. See "Refunds and Releases," below, for more details.

While the Machinery Act does not place any specific limits on the authority to waive discovery bills, governing boards are wise to seek consistency in their approaches to this issue. A lack of consistency when making waiver decisions could lead to accusations of favoritism or bias.

When a discovery bill includes municipal property taxes, that municipality's governing board retains the authority to compromise that portion of the bill. The county commissioners may compromise only the portion of the discovery bill that involves county taxes.

Evaluating the Assessor

County commissioners can choose from a variety of metrics to evaluate the performance of their assessors. One major consideration is often the cost and effectiveness of the countywide reappraisal of real property. Reappraisals are usually the most controversial activity undertaken by a county's tax office. To conduct a successful reappraisal, an assessor must possess technical appraisal skills, managerial competence, and perhaps above all, strong public relations capability. Educating taxpayers about the reappraisal and appeal process is a necessity, and the assessor cannot accomplish that key task without the ability to communicate clearly and effectively to different interest groups.

From a statistical perspective, the sales assessment ratio discussed earlier in this chapter may be the most useful figure for county commissioners to analyze. Immediately following a reappraisal, a county's sales assessment figure should be very close to 100 percent, meaning that, on average, sales prices equal tax values. If that is not the case, the reappraisal was not very accurate and the assessor should be held accountable.

The assessor should not be held accountable for changes in the tax base due to economic conditions. The fact that tax values have not risen as much as the commissioners might have hoped or have not fallen as much as taxpayers might have expected does not mean that the assessor is incompetent. More often, it means that the observers' expectations were not based on the actual conditions experienced by the county. Pre-reappraisal education is the key to minimizing unrealistic expectations on behalf of both elected officials and taxpayers.

---

37. G.S. 105-312(k).

Collection

After an assessor lists and assesses all taxable property in a jurisdiction and the jurisdiction's governing board sets the tax rate, property taxes are handed over to the tax collector for billing and, if necessary, enforced collection efforts, such as bank account attachments, wage garnishments, and real property foreclosures.

As is true of the listing and assessing process, the collection process should normally proceed with minimal involvement by the governing board. The tax collector should apply the same collection procedures to all similarly situated taxpayers, free from political pressures.

The governing board's role in the collection process is limited to

- appointing a tax collector or, for municipalities, choosing to contract with the county for property tax collection;[38]
- deciding whether to offer taxpayers a discount for early payment;[39] and
- reviewing the tax collector's performance throughout the year and after receiving the year-end settlement.[40]

Appointing the Tax Collector

Every local government that levies property taxes must appoint a tax collector who will be authorized to use the Machinery Act collection remedies of attachment and garnishment, levy and sale, and foreclosure. That tax collector can be an employee of the taxing government or an employee of another government with whom the taxing government contracts for tax collection services.

The Machinery Act creates only a few limitations on who can be appointed as tax collector. Members of the governing board are ineligible to serve as tax collector, as are local government finance officers absent special approval from the Local Government Commission. In terms of education and experience, the only requirement is that the appointee be "a person of character and integrity whose experience in business and collection work is satisfactory to the governing body." The appointee's criminal and financial history must not be so bad as to prevent the local government from being able to purchase the required bond to cover losses caused by the tax collector's misconduct or neglect. The bottom line is that the governing body has great discretion when deciding whom to appoint as tax collector.[41]

The tax collector must be appointed for a set term determined by the governing board. Most commonly these terms are two or four years in length. Once fixed by the governing board upon the tax collector's appointment, the length of the collector's term may not be changed until the term ends or the collector is removed from office. No term limits exist for collectors, meaning the governing board may reappoint a particular tax collector repeatedly. After appointment, the tax collector can be removed from office only "for cause," the same standard that is applied to the removal of the assessor.

Unlike assessors, tax collectors are not subject to mandatory state certification. However, the North Carolina Tax Collectors Association (NCTCA) operates a voluntary certification process

---

38. G.S. 105-349.
39. G.S. 105-360(c).
40. G.S. 105-373.
41. G.S. 105-349.

> ### Should Municipalities Collect Their Own Taxes?
>
> All 100 counties appoint and employ their own tax collectors. So do many municipalities. But a growing number of municipalities have decided not to employ their own tax collectors and instead have appointed the county tax collector as the municipal tax collector through interlocal agreements.
>
> The Machinery Act offers no guidance on the terms of these municipal–county collection agreements, meaning that the compensation provided by the municipality to the county for its tax collection services is up for negotiation between the parties. The compensation typically is set as a percentage of the taxes collected, usually around 1 to 2 percent and sometimes with a bonus if the collection rate exceeds a certain benchmark.
>
> From a financial perspective, relying on the county tax collector makes sense for many municipalities. The county already has the billing infrastructure in place, meaning that the cost it charges to the municipality to bill and collect municipal taxes will likely be less than the cost the municipality would incur to create its own billing system. But some municipalities prefer to retain complete control over the billing and collection process even if that approach costs more in the long run.

for tax collectors.[42] Many local governments now expect their collectors to obtain NCTCA certification as part of their required duties.

Tax Bills

Surprisingly, the Machinery Act does not require local governments that levy property taxes to send bills to their taxpayers. For obvious reasons, all do. But because tax bills are not required, a taxpayer cannot rely on failure to receive a tax bill as justification to avoid responsibility for a particular tax. The Machinery Act charges all taxpayers with notice of the fact that taxes are owed on their property even if they never receive actual notice in the form of a tax bill.[43]

Tax bills cannot be created until the tax rate is adopted along with the budget for the new fiscal year. Local governments are expected to finalize their budgets before July 1, the beginning of the fiscal year. But this deadline is far from ironclad, and plenty of local governments delay the final budget decision well into the new fiscal year. Of course, the later the budget is adopted, the later tax bills will go out, and the longer the local government will wait to receive its property tax revenue.

Because the Machinery Act is silent on the issue of tax bills, local governments have flexibility as to the form and content of those bills. Any tax, fee, fine, or other obligation can be included on a property tax bill. But billing an obligation along with property taxes does not automatically empower the local government to use property tax collection remedies to collect that obligation.

For example, some local governments include water, sewer, or stormwater fees on their tax bills. Absent special approval from the state legislature, these fees cannot be collected using property tax collection remedies even though they are included on the same bill with property taxes.

---

42. Details of the NCTCA certification process can be found at https://propertytaxnc.org/page/NCTCACerts.

43. G.S. 105-348.

An important exception to this rule concerns solid waste fees. All local governments are authorized to adopt a resolution calling for solid waste fees to be billed with property taxes and collected as property taxes.[44]

Discounts for Early Payment

The Machinery Act permits but does not require local governments to offer taxpayers a discount for paying their property taxes before September 1, the due date for property taxes other than those on registered motor vehicles.[45] Discounts are becoming less and less common. Those jurisdictions that do offer them usually set the discount at 1 or 2 percent. If a jurisdiction wishes to offer a discount, it must set the discount schedule by May and obtain approval from the N.C. Department of Revenue (NCDOR). Once adopted, a discount schedule remains in effect for all subsequent tax years unless and until it is repealed by the governing board.

Interest

Unlike discounts, interest is mandatory. On January 6 following the year in which taxes are levied, unpaid property taxes begin to accrue interest.[46] For example, taxes levied for the 2023–2024 fiscal year become delinquent and begin to accrue interest on January 6, 2024. (Different rules apply to taxes to motor vehicles—see "Registered Motor Vehicles," below.)

Interest accrues at a rate of 2 percent for the first month and 0.75 percent for every month thereafter.[47] Machinery Act interest is simple interest rather than compound interest, meaning that interest does not accrue on interest. On the first day of each month that a delinquent tax remains unpaid, another 0.75 percent of interest accrues on the principal amount of taxes owed plus any penalties and costs that have been added to that amount. For example, tax collectors are permitted to apply a 10 percent penalty for checks returned by the bank for insufficient funds. That penalty is added to the principal amount of taxes owed and will accrue interest if it remains unpaid past the delinquency date.

> ### How Is Interest Calculated?
>
> Assume Tommy TarHeel owes $1,000 in 2022 property taxes to Carolina County that became delinquent on January 6, 2023. He appears in the tax office on May 1, 2023, and asks how much he must pay to satisfy his tax obligation.
>
> The answer is $1,050, $1,000 in principal taxes and $50 in interest. The interest charge equals 5 percent: 2 percent for January plus 0.75 percent each month for February, March, April, and May.

Governing boards cannot waive interest charges unless that interest accrued illegally or due to clerical error. These are the same standards that apply to the release and refund of principal taxes. (See "Refunds and Releases," below, for more details.)

---

44. For more on collecting solid waste fees, water bills, and other taxes and charges, please see Christopher B. McLaughlin, "Beyond the Property Tax: Collecting Other Taxes and Fees," *Property Tax Bulletin* No. 174 (UNC School of Government, Jan. 2018).

45. G.S. 105-360(c).

46. G.S. 105-360(a).

47. G.S. 105-360(a).

Special Rules: Weekends, Holidays, and Postmarks

Two Machinery Act provisions affect when interest accrues in special situations.

The first is the weekend and holiday rule.[48] Whenever the last day to pay a tax without additional interest falls on a weekend or holiday, the deadline is extended to the next business day. For example, January 6, 2019, fell on a Sunday, meaning that the last day to pay 2018–2019 property taxes without interest was a Saturday (January 5). The weekend and holiday rule extended this deadline to the next business day (Monday, January 7). Interest on unpaid 2018–2019 property taxes began to accrue on Tuesday, January 8.

The second is the postmark rule.[49] The Machinery Act requires that tax offices treat property tax payments made by mail as if the payments were received on their postmark dates. Assume Tommy TarHeel pays his 2023–2024 property taxes in full by mail on Wednesday, January 3, 2024. The tax office does not receive his payment until Monday, January 8, several days after interest was to accrue on 2023–2024 property taxes. If Tommy's payment has a U.S. Postal Service postmark date of January 4 or January 5, the tax office must treat the payment as if it were actually received on either date and no interest would accrue on Tommy's property taxes. If the payment has no postmark or only a private postal meter mark, it cannot benefit from the postmark rule and Tommy must be charged interest.

Depending on the size of the locality, it may not be practical for tax office staff to check postmark dates on all payments made on or near an interest deadline. Instead, many tax offices apply a grace period of several days after each interest accrual date. Payments received by mail within the grace period do not accrue interest, without regard to postmark dates. While reasonable, tax offices should be aware that this practice satisfies only the spirit and not the letter of the postmark rule. Tax payments arriving after the grace period that have postmark dates prior to the interest accrual date should not be charged interest.

Deferred Taxes

Ten different Machinery Act provisions provide taxpayers tax relief in the form of deferred taxes. By far the largest of these deferred tax programs is the present-use value program discussed previously. But deferred taxes are also created under the circuit-breaker program as well as under exclusions that cover historic properties, working waterfront property, wildlife conservation land, and future sites for low-income housing.

Program details vary, but the general principle remains the same: some amount of taxes is deferred each year for as long as the property qualifies for the program. Interest accrues on these deferred taxes, but the local government cannot take action to collect them. When the property is sold or otherwise becomes ineligible for the program, several years (usually three) of deferred taxes plus interest become due and payable. If the deferred taxes are not paid immediately, the local government can proceed with enforced collection remedies.

---

48. G.S. 105-395.1.
49. G.S. 105-360(d).

Table 5.7 Enforced Collection Remedies

Remedy	Property Targeted
Attachment and garnishment	Wages, bank accounts, rents, or any other money owed to the taxpayer
Levy and sale	Cars, boats, planes, or any other tangible personal property owned by the taxpayer
Foreclosure	Real property subject to a lien for delinquent taxes
Set-off debt collection	State income tax refunds, lottery winnings, or any other money owed to the taxpayer by the state

Enforced Collection Remedies

Once taxes become delinquent on January 6, tax collectors can immediately begin enforced collections. The Machinery Act creates three enforced collection remedies: attachment and garnishment; levy and sale; and, for taxes that are liens on real property, foreclosure. Separate state provisions allow local governments to collect delinquent property taxes through the set-off debt collection process, which targets state income tax refunds and lottery winnings.[50] All four remedies are summarized in Table 5.7.

Local governments can also sue delinquent taxpayers in state court, but few pursue this option because the remedies available to a local government after winning such a lawsuit are essentially the same remedies it already possesses under the Machinery Act.

Unless the governing board directs otherwise, the tax collector normally may use any of these remedies in any order desired. However, once a foreclosure proceeding begins, all other Machinery Act remedies must stop.

Most local governments use all four tax collection remedies. But some refuse to employ collection remedies that taxpayers consider too intrusive, such as wage garnishment or foreclosure. Local governments that ignore any of these remedies suffer reduced collection percentages and lost revenues and do grievous harm to the perceived fairness of the property tax scheme.

Three of these remedies can be initiated without the involvement of the courts. Attachment and garnishment, levy and sale, and set-off debt collection require only notice to the taxpayer and, in the case of attachment and garnishment, notice to the party that holds the property being attached.

A court proceeding is required for foreclosure, which is available only for taxes that are a lien on real property. All taxes on real property automatically become a lien on that real property on the listing date, which is the January 1 prior to the fiscal year for which the taxes are levied. The tax lien on real property also includes the taxes owed on personal property other than registered motor vehicles that is owned by the same taxpayer in the same jurisdiction.

For example, assume that Wanda Wolfpack owns real property Parcel A, a boat, and a registered Honda Civic, all of which are listed for taxes in Carolina County. The taxes on both Parcel A and the boat are a lien on Parcel A. The county could foreclose on Parcel A for Wanda's failure to pay either the taxes on the real property itself or the taxes on the boat. The taxes on

---

50. G.S. Ch. 105A.

Table 5.8   Which Owners Can Be Held Personally Responsible for Property Taxes?

Type of Property	Original Owner	Subsequent Owners
Real property	Yes	Yes
Personal property (boats, planes, business property)	Yes	No, unless "going out of business" provision applies
Registered motor vehicles	Yes	No

the Honda Civic are *not* a lien on Parcel A, meaning that the tax collector could not foreclose on Parcel A if Wanda failed to pay the taxes on her Civic.

The Machinery Act creates a ten-year statute of limitations for all enforced collections. Foreclosures, attachments and garnishments, and levies must begin within ten years of the delinquent tax's original due date, which for all taxes other than those on registered motor vehicles is September 1 of the year the taxes were levied.

Who Can Be Targeted with Enforced Collection Remedies?

Only property of the responsible taxpayer can be targeted with enforced collection remedies. G.S. 105-365.1 creates different rules for the responsible taxpayer for taxes on personal property as compared to real property. For personal property, the responsible party is the taxpayer that listed the property for taxation, meaning the owner on the previous January 1. In other words, new owners of personal property are not responsible for old taxes on that property. For real property, the responsible parties are the owners as of the date of delinquency (January 6 of the fiscal year) and all subsequent owners. In other words, new owners of real property are responsible for old taxes on that property. Table 5.8 summarizes the rules concerning responsible taxpayers.

Here is how the rules work for real property. Assume that Dave Deacon owns Parcel A, on which taxes from 2022–2023 are delinquent. He sells Parcel A to Susie Seahawk in June of 2023. Normally, Susie (or her attorney) would require that the delinquent taxes be paid at or before the closing. But if those taxes are not paid, Susie would be personally responsible for the old taxes on Parcel A despite the fact that the taxes became delinquent while the property was owned by Dave (on January 6, 2023). Dave would also remain personally responsible. To collect these taxes, the tax collector could foreclose on Parcel A, garnish Dave's or Susie's wages, attach Dave's or Susie's bank account, or seize and sell Dave's or Susie's car or other personal property. If Susie's cash or property is taken to satisfy the taxes, Susie may have a legal action against Dave for reimbursement. But that depends on the terms of the real estate contract between Susie and Dave and has no effect on the taxing unit's right to collect the delinquent taxes using all methods permitted by the Machinery Act.

Now consider a personal property example. Assume that Mike Mountaineer owns a boat on which 2022 property taxes are delinquent. If Mike sells the boat to Wanda Wolfpack, Mike remains the only party personally responsible for the 2022 taxes on the boat. Only Mike's wages, bank accounts, and other property may be targeted with enforced collections. The tax collector cannot seize and sell the boat or target any of Wanda's other property because responsibility for taxes on that boat does not transfer to its new owner.

Although multiple collection actions are permitted for a single delinquent tax, that tax may be collected only once. For example, in the real property example above, the tax collector could simultaneously pursue wage garnishments against both Dave and Susie for the delinquent 2022–2023 taxes on Parcel A. In the personal property example, the tax collector could simultaneously attach Mike's wages and bank account for the delinquent 2022 taxes on the boat. Tax collectors are permitted to proceed with multiple collection actions for delinquent taxes simultaneously. But once the full amount of delinquent taxes plus interest and costs are collected, all collection actions must stop and any excess funds collected must be returned to the targeted taxpayer(s).

Property Taxes and the Register of Deeds

About three-quarters of North Carolina's 100 counties have received authorization from the General Assembly under G.S. 161-31 to prohibit a register of deeds from accepting a deed transferring real property unless the county tax collector first certifies that there are no property tax liens on the property that is the subject of the deed. This certification must cover all property taxes that the tax collector is responsible for collecting, which could include county taxes, municipal taxes, special service-district taxes, rural fire-district taxes, and supplemental school-district taxes. This provision provides great incentive for a closing attorney to ensure that the taxes on property being transferred are paid because, otherwise, the deed cannot be recorded, and the buyer's ownership rights may be jeopardized. Unfortunately, the provision contains a loophole that permits attorneys to record deeds if they promise to pay the delinquent taxes at closing. Too often these promises are broken and the taxes remain unpaid after the deeds are recorded.

G.S. 161-31 lists the counties with the authority to enact this requirement. If a county is not on that list and desires this authority, it should ask its state representatives to introduce legislation adding it to that list. Although the statute covers municipal taxes only if those taxes are collected by the county, at least one municipality that collects its own taxes has obtained a local modification to the law that prohibits the recording of deeds unless municipal taxes are paid along with county taxes.[51]

Advertising Tax Liens

Despite increasing questions about their effectiveness, newspaper advertisements of delinquent real property tax liens are still required every year.[52] The cost of these advertisements can be substantial, with larger counties spending tens of thousands of dollars to buy newspaper space. Tax collectors are permitted to pass these costs along to the delinquent taxpayers, and much of the advertising cost will be recaptured when the delinquent taxes are paid. But because not all of these taxes will be paid, the local government is certain to wind up eating a portion of the advertising cost.

Due to cost and to administrative burden, some local governments have considered eliminating tax lien advertisements. This course of action is not recommended for two reasons.

---

51. *See* S.L. 2010-24 (affecting Duplin County).
52. G.S. 105-369.

First, the advertisement is the mandatory initial step for an *in rem* foreclosure, the Machinery Act's expedited foreclosure process that can be accomplished without the need for attorneys. If a tax collector were to move forward with an *in rem* foreclosure without first advertising the tax lien, the taxpayer would have strong grounds for defending or reversing that collection action.

Second, local governments that do not use the *in rem* foreclosure process could place their other collection actions at risk if they intentionally ignore the advertising requirement. While the Machinery Act and state courts are generally tolerant of good faith errors in the tax collection process (see the discussion under "Immaterial Irregularities—Recapturing Lost Taxes" below), they are less likely to be forgiving of willful illegality by a local government.

Evaluating the Tax Collector: The Tax Collection Percentage

The Machinery Act requires tax collectors to make monthly reports to their governing boards about their collection results.[53] These reports, combined with the annual settlement required of tax collectors summing up their efforts and results for the entire fiscal year, give governing boards multiple opportunities to evaluate the performance of their collectors.

Perhaps the most important statistic used in the evaluation process is the tax collection percentage. Thanks to the very effective collection remedies provided by the Machinery Act, county collection percentages are very high, averaging around 99 percent for the past few years. Collections of taxes on registered motor vehicles traditionally lagged behind collections of other property taxes but have increased substantially since the 2013 implementation of the Tag & Tax Together collection system described below.

Two factors that can affect an individual local government's collection percentage are property tax assessment appeals and bankruptcies, both of which prevent a tax collector from pursuing enforced collections against the taxpayer in question.[54] If a jurisdiction experiences either a high number of property tax appeals during a reappraisal year or a bankruptcy filing by a major commercial taxpayer, the tax collector will not be able to collect the taxes involved while the proceedings are pending. As a result, the collection percentage is likely to suffer.

"Settlement" is the term the Machinery Act uses for the required annual accounting that tax collectors must provide to their local governing boards.[55] Presented after the old fiscal year ends and before the tax collector is charged with taxes for the new fiscal year, the settlement accounts for all of the funds received by the tax collector and identifies those taxes that remain unpaid. The settlement must be provided to the board in written form, but most tax collectors also make an oral presentation to the governing board so that they can answer questions in person.

As part of the settlement, the tax collector will usually provide the governing board with tax collection rates, often times broken out by year or property type.

---

53. G.S. 105-350.

54. G.S. 105-378(d) bars any enforcement action for taxes that are under appeal. The automatic stay that applies to all federal bankruptcy cases similarly bars enforcement actions for any taxes owed by a debtor who filed for bankruptcy. 11 U.S.C. § 362.

55. G.S. 105-373.

Other Performance Evaluation Measures

Although collection percentage is the most common and usually the most important criterion used to evaluate a tax collector, other aspects of the collector's performance can and should be considered by the local governing board. The collector's ability to communicate with the board and with the public is key to an effective property tax system. Taxpayer complaints and the collector's responsiveness to those complaints are related issues that may provide insight into that official's performance.

Consistency and impartiality are vital characteristics for a tax collector. The board needs proof that the collector demonstrates these traits. Does the tax collector treat all similarly situated taxpayers equally? Does he or she employ tax collection remedies in an impartial fashion against all delinquent taxpayers and not play favorites? If not, the local government is likely to face taxpayer dissatisfaction and legal exposure.

Old Taxes

The Machinery Act creates a ten-year statute of limitations that bars enforced collection actions after taxes are more than ten years past due.[56] Most counties rely on this statute of limitations to allow their tax collectors to write off taxes after they hit the ten-year mark. Technically, this approach violates the Machinery Act. The statute of limitations bars enforced collection, but it has no relevance to the tax collector's responsibility for those taxes.

The only technically correct method of writing off taxes and thereby relieving tax collectors of responsibility for them is through the "insolvents list."[57] As part of the settlement process, a tax collector should identify unpaid taxes from the just-ended fiscal year that are not a lien on real property. The governing board can then place those taxes on the insolvents list and, once those taxes are more than five years past due, can write off those taxes by relieving the tax collector of responsibility for them. Taxes on registered motor vehicles that are placed on the insolvents list can be written off after they are more than one year past due.

Note that taxes that are a lien on real property cannot be placed on the insolvents list and, therefore, technically can never be written off by the tax collector. When all other efforts fail, foreclosure remains an option for any tax that is secured by a lien on real property. The problem, however, is that property that makes it through to a foreclosure sale is often worth very little. It may be more effort than it is worth to pursue foreclosure, which is why many counties allow the tax collector to informally write off old taxes on real property despite the Machinery Act's contrary admonition.

Immaterial Irregularities—Recapturing Lost Taxes

From a local government perspective, few Machinery Act provisions are more beneficial than the "immaterial irregularity" provision. Essentially, this provision excuses errors in the listing, assessing, billing, and collecting processes and allows local governments to retroactively correct those errors and levy and collect the taxes in question as if the errors never occurred.[58]

---

56. G.S. 105-378.
57. G.S. 105-373(g).
58. G.S. 105-394.

Cities and counties have relied on the immaterial irregularity provision in a variety of situations. They have used it to retroactively bill taxes on property that was listed by the taxpayer but never assessed, to pursue taxes on property that was annexed by a municipality years ago but never taxed by it, and to collect underbillings resulting from computer errors.

About the only type of error that courts have found significant enough not to be excused is the failure to give adequate notice to owners of real property before moving forward with a foreclosure action. Local governments using the foreclosure process should take care to provide timely notice to all parties who may have an interest in the property being foreclosed upon, including lien holders and the heirs of deceased taxpayers.

Refunds and Releases

A favorite question from taxpayers, tax collectors, and governing boards across the state is: when can taxes be waived? The short answer is, very rarely. Governing boards cannot waive taxes whenever they choose.

In Machinery Act terminology, waivers are either "refunds" (for taxes that were previously paid) or "releases" (for taxes that have not been paid). Under G.S. 105-381, refunds and releases are permitted in only the following two circumstances:

1. when the tax was levied illegally or
2. when the tax was levied due to clerical error by the tax office.

If a governing board approves a refund or release that does not satisfy one of these two categories, board members can be held personally liable for the lost taxes.

Examples of illegal taxes include

- taxes on property that did not have situs in the jurisdiction,
- double taxation on the same property by the same jurisdiction, and
- taxes that were levied without the required procedural steps.

Examples of taxes levied due to clerical error include

- assessments in which digits were transposed or added (for example, a tax value of $250,000 is mistakenly recorded as $520,000 or a property's square footage is recorded as 25,000 instead of 2,500);
- tax payments applied to the wrong accounts contrary to taxpayer instructions or due to mistakes by the tax office; and
- tax bills calculated on the wrong tax rate.

Two of the most common reasons taxpayers seek refunds and releases *do not* satisfy G.S. 105-381. Governing boards should not approve tax waiver requests based on either

1. value judgments by the assessor's office or
2. clerical errors made by the taxpayer rather than by the tax office.

First, consider value judgments made by the assessor. These judgments must be challenged during the regular appeal process that closes when the county board of equalization and review adjourns. (See "Listing and Assessing," above.) Otherwise, a local government would have great difficulties budgeting each year because its tax base would always be subject to retroactive adjustments due to after-the-fact value appeals. These errors in judgment can be corrected going forward so that future tax bills are accurate, but retroactive changes are not permitted.

The best question to ask when deciding if a mistake by the tax office was a value judgment or a clerical error is: was the resulting assessment the one intended by the assessor? If so, the issue is a value judgment that cannot justify a refund or release. If not, the issue is a clerical error that can justify a refund or release.

For example, consider two houses that were each assessed at $400,000 during Carolina County's last reappraisal in 2022.

House A was intended to be assessed at a square footage of 2,500, but a data entry error resulted in the square footage being recorded at 5,200. As a result, the assessment increased from the intended $300,000 to $400,000.

House B was assessed as if it had a finished basement and third floor, as do all of the other houses in House B's development. The assessor calculated the finished square footage to be 5,200. In fact, House B has neither a finished basement nor a third floor, and its actual finished square footage is 2,500. Had the assessor known that the house did not have this extra finished space, the house's assessment would have dropped from $400,000 to $300,000.

Neither owner appealed the tax valuation in 2022. Both learned of the mistakes made by the tax office in 2023 and asked for a refund of the excess taxes they paid in 2022. How should the Carolina County board of county commissioners respond to these requests?

The Machinery Act permits the tax assessments on both houses to be adjusted for 2023 taxes and future years' taxes. But only the owner of House A is entitled to a refund of 2022 taxes. The mistake involving House A was a true clerical error because the assessor never intended to assess House A as if it had 5,200 square feet. A refund is justified.

The mistake involving House B did not produce an unintended assessment. Based on the information before the assessor at the time, the assessor intended the assessment for House B to be based on a square footage of 5,200. This was a judgment error, not a clerical error. If the taxpayer disputed this figure, he or she had the obligation to raise the issue during the 2022 appeal process. No refund is justified.

Similarly, a taxpayer should not receive a refund based on valuation errors from prior tax years. For example, assume Tommy TarHeel's house is appraised at $500,000 as part of Carolina County's 2022 reappraisal. Tommy does not appeal in 2022. But he does appeal in 2023 and produces evidence that an identical house directly across the street from his house sold in late 2021 for $400,000. The assessor agrees that Tommy's house should have been assessed at $400,000 for 2022. The assessor should change the tax value of Tommy's house to $400,000 for 2023 and subsequent years but should not provide a refund for any taxes paid by Tommy in 2022. This issue was a valuation error, not an illegal tax, and no refund is justified under G.S. 105-381.

Second, consider clerical errors made by the taxpayer. The Machinery Act permits refunds and releases when taxes are "levied due to clerical error." Because only local governments can

Table 5.9   Time Limits on Refunds and Releases under G.S. 105-381

Releases of unpaid taxes	No time limit
Refunds of paid taxes	The later of: • five years from the original due date *or* • six months from the date the taxes were paid

levy property taxes, the clerical error in question must be one by a local government and not one by a taxpayer.

A common taxpayer error concerns escrow payments. Many taxpayers escrow their property taxes with their mortgage companies and do not pay those taxes directly. If a taxpayer forgets about the escrow fund and mails a tax payment to the tax office, can that taxpayer get a refund of that payment because the mortgage company will be paying those taxes later in the year? The answer is no, because the payment was for a validly levied tax and the taxpayer's mistake cannot justify a refund. The taxpayer should seek a refund from the mortgage company, not from the tax office.

Another common error arises when a mortgage company sends tax payments for multiple parcels and mistakenly instructs the tax office to apply one of those payments to the wrong parcel. When the mortgage company learns of its mistake, is it entitled to have its payment moved to the correct parcel? Again the answer is no because moving that tax payment from one parcel to another would constitute a refund of the taxes on the original parcel. Of course, if the tax office made the mistake and applied the payment to the wrong parcel contrary to the mortgage company's instructions, a refund would be justified.

Who Makes the Decision to Authorize a Refund or Release?

The authority to approve refunds and releases lies with the local governing board, not with the tax collector. For small refunds (less than $100), the governing board can delegate the authority to approve refunds and releases to the local government's finance officer, manager, or attorney.

In practice, tax collectors often make routine refunds and seek approval from the board later. For example, if the tax office mistakenly processes a payment for taxes that have already been paid, the tax collector might refund the duplicate payment before seeking permission from the board. Governing boards should discuss this issue with their tax collectors so that all parties are clear on how to proceed before problems arise.

Time Limits on Refunds and Releases

The Machinery Act does not create a time limit for releases of unpaid taxes. But refunds of paid taxes are limited to the later of (1) five years from the date the tax was originally due or (2) six months from the date the taxes were paid (see Table 5.9).

For example, assume that Blue Devil City has been levying taxes on Tommy TarHeel's property for decades under the assumption that Tommy's property is within the municipal limits. Tommy has paid those taxes each year in a timely fashion. In July 2023, Tommy has a new survey done that demonstrates that his property is in fact outside the municipal limits. Tommy immediately asks for a refund of all of the municipal taxes he has paid since purchasing the property in 2000.

Tommy is clearly entitled to a refund because it is illegal for Blue Devil City to tax property not within its borders. But Tommy's refund is limited by the Machinery Act to those taxes that came due within five years of Tommy's refund request. Taxes on real property are due on September 1 each year. The 2018 taxes were due on September 1, 2018, which is within five years of Tommy's request for a refund in July 2023. But the 2017 taxes fall outside of that five-year window because they were due on September 1, 2017. And the six-months-from-payment provision does not apply because Tommy paid those taxes back in 2017, long before submitting his refund request. Taxes from years 2016 and earlier similarly fall outside of the refund limitations. As a result, Tommy is entitled to a refund of municipal taxes only for the years 2018 through 2023.

Registered Motor Vehicles

The Tag & Tax Together System

The taxation of registered motor vehicles (RMVs) is a world unto itself. The rules and practices described above do not necessarily apply to taxes levied on RMVs.

Under the "Tag & Tax Together" system that took effect in 2013, the N.C. Division of Motor Vehicles (DMV) collects both registration fees and local government property taxes on registered motor vehicles at the time of registration or renewal. The taxes are passed along to the appropriate local governments minus a small collection fee retained by the state. If the taxes are not paid, the DMV will not permit the motor vehicle to be registered or renewed. Local governments no longer have any collection authority for taxes on RMVs.[59]

Despite the varying collection methods, local governments must levy property taxes on RMVs at the same rate levied on other types of personal property and on real property. The uniformity provisions in the N.C. Constitution discussed in "The Property Tax Rate," above, prohibit local governments from taxing RMVs at rates different from those applied to other property within their jurisdictions.

Other Local Taxes on Motor Vehicles

In addition to property taxes, both counties and municipalities have the authority to generate other revenues from motor vehicles.[60]

Counties have the authority to levy a registration tax of up to $7 per year if the county or one of the local governments in the county operates a public transportation system. The proceeds from this tax may be used only for the creation or operation of that public transportation system.

---

59. G.S. Ch. 105, Art. 22A.
60. For more information regarding these revenues, see Chapter 4, "Revenue Sources."

All municipalities are authorized to levy taxes on the privilege of operating a motor vehicle within their borders of up to $30 per vehicle. The first $5 of that tax may be used for any legal purpose. An additional $5 of the tax may be used for the creation or operation of a public transit system. Any remaining revenue from the tax must be used for constructing, repairing, or improving public streets. Some municipalities have been exempted from these usage restrictions through local acts of the General Assembly.[61]

The DMV collects these additional local government taxes on RMVs along with property taxes at the time of registration or renewal.

---

61. G.S. 20-97.

Chapter 6

Revenue Forecasting

by Whitney B. Afonso

Introduction

> Forecasting attempts to identify the relationship between the factors that drive revenues (tax rates, building permits issued, retail sales) and the revenues government collects (property taxes, user fees, sales taxes). . . . Revenue forecasts can apply to aggregate total revenue or to single revenue sources such as sales tax revenues or property tax revenues. There is no single method for projecting revenues. Rather, different methods tend to work better depending on the type of revenue. Similarly, there is no standard time-frame over which to attempt a forecast.[1]

This chapter presents an overview of the primary ways in which local governments forecast revenues. Revenue forecasting is critical to quality financial management in both the short term and long run. The forecasted revenues are the foundation on which the budget is built and can dramatically alter the direction and scope of government services. In fact, it is reasonable to

---

1. Thomas A. Garrett and John C. Leatherman, *An Introduction to State and Local Public Finance* (Morgantown, WV: Regional Research Institute, West Virginia University, 2000), 1.

argue that "without exception, revenue forecasting is the most important task in budget preparation."[2] Although revenue forecasting is critical, there are no clear universal rules or guidelines. There is no best forecast method, nor is there any forecast method without merit or weaknesses.

Revenue forecasting is not simply a best practice, but also a necessity. In fact, North Carolina local governments are required by the Local Government Budget and Fiscal Control Act (referred to in short as the Fiscal Control Act) to forecast their revenues. This requirement, though not explicit, is present in numerous places, most clearly in two components of the Fiscal Control Act. The first is through the balanced budget requirement: "a budget ordinance is balanced when the sum of estimated net revenues and appropriated fund balances is equal to appropriations."[3] Those "estimated net revenues" are the revenue forecasts. The law does not dictate the method of estimating those revenues, but it clearly dictates that revenue forecasting must be done. The second component states that "estimated revenue shall include only those revenues reasonably expected to be realized in the budget year," indicating that the estimates or forecasts must be reasonable and reliable as well as justifiable.[4]

This chapter proceeds with a discussion of a potential administrative process for forecasting revenues.[5] It then presents descriptions and a discussion of qualitative and quantitative methods, with a focus on judgmental forecasting, trend analysis, and causal modeling. After providing a selection of the different methods available for forecasting, the chapter discusses additional issues to consider in choosing the *right* method, highlighting many concerns and best practices.

Potential Administrative Process for Revenue Forecasting

There are many ways in which a local government can structure its process for revenue forecasting; some of these choices will depend on capacity, diversity of the local government's revenue portfolio, and the stability of their local economy. However, there are four basic steps for creating and implementing a transparent, easily replicated (internally and externally) forecasting process. These steps are (1) create a revenue manual, (2) compile estimates for major

---

2. Robert L. Bland, *A Budgeting Guide for Local Government* (Washington, D.C.: International City/County Management Association, 2007).

3. Chapter 159, Section 8(a) of the North Carolina General Statutes (hereinafter G.S.).

4. G.S. 159-13(b)(7). Furthermore, forecasts can be used to improve financial management and strategic thinking. *See* Roland Calia, Salomon Guajardo, and Judd Metzgar, "Best Practices in Budgeting: Putting the NACSLB Recommended Budget Practices into Action," *Government Finance Review* 16, no. 2 (2000): 1–9; William C. Rivenbark, "Financial Forecasting for North Carolina Local Governments," *Popular Government* 73, no. 1 (2007): 6–13.

5. There are three basic types of forecasting that are distinguished by the forecast period. Short-term forecasts estimate revenues for the near future, that is, less than one year. They are most commonly used by local officials and managers to make informed operational choices. For budgeting purposes, short-term forecasts are often used to update existing forecasts as the year proceeds. Medium-term forecasts estimate future revenues for a period of one to three years. They are used when developing budgets and programs. The third type is long-term forecasting. Long-term forecasts estimate revenue over a period of longer than three years, most frequently five years. These forecasts are key to strategic planning and help to illustrate where a local government is moving or is striving to move toward.

non-departmental revenue sources, (3) compile estimates from revenue-generating entities within the local government, and (4) update all estimates.[6] Each of these steps is consistent with North Carolina law.

Step 1: Create a Revenue Manual

The first step is to create a (or to maintain an up-to-date) revenue manual.[7] A revenue manual is a complete list of all revenue sources. It often includes the following information for each revenue source: the statute authorizing the revenue source[8] and corresponding restrictions; the current rate, previous rates, and collection rates; the forecast method; what elements in the local economy affect the revenue generated (or the tax base); and the groups that pay this tax (or fee). It also is critical to determine who collects the revenue. For example, is it collected by a public utility? By the state? Another aspect of revenue that is important to include is whether it is periodic (or seasonal), for example, a community pool that collects revenue only during the summer months or property taxes where the majority of tax remittance takes place during January and February. Ultimately, a revenue manual should contain information on all revenue sources and provide any data that will be helpful in understanding trends (including fluctuations) in revenue generation.

There is a great deal of diversity in the form that a revenue manual can take. One useful example is the revenue manual created by the City of Fort Lauderdale, Florida.[9] It presents each revenue instrument, a description of it (including if the revenue is earmarked and the tax rate), historical collections, the current projection, and forecasts for the following five years. The manual also includes the legal authority that authorizes the municipality[10] to implement that revenue, the fiscal capacity, and the forecast assumptions. It is a well-done revenue manual, but there may be even more information that a local government might want to include.[11] For a local government that has not yet created a revenue manual, the most productive place to begin is with major revenue sources and with building toward a comprehensive manual.[12]

As this chapter proceeds, it will become clear that many a local government performs individual forecasts only for *major* revenue sources, while it combines all *minor* revenue sources in a separate additional forecast or via departmental forecasts. Even if a local government generates a unique forecast for only three or four revenue sources, it is considered a best practice to create a revenue manual that includes all of the sources from which it collects revenues.

---

6. Adapted from Bland, note 2 above.

7. This step is recommended as a best practice by the Government Finance Officers Association (GFOA) in their publication *Recommended Budget Practices: A Framework for Improved State and Local Government Budgeting* (Chicago: GFAO, 1999), 49.

8. A possible exception to this would be states where local governments operate under home rule, but North Carolina is not one of those states.

9. *See* City of Ft. Lauderdale, Florida, *Revenue Manual* (April 2013).

10. As used in this book, the term "municipality" is synonymous with "city," "town," and "village."

11. Other examples of revenue manuals highlighted by the GFOA are those for the City of Boise, Idaho (https://www.cityofboise.org/media/10313/fy2021_annual_budget.pdf; see page 20), and for Lee County, Florida (https://www.leegov.com/budget/Documents/Revenue/2016_Revenue_Manual.pdf).

12. *See* Whitney Afonso, "So, Your Jurisdiction is Thinking of Starting a Revenue Manual . . .," *Death & Taxes: The Public Finance Blog You Can't Avoid* (Oct. 12, 2021).

Step 2: Estimate Major Revenue Sources

In the second step, to be taken before beginning work on a proposed budget, a local government's budget office should begin to create and/or compile estimates of *major* revenue sources that are not collected directly by departments.[13] The Fiscal Control Act leaves quite a bit of discretion as to how local governments may present budgets and estimate revenues but states that the budget ordinance "shall make appropriations by department, function, or project and show revenues by major source."[14] The fact that the Fiscal Control Act dictates that local governments present forecasts of major revenue sources separately means that they must also be forecast separately, but local governments should do this regardless of legal mandate.[15]

It is important to forecast revenues separately because they likely have different tax bases and thus will react differently to changes in the economy. A good illustration of why major revenue sources need to be forecast separately are the two major revenue sources that North Carolina local governments rely on, sales and property taxes. Sales taxes are often estimated based on recent history but also are weighted by recent trends and anticipated fluctuations in the economic base. They are more reactive to these changes than property taxes; sales tax revenue grows more quickly with the economy and decreases more quickly than property taxes do. Therefore, it is unreasonable to believe that sales and property taxes will change at the same rate for forecasting purposes.[16] In fact, it is likely that a forecaster will choose different forecasting methods for these two revenue sources.

Step 3: Ask for Departmental Revenue Forecasts

In the third step, a local government's budget office reaches out to revenue-generating departments for their estimates of projected revenues.[17] In North Carolina this can include such public entities as utilities, libraries, and parks. In addition, a budget office may ask the different departments to offer estimates under different scenarios. For example, it may be helpful to have water and sewer utilities provide estimates based on changing the levels of expected rainfall. This will help elected officials understand options, likely outcomes, and how sensitive these estimates are to assumptions.

This process may be considered a best practice in other states, but local governments in North Carolina are required to solicit these forecasts from revenue-generating departments. The Fiscal Control Act dictates that "before April 30 of each fiscal year (or an earlier date fixed by the budget officer), each department head shall transmit to the budget officer the budget requests

---

13. Steps 2 and 3 happen in parallel but involve different actors and so are discussed separately. The distinction between the two steps is how the revenue is generated and who forecasts it. In step 2, the revenue forecast is done by the budget office, whereas step 3 is concerned with revenue being generated by a department and thus is forecast by the collecting department.

14. G.S. 159-13(a).

15. These estimates or forecasts should be constantly updated as new information relevant to economic and political factors as well as current revenue surfaces, as this new information will possibly reinforce or alter the forecast. Bland, note 2 above.

16. John L. Mikesell, "Consumption and Income Taxes," in *Management Policies in Local Government Finance*, John R. Bartle, W. Bartley Hildreth, and Justin Marlowe, eds. (Washington, D.C.: International City/County Management Association, 2013).

17. Bland, note 2 above.

and revenue estimates for his department for the budget year. . . . The revenue estimate shall be an estimate of all revenues to be realized by department operations during the budget year."[18]

Steps 2 and 3 are broad steps that are really comprised of many sub-steps and will take place simultaneously. Some of the sub-steps within these steps are (1) Choose a time frame over which you are going to analyze the data. Considerations may include such factors as availability of data, quality of data, and the revenue source being forecasted. (2) Perform the actual revenue forecasts/projections and document them. Not just for the major revenue sources but also for "all other" revenue generators. (3) Evaluate your forecasts for how reliable they are. Reliability can be tested by doing a sensitivity analysis, where certain assumptions are relaxed and parameters (for example, population growth) are modified. If these changes have dramatic effects on your forecasted revenue, then those projections are too sensitive to your assumptions and model and are not considered very reliable.[19]

Step 4: Update Estimates

The quality of the forecasts will improve as more (and more recent) data are collected, so it is critical to update forecasts both before the budget is adopted and after. Thus, the final step is to monitor actual revenues and compare those numbers with projections and update forecasts accordingly. There are many potential sources of information and data that may be helpful to this process, including but not limited to, changes in laws and rates, changes to the tax base, changes to the underlying growth factors that drove the initial forecasts, and actual collection numbers.

This step is especially critical for such taxes as the sales tax, which generates revenue continuously, rather than for, say, the property tax, which is collected in one period. Thus, the property tax forecast may need to be updated in March but likely not again. Actual collections, especially those of a periodic nature, need to be closely monitored and checked against the forecasts. Comparing actual collections against the forecasts provides a budget officer with early warning if collections appear to be falling short of expectations.[20] This early warning provides time for more thoughtful midyear reductions if necessary.

In North Carolina, local governments can amend their budget ordinances any time after the ordinance is adopted.[21] This is explicitly discussed in the Fiscal Control Act: "Except as otherwise restricted by law, the governing board may amend the budget ordinance at any time after the ordinance's adoption in any manner, so long as the ordinance, as amended, continues to satisfy the requirements of G.S. 159-8 and 159-13."[22] While there are more restrictions surrounding amendments to the property tax forecasts, there is still room within the Fiscal

---

18. G.S. 159-10. This is another reason why revenue manuals are useful. This information should be housed within the budget manual, adding to its administrative value.

19. Salomon A. Guajardo and Rowan Miranda, *An Elected Official's Guide to Revenue Forecasting* (Chicago: Government Finance Officers Association of the United States and Canada, 2000).

20. Mikesell, note 16 above.

21. The only exception involves certain aspects of the property tax. "However, except as otherwise provided in this section, no amendment may increase or reduce a property tax levy or in any manner alter a property taxpayer's liability, unless [a local government's] board is ordered to do so by a court of competent jurisdiction, or by a State agency having the power to compel the levy of taxes by the board" (G.S. 159-15).

22. G.S. 159-15.

Control Act for unanticipated events: "if after July 1 the local government receives revenues that are substantially more or less than the amount anticipated, the governing body may, before January 1 following adoption of the budget, amend the budget ordinance to reduce or increase the property tax levy to account for the unanticipated increase or reduction in revenues."[23] Therefore, this can all be understood as the Fiscal Control Act encouraging local governments to carefully monitor their forecasts for accuracy and to update them throughout the fiscal year (FY).

How often forecasts should be updated depends on many factors, including capacity and previous stability. For example, larger counties, on average, start four months earlier (nine versus five) than smaller counties in terms of revenue forecasting. In part, as a result of this (and of capacity), they also modify their estimates, on average, three times during the fiscal year, whereas smaller counties do so, on average, 1.3 times.[24]

Forecasting Methods

[Forecasting methods] range from relatively informal qualitative techniques to highly sophisticated quantitative techniques. In revenue forecasting, more sophisticated does not necessarily mean more accurate. In fact, an experienced finance officer can often "guess" what is likely to happen with a great deal of accuracy.[25]

In determining what method of forecasting is best for a particular local government, there are two broad categories to choose from: qualitative and quantitative. Qualitative methods revolve around expert judgment, do not rely heavily on data, and often do not clearly lay out how the final forecasted numbers were estimated and what underlying assumptions drove them, whereas quantitative methods rely heavily on quantifiable data. Ideally, the assumptions that are used to model and categorize the relationships between variables and historical values are clearly identified. Due to their technical nature, quantitative methods are also often able to present margins of error for the forecasts, revealing the level of certainty and reliability of those estimates.

There are *many* ways to forecast revenues. In this chapter, the most common methods used by local governments are discussed, but the discussion is by no means exhaustive. A list of resources that provide more information on additional methods is presented at the end of this chapter.

Qualitative Methods

Qualitative forecasting relies on the expertise of an individual or a group for forecasting revenue. This may mean that a local government has an internal expert (professional) whose judgment can be trusted, for example, a budget director or a person from the agency administering the

---

23. G.S. 159-15.

24. Dongsung Kong, "Local Government Revenue Forecasting: The California County Experience," *Journal of Public Budgeting, Accounting & Financial Management* 19, no. 2 (2007): 178–99.

25. Garrett and Leatherman, note 1 above, at 1.

tax/fee. It is also common for local governments to solicit assistance from outside experts, such as professors, economists, business people from the community, or consultants. There are two primary types of qualitative forecasting: judgmental and consensus.

Judgmental Forecasting

Judgmental forecasting, the most common form of forecasting used by local governments, involves a single individual estimating "likely" future conditions. This can lead to very good results, especially when the forecaster has experience as well as expertise with historical trends, the state of the economy, and other factors likely to affect the tax base. "Judgmental approaches tend to work best when background conditions are changing rapidly. When economic, political or administrative conditions are in flux, quantitative methods may not capture important information about factors that are likely to alter historical patterns."[26]

Consensus Forecasting

Consensus forecasting relies on a panel of experts who provide their input in either a round-table format or through a survey. Ideally, input should be solicited from experts who understand what factors are key and how those factors have been changing and are likely to change in the future. For a local government, this panel of experts may consist of people who understand the real estate market, economists who study both state and local changes to the relevant sectors of the economy, and officials from local financial institutions.[27] One study found that a survey of experts produced a more accurate long-term forecast than did advanced quantitative methods.[28]

Strengths of Qualitative Forecasting

There are many reasons why qualitative forecasting is attractive and could be the best method for local governments to use. First, qualitative forecasts are inexpensive and easy to administer. This makes them a low-resource solution, which in some cases is paramount. Second, the actual forecasted revenue numbers are easier to understand than some quantitative data, which can be so complex and mathematical that they seem intimidating. This should not be taken to imply, however, that expert judgments may not be guided by numbers, data, and quantitative models. Third, qualitative forecasting may be a local government's best choice when there is very little data to input into the quantitative models.

Weaknesses of Qualitative Forecasting

While there are many benefits to qualitative forecasting there also are shortcomings. The end forecasted revenue amount is easy to understand, but it may not be clear where that revenue projection came from and what considerations and assumptions led an expert to it. This may result in less ability to analyze the sensitivity and reliability of these forecasts. While this is an oft-cited weakness of qualitative forecasting, Salomon Guajardo and Rowan Miranda lay out eight additional weaknesses: (1) the presence of anchoring events that may cause a current event to unduly shape perceptions of what the future will bring; (2) too much emphasis given to the

---

26. Garrett and Leatherman, at 3.
27. Garrett and Leatherman.
28. Reid Dorsey-Palmateer and Gary Smith, "Shrunken Interest Rate Forecasts Are Better Forecasts," *Applied Financial Economics* 17, no. 6 (2007): 425–30.

Table 6.1 Property Tax Revenues for Alamance County, by Year

2005	2006	2007	2008	2009	2010	2011
$48,333	$55,546	$58,536	$60,794	$62,223	$63,241	$62,654

Note: Amounts are multiples of 1,000.

Table 6.2 Local Option Sales Tax Revenues for Alamance County, by Year

2005	2006	2007	2008	2009	2010	2011
$22,478	$23,952	$26,378	$27,477	$22,776	$16,658	$18,720

Note: Amounts are multiples of 1,000.

information that is available to the expert; (3) bad assumptions made about the causal mechanisms and correlations between certain indicators and fiscal outcomes; (4) changing methods/strategies over time to produce incomparable and inconsistent results (especially problematic when the assumptions and tactics are not well documented or laid out); (5) experts allowing their own worldviews to cloud their judgment or, worse, ignoring pertinent data and information when it conflicts with their opinions and perceptions; (6) letting the preferred outcome (or wishful thinking) guide their assumptions and lead to undue weight given to certain numbers and factors; (7) letting group think guide choices instead of independently assessing and evaluating the assumptions; and (8) allowing political pressures to shape assumptions and estimates.[29]

Despite these potential weaknesses of qualitative forecasting, there is largely consensus that expert(s) judgment should be incorporated into quantitative forecasts as well.

Quantitative Methods

There are many quantitative forecasting methods, from simple equations and formulas to sophisticated causal models requiring technical software and statistical knowledge in addition to high-quality data. This section of the chapter uses data from Alamance County in the pre– and post–Great Recession period for the purpose of clarifying some of these concepts.[30] This period was chosen because of the dramatic economic conditions that forecasters faced during that time and because it demonstrates some of the differences in results that emerge when selecting methods and time frames. The Alamance County property tax data are presented in Table 6.1; local option sales tax data, in Table 6.2.

Simply by looking at the revenues generated by these two tax instruments (Figure 6.1), and without applying a formal quantitative methodology, it becomes clear that property tax revenue is more stable[31] and predictable than sales tax revenue. This reinforces the earlier discussion of needing to forecast revenue sources separately.

---

29. Guajardo and Miranda, note 19 above.

30. Data is from 2014 and was taken from the North Carolina Department of the State Treasurer.

31. This is so even with tax rates changing twice over this time period and a re-evaluation in 2009. *See* Alamance County, *Historic Tax Rates, 1939–2017* (2018).

Figure 6.1 Alamance County Revenue Collections, by Year

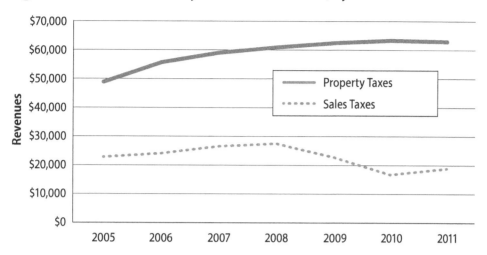

Formula-Based Projections

Formula-based projections, sometimes referred to as deterministic models, are simply mathematical formulas established for estimating future revenues. Once the formulas are created, the forecaster simply needs to plug in the various values required. If a formula-based projection is used, it and any additional information about its accuracy, assumptions, and reliability should be included in a local government's revenue manual.

The most common formula-based projections made by local governments are property tax forecasts. They often are forecasted according to the following formula:

Property tax revenue = (Total assessed value) / 100) × Tax rate.

It would be easy for local governments to forecast their property taxes using the above formula. In fact, it would most likely achieve relatively accurate results. However, it is important to be mindful of collection rates, and in North Carolina the previous year's collection rate is used in the calculation of property tax forecasts.[32] Furthermore, it is important also to incorporate any changes in assessed values into the assessed values used in the calculation of property tax forecasts. This is an excellent example of why the budget director will be updating these projections during this process. New information about collections and property assessments may make the formula look more like the following:

Property tax revenue = ((Updated total assessed value / 100) × Tax rate) × Collection rate.

For a local government considering changing its property tax rate, it is fairly apparent how changing the rate would change the amount of revenue collected.

So, for example, had Alamance County officials, in forecasting for FY 2012, used formula-based projections, they would have forecast exactly what was collected in 2011.[33] This is because they did not change their rate ($0.52 per $100), the last assessment was in 2009, and they are

---

32. G.S. 159-13(b)(6).

33. The only exception to this is if there were slight changes to the assessed value of particular parcels, such as additions and renovations, new construction, government buying land, etc.

required to use the same collection rate as in the previous year (i.e., FY 2011). So, using formula-based projections, property tax revenues for Alamance County in FY 2012 would be forecasted at approximately $62,654.

Since all of this information is available to the forecaster for property taxes, this is the most common way to forecast property taxes. Furthermore, it is also highly accurate. For a medium-term forecast, there is no reason to use alternate forecasting methods. However, a local government has the right to choose other forecasting methods. Within this section, alternate forecasting techniques are discussed, property taxes will be used again as an illustrative sample, and the outcomes will be compared to the formula-based projection calculated here. Then they will be compared to actual collections from FY 2012.

Strengths and Weaknesses of Formula-Based Projections

Formula-based projections work best when jurisdictions have a great deal of control over revenue sources[34] and those sources are stable, like the property tax, but they work less well for jurisdictions with revenue sources that fluctuate more with the economy, like sales taxes. Formula-based projections are very transparent, with their assumptions clearly laid out, which also makes them easier to understand. However, again using property taxes as an example, the method's weaknesses include not considering changes in assessments, as when new properties are added or property defaults occur. Fundamentally, formula-based projections are good for property taxes at the local level but not for more-dynamic revenues with harder to characterize (and less stable) tax bases.

Trend Analysis

Trend analysis, also referred to as time-series analysis, captures a great many methods for forecasting. It can include anything from a naive model, where the forecast is simply equal to the previous year's revenue, to an ARIMA (auto-regressive integrated moving average) model, which is as complicated as it sounds! Within this section, the discussion is limited to two basic trend analysis models: moving averages (three forms are discussed) and univariate regression. Also included is a brief discussion of a cumulative experience curve, which is often used for updating forecasts.

Moving Averages

The moving averages model captures a great many methods for forecasting. One method is simply to project that revenue will increase or decrease by the average amount it has changed over the past five years, thus giving no additional weight to recent years. A forecaster could also forecast the revenue as the average of those years. These decisions often involve assuming that the revenue source is too volatile to reasonably expect a trend to continue upward or downward.

The first form of moving averages, a *simple moving average* (SMA), is a method wherein the forecaster takes an average of historical data and uses the result as the forecast. In the initial step, the forecaster sets a window for how many years to include in the average (for the purposes of this chapter, a seven-year window is used). After the window is set, the necessary data are collected. (Of course, this is often not the order in practice, as data availability can determine

---

34. Formula-based projections are also more successful when the local government controls and has detailed information on the tax base. For property taxes, the local government quantifies it and sets it via assessments.

the size of the window.) Once the window is identified and the revenue data are collected, the forecaster takes all of the years of data, sums them, and then divides by the number of years. The reason the result is called a "moving" average is that the next year, the forecaster will drop the most-distant year included and replace it with the current fiscal year's data. So, it will always be the same number of years, just shifting forward (or moving).

For example, take the property tax revenue from Alamance County and imagine that the forecaster is creating a forecast for FY 2012.[35] Using the most-current data (up to and including FY 2011) reported by the North Carolina Department of the State Treasurer (2014), the seven-year window consists of FY 2005 to FY 2011. A simple moving average forecast for FY 2012 is accomplished by calculating the following:

$$(\$48{,}333 + \$55{,}546 + \$58{,}536 + \$60{,}794 + \$62{,}223 + \$63{,}241 + \$62{,}654) \: / \: 7 = \$58{,}761.$$

Imagine changing how large the window is, that is, how many years of historical data are being used. What happens when the window is only six years (so you drop 2005)? Five years? This should illustrate another point: that simple moving averages, like all trend forecasting, are sensitive to the size of the window the forecaster uses. Another weakness is that these moving averages treat the predictive power of previous years the same no matter how recent they are or how far in the past they are.[36]

The second form of moving averages is *arithmetic mean return* (AMR). The forecaster using AMR is most interested in calculating the growth rate, which, as defined here, is the percentage increase (or decrease) in collected revenue from the previous year.[37] Under this definition, the growth rate for FY 2006[38] is calculated as

$$\$55{,}546 \: / \: \$48{,}333 = 1.15.$$

This means that in FY 2006, Alamance County collected 115 percent of the revenue that was collected in FY 2005.[39] The growth rate is calculated as follows:

$$1.15(100){-}100 = 15\%.$$

This is done each year within the specified window. Results are reported below. Then, just like above, the growth rates are averaged.

$$\frac{15 + 5 + 4 + 2 + 2 - 1}{6} = 4.5.$$

Thus, the average growth in revenue from FY 2006 to 2011 is 4.5 percent (see Table 6.3).

---

35. Property taxes are most likely going to be forecast using formula-based projections, but to illustrate the different methodologies and to compare how close they come to forecasting actual revenues, property taxes are used as an example throughout this chapter.

36. Weighted moving averages are an example of how to use trend forecasting but give additional weight to recent observations, which many would consider to be more important indicators of future revenues.

37. This is similar to transformation moving averages wherein the forecaster simply takes the change in revenue (in dollars) and creates an average rate of change between years within the specified window. This average change would then be added to the most-recent fiscal year. For property tax revenues for FY 2012, the forecast using transformation moving averages is $65,041.

38. The growth rate for FY 2005 cannot be calculated because FY 2004 data are not included here.

39. The number 1.15 is multiplied by 100 to get the percentage.

Table 6.3 Average Growth Rates in Revenue, FY 2006–2011 (Rounded)

	2005	2006	2007	2008	2009	2010	2011	Average
Property Taxes	$48,333	$55,546	$58,536	$60,794	$62,223	$63,241	$62,654	$58,761*
Growth		15	5	4	2	2	-1	4.5**

* The forecasted revenue using simple moving averages.
** The forecasted multiplier or growth rate using AMR.

Once again, the forecaster could simply use the average revenue collected, $58,761, as the forecast for next year. However, what is more likely to be accurate is to take FY 2011 property tax collections ($62,654) and apply the average growth rate of 4.5 percent, which would result in an estimate of $65,473.43 for FY 2012. Some questions to consider are the following: Do any of the numbers stand out? Looking at the data and not just the calculations, does it seem reasonable to expect a 4.5 percent growth rate? Not really. The growth rate for property taxes decreased dramatically in 2007 and has continued to slow. In fact, by removing the change between FY 2005 and 2006, the average growth rate drops from 4.5 percent to 2.5 percent, which, in light of the trend, seems more likely. A forecaster for Alamance County might have been even more cautious and noted that property taxes experienced negative growth in the most recent year.

Third, a forecaster can create *moving means* that, once calculated, can be used with either simple moving averages or the AMR technique. Using the moving means method, the forecaster calculates an average for each year by, for example, taking the average of the year in question, the year before it, and the year after it. Then, using the three-year average as the value for that year, the forecaster conducts the same trend analysis as above. This method helps smooth bumps and "noise" from the estimates. So, if one year the revenue was particularly high or low, the influence of that data point can be minimized without it actually being removed from the analysis.

Again plugging in the property tax revenue data from Alamance County, the data point to be used for FY 2006 using a three-year window is calculated by taking the average for fiscal years 2005, 2006, and 2007.

$$\frac{\$48,333 + \$55,546 + \$58,536}{3} = \$54,138.33.$$

A forecaster who wanted to use moving means with a simple moving average could replace the actual revenue collections with these *smoothed* estimates. The calculation would include estimates for FY 2006 through 2010. Another option, which adds a slight weight to recent data, is to use the FY 2011 data but, because the forecast is for FY 2012, use the average of 2010 and 2011. This weights the two most-recent years more heavily than the previous years, which are averages of three years. That is accomplished as follows.

$$\frac{\$54,138.33 + \$58.292.00 + \$60.517.67 + \$62,086.00 + \$62,706.00 + \$62,947.50}{6} = \$60,114.58.$$

In contrast to using just the simple moving average, the above formula results in a higher revenue forecast: $60,114.58 versus $58,761. Of course, the goal is not to forecast the *most* revenue

Figure 6.2 Simple Moving Averages: Property Tax Revenue

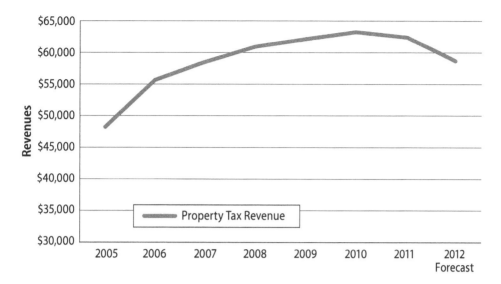

but, rather, the *most accurate*. When looking at the trend in recent years, this still appears to be a conservative estimate.

Similarly, a forecaster can take the transformation moving averages using the moving means. That calculation would look like

$$\frac{8 + 4 + 3 + 1 + 0}{5} = 3.$$

So, the expected growth using transformation moving averages in conjunction with moving means produces an expected property revenue for FY 2012 of $62,654 × 1.03 = $64,533.62. This is less than the estimate created by the transformation moving averages above, $66,181.49. This is because the $65,473.43 estimate smoothed some of the more-dramatic changes.[40]

Once again it is helpful to look at these forecasts visually (where expert judgment is useful). Using the simple moving averages method (Figure 6.2), it is apparent that there is expected to be a relatively sharp decline in property tax revenue in FY 2012. This is unlikely and would often be considered too conservative.

In contrast, when looking at the revenue forecast created by the estimate of 4.5 percent growth (Figure 6.3), it is clear that it has forecasted a relatively sharp increase in property tax revenue for FY 2012. This is likely going to be considered by a finance or budget officer as too

---

40. Something to keep in mind while considering moving means is how the amount of data shapes estimates. As mentioned in the discussion of simple moving averages, reducing or expanding the window inevitably changes the estimates. Here, because it is being taken as a given that no data are available before 2005, the window gets smaller by performing moving means. This is true also for transformation moving averages. In fact, when calculating transformation moving averages with moving means, two years get dropped—one for each method. Such would not be the case had 2003 and 2004 data been available and the seven-year window been maintained.

Figure 6.3 Arithmetic Mean Return: Property Tax Revenue

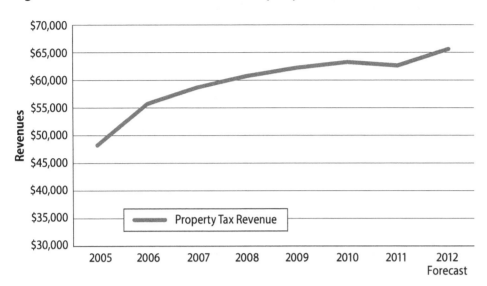

ambitious of an estimate. That is, unless the finance/budget officer applies their expert judgment and considers that growth has been slowed by the recession and that their county is expecting to start a nice rate of recovery.

Below are the forecasts for the simply moving averages (SMA) and for arithmetic mean return (AMR) using the moving means (Figure 6.4). As is apparent under both approaches, moving means do, in fact, smooth the estimates and present what is most likely a more-accurate forecast of revenue. It still seems likely, though, that one is too conservative and the other too optimistic.

Figure 6.4 Forecasted Revenues Using Moving Means

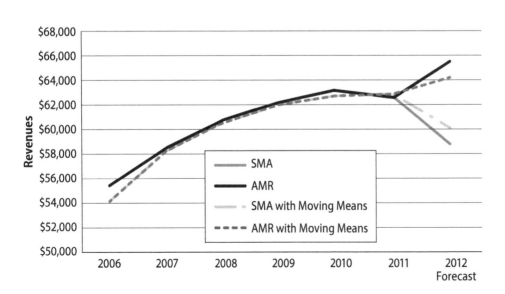

Univariate Regression

A simple way to forecast revenues using a statistical model is through univariate regression. Univariate simply means that only one independent (or control) variable is being used to predict the dependent variable. So, in the example we've been using, the independent variable is years and the dependent variable is revenue collections. The software captures the relationship between time progressing and revenue collections.

This model can be presented as $y = \propto (x) + \beta$, where y is the dependent variable, x is the independent variable, $\propto$ is the slope of the line when graphing it, and β is a constant term (or the point where the slope of the line intercepts with the y-axis on a graph). $\propto$ is how much revenue is forecasted to increase (or decrease) from the previous year based on earlier trends. Once again, some level of expert judgment is needed to confirm that there are no meaningful changes on the horizon that would affect future collections.

In this context the model can also be written as

$$Revenue = \propto (Year) + constant.$$

Univariate regression can be performed in many statistical packages, including Microsoft Excel. Here is a tip for forecasting revenue this way: look for a high R, or the correlation coefficient. R, which will be reported with the results, is measured on a scale from 0 to 1, where an R of 0 suggests no correlation and predictive ability and an R of 1 suggests perfect predictive ability. Neither situation is likely.

Reported here are estimates that are generated by performing univariate regression in Excel. The Excel regression estimates the constant [41] to be $49,898.14 and the $\propto$ to be $2,215.71.[42] In order to forecast for FY 2012, the forecaster would use these estimates in the above equation:

$$\$2,215.71(8) + \$49,898.14 = \$67,623.86.$$

Eight is used as the variable for the year because it is the eighth year of data in the window. This is only the case because the years for the regression were changed from 2005 through 2011 to 1 through 7. If left as is, the $\propto$ would have been much lower and 2012 would have been the appropriate multiplier.

In addition, the output produces an R of 0.90, so there is a great deal of predictive ability based on the time trend alone.

Once again, the forecast methodology has predicted a relatively sharp increase, in fact the largest so far (Figure 6.5). This is due to the trend of the data. The recession slowed what had been steady growth, so the forecasting methods are picking up on the earlier trend and dampening it by the slowed (and, in FY 2011, negative) growth. This clearly demonstrates, once again, the importance of always integrating some level of expert judgment into *all* methods.

Which method is most accurate for forecasting property taxes? According to the Alamance County budget for FY 2014, property tax revenue was $62,961 in FY 2012.[43] It is clear that for a

---

41. Excel uses the term "intercept."

42. The years for the recession were changed from 2005 through 2011 to 1 through 7.

43. The budget is available at www.alamance-nc.com/finance/wp-content/uploads/sites/10/2013/09/FY-2013-2014-Annual-Budget.pdf.

Figure 6.5   Univariate Regression: Property Tax Revenue

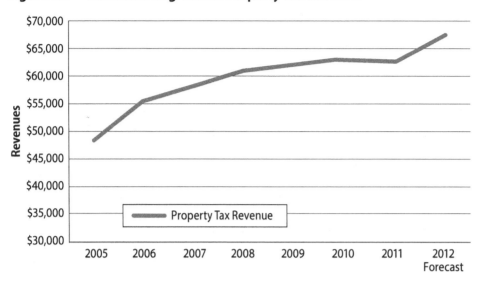

Figure 6.6   Forecasted Property Tax Revenue

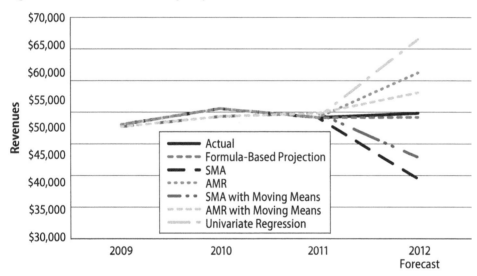

one-year property tax forecast, formula-based projection is the most accurate method. (See Figure 6.6 for a visual representation of all of the methods, including the actual revenue collected in FY 2012 for property taxes.) Now try replicating these methods for sales taxes. What stands out? Does either type of moving averages seem more reasonable for sales taxes than for property taxes? Moving means? Compare the sales tax forecasts with the actual FY 2012 revenue, which is: $17,328.

Cumulative Experience Curve

A third method of trend analysis is the *cumulative experience curve.* It is used most frequently to modify projections as revenue comes in during the fiscal year. Using a cumulative experience curve the forecaster examines monthly totals of revenue collected over a five-year period.[44] The forecaster takes the average amount collected per month and converts it into a percentage of the total amount of revenue collected. Then, once actual collections for the month in the current fiscal year are known, the forecaster can modify projections for the rest of the year. Of course, this is true only if the forecaster is willing to assume that the percentage of the total will be approximately the same. Ideally, this would be done by a local government throughout the year with the time frame and expectations clearly laid out in the unit's revenue manual.

Strengths and Weaknesses of Trend Analysis

As has been noted, a forecaster should always incorporate a level of expert judgment into creating forecasts. One reason for this is that trend analysis is fundamentally based on the idea that the past can be used as a good predictor of the future. However, if a community has experienced large economic shocks or changes this will not hold true. While these trend analyses can be valuable, research suggests that this method is most effective when used in combination with expert judgment.[45] The greatest weakness of trend analysis is not being able to anticipate coming changes or incorporate known changes into the model. This results in forecasts lagging behind changes to the economy.

Nonetheless, trend analysis is largely accurate for more-stable revenue sources. It also requires modest data and is relatively straightforward to implement. This is one reason why it is used heavily by smaller local governments.[46]

Causal Modeling

Causal modeling, also referred to as econometric modeling or multiple (multivariate) regression, models the "relationship between the revenue source and the economic variables that drive the tax base; in other words, this approach looks for what causes the collections to be what they are and creates a model of the relationship."[47] Causal modeling recognizes that demographic and economic changes to a community affect its revenues. These could include such factors as population, median income, inflation, and industry. It allows a forecaster to take data on an individual local government and determine how tax revenue is expected to change when a component of the model changes, for example, when unemployment increases, and how it is expected to affect a revenue source. Causal modeling becomes more valuable as the size and/or complications of the government, its respective economy, and its revenue portfolio grow.[48]

The section above on univariate regression uses a simple regression equation. To help explain causal modeling, that equation is going to be expanded. The dependent variable, *y*, continues to be actual revenues over multiple years; however, additional *x*'s, or independent variables,

---

44. Other time frames can be used; this is just a common one.

45. Gloria A. Grizzle and William Earle Klay, "Forecasting State Sales Tax Revenues: Comparing the Accuracy of Different Methods," *State and Local Government Review* 26, no. 3 (1994): 142–52.

46. It is also often used by larger local governments, especially for their more-minor revenue sources.

47. Mikesell, note 16 above, at 210.

48. Bland, note 2 above.

have been added. The forecaster is going to be predicting revenue based not just on the passage of time, but on its relationship with other variables. In this multivariate model revenues are dependent on these other independent variables, such as unemployment, median income, year, among others (represented by the x's below). The model can be represented by the following:

$$y = \propto (x_1) + \mu (x_2) + \gamma (x_3) + \theta (x_4) + \beta.$$

Once the model is carefully constructed and the data are input, the forecaster can generate the estimated effect of the independent variables on revenue and make assumptions (possibly from trend analysis or from expert judgment) about those independent variables, use the slopes or the coefficients (like $\propto$), multiply the projected values for those independent variables, and add the constant term (β) to get their projected revenue.

Below is a description of an academic exercise in forecasting and how the scholar chose to test forecasting methods.

> The model employed in this article identifies explanatory variables in four areas: personal income, employment, population, and inflation. From each of these four areas, multiple explanatory variables are identified. The personal income area considers county personal income, state personal income, county personal income growth rate, and county per capita personal income as candidates for explanatory variables; the employment area considers county total employment, county total unemployment, county total labor force, county unemployment rate, and state unemployment rate; the population area considers county total population and county population growth rate; and the inflation area considers the national prime interest rate, the national mortgage interest rate, the California consumer price index (CPI) for all urban customers, and the California CPI growth rate. . . . County explanatory variables are forecasted in the simplest way, mainly because including more elaborate forecasting equations for these variables would easily double the size of this model without significantly increasing the overall forecasting accuracy.[49]

This passage should clarify two aspects of causal modeling. First, that it requires a great deal of annual (if not quarterly or monthly) data. This level and quality of data are often difficult to come by, if not impossible. Using data from the last U.S. Census is simply inadequate. Second, in an applied analysis, while Dongsung Kong finds that causal modeling is effective and accurate, he also finds that sparser specifications are accurate. So, it may not be necessary to have all of these variables.

Causal models are used less frequently at the local level and can be very complex and challenging to implement. They are also very sensitive to specification and assumptions about the economy, so the forecaster must take particular care in identifying the independent variables to be included. In addition, as with univariate regression, the forecaster wants to generate a high (close to 1) R-squared. The lower the estimated R-squared, the less predictive power the model has and the less accurate it should be expected to be. An R-squared of one means that all variation between the values of the dependent variable is captured or explained by the covariates in the model, whereas a 0 would mean that none of the variation in the dependent variable is explained by the model.

---

49. Kong, note 24 above, at 183.

Strengths and Weaknesses of Causal Models

The primary reason forecasters undertake causal modeling is that it allows for taxes, which are more sensitive to the changing economic environment, to be forecasted based on those changes. This means that causal modeling is more likely to capture shocks and trends. With causal modeling it is not necessarily the case that revenue forecasts will lag behind changes to the tax base in the way they do with trend analysis.

The reason not every local government forecasts using causal modeling is that it is very difficult to do. Most local governments that use this methodology do not do it themselves. They hire economists from either a local university or a consulting firm. In addition, there is often very incomplete data, and "the absence of data on economic and structural variables at the city level" is very restricting.[50] Many of the key variables that are needed, such as personal income and population, are not available annually and potentially are not even collected for a unit of government (some data are collected just for counties; other data, just for large municipalities or even metropolitan statistical areas). Furthermore, causal models require the forecaster to also estimate the values for the independent variables in the next fiscal year. This introduces the possibility for even more error in the model. These factors make causal modeling difficult if not impossible for many local governments to use.

Overall Assessment of Quantitative Methods

In closing, quantitative forecasting methods may more accurately model future revenues than qualitative methods. When using data, it is always important to remember: garbage in, garbage out. Reliable data is critical. In addition, evidence suggests that the simple, straightforward models perform as well as the complicated models. In both the short and medium term, trend analysis models perform better than causal models. So, it should not be considered necessary for local governments to embark on heroic efforts to perform sophisticated causal models if it is not within their means and the trend analyses have been reliable for them.

Considerations on Choosing the *Right* Method

There are many factors to consider in determining what method of forecasting is best. In this section some of the more universal factors are discussed, recognizing, however, that a local government can modify these perspectives in light of its own needs, for example, in terms of local capacity and what is realistic. What the forecasting staff (or the lack thereof) are capable of doing, especially with regard to the use of quantitative methods, is a crucial consideration. There is always the question of the budget and if a local government can afford to hire experts to aid in or perform qualitative or quantitative forecasting or if that money could be better used elsewhere. In general, local governments rely heavily on expert judgment (internal and external). More than half of all counties in California, according to one study, use expert judgment as their primary method of forecasting revenues. This is especially true for small jurisdictions, where the number is closer to two-thirds.[51]

---

50. Mikesell, note 16 above, at 211.
51. Kong, note 24 above.

A forecaster should also carefully consider individual revenue instruments, that is, specific taxes, fees, and the like. Typically, a revenue forecast is created for every major revenue source (so possibly property taxes, sales taxes, and utilities). For the smaller revenue sources a local government may just look at historical numbers and establish an estimated total for each source. Even within that context, however, the same forecast method is most likely not the best choice for all of the revenues to be forecasted.

Therefore, it becomes important to ask how a forecaster decides to choose between the available methods. First, the data are examined for trends, patterns, and rates of changes. An important component of this process is considering how stable the revenue source is, not just the "trend" but how closely it follows that trend.[52] Sales taxes are more unstable than property taxes, and this makes trend analysis more problematic in light of the cyclical nature of the economy. For example, "property taxes for most local governments are levied on an assessed value base that, because of assessment lags, is known at the time that budgets are adopted and property tax rates are set, [but] there [are] no such lags for sales and income taxes; their bases are emerging as the budget is being executed."[53] Therefore, a formula-based forecast or a trend analysis may be best suited for property taxes, and a causal model may best capture sales tax revenue forecasts.

Examining the economic, political, and social influences on a particular revenue source can also be useful. Look beyond the data. Is the revenue instrument, or more accurately its base, likely to be affected by a recession? Is citizen demand for this service growing? Some of these relationships and assumptions will help guide you to the appropriate forecasting method.[54]

A third way of approaching the potentially difficult decision of selecting the proper forecasting method is simply to forecast the most recent complete year of revenue using the competing methods and see which ones work best for which instruments, as has been done here. There is an online resource included with this chapter. It presents an Excel spreadsheet and step-by-step directions for recreating the different forecasting methods highlighted in this chapter. This resource is a good initial step for a new forecaster or for someone who is reconsidering which forecasting method might work best for the revenue instrument they are responsible for forecasting. It is advisable to begin with the revenues presented here to ensure that the forecasted amounts are equivalent and that the methods are clear. A forecaster could then insert their own revenue values to begin the analysis for themselves.[55]

Finally, a forecaster may also want to know what forecasting method has been found to be the most accurate by academic researchers. Unfortunately, such studies do not provide a consensus view. Some studies have found that simple time-series models, particularly the moving average, produce the most reliable results.[56] Another study, however, found that

52. Guajardo and Miranda, note 19 above.

53. Mikesell, note 16 above, at 210.

54. Guajardo and Miranda, note 19 above.

55. *See* https://www.sog.unc.edu/pubs/978642380798.

56. Howard A. Frank, "Municipal Revenue Forecasting with Time Series Models: A Florida Case Study," *American Review of Public Administration* 20, no. 1 (1990): 45–59; Howard A. Frank and Xiao Hu Wang, "Judgmental vs. Time Series vs. Deterministic Models in Local Revenue Forecasting: A Florida Case Study," *Public Budgeting and Financial Management* 6, no. 4 (1994): 493–517; Gerasimos A. Gianakis and Howard A. Frank, "Implementing Time Series Forecasting Models: Considerations for Local Governments," *State and Local Government Review* 25, no. 2 (1993): 130–44.

judgmental methods perform better than time-series or causal models.[57] A more-recent study found that, when looking at sales taxes, causal models perform best and trend analysis does poorly even though it is the most common of those being tested.[58] In addition, that study found that "simpler, more readily communicated models generally perform at least as well as more complex methods."[59]

Best Practices in Forecasting Revenues

There are many best practices when it comes to forecasting, many of which have been mentioned in this chapter. This section focuses on many of the more-successful practices. By no means is this an exhaustive list, however, and not every method is necessarily *best* for every local government.

The first best practice is to create a revenue manual (described as step 1 in the section above titled "Potential Administrative Process for Revenue Forecasting"). This is an action that all local governments should be able to take and that should be of universal benefit. If a local government does not already have a revenue manual in place, the process of creating one may be a multi-year undertaking. The place to start is at the top, with major revenue sources.

Second, forecasters should consider creating hybrid or conditional models that can be adjusted in line with other scenarios, such as changes in tax rates or the tax base.[60] For example, adjusting the tax rate is a straightforward process in a formula-based allocation.[61] In fact, one of the common uses of forecasting beyond creating one-year revenue projections for a local government's budget is guiding tax-rate adjustments. This is helpful in trying to establish consistent tax policies so that tax rates do not have to be adjusted every year.[62] This is best when the process is transparent and the assumptions are clearly laid out. Hybrid models present alternative forecasts of possible revenues, act as a sensitivity test to assumptions in the model, and provide elected officials with options if they are considering changing elements of their policy.

It is important to remember that forecasts are projections, not predictions. While a hybrid model may be useful in testing assumptions and providing options and, in some cases, for assisting in long-term planning, it is not appropriate or acceptable for annual budget forecasts. Revenue numbers must be decided upon and used to balance the budget.

---

57. H. Naci Mocan and Sam Azad, "Accuracy and Rationality of State General Fund Revenue Forecasts: Evidence from Panel Data," *International Journal of Forecasting* 1, no. 3 (1995): 417–27.

58. Kong, note 24 above.

59. Kong, at 197.

60. "The forecast may even be conditional, in the sense that it is prepared with alternative assumptions (high/low scenarios) for certain economic or developmental factors." Mikesell, note 16 above, at 209.

61. Also, if rates have changed over time, it is critical to adjust the data to reflect that. If the forecaster is engaged in causal modeling, it may be as straightforward as controlling for rate. However, if a more basic trend analysis is being used, it would be crucial to adjust the data to reflect that rate, and not a change in the economy or tax base, is driving the change in collections.

62. Rivenbark, note 4 above.

Third, be careful when managing the data. Below are three tips for dealing with the data used to make forecasts.[63]

1. *Always graph data.* This allows for a deeper understanding of what the data are saying and ensures that the data make sense in the context of institutional knowledge.
2. *Adjust away outliers.* Some data points will not be representative. A graph helps identify such cases so that they can be removed or handled differently, for example, by using moving means.
3. *Keep records of original, unadjusted data.* It is a best practice to always keep a file with the original data before it has been modified, adjusted, or manipulated. This allows one to go back and see what the data said before adjustments were made, to look for patterns that might have been missed or that are new, for example, that an outlier was not an outlier but actually the start of a new event or period.

Fourth, consider other factors beyond the revenue forecasts that may be affected by their accuracy, for example, a local government's fund balance. It is clear that revenue projections or forecasts are not going to be completely accurate, and while it is considered best to err slightly on the conservative side of forecasting, it should nonetheless be apparent that this is one of the many reasons that maintaining a fund balance is encouraged—not just for downturns, but also for years when estimates are on the high end of the spectrum. This is especially important when there is less confidence in the forecasts. For example, if a forecast relies heavily on sales taxes, and they are volatile historically, a local government may choose to maintain larger fund-balance reserves.[64]

Fifth, create within-year monthly or quarterly targets for periodic revenues, such as sales taxes. These should be based on historical data, typically a three-year average monthly (or quarterly) collection number that reflects the expected trend for that year. So, if one-eighth of all local sales tax revenue is collected in November, on average, the target for November should be approximately one-eighth of what has been forecasted for the year.

Sixth, consider creating a long-term financial plan. The National Advisory Council on State and Local Budgeting (NACSLB) encourages local governments to develop such a plan by using a strategic process that allows for greater insights and the information necessary to establish policies surrounding both expenditures and revenues that will lead to long-term fiscal health.[65]

Finally, as noted in the section on choosing the right forecasting method, one should consider how a given revenue source is likely to be impacted by changes in the broader economy, such as a recession. The twenty-first century has demonstrated that taking stock of the cause of a recession and its anticipated impact on the economy more broadly must also be integrated into the forecasting process. In the past, it was reasonable for a forecaster operating in the midst of a recession or out of concern that one may be on the horizon to turn to previous economic downturns to inform revenue projections. As evidenced by the tremendous diversity in the three recessions of this century (the dot-com recession of the early 2000s, the Great Recession, and

---

63. Adapted from Greg C. G. Chen, Dall W. Forsythe, Lynne A. Weikart, and Daniel W. Williams, *Budget Tools: Financial Methods in the Public Sector* (Washington, D.C.: CQ Press, 2008).

64. Whitney Afonso, "Diversification toward Stability? The Effect of Local Sales Taxes on Own Source Revenue," *Journal of Public Budgeting, Accounting and Financial Management* 25, no. 4 (2013): 649–74.

65. Calia, Guajardo, and Metzgar, note 4 above.

the recession brought on by the pandemic), it is clear that the underlying cause of a recession is critical to understanding how it impacts revenues.[66] The dot-com recession behaved similarly to past recessions, as did the Great Recession in many respects, but the severity, length, and impact of these two events on property taxes were largely unprecedented. The pandemic-induced recession behaved very differently from the other two twenty-first century recessions and had forecasters during this time used numbers and trends from the Great Recession, it would not have led to accurate forecasting.[67] Trend analysis would not be able to factor in these differences or the concern of a looming economic downturn. Once again, this is where expert judgement is critical to forecasting.

Forecasting Is Not Perfect

It is important to remember that no forecast is ever completely accurate; the numbers will inevitably be wrong. The goal is to minimize how wrong they are! With that in mind, there are four additional points to be made about errors in forecasting.[68] First, the forecaster should strive to include predicted errors with the estimates. It should be clear how confident the forecaster is that these forecasts are reliable. Second, the farther out the forecast, the larger the errors are likely to be. Third, forecasts are built upon the past. This has two important implications:

---

66. The pandemic-induced recession presented unique challenges for local governments when it came to revenue forecasting. Unlike a typical recession, the one brought on by the pandemic resulted in a sudden and sharp drop in revenue, as many businesses were forced to close their doors and many people lost their jobs. This made it difficult for local governments to accurately forecast revenue and plan for the future. In addition, the uncertainty surrounding the pandemic made it difficult to predict when revenue would begin to recover.

One of the biggest differences between local government revenue forecasting during the pandemic and during a typical recession was the level of uncertainty that existed. In a typical recession, revenue declines are gradual and predictable. In contrast, the pandemic resulted in a sudden and unprecedented shock to the economy, which made it difficult to predict the impact on revenue. Local governments had to grapple with a high degree of uncertainty, as the pandemic's trajectory was uncertain, and it was difficult to predict when economic activity would resume. Among many unanswered questions, it was not clear how long stay-at-home orders would remain in place, how long it would take for people to feel comfortable and confident enough to leave their homes, how long work-from-home arrangements would be allowed to continue for many workers, or how much time it would take to create and administer vaccinations (if that occurred at all).

The nature of the pandemic and how it affected revenue streams also distinguished this latest recession from the previous two recessions. The pandemic led to the closure of businesses, which resulted in a rapid and unprecedented decline in sales tax revenues, as well as occupancy and food and beverage tax revenues. These factors made revenue forecasting more challenging and required local governments to consider multiple scenarios and potential outcomes.

67. For more information on some of these impacts, see Whitney Afonso, Monica Allen, and Richard Carey, "The Great Lockdown's Impact on the City of Charlotte's Budget," *Municipal Finance Journal* 42, no. 1 (2021); Whitney Afonso, "Planning for the Unknown: Local Government Strategies from the Fiscal Year 2021 Budget Season in Response to the COVID-19 Pandemic," *State and Local Government Review* 53, no. 2 (2021): 159–71.

68. Adapted from Kenneth A. Kriz, "Long-Term Forecasting," in *Handbook of Local Government Fiscal Health*, Helisse Levine, Jonathan B. Justice, and Eric A. Scorsone, eds. (Burlington, MA: Jones and Bartlett Learning, 2013).

(1) if the future deviates from the past in a meaningful way the forecasts will not be accurate and (2) if key data or trends from the past are ignored, more errors will be introduced into the estimates. Fourth, forecasting for a period greater than three years will be more reliable if the revenues are more aggregated. So, while it is useful to forecast individual revenue streams for the short and medium term, this is less valuable for long-term forecasting.

Because errors do inevitably occur, it is advisable to forecast on the conservative side, but just slightly so. It is not prudent to dramatically underestimate revenues because budgets do have to be balanced, which could cause budget makers to make unnecessary cuts to services or to increase taxes. "Estimates that are too high can create major crises during the execution phase, at which time expenditures must be cut so as not to exceed revenues. Low estimates also cause problems, in that programs may be needlessly reduced at the beginning of the fiscal year."[69]

Forecasting: Cautions

Beyond just the reliability of the results produced by a methodology, time frame, and data, other concerns may corrupt a forecaster's estimates, for example, when politics enters the process. Unfortunately, forecasting can quickly become political. This is why, in general, it is often considered a best practice to be slightly conservative and to estimate revenues just below where the forecaster thinks they will be.[70] However, this practice makes it harder to balance the budget and may require service cuts or increased taxes, so it is also possible that forecasters will face pressure to be more *optimistic*. It is important to stand your ground though, because "in revenue forecasting, your sins find you out, and they do have a cost."[71]

Another persistent problem in generating reliable forecasts is the cyclical nature of the economy. Taken back far enough, historical data reveals periodic dips in growth. Revenues, some more than others, are cyclical and influenced by business cycles, which can be understood as *natural* expansions and recessions (shrinking) of the economy.[72] As local governments reduce their reliance on property taxes and increase their use of user fees and sales taxes, awareness of this will become even more critical. Keep this in mind as forecasts are prepared, especially for long-term forecasts.

Conclusion

Revenue forecasting is an exercise that every local government performs. Despite that universality, there is a great deal of diversity in the methodology of those forecasts—some local governments may choose to simply forecast next year's revenue to equal the previous year's

---

69. Robert D. Lee, Ronald W. Johnson, and Philip G. Joyce, *Public Budgeting Systems* (Burlington, MA: Jones and Bartlett Learning, 2008), 125.

70. "In both larger and smaller counties, the acceptable overestimation range was lower than the acceptable under-estimation range. These findings confirm the conservative behavior among government revenue forecasters in the presence of uncertainty. And, when the county revenue forecasters were asked how conservative they are in forecasting sales taxes, 90% of the counties responded that their estimation was at least somewhat conservative." Kong, note 24 above, at 190.

71. Bland, note 2 above.

72. Garrett and Leatherman, note 1 above.

revenue, whereas others may create sophisticated causal models that attempt to capture the changing nature of the underlying tax base. These potential extremes highlight the need for transparency both internally and externally. Revenue forecasts should not just provide a number; they should also (especially if quantitative) provide the methodology and assumptions on which forecasts are based. One place for a local government to record this information is in a revenue manual.

In addition, local governments need to be thoughtful when choosing which forecasting methods are best for them and when they should employ different methods for different revenue instruments. Unfortunately, there is no one right answer. The benefit of having a more-advanced forecasting method with *slightly* more-accurate forecasts may not outweigh the additional costs of performing it.[73] These costs may be direct, such as paying outside consultants, or indirect, such as staff time and additional training. In light of the information presented in this chapter, it should not be surprising that expert and trend analyses are the most-common methods for forecasting revenues and expenditures in North Carolina and that there is no standard model or methodology because each local government develops its own catered to its particular needs.[74]

Although revenue forecasting may seem like, and often is, a challenging undertaking, there are many excellent resources available to local governments in North Carolina.[75] Below are resources to enable budget and finance officers to reach out and connect with peers and experts.

- North Carolina League of Municipalities (NCLM): www.nclm.org;
- North Carolina Association of County Commissioners (NCACC): www.ncacc.org;
- North Carolina Government Finance Officers Association (NCGFOA): www.ncgfoa.org;
- North Carolina Local Government Budget Association (NCLBA): www.nclgba.org;
- School of Government (SOG): www.sog.unc.edu.
- Excel spreadsheet on revenue forecasting (prepared by the author) and directions for using the spreadsheet: https://www.sog.unc.edu/pubs/978642380798.

For more on additional forecasting methods and a more in-depth discussion of the math behind revenue forecasting, the following resources may be helpful.[76]

- Thomas A. Garrett and John Leatherman, *An Introduction to State and Local Public Finance* (Morganton, WV: Regional Research Institute, West Virginia University, 2000), www.rri.wvu.edu/WebBook/Garrett/contents.htm.
- Dongsung Kong, "Local Government Revenue Forecasting: The California County Experience," *Journal of Public Budgeting, Accounting & Financial Management* 19, no. 2 (2007): 178–99.

---

73. Kong, note 24 above.

74. Rivenbark, note 4 above.

75. For example, the North Carolina Association of County Commissioners (NCACC) prepares a report on projections for county revenues every year. While the projections are not specific to individual counties, they can offer some insight and direction. See the County Budget, Tax, & Finance Information page of the NCACC website, https://www.ncacc.org/research-and-publications/research/county-budget-and-tax/.

Similarly, the North Carolina League of Municipalities (NCLM) also prepares a memo on municipal revenue projections for the state. For FY 2015–2016, see https://www.nclm.org/financial-consulting/revenue-forecasts.

76. The academic resources in this list may be purchased or accessed through a local college or university library.

- Gloria A. Grizzle and William Earle Klay, "Forecasting State Sales Tax Revenues: Comparing the Accuracy of Different Methods," *State and Local Government Review* 26, no. 3 (1994): 142–52.
- Shayne C. Kavanagh and Charles Iglehart, "Structuring the Revenue Forecasting Process," *Government Finance Review* (Oct. 2012), www.gfoa.org/structuring-revenue-forecasting-process.

Chapter 7

Financing Capital Projects

by Connor H. Crews

Introduction

County and municipal officials are responsible for acquiring, constructing, and maintaining the facilities, equipment, and other capital assets necessary to perform public services.[1] Units of local government in North Carolina perform a wide variety of public services—and as a result, the cost and complexity of the capital assets that a local government might need to perform a given public service (e.g., water and sewer service or operation of a courthouse), can vary substantially according to the types of public services that a unit provides. Because the useful life of a capital asset can extend for multiple fiscal years, the tools that a local government uses to budget for and finance the acquisition or construction of capital projects differ from those used to budget and finance current assets or operating expenses.[2]

This chapter focuses on funding capital assets used solely or primarily for traditional governmental purposes and explores the five primary mechanisms available to North Carolina's local governments to finance capital projects: (1) current revenues, (2) savings, (3) special levies, (4) debt, and (5) grants or partnerships.[3] Table 7.1 lists the authorized financing mechanisms within each category, and the remainder of the chapter details the legal authority of local governments to use each financing mechanism.

---

1. In broad terms, a capital asset is an asset of significant value that has a useful life of more than one year.

2. Chapter 3, "Budgeting for Operating and Capital Expenditures," discusses the capital budgeting process.

3. Several other chapters in this book discuss grants and partnerships. For more information on acquiring property through leases, see Chapter 11, "Procurement, Contracting, and Disposal of Property." For information on public-private partnerships and redevelopment, see Chapter 15, "Financing and Public-Private Partnerships for Community Economic Development."

Table 7.1   Authorized Capital Financing Mechanisms in North Carolina

Current Revenues	Savings	Special Levies	Borrowing Money	Grants and Partnerships
• General fund revenues • Enterprise fund revenues	• Fund balance • Capital reserve fund	• Special taxing districts • Traditional special assessments • Critical-infrastructure assessments • Development exactions	• General obligation bonds • Installment financings/ synthetic tax-increment financings • Revenue bonds • Special obligation bonds • Project-development financings (tax-increment financings)	• Leases • Reimbursement agreements • Redevelopment areas • Grants • Gifts/donations/ crowd-funding[a] • State direct appropriations

a. Crowd-funding involves the use of online platforms to raise private money to fund public infrastructure projects. At its core, crowd-funding simply provides a newer mechanism to accept private donations for specific public improvement projects.

Current Revenues

Current revenues are revenues that a unit of local government collects on a regular, recurring basis (e.g., each fiscal year).[4] The largest source of current revenue in a unit's general fund is typically the property (*ad valorem*) tax, followed by local sales and use taxes. Current revenues in a unit's enterprise funds typically encompass user fees and charges.

Although units typically use current revenues to fund government programs and, in particular, to cover recurring operational expenses, including salaries and benefits, utilities, and supplies, many also use a portion of current revenues to fund capital projects. Local governments typically use current revenues to fund two categories of capital expenditures: (1) those falling below a certain dollar amount and (2) those recurring on a regular basis (e.g., maintenance and repair expenditures on capital assets). Some local governments establish in their annual budget ordinance the dollar amount below which they will fund any capital expenditures with current revenues. A particular recurring capital expenditure may exceed that amount, in which case a local government may still choose to finance it using current revenues.

Savings

A unit often must save current revenues over time to finance a capital expenditure. North Carolina's local governments can do this in two ways: (1) by accumulating moneys in fund balance or (2) by allocating revenues to a capital reserve fund.

4. For more information regarding sources of local government revenue, see Chapter 4, "Revenue Sources."

Fund Balance

Local governments use fund accounting to track their assets and liabilities.[5] In a fund accounting system, each accounting fund contains its own subset of self-balancing accounts—and each fund has its own assets, liabilities, revenues, and expenses.

Several types of funds can exist in a fund accounting system, including a "general fund," which is both the most common type of fund that local governments hold and which accounts for the majority of revenues and expenditures for general government purposes. Equity within an accounting fund—the difference between its financial assets (e.g., revenues) and liabilities (e.g., expenditures)—is known as "fund balance."

Primary Purposes

Fund balance serves three primary purposes: (1) to provide sufficient cash flow to cover operating expenses, (2) to serve as an emergency or "rainy day" fund, and (3) to function as a saving mechanism for anticipated capital expenditures.

Covering Operating Expenses

Although the fiscal year for most units of local government and public authorities begins on July 1,[6] many local governments do not receive the majority of their current revenues (in the form of property tax proceeds) until late December or early January.[7] Therefore, a local government typically must rely upon cash reserves—accumulated in fund balance—from its prior fiscal year to cover expenditures in the first several months of its new fiscal year.

Maintaining an Emergency or "Rainy Day" Fund

Fund balance can also serve as an emergency or "rainy day" fund. In an economic downturn or in response to unexpected expenses (e.g., a natural disaster or pandemic), local governments may have difficulty generating additional revenues (through taxes, fees, or user charges) quickly. Fund balance can provide a local government with cash flow to cover unanticipated operating or capital expenditures.

Saving for Anticipated Capital Expenditures

Some local governments also use fund balance to save money over time for anticipated capital expenditures. For example, if a local government knows that it must finance a capital expenditure in the next several years, it might purposefully enlarge its fund balance in fiscal years preceding the expenditure. When the project begins, the local government can then appropriate moneys accumulated in fund balance to finance the project.

---

5. *See* Robert J. Freeman et al., *Governmental and Nonprofit Accounting: Theory and Practice* 8th ed. (Hoboken, NJ: Prentice Hall, Inc., 2006), 23.

6. The fiscal year for most units of local government and for public authorities begins on July 1 and ends on June 30, although the Local Government Commission (LGC) can permit a public authority to operate under an alternative fiscal year "if it determines that a different fiscal year would facilitate the authority's financial operations." G.S. 159-8(b).

7. Although property (*ad valorem*) taxes are due on September 1 of the fiscal year in which they are levied, no interest accrues on unpaid property taxes until January 6. *See* G.S. 105-360(a). Collections of property taxes therefore typically increase in December and early January.

Proper Amounts of Fund Balance

North Carolina law limits the maximum amount of fund balance that a unit may appropriate in an annually budgeted fund, but it does not force units to maintain any minimum level of fund balance. The Local Government Commission (LGC), a division of the North Carolina Department of the State Treasurer responsible for overseeing local government financial-management practices, similarly does not require units to set any minimum amount of fund balance.[8] Instead, the LGC has encouraged units of local government to "maintain a fund balance that is consistent with . . . peers that provide similar services"[9] and use LGC-published memoranda that list fund balances available for all counties and municipalities[10] to determine a unit-specific amount of fund balance to maintain on an annual basis. What may be an appropriate amount of fund balance for one unit (e.g., 8 percent of general expenditures or one month of operating expenditures) may be inappropriate for another.

The LGC recommends that each local government adopt a fund balance policy that can be used to develop operating budgets and provide for corrective action should fund balance drop below the intended level at the close of a fiscal year.[11] The LGC also has drafted a sample fund balance policy, which contemplates that certain portions of fund balance "should be contemplated as a funding source for capital needs."[12]

Using Savings Held in Fund Balance for Capital Expenditures

Appropriating portions of fund balance for a capital expenditure is relatively simple. A governing board need only amend its budget ordinance or project ordinance to account for and authorize an expenditure for one or more capital projects.[13] A governing board may need to take additional actions to authorize a unit to enter into a contract for the acquisition or construction of a capital project.[14]

---

8. N.C. Department of State Treasurer, "LGC Staff Guidance on Fund Balance Available" (blog), NCTreasurer.com (July 11, 2022).

9. "LGC Staff Guidance on Fund Balance Available."

10. See, e.g., the following memoranda issued by the N.C. Department of State Treasurer, Local Government Commission: *Memorandum 2022-04, Management of Cash and Taxes and Fund Balance Available – Municipalities – for the Fiscal Year Ended June 30, 2020* (Aug. 17, 2021); *Memorandum 2022-03, Management of Cash and Taxes and Fund Balance Available – Counties – for the Fiscal Year ended June 30, 2020* (Aug. 11, 2021). As used in this book, the term "municipality" is synonymous with "city," "town," and "village."

11. To review the LGC's sample fund balance policy, see N.C. Department of State Treasurer, Local Government Commission, *Fund Balance Policy: City of Dogwood* (2022).

12. *Fund Balance Policy: City of Dogwood*, at 2.

13. *See* G.S. 159-15 (budget ordinance amendment); 159-13.2(e) (project ordinance amendment). For more information on amending budget and project ordinances, see Chapter 3, "Budgeting for Operating and Capital Expenditures."

14. For example, state law might require a unit of local government to undertake a competitive bidding process prior to entering a contract for construction or for the acquisition of personal property. *See* G.S. 143-129(a) (formal bidding process); 143-131 (informal bidding process). For more information, see Chapter 11, "Procurement, Contracting, and Disposal of Property."

Advantages and Disadvantages of Accumulating Savings for Capital Expenditures in Fund Balance

Using fund balance to save money for future capital projects affords flexibility to a local government's governing board. Because state law does not dictate that a unit spend unrestricted fund balance on a particular project or asset, the board may use the moneys accumulated in fund balance to finance either operating or capital expenditures.[15] This flexibility can be beneficial in the face of unexpected events. For example, assume that a county wishes to expand its solid waste disposal facility in approximately five years. The county's board of commissioners begins to purposefully accumulate fund balance toward this goal, but in year three, the county suffers from an economic recession. In this case, the board may divert the accumulated fund balance—with the exception of any moneys restricted by statute, regulation, or grant condition—to meet unrelated operating expenses or more pressing capital expenditures.

Using fund balance as a mechanism to save for future capital expenditures also may create controversy. Citizens may question why a unit of local government continues to raise revenue (through taxes, fees, and other charges) when it has sufficient reserves to meet its annual cash flow needs. They also may not trust that the governing board ultimately will spend the accumulated fund balance on capital expenditures.

Capital Reserve Funds

Instead of accumulating savings for capital expenditures in fund balance, a unit of local government may establish a capital reserve fund and periodically appropriate money to it.[16] North Carolina law enables a unit of local government to establish and maintain a capital reserve fund for any purpose for which it may issue bonds.[17] Local government utilities must account for any proceeds of system development fees in a capital reserve fund, regardless of the type of capital projects that the moneys will be used to fund, unless the local government has pledged those revenues as security in a bond financing.[18] In that case, the local government may deposit the proceeds of system development fees in the funds, accounts, or subaccounts in accordance with the relevant bond order, bond resolution, trust agreement, or similar instrument that secures the relevant bonds.[19]

---

15. Fund balance often includes some components that must be used for particular purposes. For a detailed description of the components of fund balance, see Chapter 10, "Accounting, Financial Reporting, and the Annual Audit."

16. G.S. 159-18.

17. G.S. 159-48. A local government may, but is not required to, issue bonds to fund the project for which it creates a capital reserve fund.

18. G.S. 162A-211(d), (e). For a sample resolution creating a capital reserve fund for the proceeds of system-development fees, see the following blog posts from Kara Millonzi: "CRFs for SDFs (aka Capital Reserve Funds for System Development Fees)," *Coates' Canons: NC Local Government Law* blog (May 24, 2018); "2018 System Development Fee Law Changes," *Coates' Canons: NC Local Government Law* blog (June 26, 2018).

19. *See, e.g.,* City of Charlotte, North Carolina, *Official Statement for $464,680,000 Water and Sewer System Revenue Bonds, Series 2022A, and $13,405,000 Taxable Water and Sewer System Revenue Bonds, Series 2022B* (Aug. 25, 2022). Under the General Trust Indenture and Series Indenture securing these bonds, the City of Charlotte has pledged the system-development fees that it collects in connection with its water and sewer system as security for its obligation to repay these bonds. City of Charlotte Official

Creating and Amending a Capital Reserve Fund

To create a capital reserve fund, the governing board of a unit of local government must adopt a resolution or ordinance stating:

(1) the purposes for which the capital reserve fund is created,[20]

(2) the approximate periods of time during which the moneys shall be accumulated in the fund for each purpose,

(3) the approximate amounts to be accumulated for each purpose, and

(4) the sources from which moneys for each purpose will be derived.[21]

A local government's governing board may appropriate funds from its annual budget ordinance to a capital reserve fund at any time.[22] Whenever it makes an appropriation, the board must amend the capital reserve fund into which the money will be transferred to account for the additional revenue.

The board also can amend a capital reserve fund, at any time, to change the purposes for which the fund was originally created.[23] For example, assume that the governing board of a rapidly growing municipality anticipates a need to expand its water system within eight to ten years. The board establishes a capital reserve fund and allocates moneys to the fund on an annual basis for five years for the water-system expansion project. In year six, the municipality suffers from a major economic recession and its growth slows significantly, making a water-system expansion unnecessary. In that case, the governing board can amend the capital reserve fund to identify alternative capital expenditures for which it will expend funds previously accumulated for the water-system expansion (e.g., road improvements, vehicle acquisition, or construction of a new administrative building). The board could not, however, divert accumulated savings in the capital reserve fund to cover the municipality's operating expenses (e.g., salaries and benefits).

Using Savings Held in a Capital Reserve Fund for Capital Expenditures

Expending moneys held in a capital reserve fund for a capital expenditure is a simple task. The governing board of a unit of local government must adopt an ordinance or resolution authorizing the withdrawal, the transfer of moneys to another fund (e.g., the general fund or an enterprise fund), and the expenditure of moneys for one or more of the capital projects or assets identified in the resolution or ordinance creating the capital reserve fund.[24]

Statement at 25. The proceeds will be held in a "Water and Sewer Operating Fund" created under the General Indenture. City of Charlotte Official Statement at 14.

20. A unit of local government may create a single capital reserve fund for multiple, unrelated capital projects so long as the adopting resolution or ordinance separately lists each project.

21. These sources might include, among other things, property tax proceeds, utility fees, the proceeds of local sales and use taxes, and grant proceeds.

22. *See* G.S. 159-20.

23. *See* G.S. 159-19.

24. *See* G.S. 159-22.

Advantages and Disadvantages of Accumulating Savings in a Capital Reserve Fund

A capital reserve fund provides a more formal mechanism to save for future capital expenditures than fund balance. A capital reserve fund might be viewed as providing more transparency than an accumulation of fund balance because the governing board of a local unit must specify in the resolution or ordinance creating the capital reserve fund the capital projects for which it will accumulate funds. However, appropriating money to a capital reserve fund also provides a governing board with less flexibility than accumulation of fund balance. Once a governing board appropriates funds to a capital reserve fund, those moneys cannot be used to finance operating expenses—they must be used to fund capital expenditures, even in an emergency or recession.

Special Levies

Units of local government derive most of their current revenues from revenue sources held in the general fund, including the largest revenue source held in the general fund for counties and municipalities: the property (*ad valorem*) tax.[25] Owners of real and personal property subject to *ad valorem* taxes pay those taxes to a taxing county or municipality without regard to whether they benefit from the services that either jurisdiction provides. Governing boards typically feel obligated to spend the proceeds of property taxes for services that provide general benefits to the community rather than services that offer benefits to a single geographic area or users of a particular public service.

Governing boards also often feel pressure to provide and fund increasing numbers of projects and services while maintaining or reducing the property tax levy. As a result, many counties and municipalities now rely upon mechanisms for targeted revenue generation like user charges or fees, which are paid only by the citizens or property owners that benefit most directly from a service that a county or municipality provides. For example, many municipalities at one time used property tax proceeds to fund solid waste services, including disposal facilities, convenience centers, and even curbside pickup. Now, however, many local governments across the country increasingly assess user fees or charges to cover some or all of the cost to provide these types of services.[26]

Counties and municipalities commonly impose user fees or charges for wastewater utility services, recreational and cultural activities, health and mental services, ambulance services, parking, public transportation, stormwater, cemeteries, and airport usage. Many counties also rely on fee revenue to fund certain regulatory activities, including inspections and plan reviews.[27]

User charges are typically an appropriate funding source for services that have specific, identifiable beneficiaries rather than the public at large.[28] And although financing capital projects with user charges is possible, it may present challenges. Some units attempt to apportion some

---

25. For more information regarding property taxes, see Chapter 5, "Property Tax Policy and Administration."

26. *See generally* Kenneth R. Ahern, National Bureau of Economic Research, *Working Paper 28805: The Business of City Hall* (May 2021) (noting that thirty-nine of the largest cities in the United States collect an increasingly large proportion of revenues through user fees rather than taxes).

27. For more information regarding these "regulatory fees," see Chapter 4, "Revenue Sources."

28. Harry Kitchen, Melville McMillan & Anwar Shah, *Local Public Finance and Economics: An International Perspective* (London: Palgrave Macmillan, 2019), 365.

of the capital costs associated with providing a particular service among users of that service. For example, a local government that operates a water or sewer system might assess a customer a monthly charge consisting of two components: (1) a variable usage charge that increases or decreases based upon a user's actual use and (2) a fixed "overhead" charge.[29] The fixed "overhead" charge covers both operating overhead and at least some capital expenses.

In addition to user charges, North Carolina law also permits counties and municipalities to use targeted revenue generation to fund capital projects through four types of "special" levies: (1) "traditional" special assessments, (2) critical infrastructure assessments, (3) special taxing districts, and, to a limited extent, (4) development exactions.

Special Assessments

A special assessment is a charge levied against real property to pay for public improvements that benefit that property. It is neither a user charge nor a tax, but shares characteristics of each. Like a user fee, a special assessment is levied in some proportion to the benefit that the assessed property receives. Like a property tax, it is levied against property rather than individuals and creates a lien on each parcel of real property assessed.[30]

The authority to levy special assessments provides units of local government with a potentially important tool to fund capital projects. Recouping some or all of the costs of a capital project that directly benefits a defined range of property owners can make financial and political sense. Using special assessments to finance public infrastructure projects that primarily benefit a particular set of property owners also can permit a governing board to expend property tax proceeds and other revenue sources in the general fund on projects that benefit a broader subset of a unit's citizens.

Currently, North Carolina counties and municipalities have two statutory methods for imposing special assessments: (1) "traditional" special assessments and (2) "critical infrastructure" assessments. Using special assessments can permit a unit to recoup some or all of the costs of a particular project.

"Traditional" Special Assessments

North Carolina's local governments have infrequently imposed "traditional" special assessments for a number of reasons.

First, state law limits the purposes for which counties and municipalities may levy such assessments. Counties may levy assessments to finance water systems, sewage collection and disposal systems, beach erosion control and hurricane protection works, watershed improvement projects, drainage projects, water resources development projects, local costs of N.C. Department of Transportation improvements to subdivision and residential streets located outside of municipalities, and streetlight maintenance.[31] Municipalities may levy assessments to finance public improvements involving streets, sidewalks, water systems, sewage collection

---

29. *See, e.g.,* Orange Water and Sewer Authority, *Schedule of Rates, Fees and Charges: Summary of Rates Effective On and After October 1, 2022* (reflecting a fixed "water service charge" and "sewer service charge" and a variable "water volume charge" and "sewer volume charge").

30. The lien may be foreclosed in the same manner as property tax liens. For more information on enforcing property tax liens, see Chapter 5, "Property Tax Policy and Administration."

31. *See* G.S. 153A-185.

Table 7.2 "Traditional" Special Assessment Process

Step	Action Required of Governing Board
1	For street, street light, and sidewalk assessments only—the board must receive a petition from the requisite number of affected property owners.[a]
2	Adopt a preliminary assessment resolution that includes, among other things, a description and estimated cost of the project, the percentage of the cost to be funded through assessments, the basis of assessments, the terms of payment of the assessments, and the time and place for a public hearing on matters contained in the resolution.[b]
3	At least ten days prior to the date of the public hearing on the matter, publish notice of adoption of preliminary assessment resolution and the date of the public hearing, and mail a copy of the preliminary resolution to affected property owners.[c]
4	Hold a public hearing on the preliminary assessment resolution.[d]
5	Adopt a final assessment resolution setting forth the basis of the assessments, percentage of costs to be funded through assessments, and terms of payment of the assessments.[e]
6	After completion of the project, determine the project's total costs.[f]
7	Prepare preliminary assessment roll, containing a description of each property to be assessed, the amount assessed against each property, the terms of payment, and the name of the owner of each assessed lot. File roll with the clerk to the board and set the time and place for a public hearing on the roll.[g]
8	At least ten days prior to the date of the public hearing, publish notice of completion of the preliminary assessment roll and state the time and place for the public hearing.[h]
9	Hold a public hearing on the preliminary assessment roll.[i]
10	Confirm the assessments, in whole or in part. The clerk to the board must record the date, hour, and minute of confirmation, and, after confirmation, the board must deliver a copy of the confirmation to the county tax collector for collection.[j]
11	The tax collector must publish the assessment roll no earlier than twenty days from the date of confirmation of the assessment roll.[k]

a. G.S. 153A-205(c) (streets); 153A-206(d) (street lights); 160A-217(a) (street and sidewalks). Before a county may impose special assessments for street improvements, it must first receive a petition signed by at least 75 percent of the owners of the property to be assessed, who represent at least 75 percent of the lineal feet of frontage of the lands abutting the street or portion of the street to be improved. *See* G.S. 153A-205(c). Similarly, before a municipality may impose special assessments for street or sidewalk improvements, a municipality must receive a petition signed by a majority of the owners of property to be assessed, who represent at least a majority of all the lineal feet of frontage of lands abutting the street or portion of the street to be improved. *See* G.S. 160A-217(a). The General Assembly has modified the petition requirements for certain jurisdictions by local act. *See, e.g.,* S.L. 1989-611, An Act to Revise and Consolidate the Charter of the Town of Wrightsville Beach, § 5.2 (granting authority to assess the costs of sidewalk improvements or repairs without the need for a petition from affected property owners).

b. G.S. 153A-190; 160A-223.

c. G.S. 153A-191; 160A-224.

d. G.S. 153A-192; 160A-225.

e. G.S. 153A-192; 160A-225. State law establishes permissible bases of assessment. *See* G.S. 153A-186; 160A-218. The most common basis of assessment is based upon "front footage"—each property is assessed according to a uniform rate per foot for each foot of property that abuts the project. Other common bases include the size of the area benefited and the value added to each property because of the improvement. All permissible bases of assessment mandate that the assessment basis be made equally across all assessed properties. *See* G.S. 153A-186; 160A-218.

f. G.S. 153A-193; 160A-226.

g. G.S. 153A-194; 160A-227.

h. G.S. 153A-194; 160A-227.

i. G.S. 153A-195; 160A-228.

j. G.S. 153A-195; 160A-228.

k. G.S. 153A-196; 160A-229.

and disposal systems, storm sewer and drainage systems,[32] and beach erosion control and flood and hurricane protection works.[33]

Second, a county or municipality may pay all the costs of a project prior to levying special assessments. Only *after* a unit completes a capital project may it levy any special assessments,

---

32. *See* G.S. 160A-216.
33. *See* G.S. 160A-238.

and assessments often are paid in installments over a number of years (up to ten). Some units have created special assessment revolving funds, using yearly special-assessment payments from former projects to fund the initial costs of new projects.[34] But establishing a sufficient revolving fund can take several years.

Third, the process used to levy the assessments—detailed below—is onerous.

Process of Imposing "Traditional" Special Assessments

To impose a "traditional" special assessment, the governing board of a county or municipality must follow the steps in Table 7.2.[35]

Once a unit confirms the final assessment roll, the assessments become a lien on the real property assessed.[36] Although a unit may demand full payment of the assessments within thirty days of publishing the confirmation, it typically permits payment in up to ten yearly installments, with interest.[37]

"Critical Infrastructure" Assessments

Beginning in its 2008 legislative session, the General Assembly authorized counties and municipalities to finance a wide range of capital projects through special assessments for "critical infrastructure needs."[38]

The authority to impose special assessments for critical infrastructure needs, modeled on similar legislation from other states, can assist counties and municipalities in financing public infrastructure projects that benefit new, private development. A unit may impose assessments, with payments spread out over a period of years, expecting that the ultimate owners of developed property (instead of a private developer or local government) will pay the majority of those costs. Like traditional special assessments, the unit can pay the costs of the project up front and recoup its investment over time through yearly assessment payments. But unlike traditional special assessments, state law permits a unit imposing a critical infrastructure assessment to borrow the initial costs of a project, pledge the assessment revenue as security for the debt that it issues, and use yearly assessment revenues to meet its debt-service obligations.[39] Alternatively, a unit may contract with a developer to construct the capital project and use the critical infrastructure assessment revenue to reimburse the developer, over time, for costs that it incurred.[40]

A critical-infrastructure assessment is conceptually similar to an "impact fee." An impact fee is a fee that a unit of local government levies on new development (typically as a condition

---

34. Once a unit of local government receives special-assessment payments, North Carolina law does not restrict the use of those funds to reimbursement for the project for which the special assessments were initially imposed. However, a unit that establishes a revolving loan fund simply foregoes reimbursement for costs originally incurred when it uses the proceeds of special-assessment payments to finance new projects rather than to reimburse itself for previous projects.

35. For more information on the assessment process, see Kara A. Millonzi, "An Overview of Special Assessment Bond Authority in North Carolina," *Local Finance Bulletin* No. 40 (Nov. 2009).

36. *See* G.S. 153A-195; 160A-228.

37. *See* G.S. 153A-199; 160A-232. Portions of unpaid assessments may bear interest at a rate not to exceed 8 percent per year. *See* G.S. 153A-200(a); 160A-233(a).

38. *See* G.S. Ch. 153A, Art. 9A (counties); Ch. 160A, Art. 10A (municipalities).

39. *See* G.S. 153A-210.4(a)–(b), -210.6(a); 160A-239.4(a) –(b); 160A-239.6(a).

40. Note that these agreements may be subject to approval by the Local Government Commission (LGC). For more information on the types of agreements that the LGC must approve, see G.S. 159-158 and -153 and Figure 7.2.

Authorized Critical-Infrastructure Assessment Projects[a]

1. Capital costs of providing airport facilities
2. Capital costs of providing auditoriums, coliseums, arenas, stadiums, civic centers, convention centers, and facilities for exhibitions, athletic and cultural events, shows, and public gatherings
3. Capital costs of providing hospital facilities; facilities for the provision of public health services; and facilities specially designed for the diagnosis, treatment, education, training, or custodial care of individuals with intellectual or other developmental disabilities
4. Capital costs of art galleries, museums, art centers, and historic properties
5. Capital costs of on- and off-street parking and parking facilities, including meters, buildings, garages, driveways, and approaches open to public use
6. Capital costs of providing certain parks and recreation facilities, including land, athletic fields, parks, playgrounds, recreation centers, shelters, permanent and temporary stands, and lighting[b]
7. Capital costs of redevelopment through acquisition and improvement of land for assisting local redevelopment commissions
8. Capital costs of sanitary sewer systems (including septic systems)
9. Capital costs of storm sewers and flood-control facilities
10. Capital costs of water systems, including facilities for supply, storage, treatment, and distribution of water
11. Capital costs of public transportation facilities, including equipment, buses, railways, ferries, and garages
12. Capital costs of industrial parks, including land and shell buildings, to provide employment opportunities for citizens of a county or municipality
13. Capital costs of property to preserve a railroad corridor
14. Capital costs of providing community college facilities
15. Capital costs of providing school facilities
16. Capital costs of improvements to subdivision and residential streets, in accordance with G.S. 153A-205
17. To finance housing projects for persons of low or moderate income
18. Capital costs of electric systems
19. Capital costs of gas systems
20. Capital costs of streets and sidewalks (including traffic controls and lighting)
21. Capital costs of improving existing systems or facilities for transmission or distribution of telephone services
22. Capital costs of housing projects for persons of low or moderate income
23. To provide or maintain beach erosion control and flood and hurricane protection works, downtown revitalization projects, urban area revitalization projects, transit-oriented development projects, drainage projects, sewage collection and disposal systems, off-street parking facilities, watershed improvement projects, water resources development projects, and conversions of private residential streets to public streets[c]
24. Installation of distributed-generation renewable energy sources or energy-efficiency improvements that are permanently fixed to residential, commercial, industrial, or other real property[d]

a. Counties and municipalities may impose critical infrastructure assessments to assist in the arranging for payment of the capital costs of projects (1) for which project-development-financing debt instruments may be issued under G.S. 159-103 and (2) for the purpose of the installation of distributed-generation renewable energy sources or energy-efficiency improvements that are permanently fixed to residential, commercial, industrial, or other real property. See G.S. 153A-210.2(a); 160A-239.2(a). Items 1 through 23 list the projects for which project-development-financing debt instruments may be issued. Through July 1, 2022, counties had authority under general law to make critical-infrastructure assessments for certain dam repair projects. See G.S. 153A-210.2(a1); S.L. 2019-190, § 2. Due to statutory conditions limiting the dam repair to only certain types of dams, only two counties—Richmond and Moore—were likely to exercise this authority. See Nicholas Giddings, Staff Attorney, N.C. General Assembly Legislative Analysis Division, *Analysis of Second Edition of Senate Bill 190: Expand Special Assessments for Dam Repair* (June 18, 2019). As of March 1, 2023, the General Assembly has not extended the authority to impose special assessments for dam repair projects. See G.S. 153A-210.2(b).

b. G.S. 159-103(a) does not permit the issuance of project-development-financing debt instruments for certain types of parks and recreation facilities: stadiums, arenas, golf courses, swimming pools, wading pools, and marinas. Therefore, counties and municipalities may not impose critical-infrastructure assessments to pay for the cost of these parks and recreation facilities.

c. Counties may impose critical-infrastructure assessments to assist in the arranging for payment of the capital costs of projects for which project-development-financing debt instruments may be issued under G.S. 159-103. *See* G.S. 153A-210.2(a). G.S. 159-103 permits the issuance of project-development-financing instruments and the use of resulting proceeds for, among other things, "any service or facility authorized by G.S. 160A-536 to be provided in a municipal service district." G.S. 159-103(a). Counties and municipalities each have authority to create and maintain, respectively, county and municipal service districts for (1) beach erosion control and flood and hurricane protection works; (2) sewage collection and disposal systems of all types, including septic tank systems or other on-site collection or disposal facilities or systems; and (3) watershed improvement projects, drainage projects, and water-resources development projects. *See* G.S. 153A-301(a)(1), (4), (8); 160A-536(a)(1), (3), (3a), (5). However, counties lack explicit authority to provide services or facilities for five purposes listed in G.S. 160A-536: (1) downtown revitalization projects, (2) urban area revitalization projects, (3) transit-oriented development projects, (4) off-street parking facilities, and (5) conversion of private residential streets to public streets. *See* G.S. 160A-536. Even assuming that counties have authority to issue project-development-financing debt instruments under G.S. 159-103(a) and thus impose critical-infrastructure assessments for these purposes under G.S. 153A-210.2(a), it is not clear that counties have underlying authority to carry out these functions listed in G.S. 160A-536.

d. Note that G.S. 160D-1320(b) authorizes local governments to establish programs to finance the purchase and installation of distributed-generation renewable energy sources or energy-efficiency improvements that are permanently affixed to residential, commercial, industrial, or other real property. These statutes authorize a local government to (1) purchase the renewable energy sources or energy-efficiency improvements and install them on private property or (2) contract for their purchase or installation. *Renewable energy sources* include "solar electric, solar thermal, wind, hydropower, geothermal, or ocean current or wave energy resource; a biomass resource, including agricultural waste, animal waste, wood waste, spent pulping liquors, combustible residues, combustible liquids, combustible gases, energy crops, or landfill methane; waste heat derived from a renewable energy resource and used to produce electricity or useful, measurable thermal energy at a retail electric customer's facility; or hydrogen derived from a renewable energy resource." *See* G.S. 160D-1320(c) (noting that "renewable energy source" has the same meaning as "renewable energy resource in G.S. 62-133.8); 62-133.8(a)(8) (defining "renewable energy resources"). The term does not include peat, a fossil fuel, or a nuclear energy resource." *Id.* The General Statutes do not define *"energy efficiency improvements."*

of obtaining a building permit) to pay for public infrastructure costs that the new development imposes.[41] Like it may with an impact fee, a municipality or county may use the proceeds of critical-infrastructure assessments to fund public infrastructure projects that new private development requires—but the critical-infrastructure assessment method typically imposes fewer costs on a developer than an impact fee does. Assuming the developer completes the project, many, if not most, of the payments will be collected after completion.

Counties and municipalities may finance a much broader array of public infrastructure projects through critical-infrastructure assessments than through traditional special assessments. Authorized projects include a variety of traditionally "public" projects, ranging from constructing and maintaining public roads to building public schools, and encompass most capital projects in which a county or municipality is authorized to engage.[42] The sidebar on this page presents a list of authorized critical-infrastructure projects.

Advantages and Disadvantages of "Critical Infrastructure" Assessment Method

A unit may use critical-infrastructure assessment revenues to make its debt-service payments and pledge those assessment revenues to debt holders to secure the debt that it incurred. Therefore, unlike traditional special assessments, critical-infrastructure assessments allow counties and municipalities to borrow money to cover the cost of an authorized capital project without committing general fund revenues to the project.

---

41. North Carolina counties and municipalities do not have general legal authority to impose impact fees.

42. *See* G.S. 153A-210.2 (counties); 160A-239.2 (municipalities). For more information on critical infrastructure assessments, see Millonzi, note 35 above; Kara Millonzi, "Recent Amendments to Special Assessment Authority," *Coates' Canons: Local Government Law* blog (Sept. 5, 2013); Kara Millonzi, "Special Assessments for Economic Development Projects," *Coates' Canons: NC Local Government Law* blog (Oct. 31, 2013).

Table 7.3 Comparison of Authorized Special-Assessment Methods

Traditional Special-Assessment Method	Critical-Infrastructure Assessment Method
• Limited statutory purposes • Generally, no petition requirement (except for street and sidewalk projects) • Amount of assessment must be based on one or more statutory bases • Unit must follow detailed statutory procedures before levying assessments (including at least two public hearings) • Unit may borrow money to front costs of a project funded with assessments but may not pledge assessment revenue as security for debt issued • Unit must complete public improvement project before imposing assessments • Assessments may be paid in up to ten yearly installments • Statutory authority does not contain a sunset date	• Expansive statutory purposes • Petition requirement for all projects • Assessment method within discretion of governing board but must relate to benefit to properties assessed • Unit must follow detailed statutory procedures before levying assessments (including at least two public hearings) • Unit may borrow money to front costs of a project funded with assessments and may pledge the assessments as security for debt issued • Unit may impose assessments before the project is complete, based on estimated costs • Assessments may be paid in up to twenty-five yearly installments • Statutory authority *expires* July 1, 2025, for projects that have not been approved under a final assessment resolution

Of course, a unit may not be able to collect all of the assessment revenues necessary to meet its debt-service obligations. However, a unit can use the remedies available for the collection of property taxes in collecting unpaid assessments. In fact, the trust agreement under which a county or municipality issues special assessment–backed debt likely will include a covenant requiring the unit to use similar policy and effort in collecting special assessments as it does for property taxes.[43]

Even though counties and municipalities have robust authority to collect unpaid special assessments, debt backed by special assessments can pose more risk to investors than other types of local government debt (e.g., general obligation bonds). To compensate investors for this risk, special assessment–backed debt typically carries higher rates of interest than other types of borrowing.[44]

Process of Imposing "Critical Infrastructure" Assessments

With some exceptions, the process of imposing "critical infrastructure" assessments is similar to the process of imposing "traditional" special assessments as detailed in Table 7.2.

Table 7.3 summarizes the major differences between the two methods of imposition. Of particular note, before a county or municipality may impose any critical infrastructure assessment,

---

43. *See, e.g.,* Town of Hillsborough, North Carolina, *Official Statement for $4,630,000 Special Assessment Revenue Bonds*, Appendix A, Form of Trust Agreement, Art. VI(h) (Oct. 9, 2013) ("The Town will use . . . substantially similar policy and effort in the collection of the Special Assessments as it does in the collection of its generally applicable property taxes.").

44. For example, the Town of Mooresville issued general obligation bonds in February 2015 containing annual interest rates ranging from 2.125 percent to 5.0 percent. *See* Town of Mooresville, North Carolina, *Official Statement for $20,000,000 General Obligation Public Improvement Bonds, Series 2015* (Jan. 29, 2015). The town issued two special assessment–backed term bonds in June 2015 with respective interest rates of 4.375 percent and 5.375 percent. *See* Town of Mooresville, North Carolina, *Official Statement for $8,550,000 Special Assessment Revenue Bonds, Series 2015* (June 17, 2015).

it must first receive a petition signed by a majority of the owners of real property to be assessed, whose real property also represents at least 66 percent of the assessed value of all real property to be assessed.[45] In setting this requirement, the General Assembly likely envisioned that a single or just a few individuals or entities (e.g., corporate developers) would own the subject properties at the time of assessment. The petition must include a description of the public infrastructure projects to be financed, their estimated costs, and an estimate of the percentage of estimated costs to be assessed.[46] A developer owning real property to be assessed would likely negotiate all of these points with a county or municipality prior to submitting a petition. Once a county or municipality receives a petition to impose a critical-infrastructure assessment, it generally must follow the same detailed statutory process to impose the assessments as is required for traditional special assessments.

Unlike traditional special assessments, for critical-infrastructure assessments a unit need not complete a project before confirming the final assessment roll. Instead, it may base its assessments upon an estimate of the total costs to perform the project.[47] A unit also is not limited to a ten-year repayment period as it is when imposing traditional special assessments. It can instead set a repayment period of up to twenty-five years.[48]

Frequency of Use Since Initial Authorization

To date, only two units of local government—the Town of Hillsborough and the Town of Mooresville—have issued debt backed by critical-infrastructure assessments.[49] Similar mechanisms are used more frequently in other states, particularly in Florida, Georgia, and Texas.[50]

Special Taxing Districts

A municipality or county might fund a capital project using targeted revenue generation by establishing a special taxing district. Although the North Carolina Constitution requires that a local government's rates of property tax be uniform throughout the jurisdiction,[51] it also authorizes the General Assembly to permit counties and municipalities to (1) delineate one or more geographic areas within the unit as special taxing districts and (2) levy taxes within those districts to finance or provide services or facilities to a greater extent than those financed or provided in other parts of the jurisdiction.[52] The General Assembly has exercised that authority in several cases, most notably in authorizing counties and municipalities to create "service districts."[53]

---

45. G.S. 153A-210.3(a) (counties); 160A-239.3 (municipalities).

46. *See* G.S. 153A-210.3(a); 160A-239.3.

47. *See* G.S. 153A-210.3(a2); 160A-239.3(a2).

48. *See* G.S. 153A-210.5(a); 160A-239.5(a).

49. See notes 43 and 44 above.

50. *See* Adam C. Parker, "Using Special Assessments for Community Development in North Carolina," *Community and Economic Development in North Carolina and Beyond* blog (July 24, 2012).

51. *See* N.C. Const. art. V, § 2(2).

52. N.C. Const. art. V, § 2(4).

53. Counties also may establish special taxing districts for rural fire-protection services (G.S. Chapter 69, Article 3A), public schools (G.S. Chapter 115C, Article 36), and water and sewer services (G.S. Chapter 162, Article 6). These districts provide counties with additional mechanisms to fund capital and operating expenses for the statutorily specified purposes. For a county to levy a tax for rural fire protection

Like special assessments, these special taxing districts are based upon the principle that those benefitting most directly from a government function should pay for it. But unlike special assessments, which must be assessed on a project-specific basis, a county or municipality can establish a special taxing district to fund a variety of projects or services benefitting properties in the district on an ongoing basis. Chapter 4, "Revenue Sources," details what types of service districts counties and municipalities may establish, the process to establish a service district, municipal and county authority to levy taxes in service districts, and what types of projects a county or municipality may undertake in a service district.

A county or municipality may borrow money to fund capital projects located in a service district to the same extent, and in the same manner, as it funds similar capital projects located outside of a service district. In addition, a municipality may issue special obligation bonds to finance capital projects located in a municipal service district.[54]

Counties and municipalities typically are subject to an additional procedural requirement when issuing general obligation (GO) bonds to fund capital projects in service districts. If the GO bonds are subject to voter referendum, a majority of the district's voters must approve the issuance of bonds, in addition to a majority of the voters residing within the municipality or county.[55]

Development Exactions

Local governments sometimes seek to impose development exactions to finance the cost of public infrastructure projects. Exactions typically take one of two forms: (1) a requirement that a developer compensate a unit of local government for the capital costs the unit incurred to acquire or construct public infrastructure that supports the development or (2) a requirement that a developer construct public infrastructure to support its development. Local governments in North Carolina have limited statutory authority to impose development exactions.[56]

Borrowing Money

The most common method for financing costly capital projects is borrowing money. Neither current revenues nor savings or special levies are likely to generate sufficient revenues to finance the acquisition, construction, or equipping of a significant capital asset. Borrowing money allows a unit of local government to leverage future revenue streams—a unit obtains cash in the short term and uses future revenues to repay debt over time.

---

or public schools, a majority of qualified county voters voting in a referendum must approve the tax. *See* G.S. 69-25.1–.25.4 (rural fire-protection services); 115C-508(b) (public schools).

54. *See* G.S. Ch. 159, Art. 7A. *See also* "Special Obligation Bonds," below.

55. *See* G.S. 153A-308; 160A-543.

56. For more information on development exactions, see Adam Lovelady, "Exactions and Subdivision Approval," *Coates' Canons: NC Local Government Law* blog (Feb. 1, 2013); Adam Lovelady, "The *Koontz* Decision and Implications for Development Exactions," *Coates' Canons: NC Local Government Law* blog (July 1, 2013). The U.S. Supreme Court has interpreted certain provisions of the U.S. Constitution to limit the ability of local governments to impose development exactions. *See, e.g.,* Nollan v. Cal. Coastal Comm'n, 483 U.S. 825 (1987); Dolan v. City of Tigard, 512 U.S. 374 (1994).

Table 7.4 Authorized Securities for Borrowing Transactions

	Primary Security	Authorized Secondary Securities
General Obligation Bonds	• Full faith and credit (taxing power)	• Revenues generated by revenue-generating asset or system
Revenue Bonds	• Revenues generated by revenue-generating asset or system • Critical-infrastructure assessments	• Asset(s) or part of asset(s) being financed
Special Obligation Bonds	• Any unrestricted revenues other than unit-levied taxes	• Asset(s) or part of asset(s) being financed
Project-Development-Financing Bonds	• Incremental increase in property tax revenue within defined area due to new private development	• Asset(s) or part of asset(s) being financed • Any unrestricted revenues other than unit-levied taxes • Special assessments
Installment Financings	• Asset(s) or part of asset(s) being financed	

When a unit of local government borrows money, it agrees by contract—typically referred to as a "debt instrument"—to repay those that have loaned money to it. Should a local government breach its promise to repay its debt or any other promise it makes under the terms of the debt instrument, its lenders typically have legal rights to enforce repayment or force the unit to cure its default.

Debt instruments can take a variety of legal forms, but most commonly take the form of a bond. North Carolina's local governments are authorized to issue general obligation bonds, revenue bonds, special obligation bonds, project-development-financing bonds, and limited obligation bonds. North Carolina local governments also may borrow money through installment financing contracts. This section addresses each of these mechanisms for issuing debt.

Security

When a local government borrows money, its most fundamental promise is to repay the debt it incurs. But in addition, a local government also may pledge to its lenders certain legal rights to force or "secure" the repayment of its debt. Those legal rights are known as "security." Depending on the type of transaction, that security might take the form of, among other things, a right to force a defaulting local government to levy taxes to repay its debt, to require changes in the operation of a public enterprise that the local government operates, or to repossess certain property that the defaulting local government owns.

North Carolina law dictates what types of security a local government may pledge to its lenders in connection with each authorized method of borrowing. The type of security that a local government pledges can affect the form of debt instrument issued, whether a unit must obtain voter approval or approval from the Local Government Commission (LGC), and the cost of debt.

For each borrowing mechanism, Table 7.4 explains (1) the "primary" sources of security—those that a local government legally may and typically does pledge to its lenders and (2) the "secondary" sources of security—those that a local government sometimes, but less commonly, pledges in order to make a financing more attractive for lenders. The primary sources of security for each borrowing mechanism are discussed below.

Entities Involved

Borrowing money often requires a unit of local government to interact with a range of third parties. These outside entities might include bond counsel, financial advisors, underwriters, lenders, ratings agencies, trustees, and the LGC. Not all of these parties are involved in every borrowing, and local governments often complete simple, small borrowings without external guidance or oversight.

Bond Counsel

A private law firm acts as "bond counsel." When a local government issues bonds, the primary duty of bond counsel is to render a legal opinion that addresses, among other things, (1) the validity of bonds that a local government issues and (2) the taxability of interest paid to holders of the bonds under federal and state income tax laws.[57] Local governments and the purchasers of their bonds typically require receipt of this legal opinion as a condition of closing a bond transaction. Prior to issuing its legal opinion, bond counsel guides a local government—in concert with a unit's regular attorney—through the procedural steps required to issue debt under state law. Bond counsel also prepares the majority of the legal documents required to complete a bond issuance. Through its involvement throughout this process, bond counsel is able to provide its approving legal opinion when a transaction is completed.

After an issuance occurs, bond counsel also might advise a local government about how to comply with complex provisions in the federal tax code that regulate how a unit may spend or invest proceeds of "tax-exempt" bonds.[58] Bond counsel also might advise a local government about its obligations under federal securities laws to disclose certain facts affecting bonds issued or the local government's financial condition.[59] The terms of an engagement letter between a unit of local government and a private law firm providing bond counsel services will dictate whether and at what expense these services will be provided.

If a unit of local government is contemplating a bond issuance, it should hire reputable bond counsel with prior experience advising a North Carolina local government in the issuance of debt.[60] In doing so, a unit should seek to understand the specific functions that bond counsel will perform during the initial issuance of the bonds and after the debt has been issued.

---

57. National Association of Bond Lawyers (NABL), *The Function and Professional Responsibilities of Bond Counsel*, 3rd ed. (Washington, D.C.: NABL, 2011), 6. For examples of recent legal opinions issued by North Carolina bond counsel in connection with the issuance of general obligation bonds, see County of Guilford, North Carolina, *Official Statement for $41,000,000 General Obligation Public Improvement Bonds, Series 2022A*, Appendix E (March 15, 2022); County of Wake, North Carolina, *Official Statement for $287,295,000 General Obligation Bonds*, Appendix F (Feb. 15, 2022); Town of Clayton, North Carolina, *Official Statement for $13,500,000 General Obligation Parks and Recreation Bonds, Series 2021*, Appendix E (Nov. 30, 2021).

58. For more information about the distinction between "tax-exempt" and "taxable" bonds, see "The Taxability of Interest Paid to Holders of Local Government Debt," below.

59. For more information, see "Disclosure Obligations for Publicly Offered Debt," below.

60. No uniform criteria exist for determining whether bond counsel is "reputable." *See* NABL, note 57 above, at 5, n.5. However, participants in the municipal bond market typically consider public finance lawyers listed in *The Bond Buyer's Municipal Marketplace* (known as the "Red Book") to have a sufficient minimum level of expertise. *See* the Red Book (published by LexisNexis Risk Solutions). Although North Carolina law does not require a unit of local government to undertake a competitive process to select bond counsel, many units of local government issue requests for proposals to seek information about prior experiences of potential bond counsel.

Financial Advisor

Although no law requires a local government to hire a private firm to advise it or advocate for its interests when issuing debt, many local governments hire private firms as financial advisors to assist with the structuring and sale of bonds. These financial advisors might analyze, among other things, a local government's ability to add additional debt, its compliance with existing debt covenants, or the proper mechanism to finance a new capital project. A financial advisor that advises a local government in connection with the issuance of its debt—including advice with respect to the structure, timing, and similar matters of debt—must register as a "municipal advisor" with the federal Securities and Exchange Commission.[61] "Municipal advisors" have fiduciary duties under federal law to act in the best interests of their clients.[62]

A local government can engage a municipal advisor for a single debt issuance or for a range of services that extend beyond a particular transaction.[63] The staff of the Local Government Commission can and will assist a local government in considering the structure of its debt or the proper mechanism for financing a project, but unlike a private "municipal advisor," these staff may assist in the Commission's decisions to approve or deny a particular debt issuance.

Other Consultants

A local government may need to hire other consultants to complete certain types of bond issuances. In particular, a local government that issues revenue bonds—which are payable from the proceeds of certain revenue-generating assets (e.g., municipally owned water and sewer systems)—might hire a "financial feasibility consultant." Such a consultant might produce a "financial feasibility report," which projects the operating results of the revenue-generating assets securing the repayment of the bonds. The intent of this report is to demonstrate to potential investors that a local government will be able to service its debt and comply with certain financial covenants after issuing revenue-backed debt.[64]

Underwriter or Lender

An underwriter is a financial institution that purchases an issue of local government debt for resale to institutional or individual investors. An underwriter may initially acquire bonds either by (1) competitive sale or (2) negotiation with a borrowing unit.

Most general obligation bond sales in North Carolina are conducted on a competitive basis; underwriters submit sealed bids to the Local Government Commission (LGC) to buy the bonds,

---

61. *See* U.S. Securities and Exchange Commission, Registration of Municipal Advisors, Final Rule, 78 Fed. Reg. 67,468 (Nov. 12, 2013). Providing such advice while failing to register as a "municipal advisor" violates federal law. *See* 15 U.S.C. § 78o-4(a)(1)(B). For additional information regarding the obligation to register as a "municipal advisor," see U.S. Securities and Exchange Commission, *Registration of Municipal Advisors: Frequently Asked Questions* (Sept. 20, 2017).

62. *See* 15 U.S.C. § 78o-4(c)(1).

63. Although North Carolina law does not require a unit of local government to undertake a competitive process to select a municipal advisor, many units of local government issue requests for proposals (RFP) to select such a firm. The Government Finance Officers' Association has issued guidance that can assist in creating such an RFP. *See* Government Finance Officers' Association, *Best Practice: Selecting and Managing Municipal Advisors* (Feb. 28, 2014).

64. For examples of such reports, see City of High Point, North Carolina, *Official Statement for $34,755,000 Combined Enterprise System Revenue Bonds, Series 2022*, Appendix B (April 28, 2022); Town of Clayton, North Carolina, *Official Statement for $95,800,000 Water and Sewer System Revenue Bonds, Series 2022*, Appendix B (Dec. 7, 2022).

and the LGC awards the sale to the firm providing the most favorable offer.[65] Other types of bond sales (revenue bonds, special obligation bonds, project-development-financing bonds, and limited obligation bonds) occur by negotiation.[66] In a negotiated sale, a local government selects one or more underwriters at the outset of a transaction and negotiates the financing structure and borrowing costs with the selected firm.[67]

Underwriters that purchase and resell a local government's bonds to investors must comply with certain federal securities regulations, including the SEC's "Rule 15c2-12."[68] With some exceptions, these underwriters must (1) obtain certain disclosure documents from the local government that describe the bonds to be sold and certain information about the issuer of the bonds, (2) distribute these disclosure documents to potential investors, and (3) reasonably determine that the issuer has agreed to provide continuing disclosure of certain information after the bonds are issued.[69] An underwriter typically hires legal counsel to advise it on the structure of the offering and its responsibilities, and a local government typically pays for the cost of such legal counsel at closing out of bond proceeds.

In some cases, a financial institution may not purchase a local government's bond or debt in order to resell it to other investors. Instead, it may hold this debt on its own balance sheet. A financial institution participating in such a "private placement" may be referred to as a "lender" rather than an "underwriter."

Rating Agencies

A "public offering" occurs when a unit of local government sells bonds to an underwriter that will be offered publicly (i.e., resold to individual and institutional investors). As a practical matter, bonds that are sold publicly must be rated.[70] At present, three nationally recognized credit rating agencies rate local government debt: Moody's Investors Service, S&P Global Ratings, and

---

65. *See* G.S. 159-123. A unit may request that the LGC authorize a "private sale" of certain types of bonds. *See* G.S. 159-123(b), (c).

66. *See* G.S. 159-123.

67. Although North Carolina law does not require a unit of local government to undertake a competitive process to select an underwriter, many units of local government issue requests for proposals (RFP) to select such a firm. The Government Finance Officers' Association has issued guidance that can assist in creating such an RFP. *See* Government Finance Officers' Association, *Best Practice: Selecting and Managing Underwriters for Negotiated Bond Sales* (Feb. 28, 2014). A unit also should confer with the staff of the LGC during this process. Larger transactions may have multiple underwriters, which each purchase and resell a portion of the bonds sold. *See, e.g.,* City of Charlotte Official Statement, note 19 above, at 3 (reflecting five underwriters).

68. *See, e.g.,* 17 C.F.R. § 240.15c2-12 (hereinafter Rule 15c2-12).

69. *See* Rule 15c2-12(b)(1) (obligation to obtain official statement); (b)(2) (obligation to distribute certain disclosure documents to investors); (b)(5) (obligation to reasonably determine issuer's commitment to provide continuing disclosure of certain information). The exemptions to Rule 15c2-12 include, among others, primary offerings of municipal securities that will be sold in authorized denominations of $100,000 or more and are sold to no more than thirty-five sophisticated investors meeting certain criteria. *See* Rule 15c2-12(d)(1). For more information about the continuing disclosure obligations of issuers of local government bonds, see "Disclosure Obligations for Publicly Offered Debt," below.

70. The LGC will not approve a public offering of bonds without an "investment grade" rating from a nationally recognized credit rating agency. *See* N.C. Department of State Treasurer, State and Local Government Finance Division, Local Government Commission, *Guidelines on Debt Issuance (Revised)* (Sept. 4, 2019). Investment-grade ratings are those above Baa3 (Moody's) and BBB- (S&P Global Ratings and Fitch).

Fitch Ratings. A bond's rating can serve as an indication of its credit risk at a given point in time, and each credit agency has a slightly different methodology of determining a credit rating.[71]

A local government typically will submit a wide variety of information to a rating agency in order to receive a credit rating for a particular public offering of bonds. These disclosures can vary substantially but typically include information regarding the particular debt structure proposed; the unit's financial condition, demographics, and management practices; and, if applicable, the revenue sources supporting the issuance of the bonds.

Trustee

A trustee is a corporate entity—typically an arm of a financial institution—that is involved in some, but not all, issuances of local government debt.[72] Subject to the terms of the bond documents under which bonds are issued, a bond trustee usually takes several actions throughout the life of a bond. It might act on behalf of bondholders in the event a local government defaults under the terms of the bond documents, obtain certain disclosures from the local government over the life of the bonds, and, as a "paying agent," collect a local government's payments of principal and interest and ensure their proper application.[73]

Local Government Commission

The Local Government Commission (LGC), a division of the North Carolina Department of State Treasurer, is a nine-member body responsible for fiscal oversight of local governments and public authorities in North Carolina.[74] The LGC must approve each new issue of general obligation bonds, revenue bonds, special obligation bonds, and project-development-financing bonds.[75] It also must approve some installment financings, certain leases, and other financial agreements.[76]

In reviewing proposed issuances of debt, state law requires the LGC to consider certain criteria specified by statute that vary between different types of borrowing. Generally, the LGC must determine whether, considering its other debts, a unit can afford to borrow a proposed amount at a particular rate of interest.

The staff of the LGC will work with a unit throughout the borrowing process to help its officials determine the most advantageous borrowing method for a proposed project. The staff can also identify any deficiencies in the unit's financial history or management practices that might prevent LGC approval. When contemplating an issuance of debt that will require LGC approval, local officials should contact LGC staff as early as possible for assistance (preferably after the initial scope of a capital project is determined).[77]

---

71. *See* U.S. Securities and Exchange Commission, *Investor Bulletin, Municipal Bonds: Understanding Credit Risk* (December 2012), 3.

72. Trustees are most commonly involved in issuances of revenue bonds or special obligation bonds.

73. For helpful general information on the role of a bond trustee, see UMB Financial Corporation, "Defining the Role of a Bond Trustee or Paying Agent," *UMB Blog* (July 29, 2020).

74. *See* G.S. 159-3(a).

75. *See* G.S. 159-51 (general obligation bonds); 159-85(a) (revenue bonds); 159-146(k) (special obligation bonds); 159-104 (project-development-financing bonds).

76. For more information regarding the types of financial agreements that the LGC must approve, see Kara Millonzi, "Local Government Commission (LGC) Approval of Bonds, Installment Financings, Leases, and Other Contracts Involving Capital Assets (Including Recent Changes Related to Local Governments on the Unit Assistance List)," *Coates' Canons: NC Local Government Law* blog (Oct. 28, 2022). *See also* Figure 7.2, below.

77. See note 107 below. The LGC also has released guidelines for its approval of debt. See note 70 above.

Joint Legislative Committee on Local Government

In 2011, the General Assembly established the Joint Legislative Committee on Local Government as a legislative study committee.[78] The purpose of the committee is, among other things, to "review and monitor" local government capital projects (other than those relating to schools, jails, courthouses, or administrative buildings) that require both LGC approval and the issuance of local government debt exceeding $1 million.[79] The committee may only review and monitor capital projects—it has no authority to approve or reject a capital project or financing.

Any unit of local government embarking upon a capital project within the legislative committee's purview (i.e., those that require both LGC approval and the issuance of debt exceeding $1 million) must submit a letter to the chairs of the committee, its assistant, and the Fiscal Research Division of the General Assembly at least forty-five days prior to the meeting at which the LGC will consider approval of the debt.[80] The letter must include (1) a description of the project, (2) the debt requirements of the project, (3) the means of financing the project, and (4) the source or sources of repayment for project costs.[81] The LGC has encouraged units to consult their regular counsel or bond counsel when preparing this letter.[82]

The committee may meet at the discretion of its co-chairs to review a proposed capital project[83] and may send a letter of objection or support to the LGC for a particular project. In addition, the committee may make periodic reports on local government capital projects that it reviews and also recommend that the General Assembly adopt legislation relating to local government borrowing authority.[84]

Types of Authorized Borrowing

The General Assembly may only authorize units of local government to borrow money by general law—not by local act.[85] At present, North Carolina's local governments may issue seven types of debt: (1) general obligation bonds, (2) revenue bonds, (3) special obligation bonds, (4) project-development-financing instruments, (5) bond anticipation notes, (6) installment financing contracts or limited obligation bonds, and (7) bonds or notes issued to the federal

---

78. S.L. 2011-291, § 1.8(a) (codifying G.S. Ch. 120, Art. 20).

79. G.S. 120-157.2(a).

80. *See* G.S. 120-157.2(a).

81. N.C. Joint Legislative Committee on Local Government, Minutes (Oct. 10, 2011), 2. See also the following memoranda from the N.C. Department of State Treasurer, State and Local Government Finance Division and the Local Government Commission: Memorandum No. 2012-02, *Recent Enactment of Session Law 2011-291 (House Bill 595) Requiring Reporting of Certain Local Government Proposed Debt Issuances to Newly Created Joint Legislative Committee on Local Government* (July 25, 2011); Memorandum No. 2012-09, *Update on Memorandum # 2012-02 Regarding Reporting Requirements for Certain Local Government Proposed Debt Issuances to Newly Created Joint Legislative Committee on Local Government (House Bill 595)* (Oct. 18, 2011).

82. Since 2011, the committee has posted copies of these letters to its website. *See* N.C. General Assembly, Joint Legislative Committee on Local Government, Documents, Local Government Debt Submissions (last visited Jan. 30, 2023).

83. The committee's website reflects that, as of March 1, 2023, the committee last met on December 9, 2013. *See* N.C. General Assembly, Joint Legislative Committee on Local Government, Agenda (Dec. 9, 2013).

84. *See* G.S. 120-157.2(b).

85. N.C. Const. art. V, § 4.

or state government to repay a loan from an agency of either entity.[86] The General Assembly also has bestowed borrowing authority upon certain types of public authorities.[87] Summaries of each debt mechanism follow.

General Obligation Bonds

Security and Authority

The strongest form of security that a county or municipality can pledge to secure the repayment of its debt is its "full faith and credit." When a unit of local government makes such a pledge, it promises to take all actions within its power—including levying property taxes in any amount necessary—to repay the debt. Such a pledge creates a "general obligation" of the unit. For that reason, debt secured by a general obligation is called a "general obligation bond."

The Local Government Bond Act is the primary source of authority for units of local government to issue general obligation (GO) bonds.[88] The Act specifies the types of capital projects that a county or municipality may fund with the proceeds of GO bonds.[89] Counties and municipalities can use the proceeds of GO bonds to finance most of the capital projects in which they are otherwise authorized to engage.

Requirements and Limitations

Although North Carolina law authorizes units of local government to issue GO debt for a wide variety of purposes, the process it imposes to issue such debt limits its practical importance. Prior to issuing a GO bond, a unit of local government typically must (1) hold a successful voter referendum before pledging its faith and credit, (2) ensure that a borrowing not exceed its "net debt" limit, and (3) obtain approval from the Local Government Commission.

Voter Approval Requirements

Except in limited circumstances, a unit of local government may not issue GO bonds unless a majority of its voters voting in a referendum approve such an issuance.[90] Voters participating in a referendum may be unlikely to support the issuance of GO bonds to finance controversial or less-popular projects (e.g., jails or landfills), and local governments often exercise caution when proposing the issuance of GO bonds to voters. Even referenda for popular projects, such as a park, can fail. For example, from November 2012 through November 2022, six of the eleven GO bond referenda that failed across the state were to finance parks and recreation projects.[91]

---

86. A municipality has additional borrowing authority when acting as a redevelopment commission. *See* G.S. 160A-512(8).

87. *See, e.g.,* G.S. 162A-8 (revenue bond authority for water and sewer districts); 162A-90 (revenue and general obligation bond authority for county water and sewer districts); 130A-61 (general obligation bond authority for sanitary districts); 159-210 (lease-backed financings by airport authorities).

88. *See* G.S. Ch. 159, Art. 4.

89. *See* G.S. 159-48.

90. N.C. CONST. art. V, § 4(2). For a unit of local government to issue GO bonds subject to a constitutional voter-approval requirement, a majority of voters that vote in a specific referendum on the bonds—not a majority of all of a unit's registered voters—must approve the issuance.

91. N.C. CONST. art. V, § 4(2). The six failed referenda for parks and recreation bonds occurred in Hendersonville (Nov. 2013), Goldsboro (Nov. 2014), Harrisburg (Nov. 2017), Mint Hill (Nov. 2018), Cape Carteret (Nov. 2020), and Mount Holly (Nov. 2021). The other failed referenda proposed to authorized bond issuances by (1) the City of Wilmington to finance the acquisition and construction of a minor league baseball stadium, (2) Onslow County to pay for public school facilities, (3) the Village of Bald Head

From November 2012 through November 2022, North Carolina voters approved 202 of 213, or 94.8 percent, of GO bond referenda.[92] Although this high approval rate suggests that securing voter approval of a proposed GO bond issuance can generally be expected, it also suggests that local governments do not proceed with the lengthy process of issuing GO bonds and securing voter approval for projects expected to be controversial or unpopular in the community. Units of local government often use other borrowing mechanisms authorized under state law—for which no voter approval is required—to avoid the time and expense incurred in securing voter approval for a GO bond issuance.

Exceptions to the Voter Approval Requirement for General Obligation Bonds

A municipality or county need not obtain voter approval to issue certain types of GO bonds. In particular, as permitted by the North Carolina Constitution, the General Assembly has permitted the issuance of "refunding" bonds and "two-thirds" bonds without voter approval.[93]

— REFUNDING BONDS

A unit of local government issues refunding bonds to retire or "pay off" an existing debt. Most commonly, a unit will issue refunding bonds because interest rates have fallen and, as a result, the unit can issue debt at an interest rate lower than that of the debt to be paid off. If this is the case, a unit can lower its debt-service payments by issuing refunding bonds. Under North Carolina law, a unit need not obtain voter approval to issue GO refunding bonds.[94]

Municipal bond investors often seek to prohibit bond issuers from paying off existing bonds prior to their maturity date (i.e., the date upon which an issuer must pay all remaining principal and interest on a bond).[95] Therefore, GO bonds often include provisions that prohibit the early retirement—known as the "call"—of a bond issue for a certain period of time (typically ten years).[96]

In some cases, bond issuers can still take advantage of falling interest rates prior to the "call" date of a bond by using a mechanism known as "advance refunding." In an advance refunding, a unit issues refunding bonds but, instead of using the proceeds of the refunding bonds to immediately retire the outstanding obligations, places proceeds in an escrow account controlled by an independent third-party (most commonly, a trustee). The trustee invests the proceeds of the refunding bonds, makes payments to the holders of the refunded bonds in accordance with the payment schedule for those refunded bonds, and retires (i.e., pays off) the remaining principal and interest on the refunded bonds on or after their call date.

Recent changes in federal income tax laws have decreased the usefulness of advance refunding. Prior to January 1, 2018, interest paid to holders of refunding bonds was exempt from federal income tax as long as the refunding bonds were issued at least ninety days prior to the

---

Island to finance a broadband network, (4) the Town of Mint Hill to build a cultural arts center, and (5) Union County to build and equip a 4-H pavilion.

92. Data on file with author. To access historical results of referenda held between November 2012 and November 2022, see N.C. State Board of Elections, *Contest Results*.

93. N.C. CONST. art. V, § 4(2); G.S. 159-49.

94. *See* N.C. CONST. art. V § 4(2); G.S. 159-49(2).

95. They do so because an investor that holds a bond that is "called" must find an alternative investment that may carry a lower rate of return.

96. *See, e.g.,* County of Guilford, North Carolina, note 57 above, at 2 ("The Bonds maturing on or prior to March 1, 2032 will not be subject to redemption prior to maturity.").

call date of refunded bonds. In December 2017, Congress repealed that exemption for refunding bonds issued after January 1, 2018—making interest paid on refunding bonds federally taxable.[97] To compensate for the loss of the tax exemption, issuers must pay relatively higher rates of interest to holders of advance refunding bonds issued after January 1, 2018.[98]

A local government interested in retiring debt prior to its maturity date should consult bond counsel to determine what options might exist for refinancing.

— Two-Thirds Bonds

A unit of local government need not obtain voter approval to issue GO bonds in an amount equal to or less than two-thirds of the amount by which the unit reduced its outstanding indebtedness in the immediately preceding fiscal year.[99] A unit may only issue these types of GO bonds—known as "two-thirds bonds"—in the fiscal year immediately following the year in which it reduced its debt.

A unit's reduction in outstanding indebtedness is determined only by reference to its net reduction in the amount of outstanding principal in a prior fiscal year—not by any interest that the unit pays. If a unit issues debt in a prior year, it may increase its overall outstanding indebtedness and therefore lack any ability to issue two-thirds bonds in a subsequent fiscal year.

With several exceptions, a unit may use non-voted two-thirds bonds for any purposes authorized by general law.[100] When the governing board of a county or municipality announces its intention to issue two-thirds bonds without securing voter approval, the unit's citizens can force a referendum by submitting to the unit's clerk a petition signed by at least 10 percent of the unit's registered voters.[101]

Net-Debt Limitation

A unit may not issue general obligation (GO) bonds if the issuance would raise the "net debt" of a unit to 8 percent of the aggregate appraised value of property subject to taxation by the unit.[102] The General Statutes prescribe a formula for calculating a unit's "net debt," which is reflected in

---

97. *See* Pub. L. 115-97, § 13532, 131 Stat. 2154 (Dec. 22, 2017).

98. If interest rates are low enough, an issuer still might be able to issue advanced refunding bonds on a taxable basis at a lower rate than existing tax-exempt debt. *See, e.g.*, Local Government Commission, Agenda, at 12 (May 4, 2021) (reflecting intent of Johnston County to issue GO refunding bonds on a taxable basis to refund all or a portion of its $13,100,000 GO public improvement bonds and achieve a net present-value savings of $548,700); County of Johnston, North Carolina, *Official Statement for $36,000,000 General Obligation Public Improvement Bonds, Series 2021, and $13,475,000 Taxable General Obligation Refunding Bonds, Series 2021* (May 11, 2021). The Local Government Commission (LGC) has stated that the present value of savings from a refunding should exceed 3 percent of the refunded bonds in order to receive the LGC's approval. *See* Local Government Commission, note 70 above.

99. N.C. Const. art. V, § 4(2)(f).

100. G.S. 159-49. A unit must obtain voter approval prior to issuing GO bonds for the purpose of, among other things, providing auditoriums, coliseums, arenas, stadiums, civic centers, convention centers, art galleries, museums, art centers, historic properties, redevelopment through the acquisition of land and improvement thereof, public transportation facilities, or cable television systems. *See* G.S. 159-49(2).

101. *See* G.S. 159-60. The petition must be filed with the clerk of the unit within thirty days after the date of publication of the bond order, as introduced.

102. *See* G.S. 159-55(c). The statute provides for several exceptions to that general rule. This restriction also applies to installment-financing contracts. *See* G.S. 159-150.

Figure 7.1 Net-Debt-Limit Formula

$$\frac{\text{(A) Total Gross Debt} - \text{(B) Total Deductions}}{\text{(C) Total Assessed Value of Property in Unit Subject to Taxation}} \leq 8\%$$

Gross Debt

Outstanding debt evidenced by GO bonds	$
Proposed financing, and GO bonds authorized by orders introduced but not yet adopted	$
Unissued GO bonds authorized by adopted orders	$
Outstanding installment financing debt	$
Total Gross Debt (A)	**$_____**

Deductions

Funding and refunding bonds authorized by orders introduced but not yet adopted	$
Funding and refunding bonds authorized but not issued	$
Amount held in sinking funds or otherwise for the payment of gross debt other than debt incurred for water, gas, electric, light, or power purposes or sanitary sewer purposes (to the extent deductible under G.S. 159-55(b)) or two or more of these purposes	$
Bonded debt included in gross debt and incurred or to be incurred for water, gas, or electric light or power purposes, or any two or more of these purposes	$
Bonded debt included in gross debt and incurred or to be incurred for sanitary sewer system purposes (to the extent deductible under G.S. 159-55(b))	$
Uncollected special assessments levied for local improvements for which gross GO debt (that is not otherwise deducted) was or is to be incurred, to the extent it will be applied when collected, to the payment of such gross GO debt	$
Estimate of special assessments to be levied for local improvements for which any part of gross GO debt (that is not otherwise deducted) was or is to be incurred, to the extent that the special assessments when collected, will be applied to the payment of any part of the gross GO debt	$
Total Deductions (B)	**$_____**
Net Debt: (A)–(B)	**$_____**
Total Assessed Valuation (C)	**$_____**
Percentage of Net Debt: (C)/(D)	**$_____**

Figure 7.1.[103] A county or municipality is likely to repay GO and installment financing debt with the proceeds of property taxes—and this limitation seeks to ensure that a unit has sufficient taxing capacity to support the debt incurred.

For many units, this "net debt" limitation is more theoretical in its limitation than practical.[104] However, some units set a target net-debt threshold in order to bolster their credit ratings.

Bond Issuance Process

The process to issue GO bonds that require voter approval is long and requires detailed planning and coordination among a unit's staff, bond counsel, the Local Government Commission (LGC), and other third parties (e.g., financial advisors or ratings agencies).[105] Bond counsel typically assists a unit's staff in the preparation of public notices, required statements that a finance officer must prepare or file, and documents to be approved by the governing board and the LGC. The LGC must approve all issuances of GO bonds—even those that do not require voter approval.[106]

LGC Approval

State law prescribes an application process for units to follow when seeking the LGC's approval of a GO bond issuance. But even prior to that formal process, the LGC's staff—in particular, employees of the Local Debt Management Section of the North Carolina Department of State Treasurer's State and Local Government Finance Division—can meet with a unit's representatives to discuss plans for a bond issuance.[107]

— Application Process

To initiate the application process, a unit must file with the LGC an application for the approval of a GO bonds issuance.[108] The LGC may require the unit's staff to meet with LGC staff prior to the acceptance of the application.[109]

Adoption of Bond Order

After the LGC accepts the unit's application, the governing board of the unit must adopt a "bond order," which is the central document the governing board must approve prior to issuing a GO bond.[110] Among other things, a bond order authorizes the issuance of the bond and states both the purpose for which the unit will spend the proceeds of the bond and the maximum amount of bonds that may be issued under the bond order.[111] If a unit proposes to issue GO bonds for

---

103. *See* G.S. 159-55.

104. For example, Guilford County had capacity to add additional net debt of $3.27 billion as of June 30, 2021. *See* County of Guilford Official Statement, note 57 above, at A-15.

105. Form LGC-107, available from the LGC upon request, lists the major steps necessary for counties and municipalities to authorize the issuance of GO bonds requiring voter approval.

106. *See* G.S. 159-51.

107. The LGC's staff has created a web portal for local government staff members to inform the LGC of intentions to issue debt. *See* N.C. Department of State Treasurer, Local Government Commission, *LGC Debt Approval* (last visited Feb. 6, 2023). The webpage indicates that a member of the LGC's debt-management team will discuss inquiries submitted through the portal.

108. *See* G.S. 159-51.

109. *See* G.S. 159-51.

110. The bond order may be introduced after or at the same time the LGC accepts an application. *See* G.S. 159-54.

111. *See* G.S. 159-54.

unrelated purposes (e.g., schools and public parks), it must adopt a separate bond order for each purpose.[112] Bond orders authorizing the issuance of bonds for which voter approval is required do not take effect unless and until the voters approve them.[113]

Preparation of Sworn Statement of Debt and Statement of Disclosures Necessary for Bond Authorization

After a unit's governing board has introduced a bond order authorizing the issuance of GO bonds, the unit's finance officer must prepare and file with the clerk to the governing board a sworn statement of debt.[114] This statement reflects the unit's net debt, the assessed value of property subject to taxation by the unit, and the percentage of net debt compared to that assessed value.[115] As discussed previously, that percentage may not exceed 8 percent.

As of October 1, 2022, the finance officer of a unit intending to issue GO bonds also must file a statement of disclosure with the LGC and the clerk to the governing board that contains (1) an estimate of the total amount of interest that will be paid on the bonds over their expected term, if issued, and a summary of the assumptions upon which that estimate is based; (2) an estimate of the increase in property tax rate, if any, necessary to service the proposed debt; and (3) the amount of two-thirds bonds capacity the unit has available for the current fiscal year.[116]

LGC Approval Criteria

North Carolina law requires the LGC to approve a debt issuance if it finds and determines all of the following:

1. The proposed bond issue is necessary or expedient.
2. The amount proposed is adequate and not excessive for the proposed purpose of the issue.
3. The unit's debt-management procedures and policies are good or reasonable assurances have been given that its debt will henceforth be managed in strict compliance with law.
4. The increase in taxes, if any, necessary to service the proposed debt will not be excessive.
5. The proposed bonds can be marketed at reasonable rates of interest.
6. The assumptions used by the unit's finance officer in preparing the "statement of estimated interest" are reasonable.[117]

In November 2022, the LGC adopted a "safe harbor policy" to govern its assessment that a unit's finance officer used reasonable assumptions in the statement of disclosure when determining the total interest to be paid over the expected term of the bonds. Under that policy, the LGC will find such assumptions to be reasonable if they assume that (1) principal will be paid in twenty annual equal principal installments and (2) the interest rate on the bonds will

---

112. *See* G.S. 159-48(g).

113. *See* G.S. 159-54(6). Bond orders authorizing the issuance of bonds for which voter approval is not required can take effect upon adoption by a unit's governing board.

114. G.S. 159-55(a).

115. G.S. 159-55(a)(3)–(5).

116. G.S. 159-55.1(a). The statement of disclosure also must be posted online, but it need not be published in a newspaper. *See* G.S. 159-55.1(c).

117. G.S. 159-52(b). The sixth finding is effective for bond orders introduced after October 1, 2022. *See* S.L. 2022-53, §§ 1 and 10.

be equal to a Bond Buyer 20 index (BB20) rate published within twenty-five days prior to the introduction of the bond order plus 200 basis points (2 percent) or higher.[118]

Voter Approval and Issuance of the Bonds

The governing board of a unit of local government must call for a referendum on the bonds to be held within one year after the bond order's passage.[119] After the bond order is approved by voters, the unit may issue bonds authorized under the bond order within seven years of the date upon which the bond order takes effect.[120] After the unit adopts a resolution fixing the details of bonds to be issued,[121] the LGC sells GO bonds on behalf of the unit, typically on a competitive basis.[122]

Revenue Bonds

Security and Authority

The State and Local Government Revenue Bond Act authorizes certain units of local government to issue "revenue bonds."[123] Local governments issue revenue bonds to finance the acquisition, construction, or equipping of a single revenue-generating asset (e.g., a parking deck) or multiple assets contained within a revenue-generating system (e.g., water and sewer lines in a portion of a municipality's water and sewer system). Although North Carolina's local governments most commonly issue revenue bonds to finance water- and sewer-system projects, they also have legal authority to issue revenue bonds for gas or electric facilities, solid waste facilities, parking, marine facilities, auditoriums, convention centers, economic development, electric facilities, public transportation, airports, hospitals, stadiums, recreation facilities, and stormwater drainage.[124]

When a local government issues revenue bonds, its obligation to repay the proceeds of those bonds is secured by a "pledge" of the revenue generated by the financed asset (e.g., a parking deck) or system of which the debt-financed asset becomes a part (e.g., a municipal water and sewer system). By law, holders of these revenue bonds have a lien on these pledged revenues,[125] and typically, if a local government fails to pay principal and interest upon the bonds as each

---

118. N.C. Department of State Treasurer, State and Local Finance Division and Local Government Commission, *Resolution Adopting Safe Harbor Policy Related to Reasonableness of Estimated Interest Assumptions* (Nov. 1, 2022). A unit's finance officer may use alternate assumptions, and in that case, the LGC will consider the reasonableness of those assumptions when it considers the unit's application for approval.

119. *See* G.S. 159-61(b).

120. A unit may obtain a three-year extension, from seven to ten years, with approval from the LGC. *See* G.S. 159-64.

121. *See* G.S. 159-65(a).

122. *See* G.S. 159-123(a) (authorizing competitive sale); 159-127 (setting forth procedure for award of sale).

123. *See* G.S. Ch. 159, Art. 5.

124. *See* G.S. 159-83(5) (authorizing local governments "[t]o borrow money for the purpose of acquiring, constructing, reconstructing, extending, bettering, improving or otherwise paying the cost of revenue bond projects"); 159-81(3) (defining "revenue bond project"). A county or municipality also may issue revenue bonds secured by the proceeds of revenues generated by special assessments under the critical-infrastructure assessment method. See "Critical Infrastructure Assessments," above.

125. *See* G.S. 159-91.

becomes due, these bondholders can demand that a local government raise its rates or change the operations of its revenue-generating system in order to pay the debt service owed.

North Carolina law only allows units of local government to pay debt service on revenue bonds from revenues pledged as security for the bonds.[126] For example, a municipality that issues revenue bonds to finance the construction of a public parking deck may only use revenues generated by its operation of that parking deck (e.g., parking fees) to pay principal and interest to revenue bondholders. In most cases, holders of revenue bonds do not have a right to demand that a local government raise taxes or demand payment from any source other than the revenues of the financed asset or system.[127]

Requirements and Limitations

Covenants

Because the revenues of an asset or system financed with revenue bonds both secure and serve as the source of repayment for revenue bonds, lenders and underwriters that resell bonds to investors typically require that revenue bond issuers agree to abide by certain restrictions when operating financed assets. These restrictions are known as "covenants."[128]

Although the exact form of covenants will vary by transaction, almost all issuers of revenue bonds can expect to make a "rate covenant." Under a rate covenant, an issuer of revenue bonds typically agrees to set and collect the rates, fees, and charges of revenue-producing assets to ensure that the assets' net revenues exceed annual debt-service requirements by a certain percentage.[129] For example, an issuer will commonly agree to ensure that its rates and charges will generate annual net revenues of between 120 and 150 percent of either the current year's debt-service requirements or the maximum annual debt-service requirements during the life of the loan.[130] This margin of safety is referred to as "times-coverage" or a "debt service coverage ratio" and serves as a measure of the issuer to repay its debt without excess financial strain.[131] If an issuer fails to meet its debt-service coverage ratio, bondholders may have certain rights to force the issuer to change the operations of the financed assets.

Issuers of revenue bonds also typically agree to certain restrictions on their ability to issue additional revenue bonds that are secured and payable from the same source of revenues as previously issued bonds.[132] Known as an "additional bonds test," this covenant generally permits an issuer of revenue bonds to issue additional bonds that are secured by and payable from the

---

126. G.S. 159-94(a).

127. A local government has authority to pledge its taxing power as additional security for some types of revenue bond projects. *See* G.S. 159-97. Such pledges are uncommon.

128. G.S. 159-89 contains the list of covenants to which a local government may agree when issuing revenue bonds.

129. *See, e.g.*, Town of Clayton Official Statement, note 64 above, at 7–8.

130. Town of Clayton Official Statement at 7–8 (reflecting a rate covenant requiring the net revenues of a municipal water and sewer system to be no less than 125 percent of the annual debt-service requirements on issued revenue bonds).

131. Issuers of revenue bonds typically must hire a financial-feasibility consultant to project the net revenues of a financed asset or system. Among other things, that consultant produces a report that demonstrates the ability of an issuer to meet its debt-service obligations and the rate covenants. For more information and an example of a financial feasibility report, see note 64 above and accompanying text.

132. *See, e.g.*, Town of Clayton Official Statement, note 64 above, at 10–11.

same source of revenues as outstanding revenue bonds only if the issuer can demonstrate that the net revenues have been and will continue to be sufficient to service the additional debt.

Lastly, revenue bond issuers also commonly agree to maintain various funds (e.g., a revenue fund, a debt-service fund, a construction fund, and a debt-service reserve fund).[133] Each of these funds is restricted by the terms of the bond documents under which the revenue bonds are issued. An issuer will commonly agree that a third-party trustee will maintain the proceeds of the revenue bonds and will disburse the proceeds of those bonds only upon the issuer's submission of proper documentation (e.g., relevant evidence of construction pay applications).[134]

Bond Issuance Process

The procedures required to issue revenue bonds under North Carolina law are much less extensive than those required to issue general obligation (GO) bonds. Other than securing Local Government Commission (LGC) approval and adopting a bond order at the proper time, state law imposes few procedural requirements upon a local government's issuance of revenue bonds.

LGC Approval

Although a unit of local government need not obtain voter approval to issue revenue bonds,[135] it must obtain approval from the LGC to issue revenue bonds.

— APPLICATION PROCESS

A unit of local government seeking to issue revenue bonds must submit an application for approval to the LGC.[136] And, as with GO bonds, the LGC may require the unit's staff to meet with LGC staff prior to the acceptance of the application.[137] Once the LGC accepts the unit's application, it will consider whether to approve the proposed revenue bond issuance, and in doing so may consider, among other things, whether the probable net revenues of the financed assets will be sufficient to meet the debt service on the proposed revenue bonds.[138]

The LGC must approve a revenue bond issuance if it finds and determines all of the following:

1. The proposed revenue bond issue is necessary or expedient.
2. The amount proposed is adequate and not excessive for the proposed purpose of the issue.
3. The proposed project is feasible.
4. The unit's debt-management procedures and policies are good or reasonable assurances have been given that its debt will henceforth be managed in strict compliance with law.
5. The increase in taxes, if any, necessary to service the proposed debt will not be excessive.
6. The proposed bonds can be marketed at reasonable interest cost.[139]

Ordinarily, the LGC will consider the approval of a unit's application to issue revenue bonds at its regular monthly meeting.

---

133. *See, e.g.*, Town of Clayton Official Statement, at 8–10.
134. G.S. 159-89 provides a full list of covenants to which an issuer of revenue bonds may agree.
135. If a unit pledges its taxing power as additional security for a revenue bond, it must obtain voter approval. *See* G.S. 159-97.
136. *See* G.S. 159-85(a).
137. *See* G.S. 159-85(b).
138. *See* G.S. 159-86(a).
139. *See* G.S. 159-86(b).

Negotiating the Terms of a Revenue Bond Issuance

Revenue bonds are typically sold by negotiation rather than competitive bid, and a borrowing government typically selects an underwriter or placement agent at the outset of the negotiating process.[140] The terms of the bonds—in particular, the terms of an issuer's covenants—are negotiated over a series of weeks or months by representatives of an issuing local government, its regular counsel, bond counsel, one or more underwriters or placement agents and their counsel, staff members of the LGC, and, in some cases, the financial advisor to the issuing local government.

Adoption of Bond Order

With input from all of these stakeholders, bond counsel typically reduces the relevant terms to a bond order. As is the case for GO bonds, the bond order is the central document that a governing board must approve prior to issuing revenue bonds. It will, in comprehensive detail, set out the amount and purpose of the borrowing, the security for the revenue bonds issued, and the covenants to which the local government has agreed.[141]

Unlike with GO bonds, a unit's governing board may introduce a bond order for revenue bonds at any regular or special meeting and adopt it at the same meeting, as long as the unit has submitted its application for approval to the LGC.[142] To approve a revenue bond issuance, state law does not require the unit to publish notice of a referendum or take any other procedural action other than approving the bond order.

Issuance of the Bonds

The LGC sells revenue bonds on behalf of a unit of local government, typically on a negotiated basis.[143] The date of sale is fixed by consultation with the LGC, the issuing unit of local government, its underwriter, and other parties involved in the transaction.[144]

Special Obligation Bonds

Security and Authority

North Carolina law authorizes certain units of local government to issue "special obligation" bonds for a limited number of purposes.[145] In particular, counties, municipalities, and regional solid waste management authorities may issue special obligation bonds for solid waste

---

140. Although North Carolina law does not require a unit of local government to solicit competitive proposals for underwriting services when issuing revenue bonds, many units do. The Government Finance Officers' Association has issued guidance that can assist in creating such a request for proposals. *See* Government Finance Officers Association, note 67 above.

141. As a practical matter, many bond orders approve and incorporate the terms of separate trust agreements into which units of local government enter. *See, e.g.,* City of Charlotte, *Resolution Introducing and Adopting the Bond Order Authorizing the Issuance of Water and Sewer System Revenue Bonds of the City of Charlotte, North Carolina, in the Aggregate Principal Amount Not to Exceed $535,000,000* (July 11, 2022). These trust agreements can take a variety of forms, but often include (1) a "general indenture" that governs all issuances of bonds secured by a given revenue-generating system and (2) a "series indenture" that modifies the general indenture and governs the issuance of a particular set of bonds.

142. *See* G.S. 159-88(b). It may be adopted by a simple majority of those present and voting as long as a quorum is present.

143. *See* G.S. 159-123(b)(3) (authorizing private, negotiated sale).

144. *See* G.S. 159-124.

145. *See* G.S. Ch. 159, Art. 7A.

management projects; certain water supply, conservation, and reuse projects; and wastewater collection and treatment projects.[146] Municipalities also may issue special obligation bonds to finance or refinance projects that they may otherwise undertake in a municipal service district.[147]

Conceptually, a revenue bond is a type of special obligation bond because it is secured by and payable from a particular source of local government revenue. But the technical term "special obligation," as used in North Carolina law, refers to debts secured by and payable from revenue sources other than (or in addition to) revenues from the financed asset or system of assets.

A special obligation bond may be secured by and payable from almost any revenue source available to the borrowing government. However, a unit may not issue special obligation bonds secured by the unit's taxing power.[148] For example, a county could not issue a special obligation bond secured by the proceeds of local option sales and use taxes, animal taxes, or property taxes because it exercises its taxing power when it levies these taxes.[149] However, a municipality could pledge the proceeds of local option sales and use taxes that it receives from the Department of Revenue because only counties—not municipalities—have authority to levy those taxes.

Units of local government in North Carolina have issued special obligation bonds infrequently. As of July 1, 2022, only nine issues of special obligation bonds were outstanding across the state.[150]

---

146. G.S. 159-146(a) (authorizing issuance of special obligation bonds to finance or refinance a "project"); 159-146(b)(7) (defining "project").

147. *See* G.S. 159-146(b)(7). *See* Chapter 4, "Revenue Sources," for a list of projects that municipalities can undertake in municipal service districts.

148. G.S. 159-146(c).

149. *See* Chapter 4, "Revenue Sources," for a more-detailed description of each of these revenue sources.

150. *See* Local Government Commission, *Form LGC 129, Annual Principal and Interest Requirements* (Sept. 8, 2022). Two counties (Macon and Mecklenburg) and seven municipalities (Asheville, Greenville, Holden Beach, Kannapolis, Nags Head, Rocky Mount, and Winston-Salem) had outstanding special obligation bonds as of July 1, 2022. *See* Form LGC 129. Macon and Mecklenburg County each issued special obligation bonds to fund solid waste management projects. *See* Macon County, North Carolina, *Annual Comprehensive Financial Report for the Year Ended June 30, 2022* (Nov. 22, 2022), 82; County of Mecklenburg, North Carolina, *Official Statement for $12,220,000 Special Obligation Bonds, Series 2011* (Oct. 13, 2011). Although each municipality issued special obligation bonds to finance or refinance the costs of projects undertaken in a municipal service district, the revenues that each municipality pledged as security for the special obligation bonds varied. Asheville and Rocky Mount each pledged the proceeds of local option sales tax revenues and state-imposed taxes distributed to municipalities. *See* City of Asheville, North Carolina, *Official Statement for $17,140,000 Special Obligation Bonds, Series 2017* (Oct. 13, 2017), 3; City of Rocky Mount, North Carolina, *Official Statement for $36,815,000 Special Obligation Bonds, Series 2016* (Dec. 14, 2016), 2. Kannapolis and Winston-Salem each pledged the proceeds from local option sales taxes. *See* City of Kannapolis, North Carolina, *Annual Comprehensive Financial Report for the Year Ended June 30, 2021* (Nov. 30, 2021), 69; City of Winston-Salem, North Carolina, *Official Statement for $15,450,000 Special Obligation Bonds, Series 2013* (May 17, 2013), 3. Greenville and Nags Head each pledged proceeds of occupancy tax revenues that they receive, respectively, from Pitt and Dare County. *See* City of Greenville, North Carolina, *Annual Comprehensive Financial Report (ACFR) – Fiscal Year Ending June 30, 2022* (Nov. 28, 2022), 90; Town of Nags Head, North Carolina, *Resolution of the Board of Commissioners of the Town of Nags Head, North Carolina, Providing for the Issuance of a Special Obligation Bond (Town Project), Series 2019A* (June 2018), A-3. Holden Beach appears to have pledged proceeds of federal grants that the town will receive for beach renourishment. *See* Town of Holden Beach, North Carolina, *Basic Financial Statements for the Year Ended June 30, 2022* (Oct. 13, 2022), 58.

Requirements and Limitations

Because a special obligation bond is not secured by a unit's taxing power, investors typically require an issuer of special obligation bonds to make covenants similar to those required for the issuance of revenue bonds. For example, a municipality might agree that if revenues pledged to pay and secure outstanding special obligation bonds are insufficient to meet a specific debt-service coverage ratio, it will add to the pledged funds a source of revenue other than a municipally levied tax in order to meet the coverage ratio.[151]

Bond Issuance Process

North Carolina law does not prescribe a strict statutory process that a unit of local government must follow to issue special obligation bonds. The LGC must approve all special obligation bond issuances, and a unit of local government must submit an application to the LGC to approve any such issuance.[152] In considering whether to approve an application, the LGC may consider the same criteria as those applicable to a GO bond issuance, a revenue bond issuance, or both.[153] The LGC sells special obligation bonds on behalf of an issuing unit, typically in a privately negotiated sale.[154]

Project-Development Financings

Security and Authority

Since 2003, North Carolina law has authorized local governments to engage in project-development financings.[155] Project-development financing is structurally equivalent to a type of borrowing in other states known as "tax increment financing" or "TIF."[156] Public finance practitioners in North Carolina also often refer to project-development financing as "TIF."

Project-development financing seeks to increase the aggregate property value in a currently blighted, depressed, or underdeveloped area within a county or municipality. A unit borrows money to fund public improvements within a designated area (known as a "development district") with the goal of attracting private investment. The debt that a unit incurs to fund the improvements is secured and repaid by the incremental increase in property tax revenue resulting from the district's new development.

The Project Development Financing Act permits counties and municipalities to issue project-development-financing bonds and use the proceeds for many, but not all, of the purposes for which either type of unit may issue GO bonds.[157] The act also allows local governments to use the proceeds for any service or facility authorized to be provided in a municipal service district,

---

151. *See,* City of Asheville Official Statement, note 150 above, at 4–5.

152. *See* G.S. 159-146(k).

153. G.S. 159-146(k).

154. *See* G.S. 159-123(b)(3) (authorizing the private sale of special obligation bonds).

155. *See* S.L. 2003-403.

156. For more-detailed information on project-development financing in North Carolina, see William C. Rivenbark, Shea Riggsbee Denning, & Kara A. Millonzi, "2007 Legislation Expands Scope of Project Development Financing in North Carolina," *Local Finance Bulletin* No. 36 (Nov. 2007).

157. G.S. 159-103. For more information on project-development-financing authority in North Carolina, see "Tax Increment Financing Frequently Asked Questions," *Tax Increment Financing in North Carolina* (UNC School of Government microsite).

Table 7.5 Authorized Purposes for Project-Development Financing

- Capital costs of providing airport facilities
- Capital costs of providing auditoriums, coliseums, arenas, stadiums, civic centers, convention centers, and facilities for exhibitions, athletic and cultural events, shows, and public gatherings
- Capital costs of providing hospital facilities, facilities for the provision of public health services, and facilities for care of the mentally retarded
- Capital costs of art galleries, museums, art centers, and historic properties
- Capital costs of on- and off-street parking and parking facilities, including meters, buildings, garages, driveways, and approaches open to public use
- Capital costs of providing certain parks and recreation facilities, including land, athletic fields, parks, playgrounds, recreation centers, shelters, permanent and temporary stands, and lighting[a]
- Capital costs of redevelopment through acquisition and improvement of land for assisting local redevelopment commissions
- Capital costs of sanitary sewer systems
- Capital costs of storm sewers and flood control facilities
- Capital costs of water systems, including facilities for supply, storage, treatment, and distribution of water
- Capital costs of public transportation facilities, including equipment, buses, railways, ferries, and garages
- Capital costs of industrial parks, including land and shell buildings, in order to provide employment opportunities for citizens of a county or municipality
- Capital costs of property to preserve a railroad corridor
- Capital costs of providing community colleges facilities
- Capital costs of providing school facilities
- Capital costs of improvements to subdivision and residential streets
- To finance housing projects for persons of low or moderate income
- Capital costs of electric systems
- Capital costs of gas systems
- Capital costs of streets and sidewalks
- Capital costs of improving existing systems or facilities for transmission or distribution of telephone services
- Capital costs of housing projects for low- or moderate-income persons
- To provide or maintain beach erosion control and flood and hurricane protection, downtown revitalization projects, urban area revitalization projects, drainage projects, sewage collection and disposal systems, off-street parking facilities, and watershed improvement projects in a municipal service district

a. G.S. 159-103(a) specifically exempts certain types of parks and recreation facilities—stadiums, arenas, golf courses, swimming pools, wading pools, and marinas.

though no district actually need be created.[158] Table 7.5 sets forth all the purposes for which a unit may use the proceeds of project-development bonds.

Requirements and Limitations

The Project Development Financing Act sets out detailed procedural requirements for issuing project-development bonds. A unit must (1) define a financing district, (2) adopt a financing plan, and (3) secure various approvals from governmental entities.

---

158. See Chapter 4, "Revenue Sources," for a list of projects that municipalities can undertake in a municipal service district.

Financing District

At the outset of a project-development-financing project, a county or municipality must establish a development-financing district that must consist of property that is

1. blighted, deteriorated, deteriorating, undeveloped, or inappropriately developed from the standpoint of sound community development and growth;
2. appropriate for rehabilitation or conservation activities; or
3. appropriate for economic development.[159]

A municipal district must consist of property that meets at least one of the conditions set forth for a county district or that meets the criteria of an urban "redevelopment area" (as defined by G.S. 160A-503). A municipality's planning commission may designate any of the following types of property as a redevelopment area:

1. property that is blighted because of dilapidated, deteriorated, aged, or obsolete buildings; inadequate ventilation, light, air, sanitation, or open spaces; high density of population or overcrowding; or unsanitary or unsafe conditions;
2. a nonresidential redevelopment area with dilapidated, deteriorated, aged, or obsolete buildings; inadequate ventilation, light, air, sanitation, or open spaces; defective or inadequate street layout or faulty lot layout; tax or special assessment delinquency exceeding the value of the property; or unsanitary or unsafe conditions;
3. a rehabilitation, conservation, and reconditioning area in present danger of becoming a blighted or nonresidential redevelopment area; or
4. any combination of the above types of areas.[160]

The total land area within a financing district may not exceed 5 percent of the total land area of the taxing unit.[161] A county may not include in a development-financing district any land located within a municipality at the time the district is created, but a county and municipality may jointly agree to create such a district.[162] In the absence of such an agreement, any land in a municipally established development-financing district will not count against the 5 percent of unincorporated land in that county that may be included in a development-financing district.[163] If a county and municipality jointly create a development-financing district, and each unit pledges its incremental tax revenue in support thereof, the area included within the district likely counts against the 5 percent limit for both the county and the municipality.

---

159. G.S. 158-7.3(c); 160A-515.1(e).

160. Additional limitations apply to a plan for a development-financing district established pursuant to G.S. 158-7.3 and located outside a municipality's central business district. *See* G.S. 158-7.3(a)(1).

161. G.S. 158-7.3(c); 160A-515.1(b).

162. G.S. 158-7.3(c); 159-107(e).

163. Conversely, land in a county district subsequently annexed by a municipality does not count against the municipality's 5 percent limit unless the county and municipality have entered into an increment agreement; in such an agreement, the municipality agrees that municipal taxes collected on part or all of the incremental valuation in the district will be paid into the reserve increment fund for the district. G.S. 159-107(e).

Financing Plan and County Approval

Once a unit identifies a development-financing district, it must adopt a financing plan that includes the following:

- a description of the boundaries of the development-financing district;
- a description of the proposed development, both public and private;
- a listing of the costs of the proposed public activities;
- a listing of the sources and amount of funds that will be used to pay for the proposed public activities;
- a base valuation of the district;
- a projected increase in the assessed valuation of property in the district;
- an estimated duration of the development-financing district (the earlier of thirty years from the effective date of the district or when the bonds are repaid);
- a description of how the proposed public and private development of the district will benefit district residents and business owners in terms of jobs, affordable housing, or services;
- a description of appropriate ameliorative activities if the proposed projects negatively impact district residents or business owners in terms of jobs, affordable housing, services, or displacement;
- a statement that the initial users of any new manufacturing facilities included in the plan will be required to pay certain wages, unless exempted by the state Secretary of Commerce.[164]

The unit must hold a public hearing on the proposed financing plan.[165] After the public hearing, a county governing board may approve the plan, with or without amendment, unless the plan has been disapproved by the secretary of the North Carolina Department of Environmental Quality (NCDEQ). A municipal board has an additional procedural requirement: it must provide notice to the governing board(s) of the county or counties in which the proposed district is located.[166] The county governing board(s) has twenty-eight days to disapprove the plan. If it is not disapproved by the county board(s), the municipal board may proceed to adopt the plan.

LGC and State Agency Approval

The plan and the district do not become effective until the Local Government Commission (LGC) approves the issuance of project-development-financing bonds for the district. The LGC may consider any matters it deems relevant to whether the bond issuance should be approved, including

1. whether the projects to be financed from the bonds are necessary to secure significant new project development for the district;
2. whether the proposed projects are feasible (taking into account additional security, such as credit enhancement, insurance, or guarantees, as discussed below);
3. the county's or municipality's debt-management procedures and policies;

---

164. G.S. 158-7.3(d); 160A-515.1(c).

165. *See* G.S. 158-7.3(h); 160A-515.1(g). Each unit must publish notice of the public hearing in a newspaper of general circulation and mail notice to all affected property owners in the proposed district. *See* G.S. 158-7.3(h); 160A-515.1(g).

166. G.S. 160A-515.1(e).

4. whether the county or municipality is in default on any debt-service obligation;

5. whether the private development forecast in the development-financing plan is likely to occur without the public project or projects to be financed by the bonds;

6. whether taxes on the incremental valuation accruing to the development-financing district, together with any other revenues available under G.S. 159-110, will be sufficient to service the proposed project-development-financing debt instruments;

7. whether the LGC can market the proposed project-development-financing debt instruments at reasonable rates of interest.[167]

Two other state agencies must approve certain types of project-development financings. If a development-financing plan involves the construction and operation of a new manufacturing facility, the plan must be submitted to the secretary of NCDEQ. The secretary's review will determine whether the facility will have a materially adverse effect on the environment and whether the company that will operate the facility has previously complied with federal and state environmental laws and regulations.[168]

The development-financing plan also must be submitted to the Secretary of the North Carolina Department of Commerce. The secretary must certify that the average weekly manufacturing wage required by the plan to be paid to the employees of the initial users of the proposed new manufacturing facility is either above the average weekly manufacturing wage in the county in which the district is located or not less than 10 percent above the average weekly manufacturing wage paid in the state.[169] The secretary may exempt a facility if certain criteria are met.

Bond Anticipation Notes

A unit of local government may, in certain cases, elect to issue "bond anticipation notes." As the name suggests, bond anticipation notes are promissory notes that a unit issues in anticipation of a future bond issuance.[170] They are secured primarily by the proceeds of future bonds issued[171] and typically have a maturity of less than two years.

A unit might issue such notes if it has authorized a bond issue but does not wish to borrow the full sum at one time. It also might issue bond anticipation notes if it intends to use the proceeds of the notes for construction financing.[172] A unit must obtain short-term construction

---

167. G.S. 159-105(a); *see also* G.S. 159-105(b) (establishing the criteria used by the LGC to approve proposed project-development-financing bonds).

168. G.S. 158-7.3(g); 160A-515.1(f).

169. G.S. 158-7.3(e); 160A-515.1(d).

170. Bond anticipation notes may be issued as general obligation bond anticipation notes, revenue bond anticipation notes, special obligation anticipation notes, or project-development bond anticipation notes. In order to issue general obligation bond anticipation notes, a unit must follow the statutory procedures for authorization of a general obligation bond issuance in the Local Government Bond Act. *See* "General Obligation Bonds," above.

171. *See* G.S. 159-162 (security for general obligation bond anticipation notes); 159-163 (security for revenue bond anticipation notes); 159-163.1 (security for project-development-financing debt instrument anticipation notes); 159-146(c), (e) (security for special obligation notes).

172. For example, the City of Charlotte issued a Water and Sewer System Revenue Bond Anticipation Note in 2021 to provide short-term financing for the capital costs of improvements to its water and sanitary sewer system and refunded that note in 2022 by issuing Water and Sewer System Revenue Bonds. *See* City of Charlotte Official Statement, note 19 above.

financing when it intends to sell an issue of future bonds to the U.S. Department of Agriculture's Rural Development unit (USDA-RD). USDA-RD offers long-term (up to forty-year) financing for the construction or repair of certain types of public infrastructure in rural jurisdictions. To be eligible for such long-term financing, a unit typically must (1) obtain short-term construction financing from a lender other than USDA-RD (e.g., a private financial institution) and (2) substantially complete the project to be financed. A unit issues a bond anticipation note in order to obtain short-term financing, and when the unit issues a long-term bond to USDA-RD, it uses the proceeds of that financing to pay off the initial short-term loan evidenced by the bond anticipation note.[173]

A unit of local government must obtain approval from the LGC to issue bond anticipation notes,[174] and the LGC will sell any notes approved on behalf of the unit.[175]

Installment Financings

The most common method of borrowing money for the majority of North Carolina's local governments is "installment financing."[176] North Carolina law permits counties, municipalities, and certain other units of local government to borrow money by entering into installment financing agreements.[177] Because a single statute—G.S. Chapter 160A-20—contains this authority, public finance practitioners in North Carolina often refer to this type of arrangement as a "160A-20" financing.

Security and Authority

Installment financing can, but frequently does not, involve the issuance of bonds. In its most basic form, an installment finance agreement evidences a loan transaction in which a local government borrows money to finance or refinance either (1) the purchase of real or personal property or (2) the construction or repair of fixtures or improvements on real property that the local government owns.[178]

---

173. For example, the Town of Princeton obtained LGC approval in 2022 to (1) issue a water and sewer system revenue bond anticipation note to finance the construction of improvements to its water and sewer system and (2) at the completion of construction, issue a water and sewer system revenue bond to USDA. *See* N.C. Department of State Treasurer, Local Government Commission, Minutes (Oct. 4, 2022), 21–24.

174. *See* G.S. 159-161.

175. *See* G.S. 159-165.

176. As of June 30, 2022, the aggregate amount of installment-financing debt outstanding for counties and municipalities totaled $8.807 billion, while the aggregate amount of general obligation debt outstanding for counties and municipalities totaled $9.109 billion. *See* N.C. Department of State Treasurer, Division of State and Local Government Finance, *Analysis of Debt of North Carolina Counties at 6-3-22*, and *Analysis of Debt of North Carolina Municipalities at 6-30-2022* (Jan. 26, 2023). However, only counties with populations of 250,000 or more as of July 1, 2021 (Buncombe, Cumberland, Durham, Forsyth, Guilford, Mecklenburg, and Wake), had more general obligation debt outstanding ($4.364 billion) than installment purchase debt outstanding ($1.713 billion). After subtracting each form of debt incurred by those counties, the aggregate amount of installment purchase debt outstanding statewide ($7.094 billion) exceeds the amount of general obligation debt outstanding statewide ($4.745 billion) by approximately 50 percent.

177. G.S. 160A-20.

178. G.S. 160A-20(a) allows a unit of local government to "purchase, or finance or refinance the purchase of, real or personal property by installment contracts that create in some or all of the property purchased a security interest to secure payment of the purchase price." An authorized entity also may "finance or refinance the construction or repair of fixtures or improvements on real property by contracts

In an installment financing, a unit of local government must grant a security interest to its financier in the asset purchased or in the real property, fixtures, or improvements to that real property financed with borrowed funds—it may not grant a security interest in real or personal property that is not financed with the proceeds of an installment financing. For example, assume that a county uses an installment financing to finance the construction of a vehicle maintenance garage on county-owned land. The county may borrow money to finance the cost of constructing the garage and may pledge to the financing provider, as security, either the garage or the land upon which the garage is built (or both). However, the county may not pledge any other property it owns that is not acquired or improved with the financing's proceeds (e.g., the county library).

A unit of local government can only grant a security interest in real or personal property which it owns. Therefore, an installment financing agreement is valid under North Carolina law only if a unit takes legal title to the financed property when the financing term begins. The vendor, bank, or other financier may not take title to the asset at the outset of a transaction and retain title until the loan securing the purchase price is repaid.[179] For example, if a municipality purchases a vehicle and obtains vendor financing with a five-year repayment term, the municipality must acquire a certificate of title to the vehicle when it takes possession of the vehicle—not at the conclusion of the financing term.

North Carolina law does not identify particular sources of revenue that a local government must use to repay debt incurred in an installment financing arrangement. A local government may use any unrestricted funds to repay the debt.

Forms of Installment Financing

Installment financings can take one of three general forms, each of which is described in more detail below.

Vendor Financing. A contract between a seller of real or personal property and a borrowing government, under which the seller loans money to a borrowing government to purchase the seller's assets.

Lending Institution Contracts. A contract between a financial institution (i.e., a lender) and a borrowing local government, under which the financial institution loans money to a borrowing government to either (1) purchase real or personal property from a third-party seller or (2) contract to construct or repair fixtures or improvements to real property.

Bond Market Financing.
Limited Obligation Bonds. A financing in which a local government directly issues "limited obligation bonds," either to an individual purchaser (e.g., a bank) or to one or more underwriters

---

that create in some or all of the fixtures or improvements, or in all or some portion of the property on which the fixtures or improvements are located, or in both, a security interest to secure repayment of moneys advanced or made available for the construction or repair." G.S. 160A-20(b).

179. This type of transaction is known as a lease-purchase arrangement, a borrowing structure in which North Carolina's local governments are not generally authorized to engage. Even a lease-purchase arrangement that provides a local government with an option to purchase an asset at the conclusion of the lease term will not comply with G.S. 160A-20.

(which resell the limited obligation bonds to other investors), in order to (1) purchase real or personal property from a third-party seller or (2) contract to construct or repair fixtures or improvements to real property.

Certificates of Participation. A financing in which a nonprofit corporation makes a "loan" to a local government to finance the unit's (1) purchase of real or personal property from a third-party seller or (2) contract to construct or repair fixtures or improvements to real property. In a contract between a unit of local government and a nonprofit corporation, the local government agrees to repay the loan to the corporation and grant to the corporation a mortgage on any real property improved, if any. In turn, the nonprofit corporation issues "certificates of participation" in the loan (i.e., rights to receive the revenues from the unit of local government) on the public market and assigns its granted rights to a trustee for the benefit of the purchasers of the certificates.

Vendor Financing

Vendor financing is the simplest form of installment financing. In a vendor financing, a seller of real or personal property enters into a contract with a borrowing local government.[180] Under the contract, the vendor conveys real or personal property to a local government and the local government agrees to pay the purchase price of the property to the vendor through a series of installment financing payments. These payments incorporate a principal component and an interest component.

In a vendor financing, a borrowing local government also grants a security interest to the vendor in the real or personal property purchased to secure its obligations to pay the vendor for the purchase price of the property.[181] If the unit of local government fails to uphold its obligations under the contract, the vendor may repossess the personal property or foreclose upon the real property.

Lending Institution Contracts

More commonly, a local government entering into an installment financing will enter into two contracts: (1) a contract with a vendor to purchase property or improvements to real property and (2) a contract with a lending institution (commonly, a bank) under which the lender agrees to provide the borrowing government money to pay the vendor and the borrowing government agrees to repay the lender, with interest, in a series of installment financing payments. Under the first contract, a vendor conveys legal title in the real or personal property to the borrowing government. Under the second contract, the borrowing government grants a security interest in the assets purchased, improvements constructed, or land upon which improvements are constructed.

---

180. In this context, a "vendor" includes a contractor that constructs an improvement on real property that the local government owns.

181. Granting a "security interest" in real property will require a borrowing local government to record a deed of trust (i.e., a mortgage) encumbering the property in favor of the vendor.

Bond Market Financings: Limited Obligation Bonds and Certificates of Participation

Installment financings frequently involve a single financing provider. But for large financings—particularly those that require a local government to issue more than $10 million in tax-exempt debt in a calendar year—local governments often turn to the bond market.[182] In an installment financing conducted through the bond markets, a local government typically sells limited obligation bonds (LOBs) or a nonprofit corporation sells certificates of participation (COPs) to an underwriter or a syndicate of underwriters. An underwriter that participates in such a financing resells such LOBs or COPs to other institutional or individual investors.

In a limited obligation bond financing, a borrowing government directly enters into a "trust agreement" or "indenture" with a third-party trustee, under which the local government grants a security interest in the financed asset (typically land and any improvements constructed thereon) to the trustee for the benefit of the bondholders. If the borrowing government fails to make scheduled installment financing payments to the trustee, the trustee may foreclose upon the property and use the proceeds of any foreclosure to pay bondholders.[183] In this structure, each bond is considered a separate "installment purchase contract."

As noted previously, the legal structure of a certificate of participation financing is slightly more complex than other financing methods but achieves the same economic result.[184] When a unit of local government is engaged in a LOBs or COPs financing, bond counsel and a variety of other third parties will be involved.

Requirements and Limitations

Non-Appropriation Clause

An installment financing contract must include a "non-appropriation" clause. Such a clause makes clear that (1) all of a local government's obligations to repay debt incurred under the contract are subject to the decision of the unit's governing board to appropriate funds for that purpose and (2) the unit does not pledge its taxing power to secure its obligations to repay installment financing debt.[185]

In the event that a local government defaults under an installment financing contract, an installment financing provider's sole remedy is to repossess or foreclose upon the personal

---

182. In general, a local government that issues tax-exempt debt that does not exceed a total of $10 million in a calendar year is known as a "qualified small issuer" under the Internal Revenue Code. 26 U.S.C. § 265(b)(2)(C). A financial institution can typically deduct up to 80 percent of its carrying costs incurred in making a loan to a "qualified small issuer" from its federal income tax liability. *See* 26 U.S.C. § 265(b)(3); 26 U.S.C. § 291(e)(1)(B). For that reason, debt issued by a qualified small issuer is typically referred to as "bank-qualified" debt. A financial institution may not want to hold non-bank-qualified debt in its portfolio. Therefore, it may be more advantageous to structure an issuance of non-bank-qualified debt to enable its resale to other institutional or individual investors in the public markets.

183. *See, e.g.,* County of Wake, North Carolina, *Official Statement for $302,410,000 Limited Obligation Bonds, Series 2021* (Feb. 3, 2021).

184. For an example of a COPs financing, see City of Charlotte, North Carolina, *Official Statement for $107,600,000 Certificates of Participation (Governmental Facilities and Equipment), Series 2021B* (Sept. 29, 2021).

185. Subject to limited exceptions, a unit may not contract debts secured by its faith and credit without obtaining voter approval. *See* N.C. Const. art. V, § 4(2). In 1991, the North Carolina Supreme Court rejected arguments that G.S. 160A-20 unconstitutionally permitted a county to incur debt secured by its faith and credit without voter approval. *See* Wayne Cnty. Citizens Ass'n v. Wayne Cnty. Bd. of Comm'rs, 328 N.C. 24 (1991). The court noted that both G.S. 160A-20, as well as the contract at issue in the case, prohibited a county from pledging its taxing power. *Id.*

or real property in which the local government has granted a security interest—and a non-appropriation clause makes this explicit. An installment financing provider may not obtain a deficiency judgment against a defaulting local government in the event that the proceeds from a sale of foreclosed property are insufficient to repay the debt that the local government owes.[186]

Non-Substitution Clause

An installment financing contract may not include a "non-substitution" clause.[187] Such a clause restricts the right of a borrowing local government to (1) "continue to provide a service or activity" or (2) replace or provide a substitute for any fixture, improvement, project, or property financed, refinanced, or purchased pursuant to the contract.[188]

Process for Entering into an Installment Financing Contract

North Carolina law does not prescribe a strict statutory process that a unit of local government must follow to enter into an installment financing contract. At a minimum, a local government must ensure that, where required, it (1) holds a public hearing and (2) obtains Local Government Commission (LGC) approval.

Public Hearing

A unit of local government that enters into an installment financing contract that "involves real property" must hold a public hearing on the contract.[189] At a minimum, contracts to finance the acquisition of land or construction of improvements on land would "involve real property." A unit must publish notice of any required public hearing in a newspaper of general circulation in the jurisdiction at least ten days prior to the date upon which the hearing will be held.[190]

A unit of local government may, but is not required to, hold a public hearing on an installment financing contract that only concerns the acquisition of personal property.

LGC Approval

The LGC must approve some, but not all, installment financings. To determine whether the LGC must approve a particular installment financing, a unit should answer the questions posed in the flowchart contained in Figure 7.2.

If a local government's installment financing contract is subject to LGC approval, the unit's staff should contact LGC staff as soon as possible to discuss the proposed financing. The LGC may require that the unit's staff attend a preliminary conference with LGC staff to discuss the unit's need for the financing, alternative financing structures, debt-management procedures and policies, and the financing process. After initial discussions with LGC staff, a local government's governing board typically adopts a resolution authorizing its staff to file a formal application for approval to the LGC and directing its staff to request proposals for financing.

The LGC must approve the proposed financing if it finds and determines all of the following:

1. The proposed contract is necessary or expedient.
2. The contract, under the circumstances, is preferable to a bond issue for the same purpose.

---

186. *See* G.S. 160A-20(f). A deficiency judgment would entitle an installment financing provider to proceed against other assets of a defaulting local government.
187. G.S. 160A-20(d).
188. G.S. 160A-20(d).
189. G.S. 160A-20(g).
190. G.S. 160A-20(g).

Figure 7.2 Installment Financings Subject to LGC Approval

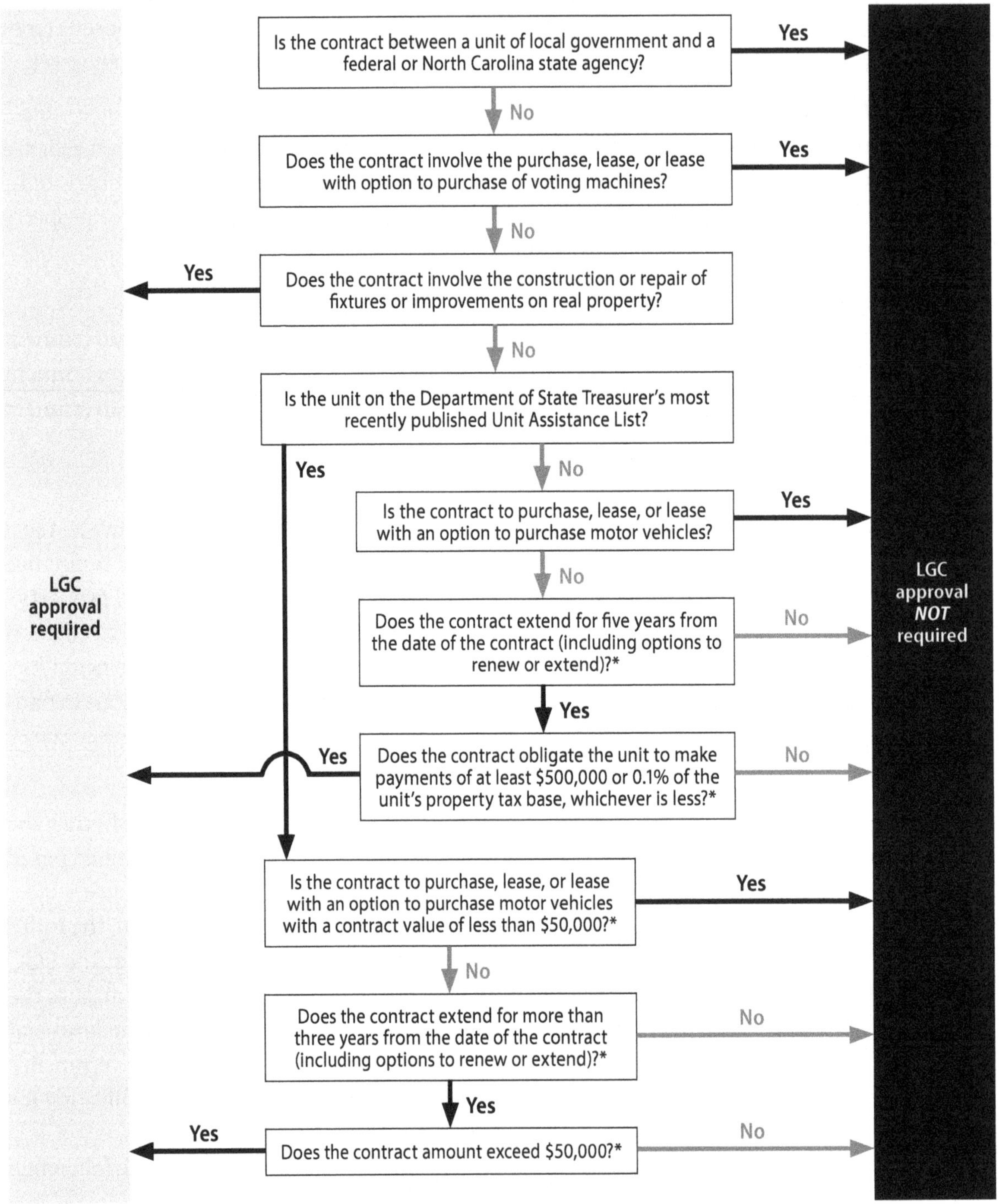

LGC approval required

Is the contract between a unit of local government and a federal or North Carolina state agency? — **Yes** →

No ↓

Does the contract involve the purchase, lease, or lease with option to purchase of voting machines? — **Yes** →

No ↓

← **Yes** — Does the contract involve the construction or repair of fixtures or improvements on real property?

No ↓

Is the unit on the Department of State Treasurer's most recently published Unit Assistance List?

Yes ↓   No ↓

Is the contract to purchase, lease, or lease with an option to purchase motor vehicles? — **Yes** →

No ↓

Does the contract extend for five years from the date of the contract (including options to renew or extend)?* — No →

Yes ↓

← **Yes** — Does the contract obligate the unit to make payments of at least $500,000 or 0.1% of the unit's property tax base, whichever is less?* — No →

Is the contract to purchase, lease, or lease with an option to purchase motor vehicles with a contract value of less than $50,000?* — **Yes** →

No ↓

Does the contract extend for more than three years from the date of the contract (including options to renew or extend)?* — No →

Yes ↓

← **Yes** — Does the contract amount exceed $50,000?* — No →

LGC approval NOT required

* Note that multiple contracts involving the same undertaking should be deemed a *single* contract. The *amount* of a contract can be determined by adding the total of all sums due under each contract entered into for a single undertaking.

3. The sums to fall due under the contract are adequate and not excessive for its proposed purpose.
4. The unit's debt-management procedures and policies are good or reasonable assurances have been given that its debt will henceforth be managed in strict compliance with the law.
5. The increase in taxes, if any, necessary to meet the sums to fall due under the contract will not be excessive.
6. The unit is not in default in any of its debt-service obligations.[191]

The LGC need not make all of these findings if it concludes that (1) the proposed project is necessary and expedient, (2) the proposed undertaking cannot be economically financed by a bond issue, and (3) the contract will not require an excessive increase in taxes.

If the LGC tentatively denies an application based upon the information that a unit provides, the LGC must notify the unit.[192] The unit may request a public hearing on its application, and the LGC may revisit its decision based upon testimony or other evidence presented at the hearing.[193] After a unit obtains LGC approval, it may proceed to close the installment financing.

"Synthetic" Project-Development Financings

Although project-development financing often is the most expensive way for units of local government to borrow money to fund public infrastructure projects, the structure is attractive to units because a unit does not pledge or obligate any of its current revenues. Instead, it pledges future revenue streams that new development will generate.

A "synthetic" project-development financing—or "synthetic TIF"—occurs when a local government determines that projected incremental revenues from new private development can justify a debt issuance to fund public infrastructure benefitting or encouraging that development. But rather than issue project-development bonds, the unit uses another form of authorized borrowing—typically, an installment financing under which the unit pledges a public asset itself as security for the loan—to fund the public improvement.

If private development occurs according to the unit's projections, the unit can use new revenue generated by the private development to repay the debt. Because local governments in North Carolina can obtain good ratings on installment financing debt sold in the public markets, synthetic project-development financing is often a cheaper and less complex alternative to formal project-development financing.

Federal and State Loans

Counties and municipalities may borrow money from an agency of the federal government or from the State of North Carolina "for constructing, expanding, maintaining, and operating any project or facility, or performing any function, which such city or county may be authorized by general law or local act to provide or perform."[194] On the state level, counties and municipalities

---

191. G.S. 159-151(b). Although not a statutory requirement, the LGC requires that the governing board of a unit of local government also make these findings in an adopted resolution prior to the submission of an application for approval of an installment financing.
192. G.S. 159-151(b).
193. G.S. 159-151(b).
194. G.S. 160A-17.1(a).

most commonly obtain loans from the North Carolina Department of Environmental Quality (NCDEQ) to finance the construction or repair of water or sewer infrastructure. On the federal level, counties and municipalities most commonly obtain loans from the U.S. Department of Agriculture to finance the construction or repair of a variety of public infrastructure in rural areas.[195] This section briefly describes the type of loans available from NCDEQ.[196]

State Loans: Clean Water State Revolving Fund, Drinking Water State Revolving Fund, Wastewater Reserve, and Drinking Water Reserve

NCDEQ, through its Division of Water Infrastructure, may make loans to eligible units of local government from the state-held Clean Water State Revolving Fund (CWSRF), Drinking Water State Revolving Fund (DWSRF), Wastewater Reserve, or Drinking Water Reserve.[197] Eligibility for a loan from the CWSRF or the DWSRF, each of which is funded in part by federal appropriations, is determined by reference to federal law.[198] Among other things, CWSRF loans can finance certain wastewater treatment and collection projects, stream restoration, and stormwater improvements, while DWSRF loans can finance water storage, treatment, or transmission and distribution systems.[199]

NCDEQ may make loans from the Wastewater Reserve for wastewater collection and treatment projects, stormwater quality projects, and nonpoint source pollution projects;[200] it may make loans from the Drinking Water Reserve for public water-system projects.[201]

A unit of local government that receives any type of loan from NCDEQ may execute a debt instrument payable to the State to evidence its obligation to repay principal and interest to the State.[202] It also may pledge as security for the loan, among other things, the revenues of any financed water or wastewater system.[203] The LGC must approve any loan into which NCDEQ and a unit of local government enter.[204]

The Taxability of Interest Paid to Holders of Local Government Debt

Units of local government in North Carolina can enjoy a substantial advantage in the capital markets when they borrow money. They may, with proper structuring, issue debt on a "tax-exempt" basis, meaning that any interest paid upon such debt is not subject to federal income

---

195. For additional information, see "Bond Anticipation Notes," above.

196. This section does not provide a comprehensive treatment of all federal and state loans available to units of local government.

197. *See generally* G.S. Ch. 159G, Art. 2.

198. *See* G.S. 159G-32(a). See also the following publications from the U.S. Environmental Protection Agency: *Overview of Clean Water State Revolving Fund Eligibilities* (May 2016); *Drinking Water State Revolving Fund Eligibility Handbook* (June 2017).

199. See the following webpages of the N.C. Department of Environmental Quality: *Clean Water State Revolving Fund* (last visited Mar. 10, 2023); *Drinking Water State Revolving Fund* (last visited March 10, 2023).

200. *See* G.S. 159G-32(b).

201. *See* G.S. 159G-32(c).

202. *See* G.S. 159G-40(d).

203. *See* G.S. 159G-40(c).

204. *See* G.S. 159G-40(a). The LGC must "consider the loan as if it were a bond proposal and review the proposed loan in accordance with the factors set out in G.S. 159-52 for review of a proposed bond issue." *Id.*

tax.[205] Because such interest is exempt from federal income tax, holders of "tax-exempt" debt will accept a lower rate of interest than comparable "taxable" debt. A local government that issues "tax-exempt" debt can lower its borrowing costs.

Issuing "tax-exempt" debt comes with administrative costs. To preserve the tax exemption, local governments must comply with complex provisions in the Internal Revenue Code (the "Code") and regulations promulgated by the Internal Revenue Service.[206] Among other things, these provisions regulate (1) the allocation and expenditure of the proceeds of tax-exempt debt, (2) the sources of and security for repayment of tax-exempt debt, (3) the investment of the proceeds of tax-exempt debt, and (4) the use and disposition of property financed by the proceeds of tax-exempt debt.[207] Bond counsel can assist a local government in understanding these provisions, but ultimately, the responsibility for compliance falls upon local government staff.

Tax Certificates

When a local government issues tax-exempt debt, bond counsel typically prepares a "tax certificate" that the unit's ranking officials execute on the unit's behalf. This document, which can be substantial in length, usually sets forth, among other things, (1) how the unit intends to expend tax-exempt bond proceeds, (2) from what sources and with what security it intends to repay and secure the tax-exempt debt, (3) how it intends to invest any proceeds of tax-exempt bonds, and (4) how it intends to operate the financed facility. In each case, bond counsel drafts such a certificate to ensure that, by strictly following its requirements, a local government can preserve the tax-exempt status of interest upon its debt.

"Taxable" Debt

A unit of local government that otherwise has authority to issue debt under North Carolina law is not necessarily required to issue "tax-exempt" debt. In some cases—and particularly when interest rates have fallen substantially—a local government may decide that an issuance of "taxable" debt in lieu of "tax-exempt" debt is worthwhile.[208] Local governments should consult with their financial advisors, the LGC, and bond counsel when seeking to issue taxable debt.

Disclosure Obligations for Publicly Offered Debt

As discussed above (see "Underwriter or Lender"), an underwriter that purchases and resells a local government's bonds to investors typically must comply with, among other regulations, U.S. Securities and Exchange Commission (SEC) Rule 15c2-12.[209] Where it applies, Rule

---

205. *See generally* 26 U.S.C. § 103(a) (noting that, with exceptions, "gross income does not include interest on any State or local bond"); 26 U.S.C. § 103(c)(1) ("The term 'State or local bond' means an obligation of a State or political subdivision thereof."). Interest paid upon an obligation of a "political subdivision of [the State], or a commission, an authority, or another agency of [the] State or of a political subdivision of [the State]" is also exempt from North Carolina state income tax. *See* G.S. 105-130.5(b)(1a)a.

206. The relevant provisions of the Code generally can be found in 26 U.S.C. §§ 103 and 141–150.

207. For a high-level overview of these provisions, see Internal Revenue Service, *Publication 4079, Tax-Exempt Governmental Bonds* (Sept. 2019). For a high-level overview of restrictions on investments of bond proceeds, see Internal Revenue Service, *Publication 5271, Complying with Arbitrage Requirements: A Guide for Issuers of Tax-Exempt Bonds* (Sept. 2019).

208. See, e.g., note 109 above for examples of issuances of taxable debt.

209. For technical references to Rule 15c2-12 and exceptions to its scope, see note 69 above.

15c2-12 prohibits an underwriter from purchasing or selling municipal securities unless it has "reasonably determined that an issuer of municipal securities . . . has undertaken [to provide certain information in Rule 15c2-12 to the Municipal Securities Rulemaking Board (an entity overseen by the SEC)] . . . in a written agreement or contract for the benefit of [the] holders of such securities."[210] In practice, public finance practitioners typically refer to this requirement as a "continuing disclosure undertaking."

The purpose of this SEC rule, on a very basic level, is to ensure that purchasers of municipal bonds can understand current risks associated with holding the bonds. Local governments that have agreed to provide such a continuing disclosure undertaking must provide certain information to the Municipal Securities Rulemaking Board through its Electronic Municipal Market Access (EMMA) system.[211] Among other things, an obligated local government must provide to EMMA (1) "annual financial information"[212] and (2) notices of sixteen specified events within ten business days after the occurrence thereof.[213] The LGC has released a variety of resources to assist local governments in complying with their disclosure obligations, and local governments may wish to consult bond counsel for advice in complying with an existing continuing disclosure undertaking.[214]

Grant Funding for Capital Projects

North Carolina law authorizes counties and municipalities to accept grants from the federal or state government to construct, expand, maintain, and operate any project or program which state law permits the unit to provide or perform.[215] Local governments commonly use these grants to finance—in whole or in part—many types of capital projects, including the acquisition, construction, and equipping of affordable housing, water and sewer facilities, parks or recreation facilities, and other types of public infrastructure. The availability of federal and state grant funding can fluctuate according to the respective willingness of Congress or the General Assembly to appropriate grant funds.

---

210. *See* Rule 15c2-12(b)(5).

211. *See* Municipal Securities Rulemaking Board, *Electronic Municipal Market Access (EMMA).* As of June 30, 2022, forty-five municipalities and fifty-seven counties were subject to continuing disclosure undertakings. *See* N.C. Department of State Treasurer, State and Local Finance Division, *Units Subject to Continuing Disclosure as of June 30, 2022* (last visited Mar. 14, 2023).

212. *See* Rule 15c2-12(b)(5)(i)(A). "Annual financial information" includes "financial information or operating data, provided at least annually, of the type included in the financial official statement with respect to [a borrower]. . . ." Rule 15c2-12(f)(9). In other words, this provision requires an issuer of local government debt to annually update the financial information it disclosed in connection with the initial sale and offering of debt.

213. *See* Rule 15c2-12(b)(5)(i)(C). These sixteen events include, among other things, ratings changes, delinquencies in the payment of principal or interest, or modifications to the rights of security holders, if material. *See id.*

214. For LGC resources, including a procedure for confirming submissions to EMMA and sample disclosure filings, see N.C. Department of State Treasurer, Local Government Commission, *Continuing Disclosure* (last visited Mar. 14, 2023).

215. *See* G.S. 160A-17.1(a).

Federal Grantmaking

Federal agencies may award a federal grant to a non-federal entity[216] only when Congress has (1) enacted legislation authorizing an agency to make a grant for a specific purpose and (2) appropriated money to the agency to provide the grant.[217] Once an agency has authority to fund a federal grant, it will announce the availability of the funding opportunity.

In most cases, an agency that awards a federal grant must release a public notice—termed a "notice of funding opportunity" or "NOFO"—that includes detailed information about the award, the types of entities eligible to apply, the evaluation criteria for selection, required components of an application, and how to apply.[218] NOFOs are accessible at grants.gov, a website maintained by the federal Office of Management and Budget. Local governments can use this website to identify and apply for federal funding opportunities.

Local Government as "Recipient"

A local government can receive grant funding *directly* from a federal awarding agency as a "recipient" of a federal grant.[219] If a federal agency selects a local government to receive a federal grant as a recipient, the agency typically will issue a notice of award, termed an "NOA," and will require the local government to execute a grant agreement. A grant agreement is a legal instrument that reflects the terms and conditions upon which a non-federal entity may use awarded funds.[220] Once a local government executes a grant agreement or accepts federal grant funds, it is contractually bound to the awarding agency to abide by the terms and conditions of the federal award.[221]

Local Government as "Subrecipient"

A local government also might receive federal grant funding in an *indirect* fashion: by obtaining a "subaward" of federal funding from another non-federal entity—a "pass-through entity"—that is a recipient of federal grant funds.[222] For example, federal agencies commonly make a variety of grants to state government agencies. In turn, these state agencies commonly act as pass-through

---

216. A non-federal entity includes, among other entities, a local government. *See* 2 C.F.R. § 200.1 (defining "non-federal entity").

217. *See generally* Robert M. Lloyd, *A Practical Guide to Federal Grants Management – From Solicitation Through Audit*, 3rd ed. (Arlington, Va.: Columbia Books, Inc., 2020), 20 (describing grant-making authority of federal agencies). For a more-detailed treatment of the appropriations process for federal grants, see U.S. Government Accountability Office (GAO), Office of the General Counsel, "Federal Assistance: Grants and Cooperative Agreements," chap. 10 in *Principles of Federal Appropriations Law* Vol. 2, 3rd ed. (Washington, D.C.: GAO, 2006).

218. *See* 2 C.F.R. § 200.204 (requiring federal awarding agencies to release notices of funding opportunities for competitive discretionary grants); 2 C.F.R. § 200.1 (defining "notice of funding opportunity").

219. *See* 2 C.F.R. § 200.1 ("*Recipient* means an entity . . . that receives a Federal award directly from a federal awarding agency.").

220. *See* 31 U.S.C. § 6304.

221. In some cases, a representative of a non-federal entity need not actually sign a grant agreement. Instead, the non-federal entity becomes bound to the terms and conditions of a grant agreement by accepting a disbursal of federal funds. *See* Lloyd, note 217 above, at 69.

222. *See* 2 C.F.R. § 200.1 ("*Subrecipient* means an entity . . . that receives a subaward from a pass-through entity to carry out part of a Federal award."). A "pass-through entity" is a "non-federal entity that provides a subaward to a subrecipient to carry out part of a Federal program." *Id.*

entities and subaward federal funds to local governments.[223] A local government acting as a subrecipient will use awarded funds to carry out the objectives of the federal grant program and is obligated to use the funds in accordance with the terms and conditions of a subaward agreement and any other applicable laws and regulations that apply to the awarded funds.[224]

Complying with the Terms and Conditions of Federal Grants

As a recipient or subrecipient of a federal grant, a local government must act as a steward of federal funds. In particular, it must administer those funds in accordance with the federal statutes that authorized the grant and other governing laws, regulations, and terms and conditions specified in the grant agreement.

Although the laws and regulations that apply to each federal grant are unique, the federal Office of Management and Budget has made recent attempts to consolidate and streamline many of the regulations that govern the expenditure of federal grants into a single title of the Code of Federal Regulations: 2 C.F.R. Part 200.[225] Entitled the "Uniform Administrative Requirements, Cost Principles, and Audit Requirements" and known popularly as the "Uniform Guidance" or "UG," 2 C.F.R. Part 200 attempts to establish a uniform framework for the administration of federal financial assistance that federal agencies and non-federal entities must follow.

The Uniform Guidance (2 C.F.R. Part 200)

Comprised of six subparts and twelve appendixes, the Uniform Guidance addresses, in significant detail, (1) the obligations of federal agencies prior to awarding federal financial assistance to non-federal entities and (2) how non-federal entities must manage the expenditure of federal financial assistance. In general, recipients and subrecipients of federal grants must adhere to applicable provisions of the Uniform Guidance unless a granting agency has established an exception to those provisions in separate regulations or in a particular grant agreement.

Basic Compliance Requirements

Local governments that receive federal financial assistance, including federal grants, must be familiar with the compliance obligations that the Uniform Guidance imposes upon their expenditure of federal monies. Among other things, the Uniform Guidance

(1) dictates and restricts which direct and indirect costs a non-federal entity may charge to a federal award;[226]
(2) requires that a non-federal entity adopt and implement internal controls to ensure proper management of federal funds;[227]

---

223. For example, the U.S. Department of Housing and Urban Development awards Community Development Block Grant (CDBG) funds to the North Carolina Department of Commerce (DOC). DOC "passes through" the CDBG grant funds to eligible subrecipients—including county or municipal governments—to enable them to undertake authorized projects with CDBG funds. For more information about the CDBG program, see Chapter 15, "Financing and Public-Private Partnerships for Community Economic Development."

224. For general requirements that pass-through entities must follow in making subawards, see 2 C.F.R. § 200.332. For a helpful discussion of managing subrecipient awards, see Lloyd, note 217 above, at 245–70.

225. *See* 2 C.F.R. Part 200.

226. *See* 2 C.F.R. §§ 200.400–.476 (outlining "cost principles" for federal awards).

227. *See* 2 C.F.R. §§ 200.302–.305. The Uniform Guidance directs non-federal entities to model their internal controls after the Standards for Internal Control in the Federal Government (Green Book) or the

(3) requires that a non-federal entity, when acquiring property or services with the proceeds of federal financial assistance, adopt and follow documented procurement procedures and a conflict of interest policy that are consistent with state law and procurement standards set forth in the Uniform Guidance;[228]

(4) mandates that a non-federal entity follow certain standards for the use, maintenance, and disposition of real property, equipment, or supplies acquired using federal financial assistance;[229]

(5) requires that a non-federal entity retain records related to an award of federal financial assistance for a minimum period of three years;[230] and

(6) requires that a non-federal entity undergo a single audit or program-specific audit if it expends $750,000 or more in federal financial assistance during a single fiscal year.[231]

Depending on the particular grant, other portions of the Uniform Guidance may apply, and prior to accepting a federal award, a local government should confirm all provisions applicable to its expenditure and management of federal funds.

Due to the complexity of complying with federal grant conditions in applicable federal laws and regulations, some units of local government that receive federal grants have started to develop and implement comprehensive grants-management compliance programs.

Remedies for Noncompliance

Failure to comply with the terms and conditions of a federal grant or with other federal laws or regulations applicable to the expenditure of federal financial assistance can have severe consequences for a local government. Among other things, a federal awarding agency may withhold cash payments from a noncompliant local government, disallow improper costs charged to a federal award, or even partially or completely terminate a federal award.[232] For more egregious acts of noncompliance, a federal awarding agency has authority to initiate suspension or debarment proceedings against a local government, which could prohibit a local government—either temporarily or permanently—from receiving federal grant funds.[233]

Opportunities to Secure State Grant Funding

In addition to passing through federal funds to units of local government across the state, the North Carolina General Assembly and various state agencies also regularly make state funds available to units of local government for a variety of purposes. The State of North Carolina regularly publishes a variety of grant opportunities and also has created a database where users

---

Internal Control-Integrated Framework issued by the Committee on Sponsoring Organizations (COSO). *See* 2 C.F.R. § 200.303. For a more-detailed discussion of implementing internal controls over federal awards, see Chapter 9, "Internal Control in Financial Management."

228. *See* 2 C.F.R. §§ 200.317–.327. Non-federal entities may award contracts only to responsible contractors and must ensure that contractors satisfactorily perform under a contract's terms. *See* 2 C.F.R. §§ 200.318(b), (h).

229. *See* 2 C.F.R. 200.310 – 200.316.

230. *See* 2 C.F.R. § 200.334 (requiring maintenance of financial records and supporting documentation pertaining to federal awards for a minimum of three years from the date of the submission of the final expenditure report).

231. *See* 2 C.F.R. §§ 200.500–.521.

232. *See* 2 C.F.R. § 200.339.

233. For more information, see 2 C.F.R. Part 180.

can explore available grant programs.[234] When expending state grant monies for capital projects, local governments may be required to execute a grant agreement with a state agency and follow principles and restrictions contained in the North Carolina Administrative Code that are similar to those in the Uniform Guidance.[235]

Conclusion

Units of local government face a variety of challenges when financing capital projects. They must understand their legal authority to finance the acquisition or construction of capital assets, decide which financing mechanisms may be appropriate for a given capital project, and balance the needs of current and future citizens in generating revenue to support each undertaking. North Carolina law provides a variety of tools to fund the initial costs of large and small capital projects, and governing boards and staff should think critically about these issues and the needs of their communities before embarking on a particular financing path.

---

234. For a list of grant opportunities and a link to the database, see NC.gov, *Grant Opportunities* (last visited April 11, 2023).

235. *See, e.g.*, Uniform Administration of State Awards of Financial Assistance, Title 09, Subchapter 3M, Sections .0101–.0802 of the N.C. Administrative Code.

III. FINANCIAL MANAGEMENT

Chapter 8

Managing and Disbursing Public Funds

by Gregory S. Allison and Kara A. Millonzi

A local government and public authority (collectively, local units) needs to pay for the personnel, supplies, infrastructure, and other expenses necessary to carry out the purposes for which it was established. Proper management and expenditure of a local unit's revenues are important both to ensure that sufficient funds are available and to maintain public trust in the government.

Internal controls are processes designed to safeguard the assets of the unit. Although the exact nature of internal controls will vary significantly from government to government due to differences in size, resources, and organizational structure, all local government entities need to take steps to ensure the proper stewardship of public funds. And that duty should take precedence over the efficiency and expediency of business processes. Internal controls introduce redundancies and, to the frustration of local government officials, may cause administrative delays of even routine transactions. They serve an invaluable function, though: to ensure that moneys are managed and spent appropriately, according to clear budget directives by the governing board. That is a necessary trade-off in the public sector.

Internal controls fall roughly into two categories—preventative (policies and procedures that do not allow certain events to occur) and detective (backup procedures to ensure that primary internal controls operate as intended). A local government needs to incorporate both categories into its financial operations. Perhaps the most common internal control is segregation of duties—so that no employee or official handles an entire transaction from start to finish. Other controls include providing oversight of financial activity by supervisors and board members, periodically rotating staff duties, doing a thorough and accurate audit of all receipts and claims, requiring that adequate records be maintained and presented for intermittent inspection by an internal audit committee, responding to deficiencies identified through the yearly external audit, educating employees and officials about detecting red flags of potential fraudulent activity, and even mandating that employees use all of their vacation time each year. Employees and officials at all levels of local government must implement, monitor, and periodically reevaluate the sufficiency of controls relating to the collection, management, obligation, and disbursement of public funds.

A local unit has a good deal of flexibility in establishing and implementing internal controls. At a minimum, internal controls must serve to detect, mitigate, and ideally prevent, the misappropriation of moneys collected or received by the unit. The Local Government Budget and Fiscal Control Act (LGBFCA)[1] specifies certain internal controls, most notably,

- accounting system requirements (G.S. 159-26);
- annual independent audit (G.S. 159-34);
- Local Government Commission/State Board of Education oversight (G.S. 159-25, -33, -33.1, -34, -36, -181, -182);
- appointment of finance officers, budget officers, and deputy finance officers (G.S. 159-9, -24, -28);
- daily deposit in official repository requirement (G.S. 159-31, -32);
- disbursement process (G.S. 159-28);
- dual signature requirement (G.S. 159-25);
- employee and official bonding requirement (G.S. 159-29);
- governing board oversight provisions (G.S. 159-25, -28, -29, -30, -31, -34);
- investment limitations (G.S. 159-30);
- preaudit process (G.S. 159-28).

This chapter reflects the law as of June 1, 2023.

1. Chapter 159, Article 3 of the North Carolina General Statutes (hereinafter G.S.). Note that the School Budget and Fiscal Control Act, G.S. Chapter 115C, Article 31, prescribes similar, and in many cases exactly analogous, requirements for local school administrative units.

These provisions in the LGBFCA set the minimum internal controls required by law. Basic legal compliance could go a long way toward preventing fiscal malfeasance but often is not sufficient to fully insulate a government entity from an employee or vendor/contractor mistake or fraud. Most units need to implement additional financial internal controls to safeguard public funds.

Some of the above-listed controls are discussed in detail in other chapters. This chapter will focus on the daily deposit requirement, investment limitations, preaudit and disbursement processes, dual signature requirement, and governing board oversight.

Daily Deposits and Official Depositories

The first statutory requirement related to the management of a local unit's revenues is that the funds be deposited and insured. Specifically, Chapter 159, Section 32 of the North Carolina General Statutes (hereinafter G.S.) states that, except as otherwise provided by law, all moneys "collected or received" by an "officer or employee" of a local unit must be deposited daily "with the finance officer or in an official depository," or must be submitted to "a properly licensed and recognized cash collection service. . . ."

Daily Deposit Requirement

"Officer or Employee"

The daily deposit requirement applies to all local government and public authority officials, even those such as sheriffs and registers of deeds who are independently elected or local board of elections personnel who are independently appointed. If an agency is part of a local unit for purposes of budget adoption and control, it and its officers and employees also are part of the local unit for purposes of the daily deposit requirement.

"Collected or Received"

The statute also makes no distinction among types of moneys. It applies to all moneys "collected or received" by a local unit, including taxes and fees, as well as moneys collected through fundraisers, state or federal appropriations, donations, grants, loans, and gifts. It applies, for example, when a sheriff's office receives a check from the federal government pursuant to a federal drug-share program. It applies when a recreation staff member of a municipality collects fees on-site for the local unit's open gym night. It applies when a social services department receives monetary donations around holiday time to support its outreach programs.[2] And it applies if a municipal library holds a used-book-sale fundraiser.[3]

---

2. Increasingly, donations to a county's social services department are being made by bank gift card instead of in the form of cash or a check. Bank gift cards are not "moneys" for purposes of the daily deposit statute but should be treated as revenue. For budget purposes, if the unit intends to use a gift card to pay for unit expenditures, its governing board must first recognize the amount of the gift card as revenue in the budget ordinance and appropriate it to a specific department, function, or project. The finance officer also should establish appropriate internal controls for accepting and securely storing bank gift cards.

3. As used in this book, the term "municipality" is synonymous with "city," "town," and "village."

Sometimes a local unit collects moneys on behalf of other governments or on behalf of private entities or individuals. For example, a unit may collect funds for a local nonprofit along with its water and sewer payments. Or a unit may contract with a private electric or gas company to accept customer payments on behalf of the private company. County prison officials typically collect and hold funds belonging to inmates. Many municipalities collect funds to maintain private cemetery plots within a municipal cemetery. A unit typically holds these funds in a fiduciary or agency capacity. They are not recognized as revenue in the unit's budget. Nevertheless, these funds are subject to the daily deposit requirement because they are "collected or received" by the unit.

Similarly, some units collect deposits on equipment or facility rentals. These deposits also are "collected or received" by the unit and thus are subject to the daily deposit requirement, even if they are held for only a brief period of time. The appropriate procedure is for the unit to deposit the funds and then cut a refund check when the equipment is returned or the facility rental period is over.

There are at least three circumstances in which a local unit possesses moneys that arguably it has not "collected or received" for purposes of G.S. 159-32—vending machine proceeds, sealed bid deposits, and certain cash seized by law enforcement.

Vending Machine Proceeds

Moneys *"received* by a [local unit] on account of operation of vending facilities" must be deposited, budgeted, appropriated, and expended pursuant to the LGBFCA.[4] The statute does not require that all proceeds from vending facilities on government property be received by that government. Rather, it simply requires that when such moneys are "received" by the government, they are to be deposited and otherwise handled pursuant to the LGBFCA's provisions. Therefore, if a unit permits others, whether a vending company or a group of employees, to place vending facilities on the unit's property and to retain the proceeds from those facilities, the moneys in question are not subject to the daily deposit requirement. If the unit itself collects and keeps the moneys, however, the funds must be deposited according to the law.

Sealed Bid Deposits

Another likely exception to the daily deposit requirement involves deposits included in sealed bids for construction projects that have yet to be opened by a local unit. It is reasonable to assume that the moneys have not been "received" or "collected" for purposes of G.S. 159-32 until the sealed bids are open.

Cash Seized by Law Enforcement

Cash seized by law enforcement as evidence of a crime also likely has not been "received" or "collected" by the local unit for purposes of G.S. 159-32. Seized cash should be handled by the law enforcement agency in the same manner as other evidence.

---

4. G.S. 159-17.1 (emphasis added).

Deposited Daily "With the Finance Officer or in an Official Depository"

The statute specifies that moneys must be deposited daily with a local unit's finance officer or in an official depository. Under the latter option, the employee or official depositing the funds must immediately notify the finance officer by means of a "duplicate deposit ticket."[5] Alternatively, moneys may be submitted to a licensed and recognized cash collection service. The finance officer may audit the accounts of any officer or employee collecting or receiving moneys at any time and may prescribe the form and detail of these accounts.[6] The finance officer must audit all such decentralized collections at least once annually. This is an internal audit; the annual independent audit does not suffice to satisfy this requirement.

Does the statute require that every dollar collected, whether at 9:00 A.M. or 4:59 P.M., be deposited the day it is collected? The answer is "probably not." A reasonable interpretation of the law is that each department that collects or receives moneys must make at least one deposit each day, either in an official depository or with the unit's finance officer. In many local units the daily deposit to an official depository is made before the cutoff time (e.g., 2:00 P.M.) set by the depository for crediting interest earnings on deposits made that day. This may result in some funds being retained overnight (or possibly even over a weekend) in a safe or other secure area within a department.

$500 Threshold

The statute also allows a unit's governing board to authorize an individual who collects or receives moneys to make the mandated deposit only when moneys on hand amount to $500 or more, though a deposit must always be made on the last business day of each month.[7] The board should adopt a resolution indicating its approval of such a policy and ensure that there are sufficient controls to safeguard the amounts outstanding.

Exemptions from Daily Deposit Requirement

G.S. 159-32 states that if another law provides for a different method of depositing moneys collected or received, the daily deposit requirement does not apply. Occasionally other statutes direct that funds collected by a unit be handled differently. For example, G.S. 1-339.70 directs a sheriff to turn over the net proceeds of an execution sale to the clerk of superior court. Similarly, G.S. 15-15 directs a law enforcement officer to disburse the net proceeds of a sale of confiscated, found, or abandoned property to "the treasurer of the county board of education of the county in which such sale is made."

---

5. G.S. 159-32.

6. G.S. 159-32. As discussed below, the accounts of each officer or employee who collects or receives moneys must be audited by the finance officer at least once annually.

7. G.S. 159-32. Only the governing board may approve the use of this exception. Managers, finance officers, other officers, or advisory boards or commissions may not authorize it.

Official Depository Requirement

Governing Board Selects Official Depositories

Who determines where collected or received moneys are deposited? This task is expressly delegated to the governing board of the unit or authority. A governing board must designate one or more banks, savings and loan associations, or trust companies in the state to serve as the unit's official depository or depositories.[8] In fact, it is "unlawful for any public moneys to be deposited in any place, bank, or trust company other than an official depository."[9] With the written permission of the secretary of the Local Government Commission (LGC) a board also may select a nationally chartered bank located in another state as an official depository. (For a number of reasons, the secretary of the LGC will approve the use of out-of-state depositories only in rare circumstances, such as when authorizing a governing board to designate a nationally or state-chartered out-of-state bank as a depository or fiscal agent for payment of debt service.) A board may not select a credit union as an official depository, even if it is located in the state.

Selection Process

Local units follow a variety of methods in selecting or designating official depositories. Some name each bank and savings institution with an office located within their jurisdiction as an official depository and open an account in each. Others maintain just one account, rotating it among each local financial institution that is qualified to serve as an official depository and changing it according to a predetermined schedule (commonly every one to three years). Although these methods demonstrate a local government's support of local banks and financial institutions, they can complicate the government's cash-management procedures, hinder its investment program, and cause it to pay more than it would otherwise for banking services. For these reasons, the majority of local units statewide follow a third method—selecting a bank or financial institution to serve as a depository through a request-for-proposals process that awards the business to the institution that offers the most services for the fees charged or the most services for the lowest compensating balance that the county or the municipality must maintain at the bank or financial institution.

Types of Accounts

Depository accounts may be non-interest-bearing accounts with unlimited check-writing privileges; interest-bearing accounts with unlimited check-writing privileges (NOW or super-NOW accounts); interest-bearing money market accounts for which check-writing privileges are restricted; or certificates of deposit (CDs) that have no check-writing privileges. Generally, the use of interest-bearing accounts is recommended.

---

8. G.S. 159-31. State law (G.S. 14-234) generally forbids governing board members and other officials involved in the contracting process to make contracts for the local governments in which they have an interest. An exception exists, however, for transacting business with "banks or banking institutions." Therefore, a county or a municipality may designate as a depository a bank or a savings institution in which a governing board member, for example, is an officer, owner, or stockholder.

9. G.S. 159-31.

Insurance and Collateralization of Deposits

Funds on deposit in an official depository (except funds deposited with a fiscal agent for the purpose of making debt-service payments to bondholders[10]) must be fully secured.[11] This is accomplished through a combination of methods. First, government funds on deposit with a bank or a savings institution or invested in a CD issued by such an institution are insured by the Federal Deposit Insurance Corporation (FDIC). If the funds that a local unit has on deposit or invested in a CD do not exceed the maximum amount of FDIC insurance—currently $250,000 per official custodian for interest-bearing accounts and an additional $250,000 per official custodian for non-interest-bearing accounts—no further security is required. For purposes of FDIC regulations, the finance officer is always the official custodian.

Uninsured funds in a bank or a savings institution may be secured through a collateral security arrangement. Under one type of arrangement the institution places securities with a market value equal to or greater than the local unit's uninsured moneys on deposit or invested in CDs into an escrow account with a separate, unrelated third-party institution (usually the trust department of another bank, the Federal Reserve, or the Federal Home Loan Bank). The escrow agreement provides that if the depository bank or savings institution defaults on its obligations to the local unit, the unit is entitled to the escrowed securities in the amount of the default less the amount of FDIC insurance coverage. Under this method, the government must execute certain forms and take certain actions to ensure that deposits are adequately collateralized. Responsibility for assuring that deposits are adequately secured under this method rests with a local unit's finance officer, who should closely supervise the collateral-security arrangement.

Alternatively, a bank or a savings institution may choose to participate in a pool of bank- and savings institution–owned securities sponsored and regulated by the state treasurer to collateralize state and local government moneys on deposit or invested in CDs with these institutions. A third-party institution, chosen by the various pooling-method banks, holds the securities in the pool. Participating depository banks and savings institutions are responsible for maintaining adequate collateral securities in the pool, though each financial institution's collateral balances are monitored by the state treasurer. In the unlikely event of defaults or similar financial troubles, the state treasurer would be considered the beneficiary of reclaimed deposits and collateral. Certain standards of financial soundness are required by the state treasurer before a financial institution is allowed to participate in this system.

Reporting Requirements

A unit must notify an official depository each time it opens a new account there that the deposits are subject to the collateralization rules. To assist the depository in keeping its records current, as of June 30 each year, the unit also must provide to each depository a Form COLL-91, "Annual Notification of Accounts by Public Depositor," which lists the current account names and numbers of all its public deposit accounts. The unit sends a duplicate of the form to the N.C. Office of State Treasurer to assist in the monitoring process. Forms are supplied to the unit by the treasurer's State and Local Government Division.[12]

---

10. Moneys in the hands of a fiscal agent need not be secured if they have been remitted to the bank no more than sixty days before the bonds or notes that are being paid mature.

11. G.S. 159-31(b).

12. *See* N.C. Department of State Treasurer, *Collateralization of Public Deposits* (last visited Feb. 27, 2023).

Liability for Losses

If deposits are adequately and legally secured, no officer or employee of a local unit may be held liable for losses sustained by the unit because of default by the depository.[13] Under the common law, a custodian of public funds is strictly liable for any such losses. Thus, this statute operates as an exception to the common law rule.

Finance Officer Manages Accounts in Official Depository

The finance officer of a local government unit is charged with oversight and management of all moneys collected or received by the unit and deposited into an official depository.[14] The finance officer also must establish all bank accounts for the local unit.[15] A manager, administrator, department head, or other officer or employee may not open an account, even if it is in an official depository.[16] The finance officer may set up separate accounts within an official depository for each department, or for each project or revenue source, or the finance officer may choose to pool moneys within a single account. Even if moneys are commingled in a single bank account, they still must be accounted for and allocated to the appropriate department according to the unit's or authority's budget ordinance. Revenues that are legally earmarked only for certain purposes also must be traceable to ensure proper expenditure.

The finance officer also is mandated by statute to periodically audit the accounts of any individual or department that collects or receives money. It must be done at least once per year. The statute does not prescribe the form or substance of this internal review. A finance officer is free to develop his or her own metrics to ensure that moneys are being accounted for appropriately. The metrics should be designed to test the sufficiency of internal controls within the department and also to verify that the amount that should be collected or received is actually accounted for in the actual deposits. A finance officer may want to have at least one unannounced spot check as well as regular scheduled reviews of departmental procedures, cash draws, and accounts.

Investments

It would be fiduciarily irresponsible for local units to let significant amounts of cash lie idle in non-interest-bearing depository accounts. Investment income can amount to the equivalent of several cents or more on the property tax rate. G.S. 159-30 prescribes allowable investment options for local units. It also makes the finance officer responsible for managing investments, subject to policy directions and restrictions that the unit's governing board may impose.

---

13. G.S. 159-31(b).

14. G.S. 159-25.

15. G.S. 159-25.

16. As discussed below, however, a unit's governing board may designate other employees or officials as deputy finance officers with authorization to disburse moneys from an account in an official depository. *See* G.S. 159-28.

Authorized Investments

Among the securities and instruments in which local units invest are CDs or other forms of time deposits approved by the Local Government Commission (LGC) that are offered by banks, savings institutions, and trust companies located in North Carolina.[17] A bank-issued CD has traditionally been the most widely used investment instrument, especially by small- and medium-sized local governments.[18] Other investments authorized by G.S. 159-30(c) are listed below. The available options reflect a policy decision by the legislature to prioritize liquidity and low-risk investments over those with higher potential yields. A local unit is directed to adopt an investment program that is managed such that "investments and deposits can be converted into cash when needed."[19]

1. **United States Treasury obligations (bills, notes, and bonds)—called Treasuries— and United States agency obligations that are fully guaranteed by the United States government**

   Because these obligations are full-faith-and-credit obligations of the United States, they carry the least credit risk—that is, risk of default—of any investment available to local units. As a result, short-term Treasuries are usually lower yielding than alternative investment securities. Long-term Treasuries and Government National Mortgage Association securities (fully guaranteed by the U.S. government) can experience significant price variations, a characteristic of long-term securities in general; therefore, such securities should be carefully evaluated and considered only for investing certain, limited funds, such as capital reserve moneys, that will not be needed for many years.

2. **Direct obligations of certain agencies that are established and/or sponsored by the United States government but whose obligations are not guaranteed by it**

   Among the agencies that issue this form of investment are the Federal Home Loan Bank Board, the Federal National Mortgage Association, and the Federal Farm Credit System. Direct debt issued by these agencies generally carries a very low credit risk, though economic conditions that adversely affect an economic sector heavily financed by the agency (e.g., housing) can create some risk for local units or for others who invest in a local unit's securities. Some securities provided by these agencies are not direct debt and therefore are not eligible investments for North Carolina governments. Moreover, even though longer-term direct debt of these agencies carries low credit risk, it can experience significant price fluctuations before maturity.

3. **Obligations of the State of North Carolina or bonds and notes of any of its local governments or public authorities, with investments in such obligations subject to restrictions of the secretary of the LGC**

   Because the interest paid to investors on these obligations, bonds, and notes is typically exempt from federal and state income taxes, they generally carry lower yields than alternative investment instruments available to local units. However, should

---

17. G.S. 159-30(b), -30(c)(5).

18. If a local unit is using a CD as an investment vehicle under G.S. 159-30, the unit is not required to invest in a CD of an official depository.

19. G.S. 159-30(a).

state and local governments in North Carolina begin to issue significant amounts of securities on which the interest paid is subject to federal income taxes, those securities would carry higher interest rates than tax-exempt state and local government obligations. This could make the taxable obligations attractive to local units as investment instruments.

4. **Top-rated commercial paper issued by domestic United States corporations**

Commercial paper is issued by industrial and commercial corporations to finance inventories and other short-term needs. Such paper is an unsecured corporate promissory note that is available in maturities of up to 270 days, though maturities from 30 to 90 days are most common. For any local unit to invest in commercial paper, the paper must be rated by at least one national rating organization and earn its top commercial paper rating. If the paper is rated by more than one such organization, it must have the highest rating given by each.

Historically, commercial paper has been relatively high yielding, and many local units have invested heavily in it over the years. In economic recessions, some commercial paper issuers are downgraded. This means that their commercial paper is no longer eligible for investment by North Carolina local governments. Occasionally the downgrade occurs after the investment is purchased but before it matures. In this situation, it is most common for the entity to continue to hold the investment to maturity, as the risk of loss is typically low. As long as a commercial paper issuer is top-rated and a local unit's finance officer closely monitors its ratings, the risk for this type of investment is small. Officials should understand, however, that eligible commercial paper issued by banks is not a deposit and, consequently, is not covered by insurance and collateralization.

5. **Bankers' acceptances issued by North Carolina banks or by any top-rated United States bank**

Bankers' acceptances are bills of exchange or time drafts that are drawn on and guaranteed by banks. They are usually issued to finance international trade or a firm's short-term credit needs and usually are secured by the credit of the issuing firm as well as by the general credit of the accepting bank. Most bankers' acceptances have maturity terms of 30 to 180 days. Local units may invest in bankers' acceptances issued by any North Carolina bank. Only the largest banks in the state issue them, and they are not as common as they once were. For a local government to invest in bankers' acceptances of a non–North Carolina U.S. bank, the institution must have outstanding publicly held obligations that carry the highest long-term credit rating from at least one national rating organization. If the bank's credit obligations are rated by more than one national organization, the bank must receive the highest rating given by each.

6. **Participating shares in the North Carolina Capital Management Trust (NCCMT)**

The NCCMT is a money market mutual fund established specifically for investments by North Carolina local governments and public authorities. It is certified and regulated by the LGC, and unlike other state-sponsored investment pools for public entity investments, it is registered with the U.S. Securities and Exchange Commission, which imposes extensive requirements on the fund to ensure the safety of moneys invested. The NCCMT currently manages the Government Portfolio, which was started in 1982 and is intended for the investment of operating cash balances and debt proceeds. The principal value of moneys invested in a share in this portfolio remains fixed at $1. Funds invested in the NCCMT may be withdrawn on the same day of notice; however, the managers of the portfolios do request that local governments provide one day's advance notice if large withdrawals will be made. The Government Portfolio may invest only in U.S. Treasury securities and U.S. government agency securities which are authorized under G.S. 159-30(c). The Government Portfolio maintains "AAA" ratings from Moody's and Standard & Poor's.

7. **Repurchase agreements**

A repurchase agreement is a purchase by an investor of a security with the stipulation that the seller will buy it back at the original purchase price plus agreed-upon interest at the maturity date. These agreements were once popular for short-term or overnight investments by North Carolina local governments. Unfortunately, some local governments in other states suffered substantial losses by buying repurchase agreements from unscrupulous securities dealers. As a result, strict laws and requirements for the safe use of these agreements have been enacted, both in North Carolina and across the country. G.S. 159-30(c) authorizes local units to invest in repurchase agreements but only under very limited conditions.[20] These conditions have greatly reduced the cost-effectiveness of local government investments in these instruments.

8. **Evidences of ownership of, or fractional undivided interests in, future principal and interest payments of stripped or zero-coupon instruments issued directly or guaranteed by the United States government**

These instruments were first authorized as a local government investment in 1987. They are sold at discount from face or par value and pay no interest until maturity. At maturity, the investor receives the face value, with the difference between that value and the discounted purchase price of the security representing the effective interest earned. Stripped or zero-coupon securities can be useful investment vehicles for certain limited moneys, such as those held in a capital reserve fund that will not be needed until after the instrument matures. However, because most "strips" or zero-coupon securities have long maturities, they are subject to considerable price

---

20. The following restrictions apply to local government investments in repurchase agreements: (1) the underlying security acquired with a repurchase agreement must be a direct obligation of the United States or fully guaranteed by the United States; (2) the repurchase agreement must be sold by a broker or a dealer recognized as a primary dealer by a Federal Reserve Bank or by a commercial bank, a trust company, or a national bank whose deposits are insured by the Federal Deposit Insurance Corporation (FDIC); (3) the security underlying the agreement must be delivered in physical or in electronic book-entry form to the local unit or its third-party agent; (4) the value of the underlying security must be determined daily and must be maintained, at least, at 100 percent of the repurchase price; (5) the local unit must have a valid and perfected first security interest in the underlying security (this can be achieved through delivery of the security to the local unit or its third-party safekeeping agent under a written agreement); (6) the underlying security acquired in the repurchase agreement must be free of any lien or third-party claim.

fluctuations before maturity and should not be used for the investment of general county funds. If investments are made in these securities and market interest rates later rise substantially, a county that has to cash in the investment before maturity may lose a significant portion of the principal invested in the securities.

9. **Certain mutual funds for moneys held by either a county or a municipality that are subject to the arbitrage and rebate provisions of the Internal Revenue Code**

The LGBFCA authorizes unspent proceeds from bonds or other financings subject to the Internal Revenue Code's arbitrage and rebate provisions to be invested, under strict procedures, in tax-exempt and taxable mutual funds. Operating moneys and proceeds from financings that are not subject to the arbitrage and rebate provisions may not be invested in these mutual funds. Because of the complexity of the federal tax code and the wide variety of available mutual funds, a local government entity should consult with its bond counsel before placing moneys in this type of investment.

10. **Derivatives issued directly by one of the federal agencies listed in G.S. 159-30(c)(2) or guaranteed by the United States government**

Derivatives are not specifically mentioned in the law, but they may be eligible investments if they are otherwise authorized in G.S. 159-30(c). The term *derivatives* refers to a broad range of investment securities that can vary in market price, yield, and/or cash flow depending on the value of the underlying securities or assets or changes in one or more interest-rate indices. Derivatives commonly include mortgage pass-through instruments issued by federal agencies, mortgage obligations guaranteed by federal agencies (but not by the U.S. government), callable step-up notes, floaters, inverse floaters, and still other securities that go by even more interesting names. It is beyond the scope of this chapter to explain these different types of derivatives. It suffices to say that derivatives are generally complex instruments, and many of them are subject to rapid and major changes in value as market interest rates change. Some local governments in other states have lost vast amounts of moneys by investing in derivatives. The volume of derivatives available to investors has grown dramatically, and investment brokers and dealers often try to sell various types of derivatives to county, municipal, and other local government finance officers. Many derivatives are not legal investment instruments for North Carolina local governments. Those that are direct debt (i.e., a balance-sheet liability) of the federal agencies listed in G.S. 159-30(c)(2) or guaranteed by the U.S. government are usually legal investments. However, many if not most of them are inappropriate as investment vehicles for counties or municipalities except in very special circumstances. Even though legal, many of them are subject to extreme price and cash flow volatility. A finance officer considering investing the local unit's moneys in one or more derivatives should do so only pursuant to a governing board investment policy that explicitly authorizes such an investment, only if the finance officer understands the nature of the security and the risks associated with it, and only for a short maturity.

Custody of Investment Securities

The LGBFCA requires that "[s]ecurities and deposit certificates shall be in the custody of the finance officer [of a local government unit] who shall be responsible for their safekeeping."[21] Investment securities come in two forms: certificated and noncertificated. Ownership of certificated investments is represented by an actual physical security. Some CDs and certain other securities are issued in certificated form. To obtain proper custody of certificated securities, a finance officer should hold the securities or the certificates in the local unit's vault or its safe deposit box at a local bank or trust company. Alternatively, certificated securities may be delivered to and held by the local government's third-party safekeeping agent, which can be the trust department of a North Carolina bank.

Many investment securities—U.S. Treasury bills, notes, and bonds; federal agency instruments; some commercial paper; and other types of securities—are not certificated. Ownership of them is evidenced by electronic book-entry records maintained by the Federal Reserve System for banks and certain other financial institutions and by the financial institutions themselves. In addition, for certain other securities, the Depository Trust Co. in New York maintains the electronic records of ownership. When a local unit buys noncertificated securities from a bank or a securities dealer, the record of ownership is transferred electronically from the seller or the seller's bank to the local government's custodial agent. To obtain proper custody of book-entry securities, a local government should have a signed custodial agreement in place with the financial institution that serves as its custodial agent. The financial institution agent should be a member of the Federal Reserve System authorized to conduct trust business in North Carolina. Local units may not use securities brokers and dealers or the operating divisions of banks and savings institutions as custodial agents for their investment securities. Generally, the trust department of a bank or financial institution that sells securities to a local unit may act as the custodial agent for the securities as long as the trust department itself did not sell the securities to the local government and provided that the institution is licensed to do trust business in North Carolina and is a member of the Federal Reserve. It is essential that a local unit or its applicable custodial agent obtain custody of all investments. Major losses from investments suffered by local governments in other states have been due to the failure of those governments to obtain proper custody of their investments.

Distribution of Investment Proceeds

Interest earned by a local government unit on deposits and investments must be credited to the fund in which cash is deposited or invested.[22] This is true even if moneys from different funds are pooled for investment purposes. In that case, a prorated share of the investment income must be allocated to each fund from which the moneys derived.

---

21. G.S. 159-30(d).
22. G.S. 159-30(e).

Finance Officer Responsible for Investments

A local unit's finance officer is statutorily charged with managing the unit's investments.[23] In conducting an investment program, a finance officer must forecast cash resources and needs, thus determining how much is available for investment and for how long. A finance officer also must investigate what types of investment securities are authorized by law and by the unit's internal investment policies and decide which ones to purchase. If an investment security is to be sold before maturity, the finance officer must make that decision.

A governing board, however, should establish general investment policies and restrictions for its finance officer to follow. Such board-adopted policies could, for example, limit the maximum maturities for investments of general fund moneys; require the use of informal competitive bidding for the purchase of securities; authorize the finance officer to invest in the cash and/ or term portfolios of the North Carolina Capital Management Trust (discussed above); and make clear that safety and liquidity should take precedence over yield in the county's or the municipality's investment program. A growing number of local governing boards are adopting such investment policies.

Guidelines for Investing Public Funds

Because of great changes and technological innovation in financial markets and challenges presented to these markets by international events as well as by the availability of many new types of investment instruments, the investment and general management of public moneys have become very complex. North Carolina local governments can avoid many of the problems that have harmed local governments in other states by adhering to the following guidelines in conducting their investment programs.

1. **An investment program should put safety and liquidity before yield.**

   A local unit should not put its investment funds at risk of loss in the interest of obtaining higher investment earnings. The temptation to sacrifice safety for yield is particularly great when interest rates are falling and local government officials are attempting to maintain investment earnings and revenues. Any local unit should always have funds available to meet payment obligations as they come due. This requires maintaining adequate liquidity in an investment portfolio and limiting most investments to securities with short-term maturities.

2. **A local government entity should invest only in securities that its finance officer understands.**

   Many investment vehicles, including most derivatives, are extremely complex. Before purchasing a security, a finance officer should thoroughly understand all of its components—especially how its value is likely to increase or decrease with changes in market interest rates. A finance officer who is considering investing in a type of security that has not been used before should obtain and study the prospectus or equivalent information for the security and talk to LGC staff and other informed, disinterested parties about the nature and risks of that security.

---

23. *See* G.S. 159-30(a), -25(a).

3. **A finance officer and other officials involved in investing a local government entity's funds should know the financial institutions, the brokers, and the dealers from which the government buys investment securities.**

   Investment transactions are made by phone, and investment funds and securities are often electronically transferred in seconds. Funds and securities can easily be lost or "misplaced" in such an environment. To protect the local government, officials conducting the investment program must be sure that they deal only with reputable and reliable institutions, brokers, and dealers. In fact, the authoritative literature that establishes generally accepted accounting principles (GAAP) also refers to the importance of knowing one's brokers or dealers. A finance officer should obtain a list of the North Carolina local government clients of any firm or person attempting to sell investment securities and obtain references from these officials. The finance officer should also obtain and evaluate current financial statements from any institution, broker, or dealer that sells or wishes to sell securities to the local government entity. Local governments in other states have lost invested funds because they placed moneys with firms that later went bankrupt and were unable to return the funds. A county should also enter into an investment trading agreement with any firm or person from which it buys investments. Model investment trading agreements are used by and are available from several of North Carolina's large counties.

4. **A county's or municipality's finance officer should ensure that the local unit adequately insures or collateralizes all investments in CDs (as well as other deposits in banks) and that it has proper custody of all investment securities.**

   Insurance and collateralization must be in accordance with statutory requirements.

5. **A local government's investment program should be conducted pursuant to the cash management and investment policy approved by its governing board.**

   Such a policy should be based on G.S. 159-30 and related statutes. It should set forth the governing board's directions and expectations about which investments will be made and how they will be made and should establish general parameters for the receipt, disbursement, and management of moneys.

6. **A local government finance officer should report periodically to the governing board on the status of the unit's investment program.**

   Such a report should be made at least semiannually—preferably quarterly or monthly—and should show the securities in the local government's investment portfolio, the terms or maturities of those investments, and their yields. If possible, average investment maturity and yield also should be calculated and shown in this report.

7. **A local government should understand that the use of investment managers does not relieve its finance officer of the responsibility of safeguarding public funds.**

   A few counties and municipalities in North Carolina have considered the engagement of outside professional investment managers to administer their routine investment functions. Obviously, there are advantages and disadvantages to this arrangement. The most obvious disadvantage is the inability of a county/municipal finance officer to have direct control of investments even though he or she has responsibility for them. Also, because of legal restrictions on the types of investments local governments can make, the return an investment manager can earn for the unit after management fees have been deducted may be lower than the return the unit can earn on its own. It also should be noted that local legislation may be required in order for an entity to engage an outside investment manager. If it is determined that an outside investment manager would be beneficial, a written agreement should be executed outlining permissible investments, safekeeping arrangements, diversification requirements, maturity limitations, the liability to be assumed by both parties, and the fees of the contract.

Obligating and Disbursing Public Funds

Article V, Section 7(2) of the North Carolina Constitution provides that "[n]o money shall be drawn from the treasury of any county, city or town, or other unit of local government except by authority of law." The LGBFCA establishes the requirements regarding disbursement of public funds. Through both the budget ordinance and project ordinances, a governing board authorizes a local unit to undertake programs or projects and to spend moneys.[24] G.S. 159-8 directs that no local unit "may expend any moneys . . . except in accordance with a budget ordinance or project ordinance." The proper functioning of the budgeting process depends on adherence to the terms of the budget ordinance and any project ordinances. For example, budget and project ordinances are required by law to be balanced. If a unit complies with these directives, deficit spending should not occur and the board's policies and priorities will be carried out.

The principal legal mechanisms for ensuring a local unit's compliance with the budget ordinance and each project ordinance are the *preaudit* and *disbursement* processes prescribed by the LGBFCA. Both processes are set forth in G.S. 159-28. The statute also specifies the forms of payment that a local unit may use to satisfy its obligations.

Preaudit Requirement

G.S. 159-28(a), (a1), and (a2), collectively referred to as the preaudit requirement, state as follows:

(a) Incurring Obligations.—No obligation may be incurred in a program, function, or activity accounted for in a fund included in the budget ordinance unless the budget ordinance includes an appropriation authorizing the obligation and an unencumbered balance remains in the appropriation sufficient to pay in the current fiscal year the sums obligated by the transaction for the current fiscal year. No obligation may be incurred for a capital project or a grant project authorized by a project ordinance unless that project ordinance includes an appropriation authorizing the obligation and an unencumbered balance remains in the appropriation sufficient to pay the sums obligated by the transaction. Nothing in this section shall require a contract to be reduced to writing.

---

24. For information on the annual budget ordinance and project ordinances, see Chapter 3, "Budgeting for Operating and Capital Expenditures."

(a1) *Preaudit Requirement.*—If an obligation is reduced to a written contract or written agreement requiring the payment of money, or is evidenced by a written purchase order for supplies and materials, the written contract, agreement, or purchase order shall include on its face a certificate stating that the instrument has been preaudited to assure compliance with subsection (a) of this section. The certificate, which shall be signed by the finance officer, or any deputy finance officer approved for this purpose by the governing board, shall take substantially the following form:

> "This instrument has been preaudited in the manner required by the Local Government Budget and Fiscal Control Act.
>
> _____
>
> (Signature of finance officer [or deputy finance officer])."

(a2) *Failure to Preaudit.*—An obligation incurred in violation of subsection (a) or (a1) of this section is invalid and may not be enforced. The finance officer shall establish procedures to assure compliance with this section, in accordance with any rules adopted by the Local Government Commission.

To fully understand the preaudit requirement, it is helpful to break the analysis down into three parts—(1) determining when the statutory provisions apply, (2) determining what the statute requires, and (3) determining what happens if the requirements are not met.

When Does G.S. 159-28(a) Apply?

G.S. 159-28(a) applies when a local unit incurs an obligation that is accounted for in the budget ordinance or in a project ordinance. An obligation is incurred when a unit commits itself to pay money to another entity. Examples include placing orders for supplies and equipment, entering into contracts for services, and even hiring an employee. There is no minimum threshold amount to trigger the requirement. If a contract, purchase order, or other agreement commits the unit to an expenditure of any amount of money, an obligation is incurred. It also does not matter if the liability is uncertain.[25] An obligation is incurred, for example, when a unit engages a law firm and agrees to pay an hourly fee for work that will be performed during the fiscal year, even though the total number of hours likely will not be known at the outset of the agreement. The form of the obligation also is irrelevant. A local unit may incur an obligation by executing a construction contract, issuing an electronic purchase order for goods, or verbally committing to pay a salary to a newly hired at-will employee.

---

25. *See, e.g.,* Transp. Servs. of N.C., Inc. v. Wake Cnty. Bd. of Educ., 198 N.C. App. 590 (2009) (holding that contract in which school board agreed to compensate transportation services provider for services on per-student-assigned basis was subject to preaudit requirement under analogous provision to G.S. 159-28); Watauga Cnty. Bd. of Educ. v. Town of Boone, 106 N.C. App. 270 (1992) (declaring that resolution passed by town requiring that 18 percent of profits of town's ABC store be given to school system was subject to preaudit requirement).

Specific Performance Obligations

A preaudit is not required, however, if a unit enters into a contract or agreement that does not commit the unit to pay money. An example is an agreement by a municipality to provide water to a commercial entity located outside its borders. Such a contract commits the unit to perform a specific task; it does not, however, commit the unit to pay money. This type of arrangement is often referred to as a contract for specific performance, and it does not trigger the preaudit requirement.[26]

Continuing (Multi-Year) Contracts

What about continuing contracts—contracts that extend for more than one fiscal year? Whether or not the preaudit is triggered depends in part on whether the appropriation authorizing the obligation is accounted for in the annual budget ordinance or in a project ordinance.

Annual Budget Ordinance Appropriations

If the appropriation authorizing the obligation is accounted for in the budget ordinance and it is certain that the unit will have to expend money under the contract in the fiscal year in which it is entered into, an obligation is incurred for purposes of G.S. 159-28(a). If, however, a local unit does not expect to expend money in the current fiscal year, or if it is certain that the unit will not have to expend money in the current fiscal year, things get a little murkier. There are a couple of North Carolina Court of Appeals cases suggesting that if there is a good chance that no resources will be expended in the year in which the contract or agreement is entered into, then a preaudit is not needed. In *Myers v. Town of Plymouth*,[27] the town entered into an employment contract with the town manager in March 1997 (fiscal year 1996–97), whereby the manager agreed to work for the town for four years. Both the town and the manager reserved the right to terminate the employment relationship with thirty days' notice. The contract provided the manager with a severance package if he was terminated by the town for any reason except felonious criminal conduct or a failure of performance that the manager failed to rectify after appropriate notice. The following December (fiscal year 1997–98) a new town council was seated, and within a few months the new council terminated the manager and refused to pay the severance package. The manager sued. Among other defenses, the town argued that the employment contract was void because it lacked a preaudit certificate (one of the requirements of G.S. 159-28(a)). The court disagreed, holding that no preaudit was needed because it was highly improbable that the town would have been required to pay the severance package in the

---

26. *Compare* Lee v. Wake Cnty., 165 N.C. App. 154 (2004) (holding that an agreement to enter into a formal settlement agreement did not require a preaudit because it was "an action for specific performance, not for the payment of money"), *and* Moss v. Town of Kernersville, 150 N.C. App. 713 (2002) (holding that a consent agreement, whereby the town agreed to make certain repairs to a dam, did not require a preaudit certificate because it was a contract for specific performance, not a contract requiring the payment of money), *with* Cabarrus Cnty. v. Systel Bus. Equip. Co., 171 N.C. App. 423 (2005) (holding that the settlement agreement at issue, which required the county to pay a specified amount of money, required a preaudit).

27. 135 N.C. App. 707 (1999); *see also* M Series Rebuild, LLC v. Town of Mount Pleasant, 222 N.C. App. 59, *review denied,* 366 N.C. 413 (2012) (noting that a preaudit was required of a "contract and obligation to pay [that were] both created in the same fiscal year."); Davis v. City of Greensboro, 770 F.3d 278 (4th Cir. 2014) (holding that a preaudit certificate was not required on law enforcement and firefighter longevity pay contracts, where no payments came due during the fiscal year in which the contracts were entered into).

fiscal year in which the contract was signed. (And, in fact, the town was not required to pay the severance package in the fiscal year in which the contract was signed.)

It is not entirely clear how broadly to read *Myers*. The holding may be limited to the unique factual scenario presented by this one case. Even if it is meant to be applied more broadly, the holding leaves many unanswered questions. For example, it is not clear how low the probability or possibility of incurring an obligation in the current fiscal year must be for the preaudit requirement not to apply. Given this ambiguity, it may be safer for a unit to comply with G.S. 159-28(a) if there is any chance it will have to expend funds under a contract, agreement, or purchase order in the current fiscal year.

If a preaudit is required for a multi-year contract, the finance officer or deputy finance officer of a local unit will only be attesting that there is a budget appropriation for the amount expected to come due in the current fiscal year. The unit is not required to re-preaudit the contract in future fiscal years. However, G.S. 159-13 generally requires a governing board to appropriate sufficient moneys each year to cover the amounts due that year under continuing contracts.

Project Ordinance Appropriations

If an appropriation authorizing an obligation is accounted for in a capital- or grant-project ordinance, the preaudit is triggered regardless of whether any amounts are expected to come due in the fiscal year in which the obligation is incurred. A project ordinance is effective for the life of the project. It does not expire at the end of each fiscal year.[28] The preaudit will be for the full amount of the obligation.

Electronic Transactions

Finally, what about when a unit places an Internet order for park equipment and pays for the equipment with a credit card? Or when a unit makes a p-card (purchase card) purchase from a local vendor for water treatment chemicals? Or when an ambulance crew member uses a fuel card at a local gas station? Do electronic payment transactions such as these require a preaudit?

A preaudit is required if

1. a unit enters into a contract or agreement or places an order for goods or services that are accounted for in the budget ordinance or a project ordinance *and*

2. the unit is obligated to pay money by the terms of the contract/agreement/order *and*

3. if the obligation is accounted for in the annual budget ordinance, the unit anticipates paying at least some of the money in the fiscal year in which the contract/agreement/order is entered into.

The answer is "yes"; the preaudit requirements do apply to these transactions. An obligation is incurred for purposes of the preaudit statute in a credit card transaction when a unit uses the credit card, p-card, or fuel card to pay for goods or services. That is when the unit is authorizing the issuing company to pay the vendor or contracting party and thereby committing the unit to

---

28. *See* G.S. 159-13.2.

pay money (to the issuing company) to cover the costs of the expenditure. When the General Assembly authorized local units to make "electronic payments" (defined as payment by charge card, credit card, debit card, or by electronic funds transfer), it specified that each electronic payment "shall be subject to the preaudit process. . . . "[29] As discussed below, a local unit must comply with any rules adopted by the Local Government Commission (LGC) in executing electronic payments.[30]

The text box above summarizes when the preaudit is triggered.

What Does G.S. 159-28(a) Require?

Before a local unit incurs an obligation subject to the preaudit, its finance officer (or a deputy finance officer approved by the unit's governing board for this purpose) must take the following actions.

1. *Ensure that there is a budget or a project ordinance appropriation authorizing the obligation.* This typically is not much of a hurdle because the budget ordinance and project ordinances often are adopted at a very general level of legal control. In fact, units are authorized to make budget appropriations only by department, function, or project.[31] (A preaudit is not performed on line-item appropriations in the unit's "working budget.")

2. *Ensure that sufficient funds will remain in the appropriation to pay the amounts that are expected to come due.* If the obligation is accounted for in the annual budget ordinance, the appropriation need cover only the amount that is expected to come due in the current fiscal year. However, if the obligation is accounted for in a project ordinance, the appropriation must be for the full amount due under the contract.

3. *If the order, contract, or agreement is in writing, affix and sign a preaudit certificate to the "writing."* If the order, contract, or agreement is not in writing—such as a telephone order or other verbal agreement—a preaudit certificate is not required.[32] In addition, as discussed below, a few types of transactions may be exempt from the preaudit certificate requirement even if they are in writing.

---

29. G.S. 159-28(d2).

30. The LGC rules ensure that the local unit properly performs the preaudit process before undertaking an electronic transaction.

31. For more information on the budgeting process, see Chapter 3, "Budgeting for Operating and Capital Expenditures."

32. Note, however, that other provisions of law may require a particular contract or agreement to be in writing. For example, all contracts entered into by a municipality must be in writing, though the governing board of the municipality may ratify a contract that violates this provision. G.S. 160A-16. All contracts involving the sale of "goods" for the price of $500 or more must be in writing. G.S. 25-2-201. And contracts for purchases and construction or repair subject to formal bidding requirements must be in writing. G.S. 143-129(c).

Complying with Preaudit Requirement

The statute envisions that all of these steps be performed before the obligation is incurred—that is, before the goods are ordered or before the contract is executed. It is not sufficient to perform the preaudit process after a contract is executed.[33] As numerous finance officers have attested, though, complying with these requirements can be very difficult.

G.S. 159-28 directs a unit's finance officer to "establish procedures to assure compliance" with the statute. Thus, a finance officer has a great deal of flexibility to design ordering and contracting processes that comply with the statute (or at least come close). The processes likely will vary depending on the size of the unit, the number of personnel, and the various needs of the departments within the unit.

One important tool that often is overlooked by units is statutory authority for the governing board to appoint one or more deputy finance officers to perform the preaudit process.[34] To the extent that individual departments in a unit need to order goods or enter into service contracts, the governing board can appoint one or more department heads (or other department employees) as deputy finance officers. The deputy finance officers then would be authorized to enter into obligations consistent with their department budget appropriations.

Even if all ordering/contracting is centralized within a unit's finance office, it may be impossible for the finance officer to actually perform the preaudit process for each obligation. Again, the governing board could appoint other finance office employees as deputy finance officers to perform the preaudit. The finance officer also could delegate the ministerial job of performing the preaudit process, including affixing the finance officer's signature to the preaudit certificate. Under the latter approach, though, it is important that the finance officer trust that the preaudit process will be performed properly because the finance officer could be held liable for any statutory violations.

Exemptions from Preaudit Certificate Requirement

Recognizing these practical difficulties, the legislature has exempted certain transactions from the preaudit certificate requirement, even if the order, contract, or agreement is in writing. There are three categories of exempt transactions. The first two apply automatically. The third applies only if the LGC adopts certain rules and the local unit follows those rules. The fourth applies only if the LGC certifies that a local government's accounting system meets statutory requirements. (It is worth emphasizing that all of these exemptions apply only to the preaudit certificate requirement. A unit still must perform the other preaudit steps before incurring an obligation pursuant to one or more of the exempt transactions.)

Exemption 1: Any obligation or document that has been approved by the LGC.[35]

This exemption from the preaudit certificate requirement applies to loan agreements, debt issuances, and other leases and financial transactions that are subject to LGC

---

33. A trial court judge invalidated an interlocal agreement between a city and a county because the preaudit certificate had been affixed to the contract after the contract was executed (that is, after it was signed by both parties). *See* Jon Hawley, "Judge Voids Water Contract," *DailyAdvance.com*, April 12, 2016.

34. *See* G.S. 159-28(a1).

35. G.S. 159-28(f)(1).

approval and have, in fact, been so approved.[36] It also likely applies to audit contracts, which must be approved by the LGC pursuant to G.S. 159-34.

Exemption 2: Payroll expenditures, including all benefits for employees of the local unit.[37]

This exemption ensures that salary and benefit changes for current employees, even if in writing, do not need to include a preaudit certificate.

Exemption 3: Electronic payments, defined as payments made by charge card, credit card, debit card, gas card, or procurement card.[38]

Electronic payments often are the most difficult to preaudit. The point of transaction often occurs off-site or on the vendor's proprietary software. A local unit, therefore, is not easily able to include a signed preaudit certificate. This exemption eliminates the problem. It only applies, however, if the local unit follows the rules adopted by the LGC. The LGC rules are considered a safe harbor. In other words, the law presumes compliance with the statutory preaudit requirements if a finance officer or deputy finance officer follows the LGC rules. The rules must ensure that a local unit properly performs the other steps in the preaudit process before undertaking an electronic transaction.[39]

The LGC rules are part of the North Carolina Administrative Code (Title 20, Chapter 03, Section .0409). These rules require the following:

Resolution

A local unit's governing board must adopt a resolution authorizing the unit to engage in electronic transactions. That resolution authorizes the unit's employees and officials to use p-cards, credit cards, and/or fuel cards, and it either incorporates (by reference) the unit's written policies related to the use of those cards or authorizes the finance officer to prepare those policies.

Encumbrance System

State law requires that certain local units that meet certain population thresholds (municipalities with a population over 10,000 and counties with a population over 50,000) incorporate encumbrance systems into their accounting systems. In order to comply with the new LGC regulations, all units will need to implement encumbrance systems. For units under the population thresholds listed above, the encumbrance system does not have to be incorporated into the unit's accounting system. In fact, for small units, it can be as simple as tracking expenditures against budget appropriations in a spreadsheet or even on index cards. To facilitate individual transactions, though, a unit might want to create a shared electronic document that can be accessed by anyone authorized to make purchases.

---

36. To determine the types of contracts that are subject to LGC approval, see Kara Millonzi, "Local Government Commission (LGC) Approval of Bonds, Installment Financings, Leases, and Other Contracts Involving Capital Assets (Including Recent Changes Related to Local Governments on the Unit Assistance List)," *Coates' Canons: NC Local Government Law* blog (Oct. 28, 2022).

37. G.S. 159-28(f)(2).

38. G.S. 159-28(f)(3).

39. G.S. 159-28(d2).

Policies and Procedures

A local unit's governing board or finance officer must adopt written policies that outline the unit's procedures for using p-cards, credit cards, and/or fuel cards. At a minimum, the policies need to provide a process to ensure that *before each transaction is made*, the individual making the transaction

1. ensures that there is an appropriate budget ordinance or project/grant ordinance appropriation authorizing the obligation (for school units, the reference should be to the budget resolution);
2. ensures that sufficient moneys remain in the appropriation to cover the amount expected to be paid out in the current fiscal year (if the expenditure is accounted for in the budget ordinance/resolution) or the entire amount (if the expenditure is accounted for in a project/grant ordinance);
3. records the amount of the transaction in the unit's encumbrance system or reports the amount to another individual (either within the individual's department or within the finance department) to encumber; as stated above, in order to comply with this requirement, each unit must have an encumbrance system.

In addition to these requirements, a unit's p-card, credit card, and/or fuel card policies should address who has custody of the cards, who has access to the cards, what dollar limits are placed on the cards and individual transactions, what expenditure category limits are placed on the cards, and how transactions must be documented for reconciliation with the monthly bills. They should also state the consequences for failure to comply with these policies. The local unit's finance officer is responsible for overseeing all electronic payments, and the policies must build in sufficient controls to allow the finance officer to carry out his or her duties.

Policies will vary significantly by local unit and by type of transaction. They need to address all the different ways in which p-card, credit card, or fuel card transactions may occur and be detailed enough to inform individual employees and officials of the exact steps they must take (and how to take them) before initiating a p-card, credit card, or fuel card transaction. At the same time, they need to be flexible enough to allow local officials to carry out their day-to-day responsibilities effectively. Finance officers may be well advised to consult with department heads and others in their units and formulate policies that track existing business practices as much as possible.

These new rules do not supplant the preaudit process in its entirety. They merely provide a workable alternative to affixing the preaudit certificate to an electronic payment. And these policies, alone, may not provide sufficient internal controls. Finance officers are well advised to implement additional controls in areas where misappropriations are more likely to occur.

Training

Once the policies are enacted, the local unit must provide training to all personnel about the policies and procedures to be followed before using a p-card, credit card, or fuel card. Training should be repeated at regular intervals and presented to all new employees and officials early in their tenures. And the local unit's governing board needs to set an expectation of full compliance with the preaudit policies by all employees and officials.

Quarterly Reports

A local unit's staff must prepare and present to the unit's governing board a budget-to-actual statement by fund at least quarterly. The statement needs to include budgeted accounts, actual payments made, amounts encumbered, and the amount of the budget that is unobligated. It is incumbent on the board to gain sufficient training on how to properly interpret these reports in order to carry out the board's fiduciary responsibility to the unit.

If a local government unit uses p-cards, credit cards, and/or fuel cards it must follow the new regulations. The reason is that it is impossible to affix the signed preaudit certificate to p-card, credit card, or fuel card transactions. It is not sufficient to perform the preaudit after the transaction is completed. Because a transaction is void if the preaudit is not followed, a local unit will need to follow the new rules to come into legal compliance.

Exemption 4: Automated accounting system.

A local unit may perform its preaudit process using an automated accounting system.[40] The system must do all of the following:

1. embed functionality that determines that there is an appropriation to the department, function code, or project in which the transaction appropriately falls;
2. ensure that unencumbered funds remain in the appropriation to pay out any amounts that are expected to come due during the budgeting period; and
3. provide real-time visibility to budget compliance, alert threshold notifications, and rules-based compliance measures and enforcement.[41]

If a local unit's accounting system performs these functions, the unit is not required to include a signed preaudit certificate on any contract, agreement, purchase order, or other writing evidencing a transaction subject to the preaudit requirement. Within thirty days of the start of each fiscal year, a local unit's finance officer must certify to the LGC that the unit's accounting system meets these requirements.[42] The LGC's Secretary may reject or revoke the finance officer's certification if the prior year's annual audit includes a finding of budgetary noncompliance or if the LGC's Secretary determines that the automated financial computer system fails to meet the statutory requirements.[43]

It is worth emphasizing that all of these exemptions apply only to the preaudit certificate requirement. A unit still must perform the other preaudit steps before incurring an obligation pursuant to one or more of the exempt transactions.

What Happens if a Unit Does Not Comply with the Preaudit Requirements?

As the statute makes clear, failure to perform any of the applicable preaudit requirements makes a contract, agreement, or purchase order connected with a local government transaction void.[44] That is the equivalent of saying that it was never entered into to begin with. It does not matter

---

40. G.S. 159-28(a3).
41. G.S. 159-28(a3).
42. G.S. 159-28(a4). The certification form is available from the N.C. Department of State Treasurer.
43. G.S. 159-28(a4).
44. *See, e.g.,* L&S Leasing, Inc. v. City of Winston-Salem, 122 N.C. App. 619 (1996); Cincinnati Thermal Spray, Inc. v. Pender Cnty., 101 N.C. App. 405 (1991).

if either or both parties have performed under the contract. The court of appeals has further held that parties may not recover against government entities under a theory of estoppel when a contract is deemed invalid for lack of compliance with the preaudit requirements.[45]

The statute also provides that if "an officer or employee [of a local unit] incurs an obligation or pays out or causes to be paid out any funds in violation of [the preaudit statute], he [or she] and the sureties on his [or her] official bond are liable for any sums so committed or disbursed."[46] This means that if any officer or employee orders goods or enters into a contract or agreement subject to a preaudit before the process is completed, he or she could be held personally liable by the unit's governing board for the amounts obligated, even if the unit never actually incurs the expense.

If a finance officer or a deputy finance officer gives a false certificate, he or she also may be held liable for the sums illegally committed or disbursed. It is a Class 3 misdemeanor, and may result in forfeiture of office, if a finance officer, or a deputy finance officer, knowingly gives a false certificate.[47]

Disbursement Requirement

When a unit receives an invoice, bill, or other claim, it must perform a disbursement process before making payment. Specifically, G.S. 159-28(b) requires that

> [w]hen a bill, invoice, or other claim against a local government or public authority is presented, the finance officer shall either approve or disapprove the necessary disbursement. If the claim involves a program, function, or activity accounted for in a fund included in the budget ordinance or a capital project or a grant project authorized by a project ordinance, the finance officer may approve the claim only if both of the following apply:
>
> (1) The finance officer determines the amount to be payable.
> (2) The budget ordinance or a project ordinance includes an appropriation authorizing the expenditure and either (i) an encumbrance has been previously created for the transaction or (ii) an unencumbered balance remains in the appropriation sufficient to pay the amount to be disbursed.
>
> The finance officer may approve a bill, invoice, or other claim requiring disbursement from an intragovernmental service fund or trust or agency fund not included in the budget ordinance, only if the amount claimed is determined to be payable.

---

45. *See, e.g.,* Transp. Servs. of N.C., Inc. v. Wake Cnty. Bd. of Educ., 198 N.C. App. 590 (refusing to allow claim against school based on estoppel in absence of valid contractual agreement because of lack of preaudit certificate); Finger v. Gaston Cnty., 178 N.C. App. 367 (2006) ("To permit a party to use estoppel to render a county contractually bound despite the absence of the [preaudit] certificate would effectively negate N.C. Gen. Stat. Sect. 159-28(a)."); Data Gen. Corp. v. Cnty. of Durham, 143 N.C. App. 97 (2001) ("[T]he preaudit certificate requirement is a matter of public record . . . and parties contracting with a county within this state are presumed to be aware of, and may not rely upon estoppel to circumvent, such requirements.").

46. G.S. 159-28(e). The governing board must "determine, by resolution, if payment from the official bond shall be sought and if the governing board will seek a judgment from the finance officer or duly appointed deputy finance officer for any deficiencies in the amount." *Id.*

47. G.S. 159-181.

A bill, invoice, or other claim may not be paid unless it has been approved by the finance officer or, under subsection (c) of this section, by the governing board. The finance officer shall establish procedures to assure compliance with this subsection, in accordance with any rules adopted by the Local Government Commission.

G.S. 159-28(d1) further provides,

Except as provided in this section, each check or draft on an official depository shall bear on its face a certificate signed by the finance officer or a deputy finance officer approved for this purpose by the governing board (or signed by the chairman or some other member of the board pursuant to subsection (c) of this section). The certificate shall take substantially the following form:

"This disbursement has been approved as required by the Local Government Budget and Fiscal Control Act.

_____

(Signature of finance officer)."

The disbursement requirement is often confused (or conflated) with the preaudit requirement. Although the processes appear similar, they are not interchangeable. G.S. 159-28 envisions that most obligations will be subject to both the preaudit and the disbursement process. The disbursement process occurs when a local unit actually disburses public funds, that is, when the unit pays for the goods or services. (By contrast, the preaudit process is triggered when the goods are ordered or a contract is entered into.)

Complying with the Disbursement Process

The law requires a local unit's finance officer (or a deputy finance officer designated by the unit's governing board for this purpose) to do the following before paying a bill, invoice, or other claim that is accounted for in the budget ordinance or in a project ordinance:

1. Verify that the amount is due and owing. If the amount claimed is not due and owing because, for example, the goods did not arrive or the services were not performed, then the finance officer or deputy finance officer may not authorize the disbursement. (Part of performing this process requires that the officer verify that the preaudit process was properly performed when the obligation was incurred. G.S. 159-181 makes it a Class 3 misdemeanor for any officer or employee to approve a claim or bill knowing it to be invalid.)[48]
2. Make sure that there is (still) an appropriation authorizing the expenditure.
3. Make sure that sufficient funds remain in the appropriation to pay the amount due. If there is no budget appropriation for the expenditure, or more commonly, if sufficient unencumbered funds do not remain in the appropriation, the finance officer or deputy finance officer may not authorize the disbursement. The governing board must first amend the budget (or project/grant) ordinance to make (or increase) the appropriation.

---

48. *See* G.S. 159-181. It could result also in forfeiture of office and a statutory fine.

4. Include a signed disbursement certificate on the face of the check or draft.[49] Note that the text of the disbursement certificate varies slightly from the text of the preaudit certificate. It states "This disbursement has been approved as required by the Local Government Budget and Fiscal Control Act." This is yet another reminder that these are two separate processes.

Exemptions from Disbursement Certificate Requirement

Certain transactions may be exempt from the disbursement certificate requirement. There are three categories of exempt transactions. The first two apply automatically. The third applies only if the LGC adopts certain rules and the local unit follows those rules.

1. **Any disbursement related to an obligation that has been approved by the LGC**

   This exemption from the disbursement certificate requirement applies to any payments related to loan agreements, debt issuances, and other leases and financial transactions that are subject to LGC approval and have, in fact, been so approved.[50] It also likely applies to audit contract payments.

2. **Any disbursement related to payroll or other employee benefits**

   This exemption applies to payroll checks or payroll direct deposits. It also exempts any payments related to employee benefits, whether disbursed to the employee directly or to another entity on behalf of an employee.

3. **Any disbursement done by electronic funds transfer, as long as the local unit follows rules adopted by the LGC**

   An electronic funds transfer is defined as "a transfer of funds initiated by using an electronic terminal, a telephone, a computer, or magnetic tape to instruct or authorize a financial institution or its agent to credit or debit an account."[51] A local unit is not easily able to include a signed disbursement certificate on its electronic funds transfers. This exemption would eliminate the problem. It only applies, however, if the local unit follows rules adopted by the LGC governing electronic payments. The rules must ensure that the unit's finance officer or a deputy finance officer has performed the other steps in the preaudit process before the transaction occurs. Following the LGC rules is considered a safe harbor. In other words, the law presumes compliance with the statutory disbursement requirements if a finance officer or deputy finance officer follows the LGC rules.

The LGC rules became effective on November 1, 2017, and are part of the North Carolina Administrative Code (Title 20, Chapter 03, Section .0410). They require the following:

Resolution

A local unit's governing board must adopt a resolution authorizing the unit to engage in electronic funds transfer, defined in G.S. 159-28(g) as "[a] transfer of funds initiated by using an electronic terminal, a telephone, a computer, or magnetic tape to instruct or authorize a

---

49. A disbursement certificate is not required for certain electronic funds transfers.
50. To determine the types of contracts that are subject to LGC approval, see Millonzi, note 36 above.
51. G.S. 159-28(d2).

financial institution or its agent to credit or debit an account." A common means of making an electronic funds transfer is through an ACH (automated clearinghouse) payment. ACH payments occur when a local government gives an originating institution, corporation, or other originator authorization to debit directly from the local unit's bank account for purposes of bill payment. The resolution should incorporate written policies for making electronic fund transfers or delegate the responsibility for creating such policies to the unit's finance officer.

Policies and Procedures

A local unit's governing board or finance officer must adopt written policies that outline the procedures for making electronic fund transfers to disburse public funds. At a minimum, the policies need to

1. ensure that the amount claimed is payable;
2. ensure that there is a budget ordinance or project/grant ordinance appropriation authorizing the expenditures;
3. ensure that sufficient moneys remain in the appropriation to cover the amount that is due to be paid out;
4. ensure that the unit has sufficient cash to cover the payment.

The first three steps mirror those laid out in the statute itself (G.S. 159-28(b)). The last step simply makes sure that the local unit does not "bounce a check," so to speak. There must be sufficient cash in the account to transfer out to cover the payment.

These exemptions apply only to the disbursement certificate requirement. A unit still must perform the other disbursement process steps before disbursing funds for (or by) one or more of the exempt transactions.

What Happens if a Unit Does Not Comply with the Disbursement Requirements?

As with the preaudit, "if an officer or employee . . . pays out or causes to be paid out any funds in violation [of G.S. 159-28], he and the sureties on his official bond are liable for any sums . . . so disbursed."[52] Moreover, if a finance officer or a deputy finance officer gives a false disbursement certificate, he or she also may be held liable for the sums illegally committed or disbursed. It is a Class 3 misdemeanor, and may result in forfeiture of office, if the officer knowingly gives a false certificate.[53]

Governing Board Override

If a local unit's finance officer or deputy finance officer disapproves a bill, invoice, or other claim, the unit's governing board may step in to approve payment.[54] The board may not approve payment, however, if there is not an appropriation in the budget ordinance or in a project ordinance or if sufficient funds do not remain in the appropriation to pay the amount due. The

---

52. G.S. 159-28(e). The governing board must "determine, by resolution, if payment from the official bond shall be sought and if the governing board will seek a judgment from the finance officer or duly appointed deputy finance officer for any deficiencies in the amount." *Id.*

53. G.S. 159-181.

54. *See* G.S. 159-28(c).

board must adopt a resolution approving the payment, which must be entered in the board's meeting minutes along with the names of the members voting in the affirmative. The board's chairperson, or designated member, may sign the disbursement certificate.

If the board approves payment and it results in a violation of law, each member of the board voting to allow payment is jointly and severally liable for the full amount of the check or draft.

Forms of Payment

G.S. 159-28(d) directs that all bills, invoices, salaries, or other claims be paid by check or draft on an official depository, bank wire transfer from an official depository, electronic payment or electronic funds transfer, or cash. Wire transfers are used, for example, to transmit the money periodically required for debt service on bonds or other debt to a paying agent, who in turn makes the payments to individual bondholders. Automated Clearing House (ACH) transactions are used by local governments to make retirement system contributions to the state, to make payroll payments, and to make certain other payments. The state has extended the use of the ACH system to most transfers of moneys between the state and local governments that are related to grant programs and state-shared revenues. A local unit may pay with cash only if its governing board has adopted an ordinance authorizing it as a payment option and specifying when it is allowed.[55]

Dual Signature Requirement on Disbursements

G.S. 159-25(b) requires each check or draft from a local unit to "be signed by the finance officer or a properly designated deputy finance officer and countersigned by another official . . . designated for this purpose by the [unit's] governing board." The finance officer's (or deputy finance officer's) signature attests to completion of review and accompanies the disbursement certificate described above. The second signature may be by the chair of the board of commissioners, the mayor of the municipality, the manager, or some other official. (If the governing board does not expressly designate the countersigner, G.S. 159-25(b) directs that for counties it should be the board chair or the chief executive officer (i.e., the manager, administrator, or director of the unit).)

The purpose of requiring two signatures is internal control. The law intends that the finance officer review the documentation of the claim before signing the certificate and check. The second person can independently review the documentation before signing and issuing the check. The fact that two persons must separately be satisfied with the documentation should significantly reduce opportunities for fraud.

In many local government entities, however, the second signer does not exercise this independent review, perhaps relying on other procedures for the desired internal control. Recognizing this, G.S. 159-25(b) permits a local unit's governing board to waive the two-signature requirement (thus requiring only the finance officer's signature or a properly designated deputy finance officer's signature on the check) "if the board determines that the internal control procedures of the unit or authority will be satisfactory in the absence of dual signatures."

---

55. G.S. 159-28(d)(4).

Electronic Signatures

As an alternative to manual signatures, G.S. 159-28.1 permits the use of signature machines, signature stamps, or similar devices for signing checks or drafts. In practice, these are widely used in local units all across North Carolina. To do so, a unit's governing board must approve the use of such signature devices through a formal resolution or ordinance, which should designate who is to have custody of the devices. For internal control purposes, it is essential that this equipment be properly secured. A unit's finance officer or another official given custody of the facsimile signature device(s) by the governing board is personally liable under the statute for illegal, improper, or unauthorized use of the device(s).

Local Internal Controls

As stated in the introduction to this chapter, the LGBFCA provides a minimum set of procedures that local units must follow in depositing, investing, obligating, and disbursing public funds. Local units also must establish additional internal controls to ensure proper management of these moneys.

One of the reasons that the LGBFCA need not provide for all aspects of accounting for and managing of cash and other assets is because it commits to the Local Government Commission (LGC) broad powers over these functions. G.S. 159-25(c) authorizes the LGC to issue "rules and regulations having the force of law governing procedures for the receipt, deposit, investment, transfer, and disbursement of money and other assets." Thus, if necessary, any gaps in the act can be filled by commission regulations. In addition, the same section authorizes the commission to look into the internal control procedures of particular units or authorities and to require any modifications to those procedures that it finds to be "necessary or desirable to prevent embezzlement or mishandling of public moneys."

Within a local unit, the finance officer is charged with supervising the receipt and deposit of money that belongs to the unit.[56] He or she prescribes the form and detail of the accounts for each officer or employee who collects money and may audit those accounts at any time.[57] The finance officer establishes the policies and procedures for carrying out the preaudit and disbursement processes.[58] In addition to the statutory duties, the finance officer also should devise and implement organizational plans and operating procedures to maintain adequate controls. For example, duties may be divided so that whoever collects cash does not record collections in the accounting system. Pre-numbered receipts may be used for collections. Employees handling public funds may be required to periodically rotate duties.

The above are just a few examples. What internal controls are sufficient will vary by unit and may change over time. Finance officers must continually evaluate and adjust to changing situations.[59]

---

56. G.S. 159-25(a)(4).
57. G.S. 159-32.
58. G.S. 159-28.
59. See Chapter 9, "Internal Control in Financial Management."

Governing Board Oversight

Finally, it is important to note that the governing board of a local unit plays a critical role in overseeing compliance with all financial laws and internal policies. In addition to the roles specifically assigned to it by the LGBFCA, such as adopting the budget; selecting the official depository or depositories; setting the amount of, and paying for, performance bonds; and hiring the independent auditor/receiving the audit report, the board is charged generally with the proper stewardship of public funds. The board must set the expectation that all employees and officials of the unit are to follow both statutory and other internal rules related to the collection, management, and disbursement of public funds. In some cases, the board may need to be more involved in developing internal control policies and practices and in compelling compliance by all employees or officials by instituting meaningful consequences for nonconformance. And, of course, proper board member training on how to read and interpret budgets, financial statements, audits, and other financial documents is essential to allow the board to carry out its fiduciary duty effectively.

Chapter 9

Internal Control in Financial Management

by Rebecca Badgett

Introduction

Local governments have a duty to be good stewards of public moneys and assets. To accomplish this, units must take measures to safeguard moneys and assets and ensure that they are used for authorized and lawful purposes. Chapter 8 discusses the statutory internal controls mandated by the Local Government Budget and Fiscal Control Act (LGBFCA) that relate to depositing, investing, obligating, and disbursing public funds. This chapter explores a step-by-step process that local units can use to design and implement a strong system of internal control over financial-management operations, recognizing that each internal control system should be uniquely tailored to each local unit's needs and capabilities.

Establishing a Framework of Internal Control

There are two widely accepted frameworks of internal control on which a local government may choose to base its internal control system. The first is the *Internal Control–Integrated Framework*, issued by the Committee of Sponsoring Organizations of the Treadway Commission (COSO). COSO is a voluntary organization dedicated to improving the quality of financial reporting and strengthening internal control in private-sector organizations. The second framework is the Government Accountability Office's *Standards for Internal Control in the Federal Government*, known as the "Green Book."[1] The Green Book is the legally

---

1. United States Government Accountability Office (GAO), *Standards for Internal Control in the Federal Government*, GAO 14-704G (September 2014) (hereinafter *Standards for Internal Control*).

required internal control framework for federal entities, but it may be adopted by other public-sector organizations, including state and local governments, quasi-governmental agencies, and not-for-profit organizations.[2]

The guidance and approach to internal control offered in the Green Book and in the COSO *Internal Control–Integrated Framework* are similar. Both frameworks structure the approach to internal control by using five key components that are supported by seventeen underlying principles. While either framework may form the basis of a local government's internal control system, this chapter summarizes the guidance stipulated in the Green Book because the Green Book model is intended for use by public-sector organizations, including local governments.

Internal Control Defined

The Green Book defines internal control as a "process effected by an entity's oversight body, management, and other personnel that provides reasonable assurance that the objectives of an entity will be achieved."[3] An entity's objectives should be classified under one or more of the following categories:

- Operations—Effectiveness and efficiency of operations
- Reporting—Reliability of reporting for internal and external use
- Compliance—Compliance with applicable laws and regulations[4]

This definition highlights a few key points. First, internal control is a process; it is not one event but is, rather, a series of actions that will prove to be most effective when operationalized into daily business operations. This process must be consistently monitored, evaluated, and updated to ensure that it is functioning at the optimal level. Second, even the strongest internal control system provides only *reasonable assurance* that a unit's objectives will be met. Absolute assurance is not possible due to the inherent limitations of internal control, such as unintentional mistakes and errors, management override of established controls, and external factors like natural disasters, cybersecurity breaches, a pandemic, or other events outside of a unit's control. Lastly, the underlying objective of internal control is to safeguard public moneys and assets from loss.[5] A local unit must design its control system to limit opportunities for fraud and must put controls in place that prevent or promptly detect mistakes, errors, and acts of fraud by employees.

---

2. *Standards for Internal Control*, at 20.
3. *Standards for Internal Control*, at 5.
4. *Standards for Internal Control*, at 5.
5. *Standards for Internal Control*, at 14.

Responsibility for Internal Control

The Green Book's definition of internal control places responsibility for internal control on "management" and the "oversight body." A third category, "personnel," includes employees who assist management with the implementation of controls and must report any functional issues to management.[6]

Management

Management is responsible for the design and implementation of a unit's internal control system. The term "management" generally includes persons in upper-management positions such as the senior finance officer(s), the county or municipal manager, department heads, and possibly the unit's attorney. Although the auditor may suggest changes to improve the effectiveness of established controls, the unit's auditor is not responsible for implementing internal controls and should not be included in the internal control "management" team.

Management should keep in mind that there is no one-size-fits-all approach to internal control. Every unit's internal control system should be tailored to meet the unique needs and capabilities of the unit. It is helpful to consider factors such as size, organizational structure, operating style, number of personnel, or other special circumstances that may impact the overall function of the control system. For example, in small units, the manager may play a key role in carrying out certain responsibilities that a manager in a larger unit is not expected to perform.[7] Small units also face certain challenges, such as having limited staff, which can make it difficult to ensure adequate segregation of duties.

Oversight Body

The oversight body is responsible for overseeing management's design and implementation of the unit's internal control system.[8] In local government, the elected governing board is by default the acting oversight body. The governing board may appoint a separate committee to act as the oversight body if the full board does not want to assume oversight responsibility. In such instances, the appointed oversight committee may include a mix of governing board members and senior management. In small units, the oversight body may need to take a more active role in the internal control process by helping management design effective controls or by compelling compliance by instituting and enforcing meaningful consequences for noncompliance.

---

6. *Standards for Internal Control*, at 12.

7. *Standards for Internal Control*, at 18

8. *Standards for Internal Control*, at 11.

Components of Internal Control

The Green Book approaches internal control through a hierarchical structure of five components and seventeen principles (see Figure 9.1). The five components of internal control are:

1. control environment,
2. risk assessment,
3. control activities,
4. information and communication, and
5. monitoring.

The seventeen principles explain the requirements necessary to implement the associated components. In general, every component and principle is necessary and should be operationalized to help establish the most effective internal control system.

1. Control Environment

The first component of the Green Book's internal control framework is control environment. This component serves as the foundation of the internal control system. It is sometimes called the "tone at the top" or, in the private sector, "corporate culture." A strong control environment is fostered when management and the governing board communicate to employees the importance of ethical behavior and competence in the workplace and the need to follow established internal control processes.[9] The principles that support the control environment, set out in the paragraphs below and identified by their number in the Green Book's listing (see Figure 9.1), can serve as a road map to help create a strong control environment.

- **The Oversight Body and Management Should Demonstrate a Commitment to Integrity and Ethical Values (Green Book Principle 1).** To satisfy this principle, the local unit's oversight body and management should adopt a code of conduct to communicate expectations concerning integrity and ethical values. Management may rely on the code to help evaluate the attitudes and behaviors of employees and departments and to determine the tolerance level for deviations.[10]
- **The Oversight Body Should Oversee the Unit's Internal Control System (Green Book Principle 2).** To satisfy this principle, the oversight body must oversee management's design, implementation, and operation of the internal control system. The oversight body should test controls and consider whether the current internal control system is adequate to mitigate risks and guard against potential acts of fraud. The oversight body may provide guidance and offer suggestions on how to remediate any apparent weaknesses or deficiencies in the internal control system.[11]
- **Management Should Establish an Organizational Structure, Assign Responsibility, and Delegate Authority to Achieve the Unit's Objectives (Green Book Principle 3).** To satisfy this principle, management will want to (a) consider how the departments within the unit interact to fulfill the unit's overall responsibility and (b) establish clear reporting

---

9. *Standards for Internal Control,* at 22.
10. *Standards for Internal Control,* at 23.
11. *Standards for Internal Control,* at 24–26.

Figure 9.1 The Greenbook's Five Key Components of Internal Control and Seventeen Principles Underlying Internal Control

Control Environment	1. Demonstrate commitment to integrity and ethical values
	2. Exercise oversight responsibility
	3. Establish structure, responsibility, and authority
	4. Demonstrate commitment to competence
	5. Enforce accountability
Risk Assessment	6. Define objectives and risk tolerances
	7. Identify, analyze, and respond to risk
	8. Assess fraud risk
	9. Analyze and respond to change
Control Activities	10. Design control activities
	11. Design activities for the information system
	12. Implement control activities
Information and Communication	13. Use quality information
	14. Communicate internally
	15. Communicate externally
Monitoring	16. Perform monitoring activities
	17. Remediate deficiencies

lines with the unit's organizational structure. Organizational charts are helpful in establishing reporting lines. For example, an organizational chart for the finance department could illustrate the reporting lines and level of authority between the various finance-related positions, such as the finance officer, deputy finance officer, accountant, payroll specialist, treasurer, and other positions. When advertising a new finance position, the position description should match the level of authority designated in the organizational chart. Management can use the organizational chart to delegate internal control responsibilities to personnel down the reporting chain of command.[12]

- **Management Should Demonstrate a Commitment to Recruit, Develop, and Retain Competent Employees (Green Book Principle 4).** Management must recruit and hire qualified personnel to fill vacant positions and provide current employees with training opportunities to help ensure that the employees maintain the level of competence necessary to accomplish assigned responsibilities.[13] This requires management to have a clear understanding of job duties and position responsibilities.

- **Management Should Evaluate Performance and Hold Individuals Accountable for Their Internal Control Responsibilities (Green Book Principle 5).** To satisfy this principle, periodic

---

12. *Standards for Internal Control*, at 28.
13. *Standards for Internal Control*, at 31.

performance reviews should be conducted to evaluate whether employees are competent and performing assigned internal control responsibilities. For example, if the unit has a policy that requires the deputy finance officer to attach the preaudit certificate to contracts or purchase orders, management should review whether the employee is in fact meeting this expectation. Disciplinary action may be taken when instances of noncompliance are identified.

2. Risk Assessment

The second key component of internal control is risk assessment. Risk assessment is a process undertaken by management to identify risks facing the unit as it seeks to achieve its objectives.[14] Conducting a risk assessment allows management to identify areas in need of control activities. The goal of the risk assessment is not to eliminate all risks facing the unit, as this would be impossible. Instead, management should determine an acceptable level of risk and consider how to keep risk factors within agreed-upon confines. Management should strive to identify internal and external risks that may affect unit-wide operations, department operations, and process- or activity-level operations. It can be effective to approach the risk assessment as a three-step process:

Step 1: Management defines operational, reporting, and compliance objectives.
Step 2: Management identifies risks related to achieving the identified objectives.
Step 3: Management assesses the risks based on likelihood and impact to determine a response.

Step 1: Identify Objectives (Green Book Principle 6). Management within the finance department should begin the risk assessment by identifying objectives related to general financial operations and for each significant transaction cycle, such as budgeting, cash receivables, accounts receivable, accounts payable, capital assets, debt, and investments.

There are three categories of objectives that management should strive to identify: *operational objectives* (what must happen to ensure that business operations are running efficiently?); *reporting objectives* (what must happen to ensure that financial statements, budgets, and other financial records are accurate and timely?); and *compliance objectives* (what must happen to ensure compliance with the LGBFCA and other governing federal, state, or local laws?). The more specific the objectives, the easier it will be for management to identify risks to achieving those objectives in the next step. Examples of objectives related to a unit's financial process include the following:

- Financial reports that include updated budget-to-actual revenues and expenditures should be prepared and presented to the governing board monthly.
- Cash receipts are accurately recorded in the Daily Collection Report.
- Accounts receivables are accurately credited to the correct user account.
- A preaudit is performed as required by law and the preaudit certificate is attached to each contract or agreement that obligates the unit to expend public moneys.
- Access to the payroll system is restricted to authorized users.
- All journals, ledgers, and other accounting records are reconciled as part of the month-end closeout procedure.

---

14. *Standards for Internal Control*, at 34.

Step 2: Identify Risks (Green Book Principle 7). During the second step of the risk-assessment process, management should take steps to identify the risks that, should they occur, may negatively impact the unit's ability to achieve its objectives. It is important to understand the different types of risk and the internal and external factors that can impact those risks.

Inherent risk. Some transactions or operations are by their nature inherently risky. For example, the acceptance of cash payments always carries with it an inherent risk of loss, as cash can easily be stolen or misappropriated. This is also true for transactions involving the storage or exchange of personal property such as laptop computers and other electronic equipment. In addition, risk generally increases when the unit undertakes new or complex programs or activities, such as the administration of a new federal grant award. For example, under the American Rescue Plan Act of 2021, every municipality and county in North Carolina was eligible to receive distributions of federal financial assistance (i.e., a federal grant award) from the Coronavirus State and Local Fiscal Recovery Fund (CSLFRF).[15] The acceptance of CSLFRF funds obligated local government recipients to administer the award in compliance with the U.S. Department of Treasury CSLFRF Award Terms and Conditions and other Treasury regulations and guidance.[16] Due to the complexity of the CSLFRF award's compliance and reporting requirements, there is an inherent risk of error or noncompliance, whether intentional or not.

Change risk. Any change in business operations or personnel may increase risk. For example, the use of new technology or software is an operational change risk. The hiring of new employees or the retirement of a long-term employee may also increase risk—new hires must overcome a learning curve associated with every new position, and institutional knowledge can be lost when an employee retires or leaves.

Fraud risk. Management must always consider where there may be opportunities for an employee to commit fraud against the unit. There are three primary types of fraud to look for during the risk assessment: (1) *corruption* (e.g., bribery, bid rigging, or collusion); (2) *asset misappropriation* (e.g., embezzlement, lapping, and other fraudulent disbursement schemes); and (3) *fraudulent financial reporting*, which involves the intentional misstatement or the omission of amounts in financial statements or accounting records with the intent to deceive the financial statement user.[17]

The following questions may serve as a starting point to help management identify areas of risk within financial operations.

- Are finance employees qualified and trained to perform basic accounting functions and to create and maintain financial reports?
- Are unit policies and procedures properly documented and updated to reflect current practices?

---

15. *See* American Rescue Plan Act of 2021, Pub. L. No. 117-2, § 603, 135 Stat. 4, 228 (2021); *see also* N.C. Pandemic Recovery Office, *Funding Totals: State and Local Fiscal Recovery Funds* (last visited March 21, 2023).

16. U.S. Department of the Treasury, *Coronavirus State and Local Fiscal Recovery Funds: Award Terms and Conditions*; *see also* U.S. Department of the Treasury, *Coronavirus State and Local Fiscal Recovery Funds* (policy webpage) (last visited April 21, 2023).

17. *Standards for Internal Control*, at 40. *See also* Association of Certified Fraud Examiners, *The Fraud Tree: Occupational Fraud and Abuse Classification System* (Fraud Tree illustrates the types of occupational fraud falling under each of the three categories of fraud listed in the text), Association of Certified Fraud Examiners, *Fraud 101: What Is Fraud?* (last visited March 21, 2023).

- Does the unit have budget violations in its audit findings?
- Is the unit current with its audits? If not, why?
- How could accounting errors occur and remain undetected?
- Which assets are most liquid and prone to theft?
- If an unauthorized purchase is made, how will it be detected?
- Could a payment be made for goods or services before it is verified that the goods or services were received?
- Are bank accounts and financial records regularly reconciled?
- Are passwords/IT system-access controls sufficient to protect unauthorized access to electronic records and databases?
- Is there a process to ensure that employees who leave no longer have electronic access to records or databases?

Step 3: Assess Risk and Determine a Response (Green Book Principles 8 and 9). Once a local unit's management has identified risks, it must decide how to respond. Not all risks are created equal. Some risks may be so remote, or the effects of such risks so inconsequential, that the unit may decide simply to accept those risks without developing controls to address them. Some risks, like natural disasters, may have such significant negative impacts that, even if unlikely, the unit must limit the risk through the purchase of insurance. For all other risks, management can implement control activities to help reduce the likelihood or impact of identified risks.

To help determine which risks should be limited through control activities, management should evaluate each risk using a likelihood/impact scale to determine priority (see Figure 9.2). Those risks that rank "very high" or "high" on the unit's risk-priority scale should be reduced through the implementation of control activities. Management must weigh the cost (time, money, effort) of implementing a control activity with the resulting benefit, keeping in mind that the cost of mitigating the risk should not exceed the cost to the unit if the risk occurred.

3. Control Activities

The third key component of the Green Book's internal control framework involves control activities. Control activities are the processes, procedures, and techniques designed by a unit's management team to help provide reasonable assurances that the unit's objectives will be met. Control activities are generally either preventative or detective.[18] *Preventive controls* are designed to deter the occurrence of an undesirable event, while *detective controls* help identity when an undesirable event has occurred. In addition to reducing identified risks, all control activities should promote an effective and efficient workplace. It is important to note that control activities can stand alone or be used in combination with other measures. Green Book Principle 10 addresses how to design control activities; Principle 12 covers the implementation of these activities. The following list describes some of the most common control activities.[19]

- **Written policies and procedures.** Written policies and procedures are a key internal control activity. These written tools can be used to communicate behavioral

---

18. *Standards for Internal Control*, at 48.

19. *Standards for Internal Control*, at 45–57. The Green Book includes examples of common control activities and describes ways in which management can operationalize the controls into daily operations.

Figure 9.2 Model Risk-Priority Rating System

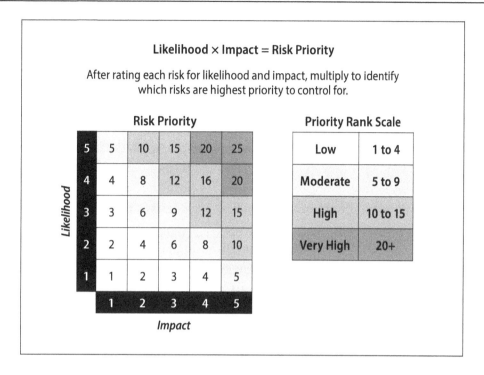

Likelihood × Impact = Risk Priority

After rating each risk for likelihood and impact, multiply to identify which risks are highest priority to control for.

Risk Priority

Likelihood					
5	5	10	15	20	25
4	4	8	12	16	20
3	3	6	9	12	15
2	2	4	6	8	10
1	1	2	3	4	5
	1	2	3	4	5

Impact

Priority Rank Scale

Low	1 to 4
Moderate	5 to 9
High	10 to 15
Very High	20+

expectations, establish workflow processes, and define internal control responsibilities. Policies and procedures help operationalize control activities, and written procedures should be used to describe all major financial transaction cycles, such as accounts receivable, accounts payable, payroll, investments, cash receipts, and capital assets. A strong control environment is fostered when management requires written policies and procedures that are communicated, followed, and regularly updated to reflect current business processes.

- **Authorization and approval.** The establishment of clear authorization and approval authority helps facilitate smooth workflow processes and ensure that financial transactions are lawful and consistent with a local unit's objectives. "Authorization" involves a delegation of authority to an employee granting that employee the right to perform a specific task or responsibility. For example, a purchasing officer may be authorized to make small purchases without supervisory approval. "Approval" is the confirmation of an event or transaction based on an independent review by an employee with approval authority. Approval indicates that the approver has reviewed supporting documentation and has verified that the transaction is accurate and complies with applicable laws and regulations. For example, a department head may approve a purchase order, indicating that the purchase is necessary and lawful.

- **Segregation of incompatible duties.** Segregation of incompatible duties is often described as implementing a system of checks and balances. This control is beneficial because it minimizes the risk that a single employee will be able to commit fraud or conceal errors. Segregation of incompatible duties involves separating job duties so that no one employee can (1) *authorize* a transaction, (2) *record* the transaction in the accounting records, (3) maintain *custody* of the asset resulting from that transaction, and (4) reconcile records that reflect the transaction. For example, if a unit's purchasing department plans to purchase ten new laptop computers, a supervisor could *authorize* the purchase via a purchase order, another employee should pay the invoice and *record* the transaction in the unit's accounting records, a third employee should verify the receipt of the computers and maintain *custody* of the assets, and a fourth employee should *reconcile* accounting records to ensure that the transaction has been accurately recorded. In small units, full segregation of incompatible duties may not be practical due to limited staff and overlapping job duties. In that case, it is recommended that a minimum of at least two employees complete any transaction. The same employee should not be responsible for both the recording and reconciliation functions. Small units should adopt compensating controls to ensure extra review of the unit's financial transactions.[20]

- **Compensating controls.** When adequate segregation of duties is not possible, a local unit should adopt compensating controls. Compensating controls involve the additional review of financial records and transactions by someone in management or by a governing board member. For example, if only two employees handle the accounts payable process, a governing board member, an internal auditor, or a member of senior management can review accounting records, bank statements, and financial reports to ensure that the accounts payable transactions are accurate, and that fraud is not going undetected. In some instances, two small units may decide to "swap" reconciliation duties to ensure an independent review of financial transactions when there is limited capacity.

- **Documentation.** Management must ensure that employees create and retain written documentation that evidences all financial transactions and facilitates the budgeting, financial reporting, and audit processes. Financial records, reports, and supporting documentation should be easily identified and be readily available to the governing board and to any auditor with whom the unit has contracted to perform auditing services.[21]

- **Reconciliation.** Account reconciliation is used to verify the accuracy of financial records through the periodic comparison of source documents and accounting records. Account reconciliations should be performed regularly, ideally after each month-end closeout.

---

20. See the North Carolina Department of State Treasurer's 2015 publication *Internal Controls for Small Units of Government* for more information on how to segregate incompatible duties for small local governments, available at https://www.nctreasurer.com/internal-controls-small-unit-government.

21. Each local government unit must retain records in accordance with the State Archives of North Carolina's *Record Retention and Disposition Schedule for Local Government Agencies*, available at: https://archives.ncdcr.gov/government/local. If a unit has received a federal grant, it likely must comply with the documentation and record retention requirements set forth in 2 C.F.R. § 200.334 (a provision of the Uniform Administrative Requirements, Cost Principles, and Audit Requirements for Federal Awards). Some federal grants impose a different record-retention period as part of that grant's award terms and conditions. In that case, a unit should follow the retention requirements set forth in those award terms and conditions. For example, recipients of Coronavirus State and Local Fiscal Recovery Funds (CSLFRF) are required, pursuant to the governing award terms and conditions, to retain records for a period of five (5) years after the award's period of performance. *See* U.S. Department of the Treasury, *Award Terms and Conditions*, note 16 above.

A local unit should not wait until the end of a fiscal year to reconcile its accounting records or rely on the auditor to perform reconciliations.

- **Physical controls.** Physical controls include the steps taken to protect real and personal property, including IT equipment, cash, checks, supplies, materials, and any other type of tangible asset from the risk of loss, misappropriation, or misuse. Physical controls include physical barriers, such as storing cash and valuables in locked cash boxes or safes, storing electronic equipment in locked storage rooms, or restricting access to public buildings and facilities to authorized employees.

- **Information-system controls (Green Book Principle 11).** Information-system controls facilitate the proper operation of information systems and help ensure the validity, completeness, accuracy, and confidentiality of transactions. Management is responsible for designing the unit's information system to respond to the unit's objectives and risks.[22] The information system includes both manual and technology-related information processes. General system-access controls facilitate the proper operation of the information system and include security management and access controls, such as requiring dual authentication to access certain electronic records or databases. This is a complex control area, and management should ensure that it has adequately addressed threats of cyber attacks and other issues that may result from insufficient cybersecurity controls.

- **Education and training.** Management has a duty to hire and retain competent personnel who have the proper education and training to perform job duties effectively. To ensure that employees have the necessary skills and training, employees should be allowed, or in some cases required, to attend supplemental training, conferences, or other educational events to advance skillsets and learn new competencies.

4. Information and Communication

The fourth key component of internal control under the Green Book framework is information and communication. While sometimes overlooked, this component is essential to the creation of a strong internal control system. A local government's management team should establish communication channels within the unit (Green Book Principle 14; Principle 15 deals with external communications) that provide timely and accurate information and updates (Principle 13 states that quality information should be used); inform employees of their internal control duties and responsibilities; allow employees to suggest ways to improve the system's operation; and convey a commitment by management and the unit's oversight body to the adherence of established internal control processes.[23] These communication channels can take many forms and may include emails, meetings, casual conversations, or training on how to perform specific internal control activities. Management may want to periodically verify that communication channels are effective and that employees are receiving and sharing information as intended.

---

22. *Standards for Internal Control*, at 51.
23. *Standards for Internal Control*, at 61.

5. Monitoring

Monitoring is the fifth and final key component of internal control. Effective monitoring of a unit's internal control system allows management to determine whether policies, procedures, and other control activities designed and implemented by management are being conducted effectively by employees. When monitoring techniques are built into the unit's business operations (Green Book Principle 16), control deficiencies may be more readily identified and corrected in a timely manner. Management is not required to review every transaction or financial report to determine whether controls are properly functioning. Instead, management can spot-check transactions, financial reports, and account reconciliations for timely completion and accuracy. For example, management can spot-check paid invoices to determine if the goods or services covered by the invoices were certified as having been received prior to authorizing payment. Management can monitor whether employees are properly segregating incompatible duties and performing other control activities as assigned. It may be helpful for management to solicit feedback from those employees responsible for carrying out the control activities in the unit to help determine if they are effective. Efforts should be made to document the performance of monitoring activities. If a breakdown in the system is identified, management may change the design of the controls to improve the operating effectiveness of the system (Principle 17 involves remediating deficiencies).[24]

Internal Control over Federal Awards

As a condition of receiving a federal award,[25] a non-federal entity, including a local government recipient and any subrecipients, must agree to maintain a system of internal control over the federal award that provides reasonable assurance of compliance with applicable laws and regulations and with the terms and conditions of the award.[26] A non-federal entity's internal control system should be modeled after the guidance offered in the Green Book or after the Internal Control-Integrated Framework issued by the Committee of Sponsoring Organizations of the Treadway Commission (COSO).[27] Accordingly, a non-federal entity should use the five key components and seventeen principles of internal control outlined in the Green Book, and discussed herein, as the basis for the design and implementation of its internal control system over federal awards.

When it comes to managing the financial aspects of federal awards, non-federal entities must design and implement strong and robust systems of internal control. These controls should help

---

24. *Standards for Internal Control*, at 65.

25. 2 C.F.R. § 200.1 defines "federal award" as "the federal financial assistance that a recipient receives directly from a federal awarding agency or indirectly from a pass-through entity." "Federal financial assistance" includes federal grants and cooperative agreements.

26. 2 C.F.R. § 200.303.

27. 2 C.F.R. § 200.303 (stating that internal controls over the federal award "should be in compliance with guidance in 'Standards for Internal Control in the Federal Government' issued by the Comptroller General of the United States or the 'Internal Control Integrated Framework', issued by the Committee of Sponsoring Organizations of the Treadway Commission (COSO)").

ensure compliance with the financial management standards set forth in 2 C.F.R. § 200.302.[28] These standards require, among other things, that non-federal entities retain records that adequately identify the source and application of award funds. In addition, non-federal entities must create and retain accounting records that adequately track authorizations, obligations, unobligated balances, assets, expenditures, income and interest, and these records must be supported by source documentation.[29]

Any non-federal entity that expends $750,000 or more in federal awards during a fiscal year must undergo a federal single audit. As part of the single audit, the auditor will test the effectiveness of the non-federal entity's internal controls over the federal award.[30] The Office of Management and Budget's annual *Compliance Supplement* is a resource intended for auditors, but it is also a helpful tool for non-federal entities that have triggered a single audit.[31] The *Compliance Supplement* includes a Matrix of Compliance Requirements for each major federal program that indicates which of the twelve compliance requirements the auditor will test during the single audit. Part 6 of the *Compliance Supplement* includes two appendixes that provide illustrative examples of internal control—Appendix I contains examples of entity-wide controls over federal awards, and Appendix II provides examples of internal controls specific to each compliance requirement. These appendixes can serve as a starting point as the non-federal entity starts to design and implement internal controls over federal awards.

Summary

A strong internal control system is necessary to help ensure that the unit is operating at the optimal level and will achieve its goals and objectives. Properly designed and functioning controls over key financial transactions and processes will significantly reduce the likelihood that errors or fraud will occur and remain undetected. When a local unit's management team and governing board take time to implement the internal control framework outlined in the Green Book, they are signaling to all unit employees and to external stakeholders that the unit values internal control and has taken the steps required to be a good steward of public moneys and assets.

---

28. 2 C.F.R. § 200.302 (setting forth financial management standards with which non-federal entities must comply in managing the federal award).

29. 2 C.F.R. § 200.302(b)(3).

30. 2 C.F.R. § 200.501(a) (a single audit is required for any non-federal entity that expends $750,000 or more during its fiscal year, except when the non-federal entity elects to undergo a program-specific audit.); 2 C.F.R. § 200.514 (the auditor who performs the single audit is required to gain an understanding of the non-federal entity's internal control over a federal program or programs sufficient to (1) plan the audit to support a low assessed level of control risk for major programs, (2) plan the testing of internal control over major federal programs, and, unless internal control is likely to be ineffective, and (3) perform testing of internal control as planned).

31. Executive Office of the President, Office of Management and Budget, 2 C.F.R. Part 200, Appendix XI, 2022 Compliance Supplement (April 2022).

Chapter 10

Accounting, Financial Reporting, and the Annual Audit

by Gregory S. Allison

Public confidence in government depends on proper stewardship of public moneys. The North Carolina Local Government Budget and Fiscal Control Act (LGBFCA)[1] sets forth requirements for fiscal control that provide a framework for ensuring accountability in a local government's budgetary and financial operations. This chapter focuses on these requirements, which generally are equally applicable both to county governments and municipal governments.[2] They pertain to the appointment and the role of a unit's finance officer, the accounting system, control of expenditures, cash management and investments, the annual audit, and audits of federal and state financial assistance.

A short discussion of the role of the North Carolina Local Government Commission and its relationship to North Carolina local government entities will facilitate understanding of references that occur throughout this chapter. Often referred to simply as the LGC, the Local Government Commission is discussed in Chapter 2, "The Local Government Budget and Fiscal Control Act," and in Chapter 7, "Financing Capital Projects."

The LGC, established by Chapter 159, Section 3 of the North Carolina General Statutes (hereinafter G.S.), operates as a division of the Department of State Treasurer. The commission itself consists of nine members. The state treasurer, the state auditor, the secretary of state, and the secretary of revenue serve as ex officio members; the remaining five members are appointed by the governor (three members) and the General Assembly (two members). The commission's primary responsibility is to provide fiscal and debt management oversight to local government

---

1. The LGBFCA is set out in Article 3 of Chapter 159 of the North Carolina General Statutes (hereinafter G.S.).

2. As used in this book, the term "municipality" is synonymous with "city," "town," and "village."

entities in North Carolina. The commission's policy directives are carried out on a day-to-day basis by the staff of the LGC, who are employees of the Department of State Treasurer.

The LGC's oversight of North Carolina counties and municipalities is extensive. A local government's financial condition, cash management practices, and audit procurement procedures are all subject to LGC review and approval. As a general rule, counties and municipalities are not allowed to enter into most types of indebtedness without the express permission of the LGC. Counties and municipalities in North Carolina have benefited extensively from this level of oversight; their financial condition and reputation in the national debt markets are among the best in the nation.

The Finance Officer

G.S. 159-24 requires that each county and municipal government have a finance officer who is legally responsible for establishing the unit's accounting system, controlling expenditures, managing cash and other assets, and preparing financial reports. The LGBFCA does not specify who is to appoint this official, leaving the decision to each jurisdiction. In many counties and municipalities, the manager appoints the finance officer.[3] In counties and municipalities that do not have a manager, the governing body typically makes the appointment. According to G.S. 159-24, the finance officer serves at the pleasure of the appointing board or official.

In most counties, the official exercising the statutory duties of finance officer carries that title; in most municipalities, the official exercising these same duties carries the title of finance director. In some of the larger counties and municipalities, the title of chief financial officer (CFO) is used. Other titles, such as accountant or treasurer, may be used by some jurisdictions, but this is less common. There are also other derivations in some smaller counties. For example, the county manager may also be the legally designated finance officer, or the finance officer may also serve as an assistant county manager. The LGBFCA permits the duties of the budget officer and finance officer to be conferred on one person. In contrast, G.S. 105-349(e) specifies that the duties of tax collector and those of the "treasurer or chief accounting officer," which should be understood to mean the finance officer, may not be conferred on the same person except with the written permission of the secretary of the LGC. This limitation recognizes both the hazards to internal control of one person holding the two offices and the fact that some local government entities are too small to make any other arrangement. While it is currently very rare for one person to serve as both the finance officer and the tax collector in a county, the commission has allowed a number of municipalities to operate under this arrangement. However, these approvals have typically been made with restrictions, such as suggesting that the municipality contract with the county for property tax billing and collection.

The finance officer's duties are summarized in G.S. 159-25(a): establish and maintain the accounting records, disburse moneys, make financial reports, manage the receipt and deposit of moneys, manage the county's or the municipality's debt service obligations, supervise investments, and perform any other assigned duties.

---

3. G.S. 153A-82 (counties) and 160A-148 (municipalities).

Official Bonds

A unit's finance officer must give "a true accounting and faithful performance bond" of no less than the greater of the following:

1. $50,000 or
2. an amount equal to 10 percent of the unit's annually budgeted funds, not to exceed $1,000,000.[4]

The term "annually budgeted funds" has been interpreted by the staff of the LGC as

1. including budgeted expenditures in a unit's or public authority's originally adopted annual budget ordinance in the fiscal year the bond is obtained and
2. excluding expenditures for which a unit or public authority budgeted in a multi-year project ordinance.

The bond must be given on the individual, not the position. The usual public official's bond covers faithful performance as well as true accounting. The bond insures a county or a municipality for losses it suffers as a result of the actions or negligence of its finance officer; it offers no insurance or protection to the officer. The county or the municipality must pay the bond's premium. If a candidate for a finance officer position is unable to obtain a performance bond in accordance with these minimum guidelines, the individual is disqualified from an appointment as a local government finance officer.

G.S. 159-29 also requires that each "officer, employee, or agent . . . who handles or has in his custody more than one hundred dollars . . . at any time, or who handles or has access to [a unit's] inventories" be bonded for faithful performance. If separate bonds for individuals are purchased, the $100 minimum should be understood to mean that the bonding requirement applies only to those persons who frequently or regularly handle that amount or more. The governing board of a county or a municipality fixes the amount of each such bond, and the unit may (and normally does) pay the premium.

In lieu of requiring a separate bond for each employee, a county or municipality may purchase a "blanket" faithful-performance bond, and nearly all counties and municipalities do (primarily for cost reasons, as blanket bonds are more economical than the total cost of separate bonds). The blanket bond does not substitute for the separate bond required for the finance officer or other county officials (tax collector, sheriff, and register of deeds) or municipal officials (tax collector), who must still be bonded individually and separately.

The Accounting System

An accounting system exists to supply information. It provides a county's or a municipality's manager and other officials with the data needed to ascertain financial performance and to plan and budget for future activities with projected resources. The accounting system is also an essential part of internal control procedures.

---

4. G.S. 159-29. *See also* Connor Crews, "Impending Changes to Bonding Requirements for Finance Officers: Prepare Now for January 1, 2023, and Beyond," *Local Finance Bulletin* No. 62 (Nov. 23, 2022).

The governing board of a unit depends on accounting information in making its budgetary and program decisions and in determining whether or not they have been carried out. This kind of information is valuable also to outside organizations. The investment community and bond-rating agencies rely on it as they assess a county's or a municipality's financial condition. Also, in counties and municipalities where bonds have recently been issued, the local government is often required to provide various types of annual financial information to meet continuing disclosure requirements. State regulatory agencies, such as the LGC, review data generated by the accounting systems to determine whether counties and municipalities have complied with the legal requirements regulating accounting and finance. Federal and state grantor agencies use the information to monitor compliance with the requirements of the financial assistance programs they administer. The media and the public depend on the information to evaluate a local government's activities.

County and municipal accounting practices are formed in response to the general statutory requirements set forth in G.S. 159-26, which are generally accepted accounting principles (GAAP) promulgated nationally by the Governmental Accounting Standards Board (GASB). In North Carolina, the rules and regulations of the LGC as well as the local government's own needs and capabilities directly impact its accounting practices.

Statutory Requirements

G.S. 159-26 requires that each county and municipality maintain an accounting system, which must do the following:

1. *Show in detail its assets, liabilities, equities, revenues, and expenditures.*
2. *Record budgeted as well as actual expenditures and budgeted or estimated revenues as well as their collection.*
3. *Establish accounting funds as required by G.S. 159-26(b).* A *fund* is a separate fiscal and accounting entity having its own assets, liabilities, equity or fund balance, revenues, and expenditures. Government activities are grouped into funds to isolate information for legal and management purposes. The types of funds that are set forth in G.S. 159-26(b) for use by counties and municipalities are discussed later in this chapter.
4. *Use the modified accrual basis of accounting. Basis of accounting* refers to criteria for determining when revenues and expenditures should be recorded in an accounting system.[5] The *modified accrual basis* requires that expenditures be recorded when a liability is incurred (time of receipt) for a good or service provided to a local government. The expenditure should be recorded then, usually before the funds are disbursed. This type of accounting also requires that revenues be recorded when the

---

5. Although the LGBFCA requires the use of the modified accrual basis of accounting, it also requires that financial reporting be in conformity with GAAP. Enterprise, internal service, and certain trust funds primarily follow accrual accounting standards for reporting in accordance with GAAP, similar to the commercial sector. A county's annual financial report must both demonstrate compliance with legal requirements (i.e., the LGBFCA) and report on operations in conformity with GAAP. Therefore, enterprise funds should be reported on both the modified accrual and the accrual basis in a county's financial statements, and internal service and certain trust funds should also be reported on the accrual basis in the county's annual financial report.

revenues are measurable and available. *Measurable* means that they can be reasonably estimated, and *available* means that they will be received within the current fiscal year or soon enough thereafter to be able to pay liabilities of the current fiscal year. In actual practice, for various reasons some revenues are recorded when they are received in cash. For example, in North Carolina, property tax revenues are generally recorded on a cash basis because taxes receivable are not considered to be collectible soon enough after the year's end to meet the availability criterion. Permits and fees also are recorded on a cash basis because they are not considered to be measurable at year's end. However, certain revenues collected after the fiscal year ends but soon enough thereafter to pay liabilities outstanding as of June 30 would be reflected as revenue for the year ending June 30 because they would be considered measurable and available. For example, the monthly sales tax payments received by counties and municipalities in July, August, and September are recorded by most local governments as revenue for the year ending June 30 because the payments can be measured; they are directly related to sales that occurred during the previous fiscal year (i.e., the July distribution is related to the previous April's sales, the August distribution is related to the previous May's sales, and the September distribution is related to the previous June's sales); and they are received soon enough after June 30 to be able to pay liabilities at the fiscal year's end.

The modified accrual basis of accounting helps keep financial practices on a prudent footing: expenditures are recorded as soon as the liabilities for them are incurred, and some revenues are not recorded until they have actually been received in cash. In addition, the modified accrual basis enhances the comparability of financial reporting for counties and reduces the opportunity for manipulation of financial information.

5. *Record encumbrances represented by outstanding purchase orders and contractual obligations that are chargeable against budgeted appropriations.* An *encumbrance* is created when a contract that will require a county or a municipality to pay money is entered into or when a purchase order is issued.

Although the LGBFCA does not explicitly mention any exceptions, in practice, expenditures for salaries and wages, fringe benefits, and utilities are usually not encumbered. Salaries, wages, and fringe benefits are not encumbered because they generally are budgeted at the full amounts expected for all positions, and this significantly reduces the risk of over-expenditure. Utilities expenditures are normally not encumbered because the amounts are generally not known in advance.

An encumbrance exists as long as a contractor or supplier has not delivered goods or services and the contract or purchase order is outstanding. While this is the case, the local government is not yet liable to pay for the goods or the services and has not yet incurred an expenditure for them. G.S. 159-26(d) requires that a county's or a municipality's accounting system record encumbrances as well as expenditures. This recognizes that an encumbrance is a potential liability, and once a purchase order is filled or a contract fulfilled, a liability for payment is created and an expenditure is incurred. Although this requirement applies only to counties with more than 50,000 citizens or municipalities with more than 10,000 citizens, nearly all counties and municipalities record encumbrances in their accounting systems.

Generally Accepted Accounting Principles for Governments

Governmental accounting, as a branch of general accounting practice, shares basic concepts and conventions with commercial accounting. However, because of major differences in the governmental environment, a distinct set of national accounting and financial reporting principles has evolved in this field. They are promulgated by the GASB. Established in 1984, the GASB is responsible for the establishment of GAAP for county and municipal governments as well as state governments. The GASB succeeded the National Council on Governmental Accounting (NCGA), which had formerly established GAAP for government entities. Although the GASB at its creation accepted the existing NCGA pronouncements, it has actively set forth standards in areas of accounting and finance that the NCGA did not formally consider. Likewise, it has updated and modified much of the guidance that it initially accepted.

The LGC plays a key role in defining and interpreting accounting standards and procedures for local governments in North Carolina. It issues rules and regulations that interpret state statutes as well as national professional standards, and it provides advice about requirements and improvements in accounting and financial reporting practices. The commission's staff has focused much attention in recent years on annual financial reports, working closely with local officials and the state's public accounting profession to keep local government accounting systems up to date with the increasingly more rigorous reporting and disclosure standards being promulgated by the GASB.

Counties' and Municipalities' Own Needs and Capabilities

Counties' and municipalities' own needs and capabilities also shape their accounting and financial reporting systems. For example, a growing number of counties and municipalities have improved their annual financial reports to the point that they have earned the Certificate of Achievement for Excellence in Financial Reporting, awarded by the Government Finance Officers Association (GFOA) of the United States and Canada to recognize outstanding achievement in governmental financial reporting. While all North Carolina local governments issue professionally acceptable annual financial reports, those winning the Certificate of Achievement provide full disclosure above and beyond the minimum standards set by GAAP and relate current financial conditions and performance to past financial trends. Approximately five thousand local governments in the United States participate in the Certificate of Achievement program, which offers a tremendous resource to help local governments continually improve their financial reporting.

Nationwide, capital asset accounting and reporting continues to be one of the more significant challenges in state and local government accounting. In recent years, the LGC and the independent public accountants auditing local governments, as well as the aforementioned GFOA, have placed increased emphasis on capital asset records. If these records are inadequate, the annual auditor's opinion may be modified, and this may adversely affect a county's or a municipality's bond rating. Also, a modified audit opinion may affect a county's or a municipality's ability to obtain approval from the LGC for debt issuance. In addition, an adequate capital asset accounting system can provide significant advantages. It places responsibility for the safekeeping of such assets with a unit's management, thereby improving internal control. It also serves as a basis for establishing maintenance and replacement schedules for equipment and for determining the level of fire and hazard insurance that should be carried on buildings and other capital assets.

It should be noted that the capitalization threshold that management establishes for financial reporting purposes should *not* be presumed to be directly correlated to adequate internal control of government property. For years, there has often been the misconception that the lower the capitalization threshold, the less likely it is that the capital asset will be lost, misplaced, or misused. However, low capitalization thresholds simply clutter the internal capital asset records with immaterial items and actually make them less useful. The external financial statements should focus on material items, and there is a significant internal cost to maintaining unusually low capitalization thresholds. For North Carolina governments, it is recommended that capital asset thresholds be no less than $1,000, and thresholds up to $5,000 are preferable. The threshold is used only to determine *where* on the external financial statements capital assets will be reported. The threshold does *not* mitigate the need for management at the departmental level to maintain adequate internal controls and records to safeguard *all* government property. Also, it should be noted that, as a general rule, capitalization thresholds for financial reporting purposes are a management responsibility and there is no required official action by governing boards to establish or modify them.

The Annual Audit

Contents of the Annual Comprehensive Financial Report

G.S. 159-34 requires local governments to have their accounts audited by independent auditors after the close of each fiscal year. The auditor's opinion is set out in an annual financial report, which must include "the [county's/municipality's] financial statements prepared in accordance with generally accepted accounting principles, all disclosures in the public interest required by law, and the auditor's opinion and comments relating to [the] financial statements."

Preparation of the report's financial statements and their accompanying notes is the responsibility of a local government's management. There are units that may not have the internal staff or expertise to prepare the annual financial statements. In those situations, the local government may contract with an independent third party to assist in their preparation. The independent auditor may only provide limited assistance in order not to impair their independence. Professional standards for auditors have greatly enhanced the requirements for independence in recent years, which has limited auditors' ability to provide significant report preparation services.

More and more local governmental entities are preparing an annual comprehensive financial report (ACFR). ACFRs are not required by GAAP or by state statute, but they are very useful to external users of a government's financial statements. These reports go above and beyond the minimum external reporting requirements and provide useful financial and nonfinancial data about a local government. An ACFR contains three primary sections: introductory, financial, and statistical. A fourth section consisting of the compliance or single-audit reports and schedules may be included, but this is not required. Table 10.1 summarizes the contents of the ACFR. If a local government does not prepare an ACFR, only the financial section, including financial statements and notes, will be found in that unit's annual financial report.

Table 10.1   Contents of an Annual Comprehensive Financial Report (ACFR)

Section	Description
Introductory Section	
Letter of transmittal	Overview of the unit's operations and financial statistics
Organizational chart	Diagram of the unit's organizational structure
List of principal officials	List of elected and appointed officials
Financial Section	
Auditor's opinion	Independent auditor's opinion on the financial statements
Management's discussion and government analysis	Overview of the government-wide and fund financial statements and condition of the local government unit during the reporting year
Government-wide financial statements	Statement of net position and statement of activities for the unit's governmental activities and its business-type activities
Fund financial statements	Information on a unit's fund activity (e.g., General, Special Revenue, Enterprise), with a focus on the major funds
Notes to the financial statements	Explanations of accounting policies and statutory violations and detailed explanations of financial statement items (e.g., cash and investments, capital assets, receivables, long-term liabilities)
Combining statements	Detailed information supporting columns reported in the fund financial statements that include more than one fund
Individual fund statements	Detailed information about individual funds (e.g., prior year amounts, budgeted amounts, actual amounts)
Required supplementary information	Trend data for funding of pension trust funds
Statistical Section	
Statistical tables	Tables, usually on multi-year basis (e.g., ten years), showing information on financial trends, revenue capacity, debt capacity, demographic and economic information, and operating information of the reporting unit
Compliance Section (optional)	
Single audit reports	Reports from independent auditor on compliance and internal control
Schedule of findings and questioned costs	Listing of grant findings and questioned costs
Schedule of expenditures of federal and state awards	Listing of federal and state financial assistance programs

Introductory Section

The introductory section of an ACFR includes the transmittal letter, which is primarily an overview of the report, a brief introduction of the local government, and the official transmission of the report to external users; an organization chart; and a list of principal elected and nonelected officials. The transmittal letter should provide useful information to members of the public and the business community who may not be aware of all the local government's functions and services.

Financial Section

The financial section of an ACFR contains financial statements, which present information in various formats and levels of detail. The financial section includes the financial statements required by GAAP—known as the basic financial statements—as well as financial presentations in greater levels of detail that often are used to exhibit budgetary compliance or to provide opportunities for more detailed analysis.

An independent auditor's opinion is the first item in the financial section of an ACFR prepared by a local government. The opinion should be printed on the auditor's letterhead, further emphasizing that it is not a representation made by the unit's management. The next presentation in the financial section is the management's discussion and analysis (MD&A), a written summary and overview of the local government's financial condition and the ways in which its financial condition has changed during the year. Governmental entities are required to prepare an MD&A even if they are not preparing an ACFR.

The basic financial statements are presented after the MD&A. As noted earlier, these statements represent the minimum information required in the external financial statements for them to be in accordance with GAAP. The basic financial statements are broken down into two main sections—the government-wide financial statements and the fund financial statements. A comprehensive set of note disclosures supports each section. The government-wide financial statements, which include a statement of net position and a statement of activities, focus on the two broad *activities* of a local government—the governmental activities and the business-type activities. The fund financial statements, however, focus on the *funds* that are reported by and are unique to local governments. The three main categories of funds—governmental, proprietary, and fiduciary—include numerous fund types. The fund types most common to counties and municipalities in North Carolina include the general fund, special revenue funds, capital projects funds, enterprise funds (e.g., utility funds), and pension trust funds.

The notes to the financial statements immediately follow the government-wide and fund financial statements and are considered an integral part of the basic financial statements. The content and form of the notes are prescribed by GAAP. Through written advisory memoranda and illustrative financial statements interpreting GAAP, the LGC provides guidance to local officials and their independent auditors on the content of the note disclosures. These disclosures contain significant information for anyone attempting to interpret the financial statements and understand the finances of a local government entity. While all disclosures are important for a good understanding of information presented in the financial statements, the note disclosures related to the definition of the reporting entity, statutory violations (if any), the collateralization of deposits and investments, capital assets, and types and terms of long-term liabilities should be of particular interest to users of the financial statements.

Statistical Section

The statistical section of an ACFR follows the financial section. It includes multi-year information on financial trends of a government, its revenue and debt capacity, relative demographic and economic information, and various operating information. The statistical section is considered an invaluable tool for bond-rating agencies and potential investors and creditors. As a general rule, the statistical tables in this section include ten years' worth of comparative data. In a few cases, the comparisons are not for a complete ten years but are comparisons of the current year with nine years prior, thus exhibiting a ten-year spread.

The Auditor's Opinion

The auditor's task is to render an independent opinion on the accuracy and reliability of the basic financial statements and the related note disclosures as well as on their conformity with GAAP. The auditor opines not that the financial statements and disclosures are always exact but that they are reliable enough for a knowledgeable reader to use them to make informed judgments about a local government entity's financial position and operations.

The auditor's opinion most commonly takes one of two forms. First, it may be *unmodified* (frequently referred to as a "clean" opinion). With an unmodified audit opinion, the auditor is opining that the financial statements present fairly the unit of government's financial position at the close of the fiscal year, in conformity with GAAP. Thus, there is no *modification* placed on the opinion (i.e., there are no exceptions noted). All North Carolina local governments should strive for an unmodified opinion.

A *modified* opinion is a second possibility. If in some way a local government's practices materially vary from GAAP, the auditor's opinion may state that the statements fairly present the local government's financial position except for any such deviation. For example, the most common type of problem that may result in a modified auditor's opinion is inadequate records supporting the valuation of a government's capital assets in its financial statements. An opinion modification also may be due to a *scope limitation*. This occurs when the independent auditor is unable to perform certain tests that are an essential part of the audit. For example, a local government's accounting system may fail to provide adequate documentation for some revenue and expenditure transactions, in which case the auditor's ability to test such transactions would be limited.

Auditors are required to present the audited financial statements and the overall results of the audit to the local government's governing board in an official open meeting. This presentation should occur no later than forty-five days after the audited financial statements have been submitted to the LGC. The presentation should address, if applicable, any significant deficiencies, material weaknesses, or other findings, including financial indicators of concern as defined by the LGC. Consequently, the unit's governing board must respond to the LGC, within sixty days of the auditor's presentation, to these findings and concerns. The response should include the board's detailed plans of corrective action and should be signed by the majority of the board members.

In addition, the auditor normally suggests improvements to the local government entity's internal control procedures and operations in a *management letter* that accompanies the audit report. This letter is a public document addressed to the unit's governing board and typically makes various specific suggestions for improving internal control and financial procedures. These suggestions normally arise from the audit but do not meet the threshold of the aforementioned deficiencies or weaknesses. The management letter is delivered at the same time as the audited financial statements. Often the auditor's suggestions have been informally made earlier, and some may already have been addressed at the time of the formal presentation.

In addition to providing the management letter, the independent auditor can often be an excellent source of advice on accounting system design, internal control procedures, and finance in general.

Selection of an Independent Auditor

G.S. 159-34 establishes certain requirements and procedures regarding contracting for a local government's annual audit. First, the auditor must be selected by and report to the unit's governing board. The auditor should not report to the unit's manager, budget officer, or finance officer.

Second, the governing board may choose any North Carolina certified public accountant (CPA) or any accountant certified by the LGC as qualified to audit local government accounts. In practice, no non-CPA accountants have requested certification or met the requirements for certification to perform local government audits in recent years. Governing board members should assure themselves that the person or firm selected is familiar with the particular features of government accounting and auditing. Auditors should be engaged early in the fiscal year so that they can become familiar with the local government's procedures and can complete some of the necessary testing before the fiscal year's end. This also ensures that the auditor can plan the audit engagement and complete it in a timely manner.

Many counties and municipalities select the auditor through a *request for proposals* (RFP) process. Although this is not required by state statute, using an RFP is recommended by LGC staff to secure the best audit proposal. Also, selecting an independent auditor through a competitive procurement process is often required by federal regulations in many grant agreements where audit costs are chargeable to the grant. It is most common for audit agreements procured through an RFP process to range from three- to five-year terms. The RFP should cover both the technical qualifications of a potential audit firm and the firm's cost proposals. Local officials should give more weight to an auditor's technical skills than to the firm's proposed audit fees. References from other local government clients should be requested from an auditor. These references should be contacted so that local government officials may obtain information on other local governments' experiences with a potential auditor.

Contrary to popular belief, government entities are not required to rotate auditors periodically. As mentioned earlier, the LGC recommends that governments issue an RFP process at least every three to five years. This does not, however, preclude any current auditors from retaining their engagements if they continue to meet the service and price requirements established in an RFP. Many government entities have retained the same audit firm for years. Some benefits of these established relationships are the auditor's familiarity with the government's environment and the government's avoidance of costs (particularly in staff time) incurred in changing auditors. On the other hand, some governing boards choose to contract with different auditors to provide a fresh look or to allocate the work to other qualified auditors in the region. Both approaches have merit, and the LGC has not encouraged or endorsed either method. It should again be noted that rotation is not statutorily required but is a policy left to the discretion of each entity's governing board.

Finally, a local government's contract with an auditor must be approved by the LGC. Payment may not be made for any auditor services until the secretary of the commission has approved the billing.

Audits of Federal and State Grants

Federal and state grants and other financial assistance programs provide moneys to support county and municipal programs. In the past, individual federal and state agencies providing these moneys audited the recipient government's expenditure of them to verify that the moneys were spent for the purposes intended and in accordance with prescribed procedures. Since the mid-1980s, however, the federal government has required local governments to procure a *combined financial and compliance audit,* or single audit, of all federal financial assistance programs that meet certain expenditure thresholds.

To build on the federal single audit, the 1987 General Assembly, with the support of local officials, passed a law requiring state financial assistance programs to be included with federal programs in a combined single audit. In North Carolina, this combined single audit is performed in conjunction with the annual financial audit by a local government's independent auditor. Federal and state agencies are allowed to build on single audits and perform monitoring work on the programs they administer. However, they should not duplicate the work performed by independent auditors.

The independent auditor issues a number of compliance and internal control reports to disclose findings from the single audit. These reports usually are included in the last section of a local government's annual financial report or in a fourth section of an ACFR. The most significant items for local officials in these reports are the internal control weaknesses, findings, and questioned costs identified by the auditor. Internal control weaknesses are usually significant deficiencies and should be corrected unless corrective actions would not be cost-effective. For example, an internal control weakness commonly cited is the lack of proper segregation of duties. However, especially for small governments, complete correction of the problem could involve additional hirings, the costs of which could outweigh the benefits. In these situations, mitigating controls can be put into place to lessen the risks and weaknesses involved. Otherwise, findings and questioned costs almost always require corrective action, which may necessitate the repayment of grant funds. County and municipal officials' formal responses to findings and questioned costs and material internal control weaknesses are included in the single-audit reports.

The LGC monitors the single audit of grant funds as part of its review of a local government's annual financial report. If the commission determines that the single-audit reports and schedules are not prepared according to applicable standards, the independent auditor may be required to revise them before the annual financial report can be accepted. If the LGC finds that the single audit is satisfactory, then all state grantor agencies must accept the audit. If the commission determines subsequent to its approval of the annual financial report that the single audit is not reliable, it may revoke its approval. This opens a county or a municipality up to individual federal and state agency audits.

Additional Resources

Government Finance Officers Association (GFOA). *2022 eGAAFR (Governmental Accounting, Auditing, and Financial Reporting).* 2022 ed. Chicago: GFOA, 2022.

Governmental Accounting Standards Board (GASB). *Codification of Governmental Accounting and Financial Reporting Standards as of June 30, 2022.* Norwalk, Conn.: GASB, 2022.

Chapter 11

Procurement, Contracting, and Disposal of Property

by Crista M. Cuccaro

Obtaining the goods and services for the operation of counties and municipalities is a major administrative responsibility.[1] In a legal sense, this responsibility involves questions of proper authority, adequate authorization for expending funds, and entering into contracts in accordance with statutory requirements. Administratively, the organizational arrangements should be both efficient and legally sufficient. Contracting procedures must also be designed to avoid violation of state and federal conflict-of-interest laws, promote fairness and objectivity, and avoid the appearance of impropriety in contracting decisions.

Similar legal and administrative considerations apply when disposing of surplus property, which must be done according to statutory requirements intended to recoup taxpayer dollars expended to purchase the property.

This chapter outlines the state law requirements applicable to procurement, contracting, and property disposal. Additionally, the Uniform Guidance requirements are incorporated throughout this chapter. The Uniform Guidance is the comprehensive set of requirements applicable to federal award recipients, including local governments. The Uniform Guidance dictates federal grants administration, from pre-award to audit, and is codified in the Code of Federal Regulations (C.F.R.).[2] Local governments, as non-federal entities (NFEs),[3] must have and use written procurement policies and procedures that comply with state law, local policies, and the Uniform Guidance.[4] This means that local governments must follow the "most restrictive" requirements of federal, state, and local regulations.[5]

The author would like to acknowledge School of Government faculty member Norma R. Houston for her prior authorship of this chapter.

1. As used in this book, the term "municipality" is synonymous with "city," "town," and "village."

2. Specifically, the Uniform Guidance is located in Title 2, Part 200 of the C.F.R. The Guidance is divided into six subparts, including definitions, general provisions, and audit requirements. Subpart D, entitled "Post Federal Award Requirements," includes many of the administrative requirements related to procurement, and, notably, these procurement standards differ from North Carolina law. An explanation of these standards is incorporated into this chapter, except for those covering conflicts of interest under the Uniform Guidance, which are found in Chapter 12, "Ethics and Conflicts of Interest."

3. Per 2 C.F.R. § 200.1, a non-federal entity is a state, local government, Indian tribe, institution of higher education (IHE), or nonprofit organization that carries out a federal award as a recipient or subrecipient. For consistency with the Uniform Guidance language and in the context of explaining applicable federal regulations, this chapter will refer to units of local government as non-federal entities (NFEs).

4. *See* 2 C.F.R. § 200.318(a).

5. *See* " 'Most Restrictive Rule' Procurement Requirements under the Federal Uniform Guidance for North Carolina Local Governments" (UNC School of Government, June 2018).

General Public Contract Requirements

Contracting Authority and Authorized Purposes

The statutes that delegate to counties and municipalities broad corporate powers necessary to govern and to conduct basic activities include a delegation of authority to contract.[6] Other statutes authorize counties and municipalities to perform particular functions and contain specific contracting powers.[7] These specific authorizations do not limit the general authority to contract. Indeed, parallel statutes for counties and municipalities authorize each to contract with a private entity to perform any activity in which the county or municipality has authority to engage.[8]

An important legal requirement for local government contracts is that the person or persons who make the contract must have authority to contract on behalf of the entity that will be bound by the contract. A local government is not bound by a contract entered into by an individual who does not have authority to contract on its behalf. North Carolina law provides that the governing board of a county or municipality is the body that has authority to act for the local government, and this includes the authority to contract.[9] The governing board may delegate its authority to others within the organization, unless a statute specifically requires action to be taken by the governing board or by another named official. For example, the state competitive bidding laws require the governing board to award construction or repair contracts that are subject to formal bidding requirements[10] and to approve a contract under certain exceptions to the bidding requirements,[11] so the board is not permitted to delegate authority to award these contracts. Similarly, most methods of surplus property disposal require governing board action.[12] For contracts that are not subject to these types of limitations, however, the county or municipality governing board has discretion to delegate its contracting authority under state law. As a general matter, the Uniform Guidance does not require governing board approval for any specific procurement or disposal actions.

A delegation of authority to contract may be either explicit or implicit. An example of explicit delegation might be found in a municipal charter, a local act of the General Assembly, or a county or municipal policy adopted by a unit's governing board delegating to its manager or some other official the authority to enter into contracts on behalf of the local government. A governing board might also adopt a resolution explicitly delegating authority for awarding purchase contracts, as permitted under the formal bidding statute, or in other circumstances, including awarding informal contracts where the statutes do not require the governing board to award these contracts. In addition, a job description or personnel policy could constitute

---

6. Chapter 153A, Section 11 and Chapter 160A, Section 11 of the North Carolina General Statutes (hereinafter G.S.).

7. For example, G.S. 153A-275 and 160A-312 authorize counties and municipalities, respectively, to contract for the operation of public enterprises.

8. G.S. 153A-449 (counties); 160A-20.1 (municipalities).

9. G.S. 153A-12; 160A-12.

10. G.S. 143-129(b). G.S. 143-129(a) authorizes the board to delegate the authority to award purchase contracts in the formal range.

11. G.S. 143-129(e)(6) (sole sources); -129(g) (previously bid contracts/"piggybacking").

12. See the section below entitled "Property Disposal" for a discussion of property disposal procedural requirements.

an explicit delegation of contracting authority if it has been approved by the governing board. Thus, a purchasing agent or department head may have authority to contract if doing so is part of his or her job responsibilities as defined by the board. Implicit authority might be found in cases where employees regularly make contracts with the knowledge and tacit approval of the board but without a formalized policy. Many local government contracts are made by local employees with implicit authority based on historical patterns of activity and consistent with assigned job responsibilities.

The extent to which contracting is delegated within a county or municipality is a function of local policy, management philosophy, and administrative organization. Responsibility for contracting should be allocated in a manner that best balances the need for efficiency and flexibility with the need to comply with legal contracting and fiscal internal control requirements. Centralization of contracting for items that require bidding or that involve commonly used items helps to ensure compliance with legal requirements and can provide better value through economies of scale and consistency in administration.

Multi-Year Contracts

Counties and municipalities have specific authority to enter into contracts that extend beyond the current fiscal year.[13] The statutes allow a unit to enter into continuing contracts and require the unit's board to appropriate the amount due in each subsequent year for the duration of that contract.

Contracts generally continue to bind the unit despite changes in board membership or philosophy. Courts have held that this rule does not apply, however, to any contract that limits essential governmental discretion, such as a contract that promises not to annex property or a contract in which the unit promises not to raise taxes.[14] Most county and municipal contracts, however, involve basic commercial transactions and, assuming all other requirements for a valid contract are met, will be enforceable against the unit for the duration of the contract.

Because a multi-year contract imposes an ongoing fiscal obligation on a unit for the duration of the contract, the unit may include a non-appropriation clause that makes continuation of the contract in subsequent years contingent on the governing board's appropriation of funds for that contract. A non-appropriation clause is required for all installment financings.[15] It also may be required on any other contract, agreement, or lease that could be construed as a borrowing by the unit. Whether a non-appropriation clause should be included in a contract is a matter of policy and is subject to negotiation with, and agreement by, the contractor or vendor that is a party to the contract.

Expenditures Supported by Appropriations and Preaudit Certifications

State laws governing local government finance require counties and municipalities to establish internal procedures designed to ensure that sufficient appropriated funds are available to pay contractual obligations. Contracts involving the expenditure of funds that are included in a unit's budget ordinance must be "preaudited" to ensure that they are being spent in accordance

---

13. G.S. 153A-13 (counties); 160A-17 (municipalities).

14. *See* David M. Lawrence, "Contracts That Bind the Discretion of Governing Boards," *Popular Government* 56, no. 1 (1990): 38–42.

15. *See* Wayne Cnty. Citizens Ass'n v. Wayne Cnty. Bd. of Comm'rs, 328 N.C. 24 (1991).

with a budget appropriation and that sufficient funds remain available in the appropriation to pay the obligation created by the contract. All written contracts must contain a certification by a unit's finance officer, as specified in Chapter 159, Section 28(a1) of the North Carolina General Statutes (hereinafter G.S.), stating that the instrument has been "preaudited in the manner required by the Local Government Budget and Fiscal Control Act."[16] Under that statute, a person who incurs an obligation or pays out funds in violation of the statute is personally liable for the funds committed or disbursed.[17] Obligations incurred in violation of this requirement are void and are not enforceable against the unit.[18]

Most local governments use computerized financial systems that automatically conduct the preaudit procedure. These programs keep track of appropriated funds by category or account and encumber obligations as they are created by removing them from the pool of available funds. In 2021, the preaudit statute was amended to explicitly allow local governments to use an automated system for the preaudit process if the system meets certain statutory requirements.[19] Additionally, in order to use the automated preaudit system, a local government, through its finance officer(s), must also file an annual certification with the Secretary of the Local Government Commission.

For more information on preaudit and disbursement requirements, see "Obligating and Disbursing Public Funds" in Chapter 8, "Managing and Disbursing Public Funds."

Contract Execution

As noted above, counties and municipalities have broad authority in allocating responsibility for contract approval. It is very important to distinguish, however, between the authority to approve a contract and the authority to execute (sign) a contract. Execution of the contract is a formality that is used to prove assent. Contracts are sometimes executed at the same time they are approved. In other cases, the contract is executed after approval, such as when a unit's governing board approves a contract that is later executed by the unit's manager. Even if a contract is properly executed, it is not enforceable against the unit if it was not approved or authorized by someone with authority to contract on behalf of the unit. The fact that someone has authority to execute a contract does not necessarily mean that he or she also has authority to approve a contract, though it may constitute evidence of implicit authority if there is no explicit delegation. Except for the preaudit certification by the finance officer of a unit, state laws do not dictate who must sign county and municipal contracts, so this is left to local discretion. As with the authority to award, the authority to execute is best delegated through a written policy, job description, or resolution approved by the governing board. Ensuring compliance with legal requirements does not end once a contract is executed, though. Local governments must monitor performance pursuant to the contract, and, in fact, the Uniform Guidance states

---

16. The Act comprises Article 3 of G.S. Chapter 159.

17. G.S. 159-28(a2).

18. G.S. 159-28(a); *see also* L & S Leasing, Inc. v. City of Winston-Salem, 122 N.C. App. 619 (1996).

19. G.S. 159-28(a3) specifies that the system must have all of the following: (1) embedded functionality that determines that there is an appropriation to the department, function code, or project in which the transaction appropriately falls; (2) functionality ensuring that unencumbered funds remain in the appropriation to pay out any amounts that are expected to come due during the budgeted period; and (3) real-time visibility to budget compliance, alert threshold notifications, and rules-based compliance measures and enforcement.

that NFEs "must maintain oversight to ensure that contractors perform in accordance with the terms, conditions, and specifications of their contracts or purchase orders."[20]

Form of Contracts and Electronic Contracts

In addition to the specific rules that apply to public contracts, all contracts must be enforceable under general common law and state statutory requirements. Most importantly, contracts must be supported by adequate consideration,[21] and there must be evidence to support any claim that the county or municipality, as a party to a contract, actually agreed to be bound by the terms of an alleged contractual commitment.

Whether a contract must be in writing depends on the type of contract and the unit of government entering into that contract. A state statute requires that all contracts made by or on behalf of municipalities must be in writing.[22] A municipal contract that is not in writing is void, but the governing board of the municipality can cure this defect by expressly ratifying the written contract. The North Carolina Supreme Court has held that the board's actions as recorded in its minutes do not satisfy the statutory requirement that a contract be in writing.[23] There is no parallel statute that requires county contracts to be in writing. The formal bidding statute, G.S. 143-129, however, requires all local government contracts that are within its scope to be in writing. (See Appendix 11.1, "Dollar Thresholds in North Carolina Public Contracting Statutes," for information on which contracts are subject to formal bidding.)

Another important writing requirement is contained in the Uniform Commercial Code (UCC). The UCC was developed to modernize and standardize the law governing commercial transactions, eliminating variations from state to state and removing many of the technicalities in the common law of contracts. In North Carolina, the UCC has been adopted as G.S. Chapter 25. The provisions governing contracts for the sale of goods are contained in Article 2, beginning at G.S. 25-2-101. Article 2 requires that all contracts (not just local government contracts) for the sale of goods exceeding $500 must be in writing.[24] In addition, while the common law requires that a contract specify all the essential terms of the agreement, the UCC modifies common law contract requirements relating to the contents of a writing and the formalities for a valid signature.[25]

Other writing requirements are found in G.S. Chapter 22. Of greatest significance to local governments is the requirement of a writing for any contract or deed evidencing the sale of land or for any interest in land, including an easement; for any sale or lease of mining rights; and for any other lease of more than three years in length.[26]

Even when it is not required by statute or when the agreement at issue does not involve the expenditure of public funds (such as a lease of government property for a term of less than three years), a writing serves important purposes, the most significant being the clear expression of

---

20. 2 C.F.R. § 200.319(b).

21. That is, by something of value exchanged between the parties on each side of the contract.

22. G.S. 160A-16.

23. Wade v. City of New Bern, 77 N.C. 460 (1877). In addition, board minutes would not satisfy the preaudit certificate requirement under G.S. 159-28(a).

24. G.S. 25-2-201(1).

25. G.S. 25-1-201(b)(37) (a contract can be signed "using any symbol executed or adopted with present intention to adopt or accept a writing").

26. G.S. 22-2.

the agreement between the parties. In addition, for local governments the written document, usually a purchase order, incorporates the fiscal and departmental approvals required by statute and by local policy, and it provides documentation for the annual audit.

State and federal laws address the acceptability of electronic contracts, providing broad authority for the use of electronic transactions in general and in governmental contracting.[27] These laws generally provide that a contract may not be denied legal effect or enforceability solely because it has been created as an electronic document or has been affixed with an electronic signature. It is up to each county or municipality to determine whether it wishes to use or accept electronic contracts and to develop systems for assuring their authenticity and enforceability.

Contract Limitations and Required Clauses

State law and federal regulations place a number of limitations and requirements on certain categories of public contracts, including the following:

State Law Restrictions

- *Construction indemnity agreements*—prohibits a party from insulating itself from its own negligence. (G.S. 22B-1)
- *Real property improvement dispute venue*—prohibits making a contract subject to the laws of another state or setting exclusive venue in other state. (G.S. 22B-2)
- *Forum selection*—prohibits requiring prosecution of an action or arbitration of a dispute in another state. (G.S. 22B-3)
- *Jury trial waiver*—prohibits requiring a party to waive its right to a jury trial (does not prohibit mutually agreed-to mediation, arbitration, or other alternative dispute resolution processes). (G.S. 22B-10)
- *Incurring third-party debt*—violates constitutional limitations on local government indemnifying obligations of other parties, which is a form of incurring debt. (N.C. CONST. art. V, § 4)
- *Organized labor restrictions*—prohibits discriminating against a bidder or contractor for adhering or not adhering to an organized labor agreement. (G.S. 143-133.5)
- *Employment-related and public accommodation requirements*—prohibits cities and counties from imposing employment-related requirements on bidders and contractors as a condition of bidding on a contract. (G.S. 153A-449(a) for counties; 160A-20.1(a) for cities)
- *E-Verify*—prohibits local governments from contracting with contractors and subcontractors who are not compliant with the state's E-Verify hiring requirement. (G.S. 143-133.3)
- *Iran Divestment Act*—prohibits local governments from contracting with an entity that has been identified by the office of the N.C. State Treasurer as engaging in Iranian investment activities. (G.S. 147-86.60)

---

27. At the federal level, see the Electronic Signatures in Global and National Commerce Act (E-SIGN), 15 U.S.C. § 7001; at the state level, see the Uniform Electronic Transactions Act (UETA), G.S. Chapter 66, Article 40 (G.S. 66-311 through -330), and the Electronic Commerce in Government Act, G.S. Chapter 66, Article 11A (G.S. 66-58.1 through -58.12).

- *Israel boycott contracting prohibition*—prohibits local governments from contracting with a company that has been identified by the office of the N.C. State Treasurer as boycotting Israel. (G.S. 147-86.82)

Federal Restrictions and Required Clauses

The Uniform Guidance requires that NFEs include certain applicable provisions in their contracts.[28] These required contract clauses can be found in Appendix II to Part 200 of the Uniform Guidance ("Contract Provisions for Non-Federal Entity Contracts Under Federal Award") and include the following:[29]

- *Remedies for contract breach*—contracts above the Simplified Acquisition Threshold must address administrative, contractual, or legal remedies for violations of the contract. (Appendix II to Part 200 (A))
- *Termination for cause and for convenience*—contracts of $10,000 or more must explain the trigger and process for termination of the contract. (Appendix II to Part 200 (B))
- *Equal employment opportunity*—federally assisted construction contracts must include a specific equal opportunity clause. (Appendix II to Part 200 (C))
- *Davis-Bacon and Copeland Anti-Kickback Acts*—prime construction contracts of $2,000 or more must include provisions for compliance with the Davis-Bacon Act, when required by federal program legislation, and with the Copeland Anti-Kickback Act. (Appendix II to Part 200 (D))
- *Contract work hours and safety standards*—contracts of $100,000 or more that involve employment of mechanics or laborers must include provisions that involve computation of wages based on a forty-hour work week and impose health and safety standards for applicable work. (Appendix II to Part 200 (E))
- *Rights to inventions*—contracts for the performance of experimental, developmental, or research work funded in whole or in part by the federal government must include the standard patent clause found in 37 C.F.R. 401.14. (Appendix II to Part 200 (F))
- *Clean Air and Federal Water Pollution Control Acts*—contracts and subgrants of amounts in excess of $150,000 must contain a provision that requires compliance with these regulations. (Appendix II to Part 200 (G))
- *Byrd anti-lobbying amendment*—contractors that apply or bid for an award exceeding $100,000 must file a certification about lobbying related to the contract. (Appendix II to Part 200 (I))
- *Procurement of recovered materials*—for purchases by state or local governments of specific items designated by the U.S. Environmental Protection Agency and costing $10,000 or more, such items must be made from recovered materials consistent with maintaining a satisfactory level of competition.[30] (Appendix II to Part 200 (J))

---

28. See 2 C.F.R. § 200.327.

29. This list summarizes the basic requirements of required contract provisions in Appendix II to Part 200. School of Government faculty member Connor Crews drafted a detailed contract addendum that incorporates all of these required clauses; *see* Connor H. Crews, "Using the Coronavirus State and Local Fiscal Recovery Funds Model Addendum: Purpose, Usage, Questions and Answers," *Local Finance Bulletin* No. 60 (April 2022): § XI.

30. *See also* 2 C.F.R. § 200.323.

- *Telecommunications and video surveillance services or equipment*—NFEs are prohibited from procuring, obtaining, or contracting for equipment, services, or systems that use certain covered telecommunications equipment, primarily affiliated with two identified companies. (Appendix II to Part 200(K))
- *Domestic preferences*—NFEs should provide a preference for the purchase, acquisition, or use of goods, products, or materials produced in the United States, to the greatest extent practicable, and must include this requirement in all contracts.[31] (Appendix II to Part 200 (L))

In addition to the federally mandated procurement and contracting clauses noted above, NFEs are prohibited from contracting with certain entities. Specifically, federal fund recipients and subrecipients, and the contractors of each, must not enter into federal-grant-funded contracts with entities that have been "debarred, suspended, or otherwise excluded" from receiving benefits from the federal government.[32] Federal regulations provide that an entity's exclusion status can be verified in one of three ways: (1) searching for government-wide exclusions in the System for Award Management (SAM) and documenting the search, (2) collecting a certification about exclusion status from the contracting entity, or (3) adding a contract clause or condition about exclusion status to the covered transaction with the entity.[33] Practically speaking, many governmental units use more than one method to verify an entity's exclusion status.

Furthermore, the Uniform Guidance discourages the use of time-and-materials contracts. A time-and-materials contract specifies the cost of materials and labor hours at fixed hourly rates rather than a fixed price for an entire project. If an NFE desires to use a time-and-materials contract, it must determine that no other contract type is suitable, and the contract must include a ceiling price that the contractor exceeds at its own risk.[34] Additionally, the Uniform Guidance prohibits the use of a cost plus a percentage of cost contract and a percentage of construction cost methods contract.[35]

General Competitive Bidding Requirements

Contracts Covered by Bidding Laws

State and federal laws require local governments to obtain competitive bids before awarding certain types of contracts. The competitive bidding process is designed to prevent collusion and favoritism in the awarding of contracts and to generate favorable pricing to conserve public funds. As discussed in this section, the law does not always require that contracts be awarded to the lowest-cost bidder, and the bidding requirements themselves are best viewed as requiring

---

31. For a detailed explanation of domestic preferences imposed by the Uniform Guidance, see Connor H. Crews, "Buy American? Buy America? Build America? An Introduction to Domestic Procurement Preferences in Federal Financial Assistance for North Carolina's Counties and Municipalities," *Local Finance Bulletin* No. 63 (March 2023): § IV.

32. *See* 2 C.F.R. § 200.214 and 2 C.F.R. pt. 180.

33. 2 C.F.R. § 180.300.

34. 2 C.F.R. § 200.318(i).

35. 2 C.F.R. § 200.324(d).

prudent investment of public dollars. This means that quality and value can be as important as initial price in evaluating competitively bid contracts.

Under state law, the two key bidding statutes, G.S. 143-129 (formal bidding) and -131 (informal bidding), apply to two categories of contracts: (1) contracts for the purchase or lease-purchase of "apparatus, supplies, materials, or equipment" (hereinafter purchase contracts) and (2) contracts for construction or repair work. As discussed in the next section, many contracts do not fall within either of these categories and thus are not subject to any mandatory competitive bidding requirements. Bidding requirements are triggered when expenditures of public funds for the two specified categories of contracts occur at the dollar thresholds specified in the statutes. These dollar amounts correspond to the cost of the contract itself as opposed to the cost of individual items under the contract or the budgeted amount available for the expenditure. Current North Carolina dollar thresholds are set forth in Appendix 11.1.

The Uniform Guidance classifies procurements differently than state law and divides procurements into the following three methods: informal procurement, formal procurement, and noncompetitive procurement.[36] Within these three categories, competitive procurement processes are required for what the Uniform Guidance labels as small purchases, sealed bids, and proposals.

Small purchase procedures are used for the acquisition of property or services when the aggregate dollar amount is higher than the micro-purchase threshold but lower than the simplified acquisition threshold.[37] At the time of publication of this edition of *Introduction to Local Government Finance*, the micro-purchase threshold is $10,000. However, through an annual self-certification process, governmental units can increase the micro-purchase threshold up to $50,000 depending on state law thresholds.[38] Sealed bids and competitive proposals are used when the value of property or services being procured exceeds either the simplified acquisition threshold or a lower threshold established by a non-federal entity (NFE). Note that where state law imposes competitive requirements at a lower threshold than the simplified acquisition threshold, an NFE must apply the Uniform Guidance requirements—along with state law requirements—at that lower threshold.[39] Sealed bids are intended to be used for firm fixed-price contracts and are the preferred method for procuring construction services. Competitive proposals are intended for use when conditions are not appropriate for a sealed bid.

North Carolina competitive bidding requirements apply to counties, municipalities, local school units, and other local government agencies. With respect to purchase contracts, state agencies, including universities and community colleges, are governed by Article 3 of

---

36. 2 C.F.R. § 200.320.

37. 2 C.F.R. § 200.320(a)(2). These thresholds are defined in 2 C.F.R. § 200.2, and at the time of publication of this edition, the micro-purchase threshold is $10,000 and the simplified acquisition threshold is $250,000.

38. For an explanation of the annual self-certification allowed under the Uniform Guidance, see Connor H. Crews, "Raising the Federal Micro-Purchase Threshold: Self-Certification for Units of Local Government in North Carolina," *Coates' Canons: NC Local Government Law* blog (April 23, 2021).

39. For example, North Carolina competitive bidding laws impose formal bidding requirements for purchases of goods starting at $90,000, which is a lower threshold than the current simplified acquisition threshold of $250,000. Thus, if federal financial assistance is being used for the purchase of goods valued at $90,000 or more, an NFE must apply the most restrictive rules of the Uniform Guidance and state law to that purchase, thereby requiring sealed bids for the purchase according to state law.

G.S. Chapter 143 and by the rules and policies of the State Department of Administration, Division of Purchase and Contract. With respect to contracts for construction or repair work, state agencies, including universities and community colleges, are governed by the statutes described here, along with rules and policies of the State Construction Office.

Private entities, whether nonprofit or for-profit, that contract with counties or municipalities are generally not required to comply with North Carolina bidding statutes, even when they are spending funds awarded to them by counties or municipalities. The funds are no longer considered public once they are received by the private entity under a contract or grant of local funds from a public agency. A local government contracting with a private entity may, however, require compliance with bidding requirements as a condition of receipt of the funds. On the other hand, federal or state agencies administering grant programs often require as a condition of a grant that private subrecipients use competitive bidding procedures when expending grant funds. Determining whether a private party needs to comply with the competitive bidding procedures in the Uniform Guidance requires evaluating whether the private party is a subrecipient or contractor.[40] In most cases, subrecipients must follow the procurement standards of the Uniform Guidance, whereas contractors are not required to comply with the Uniform Guidance and instead an NFE applies the procurement standards when selecting the contractor.

Contracts Not Covered by Bidding Requirements and Optional Procedures

Under North Carolina law, contracts for services, such as janitorial, grounds maintenance, and solid waste collection, fall outside the scope of the competitive bidding statutes. In comparison, contracts for services are subject to the competitive procurement requirements of the Uniform Guidance when the cost exceeds the micro-purchase threshold. As discussed later, special rules apply to contracts for architectural, engineering, and land surveying services (sometimes referred to as professional services) and alternative construction delivery services.

Contracts for the purchase of real property and contracts for the lease (rental) of real or personal property also fall outside the scope of North Carolina laws that require competitive bidding. However, it is important to note that contracts for the lease-purchase of personal property, the installment-purchase of personal property, or the lease with option to purchase of personal property *are* subject to competitive bidding under North Carolina law.[41] Under the Uniform Guidance, rental costs of real property and equipment are not subject to competitive procurement, but the rental costs must be reasonable and are subject to other limitations, such as those addressing maximum price and specific conflicts of interest.[42]

Finally, under North Carolina law, purchase contracts and contracts for construction or repair work that fall below the informal bidding threshold are not subject to competitive bidding, though many local policies require bidding even at these lower levels. Likewise, purchase and service contracts that fall below the micro-purchase threshold set forth in the Uniform Guidance are not subject to competitive bidding.

It is also common for counties and municipalities to seek competitive bids on contracts even when laws do not require it, such as by issuing a request for proposals for solid waste services.

---

40. 2 C.F.R. § 200.330 provides factors for distinguishing subrecipients from contractors.
41. G.S. 160A-19.
42. *See* 2 C.F.R. § 200.465.

This is a good practice to ensure fair pricing whenever there is competition for a particular service or product. Counties and municipalities often use the statutory procedures when seeking competition voluntarily, but this is not required under state law. It is important for a unit to specify what procedures and standards it will use for awarding contracts in solicitations that are not subject to state statutes, especially if the procedures will be different from those set forth in the statutes. The unit is legally bound to adhere to the procedures it opts to use when bidding is not required by statute, or it may terminate the procedure and contract using some other procedure if it deems this to be in its best interest. The decision to competitively bid a contract when it is not statutorily required does not obligate the unit to use bidding in the future for that contract or for that type of contract.

Exceptions to Bidding Requirements

State and federal bidding laws contain a number of exceptions. County and municipal officials should be cautious when contracting without bidding to make sure that the contract falls within an exception. Courts have recognized the importance of the public policy underlying the bidding requirements and have strictly scrutinized local government justifications for claiming an exemption from bidding. Except as identified below, no specific procedures apply to contracts made under these exceptions.

The exceptions to the competitive bidding requirements pursuant to state law are as follows:[43]

- *Purchases from other governments*—G.S. 143-129(e)(1). Local governments may purchase items directly from any other unit of government or from a government agency (federal, state, or local) and may purchase at government surplus sales. This exception applies to purchase contracts only.
- *Emergencies*—G.S. 143-129(e)(2). An exception applies in "cases of special emergency involving the health and safety of the people or their property." The only North Carolina case interpreting the emergency exception indicates that it is very limited, applicable only when the emergency is immediate, unforeseeable, and cannot be resolved within the minimum time required to comply with the bidding procedures.[44] This exception applies to both purchase and construction or repair contracts.
- *Competitive group-purchasing programs*—G.S. 143-129(e)(3). A group-purchasing program is created by a separate organization on behalf of public agencies, or by one or more public agencies, in order to take advantage of economies of scale for commonly purchased items. Local governments may purchase without bidding items available under contracts that have been established using a competitive process undertaken as part of a group-purchasing program. This exception applies to purchase contracts only.[45]

---

43. See *Exceptions to State Competitive Bidding Requirements For North Carolina Local Governments*, a chart published by the School of Government that summarizes competitive bidding exceptions under state law.

44. Raynor v. Comm'rs of Louisburg, 220 N.C. 348 (1941).

45. The "exceptions" to non-competitive procurement under the Uniform Guidance are discussed later in this section, but a common question is whether the Uniform Guidance allows for purchases from group-purchasing programs. Although 2 C.F.R. § 200.318(e) encourages shared procurement processes among public entities and entities receiving federal funds, this language does not contemplate the group-purchasing arrangement allowed by North Carolina state law. Therefore, local governments should

- *Change-order work*—G.S. 143-129(e)(4). For construction or repair work, competitive bidding is not required for work undertaken "during the progress" of a construction or repair project initially begun pursuant to the formal bidding statute if the additional work was unforeseen at the time the contract was awarded. Change-order work that is not within the scope of the original project could be challenged as an unlawful evasion of the bidding requirements.
- *Gasoline, fuel, or oil*—G.S. 143-129(e)(5). Purchases of gasoline, diesel fuel, alcohol fuel, motor oil, fuel oil, or natural gas are exempt from the formal bidding procedures but must be carried out using the informal procedures under G.S. 143-131.
- *Sole source*—G.S. 143-129(e)(6). This exception applies to purchase contracts only, when performance or price competition is not available, when a needed product is available from only one source of supply, or when standardization or compatibility is the overriding consideration. Note that this exception applies when there is only one source for the item; simply being available from one manufacturer does not necessarily qualify the purchase under this exception if that item is available from more than one vendor or retailer. The governing board of a unit must approve each contract entered into under this exception, even if the board has delegated authority to award purchase contracts under G.S. 143-129(a).
- *State and federal contract purchases*—G.S. 143-129(e)(9), (9a). Local governments may purchase items from contracts awarded by any North Carolina state agency or federal agency if the contractor is willing to extend to the local unit the same or more favorable prices, terms, and conditions established in the state or federal contract.[46] This includes purchases of information technology from contracts established by the State Office of Information Technology Services (G.S. 143-129(e)(7)).
- *Used apparatus, supplies, materials, or equipment*—G.S. 143-129(e)(10). Competitive bidding is not required for the purchase of used items. The exception does not define what constitutes a used item, but it specifically excludes items that are remanufactured, refabricated, or "demo" (demonstration) items.
- *Previously bid contracts* ("piggybacking")—G.S. 143-129(g). Local governments may purchase from a contractor who has entered into a competitively bid contract with any other unit of government or with a government agency (federal, state, or local), anywhere in the country, within the past twelve months. The contractor must be willing to extend to the local government the same or more favorable prices and terms as contained in the previously bid contract. This exception applies to purchase contracts in the formal bidding range only. A North Carolina local government's governing board must approve each contract entered into under this exception at a regular board meeting on ten days' public notice, even if the board has delegated authority to award purchase contracts under G.S. 143-129(a).

---

consult with their attorneys and proceed with extreme caution when purchasing from a cooperative purchasing program using federal funds.

46. *But see* 2 C.F.R. § 200.318(f). While the Uniform Guidance encourages the purchase of federal excess and surplus property in lieu of purchasing new equipment or property, it is not clear that this relieves an NFE from complying with the procurement methods in 2 C.F.R. § 200.320.

- *Force-account work*—G.S. 143-135. For construction or repair work, bidding is not required for projects to be completed using the local government's own employees. This exception actually operates as a limitation on the amount of work that may be done by local government employees. The exception limits such work to projects estimated to cost no more than $500,000, including the cost of labor and materials, or to projects on which the cost of labor does not exceed $200,000. The competitive bidding statutes still apply to materials to be used on such force-account projects. Some have argued that the exception to the bidding requirements does not limit the use of the unit's own forces as long as the local unit itself submits a bid. There does not appear to be any authority in the statutes for a local government to submit a bid to itself as a way of complying with bidding requirements and avoiding application of the force-account limits.
- *School food services and publications*—G.S. 115C-264 (food services); 115C-522(a) (publications). Local boards of education may purchase without competitive bidding supplies and food for school food services programs and published books, manuscripts, pamphlets, and periodicals used by public schools.
- *Voting systems*—G.S. 163-165.8. Counties may purchase without competitive bidding voting systems that have been approved by the State Board of Elections.
- *Alternative procedures*—Requests for Proposals (RFP). Several types of contracts that involve a combination of goods and services may be entered into using alternative—usually more flexible—competitive procedures. A more flexible RFP procedure is authorized for contracts for information technology goods and services, including computer software, hardware, and related services (G.S. 143-129.8); guaranteed energy-savings contracts (G.S. 143-129(e)(8)); and contracts involving solid waste and sludge management facilities (G.S. 143-129.2). Unless specifically authorized under an exception, local governments do not have authority to use an RFP procedure for contracts that are subject to the competitive bidding statutes.

Unlike state law, which allows for exceptions to competitive bidding procedures based largely on the subject matter or context of the contract or the place from which an item is purchased, the Uniform Guidance permits non-competitive procurement in only five instances: (1) procurement under the micro-purchase threshold, (2) single source (which is synonymous with sole source), (3) public emergency, (4) express permission from the federal awarding agency or pass-through entity, or (5) when competition is deemed inadequate after solicitation of a number of sources.[47] Micro-purchases may be awarded without soliciting any competitive quotations if an NFE considers the costs to be reasonable, but these purchases must be distributed equitably among qualified suppliers, to the extent practicable.[48] The Uniform Guidance does not elaborate on the definitions or processes for the remainder of the non-competitive procurements, and NFEs should look to the federal awarding agency for further guidance.

---

47. *See* 2 C.F.R. § 200.320(c).
48. 2 C.F.R. § 200.320(a)(1).

Specifications

Specifications describe the performance requirements, criteria, and characteristics of the item, construction project, or service being procured. While competitive specifications are an essential element of the bidding process, no statutory procedures govern the preparation of specifications for purchases. Local officials may develop specifications that are most appropriate for their respective units. Specifications cannot, however, intentionally or unjustifiably eliminate competition by using overly restrictive specifications.[49] The Uniform Guidance requires that solicitations include a clear description of the technical requirements for the material, product, or service to be procured; how proposers can meet the requirements of the solicitation; and how proposers will be evaluated.[50] Federal rules further explain and prohibit situations that are considered restrictive of competition, such as requiring unnecessary experience and excessive bonding or noncompetitive contracts to consultants that are on retainer contract.[51]

Under state law, if only one brand of product is suitable, the specification can be limited to that brand; however, specifications for materials included in construction projects must be described in terms of performance characteristics and brands can be specified only when performance specification is not possible. In such cases, at least three brands must be specified, unless it is impossible to do so, in which case the specifications must include as many brands as possible. A unit must specifically approve in advance of the bid opening preferred products that are to be listed as alternates in specifications for construction projects. A brand-specific specification is not necessarily a sole-source purchase since there may be more than one supplier of a particular brand. Similarly, the Uniform Guidance characterizes specifying brand names as restrictive of competition and prompts NFEs to allow for an equal product to be offered and to describe the performance or other relevant requirements of the procurement.[52] However, the Uniform Guidance notes that if describing the technical requirements of a product is impractical or uneconomical, a "brand name or equivalent" description may be used.[53]

In order to promote full and open competition, some individuals are prohibited from participating in the procurement process. Under North Carolina law, architects and engineers providing design services on public projects are prohibited from specifying any materials, equipment, or other items in which the designer has a financial interest.[54] Similarly, manufacturers cannot be involved in drawing plans or specifications for public construction projects.[55] The Uniform Guidance prohibits contractors that develop or draft specifications, requirements, statements of work, or invitations for bids or requests for proposals from competing for such procurements.[56]

Contracts for the construction or repair of buildings are subject to additional statutory requirements for specifications. Depending on the cost, some project specifications must be

---

49. *See* 2 C.F.R. § 200.319(b).

50. 2 C.F.R. § 200.319(d)(2).

51. For the list of situations identified in the Uniform Guidance as restrictive of competition, see 2 C.F.R. § 200.319(b). Note that the list is not comprehensive, and federal agencies could interpret other actions as restrictive of competition.

52. *See* 2 C.F.R. § 200.319(b).

53. *See* 2 C.F.R. § 200.319(d)(1).

54. G.S. 133-1.

55. G.S. 133-2.

56. 2 C.F.R. § 200.319(b).

drawn by a licensed architect or engineer.[57] If the building project is estimated to cost $300,000 or more, separate specifications must be prepared for heating, plumbing, and electrical work as well as general construction work.[58]

Trade-Ins

G.S. 143-129.7 authorizes local governments to include in bid specifications for a purchase an allowance for the trade-in of surplus property and to consider the price offered, including the trade-in allowance, when awarding a contract for the purchase. This statute effects an exemption from otherwise applicable procedures for disposing of surplus property. (See the section below titled "Property Disposal" for a full description of procedures for disposing of property.)

Summary of Bidding Procedures

Informal Bidding

For North Carolina local governments, informal bidding under G.S. 143-131 is required for contracts for construction or repair work and for the purchase of apparatus, supplies, materials, or equipment costing between the minimum informal bid threshold and the formal bidding limit (see Appendix 11.1 for current threshold amounts). No specific method of advertisement is required, and the statute does not specify a minimum number of bids that must be received. Informal bids can take the form of telephone quotes, faxed bids, or other electronic or written bids. The statute does require a county or municipality to maintain a record of informal bids received and specifies that such records are subject to public inspection after the contract is awarded. This prevents bidders from having access to bids already submitted when preparing their bids, a situation not present in formal bidding because bids are sealed until the bid opening. The standard for awarding contracts in the informal range is the same as the standard for formal bids—the lowest responsive responsible bidder—and is discussed later in this chapter. As noted below, for building construction or repair contracts in the informal range, the informal bidding statute requires counties and municipalities to solicit bids from minority firms and to report to the state Department of Administration on bids solicited and obtained for contracts in this dollar range.

Under the Uniform Guidance, informal bidding procedures apply to "small purchases," which involve the acquisition of property or services when the aggregate dollar amount is higher than the micro-purchase threshold but lower than the simplified acquisition threshold. At its upper limits and due to the interplay with state law, small-purchase procedures currently apply when federal funds are used for procuring goods up to $90,000, construction or repair up to $250,000, and services up to $250,000. Procurement of professional services, which are procured using qualifications-based selection, is covered later in this chapter. Procedurally, the Uniform Guidance requires that an NFE obtain price or rate quotations from an adequate number of qualified sources. This language gives an NFE discretion to determine the

---

57. G.S. 133-1.1(a).
58. G.S. 143-128(a).

"adequate" number of qualified sources but implies that the number must be greater than one. Moreover, the methods of obtaining the price or rate quotations are left up to the NFE. The quote could be obtained in writing, orally, from a vendor price list on a website, or generated via online search engine, but these quotes and the basis for the contractor selection and contract price must be documented.[59] Similar to state law, the Uniform Guidance also imposes requirements for contracting with small and minority businesses, women's business enterprises, and labor-surplus-area firms; these requirements, known as affirmative steps, are discussed later in this chapter.[60]

Formal Bidding

The requirements for formal bidding are more rigorous than informal bidding procedures. When local governments are spending public funds at the formal bidding thresholds established by state and federal law, the formal bidding procedures are designed to ensure fairness and transparency in the expenditure of public funds and make available opportunities for contractors. This section describes the elements of state and federal formal bidding processes, including advertisement, the format of the bid, and bonding requirements.

Under state law, formal bidding is synonymous with sealed bidding. The Uniform Guidance, however, classifies two types of procurement methods as formal bidding methods: sealed bids and proposals, referred to in this chapter as "competitive proposals." Sealed bids must be used for solicitations that exceed the simplified acquisition threshold and are the preferred method for procuring construction. When federal funds are being used and due to the interplay with state law, sealed bids are required for purchases of goods starting at $90,000 and for construction or repair starting at $250,000. Competitive proposals can be used at a dollar amount deemed appropriate by an NFE. This means that soliciting for services could be accomplished by a competitive proposal starting at $250,000, although an NFE could opt for a lower threshold. Additionally, when federal funds are being used, solicitations for architectural or engineering services by competitive proposal must also comply with the North Carolina Mini-Brooks Act, which is discussed later in this chapter.

Advertisement

The North Carolina formal bidding statute, G.S. 143-129, requires counties and municipalities to advertise opportunities to bid on contracts for construction or repair, or for the purchase of apparatus, supplies, materials, and equipment, within the formal bid thresholds as described in Appendix 11.1. The minimum time period for advertisement under the statute requires that a full seven days pass between the day of the advertisement and the day of the bid opening. It is common practice to place the advertisement more than once or for a longer period of time prior to the bid opening in order to provide sufficient opportunity for response. The advertisement must list the date, time, and location of the bid opening; identify where specifications may be obtained; and contain a statement that the unit's governing board reserves the right to reject any or all bids. For construction projects, the advertisement may also contain information about contractor licensing requirements that apply to the project. The formal bidding statute requires the advertisement to be published in a newspaper of general circulation within the

---

59. *See* 2 C.F.R. § 200.318(i).
60. *See* 2 C.F.R. § 200.321.

given county or municipality. The statute also authorizes the governing board to approve the use of electronic advertising of bidding opportunities instead of published notice.[61] On the other hand, the Uniform Guidance does not require anything more than "public advertising" that provides a sufficient time for responses to a sealed bid procurement. Likewise, competitive proposals must be "publicized" under the Uniform Guidance.

Sealed Bids

Bids must be sealed and submitted prior to the time of the bid opening. Both state law and federal rules require sealed bids to be opened in public. State law allows sealed bids to be opened before the advertised time with the permission of the bidder. Under the "dual-bidding" method of construction contracting authorized under state law (discussed later), separate-prime bids must be received (but not opened) one hour before single-prime bids. Unit staff generally conduct bid openings, but contracts must be awarded by the governing board, except for purchase contracts in jurisdictions where the board has delegated the authority to award these contracts as authorized in G.S. 143-129(a).

Once formal bids are opened, they become public records and are subject to public inspection under North Carolina's public records laws. The only exception to this rule is contained in G.S. 132-1.2, which allows a bidder to identify trade secrets that are contained in a bid and protects that information from public disclosure.[62]

Competitive Proposals

The Uniform Guidance identifies competitive proposals as an additional formal procurement method, generally used when conditions are not appropriate for the use of sealed bids. The Uniform Guidance does not elaborate on circumstances where sealed bids are not appropriate, but a competitive proposal is beneficial where price is not the primary factor for selecting a bidder. There are two ways in which competitive proposals can be used. First, a competitive proposal can be designed as a Request for Proposals (RFP), whereby proposers are evaluated based on evaluation factors, including price, and an award is made to the most advantageous proposal. Second, competitive proposals can be used for procuring architectural and engineering services, whereby price is *not* used as a selection factor and the award is made to the "most qualified offeror." This second option is similar to the qualifications-based selection required for procuring architectural, engineering, and land surveying services under North Carolina's Mini-Brooks Act. When an NFE is using an RFP, the Uniform Guidance imposes a few additional requirements. The RFP must identify all of the factors that will be used for evaluation and their relative importance.[63] Additionally, an NFE must have a written method for conducting

---

61. The governing board may authorize electronic advertisement of bids for particular contracts or for contracts in general. Action to approve electronic notice of bidding must be taken by the county or municipal governing board at a regular meeting. No specific action is required to provide electronic notice in addition to published notice.

62. A "trade secret" is defined under G.S. 66-152(3). For further discussion of when bid documents become open to public inspection, see Eileen Youens, "When Are Bids and Proposals Subject to Public Inspection?," *Local Government Law Bulletin* No. 119 (Feb. 2009), downloadable at https://www.sog.unc.edu/publications/bulletin-series/local-government-law-bulletin.

63. 2 C.F.R. § 200.320(b)(2)(i).

its evaluations of proposals. Finally, proposals must be solicited from an adequate number of qualified offerors.

Electronic Bids

Counties and municipalities have several alternatives to receiving paper, sealed bids for purchase contracts in the formal bidding range. This option is not available for contracts for construction or repair in the formal range. Under G.S. 143-129.9, formal bids for purchase contracts may be received electronically[64] or through the use of a "reverse-auction" process.[65] An electronic bidding system must be designed to ensure the security, authenticity, and confidentiality of bids at least to the same extent as with sealed paper bids. Under a reverse-auction procedure, bidders compete to provide goods at the lowest selling price in an open and interactive electronic auction process. An electronic bid or reverse-auction process can be conducted by a unit itself or by a third party under contract with the unit. The statute does not allow the use of reverse auctions for the purchase of construction aggregates, including crushed stone, sand, and gravel, nor does it authorize the use of electronic bids or reverse auctions for construction contracts in the formal bidding range.

Number of Bids

According to G.S. 143-132, three bids are required for construction or repair contracts subject to formal bidding procedures. If three bids are not received after the first advertisement, the project must be re-advertised for at least the minimum time period listed under the formal bidding statute (seven days, not including the day of advertisement and the day of the bid opening) before the next bid opening. Following the second advertisement, a contract can be awarded even if fewer than three bids are received.

Note that the three-bid minimum requirement applies only to contracts for construction or repair work in the formal bidding range. This means that three bids are not required for purchase contracts in the formal range or for any contracts in the informal range. Some local governments have local policies that require a minimum of three bids for all contracts, but this is not required by state law.

In comparison, the Uniform Guidance requires that, for sealed-bid procurement, at least two bids be received, but the Uniform Guidance does not impose a minimum number of proposals for competitive proposals. Determining the required number of bids is an instance where local governments may need to apply the "most restrictive rule." For example, if only two bids are received for a federally funded construction project that is above the North Carolina threshold for formal bidding, the procurement process cannot proceed because the three-bid minimum under state law has not been met, even though two bids are sufficient under the Uniform Guidance.

---

64. G.S. 143-129.9(a)(1).
65. G.S. 143-129.9(a)(2).

Bid, Performance, and Payment Bonds

Bonds or statutorily authorized bond substitutes are required for construction or repair contracts in the formal bid range. A bid for construction or repair work submitted in response to a formal bidding procurement—whether under state law or federal rules—must be accompanied by a bid deposit or bid bond of at least 5 percent of the bid amount. The bid bond or deposit guarantees that the bidder to whom a contract is awarded will execute the contract and provide performance and payment bonds prior to the commencement of work on the project. North Carolina law specifies the forms in which the bid security may be submitted: a bid bond, a bid deposit in cash, a cashier's check, or a certified check. No other form of security, such as a letter of credit, is authorized under state law. The Uniform Guidance contemplates the bid security in the form of a bid bond or cashier's check but also allows for other negotiable instruments.

Specific procedures are set forth in G.S. 143-129.1 for the withdrawal of a bid. A bid may be withdrawn under those procedures without forfeiting the bid bond only if the bidder can demonstrate that he or she has made an unintentional and substantial error, as opposed to an error in judgment. The law does not allow a bidder to correct a mistake, only to withdraw a bid if proof of an unintentional error is shown. If the bidder can demonstrate that the error was substantial and unintentional, the bid may be withdrawn without the bid bond being forfeited so long as the request for withdrawal is made within seventy-two hours of the bid opening.[66]

State law requires that counties and municipalities obtain performance and payment bonds from the successful bidder on major construction or repair projects exceeding the formal bidding threshold, and the Uniform Guidance requires the same for construction or facility improvements contracts above the simplified acquisition threshold. A performance bond guarantees the contractor's performance under the contract and provides the county or municipality with security in the event the contractor defaults and cannot complete the project. The payment bond protects the subcontractors who supply labor or materials to the project and provides a source of payment to those subcontractors in the event they are not paid by the general contractor. North Carolina law authorizes counties and municipalities to accept deposits of cash, certified checks, or government securities in lieu of bonds.[67]

Evaluation of Bids and Responsiveness

Once received, bids must be evaluated to determine whether they meet the specifications and are eligible for award—that is, whether they are responsive bids. The bid evaluation process is important to maintaining the integrity of the bidding process as a whole. If a county or municipality accepts bids that contain significant deviations from the specifications, other bidders may object. Indeed, courts have recognized that a governmental unit receiving bids does not have unlimited discretion in waiving deviations from specifications. North Carolina courts have held that a unit must reject a bid that contains a "material variance" from specifications, defined as a variance that gives the bidder "an advantage or benefit which is not enjoyed by other

---

66. *See* G.S. 143-129.1; the statute allows local governments to establish a longer period for bid withdrawal so long as the period was specified in the instructions to bidders. *See also* Ralph Hodge Constr. Co. v. Brunswick Reg'l Water & Sewer H2GO, 284 N.C. App. 419, 421 (2022).

67. The performance and payment bonds required under the formal bidding statute are governed by Article 3 of G.S. Chapter 44A.

bidders."[68] Even though specifications may reserve to a unit the ability to "waive minor irregularities," the unit's assessment of what constitutes a minor irregularity must be based upon the legal standard established by the courts. Thus, if the low bid omits a required feature that the unit feels it cannot live without, the unit must reject the defective bid. Similarly, if waiving the irregularity would give that bidder an unfair competitive advantage over other bidders (such as saving that bidder time or money in compiling the bid proposal), the unit must reject the bid. When the low bid is rejected, the unit then has the option of accepting the next-lowest responsive, responsible bid or rejecting all the bids, revising or clarifying the specifications, if necessary, and rebidding the contract.

A bid must also be rejected as nonresponsive if it fails to satisfy a statutory requirement applicable to the particular contract. For example, a bid in the formal range that is submitted after the advertised bid deadline, or a formal bid for a construction project that is submitted without the required bid bond, must be rejected. While a unit has the discretion to waive minor irregularities, it does not have the authority to waive statutory requirements.

Cost and Price Analysis

When using federal funds, a non-federal entity (NFE) must perform a cost or price analysis before awarding a contract for every procurement action exceeding the simplified acquisition threshold.[69] The independent cost estimate serves as a tool for evaluating the reasonableness of a contractor's proposed costs or prices. Price analysis is essentially price comparison. It is the evaluation of a proposed price without analyzing any of the separate cost elements. Conversely, cost analysis is the evaluation of the separate elements (e.g., materials) that make up a contractor's total cost proposal to determine if the costs are reasonable. A cost analysis is used when price competition does not exist—for example, when negotiating a sole-source contract, or after soliciting competitive bids, only one bid is received. The method and degree of analysis required for each procurement situation varies, and federal agencies usually issue specific guidance on conducting the appropriate analysis.

Standard for Awarding Contracts

Under state law, both the formal and informal bid statutes require that contracts be awarded to the "lowest responsible bidder or bidders, taking into consideration quality, performance and the time specified in the proposals for the performance of the contract."[70] Similarly, the Uniform Guidance dictates that NFEs award contracts only to "responsible contractors possessing the ability to perform successfully under the terms and conditions of a proposed procurement," and NFEs can consider matters such as contractor integrity, public policy, past performance, and

---

68. Pro. Food Servs. Mgmt. v. N.C. Dep't of Admin., 109 N.C. App. 265, 269 (1993) (internal quotation marks, citation omitted). *See also* Frayda S. Bluestein, "Understanding the Responsiveness Requirement in Competitive Bidding," *Local Government Law Bulletin* No. 102 (May 2002).

69. 2 C.F.R. § 200.324. Note that some federal granting agencies, such as the Federal Transit Administration, may also require an Independent Cost Estimate (ICE) to establish a reasonable price for goods or services prior to a procurement action, and NFEs should always consult agency guidance to determine if additional requirements apply.

70. *See* G.S. 143-129(b) and -131(a).

financial and technical resources.[71] Pursuant to federal rules, small purchases can be awarded to a contractor so long as the price is fair and reasonable.

Although the "lowest responsible, responsive bidder" standard probably creates a presumption in favor of the bidder who submits the lowest dollar bid, it clearly does not require an award to the lowest bidder in all cases. The North Carolina Court of Appeals has held that the formal bid statute authorizes a local government to request information from bidders about their experience and financial strength and to consider this information in determining whether the low bidder is responsible.[72] The court found that the term "responsibility" refers to the bidder's capacity to perform the contract and that the statute authorizes the board to evaluate the bidder's experience, training and quality of personnel, financial strength, and any other factors that bear on the bidder's ability to perform the work.

A local government must carefully document the factual basis for any award to a bidder who did not submit the lowest bid and be diligent in investigating the facts to make sure that the information it relies upon is accurate and reliable. The county or municipality does not necessarily have to demonstrate that a contractor is not responsible generally, only that the contractor does not have the skills, experience, or financial capacity for the contract in question.

Additionally, under state law, construction or repair contracts that are subject to the formal bidding requirements must be awarded by a unit's governing body. For purchase contracts in the formal range, G.S. 143-129(a) authorizes the board to delegate to the unit's manager, chief purchasing official, or another employee the authority to award contracts or to reject bids and re-advertise the contract and opportunity to bid. The informal bidding statute does not dictate who must award contracts. This responsibility is usually delegated to the unit's purchasing agent or to other employees responsible for handling informal contracts.

Local governments also have broad authority under state law to reject any or all bids for any reason that is not inconsistent with the purposes of the bidding laws.[73] Likewise, the Uniform Guidance states that any or all sealed bids may be rejected if there is a "sound documented reason."[74]

Local Preferences

Local governments in North Carolina do not have specific statutory authority to establish preferences in awarding contracts, such as preferences for local or minority contractors.[75] A local preference would conflict with the legal requirement in both the formal and informal bidding range that contracts be awarded to the lowest responsive, responsible bidder. Although some may think it economically or politically desirable, it is not legal to assume that a local contractor is more responsible than others under this standard for awarding contracts.[76] The Uniform

---

71. 2 C.F.R. § 200.318(h).

72. Kinsey Contracting Co., Inc. v. City of Fayetteville, 106 N.C. App. 383, 386 (1992).

73. G.S. 143-129(a).

74. 2 C.F.R. § 200.320(b)(1)(ii)(E).

75. However, several jurisdictions in North Carolina have received authorizing legislation through local bills for small business enterprise programs, which allow those local governments to consider compliance with the programs when selecting a bidder under G.S. 143-129 or -131.

76. Unlike other local governments, local school boards are authorized to adopt policies authorizing an in-state percentage-price preference in competitive bidding for the purchase of food grown or produced in North Carolina pursuant to G.S. 115C-264.4.

Guidance explicitly prohibits the use of geographical preferences unless federal statutes mandate or encourage the preference.[77]

Under state law, preferences or targeted contracting efforts may be permissible, however, for contracts that are not subject to the competitive bidding requirements, such as service contracts or contracts below the minimum bid threshold (see Appendix 11.1). Counties and municipalities can also establish procedures to identify local and minority contractors and notify them of contracting opportunities.

Special Rules for Building Contracts

Bidding and Construction Methods

In addition to the bidding requirements for contracts involving construction or repair work described above, there are several special requirements under state law for construction and repair contracts involving buildings. First, state law limits the bidding and construction methods counties and municipalities may use for major building construction. For building construction projects that are above the dollar threshold contained in G.S. 143-128 (see Appendix 11.1), local governments may use any of the following contracting methods: separate prime,[78] single prime,[79] construction management at risk,[80] design-build,[81] design-build bridging,[82] or public-private partnership.[83]

Under traditional construction delivery methods, the prime contract is the contract directly between the owner—the unit of government—and the contractor. These contracts are customarily arranged as either single-prime or separate-prime contracts. In a single-prime contract, the general contractor has the prime contract with the owner and all other contracts are subcontracts with the general contractor. Under the separate-prime (also called multiple-prime) system, contractors in the major trades[84] submit separate bids to and contract directly with the public owner. Bids also may be received on a "dual-bidding" basis, under which both separate-prime and single-prime bids are solicited. Under dual bidding, the unit may consider the cost of construction oversight, time for completion, and other factors it deems appropriate in determining whether to award a contract on a single-prime or separate-prime basis, and it may award to the lowest responsive, responsible bidder under either category.

The procurement process for alternative construction-delivery methods—construction management at risk, design-build, design-build bridging, and public-private partnership—is

---

77. 2 C.F.R. § 200.319(c). As an example, Section 25019(a) of the Infrastructure Investment and Jobs Act (Pub. L. No. 117-58, 135 Stat. 429 (November 15, 2021)) allows NFEs to utilize local or other geographic and economic hiring preferences on their federally funded highway projects, subject to state and local laws, policies, and procedures.

78. G.S. 143-128(b).

79. G.S. 143-128(d).

80. G.S. 143-128.1.

81. G.S. 143-128.1A.

82. G.S. 143-128.1B.

83. G.S. 143-128.1C.

84. These trades are general contracting, plumbing, electrical, and heating, ventilating, and air-conditioning (HVAC).

substantially different from that for traditional construction-delivery methods.[85] Generally, contracts for alternative construction-delivery methods are procured pursuant to state law using the qualification-based process that applies to design and surveying services (described below) and may be used only after the local government has determined that using an alternative construction delivery method over a traditional delivery method is in the best interest of the project.

The alternative construction-delivery methods vary in the applicable procurement and contracting processes.[86] Under the construction management at risk method, the construction manager contracts to oversee and manage construction and to deliver the completed project at a negotiated guaranteed maximum price. The construction manager is required to solicit bids and award contracts for all of the actual construction work (including general contracting work) to prequalified subcontractors. Under the design-build method, the unit enters into one contract with a team comprised of design professionals and contractors (design-build team) to both design and build the project. The design-build bridging method involves a two-contract process under which the unit first contracts with a design professional to design 35 percent of the project and then contracts with a design-build team to complete the design and perform the construction. While the contract with the design professional is procured using the qualification-based selection method, the contract with the design-build team is awarded under the lowest responsive, responsible bidder standard. A public-private partnership contract involves one contract between the unit and a private developer in which the developer finances at least 50 percent of the project and where the roles and responsibilities of the unit and the developer are delineated in a negotiated development contract.

The use of alternative construction-delivery methods in compliance with the Uniform Guidance is challenging, at best, because a conflict exists between selection processes under North Carolina law and the federal procurement standards. In selecting a construction manager at risk or design-builder, a unit must employ a qualifications-based selection process in compliance with the North Carolina Mini-Brooks Act. However, the federal procurement standards contained in the Uniform Guidance specifically limit an NFE's use of qualifications-based selection to the procurement of "architectural/engineering (A/E) professional services" and note that qualifications-based selection "cannot be used to purchase *other types of services through A/E firms* that are a potential source to perform the proposed effort."[87] Because units must abide by this Uniform Guidance provision when using federal funds, this restriction likely prohibits a unit of local government from employing the state-mandated qualifications-based selection process required to choose a construction manager at risk or design-builder.[88]

---

85. For a comparison of various construction methods, see Valerie Rose Riecke, "Public Construction Contracting: Choosing the Right Project-Delivery Method," *Popular Government* 70, no. 1 (2004): 22–31.

86. Other construction methods not specifically authorized by statute may be used only for projects below the threshold set out in the statute or with special approval from the State Building Commission or by authority of local legislation enacted by the General Assembly.

87. 2 C.F.R. § 200.320(b)(2)(iv) (emphasis added).

88. Note that the North Carolina General Assembly enacted temporary legislation, S.L. 2021-189, which authorizes local governments to consider "price" when issuing a request for qualifications for design-build services when federal funds are being used. The temporary authorization is scheduled to expire on December 31, 2025. You can read an analysis of Section 1.6 of the Session Law in School of Government faculty member Connor Crews' blog post, "Design-Build Contracting in North Carolina Using

Historically Underutilized Business and Minority and Women-Owned Business Enterprise (MWBE) Participation

Public agencies, including counties and municipalities, are required under G.S. 143-128.2 to establish a percentage goal for participation by historically underutilized business (HUB) contractors in major building construction or repair projects, to make efforts to include these contractors in these projects, and to require prime contractors to either meet or make good-faith efforts to attain the established HUB participation goal.[89] The law does not establish or authorize a quota or set-aside of particular contracts for HUB contractors or a preference for HUB contractors in awarding contracts. Failure to make the statutorily mandated minimum good-faith efforts is grounds for rejection of a bid.[90] The statute specifically states, however, that contracts must be awarded to the lowest responsible, responsive bidder and prohibits consideration of race, sex, religion, national origin, or handicapping condition in awarding contracts. Counties and municipalities are required to establish a minority business participation outreach plan and to report data regarding minority outreach and participation on specific projects to the State Department of Administration. Counties and municipalities also have authority under G.S. 160A-17.1 to comply with minority/women business enterprise program requirements that may be imposed as a condition of receiving federal or state grants and loans.

The Uniform Guidance requires that NFEs take all necessary affirmative steps to assure that minority businesses, women's business enterprises, and labor-surplus-area firms are used when possible.[91] This requirement applies regardless of contract type and dollar amount. The required affirmative steps can be found in 2 C.F.R. § 200.321 and are similar to the good-faith efforts required of local governments under North Carolina state law. Generally speaking, NFEs are not required to meet any federal MWBE goals when using federal funds. However, some federal agencies, such as the Department of Transportation, impose Disadvantaged Enterprise (DBE) goals, and in North Carolina, the North Carolina Department of Transportation administers the DBE program.

Requirements for Design and Surveying Services

State law specifies when plans and specifications for public building projects must be prepared by a registered or licensed architect or engineer.[92] The statutory thresholds (set forth in Appendix 11.1), vary depending on whether the project involves new construction or renovation that calls for foundation or structural work or that affects life safety systems. This requirement applies even if the work is to be done by a unit's own forces, subject to the force-account limits discussed earlier.

Coronavirus State and Local Fiscal Recovery Funds," *Coates' Canons: NC Local Government Law* blog (April 14, 2022).

89. G.S. 143-128.2(a), (b). The current dollar thresholds for HUB participation requirements are set forth in Appendix 11.1. *See also* Norma R. Houston and Jessica Jansepar Ross, "HUB Participation in Building Construction Contracting by N.C. Local Governments: Statutory Requirements and Constitutional Limitations," *Local Government Law Bulletin* No. 131 (Feb. 2013).

90. G.S. 143-128.2(c).

91. 2 C.F.R. § 200.321.

92. G.S. 133-1.1(a).

When selecting architects, engineers, surveyors, and alternative construction-delivery methods (construction manager at risk, design-build, design-build bridging, and public-private partnership), G.S. 143-64.31 requires public agencies to do so based on qualifications instead of bid prices. The statute prohibits public agencies from asking for pricing information, other than unit prices (understood to mean hourly rates), until after the best-qualified person or firm is identified. Fees are then negotiated to develop a final contract. Local government units that do not wish to use the qualification-based process required under the statute have the ability under G.S. 143-64.32 to approve an exemption for any particular project where the fee is less than $50,000. While approval by a unit's governing board is not required, the statute does require the unit to exempt itself in writing. Once exempt, the unit can either negotiate a contract or conduct a competitive bidding or other process under which it solicits fee pricing to select the design professional for services in these categories.

Similarly, under the Uniform Guidance, an NFE may use competitive proposal procedures for qualifications-based procurement of architectural/engineering (A/E) professional services. Using this method, price is not a selection factor and an offeror's qualifications are evaluated, and the most-qualified offeror is selected, subject to the negotiation of fair and reasonable compensation.

Protests and Legal Challenges

Unlike the laws governing state contracting, North Carolina laws governing local government contracting do not require local governments to establish bid protest procedures. North Carolina courts have held that if a contract is subject to the statutory competitive bidding procedures and those procedures are not followed, the contract is void.[93] If a bidder is dissatisfied with a decision of a county or municipality—for example, to award a contract to the second-lowest bidder or to accept a bid that does not meet specifications—the bidder can attempt to resolve these concerns by registering a complaint with the local official responsible for the contract or directly with the unit's governing board. As a practical matter, it is best for the unit to attempt to resolve the matter, but there is no legal requirement for a hearing or other formal disposition of the complaint. If the matter is not resolved administratively, the only legal option is for the aggrieved party to sue the unit of government, typically for an injunction to prevent the unit from going forward with an alleged illegal contract.[94] It is not unusual for protests to be lodged with local government officials or with governing boards, though legal challenges are rare.

If an issue arises under a contract supported with federal funds, the Uniform Guidance places the sole burden on the NFE to manage the issue.[95] Moreover, because NFEs must have written procedures regarding procurement transactions that address all applicable law, NFEs necessarily must have written procedures to address procurement and contracting disputes, such as source evaluation, protests, and claims. However, the Uniform Guidance does not require any specific procedures for resolution of procurement or contracting issues, and the federal government will not substitute its judgment unless the matter is primarily a federal concern.

---

93. Raynor v. Comm'rs of Louisburg, 220 N.C. 348, 353 (1941).

94. *See* Frayda S. Bluestein, "Disappointed Bidder Claims Against North Carolina Local Governments," *Local Government Law Bulletin* No. 98 (May 2001).

95. 2 C.F.R. § 200.318(k).

Property Disposal

Under state law, county and municipal governments generally dispose of both real and personal property in accordance with the procedures set forth in G.S. Chapter 160A, Article 12, though there are a few other disposition procedures set out in other statutes applicable to special situations.[96] These various statutes authorize several methods for selling or disposing of property and set forth the procedures for each one. This section discusses state law property-disposal methods and includes a separate section that briefly examines the disposition of property that was acquired with federal funds. However, before examining property-disposal methods and rules, it is useful to discuss one introductory matter: the need for consideration when disposing of local government property.

Consideration

Under the North Carolina Constitution, it is generally unconstitutional for a local government to dispose of property for less than its fair market value.[97] A gift of property or a sale at well below market value constitutes the granting of an "exclusive privilege or emolument" to the person receiving the property, which is prohibited by Article 1, Section 32, of the state constitution. Most of the procedures by which a local government is permitted to sell or otherwise dispose of property are competitive, and the North Carolina Supreme Court has indicated that the price resulting from an open and competitive procedure will be accepted as the market value.[98] If a sale is privately negotiated, the price will normally be considered appropriate unless strong evidence indicates that it is so significantly below market value as to show an abuse of discretion.[99]

It is not always constitutionally necessary that a local government receive monetary consideration when it conveys property. If the party receiving the property agrees to put it to some public use, that promise constitutes sufficient consideration for the conveyance.[100] (The recipient in this case is often, but not always, another government unit.) The General Statutes expressly permit the following such conveyances: those made to the state and to local governments within North Carolina (G.S. 160A-274); to volunteer fire departments and rescue squads (G.S. 160A-277); to nonprofit preservation or conservation organizations (G.S. 160A-266(b)); to nonprofit agencies to which the county or municipality is authorized to appropriate money (G.S. 160A-279); and to governmental units within the United States, nonprofits, charter schools, and sister cities (G.S. 160A-280).

Disposal Methods under North Carolina State Law

G.S. Chapter 160A, Article 12 sets out three competitive methods of sale, each of which is appropriate in any circumstance for disposing of both real and personal property of any value: sealed bid, negotiated offer and upset bid, and public auction. Article 12 also permits privately negotiated exchanges of property in any circumstance (so long as equal value changes hands)

---

96. G.S. 153A-176 requires counties to comply with the procedures for property disposal in Article 12 of G.S. Chapter 160A.

97. *See* Redevelopment Comm'n v. Sec. Nat'l Bank, 252 N.C. 595 (1960).

98. *Redevelopment Comm'n*, 252 N.C. 595.

99. Painter v. Wake Cnty. Bd. of Educ., 288 N.C. 165 (1975).

100. Brumley v. Baxter, 225 N.C. 691 (1945). However, see note 104 below regarding the limitation on disposal of local school property.

and privately negotiated sales or other dispositions of property in a number of limited circumstances. In addition, a few other statutes permit privately negotiated sales or other dispositions of property, again in limited circumstances. These various methods of disposition are summarized in the following sections. In undertaking any of them a local government must remember that the statutory procedure must be followed exactly or the transaction may be invalidated by a court.[101]

Sealed Bids

A local government may sell any real or personal property by sealed bid (G.S. 160A-268). The procedure is based on that set forth in G.S. 143-129 for entering into purchase contracts in the formal bidding range, with one modification for real property. An advertisement for sealed bids must be published in a newspaper that has general circulation in the county (for a county government) or in the county in which the municipality is located (for a municipal government). When selling personal property, publication must occur seven full days (not counting the day of publication or the day of bid opening) before the bids are opened; when selling real property, publication must occur thirty days before the bids are opened. The advertisement should generally describe the property; tell where it can be examined and when and where the bids will be opened; state whether a bid deposit is required and, if so, how much it is and the circumstances under which it will be retained; and reserve the governing board's right to reject any and all bids. Bids must be opened in public, and the award is made to the highest responsible bidder.

The sealed-bid procedure appears to be designed to obtain wide competition by providing public notice and good opportunity for bidders to examine the property being sold. In addition to formal advertising, invitations to bid may be mailed directly to prospective buyers, just as they are typically sent to prospective bidders in the formal purchasing procedures for personal property.

Negotiated Offer and Upset Bids

A local government may sell any real or personal property by negotiated offer and upset bid (G.S. 160A-269). The procedure begins when the local government receives and proposes to accept an offer to purchase specified government property. The offer may either be solicited by the local government or made directly by a prospective buyer on his or her own initiative. The governing board then requires the offeror to deposit a 5 percent bid deposit with its clerk and publishes a notice of the offer. The notice must describe the property; specify the amount and terms of the offer; and give notice that the bid may be raised by not less than 10 percent of the first $1,000 originally bid, plus 5 percent of any amount above $1,000 of the original bid. Upset bids must also be accompanied by a 5 percent bid deposit. Prospective bidders have ten days from the date on which the notice is published to offer an upset bid. This procedure is repeated until ten days have elapsed without the local government receiving a qualifying upset bid. After that time the board may sell the property to the final offeror. At any time in the process, it may reject any and all offers and decide not to sell the property.

---

101. Bagwell v. Town of Brevard, 267 N.C. 604 (1966). Some government boards routinely declare as surplus any property that is to be sold. No statute requires such a declaration, however, and it does not appear to be necessary. A municipality or county evidences its conclusion that property is surplus by selling it.

Public Auctions

A local government may sell any real or personal property by public auction under G.S. 160A-270. The statute sets out separate procedures for the auctioning of real and personal property and authorizes electronic auctions. For real property, the unit's governing board must adopt a resolution that authorizes the sale; describes the property; specifies the date, time, place, and terms of the sale; and states that the board must accept and confirm the successful bid. The board may require a bid deposit. A notice containing the information set out in the resolution must be published at least once and not less than thirty days before the auction. The highest bid is reported to the governing board, which then has thirty days to accept or reject it.

For personal property, the same procedure is followed except that (1) the governing board may in the resolution authorize an appropriate official to complete the sale at the auction and (2) the notice must be published not less than ten days before the auction.

G.S. 160A-270(c) permits a local government to sell either real or personal property by electronic auction. The governing board must follow the same procedures as set out above, but in addition the notice must specify the electronic address where information about the property to be sold can be found and the electronic address at which electronic bids may be posted. In recent years, electronic auctions through such sites as GovDeals.com[102] have largely replaced live public auctions and have become the most common method of competitive sale disposal for personal property.

Exchange of Property

Under state law, a local government may exchange any real or personal property for other real or personal property if it receives full and fair consideration for the property.[103] After the terms of the exchange agreement are developed by private negotiations, the governing board will authorize the exchange by resolution adopted at a regular meeting. A notice of intent to make the exchange must be published at least ten days before the board meeting at which the resolution will be adopted. The notice must describe the properties involved; give the value of each, as well as the value of other consideration changing hands; and cite the date of the regular meeting at which the board proposes to confirm the exchange.

Trade-In

A local government may convey surplus property as a "trade-in" as part of a purchase contract (G.S. 143-129.7). The local government must include a description of the surplus property in its bid specifications, and the amount offered by bidders for the surplus property is taken into account when evaluating bids. The unit awards one contract to the winning bidder for both the sale of the surplus property and the purchase of the new property. While the purchase contract must comply with the applicable competitive bidding requirements, the transaction need not comply with the disposal procedures of G.S. 160A-271 (exchange of property).

---

102. *See* www.govdeals.com.

103. G.S. 160A-271. For a more detailed discussion of exchanging property, see David M. Lawrence, *Local Government Property Transactions in North Carolina*, 2nd ed. (Chapel Hill, N.C.: UNC Institute of Government, 2000).

Private Negotiation and Sale: Personal Property

A local government may use private negotiation and sale to dispose of personal property valued at less than $30,000 for any one item or any group of similar items (G.S. 160A-266, -267). Note that this procedure may not be used to dispose of real property. Under G.S. 160A-266(b) and -267, the unit's governing board, by resolution adopted at a regular meeting, may authorize an appropriate official to dispose of identified property by private sale. The board may set a minimum price but is not required to do so. The resolution must be published at least ten days before the sale.

Alternatively, G.S. 160A-266(c) authorizes a governing board to establish procedures under which county or municipal officials may dispose of personal property valued at less than $30,000 for any one item or any group of similar items without further board action and without published notice. The procedures must be designed to secure fair market value for the property disposed of and to accomplish the disposal efficiently and economically. The procedures may permit one or more officials of a unit to declare qualifying property to be surplus, to set its market value, and to sell it by public or private sale. The board may require the official to use one of the statutory methods, including an electronic auction, or may permit other sorts of procedures, such as a consignment agent or a surplus property warehouse. The statute requires the selling official to maintain a record of property sold under any such procedures. It is important to note that this delegated authority only applies to personal property valued at less than $30,000. If the property is to be sold for an amount of $30,000 or more, one of the competitive disposal procedures described above must be used, unless another statutorily authorized disposal method applies.

Private Negotiation and Conveyance to Other Governments

G.S. 160A-274 authorizes any governmental unit in the state, on terms and conditions it "deems wise," to sell to, purchase from, exchange with, lease to, or lease from any other governmental unit in North Carolina any interest in real or personal property that one or the other unit may own. "Governmental unit" is defined to include municipalities, counties, the state, school units, and other state and local agencies. The only limitations on this broad authority is that before a local board of education may lease real property that it owns, it must determine that the property is unnecessary or undesirable for school purposes, and it may not lease the property for less than $1 per year.[104] While governing board approval is required, bids and published notices are not. Thus, when reaching agreements on conveying property to another governmental unit, a unit's governing board has full discretion concerning the procedure for and the terms and conditions of the conveyance.

---

104. Although in general local governments may transfer property among themselves without monetary consideration, the North Carolina Supreme Court has held that a local school board must receive fair consideration whenever it conveys property for some non-school use, including some other governmental use. Boney v. Bd. of Trs., 229 N.C. 136 (1948). The $1 requirement for leases of school property presumably is a legislative determination that this amount is adequate consideration when title to the property remains with the school administrative unit.

Other Negotiated Conveyances: Real and Personal Property

A municipality or county may, in limited circumstances, convey real and personal property by private negotiation and sale, sometimes without monetary consideration.

Economic Development

G.S. 158-7.1(d) permits a county or municipality (but no other form of local government) to convey interests in property suitable for economic development by private sale. Before making such a conveyance, a unit's governing board must hold a public hearing with at least ten days' published notice of the hearing. The notice must describe the interest to be conveyed, the value of the interest, the proposed consideration the government will receive, and the board's intention to approve the conveyance. In addition, before making the conveyance the board must determine the probable average wage that will be paid to workers at the business to be located on the property.

The statute requires the governing board to determine the fair market value of the property and prohibits the board from conveying the property for less than that value. The county or municipality, in arriving at the amount of consideration it will receive, may count prospective tax revenues for the next ten years from improvements added to the property after the conveyance, prospective sales tax revenues generated by the business located on the property during that period, and any other income coming to the government during the ten years as a result of the conveyance.

Community Development

G.S. 160D-1312 permits a municipality (but not a county or any other unit of local government) to convey interests in property by private sale when such property is within a community-development project area. The property must be sold subject to covenants that restrict its eventual use to those consistent with the community-development plan for the project area. The statute requires that the property be appraised before it is sold and prohibits the municipality from selling it for less than the appraised value.

Once a municipality has reached agreement on a conveyance pursuant to this statute, it must publish notice of a public hearing on the transaction for the two weeks running up to the hearing. The notice should describe the property, disclose the terms of the transaction, and give notice of the municipality's intention to convey the property. At the hearing itself, the municipality must disclose the appraised value of the property.

Nonprofit Agencies

G.S. 160A-279 permits a county or municipality to convey real or personal property to any nonprofit agency to which it is authorized by law to appropriate funds, although property acquired through condemnation may not be so conveyed. The same procedures must be followed as are required by G.S. 160A-267 for other private sales. In making a conveyance under this statute, a county or municipality may accept as consideration the nonprofit agency's promise to put the property to some public use. In such instances, the county or municipality must put a covenant or condition on the conveyance guaranteeing that the nonprofit will put the property to public use.

Property for Affordable Housing

Both counties and municipalities may convey property by private sale in order to provide affordable housing (i.e., housing for persons of low or moderate income) pursuant to G.S. 160D-1316. This statute allows local government to make two sorts of conveyances. First, a local government may convey residential property directly to persons of low or moderate income and if it does so, it must follow the same procedures as are required by G.S. 160A-267 for other private sales. Second, a local government may convey property to a public or private entity that provides affordable housing for others, so long as the local government imposes conditions or covenants to ensure that the property will be used as affordable housing.

A complicated series of statutes permits municipalities to convey property specifically to nonprofit entities that will construct affordable housing. First, G.S. 160D-1311 permits a city council to exercise any power granted by law to a housing authority. Second, G.S. 157-9 authorizes a housing authority to provide "housing projects," a term defined in G.S. 157-3 to include programs that assist developers and owners of affordable housing. Third, G.S. 160A-20.1 permits a municipality to appropriate money to a private organization to do anything a municipality is authorized to do, including providing affordable housing. And fourth, G.S. 160A-279, summarized in the subsection on nonprofits above, authorizes a municipality to convey property to any nonprofit agency to which it may appropriate money.

Fire or Rescue Services

G.S. 160A-277 permits counties and municipalities to lease or convey to volunteer fire departments or rescue squads serving their jurisdictions land to be used for constructing or expanding fire or rescue facilities. The governing board of a unit must approve the transaction by adopting a resolution at a regular meeting after ten days' published notice. The notice should describe the property, state its value, set out the proposed monetary consideration or the lack thereof, and declare the board's intention to approve the transaction. (Almost all fire or rescue organizations are nonprofit in nature, so a local government may also use G.S. 160A-279 to convey property to them, including personal property; G.S. 160A-280 also provides authority for conveying personal property to these nonprofit organizations.)

Architectural and Cultural Property

G.S. 160A-266(b) permits a county or municipality to convey, after private negotiation, real or personal property that is significant for archaeological, architectural, artistic, cultural, or historic reasons; for its association with these types of properties; or for its natural, scenic, or open condition. The conveyance must be to a nonprofit corporation or trust whose purposes include the preservation or the conservation of such property, and the deed must include covenants and other restrictions securing and promoting the property's protection.[105] A local government making a conveyance under this provision must follow the same procedures as described earlier for the private sale of real or personal property under G.S. 160A-267.

---

105. These deed restrictions must be in the form of a preservation agreement or conservation agreement as defined in G.S. 121-35.

Open Space

G.S. 160D-1303 permits a local government to conserve open space by acquiring title to property and then conveying it back to the original owner or to a new owner, in either case subject to covenants requiring that the property be maintained as open space. If the conveyance is back to the original owner, the statute permits it to be made by private sale pursuant to G.S. 160A-267. Otherwise, however, the government must use one of the competitive sale methods.

Other Private Conveyances

A number of other statutes permit private sales of property in narrow circumstances; only one of these statutes sets out required procedures.

1. G.S. 160A-321 permits the private sale of any entire municipal enterprise. Unless the enterprise is conveyed to another government, however, the statute requires voters of the municipality to approve the conveyance for the following kinds of enterprises: electric power distribution; natural gas distribution; public transportation; cable television; and stormwater management.

2. G.S. 105-376(c) permits a government that has acquired property through a tax foreclosure to convey the property back to the original owner or to any other person or entity that had an interest in the property (such as a deed of trust).

3. G.S. 153A-163 permits a government that has acquired property through a loan foreclosure to sell the property by private sale, so long as it receives at least as much as it paid for the property.

4. G.S. 153A-177 permits a government that has been given property for a specified purpose to give the property back to the donor if it will not use the property for the specified purpose.

5. G.S. 40A-70 permits a government that has acquired property through eminent domain which it no longer needs to convey the property back to the condemnee, so long as the government receives in return its original purchase price, the cost of any improvements, and interest.

6. G.S. 160A-342 permits a municipality that operates a cemetery to convey it to a private operator of cemeteries upon the condition that the property will continue to be used as a cemetery.

7. G.S. 20-187.2 permits a unit's governing board to convey a law enforcement officer's badge and service side arm to a retiring law enforcement officer or to the family of an officer killed in the line of duty.

8. G.S. 20-187.4 authorizes government agencies to convey a retiring law enforcement service animal to the animal's handler or to an organization that provides services for retired service animals at a price and under terms and conditions set by the local government.

Lease of Property

A county or municipality may lease any real or personal property it owns that its governing board finds will not be needed during the term of the lease—in essence, the county or municipality is permitted to make a temporary disposal of the property since the lease agreement gives exclusive use of the property to the lessee (G.S. 160A-272). The procedure to be followed depends on the length of the lease. The board may, by resolution at any meeting, make leases for one year or less. It may also authorize the unit's manager or some other administrative officer to take similar action concerning a lease of government property for the same period.

The governing board may lease government-owned property for periods longer than one year and up to ten years by a resolution adopted at a regular meeting after thirty days' published notice of its intention to do so. The notice must describe the property to be leased, specify the annual lease payment, and give the date of the meeting at which the board proposes to approve the action.

A lease for longer than ten years must be treated, for procedural purposes, as if it were a sale of property. It may be executed by following any procedure authorized for selling real property.[106]

Grant of Easements

A county or municipality may grant easements over, through, under, or across any of its property (G.S. 160A-273). The authorization should be by resolution of the unit's governing board at a regular meeting. No special published notice is required, nor is the grant subject to competition.

Sale of Stocks, Bonds, and Other Securities

A county or municipality that owns stocks, bonds, or other securities that are traded on the national stock exchanges or over the counter by brokers and securities dealers may sell them in the same way and under the same conditions as a private owner would (G.S. 160A-276).

Property Disposal Under the Uniform Guidance

Disposition by a non-federal entity (NFE) of federally funded property must follow the rules found in the Property Standards section within Subpart D of the Uniform Guidance. The Property Standards classify four major categories of property: real property, equipment, supplies, and intangible property. [107] If federal funds have been used to purchase property, title to the property typically vests in the NFE. However, the Uniform Guidance establishes a "property trust relationship" for real property, equipment, and intangible property acquired or improved using federal funds. This means that for those specific property types, the property is held in trust by the NFE as trustee for the beneficiaries of the program under which the property was acquired or improved.[108] This section focuses on the disposition rules for real property and equipment and supplies. In any instance, disposition of federally funded property must also comply with disposition rules in North Carolina state law, meaning, for example, that even if a federal awarding agency allows an NFE to sell real property, a unit of local government must

---

106. Leases of government property for siting and operation of renewable energy facilities, communications towers, and components of wired or wireless networks in limited circumstances may be for a term of up to twenty-five years without having to be treated as a sale of property.

107. There is an additional category of "exempt property" in the Uniform Guidance. Exempt property is property acquired under a federal award where the federal awarding agency has chosen to vest title to the property to the NFE without further responsibility to the federal government.

108. 2 C.F.R. § 200.316. The U.S. Department of Commerce has further explained that the federal awarding agency retains an undivided equitable reversionary interest in the property and that an agency may assert its equitable reversionary interest in the project if an NFE is failing to meet its obligation of using the property to serve the purpose of the federal program. *See* U.S. Department of Commerce, *Grants and Cooperative Agreements Manual* (2021).

still follow the procedures required for the sale of real property under Article 12 of Chapter 160A of the General Statutes, discussed earlier in this chapter.

Real Property

When real property is no longer needed by an NFE for its original federally funded purpose, the Uniform Guidance provides NFEs with three disposition options: paying the federal awarding agency and retaining title to the property, selling the property and compensating the federal awarding agency, or transferring title of the property to the federal awarding agency.[109] The formula for calculating the actual amount to be paid to the federal awarding agency varies depending on the option but generally involves paying the awarding agency an amount proportional to the agency's contribution toward the property acquisition or improvement.

Equipment and Supplies

Disposition of federally funded equipment is required when it is no longer needed for the original project or for activities funded by the federal award.[110] An NFE will need to request disposition instructions from the federal awarding agency unless such instructions are identified in the federal award's terms and conditions. If the federal awarding agency fails to provide disposition instructions within 120 days of the request, or if the items of equipment have a current per-unit fair market value of $5,000 or more, an NFE may either retain or sell the federally funded equipment.[111] Proper sales procedures must be established to ensure the highest possible return. The federal awarding agency is entitled to an amount calculated by multiplying the current market value or proceeds from the sale by the federal percentage of participation in the cost of the original purchase.[112] Items of equipment with a current per-unit fair market value of $5,000 or less may be retained, sold, or otherwise disposed of with no further obligation to the federal awarding agency, but an NFE must still request disposition instructions from that agency.[113]

Once supplies that were purchased with federal funds are no longer needed for any federal award and the aggregate value of the unused supplies exceeds $5,000, an NFE must retain or sell the supplies and must compensate the federal awarding agency for its share.[114] The compensation due to the awarding agency is calculated in the same manner as equipment under 2 C.F.R. § 200.313(e)(2).

---

109. 2 C.F.R. § 200.311. The Uniform Guidance defines real property as land, including land improvements, structures, and appurtenances but excluding moveable machinery and equipment. *Id.* § 200.1.

110. 2 C.F.R. § 200.313(e). The Uniform Guidance defines equipment as tangible personal property (including information technology systems) having a useful life of more than one year and a per-unit acquisition cost which equals or exceeds $5,000. *Id.* § 200.1.

111. 2 C.F.R. § 200.313(e)(2).

112. 2 C.F.R. § 200.313(e)(2). The federal awarding agency may permit the NFE to deduct and retain from the federal share $500 or 10 percent of the proceeds, whichever is less, for its selling and handling expenses. The Uniform Guidance does not explain how an NFE can accomplish this deduction, but presumably an NFE should ask for this deduction in its request for disposition instructions.

113. 2 C.F.R. § 200.313(e)(1).

114. 2 C.F.R. § 314. *Supplies* means all tangible personal property other than property described in the definition of equipment.

Additional Resources

Bluestein, Frayda S. *A Legal Guide to Purchasing and Contracting for North Carolina Local Governments*. 2nd ed. Chapel Hill: UNC Institute of Government, 2004.

Houston, Norma R. *A Legal Guide to Construction Contracting for North Carolina Local Governments*. 5th ed. Chapel Hill: UNC School of Government, 2015.

Houston, Norma R. *North Carolina Local Government Contracting: Quick Reference and Related Statutes*. Chapel Hill: UNC School of Government, 2014.

Lawrence, David M. *Local Government Property Transactions in North Carolina*. 2nd ed. Chapel Hill: UNC Institute of Government, 2000.

The School of Government's Local Government Purchasing and Contracting microsite, under the headings "REFERENCE MATERIALS" and "RESOURCES," offers materials on purchasing, construction contracting, and property disposal. www.sog.unc.edu/resources/microsites/local-government-purchasing-and-contracting.

Appendix 11.1   Dollar Thresholds in North Carolina Public Contracting Statutes

Dollar Thresholds in North Carolina
Public Contracting Statutes

Dollar limits and statutory authority current as of November 1, 2015

Requirement	Threshold	Statute
Formal bidding	*(Estimated cost of contract)*	
Construction or repair contracts	$500,000 *and above*	G.S. 143-129
Purchase of apparatus, supplies, materials, and equipment	$90,000 *and above*	G.S. 143-129
Informal bidding	*(Actual cost of contract)*	
Construction or repair contracts	$30,000 to formal limit	G.S. 143-131
Purchase of apparatus, supplies, materials, and equipment	$30,000 to formal limit	G.S. 143-131
Construction methods authorized for building projects	*(Estimated cost of project)*	
Separate Prime	*Over $300,000*	G.S. 143-128(a1)
Single Prime		
Dual Bidding		
Construction Management at Risk *(G.S. 143-128.1)*		
Design-Build and Design-Build Bridging *(G.S. 143-128.1A; 143-128.1B)*		
Public Private Partnership (P3) *(G.S. 143-128.1C)*		
Historically Underutilized Business (HUB) requirements		
Building construction or repair projects		
– Projects with state funding *(verifiable 10% goal required)*	$100,000 *or more*	G.S. 143-128.2(a)
– Locally funded projects *(formal HUB requirements)*	$300,000 *or more*	G.S. 143-128.2(j)
– Projects in informal bidding range *(informal HUB requirements)*	$30,000 to $500,000*	G.S. 143-131(b)
Note: Formal HUB requirements should be used for informally bid projects costing between $300,000 and $500,000		
Limit on use of own forces (force account work)	*(Not to exceed)*	G.S. 143-135
Construction or repair projects	$500,000 *(total project cost)* <u>or</u> $200,000 *(labor only cost)*	
Bid bond or deposit		
Construction or repair contracts *(at least 5% of bid amount)*	Formal bids *($500,000 and above)*	G.S.143-129(b)
Purchase contracts	Not required	
Performance/Payment bonds		
Construction or repair contracts *(100% of contract amount)*	Each contract *over $50,000* of project costing *over $300,000*	G.S. 143-129(c); G.S. 44A-26
Purchase contracts	Not required	
General contractor's license required	$30,000 *and above*	G.S. 87-1
Exemption	Force account work *(see above)*	
Owner-builder affidavit required	Force account work *(see above)*	G.S. 87-14(a)(1)
Use of licensed architect or engineer required		
Nonstructural work	$300,000 *and above*	G.S. 133-1.1(a)
Structural repair, additions, or new construction	$135,000 *and above*	
Repair work affecting life safety systems	$100,000 *and above*	
Selection of architect, engineer, surveyor, construction manager at risk, or design-build contractor		
"Qualification-Based Selection" procedure (QBS)	All contracts unless exempted	G.S. 143-64.31
Exemption authorized	Only projects where estimated fee is *less than* $50,000	G.S. 143-64.32

Chapter 12

Ethics and Conflicts of Interest

by Kristina M. Wilson and Crista M. Cuccaro

Ethics in Government: Why It's Important

The conduct of local government officials and public employees affects public perceptions of and trust in government. Citizens expect local officials and public employees to act in the best interest of the public and not to use their office for their personal benefit. Laws restrict the conduct of local public officials, but in many cases, they have a choice in how to act, such as when deciding whom to hire, when to contract, and how to vote. North Carolina laws governing the conduct of local officials focus on financial interests in voting and contracting, as well as on other ways in which government decision makers might personally benefit from the actions they take. Similarly, when federal financial assistance is involved, the Uniform Guidance defines and prohibits certain conflicts of interest and benefits for employees, officers, or agents of a governmental unit. Additionally, constitutional due process requirements focus on the need for fair and unbiased decision making when certain types of private rights are at stake.

This chapter will begin by describing state law requirements for elected officials, including when elected officials have a duty to vote and when elected officials are prohibited from voting.

Next, the chapter will explore statutory prohibitions on receiving a benefit related to a governmental contract. Finally, the chapter will explain the conflict-of-interest rules applicable when governmental units use federal financial assistance.

Requirements for Local Elected Officials

Ethics Education Requirement

North Carolina law requires elected and appointed members of the governing boards of municipalities and counties, unified governments, consolidated municipalities-counties, sanitary districts, and local boards of education to receive at least two clock hours of ethics education within twelve months after each election or reelection (or appointment or reappointment) to office.[1] The education program must cover laws and principles that govern conflicts of interest and ethical standards of conduct at the local government level; it is designed to focus on both legal requirements and ethical considerations so that key governmental decision makers will have the information and insight needed to exercise their authority appropriately and in the public interest. The ethics education requirement is an ongoing obligation triggered by reelection or reappointment to office.[2]

While state law does not require ethics education for local employees and members of local appointed boards (such as boards of adjustment or advisory committees), a local governing board may impose this requirement on these groups under the board's local ethics code or other ordinance or policy.

Local Codes of Ethics

North Carolina law also requires governing boards subject to the ethics education requirement to adopt ethics resolutions or policies (often referred to as "codes of ethics") to guide board members in performing their duties.[3] The ethics resolution or policy must address at least five key responsibilities of governing board members enumerated by statute:

1. to obey all applicable laws about official actions taken as a board member,
2. to uphold the integrity and independence of the office,
3. to avoid impropriety in the exercise of official duties,
4. to faithfully perform duties,
5. to act openly and publicly.[4]

The statute does not impose or authorize sanctions for failure to comply with ethics codes. Governing boards have no explicit authority to sanction their members as a means of enforcing

---

1. As used in this chapter, the term "municipality" is synonymous with "city," "town," or "village."

2. Chapter 160A, Section 87 and Chapter 153A, Section 53 of the North Carolina General Statutes (hereinafter G.S.).

3. G.S. 160A-86; 153A-53.

4. G.S. 160A-86; 153A-53.

an ethics code or for other purposes. However, failure to adopt a code or to comply with its provisions may elicit citizen and media criticism and may itself be considered unethical.

As with the ethics education requirement, state law does not require that ethics codes be applied to local employees and members of local appointed boards (such as boards of adjustment or advisory committees), but a local governing board may choose to extend the provisions of its code of ethics to these groups.

Some state government officials and senior employees are subject to the State Government Ethics Act,[5] which establishes ethical standards of conduct for those covered under the act and regulates individuals and entities that seek to influence their actions. The North Carolina State Ethics Commission is responsible for enforcing the act, including investigating alleged violations. Most local government officials and employees are not subject to the State Government Ethics Act by virtue of their local government positions.[6] Consequently, the State Ethics Commission does not have the authority to investigate allegations of unethical conduct by local government officials.

Censuring Board Members

Although state law does not provide specific authority for boards to sanction their members for ethical violations, elected boards do have general authority to pass resolutions or motions, and some boards use a motion or resolution of censure to address ethical or legal transgressions by board members, including violations of the board's code of ethics. This type of censure has no legal effect other than to express dissatisfaction or disapproval by the board (or a majority of the board) of the actions or behavior of one of its members. There are no specific procedural requirements for such an action. The School of Government's model code of ethics includes recommendations for a censure process.[7]

---

5. G.S. Ch. 138A.

6. Individual officials and employees may be subject to the act if they also serve in a state-level capacity covered under it, such as serving on a covered state board or commission. In addition, voting members of the policy-making boards of Metropolitan Planning Organizations (MPOs) and Rural Transportation Planning Organizations (RPOs) (these boards are often referred to as "transportation advisory committees" or "TACs") are subject to specific ethics requirements related to their service on the MPO or RPO TAC (G.S. 136-200.2(g)–(k) for MPOs and 136-211(f)–(k) for RPOs). For more information about the state ethics and lobbying laws that apply to state officials, see Norma R. Houston, "State Government Ethics and Lobbying Laws: What Does and Does Not Apply to Local Governments," *Local Government Law Bulletin* No. 135 (March 2014).

7. A. Fleming Bell, II, *A Model Code of Ethics for North Carolina Local Elected Officials* (Chapel Hill, N.C.: UNC School of Government, 2010).

Conflicts of Interest in Voting

Ethical and conflict-of-interest issues often arise as questions about whether a board member may, must, or must not vote on a particular matter in which he or she has some personal interest. In general, a governing board member has a duty to vote and may be excused from voting only in specific situations as allowed by statute.[8]

The statutes governing voting by county and municipal board members are slightly different, and, especially for municipalities, there is some ambiguity about the proper procedure for excusing a member. The county statute, G.S. 153A-44, provides that the board may excuse a member, whereas the municipal statute, G.S. 160A-75, simply says that a member "shall be excused" in cases of conflict without specifying who does the excusing. Another important difference is that the municipal statute enforces the duty to vote by providing that if a person is present at a meeting, does not vote, and has not been excused, that person is considered to have voted "yes."[9] The county statute does not contain this provision. Both statutes are specific, however, about the reasons for which a person may be excused from voting. In addition, four other statutes prohibit board members from voting in situations involving contracting, land use decisions, and quasi-judicial decisions.

The Duty to Vote

Board members are often advised to avoid even the appearance of a conflict of interest, and in many situations a board member may choose to act or to refrain from acting due to a concern about such an appearance. When it comes to voting, however, a board member's duty to vote overrides this choice, in some cases requiring a person to vote, while in only limited circumstances is a person required to refrain from voting. The general voting statutes—G.S. 153A-44 (counties) and 160A-75 (municipalities)—allow governing board members of municipalities and counties to be excused from voting *only* on

1. matters involving the consideration of the member's own official conduct or financial interest[10] or
2. matters where a member is explicitly prohibited from voting under
   a. one of the exemptions in G.S. 14-234(d1)(2), which addresses a public officer's obligations when the officer is directly benefiting under a public contract;
   b. G.S. 160D-109(a), which covers legislative decisions concerning land use and development; and
   c. G.S. 160D-109(d), which pertains to quasi-judicial decisions.[11]
      Additionally, a recently enacted conflict of interest law, G.S. 14-234.3, also prohibits public officials from voting or otherwise participating in making or

---

8. In 2015, the state legislature amended the municipal voting statute to allow a member to abstain from voting on legislative rezonings and text amendments. S.L. 2015-160.

9. The 2015 amendment described in note 8 amended G.S. 160A-75 to exempt votes taken under G.S. 160A-385 (now repealed) from this "automatic yes" rule, in effect allowing a member to abstain on zoning amendment matters.

10. Note that board member compensation does not fall under the definition of official conduct or financial interest.

11. G.S. 160D-109 also excuses members of **appointed** boards from voting when they have financial or other interests in an advisory or legislative decision regarding a development regulation or zoning amendment.

administering contracts with certain nonprofits.[12] While the above-referenced general voting statutes do not yet include specific exceptions for G.S. 14-234.3, the language of the latter statute is mandatory, and violating it results in criminal penalties.[13] As a result, G.S. 14-234.3 likely implicitly trumps the statutory duty to vote.[14]

When there is a question about whether a board member has a conflict of interest in voting, the first thing to determine is what type of matter is involved. Specific statutes govern the standard to be applied, depending on the nature of the matter before the board for decision. The following is a short list of circumstances that will help identify the appropriate standard to apply.

1. If the matter involves a development regulation in a legislative land use matter, a board member *shall not* vote where the outcome of the matter is reasonably likely to have a direct, substantial, and readily identifiable personal financial impact on the member. G.S. 160D-109(a). If the matter involves a zoning amendment, the board member *shall not* vote if the landowner of the property subject to rezoning or the applicant for a text amendment is someone with whom the board member has a close familial, business, or other associational relationship. *Id.* Examples of close familial relationships are spouses, parents, children, siblings, grandparents, and grandchildren, including step and half relationships under G.S. 160D-109(f).

2. If the matter involves a quasi-judicial function (such as the issuance of a special-use permit or an appeal of a personnel decision), the standard is as follows: a board member *shall not participate or vote* if the member has a fixed opinion (not susceptible to change) prior to the hearing; undisclosed ex parte communications; a close familial, business, or other associational relationship with an affected person; or a financial interest in the outcome. G.S. 160D-109(d). Note that this provision applies to any person (not just a governing board member) who serves on a board and exercises quasi-judicial functions.

3. If the matter involves a contract from which the board member derives a direct benefit and a statutory exception allows the contract,[15] the member is *prohibited from participating or voting*. G.S. 14-234(b1).

4. If the matter involves a contract with a nonprofit organization with which a public official is associated, the public official *is prohibited from participating or voting*. G.S. 14-234.3(a).

5. For all other matters that come before the governing board for a vote, the standard is as follows: for counties, the board member *may be excused* if the matter involves the member's own financial interest or official conduct. G.S. 153A-44. For cities, the board member *shall be excused* if the matter involves the member's own financial interest or official conduct. G.S. 160A-75.

---

12. Effective as of Jan. 1, 2022.

13. G.S. 14-234.3(a), (b).

14. Kristina M. Wilson, "Conflicts of Interest for Public Officials on Nonprofit Boards: An Analysis for North Carolina G.S. 14-234.3," *Local Government Law Bulletin* No. 142 (Nov. 2022) (hereinafter "Conflicts of Interest for Public Officials"): 14.

15. The statutory exceptions, found in G.S. 14-234(b), are discussed later in this chapter.

Note that each of the first four specific statutes *prohibits* the member from voting. Under the final category, however, it is unclear whether use of the word "may" in G.S. 153A-44 is intended to make excusing a county governing board member from voting optional or whether it simply describes the permissible grounds for being excused. G.S. 160A-75 has less ambiguous wording, providing that "[n]o member shall be excused except . . ." for cases involving the delineated statutory conflicts of interest or financial interest and official conduct. The use of the word "shall" clarifies that for city governing boards, excusals for financial interest and official conduct are mandatory.[16]

What Constitutes Financial Interest

North Carolina courts have often ruled on matters involving conflicts of interest. School of Government professor Fleming Bell fully explores the case law in *Ethics, Conflicts, and Offices: A Guide for Local Officials* (2nd edition, 2010). It's important to note, however, that some conflict-of-interest cases arise in the context of constitutional due process considerations or contracting issues, matters currently governed by specific statutes that incorporate standards from the cases. School of Government professor David Owens analyzes the case law on conflicts of interest in land use matters in *Land Use Law in North Carolina* (fourth edition in production at the time of this writing).

Other matters are governed by the general voting statutes, which contain the more broadly stated "own financial interest" standard. Several cases involving legislative and administrative decisions suggest that courts use a deferential standard when evaluating what constitutes a financial interest. For example, in *Kistler v. Board of Education of Randolph County*,[17] board members' ownership of property near the area in which a school site was located was considered insufficient to constitute a conflict of interest. Similarly, in *City of Albemarle v. Security Bank & Trust Co.*,[18] city council members' direct ties to competing financial institutions did not require them to abstain from voting on a proposed condemnation of a portion of the bank's land. These holdings seem appropriate given the underlying obligation to vote as well as the usual judicial deference given to local government decisions in the absence of a clear abuse of discretion.

The following factors, based on case law and the statutes, can be useful in determining when a person may be excused from voting under the general voting statutes.

Number of People Affected

The range of financial impact on governing board members of a local unit can be thought of as a continuum based on the extent to which the effect is unique to a board member, on one end of the spectrum, or experienced by many or most citizens, on the other end. If the effect on the board member is the same as the effect on a significant number of citizens, then it is fair to allow the individual to vote. The board member is affected as part of a larger group of citizens,

---

16. City of Albemarle v. Sec. Bank & Tr. Co., 106 N.C. App. 75, 79 (1992) ("G.S. 160A-75 provides that a member of a city council may not be excused from voting unless the vote concerns matters involving the council member's personal financial interest or official conduct.").

17. 233 N.C. 400 (1951).

18. 106 N.C. App. 75 (1993).

and the vote can serve to represent that group. This is perhaps the most important factor. Even a significant financial effect may not be disqualifying if it is one that is universally or widely experienced by citizens in the jurisdiction.

Extent of the Financial Interest (Benefit or Detriment)

The general voting statutes refer to financial *interest*, not financial *benefit*, as some of the other statutes do. This means that a positive or a negative financial impact may be a basis for excusing a governing board member from voting. An insignificant financial interest, however, whether positive or negative, is not enough to sway a person's vote and should not be used to avoid the duty to vote. Obviously, the significance of a financial interest must be considered in relation to the individual's particular situation, though it might be assessed based on what a reasonable person would do in that situation.

Likelihood That the Financial Impact Will Actually Occur

Sometimes several actions in addition to the specific vote in question are needed for an alleged financial interest to materialize. For example, a governing board member who is a real estate agent votes in favor of a loan which will facilitate a project that the real estate agency that employs the agent might have the opportunity to offer for sale. Without more to suggest that the sales opportunity will actually arise and be available to the board member, such a chain of events is probably too speculative to form a basis for being excused from voting.

Conflicts of Interest in Contracting

Several state laws limit state and local government elected officials' and public employees'[19] ability to personally benefit from contracts with the governmental units they serve. Additionally, another statute limits public officials' ability to contract with nonprofit organizations on behalf of the governmental units they serve when certain conditions are met.[20] These laws reflect the public's need to ensure that contracting and other decisions are made in a neutral, objective way based on the public's interest and not in consideration of actual or potential benefit to the decision maker. However, these laws do not prohibit all activity the public might consider improper. Instead, they identify particular activities the legislature has identified as serious enough to constitute a criminal offense. Situations that are not illegal may nonetheless be inappropriate, so public officials should always consider the public perception of their actions in addition to the legal consequences. This section will address conflict of interest laws both in the personal benefit context and in the nonprofit context.

---

19. While the statutes discussed in this section apply to all state and local government officials and employees, certain senior-level state officials and employees are subject to specific standards of conduct under the State Government Ethics Act, G.S. Chapter 138A. This act does not generally apply to local government officials and employees unless they also serve in a state capacity, such as serving on a state board or commission covered under the act. Similarly, local government officials and employees are generally exempt from G.S. Chapter 120C, which regulates lobbying by senior-level state officials and employees.

20. G.S. 14-234.3.

Contracts for Personal Benefit

A criminal statute, G.S. 14-234, prohibits an elected or appointed public officer or a public employee from deriving a direct benefit from any contract in which he or she is involved on behalf of the public agency he or she serves. The statute contains two additional prohibitions. Even if a public official or employee is not involved in making a contract from which he or she will derive a direct benefit, the official or employee is prohibited from influencing or attempting to influence anyone in the public agency who is involved in making the contract. In addition, all public officers and employees are prohibited from soliciting or receiving any gift, reward, or promise of reward, including a promise of future employment, in exchange for recommending, influencing, or attempting to influence the award of a contract, even if they do not derive a direct benefit under the contract. Violation of this statute is a Class 1 misdemeanor. Key definitions contained in the statute, along with several important exceptions, are discussed below.

As defined in the statute, a person "derives a direct benefit" from a contract if the person or *his or her spouse* (1) has more than a 10 percent interest in the company that is a party to the contract, (2) derives any income or commission directly from the contract, or (3) acquires property under the contract.[21] Note that while the prohibition includes a direct benefit to a spouse, it does not extend to other family members or friends, or to unmarried partners. If the employee or official or his or her spouse does not derive a direct benefit from it, a contract between a public agency and a family member, friend, or partner of a governing board member or employee does not violate the law. Another important aspect of the statutory definition is that it does not make illegal a contract with an entity in which a county or municipal official is an employee, as long as no income or commission is derived from the contract.

Since the definition of direct benefit includes the acquisition of property, governing board members and employees (and their spouses) who are involved in the disposal of surplus property are prohibited from purchasing that surplus property from their unit of government. An elected or appointed official (but not an employee) may be able to do so if the unit the official serves falls within the "small jurisdiction exception" described below.

G.S. 14-234 also specifies what it means to be involved in "making or administering" a contract, which is a necessary element in the statutory prohibition. Individuals who are *not* involved in making or administering contracts are not legally prohibited from contracting with their units of government. Activity that triggers the prohibition includes participating in the development of specifications or contract terms or in the preparation or award of a contract, as well as having the authority to make decisions about or interpret the contract.[22] Performing purely ministerial duties, such as a clerk providing an attestation on a contract, is not considered "making or administering" the contract.[23] The statute also makes clear that a person is involved in making a contract when the board or commission on which he or she serves takes action on the contract, even if the official does not participate. Simply being excused or recusing one's self from voting on a contract does not absolve a person with a conflict of interest from potential criminal liability. Stated differently, unless an exception applies, there is no means or mechanism that allows a public official with a conflict of interest to contract with the public

---

21. G.S. 14-234(a1)(4).
22. G.S. 14-234(a1)(2), (3).
23. G.S. 14-234(a1)(5).

agency that he or she serves. If an exception applies, as discussed below, the interested party may be excused from voting and legally contract with the unit.

The broad prohibition in G.S. 14-234 is modified by several exceptions. In any case where an exception applies, a public officer who will derive a direct benefit is prohibited from deliberating or voting on a contract or from attempting to influence any other person who is involved in making or administering the contract.[24] Contracts with banks, savings and loan associations, and regulated public utilities are exempt from the limitations in the statute,[25] as are contracts for reimbursement for providing direct assistance under state or federal public assistance programs under certain conditions.[26] An officer or employee may, under another exception, convey property to the unit he or she serves, but only through a condemnation proceeding initiated by the unit.[27] An exception in the law also authorizes a county or municipality to hire as an employee the spouse of a public officer; however, this exception does not apply to public employees.[28]

A final exception, sometimes referred to as the "small jurisdiction exception," applies only in municipalities with a population of less than 20,000 and in counties with no incorporated municipality with a population of more than 20,000.[29] In these jurisdictions, governing board members of the local unit as well as certain members of (1) the social services, local health, or area mental health boards; (2) the board of directors of a public hospital; and (3) the local school board may lawfully contract with the units of government they serve, subject to several limitations contained in the exception.[30] First, the contract (or contracts) between a governing board member and the unit he or she serves may not exceed $20,000 for medically related services and $60,000 for other goods or services in any twelve-month period. In addition, the exemption does not apply to any contract that is subject to the competitive bidding laws, which includes purchase and construction or repair contracts with an estimated cost of $30,000 or more.[31] Contracts made under the small-jurisdiction exception must be approved by special resolution of a unit's governing board in open session.[32] The statute imposes additional public notice and reporting requirements for these contracts and prohibits an interested board member from participating in the development of or voting on such a contract.[33] A contract entered into under the small-jurisdiction exception that does not comply with all the statutory procedural requirements violates the statute.

---

24. G.S. 14-234(b1).

25. G.S. 14-234(b)(1).

26. G.S. 14-234(b)(4).

27. G.S. 14-234(b)(2). The statute specifically authorizes the conveyance to be undertaken under a consent judgment, that is, without a trial, if approved by the court.

28. G.S. 14-234(b)(3).

29. G.S. 14-234(d1). Population figures must be based on the most recent federal decennial census. The population threshold was increased from 15,000 to 20,000 in 2021 by Session Law 2021-117.

30. Note that the small jurisdiction exception only applies to an elected official or person appointed to fill an elective office; the exception does not extend to public employees.

31. G.S. 14-234(d2).

32. G.S. 14-234(d1)(1).

33. Specifically, a unit shall note the total annual dollar amount of contracts with each official in the unit's audited annual financial statement, and any governing board that contracts with any officials of its unit shall summarize such transactions quarterly for the preceding twelve-month period and post the summary in a conspicuous place in a specified public facility. *See* G.S. 14-234(d1)(3), (4).

Contracts entered into in violation of G.S. 14-234 violate public policy and are not enforceable. There is no authority to pay for or otherwise perform a contract that violates the statute unless the contract is required to protect the public health or welfare and limited continuation is approved by the Local Government Commission.[34] Prosecutions under the statute are not common—although some have occurred—but situations in which governing board members or public officials stand to benefit from public contracts often make headlines.

Contracts with Nonprofits

In January 2022, the legislature enacted a criminal contracting statute focused on nonprofits.[35] Under G.S. 14-234.3(a), public officials may not knowingly participate in making or administering contracts with nonprofits with which they are associated. Three things need to be present for G.S. 14-234.3 to apply: (1) there must be a public official as defined in the statute, (2) there must be a contract at issue, and (3) the contract at issue must be with a covered nonprofit. If all of these elements are present, a conflicted public official must record his or her recusal with the governing board's clerk and cease to have any involvement with the contract at issue.[36] Once a conflicted public official records his or her recusal, the governmental unit can proceed to execute the contract.[37] If a conflicted public official fails to record his or her recusal in violation of the statute, both the public official and the unit he or she serves could face Class 1 misdemeanors.[38] The contract at issue could also be deemed void.[39]

When examining the issue of when public officials are prohibited from making or administering contracts with nonprofit entities, several questions arise. First, which individuals in a local governmental unit are considered public officials under G.S. 14-234.3(a)? Under the statute, a "public official" is "any individual who is elected or appointed to serve on a governing board of a political subdivision of this State, [excluding] employee[s] and independent contractor[s]."[40] Note that unlike the personal benefit contracting statute, the nonprofit contracting statute does not extend to employees or their spouses or to the spouses of public officials. At a minimum, the statute's definition of "public official" covers members of city councils, boards of county commissioners, boards of aldermen, and the like.[41] However, the exact scope of the definition is unclear, so if there is any argument in statute or case law that an individual serves on a governing board of a political subdivision, it may be wise for practitioners to assume that the individual is a covered public official for purposes of G.S. 14-234.3.[42]

Second, there must be a contract at issue for the statute to apply. G.S. 14-234.3(a) regulates any public official who participates in making and administering a "contract." In particular, it prohibits a public official from "making or administering a contract, *including* the award of money in the form of a grant, loan, or other appropriation" (emphasis added). As the plain language suggests, G.S. 14-234.3(a) is triggered only if a proposed transaction involves a contract.

---

34. G.S. 14-234(f).
35. G.S. 14-234.3.
36. G.S. 14-234.3(a).
37. G.S. 14-234.3(a).
38. G.S. 14-234.3(b), (c).
39. G.S. 14-234.3(b), (c).
40. G.S. 14-234.3(d)(3).
41. "Conflicts of Interest for Public Officials," at 3.
42. "Conflicts of Interest for Public Officials," at 4–5.

The legislature used the term "including" to illustrate the types of contracts that fall under this statute (i.e., contracts involving "the award of money in the form of a grant, loan, or other appropriation"), but if a public entity does not enter into a "contract," the statute does not apply.[43]

Finally, the contract at issue must be with a covered nonprofit. With the exclusion of boards, entities, or organizations created by the state or its political subdivisions, a covered nonprofit organization (1) is a "nonprofit corporation, or association, incorporated or otherwise, that is organized or operating in North Carolina primarily for educational, charitable, religious, scientific, literary, or public health and safety purposes" (2) "of which the [involved] public official serves as a director, officer, or governing board member."[44] Using the statutory definition, practitioners must first analyze whether the contracting nonprofit entity is organized or operating in the state primarily for educational, charitable, religious, scientific, literary, or public health and safety purposes. Assessing whether a nonprofit operates for one of the enumerated purposes will likely require a case-by-case analysis of the specific nonprofit at issue.[45] If such an analysis determines that the nonprofit does in fact operate for a purpose listed in the statute, the next factor to look at is whether the entity was created by the state or its political subdivisions. If the state or its political subdivisions created the contracting nonprofit entity, G.S. 14-234.3 does not apply. Finally, practitioners should ask whether the involved public official holds a leadership position with the contracting nonprofit organization. The public official must be a director, executive, officer, or governing board member of the nonprofit for the statute to apply. A public official who is merely a volunteer, low-ranking member, or informal participant will not have a conflict under this statute.[46]

Stated differently, there are three ways that a nonprofit may fall outside of G.S. 14-234.3's scope:

- the nonprofit does not operate primarily for the enumerated purposes,
- the state or its political subdivisions created the nonprofit, or
- the involved public official does not hold a leadership position with the nonprofit.

As noted above, if practitioners conclude that G.S. 14-234.3 applies to a given transaction, the conflicted public official must record his or her recusal with the clerk to the unit's governing board.[47] After the clerk records the recusal, the board can legally execute the contract.[48] What does it mean to record a recusal with the clerk? The statute provides no procedural guidance for recusal. Its plain language does not require formal board action or approval to excuse a conflicted public official, and the public official seemingly can recuse without declaring the conflict or otherwise notifying the rest of the board. However, while the statute apparently permits public officials to recuse themselves, this is not the most transparent procedure. The better approach would be for public officials to declare their conflicts and have boards formally excuse them via majority vote. The vote and the recusal could then be recorded in the board's meeting minutes. Recording recusals in meeting minutes is likely more efficient than creating a separate recusal document outside of any formal context. Since the statute does not specify

---

43. "Conflicts of Interest for Public Officials," at 7.
44. G.S. 14-234.3(d)(1).
45. "Conflicts of Interest for Public Officials," at 8.
46. "Conflicts of Interest for Public Officials," at 8.
47. G.S. 14-234.3(a).
48. G.S. 14-234.3(a).

any format for the recusal recording, documenting recusals in meeting minutes appears to be a safe-harbor approach that increases transparency and clarity.[49]

After recording a recusal with the clerk, a conflicted public official should cease all involvement with the contract at issue. The official must not deliberate or vote on the contract, attempt to influence others who are deliberating or voting on the contract, or solicit gifts or favors in exchange for attempting to influence those deliberating or voting on the contract.[50] Given the broad wording of the statute, it is likely wise for a conflicted public official to refrain from discussing the contract or the nonprofit at issue with anyone deliberating or voting on the contract. While G.S. 14-234.3 does not seem to require conflicted public officials to physically leave the room during deliberations, they may choose to do so, especially if they know that their mere presence may be interpreted as an attempt to influence deliberations or voting.[51]

Notably, G.S. 14-234.3(b) incorporates several exceptions from the contracting-for-personal-benefit statute (G.S. 14-234), including the "small jurisdiction" exception. As noted above, these exceptions apply to a governmental unit's ability to contract, not to a conflicted public official's ability to be involved with a particular contract. In other words, in the personal benefit context, these exceptions allow the governmental unit to proceed with a contract even when a public official, employee, or spouse has a conflict. The conflicted public official or employee, however, still cannot have any involvement with the contract at issue. What do these exceptions mean, then, as incorporated into the G.S. 14-234.3 context?

They do not appear to have any practical effect.[52] G.S. 14-234.3(a) already allows a unit to proceed with a contract once a conflicted public official's recusal is recorded. Thus, the G.S. 14-234 exceptions do not seem to serve any purpose. There is no exception that allows a conflicted public official to participate. Without additional clarification regarding the purpose of these exceptions, local governments should rely exclusively on the exception in G.S. 14-234.3(a) that allows a governing board to contract upon the recording of a conflicted public official's recusal.[53]

At first glance, the statutory restrictions on contracting for personal benefit and contracting with nonprofits may seem very similar. Both require contracts to be at issue and both can result in criminal penalties and void contracts. Importantly, both statutes prohibit the conflicted individual from having any involvement with the contract at issue, even when an exception might apply. However, there are important differences to keep in mind. The contracting-for-personal-benefit statute applies to public officials, public employees, and their spouses, while the nonprofit statute applies only to public officials. The personal-benefit statute has several exceptions, while the nonprofit statute has only one exception in practice. Though part of the same statutory Chapter, it is important for practitioners to pay close attention to the requirements of each distinct contracting statute.

---

49. "Conflicts of Interest for Public Officials," at 10–11.
50. G.S. 14-234.3(d)(2).
51. "Conflicts of Interest for Public Officials," at 11.
52. "Conflicts of Interest for Public Officials," at 10.
53. "Conflicts of Interest for Public Officials," at 10.

Gifts and Favors

Another criminal statute, G.S. 133-32, is designed to prevent the use of gifts and favors to influence the award and administration of public contracts. The statute applies to any contractors, subcontractors, or suppliers who are current contractors, subcontractors, or suppliers; have performed under a contract with a public agency within the past year; or who anticipate bidding on a contract in the future. For these individuals, giving any gift or favor to public officials and employees who have responsibility for preparing, awarding, or overseeing contracts, including inspecting construction projects, is a Class 1 misdemeanor. The statute also makes it a Class 1 misdemeanor for those officials to receive the gift or favor.

The statute does not define gift or favor. A reasonable interpretation is that the prohibition applies to anything of value acquired or received without fair compensation unless it is covered by a statutory exception. These exceptions include advertising items or souvenirs of nominal value, honoraria for participating in meetings, and meals at banquets. Inexpensive pens, mugs, and calendars bearing the name of the donor firm clearly fall within the exception for advertising items and souvenirs. Gifts of a television set, use of a beach cottage, or tickets to a professional sports event probably are prohibited. Although meals at banquets are allowed, free meals offered by contractors under other circumstances, such as lunch, should be refused. Some local governments have adopted local policies establishing a dollar limit for gifts that may be accepted; however, a gift allowed under a local policy must still be refused if it violates state law.

The statute also allows public officials and employees to accept customary gifts or favors from friends and relatives as long as the existing relationship, rather than the desire to do business with the unit, is the motivation for the gift. Finally, the statute specifically does not prohibit contractors from making donations to professional organizations to defray meeting expenses, nor does it prohibit public officials who are members of those organizations from participating in meetings that are supported by such donations and are open to all members—for example, sponsorship of a conference event that is open to all conference attendees.

It is important to distinguish between gifts to individuals and gifts to the government entity itself. A contractor may legally donate goods and services to the local government for use by the unit. For example, a local business can legally donate products to the unit for its own use or for the unit to raffle to employees for an employee appreciation event. Gifts or favors delivered directly to individuals for their personal use should be returned or, in some cases, may be distributed among employees such that each person's benefit is nominal. The latter approach is common for gifts of food brought to a department by a vendor. Public officials should inform contractors and vendors about the existence of the gifts-and-favors statute and about any local rules in effect within the unit addressing this issue.

Misuse of Confidential Information

G.S. 14-234.1 makes it a Class 1 misdemeanor for any state or local government officer or employee to use confidential information for personal gain, to acquire a pecuniary benefit in anticipation of his or her own official action, or to help another person acquire a pecuniary benefit from such actions. Confidential information is any non-public information that the officer or employee has learned in the course of performing his or her official duties.

Other Financial Gain

In 2021, G.S. 14-234.3 was added to the criminal statutes governing conflicts of interest for public officers. The statute makes it a Class H Felony for an elected official of a political subdivision of the state to solicit or receive personal financial gain from the political subdivision for which that elected official serves by means of intimidation, undue influence, or misuse of the employees of that political subdivision. G.S 14-234.3 does not define "personal financial gain," but this term is used (although not defined) in the State Government Ethics Act, G.S. 138A-1 *et seq.* The financial-interest analysis discussed earlier in this chapter may be useful when evaluating a scenario under this statute. As a general principle, personal financial gain is not limited to money; it could also include any forbearance, forgiveness of indebtedness, gift, or other thing of value.[54] This statute does not apply if the governing board of the political subdivision for which the involved official serves approves the financial gain, or if the financial gain is received by the elected official acting in his or her official capacity.

Conflicts of Interest for Specific Categories of Officials and Public Employees

In addition to the statutes discussed above that apply to all local officials and employees, specific conflict-of-interest prohibitions apply to certain groups of officials and employees, including those discussed briefly below.

Building Inspectors

G.S. Chapter 160D describes several conflicts of interest for members of local government inspection departments. First, no member of an inspection department may have a financial interest or be employed by a business that furnishes labor, materials, or appliances for building construction or repair within the local government's planning and development regulation jurisdiction. An inspection department member also cannot have a financial interest in the making of plans or specifications for any building within the local government's planning and development regulation jurisdiction unless the member owns the building in question. All inspection department members are prohibited from engaging in any work that is inconsistent with their public duties. In addition to these general prohibitions, the statute requires local governments to find a conflict of interest if the individual, company, or employee of a company contracting to perform building inspections for the local government has a financial or business interest in the project being inspected or has a close relationship with or has previously worked within the past two years for the project's owner, developer, contractor, or manager.[55]

---

54. *See, e.g.,* Colo. Rev. Stat. Ann. § 24-18.5-101.
55. G.S. 160D-1108.

Project Designers

Architects and engineers performing work on public construction projects are prohibited from specifying any materials, equipment, or other items manufactured, sold, or distributed by a company in which the project designer has a financial interest.[56] Project designers are prohibited also from allowing manufacturers to draw specifications for public construction projects.[57] A violation of these restrictions is punishable as a Class 3 misdemeanor; violators lose their licenses for one year and pay a fine of up to $500.[58]

Public Hospital Officials and Employees

Boards of directors and employees of public hospitals and hospital authorities and their spouses are prohibited from acquiring a direct or indirect interest in any hospital facility, property planned to be included within a hospital facility, or a contract or proposed contract for materials or services provided to a hospital facility. Limited exceptions to this prohibition apply; a contract entered into in violation of these prohibitions is void and unenforceable.[59]

Local Management Entity (LME) Board Members

Local management entity (LME) board members cannot contract with their LME for the delivery of mental health, developmental disabilities, and substance abuse services while serving on the board (and are not eligible for board service so long as such a contract is in effect).[60] Nor can an individual who is a registered lobbyist serve on an LME board.

Housing Authorities

Commissioners and employees of a housing authority, or of a municipal or county when acting as a housing authority, are prohibited from having or acquiring any direct or indirect interest in any housing project, property included or planned to be included in any project, or a contract or proposed contract for materials or services to be furnished or used in connection with any housing project.[61]

Conflicts of Interest Applicable to Federal Grant Funds

When governmental units are using federal financial assistance, the Uniform Guidance imposes additional administrative requirements, including rules governing conflicts of interest and gifts in contracting.[62] Additionally, the Uniform Guidance obligates federal awarding agencies (e.g., the Environmental Protection Agency) to establish conflict-of-interest policies for federal

---

56. G.S. 133-1.
57. G.S. 133-2.
58. G.S. 133-4.
59. G.S. 131E-14.2 (public hospitals); 131E-21 (hospital authorities).
60. G.S. 122C-118.1(b).
61. G.S. 157-7.
62. 2 C.F.R. pt. 200.

awards.[63] Thus, with any federal financial assistance, a governmental unit may need to look to both the Uniform Guidance and the federal granting agency's conflict-of-interest rules to understand what is permissible.

To complicate matters, the rules about conflicts of interest and gifts found in the Uniform Guidance differ significantly from those found in state law. In order to comply with both state law and federal rules, local governments must have and use "documented procurement procedures, consistent with State, local, and tribal laws and regulations and the standards of [2 C.F.R. § 200.318.1], for the acquisition of property or services required under a Federal award or subaward."[64] In other words, local governments must follow the "most restrictive" requirements of both federal and state law as well as their own local policies.

Maintaining Written Conflict-of-Interest Standards

2 C.F.R. § 200.318(c)(1) requires a non-federal entity[65] to maintain "written standards of conduct covering conflicts of interest and governing the actions of its employees engaged in the selection, award and administration of contracts." While the Uniform Guidance does not prescribe any specific form for the written conflict-of-interest and contracting standards, the written standards must comply with 2 C.F.R. § 200.318 and include disciplinary actions for violations of such standards by officers, employees, or agents of the NFE. The following sections explain the federal rules governing conflicts of interests and contracting that are found in the Uniform Guidance.[66]

Conflicts of Interest Related to the Selection, Award, and Administration of Contracts

Like state law, the Uniform Guidance prohibits an individual from participating in the selection, award, or administration of a contract supported by federal financial assistance if that person has a real or apparent conflict of interest.[67] Unlike state law, though, the applicability of this prohibition is much broader.

First, the individuals prohibited from participating in the contracting process when they have a conflict of interest include not only employees and officers of the NFE, but also agents of the NFE. The Uniform Guidance does not define the term "agent," but the plain meaning of the term suggests that it probably encompasses individuals that are directly under contract

---

63. *See* 2 C.F.R. § 200.112.

64. 2 C.F.R. § 200.318(a).

65. Per 2 C.F.R. § 200.1, a non-federal entity is "a State, local government, Indian tribe, Institution of Higher Education (IHE), or nonprofit organization that carries out a Federal award as a recipient or subrecipient." For consistency with the Uniform Guidance language, the remainder of this chapter will refer to units of local government as non-federal entities, abbreviated as NFEs.

66. *See* Connor Crews, *Conflict of Interest Policy Applicable to Contracts and Subawards of [Unit] Supported by Federal Financial Assistance* (March 2022) (a model federal conflict-of-interest policy drafted by a School of Government faculty member).

67. 2 C.F.R. § 200.318(c)(1). This chapter section focuses on real conflicts of interest. The Uniform Guidance does not define apparent conflicts of interest. However, some federal agencies have interpreted an apparent conflict of interest as when the circumstances are such that a reasonable person with knowledge of the relevant facts would question a public employee, official, or agent's impartiality in the matter. *See* National Institutes of Health, NIH Ethics Program, *Recusals (Disqualifications)* (last visited May 12, 2023).

with an NFE and that act on behalf of or provide advice to a unit.[68] Arguably, the term could also include individuals who have an ownership interest in a legal entity under contract with a unit.[69] Without specific guidance from a federal granting agency, an NFE may wish to extend this prohibition to the beneficial owners of a legal entity under contract with a unit.[70]

Second, the language of the Uniform Guidance prohibiting "real or apparent" conflicts of interest is more expansive than the "direct benefit" language of G.S. 14-234, regarding both the scope of interpersonal relationships and the breadth of what is considered an "interest." The Uniform Guidance instructs that a real conflict of interest arises when an employee, officer, or agent of an NFE, or any member of his or her immediate family,[71] his or her partner, or an organization which employs or is about to employ any of the aforementioned parties, has a financial or other interest in or a tangible personal benefit from a firm considered for a contract. Hence, when federal financial assistance is involved, NFEs must evaluate many more relationships than state law requires. Instead of simply understanding benefits bestowed upon public officials and their spouses as G.S. 14-234 requires, NFEs must look at the interests of and benefits to its employees, officials, and agents and their immediate family members, business partners, employers, and future employers. Furthermore, an impermissible interest under the Uniform Guidance is broader than it is under state law; it includes any financial or other interest in or a tangible personal benefit from a firm considered for a contract. While the term "financial interest" is not defined in the Uniform Guidance, federal agencies have interpreted it to include the potential for gain or loss to any individual or entity covered by 2 C.F.R. § 200.318(c)(1).[72] Likewise, "tangible personal benefit" is not defined in the Uniform Guidance, but federal agencies have opined that it is non-financial in nature and results in a personal benefit for an individual, such as improved employment opportunities, business referrals, or political influence.[73]

Gifts and Favors from Contractors or Parties to Subcontracts

The Uniform Guidance prohibits the officers, employees, and agents of an NFE from soliciting or accepting gifts, favors, or anything of monetary value from contractors or parties to subcontracts.[74] This prohibition applies to *all* officers, employees, and agents of an NFE, not just those individuals involved in the contracting process. In this way, the Uniform Guidance prohibition on gifts and items of value is more far-reaching than state law, which applies only

---

68. Crews, note 66 above, at note 5.
69. Crews, note 66 above, at note 5.
70. Crews, note 66 above, at note 5.
71. The Uniform Guidance does not define "immediate family," and in fact, the Council on Governmental Relations has identified the dilemmas created by the lack of this and other definitions, resulting in inconsistent interpretations and application by various federal agencies. *See* "Subject: Conflict of Interest under [ ] Uniform Guidance," Letter from Anthony DeCrappeo, President, Council of Governmental Relations, to employees at the Office of Management and Budget (July 8, 2016).
72. Examples of financial interests identified by the Federal Emergency Management Agency (FEMA) that would constitute a real conflict of interest include ownership of certain financial instruments or investments such as stock, bonds, or real estate, or a salary, indebtedness, job offer, or similar interest. *See* FEMA, *Procurement Disaster Assistance Team (PDAT) Field Manual: Procurement Information for FEMA Award Recipients and Subrecipients* (Oct. 2021), § 1.4.2.
73. *See* U.S. Department of Education, *Questions and Answers Regarding 2 CFR Part 200* (Dec. 1, 2016).
74. 2 C.F.R. § 200.318(c)(1).

to public employees or officers who prepare plans, award or administer contracts, or inspect or supervise construction.

NFEs are authorized to set standards for situations where a financial interest is not substantial or a gift is an unsolicited item of nominal value. Of course, "the Uniform Guidance does not define when a financial interest is 'not substantial,' . . . and no other guidance from the Office of Management and Budget ("OMB") . . . has directly addressed this question. . . . [Some] federal agencies have robust conflict-of-interest regulations that distinguish between 'significant' and 'insignificant' financial interests."[75] Ultimately, unless dictated by a federal granting agency, an NFE has discretion to define financial interests that are "not substantial" and gifts of nominal value. In doing so, an NFE may consider consulting federal agency guidance or look to the standards applicable to employees of the executive branch.[76]

Consequences of a Violation

If an NFE identifies a potential conflict of interest that may violate 2 C.F.R. § 200.318, the NFE must notify the federal granting agency in writing.[77] However, it is unclear whether there is a mechanism to resolve potential conflicts of interest other than avoiding the conflict altogether. The OMB has not addressed whether a prohibited "apparent" conflict of interest can be cured by a governing board member's recusal from action on, or from the administration of, a contract with an entity in which the member has a financial interest under 2 C.F.R. § 200.318(c)(1). Some federal granting agencies allow recipients to disclose potential conflicts of interest to the agency, propose mitigation measures, and receive an agency determination on the effectiveness of those measures.[78] Unless explicit procedures allow for an NFE to proceed when a potential conflict of interest exists, NFEs should exercise caution because the consequences for violation can be severe. If an NFE violates the Uniform Guidance or any federal award conditions, the federal awarding agency may impose additional award conditions, such as requiring additional, more-detailed financial reports or additional project monitoring.[79] However, if additional conditions cannot remedy noncompliance, federal agencies are authorized to take more substantial action, ranging from withholding payments to the NFE to initiating suspension or debarment proceedings against the NFE or terminating the federal award.[80]

---

75. Crews, note 66 above, at § IV.a.i. *See also* 42 C.F.R. § 50.603 (defining "significant financial interest" in the context of Department of Health and Human Services grants to include, among other things, any remuneration in the preceding twelve months or holding equity interest valued at $5,000 or more).

76. Federal employees are allowed to accept unsolicited gifts with a fair market value of no more than $20 per occasion, with an annual limit of $50 per source. 5 C.F.R. § 2635.204.

77. If the activity violates federal criminal laws, 2 C.F.R. § 200.113 imposes mandatory disclosure of the activity.

78. *See, e.g.*, U.S. Environmental Protection Agency (EPA), EPA's Revised Interim Financial Assistance Conflict of Interest [COI] Policy § 9.0(b) ("The agency will review COI disclosures . . . and measures applicants/recipients propose to resolve the COI and advise applicants/recipients of EPA's determination on the effectiveness of the measures within 30 calendar days of disclosure unless a longer period of time is necessary due to the complexity of the situation.").

79. 2 C.F.R. § 200.208.

80. 2 C.F.R. §§ 200.339–.343.

Additional Resources

Bell, A. Fleming, II. *Ethics, Conflicts, and Offices: A Guide for Local Officials.* 2nd ed. Chapel Hill: UNC School of Government, 2010.

_____. *A Model Code of Ethics for North Carolina Local Elected Officials.* Chapel Hill: UNC School of Government, 2010.

Bluestein, Frayda S. *A Legal Guide to Purchasing and Contracting for North Carolina Local Governments.* 2nd ed. with supplement. Chapel Hill: UNC School of Government, 2007.

Ethics for Local Government Officials, UNC School of Government microsite, www.sog.unc.edu/programs/ethics.

"Ethics & Conflicts." *Coates' Canons: NC Local Government Law* blog, https://canons.sog.unc.edu/ethics-and-conflicts.

Houston, Norma R. "State Government Ethics and Lobbying Laws: What Does and Does Not Apply to Local Governments." *Local Government Law Bulletin* No. 135 (March 2014).

Owens, David W. *Land Use Law in North Carolina.* 3rd ed. Chapel Hill, N.C.: UNC School of Government, 2020. (*Authors' Note*: The fourth edition of this book is currently in production; the estimated publishing date is July 2023.)

Wilson, Kristina M. "Conflicts of Interest for Public Officials on Nonprofit Boards: An Analysis for North Carolina G.S. 14-234.3." *Local Government Law Bulletin.* No. 142 (Nov. 2022).

IV. SELECT EXPENDITURE CATEGORIES

Chapter 13

Financing Public Enterprises

by Kara A. Millonzi

Introduction

North Carolina counties and municipalities (collectively, local units) are authorized to engage in certain public enterprise activities.[1] A *public enterprise* is an activity of a commercial nature. When a local unit owns or operates a public enterprise, it acts in a proprietary capacity and has more flexibility to treat the enterprise like a private business venture than a traditional government function. Many public enterprises are funded with user charges and are self-supporting (or predominantly self-supporting). That means that each year the local government generates enough income from the user charges to support the operating and capital expenses of the enterprise.

A local unit is not required to provide any public enterprise services. Further, if a local government chooses to provide one or more of the authorized public enterprises, it need not

---

This chapter reflects the law as of June 1, 2023.

1. As used in this book, the term "municipality" is synonymous with "city," "town," and "village." Note that, as discussed below, in addition to counties and municipalities, a handful of special-purpose local government entities also are authorized to provide certain public enterprise services.

make them available to all citizens or property owners within the unit. There is no duty of equal service.[2] Generally, as long as it is not unlawfully discriminating against a protected class of citizens, a local government can choose where, and under what circumstances, it will provide the services. If, however, a municipality involuntarily annexes property into its jurisdiction, the annexation triggers special statutory requirements regarding the provision of water and sewer services. Under certain circumstances, a municipality may be required to provide these services to newly annexed properties.[3]

Authorized Types of Public Enterprise Services

The most common types of public enterprises are water and sewer utility services, but the North Carolina General Statutes (hereinafter G.S.) authorize both counties and municipalities to operate public enterprises for all of the following purposes:

- water supply and distribution,
- sewage collection and treatment,
- solid waste collection and disposal,
- airports,
- public transportation,
- off-street parking,
- stormwater-management programs and structural and natural stormwater and drainage systems.[4]

Municipalities are authorized also to operate enterprises for the following purposes:

- cable television (and broadband),[5]
- electric power generation and distribution,
- gas production and distribution.[6]

---

2. *See* Ramsey v. Rollins, 246 N.C. 647 (1957).

3. *See* Frayda Bluestein, "Water and Sewer Extensions 'At No Cost'—Analyzing the New Annexation Law," *Coates' Canons: NC Local Government Law* blog (Aug. 2, 2011).

4. *See* Chapter 153A, Section 274 (counties) and Chapter 160A, Section 311 (municipalities) of the North Carolina General Statutes (hereinafter G.S.). Note that counties are authorized also to establish county water and sewer districts to provide water supply and distribution and sewage collection and treatment services. G.S. Chapter 162A, Article 6. A county that establishes a water or sewer district also may use its public enterprise authority under G.S. Chapter 153A, Article 15 to regulate the services and set user fees. *See* McNeill v. Harnett Cnty., 97 N.C. App. 41 (1990).

5. In *BellSouth Telecommunications, Inc. v. City of Laurinburg*, 168 N.C. App. 75 (2005), the North Carolina Court of Appeals held that the authority to provide cable television services included the authority to provide broadband services.

Counties have limited authority to provide grants to certain unaffiliated or nonprofit Internet providers to expand service in unserved areas. *See* G.S. 153A-459.

6. *See* G.S. 160A-311.

Scope of Authority

Local government authority to operate public enterprises is broad—the statutes allow a county or municipality to "acquire, lease as lessor or lessee, construct, establish, enlarge, improve, extend, maintain, own, operate, and contract for the operation of" the above-listed functions.[7] A county and municipality may provide the enterprise services both inside and outside its territorial boundaries. A county may provide the services in its unincorporated and incorporated areas.[8]

The authority is not absolute, though. State law often imposes limitations on enterprise activities. For example, a unit of local government may not "displace" a private company that is providing collection services for solid waste or recycled materials without providing appropriate notice and waiting at least fifteen months or providing due compensation to the displaced company.[9] Displacement of a private provider occurs when a local government either (1) takes any formal action to prohibit a private company from providing all or a portion of the collection services that the company is providing in the affected area or (2) uses availability fee or tax revenue to fund competing collection services. Similarly, the General Assembly has significantly limited the authority of municipalities to provide cable television and broadband services in competition with the private sector.[10] And, as detailed below, state law limits the authority of local units to charge certain fees for enterprise activities.

Governments also must be careful not to exceed the scope of an authorized enterprise function. In *Smith Chapel Baptist Church v. City of Durham*,[11] the City of Durham had established a stormwater enterprise and assessed a fee on all properties within the unit. The fee revenue funded, among other things, educational programs and other outreach efforts associated with the city's comprehensive stormwater-management program. The city established the program to satisfy state and federal regulatory requirements. The North Carolina Supreme Court held that the city had exceeded its public enterprise authority when it used revenue generated from the stormwater fee to fund the stormwater-quality management program because the relevant statute at the time specified that a unit could establish a public enterprise only for structural and natural stormwater and drainage systems. Note that the General Assembly subsequently amended the statute to allow a unit to establish an enterprise to fund a comprehensive stormwater-quality management program.[12]

---

7. *See* G.S. 153A-275(a) (counties); 160A-312(a) (municipalities).

8. Note that a county does not need a municipality's governing board's permission to construct utility lines or other infrastructure within the municipal boundaries. The county may negotiate with private property owners to obtain the necessary easements and other property rights. A municipality, however, may use its franchise authority to limit a county's ability to provide utility services within the municipality or to prohibit it altogether. *See* G.S. 160A-319.

9. *See* G.S. 160A-327.

10. *See* G.S. Chapter 160A, Article 16A.

11. 350 N.C. 805 (1999).

12. *See* G.S. 160A-311 (municipalities); 153A-274 (counties); *see also* G.S. 160A-459; 153A-454.

Interlocal Cooperation to Provide Enterprise Services

Counties and municipalities have largely coextensive authority to provide most public enterprise services. And, as discussed below, there are a handful of other local government entities authorized to provide certain public enterprise services, often on a regional basis. Two or more of these local governments may enter into interlocal agreements authorizing one unit to provide services to citizens in the other unit or authorizing the units to jointly engage in the provision of services.[13] An interlocal agreement is a contract that sets forth the terms or conditions of service and payment and, as long as it does not conflict with state or federal law, governs the parties' relationship. State law limits a municipality to a forty-year contract for the supply of water and a thirty-year contract for the supply of other public enterprise services.[14] A county is not subject to the same term limits. Use of interlocal agreements to contract for water and sewer services between and among local governments is common practice. The Environmental Finance Center at the University of North Carolina has documented numerous interlocal agreements related to the provision of water and wastewater across the state.[15] The agreements represent a variety of interlocal structures, including joint provision of services, bulk water purchases, and backup resources for emergency purposes only.

The authority to enter into interlocal agreements, however, applies only to the services that all parties to an agreement are allowed to provide. For example, a county could execute an interlocal agreement to provide solid waste services to one or more other counties or municipalities, but it could not contract through an interlocal agreement to provide cable television (broadband) services.

Franchise Agreements

In addition to interlocal agreement authority, a municipality also may enter into one or more franchise agreements with another government entity or a private entity[16] to provide any of the authorized public enterprise services (except cable television and broadband).[17] A county may enter into franchise agreements only for solid waste collection and disposal.[18] The franchise authority includes the ability to prohibit any government or private provider from furnishing a public enterprise service within a unit's territorial boundaries without a franchise. A municipal or county governing board may use a franchise agreement to impose reasonable terms of

---

13. *See* G.S. Chapter 160A, Article 20.

14. G.S. 160A-322.

15. *See* Environmental Finance Center, *Interactive Map of Community Water System Interconnections in North Carolina* (July 2015).

16. A privately owned public utility corporation may petition the state's Public Utilities Commission to provide services in a designated area. *See* G.S. Chapter 62, Article 6.

17. G.S. 160A-319.

18. G.S. 153A-136.

service on a provider, and except for solid waste, an agreement may authorize the operation of the franchised activity for up to sixty years.[19] (A solid waste franchise agreement may not exceed thirty years.)[20]

Other Local Government Public Enterprise Service Providers

Counties and municipalities are not the only authorized government providers of public enterprises. There are a number of limited-purpose government entities that can provide one or more of the authorized public enterprise services. These other government entities often are created to serve regional populations that cut across municipal or county boundaries. For example, there are several government entities that are authorized to provide water and sewer services: (1) counties or two or more political subdivisions (such as municipalities or sanitary districts) can organize water and sewer authorities;[21] (2) any two or more political subdivisions in a county can petition the board of commissioners to create a metropolitan water or sewer district;[22] and (3) the Commission for Health Services can create a sanitary district to operate sewage collection, treatment, and disposal systems and water supply systems for the purpose of preserving and promoting public health and welfare, without regard for county or municipal boundary lines.[23] (Sanitary districts also may provide solid waste collection, fire protection, recreation, and rescue services.) There also are parking authorities,[24] public transportation authorities,[25] regional natural gas districts,[26] regional solid waste management authorities,[27] and various airport authorities and commissions.[28] The authorities, districts, and commissions may serve customers within a county or municipality directly or may contract with the unit of local government to furnish the utilities.

---

19. Note that if a municipality is providing the services to another municipality under a franchise agreement, it is subject to G.S. 160A-322, which limits the time periods for contracts for the provision of water services to forty years and the provision of other public enterprise utility services to thirty years.
20. G.S. 160A-319; 153A-136.
21. *See* G.S. Chapter 162A, Article 1.
22. *See* G.S. Chapter 162A, Articles 4 and 5.
23. *See* G.S. Chapter 130A, Article 2, Part 2.
24. *See* G.S. Chapter 160A, Article 24.
25. *See* G.S. Chapter 160A, Articles 25, 26, and 27.
26. *See* G.S. Chapter 160A, Article 28.
27. *See* G.S. Chapter 153A, Article 22.
28. *See* G.S. 63-4.

Regulating Public Enterprises

Local Government Regulatory Authority

When public enterprise services are provided by counties and municipalities, or by the other local government entities listed above, they are *not* subject to regulation by the state's Public Utilities Commission. The Public Utilities Commission has jurisdiction only over privately owned utility companies (which, confusingly, are referred to as public utilities). The General Assembly has accorded a county or municipal board "full authority to protect and regulate any public enterprise system belonging to or operated by it by adequate and reasonable rules."[29] The rules must be adopted by ordinance and must apply throughout the area in which the public enterprise service is provided. (The limited-purpose government entities discussed in the section immediately above have similar authority with respect to the public enterprise service(s) they are authorized to provide.)

A local governing board may impose reasonable restrictions on who may connect to its public enterprise systems and how those connections are made. Furthermore, a unit may specify terms of continued service and may discontinue service to any customer if those conditions are not met. All regulations must be adopted by ordinance, and because most public enterprise services are provided under contract with a customer, regulations, restrictions, and other terms of service should be memorialized in a written contract as well. In fact, the more detailed the provisions in an enterprise service contract, the more protection afforded to a local government to deal with a customer who fails to live up to the terms of service.

Local Government Commission Oversight

The legislature has bestowed on the state's Local Government Commission (LGC) some oversight authority over the financial management of a county's, municipality's, or other local entity's water or sewer system. The LGC is a nine-member state body within the Department of State Treasurer that approves most local government borrowing transactions and issues bonds on behalf of local units.[30] The LGC monitors the fiscal health of local units in the state. It is empowered to "issue rules and regulations having the force of law governing procedures for the receipt, deposit, investment, transfer, and disbursement of money and other assets by units of local government. . . ."[31] The LGC also "may inquire into and investigate [a local unit's] internal control procedures" and issue warnings to units of any internal control deficiencies or violations of the Local Government Budget and Fiscal Control Act.[32]

Under certain circumstances, the LGC is empowered to take more drastic action, including assuming "full control of [a local unit's] financial affairs. . . ."[33] The LGC becomes "vested with all the powers of the governing board as to the levy of taxes, expenditure of money, adoption of budgets, and all other financial powers conferred upon the governing board by law."[34]

---

29. G.S. 160A-312(b); *see also* G.S. 153A-275(b).
30. G.S. Chapter 159, Article 2.
31. G.S. 159-25(c).
32. G.S. 159-25(c).
33. G.S. 159-181(c).
34. G.S. 159-181(c).

The LGC may assume full control of a unit's water or sewer system and assume all powers of the governing board as to the operation of the public enterprise if the system, for three consecutive fiscal years, experiences negative working capital, has a quick ratio of less than 1.0, or experiences a net loss of revenue.[35] Working capital is defined as "current assets, such as cash, inventory, and accounts receivable, less current liabilities. . . . "[36] A quick ratio of less than 1.0 "means that the ratio of liquid assets, cash and receivables, to current liabilities is less than 1.0."[37] Before the LGC assumes full control of a local unit's public enterprise system, it must find that the financial stability of the unit is threatened and that the unit has failed to make corrective changes in its operation after having received notice and warning from the LGC.[38]

Mandating Participation in Public Enterprise Services

Water and Sewer Enterprises

Under certain circumstances, a county's, municipality's, sanitary district's, or water and sewer authority's governing board may mandate that a property owner connect his or her property to the unit's water and/or sewer system. Specifically, a local unit's board may adopt an ordinance requiring the owner of any property that is developed or improved, and that is located within a reasonable distance of the unit's water and/or sewer lines, to connect.[39] The local unit may assess the property owner any costs associated with connecting the property to its water and/or sewer system.[40]

There is a notable exception to this authority for water connections. If a property owner has a permitted, functioning drinking water–well permit, a local unit may not mandate connection to the unit's water system.[41]

A local unit *must* issue a drinking water–well permit if

1. the property is undeveloped or unimproved, even if the property could be served by a government water system;[42]
2. the property is developed or improved **and** (a) a government water system has not yet installed water lines directly available to the property **or** (b) the government water system cannot provide water service to the property at the time the property owner desires service.[43]

---

35. S.L. 2013-150.

36. S.L. 2013-150.

37. S.L. 2013-150.

38. S.L. 2013-150.

39. G.S. 153A-284 (counties); 160A-317 (municipalities); 162A-6(a)(14d) (water and sewer authorities); 130A-55(16) (sanitary districts).

40. G.S. 153A-284; 160A-317; 162A-6(a)(14d); 130A-55(16). The fees are often referred to as connection fees or tap fees.

41. *See* G.S. 87-97.2(c). The same limitations apply to water systems owned or operated by water and sewer authorities and sanitary districts.

42. G.S. 87-97.2(a).

43. G.S. 87-97.2(b).

Even if a property owner has a drinking water–well permit, there are a few situations in which a local unit still may mandate connection to the unit's water system.[44] Under G.S. 87-97.2, a government utility may still require a property for which a permit has been issued to connect to its water system if one or more of the following apply.

1. "The private drinking water well serving the property has failed and cannot be repaired." The statute does not specify who determines whether or not the well can be repaired. It is up to the government utility to establish a process for verifying the functionality of each private drinking well.
2. "The property is located in an area where the drinking water removed by the private drinking water well is contaminated or likely to become contaminated due to nearby contamination." This determination is made or confirmed by the local health department.
3. Operation of the government utility "is being assisted by" the LGC. The statute does not define the circumstances under which the LGC would be deemed to be assisting the government utility. Arguably, all local governments and public authorities are assisted to some extent by the LGC, inasmuch as the LGC monitors the fiscal health of each unit by reviewing its annual audit. But to read "assisted by" this broadly would cause the exception to swallow the rule. It is likely, therefore, that the legislature intended the phrase to mean something more.

It is possible that for purposes of this statute, "assisted by" means that the LGC has issued debt on behalf of the government utility. When a local government or public authority borrows money through general obligation bonds, revenue bonds, special obligation bonds, or project-development bonds, it is the LGC that actually issues the bonds. Even this interpretation of "assisted by" seems broader than what the legislature likely intended, though.

In an extreme case, the LGC has the authority to impound the books and records associated with a government utility, assume full control of all its affairs, or take any other actions deemed necessary by the LGC to deal with a government utility that is in financial trouble.[45] Thus, "assisted by" could refer only to situations in which the LGC takes action under this statute or when it compels a government utility to make its debt-service payments pursuant to G.S. Chapter 159, Section 36. That seems too restrictive of an interpretation, though. If the legislature intended this result, it could simply have stated that the exception applies only when the LGC takes action under G.S. 159-181 or 159-36. By instead using the phrase "assisted by," it appears that the legislature intended for the exception to apply to a broader set of circumstances.

In fact, viewing the exception in the context of the whole statute, it is likely that the legislature intended it to apply when a government utility is in financial trouble, or on the verge of financial trouble, such that prohibiting the utility from mandating connections might affect the utility's continued viability. Thus, I think the most likely interpretation of "assisted by" is that the LGC has placed the unit on its Unit Assistance List.[46]

---

44. *See* G.S. 87-97.2(e).

45. *See* G.S. 159-181(c).

46. The Unit Assistance List (UAL) is developed by LGC staff to assist in prioritizing the allocation of staff resources, developing guidance and resources for units, and engaging in enhanced fiscal monitoring. The list is published periodically throughout the year based on audited financial statements and

Figure 13.1 Local Government Authority to Mandate Connection to Its Water System

Mandate Connection to Local Government Water System?	Drinking Well Permit Issued	Drinking Well Permit Not Issued
Property is developed or improved	No*	Yes
Property is undeveloped and unimproved	No*	No*

*Unless one of the exceptions in G.S. 87-97.2(e) applies.

Figure 13.2 Local Government Authority to Mandate Connection to Its Wastewater System

Mandate Connection to Local Government Wastewater System?	Property Has Functioning Septic System	Property Does Not Have Functioning Septic System
Property is developed (with at least one residential or commercial unit)	Yes	Yes
Property is undeveloped (without any residential or commercial units)	No	No

Figure 13.1 illustrates when a local unit may mandate connection to its water system, and Figure 13.2 illustrates when a local unit may mandate connection to its wastewater system.

Solid Waste Enterprise

A municipality also has authority to compel certain property owners to participate in the municipality's solid waste collection service. If a property owner has not contracted for solid waste collection services with a private hauler or another government hauler, a municipality may require that the property owner use the municipality's hauler. (A municipality may collect the solid waste itself or contract with one or more private or government haulers to act on its behalf.) A county does not have analogous authority. And neither a municipality nor a county may require that a property owner participate in the local unit's collection of recyclables.[47]

---

associated data submitted to the LGC as required under G.S. 159-34(a). It identifies units (1) with concerns related to units' general fund, water/sewer quick ratio, income, cash flow, and internal controls or (2) that have not yet submitted their audited financial statements (due four months following the end of the fiscal year).

47. *See* G.S. 153A-136(a)(6) (counties); 160A-317(b)(3) (municipalities). Recyclables are defined in G.S. 130A-290(a)(24). Note that a municipality and a county may prohibit a property owner from placing recyclables within solid waste that is disposed of in the local unit's disposal facilities. *See* G.S. 153A-136; 160A-317.

Using Public Enterprise Authority to Enforce Other Laws and Regulations

Questions often arise about whether a local unit may use its relationship with public enterprise customers to enforce other state or local rules or requirements. For example, if a unit provides water services to a customer who has not paid his or her property taxes, may the local government discontinue the water services until the property taxes are satisfied? Or, may a unit refuse to provide sewer services to a business that is operating without a required privilege license or to one that is not in compliance with the fire code? The answer to all of these questions is "no." That is because when a local government owns, operates, or contracts for the provision of public enterprise services, it is acting in a proprietary capacity (as opposed to a governmental capacity).[48] The North Carolina Supreme Court has distinguished between the two functions as follows:

> Any activity . . . . which is discretionary, political, legislative or public in nature and performed for the public good in behalf of the State, rather than to itself, comes within the class of governmental functions. When, however, the activity is commercial or chiefly for the private advantage of the compact community, it is private or proprietary.[49]

The North Carolina Supreme Court has held that a local government must not comingle its proprietary and governmental functions. Specifically, in *Dale v. City of Morganton*,[50] the court specified that the municipality's right to refuse a service it renders in its capacity as a public enterprise utility provider must be determined separately from the functions it performs in its role as a unit of local government. In that case, the municipality had supplied electricity and water to a certain house in a newly annexed area but later inspected the dwelling and found it unfit for human habitation. It subsequently cut off the electrical supply to the house and refused to reconnect the service. In its review of a challenge to the municipality's actions, the court concluded that a municipality could not deprive an inhabitant "otherwise entitled thereto, of light, water or other utility service as a means of compelling obedience to its police regulations, however valid and otherwise enforceable those regulations may be."[51]

There is an apparent exception to this general principle, and that is when a municipality uses its public enterprise authority to compel voluntary annexation. Municipalities generally are authorized to provide utility services outside their territorial boundaries. They are under no obligation to do so, though. A municipality is free to negotiate with utility customers outside municipal borders and to define by contract the conditions under which services will be

---

48. This distinction has two significant consequences. The first is that it allows a government more flexibility to operate a public enterprise like a private business entity. A local government must continue to operate within the confines of statutory authority, but often that authority is much broader in the public enterprise context, affording a unit much discretion in setting service terms. The second is that it may raise liability issues. When a local unit acts in a governmental capacity, it generally is immune from civil liability for torts arising out of the negligence of the unit's employees when acting within the scope of their employment. The state does not grant governmental immunity to a local government when it acts in a proprietary capacity.

49. Millar v. Town of Wilson, 222 N.C. 340 (1942).

50. 270 N.C. 567 (1967).

51. 270 N.C. at 573.

provided and the terms of those services. Some municipalities agree to provide utility services to "outside" properties only if the property owners contractually agree to voluntarily petition for annexation into the municipality when future criteria are met. The North Carolina Court of Appeals recently held that a municipality had authority to cease providing wastewater services to a customer located outside the municipality's territorial boundaries because the property owner refused to honor its contractual commitment to voluntarily annex the property into the city limits.[52]

Funding Public Enterprises

User Fee Authority

As stated above, public enterprises tend to be funded primarily by the collection of user fees. Both counties and municipalities, as well as most of the other local government utilities, have the same authority to impose "schedules of rents, rates, fees, charges, and penalties for the use of or the services furnished, or to be furnished, by a public enterprise . . . ."[53] This authority is very broad. And the fees may be assessed on all users of the enterprise services, regardless of their property status. Unlike with property taxes, there are no statutory exemptions from paying user fees for government property or property used for educational, charitable, or religious purposes.[54] The authority is not limitless, though. State law imposes restrictions on the types of upfront charges that may be assessed on new development.[55]

Units almost always assess periodic (monthly or bimonthly) user charges on public enterprise service customers to fund operational elements of an enterprise system. The periodic charges usually constitute a variable component based on actual usage as well as a fixed component to cover operating and capital overhead costs. Many local governments also have implemented various block-rate fee structures—either charging increased (increasing-block) or decreased (decreasing-block) rates based on additional units of usage of an enterprise service. In addition, local units have targeted revenue-generating options for certain public enterprise capital

---

52. U.S. Cold Storage, Inc. v. Town of Warsaw, 246 N.C. App. 781, 788 (2016) (Hunter, J., dissenting). In a dissenting opinion, Judge Robert Hunter Jr. argued that *Dale v. City of Morganton* prohibited the town from discontinuing wastewater service "on the basis of a collateral dispute" not related to the provision of utility service.

53. *See, e.g.*, G.S. 153A-277 (counties); 160A-314 (municipalities).

54. Note that a local government may have difficulty collecting stormwater fees from certain state entities. That is because unlike other enterprises, a unit need not have a contractual agreement with a "customer" before imposing a stormwater fee. The fee may be imposed on all real properties within the unit. Several state agencies have argued that they are shielded from paying the stormwater fee under the doctrine of sovereign immunity in the absence of a written contractual agreement with the local government.

55. *See* S.L. 2017-138. For more information on these limitations, see the following blog posts by the author (Kara A. Millonzi): "System Development Fees are the New Impact Fees," *Coates' Canons: NC Local Government Law* blog (Aug. 15, 2017); "2018 System Development Fee Law Changes," *Coates' Canons: NC Local Government Law* blog (June 26, 2018); "Assessing System Development Fees (SDFs): It's All About the Timing," *Coates' Canons: NC Local Government Law* blog (Apr. 12, 2021).

projects, such as special assessments,[56] critical-infrastructure assessments,[57] special taxing districts, and system-development fees.[58] Finally, most local governments have categorized consumers into various classes for purposes of setting rate schedules that closely track the costs of providing the enterprise services.

User fee schedules are influenced by the policy prerogatives of a local government's governing board. Consequently, the numbers and types of classifications vary greatly among North Carolina's counties and municipalities. A local government that wishes to promote conservation may impose a different rate structure from that of a local unit hoping to foster commercial or industrial development. Municipalities also may configure rates so as to encourage or discourage annexation of extraterritorial property.

User-Fee Rate Classifications

A unit may establish service classifications for purposes of charging different rates to different customer groups.[59] These classifications are subject to the common law of utilities, though.[60] Under the common law, different rate classifications may reflect differences in the costs of providing services to certain customer groups. In addition, rate classifications may be "based upon such factors as . . . the purpose for which the service or the product is received, the quantity or the amount received, the different character of the service furnished, the time of its use or any other matter which presents a substantial ground of distinction."[61] In other words, courts have upheld classifications for purposes of assessing different utility rates when there is a utility-based reason for the differentiation. However, classifications based on the type— or status—of the customer, or customer group, that do not relate to one of the above-listed purposes are not valid. For example, a local unit may assess a different rate for water used for irrigation purposes than for household or other commercial purposes (classification based on the purpose for which the water is used), but it cannot charge a different rate to all farmers (classification based on status). A unit may vary its sewer rates based on the size of a house or the number of bathrooms (proxies for different costs or capacity demands), but it may not charge a different rate based on customer income levels (classification based on status). A unit may charge all its commercial customers a solid waste collection fee rate that is different from the rate it charges residential customers (proxy for different capacity demands), but it may not charge a different rate to all churches or all nonprofit organizations (classification based on status). Or, a unit may assess a different rate to customers who request service after a certain date (again, proxies for different costs or capacity demands), but it may not set rates based on the age of its customers (classification based on status).

---

56. *See* G.S. Chapter 153A, Article 9 (counties); Chapter 160A, Article 10 (municipalities).

57. *See* G.S. Chapter 153A, Article 9A (counties); Chapter 160A, Article 10A (municipalities).

58. *See* G.S. Chapter 153A, Article 16 (counties); Chapter 160A, Article 23 (municipalities); Chapter 162A, Article 8 (all government utilities).

59. G.S. 160A-314 (municipalities); 153A-277 (counties).

60. For more information on utility ratemaking, see the following bulletins by the author (Kara A. Millonzi): "Lawful Discrimination in Utility Ratemaking, Part 2: Classifying Extraterritorial Customers," *Local Finance Bulletin* No. 34 (Oct. 1, 2006); "Lawful Discrimination in Utility Ratemaking, Part 1: Classifying Customers within Territorial Boundaries," *Local Finance Bulletin* No. 33 (Oct. 1, 2006).

61. *See* Wall v. City of Durham, 41 N.C. App. 649 (1979).

One further statutorily sanctioned rate differentiation is between customers located within a unit's territorial boundaries and customers residing outside these boundaries. This authority applies to all public enterprise activities, though it is used primarily for water and sewer services. Counties and municipalities typically assess higher fees on extraterritorial customers. For municipalities, the rate differential often serves as an incentive for voluntary incorporation by customers in surrounding unincorporated communities.

Special Limitations on User-Fee Rates

The law imposes a few additional limitations on user-fee rates for certain public enterprise services. For stormwater services, the fees assessed by a local government unit may not exceed the costs of the unit's stormwater-management program. Fee schedules must apply throughout the unit and may vary only

> according to whether the property served is residential, commercial, or industrial property, the property's use, the size of the property, the area of impervious surfaces on the property, the quantity and quality of the runoff from the property, the characteristics of the watershed into which stormwater from the property drains, and other factors that affect the stormwater drainage system.[62]

Both counties and municipalities have authority to impose three different types of solid waste fees—collection fees, disposal use fees, and availability fees.[63] Each fee may be charged only under certain circumstances. And the aggregate revenue from each fee may not exceed the costs of providing the specific solid waste services for which the fee is authorized.[64]

Process for Adopting Public Enterprise User Fees

Generally, the process for adopting public enterprise fees is simple. The governing board of a local unit sets the fees in its annual budget ordinance or in a separate ordinance. With a few exceptions, there are no notice, public hearing, or other formal public comment requirements. The governing board also is free to change the fees at any time during the fiscal year.

There are additional procedural requirements to adopt a stormwater fee. The governing board must hold a public hearing and provide sufficient notice of that hearing.[65] There also are added procedural requirements for water and sewer charges that apply to new subdivision development. Unless the applicable fees are adopted in the unit's annual budget ordinance, the unit must give notice of the fees and provide an opportunity for public comment.[66] Finally, a separate set of procedural requirements applies to the adoption of water and wastewater system-development fees.[67]

---

62. G.S. 153A-277; 160A-314.

63. *See* G.S. 153A-292; 160A-314.1.

64. For more information on solid waste fees, see Kara Millonzi, "Funding Solid Waste Services," *Coates' Canons: NC Local Government Law* blog (Oct. 7, 2010; updated 2013).

65. G.S. 160A-314; 153A-277.

66. G.S. 160A-4.1; 153A-102.1.

67. *See* G.S. Chapter 162A, Article 8.

General Fund Subsidies for Certain Utility Customers

Note that there are methods by which a local government may accomplish a purpose similar to discounting public enterprise rates, at least for certain customer groups. First, counties and municipalities are to "undertake programs for the assistance and care of [their] senior citizens" (defined as citizens who are at least 60 years of age).[68] Under this authority, a county or municipality may establish a utility rate subsidy program for its senior citizens. The program must be established in the unit's general fund (not its enterprise fund) but can be structured in a number of different ways. For example, the program may authorize a unit to transfer moneys from the general fund to the enterprise fund to pay all or a portion of a qualifying senior citizen's utility bill. It also may set up a reimbursement system for utility customers from the general fund. In addition, a county or municipality may apply a rate subsidy program to all its senior citizens, or it may limit the program to senior citizens at or below a certain income level or senior citizens who are disabled.

Second, counties and municipalities may undertake community-development programs "concerned with . . . welfare needs of persons of low and moderate income."[69] Under this authority, a local unit likely may establish a utility rate subsidy program similar to the one described above but for low- or moderate-income citizens. Again, the unit must use general fund moneys, not enterprise fund proceeds, to fund the subsidy program. Although the authorizing statute does not expressly define "low or moderate income," it does reference the Housing Authorities Law (G.S. Chapter 157, Article 1) and, by extension, local officials can reasonably employ the definitions of "persons of low income" and "persons of moderate income" found in that law (G.S. 157-3) when interpreting the statute's scope. Local officials might also consult the Section 8 income limits established by the federal Department of Housing and Urban Development for guidance in determining qualifying income limits.

Third, G.S. 158-7.1 provides broad authority for counties and municipalities "to make appropriations for economic development purposes." Under this authority, as part of a properly structured economic-development incentive, a local government may provide a cash grant to a prospective commercial or industrial entity that reimburses the entity for all, or for a portion, of its utility fees over a period of time.[70] A unit also may fund the extension of utility lines or facilities to serve the entity. Again, appropriations for such incentive programs should derive from the general fund, not an enterprise fund.

Additional Financing Sources

In addition to imposing user fees, a local government is authorized to finance the cost of any public enterprise "by levying taxes, borrowing money, and appropriating any other revenues therefor, and by accepting and administering gifts and grants from any source on behalf

---

68. G.S. 160A-497.

69. G.S. 160D-1311(a)(2) (formerly contained within G.S. 153A-376 and 160A-456).

70. For more information on legal economic-development incentive options, see the following blog posts by UNC School of Government faculty member Tyler Mulligan: "Local Government Economic Development Powers 'Clarified,' " *Coates' Canons: NC Local Government Law* blog (Oct. 26, 2015); "When May NC Local Governments Pay an Economic Development Incentive?," *Coates' Canons: NC Local Government Law* blog (Dec. 17, 2013).

thereof."[71] For accounting purposes, enterprise services often are budgeted and accounted for in an enterprise fund, whereas general government activities and revenues are accounted for in the general fund.[72] Local governments are free to transfer any property tax proceeds or unrestricted revenues from the general fund to an enterprise fund to finance the capital or operating costs of an enterprise activity.

Transferring Moneys from an Enterprise Fund to the General Fund

What about transferring moneys the other way? May a unit transfer funds from an enterprise fund to the general fund? The answer is a little more complicated. There are two types of transfers. The first is a transfer of funds from the enterprise fund to the general fund to reimburse the general fund for administrative overhead expenses to support a public enterprise activity, such as covering a portion of the unit's manager's and finance officer's salaries (which are paid out of the general fund). A reimbursement is allowed to the extent that it represents actual expenses incurred (or reasonable approximations thereof) on behalf of the public enterprise. (Note that for accounting and financial reporting purposes a local unit should refer to these appropriations as "reimbursements," not "transfers.")

The second type of transfer involves using revenue generated by a public enterprise activity to support other general government programs and functions. As to this type of transfer, G.S. 159-13 specifies that

> [n]o appropriation may be made from a utility or public service enterprise fund to any other fund than the appropriate debt service fund unless the total of all other appropriations in the fund equal or exceed the amount that will be required during the fiscal year, as shown by the budget ordinance, to meet operating expenses, capital outlay, and debt service on outstanding utility or enterprise bonds or notes.[73]

Although the statute is written as a prohibition, it actually allows a local government to transfer moneys from an enterprise fund to the general fund to support general government functions as long as all of the enterprise activity expenses that will come due during the fiscal year are covered. In essence, it allows a unit to transfer profits generated by the enterprise activity to the general fund to supplement other general fund revenue sources.

There are some limits to the authority to transfer money from an enterprise fund. The authority to transfer must be read in conjunction with the authority to set rates for the particular enterprise service. There are a few enterprise activities for which the ratemaking authority of a local unit's governing board is much more constrained. And those constraints affect the unit's ability to appropriate or loan money from an enterprise fund. For example, solid waste fees must be used only to fund solid waste activities.[74] In *Manning v. County of Halifax*,[75] the North Carolina Court of Appeals held that the county's practice of setting solid waste availability fees such that the aggregate revenue generated exceeded the aggregate costs of operating

---

71. G.S. 160A-313; *see also* G.S. 153A-276.

72. *See* G.S. 159-26. If a local unit funds an enterprise service exclusively with property tax proceeds, or with other general fund revenues, it may budget for the services in the general fund.

73. G.S. 159-13(b)(14).

74. *See* G.S. 160A-314.1, -317 (municipalities); 153A-292 (counties).

75. 166 N.C. App. 279 (2004).

the county's disposal facilities was unlawful. And the reason the court knew that the fee revenue exceeded the costs of the solid waste program was that the county had transferred the "profit" from the solid waste fund to the general fund and used the money to support general government activities.

In determining whether or not a transfer from an enterprise fund is lawful, a unit must first examine any earmarks on the money being transferred. If the money itself may be spent only to support the enterprise activity, it may not be appropriated or loaned to another fund to pay for an unrelated expenditure. Thus solid waste–fee revenue may be transferred to the general fund or to the debt-service fund to make debt-service payments on a borrowing incurred for a solid waste project. It may be moved to the general fund to cover legitimate reimbursements for services provided to the solid waste enterprise but financed in the general fund. The revenue, however, may not be appropriated to the transportation fund to purchase a new bus. It may not be appropriated to the general fund to pay for parks improvements. And it may not be loaned to the general fund to help balance the current year's budget.[76]

In addition to the statutory earmark on solid waste fees, state law requires stormwater-fee revenue to be used only to support stormwater management.[77] And transfers from electric funds of certain ElectriCities may not exceed the greater of (1) 3 percent of the gross capital assets of the electric system or (2) 5 percent of the gross annual revenues of the preceding fiscal year.[78] There may also be restrictions imposed on other enterprise revenue by contract, bond covenants, local acts, or grant agreements. None of these restrictions prohibits a local unit from using the enterprise revenue to compensate the general fund for any reasonable overhead expenses allocated to the enterprise activity. But they do constrain a unit's ability to transfer the money from the enterprise fund.

Even if legally allowed, a local unit should carefully consider whether a transfer from an enterprise fund (by means of an appropriation or loan) is appropriate. Transfers that occur frequently, or that involve a large amount of money, might be masking a problem with the unit's financial condition. Relying on enterprise ratepayers to fund general government expenditures also may raise issues of equity, fairness, and accountability. This argument resonates particularly in jurisdictions where ratepayers compose only a subset of taxpayers of the unit or where ratepayers come from outside the unit's territorial boundaries. Moreover, this practice could have negative financial implications for the unit, particularly related to issuing debt. Credit-rating agencies are likely to look unfavorably upon any effort that destabilizes an enterprise fund.

In recent years the General Assembly has indicated that it strongly disfavors transfers from an enterprise fund. In 2014, it enacted G.S. 159G-37(b), which prohibits a local government from receiving loans or grants for water or wastewater purposes from the Clean Water State Revolving Fund (CWSRF), Wastewater Reserve, Drinking Water State Revolving Fund (DWSRF), or Drinking Water Reserve if the unit has transferred money from its water or sewer enterprise fund to the general fund to supplement the resources of the general fund. The prohibition

---

76. A municipality that has a fund balance in its solid waste fund that exceeds the costs of funding a landfill, including closure and post-closure costs, may transfer excess funds accruing due to the imposition of a surcharge imposed on another local government in the state to the municipality's general fund to support other services. *See* G.S. 160A-314(a2) (municipalities).

77. *See* G.S. 160A-314(a1)(2) (municipalities); 153A-277(a1)(2) (counties).

78. G.S. 159B-39.

applies only to transfers. It does not apply to legitimate reimbursements of the general fund for "expenses paid from that fund that are reasonably allocable to the regular and ongoing operating of the utility, including, but not limited to, rent and shared facility costs, engineering and design work, plan review, and shared personnel costs."[79]

The statutory language, however, does not contain a specific time period limitation on transfers. The Department of Environmental Quality requires that a local unit certify that it has not transferred funds from an enterprise fund since the law's effective date, July 1, 2014.[80]

Collection Methods for Public Enterprise Revenues

Because most public enterprise services are voluntary, they often are governed by an express or implied contract between the government and each enterprise customer. And it is the contracting party that the government must look to for payment for enterprise services. Sometimes payment is collected before services are rendered. In many cases, however, and particularly for utility services, customers are billed after the services are received. What happens when a customer fails to pay? The following collection remedies are at a local unit's disposal.

Disconnecting Services

A local unit generally may disconnect public enterprise services at the property or premises where the delinquency occurred.[81] A county- or municipal-owned or -operated enterprise must wait ten days from the date the account becomes delinquent to suspend service. If a government operates more than one public enterprise and includes the fees for multiple public enterprises on the same bill, its governing board may adopt an ordinance ordering partial payments. That means that if a customer does not satisfy the bill in full for all enterprise services, the governing board determines what fees are paid first, and a unit may disconnect any services that remain unpaid (after the ten-day waiting period). Typically, a unit organizes payments such that water service is paid for last because it is more essential than other public enterprise services.

Civil Suit

A local unit may institute a civil suit against the contracting party to recover the amounts owed. The statute of limitations for collecting delinquent water, electric, and natural gas payments is four years.[82] The statute of limitations for collecting delinquent sewer, cable television, stormwater, and solid waste payments is three years.[83] The statute of limitations is the time period during which the unit must institute suit in order to collect on the debt.

---

79. G.S. 159G-37(b).

80. *See* N.C. Department of Environmental Quality, Division of Water Infrastructure, Fund Transfer Certification form (rev. June 2019).

81. G.S. 153A-277(b); 160A-314(b). A water and sewer authority must wait thirty days. G.S. 162A-9. Note that if a customer has filed for bankruptcy, a utility provider may not disconnect service, at least for a period of time. *See* 11 U.S.C. § 366.

82. *See* G.S. 25-2-725.

83. *See* G.S. 1-52. State law allows solid waste fees to be billed on the property tax bill. *See* G.S. 153A-293; 160A-314.1. If a unit chooses this billing method, the unit may use the same collection remedies

Debt Set-Off

Another option for a local unit seeking to collect on a delinquent public enterprise service account is to submit the claim to the state's debt set-off program for recovery against the contracting party's state income tax return or state lottery winnings, if any.[84] The amount owed must exceed $50 to be eligible for debt set-off, and the unit must follow the detailed statutory procedural requirements to participate in the program.

Prohibited Collection Methods

A local utility provider is legally prohibited from taking some collection actions. A local government may not place a lien on the property where enterprise services are provided. It also may not hold anyone other than the contracting party liable for the enterprise debts.[85] If, for example, a tenant establishes an account for water service with the local government, the tenant is the contracting party. That means that if the tenant defaults on his or her water payments, the local government may enforce collection only against the tenant. It may not proceed against the property owner. The unit also may not refuse service to a new tenant at the property where the delinquency occurred. This action would be akin to holding the new tenant liable for the former occupant's debt.

Finally, a local government generally may not refuse service to a delinquent former customer at a new property or premises. Although there is very little case law addressing this issue, a unit may be able to refuse future service if it has adopted a detailed written policy stating that the public enterprise service is conditioned on satisfaction of all previously owed (and still legally collectible) debts to the government.

Discontinuing a Public Enterprise Service Altogether

As stated above, a local government is not required to provide any public enterprise services. If, however, a municipality chooses to furnish one or more of these services, it is restricted from discontinuing the services altogether. State law prohibits a municipality from selling, leasing, or discontinuing an electric power generation, transmission, or distribution system; a gas production, storage, transmission, or distribution system; or a public transportation system, unless the proposed transaction is first approved in a voter referendum.[86] A municipality may, but is not required, to hold a referendum on a sale, lease, or discontinuance of a water treatment or

---

available to collect delinquent property taxes, and the statute of limitations for civil suits is ten years.

84. *See* G.S. Chapter 105A. For more information on the state's debt set-off program, see Chris McLaughlin, "Suped-Up Set-Off Debt Collection," *Coates' Canons: NC Local Government Law* blog (July 29, 2010).

85. Under very limited circumstances, a local government may add the amount owed by the delinquent former customer to the bill for services provided at a new property (and disconnect services at the new property for nonpayment) if the former customer resides at the new property receiving the services, even if the former customer is not the contracting party for services at the new property. *See* G.S. 160A-314; 153A-277.

86. G.S. 160A-321(a).

distribution system or a wastewater collection or treatment system.[87] A voter referendum is not required (or authorized) before the sale, lease, or discontinuation of airports, off-street parking systems, solid waste collection or disposal systems, or cable television services.[88] A county is free to sell, lease, or discontinue any of its public enterprise functions without voter approval.[89]

---

87. G.S. 160A-321(b).

88. *See* G.S. 160A-321; 160A-340.1(b).

89. *Cf.* G.S. 153A-283 ("In no case may a county be held liable for damages for failure to furnish water or sewer services.").

Chapter 14

Financing Public Schools

by Kara A. Millonzi

The importance of public education was recognized in North Carolina's first constitution in 1776. Specifically, Article XLI, Section 41 provided that "a school or schools shall be established by the legislature, for the convenient instruction of youth, with such salaries to the masters, paid by the public, as may enable them to instruct at low prices; and, all useful learning shall be duly encouraged and promoted in one or more universities." The constitution thus required the General Assembly to establish schools staffed by teachers paid from public funds. The legislature took its first step toward carrying out that mandate in 1825 when it created the Literary Fund as a source of revenue for public schools. Public schools began to function as a statewide system in 1839.

The contours and scope of that public education system have evolved over time. The current state constitution provides that North Carolinians "have a right to the privilege of education, and it is the duty of the State to guard and maintain that right."[1] It further commands the General Assembly to provide "for a general and uniform system of free public schools, which shall be maintained at least nine months in every year, and wherein equal opportunities shall be provided for all students."[2]

The North Carolina Supreme Court has interpreted these provisions to guarantee "every child of this state an opportunity to receive a sound basic education in our public schools."[3] This interpretation has arisen out of a long-running funding dispute, commonly referred to as the *Leandro* litigation. The case began in the mid-1990s as a fight over funding disparities among counties but has since evolved into an argument about what it means to provide each child with the opportunity for an adequate, or "sound basic," education.[4]

Whether or not the state of North Carolina is meeting its responsibility to ensure that every student is given an opportunity to receive a sound basic education is the subject of ongoing judicial interpretation and legislative debate. The current public school system is the product of a patchwork of efforts by the state to adapt to changing economics, demographics, and policy prerogatives.[5] It involves an intricate division of policy and funding responsibilities among state and local entities. Each entity plays an integral part in carrying out the constitutional mandate to provide a public education.[6]

This chapter analyzes the current funding framework for public elementary and secondary schools, focusing first on the state's and counties' funding responsibilities and funding sources. It then details the local budgeting process, briefly discussing additional powers of a county board that enable it to play an increasing role in shaping local education policy. Finally, it summarizes the current funding scheme for charter schools.

This chapter reflects the law as of June 1, 2023.

1. N.C. CONST. art. I, § 15.

2. N.C. CONST. art. IX, § 2(1).

3. Leandro v. State, 346 N.C. 336, 346 (1997).

4. *See, e.g.,* Hoke Cnty. Bd. of Educ. v. State, 358 N.C. 605 (2004).

5. A more detailed history of how public education has evolved in North Carolina is available at NCPEDIA, https://www.ncpedia.org/education-public (last visited June 1, 2023).

6. For more information on the current governance structure of the public school system, see Kara A. Millonzi, "The Governance and Funding Structure of North Carolina Public Schools," in *County and Municipal Government in North Carolina*, 2nd ed., edited by Frayda S. Bluestein (Chapel Hill, N.C.: UNC School of Government, 2014).

Funding Framework

Funding public schools is a responsibility of both state and county governments. (The federal government also provides limited funding for certain targeted programs).[7] In 1839, the first year that North Carolina's public schools began to function as a statewide system, the General Assembly made $40 available to each school district that raised $20 locally.[8] That was the legislature's first stab at dividing the fiscal burden of public education between the state and local governments. The struggle to find a proper division while ensuring fairness in the financial burden, equity in educational opportunities, and quality in education has continued for the ensuing 184 years.

In the early to mid-1930s, largely as a reaction to the fiscal chaos of the Great Depression—a significant number of local governments had defaulted on debt and were in rough financial shape—the state adopted the current fiscal framework of centralizing policy making and funding responsibility for public education at the state level. It enacted the School Machinery Act,[9] which made the state responsible for paying all current expenses necessary to finance a minimum six-month school term, leaving the counties responsible for constructing and maintaining school buildings.

The basic structure of school finance has not changed since the 1930s. The state continues to be responsible for the majority of current expenses necessary to maintain the minimum nine-month term, while counties are responsible for financing construction and the maintenance of school facilities. In this respect, North Carolina's approach to financing its public schools differs from that of most other states, where the basic financial backing for public schools comes from local rather than state revenues. In North Carolina, state income and sales taxes, rather than local property taxes, constitute the primary revenue sources for financing schools. In 2018,

---

7. Although public education is a state and local responsibility, since the 1950s the federal government has assumed a significant role in public education, primarily by providing funds to states. Congress generally conditions a state's receipt of federal funds on the state's compliance with federally defined conditions.

For example, the No Child Left Behind Act of 2001, 20 U.S.C. §§ 6301 *et seq.*, created rigorous testing, reporting, and academic progress requirements for all states receiving Title I funds (all fifty states). Title I, which is aimed at raising the academic achievement of low-income children, is the largest source of federal education funds. Significant federal funding also goes to programs for children with disabilities and to the school breakfast and lunch program. More recently, the U.S. Department of Education initiated the Race to the Top program, which provided competitive grants to spur innovation and reforms in state and local education. (The Race to the Top program was funded as part of the American Recovery and Reinvestment Act of 2009, Pub. L. No. 111-5, 123 Stat. 115.) States were awarded points for satisfying certain educational policies, such as performance-based standards for teachers and principals; complying with Common Core; lifting caps on charter schools; turning around the lowest-performing schools; and building data systems. North Carolina received a Race to the Top grant of nearly $400 million in 2010. In 2015, Congress enacted the Every Student Succeeds Act (ESSA), which, among other things, requires every state to measure performance in reading, math, and science and develop a "State Report Card" that is accessible online and provides parents with information on test performance.

Most federal moneys are categorical funds, which means they are appropriated by Congress to the states for specific educational purposes. These funds are channeled through the State Board of Education for distribution to local units, but the board has little control over the programs themselves. In general, poorer school units receive more federal dollars relative to their enrollment than wealthier units do.

8. 1839 N.C. Pub. Laws ch. 8.

9. 1931 N.C. Pub. Laws ch. 728.

however, the General Assembly authorized municipalities to fund public schools that are within their territorial boundaries or that serve municipal residents.[10] Over time, this could cause a significant shift of funding responsibility from the state to local governments.

It is also the case, though, that there has been a blending of funding responsibilities over time. The state often appropriates funds for school construction, and counties increasingly must provide funds for current expenses. In fact, the county share of funding has increased significantly in recent years.

State Funding

State Funding Responsibilities

The state allocates its funding to the public school system in a few different ways. The majority of funds are used to cover the operational expenses of each local school administrative unit.[11] The General Assembly, however, typically provides some funds each year to fund school facility projects.

Operational Expenses

The state appropriates its operational funding for schools in its annual budget. North Carolina differs from most other states in that it does not distribute money for the general education program on the basis of a local unit's financial ability to operate schools. The bulk of state funding for public education is essentially a flat grant to a school system based on the number of students enrolled and the general costs of operation. The primary unit of allocation is average daily membership (ADM). The ADM for each school month is calculated by dividing the number of non-violating membership days by the number of days in a school month, rounded to the nearest whole number. ADMs are calculated for each grade level and then added together to determine the school's ADM. Finally, each school's ADM in the school administrative unit is added together to determine the school unit's ADM.[12]

State appropriations typically are allocated among counties and school units through three different methods—position allotments, dollar allotments, and categorical allotments.

Position Allotments

The largest component of the state budget for schools is teacher salaries. In FY 2020–21, for example, 94.8 percent of state expenditures supported salaries and benefits.[13] The majority of this appropriation is reflected in position allotments. Each year the state appropriates funds to pay teachers, instructional personnel, and school administrators. Salaries are funded on a position basis—the state allots a certain number of teachers and support personnel to each

---

10. Chapter 160A, Section 700 of the North Carolina General Statutes (hereinafter G.S.).

11. The state's public schools are divided into 115 local school administrative units and one regional school. Each county has at least one local school administrative unit; some counties have up to three. Local school administrative units are often referred to as local education agencies or LEAs.

12. N.C. Department of Public Instruction, *School Attendance and Student Accounting Manual, 2020–2021* (last visited Feb. 2, 2023), 32–35.

13. N.C. Department of Public Instruction, *Highlights of the North Carolina Public School Budget* (March 2022), 5.

school unit based on grade-level ADMs. The current teacher-student ratios for kindergarten through grade three are as follows:

Kindergarten: 1 teacher per 18 students,
First grade: 1 teacher per 16 students,
Second grade: 1 teacher per 17 students,
Third grade: 1 teacher per 17 students.[14]

For each position allotment, the state pays the costs to fund a particular person in a particular teaching position, based on the State Salary Schedule. That allows a school unit to hire experienced teachers or instructional support personnel based on the unit's needs without being limited to a specific dollar total. A school unit also has some flexibility to use the allocated funds to cover other expenditures.[15]

Dollar Allotments

Each school unit also receives a per-ADM dollar allotment that can be used to fund textbooks, supplies, materials, and some personnel, such as teacher assistants and central office administration positions. For example, in FY 2020–21, the state allocated $30.12 per ADM for classroom materials/instructional supplies/equipment and $32.26 per ADM for textbooks.[16] A school unit may use dollar allotments to cover certain other expenditures.[17]

Categorical Allotments

The General Assembly has targeted some state appropriations to aid smaller and lower-wealth counties and to assist school units that serve student populations with unique needs. These moneys are not allocated on a straight ADM basis. Instead, they are disbursed according to detailed formulas set forth in the state's annual budget. Common categorical allotments are children with disabilities, academically gifted children, at-risk children, low-wealth counties, and small school systems.[18] Some of these allocation formulas factor in a county's appropriation to a school unit. For example, the low-wealth formula is based in part on the county's wealth and whether the county's appropriation to the school unit meets a certain minimum-effort threshold.[19] Furthermore, the low-wealth funds may not be used to supplant county appropriations.

The state also provides funds to local school units to replace buses according to a statutory replacement schedule.[20]

---

14. *See* G.S. 115C-301.

15. *See* G.S. 115C-105.25. A local school unit must publish information on its website about its state appropriations and any allotment transfers.

16. N.C. Department of Public Instruction, *Highlights of the North Carolina Public School Budget* (March 2022), 9.

17. *See* G.S. 115C-105.25. A local school unit must publish information on its website about its state appropriations and any allotment transfers.

18. *See* N.C. Department of Public Instruction, note 16 above, at 9.

19. N.C. Department of Public Instruction, note 16 above.

20. *See* G.S. 115C-249.

Capital Expenditures

Counties have been responsible for financing school construction since the state's public school system was established. Over the years, however, the state has offered direct and indirect assistance for construction costs—through state general obligation bonds, local sales and use tax authority, and direct appropriations of corporate income tax and state lottery proceeds.

State Bonds

In the past, the state has issued numerous bonds to finance construction grants to local school boards. In recent years, however, the state has chosen other forms of funding assistance for school construction. The last state bond for public-school construction was in 1996.[21]

Local Sales and Use Tax Authority

The state also has provided alternative relief for financing school construction. In 1983, it authorized counties to levy a one-half-cent sales and use tax[22] with a specified percentage of the resulting revenue earmarked for school capital outlay, including retirement of existing school indebtedness (30 percent of the proceeds are currently so earmarked). In 1986, the legislature authorized counties to levy another one-half-cent tax, this time with 60 percent of the revenue earmarked for school capital outlay expenses.[23] Because traditionally sales and use taxes have been a state revenue source, these local sales taxes may reasonably be viewed as a form of state revenue-sharing for school construction. All counties levy both taxes.[24] Counties may hold the moneys generated from the earmarked portion of the taxes in a capital reserve fund for future projects; any interest earned must be earmarked for school capital outlays.[25] Counties also are free to allocate the unrestricted portion of their local sales and use taxes proceeds to fund public-school capital and operating expenses.[26] In 2007, counties received authority to levy an additional quarter-cent tax, subject to voter approval.[27] The proceeds of the tax can be used for any county expenditure item, including public schools. Beginning in July 2016, certain counties began receiving additional sales and use tax revenues, pursuant to G.S. 105-524. This revenue results from a redistribution of a portion of the proceeds generated from county sales and use taxes. A county may use this additional revenue to fund public-school capital and operating expenses, community colleges, or economic development.

---

21. *See* 1995 N.C. Sess. Laws ch. 631.

22. G.S. Chapter 105, Article 40.

23. G.S. Chapter 105, Article 42.

24. Counties have additional sales and use tax authority. All counties levy a one-cent tax pursuant to G.S. Chapter 105, Article 39. Several counties also levy a quarter-cent tax pursuant to G.S. Chapter 105, Article 46. Neither of these taxes is earmarked for school funding, though.

25. A county may petition the North Carolina Local Government Commission (LGC) for authorization to use part or all of the earmarked revenues for other purposes. The LGC will approve a petition only if the county demonstrates that it can provide for school capital needs without the earmarked revenue. A local board of education also may petition the LGC if it believes that the county has not complied with the intent of sales and use tax laws. G.S. 105-502 and -487.

26. For more information on local sales and use taxes, see Chapter 4, "Revenue Sources."

27. G.S. Chapter 105, Article 46.

State School Construction Funds

In 1987, the legislature enacted the School Facilities Act, which created the Critical School Facility Needs Fund (CSFNF) and the Public School Building Capital Fund (PSBCF).[28]

The CSFNF, funded by corporate income tax proceeds, aided counties and school units with the most pressing needs in relation to their resources, as determined by the CSFNF Commission. Moneys were distributed to high-need counties from 1988 through 1994, at which time the fund was abolished.[29]

The PSBCF was established to provide aid to all counties for school construction projects. It too was originally funded by a portion of the state's corporate income tax proceeds,[30] which were allocated among the 100 counties on the basis of ADM. A county and its local school administrative unit(s) could jointly apply to the Department of Public Instruction to use the county's allocation for capital outlay and technology projects. A county was required to match moneys allocated for capital outlay projects on the basis of $1 of local funds for every $3 of state funds.

Beginning in 2005, the legislature also allocated a portion (roughly 40 percent) of the state's lottery proceeds to the PSBCF.[31] These funds could be used to fund capital outlay projects for school buildings and were allocated among the counties according to a detailed statutory formula.[32] No local match was required.

In 2013, the General Assembly repealed the statutory distributions of both corporate income tax proceeds and lottery proceeds to the PSBCF.[33] New appropriations to the PSBCF will be subject to yearly state budget appropriations. According to G.S. 115C-546.2(d), if funds are appropriated to the PSBCF from the state lottery, those moneys must be allocated for school construction projects based on ADM.[34] A county and its local school administrative unit(s) jointly apply to the Department of Public Instruction for a distribution of the moneys "to fund school construction projects and to retire indebtedness incurred for school construction projects."[35] No county matching funds are required. For FY 2021–22 and 2022–23, the legislature appropriated $100 million to the fund.[36] It has appropriated this same amount for many years.

In 2017, the General Assembly established a second public-school capital fund, known as the Needs-Based Public School Capital Fund (NBPSCF).[37] It appropriated to the fund $145,252,612 in FY 2021–22 and $208,252,612 in FY 2022–23.[38] This fund is used to award grants to eligible counties to assist with critical public-school building capital needs. An eligible county is a county with an adjusted market value of taxable real property of less than forty billion dollars ($40,000,000,000).[39]

---

28. 1987 N.C. Sess. Laws ch. 622.
29. 1995 N.C. Sess. Laws ch. 631, § 14.
30. G.S. 115C-546.1(b) (repealed 2013).
31. G.S. 18C-164(d) (repealed 2013).
32. G.S. 115C-546.2(d)(1), (2) (repealed 2013).
33. S.L. 2013-360, § 6.11.
34. G.S. 115C-546.2(e) allows the State Board of Education to use up to $1.5 million of the funds appropriated each year to support positions in the Department of Public Instruction.
35. G.S. 115C-546.2(d)(4).
36. S.L. 2022-74, § 4.2.(a).
37. G.S. Chapter 115C, Article 38B.
38. G.S. Chapter 115C, Article 38B.
39. G.S. 115C-546.11.

The Superintendent of Public Instruction must award grants according to the following priorities: (1) counties designated as development tier one areas, (2) counties with greater need and less ability to generate sales tax and property tax revenue, (3) counties with a high debt-to-tax revenue ratio, (4) the extent to which a project will address critical deficiencies in adequately serving the current and future student population, (5) projects with new construction or complete renovation of existing facilities, (6) projects that will consolidate two or more schools into one new facility, and (7) counties that have not received a grant from this fund in the previous three years.[40] The grant funds are subject to a county match based on adjusted market value of taxable real property, as specified by statutory formula.[41]

There are some significant restrictions in the NBPSCF grant program. First, the grant moneys may only be used for the "construction of new school buildings and additions, repairs, and renovations."[42] They may not be used to reimburse a county for past projects or to make debt-service payments on past projects. The moneys also may not be used "for real property acquisition or for capital improvements to administrative buildings."[43] They may be used to enter into certain capital leases for school facilities, though.[44] There are maximum grant amounts based on school purpose. In FY 2022-23, these amounts are up to $30 million for elementary schools, up to $40 million for middle schools and combination elementary and middle schools, and up to $50 million for high schools.[45] Finally, there are detailed grant agreement requirements, specified in G.S. 115C-546.12.[46]

In 2021, the General Assembly established the Public School Repair and Renovation Fund. It appropriated $30 million to the fund in FY 2021–22 and $50 million in FY 2022–23.[47] The funds are distributed equally among the 100 counties and used by counties "for enlargement, improvement, expansion, repair, or renovation of classroom facilities at public school buildings within local school administrative units located in [a] county."[48] The funds may not be used for the retirement of indebtedness.[49]

State Funding Sources

The primary funding source for public schools is the state income tax. There are a handful of other revenue sources, though, including state lottery proceeds, fines and forfeitures proceeds, state sales and use tax proceeds, and pass-through federal and private grants.

---

40. G.S. 115C-546.10.
41. G.S. 115C-546.11(a).
42. G.S. 115C-546.11(b).
43. G.S. 115C-546.11(a).
44. G.S. 115C-546.13.
45. G.S. 115C-546.11(c).
46. G.S. 115C-546.12.
47. S.L. 2022-74, § 4.2.(a).
48. G.S. 115C-546.21.
49. G.S. 115C-546.21.

Local Funding

Another significant difference between North Carolina's funding scheme for public education and that in other states is that local boards of education do not have authority to levy taxes to support schools.[50] Instead, this authority resides with county governments. Counties use property taxes and local sales and use taxes to fund most school capital needs and a growing percentage of operational needs as well. As of July 1, 2018, municipalities are authorized to supplement state and county funding. A few other local revenue sources are available to support public schools.

County Funding

County Funding Responsibilities

Although the state bears primary responsibility for establishing a public school system, the North Carolina Constitution authorizes the General Assembly to "assign to units of local government such responsibility for the financial support of the free public schools as it may deem appropriate."[51] It further provides that the "governing boards of units of local government with financial responsibility for public education may use local revenues to add to or supplement any public school or post-secondary school program."[52]

The legislature has not been entirely clear in delineating the public-school funding duties of the state from those of county governments. Significant confusion about the contours of a county's obligation for public schools has resulted, forcing counties and local school boards to turn to the courts for guidance.

G.S. 115C-408 specifies that "it is the policy of the State of North Carolina to provide from State revenue sources the instructional expenses for current operations of the public school system as defined in the standard course of study. It is the policy of the State of North Carolina that the facilities requirements for a public education system will be met by county governments." On its face, this statute articulates a clear demarcation of funding responsibility between the state and county governments. The statute, by its terms, is merely aspirational, however. It does not actually assign any specific funding responsibilities. Neither does it reflect funding realities.

Specified Funding Requirements

A handful of statutory provisions assign funding responsibility to counties for specific expenditure items. These statutes assign to counties responsibility for funding most capital outlay expenditures, including school facilities, furniture, and apparatus;[53] buildings for bus and vehicle storage;[54] library, science, and classroom equipment;[55] water supply and sanitary facilities;[56] and maintenance and repair of school buildings.[57] In addition, the statutes explicitly assign to counties responsibility for funding some operational expenditures—specifically, school

---

50. There are a few exceptions. At least two school administrative units—Roanoke Rapids Graded School District and Mooresville Graded School District—have authority to levy property taxes.

51. N.C. CONST. art. IX, § 2(2).

52. N.C. CONST. art. IX, § 2(2).

53. G.S. 115C-521.

54. G.S. 115C-249.

55. G.S. 115C-522(c).

56. G.S. 115C-522(c)

57. G.S. 115C-524(b).

maintenance and repairs,[58] instructional supplies and reference books,[59] school property insurance,[60] and fire inspections.[61]

If the funding framework ended there, it might not be such a knotty issue. A county would be required to fund the public-school capital and operational expense items explicitly delegated to it by statute. And, a county could choose to supplement its required appropriations in any given year, within the discretion of its governing board. The state would be required to fund any other expenditure necessary to enable a local school administrative unit to provide each student with the "opportunity to receive a sound basic education" (considering, of course, money the local school administrative unit receives from other sources, such as the federal government).

Additional Funding Requirements

The funding framework does not end there, however. The statute that sets forth the uniform budget standard for public schools also requires that a local school administrative unit maintain at least three funds to account for budgeted moneys.[62] The statute identifies the types and sources of funds that must be appropriated to each fund. One of the funds, the Capital Outlay Fund, includes appropriations from, among other sources, "revenues made available for capital outlay purposes by the State Board of Education and the board of county commissioners."[63]

Another fund, the local current expense fund, must "include appropriations sufficient, when added to appropriations from [the State], for the current operating expense of the public school system in conformity with the educational goals and policies of the State and the local board of education, within the financial resources and consistent with the fiscal policies of the board of county commissioners."[64] It further indicates that the appropriations must be funded by, among other revenue sources, "moneys made available to the local school administrative unit by the board of county commissioners."[65] Thus, despite the "policy" statements in G.S. 115C-408, the state provides some funding for capital expenses and counties are required to provide some funding for operational expenses. But the uniform budget statute still leaves ambiguity as to what the state is responsible for and what is left to counties.

To further complicate the analysis, G.S. 115C-431(a) authorizes a local board of education to initiate a dispute-resolution process[66] with the county if the local board of education determines that in any given year "the amount of money appropriated to the local current expense fund, or the capital outlay fund, or both, by the board of county commissioners is not sufficient to support a system of free public schools. . . . " The North Carolina Supreme Court has interpreted G.S. 115C-431 to "itself assign to the local government responsibility for funding 'a system of free public schools'. . . . "[67] In 2018, the legislature altered the dispute-resolution statute. With

---

58. G.S. 115C-524.

59. G.S. 115C-522(c).

60. G.S. 115C-534.

61. G.S. 115C-525(b).

62. G.S. 115C-426.

63. G.S. 115C-426(f).

64. G.S. 115C-426(e).

65. G.S. 115C-426(e).

66. The dispute-resolution process is discussed in greater detail below. *See* note 108 and accompanying text below.

67. Beaufort Cnty. Bd. of Educ. v. Beaufort Cnty. Bd. of Comm'rs, 363 N.C. 500, 507 (2009).

the changes, it is clear that a county is responsible for funding certain operational and capital expenses each year.[68] (The dispute-resolution process is discussed in detail below.) In any given year a county may be required to fund operational and capital expenditure items in addition to those explicitly specified by the statutory provisions listed above.

County Funding Sources

County Appropriations of Unrestricted Revenue

A county may appropriate any unrestricted county revenue to fund the capital and operating expenses of its school unit(s). At least to some extent, a county's governing board has discretion in determining the amount of unrestricted revenue to appropriate to support its schools. A school unit, however, may challenge a county's appropriations if it believes that the amount allocated for either capital or operating expenditures (or both), when combined with moneys made available to it through other sources, is not sufficient to provide each student with an opportunity to receive a sound basic education that year. As discussed below, a county board may exercise some control over how the appropriated funds are spent by the local school unit(s).[69]

County Appropriations of Earmarked Local Sales and Use Tax Proceeds

As discussed above, a portion of a county's local sales and use tax revenue is earmarked for certain public-school expenditures.[70] A county has discretion to determine how much of these earmarked funds to appropriate each year and for what capital projects. A county board may appropriate all the available funds each fiscal year, or it may place the money into a capital reserve fund for future expenditure. This allows a county to save moneys over several years to finance large capital outlays for its school unit(s). As with county appropriations of other general fund revenues, a county board may exercise some control over how its local school unit(s) expends these funds.[71]

A county may seek permission from the Local Government Commission (LGC) to use part or all of the earmarked local sales and use tax proceeds for any lawful purpose if the county demonstrates that it can satisfy all of the capital outlay needs of its school unit(s) from other sources. In order to apply to the LGC for an exemption from the statutory earmarks on the G.S. Chapter 105, Articles 40 and 42 tax proceeds, a board of county commissioners must adopt a resolution and then submit it to the LGC. The resolution must indicate that the county can provide for its public-school capital needs without restricting the use of part or the entire designated amount. The LGC must consider both the school unit's capital needs and those of the county generally in making its decision. The LGC must issue a written decision detailing its findings and specifying what percentage, if any, of the earmarked proceeds may be used by the county for any lawful purpose.

---

68. G.S. 115C-431.

69. *See* notes 100–102 and accompanying text below.

70. *See* notes 22–27 and accompanying text above.

71. *See* notes 100–102 and accompanying text below.

Municipal Funding

A municipality is authorized to make appropriations to "supplement funding for elementary and secondary public education" that benefit the residents of the municipality.[72] In some respects, this funding authority is broader than that afforded to county governments. It comes with some limitations, though.

Public Schools

A municipality may appropriate money to a *public school* that serves the residents of the municipality to fund the school's current operating expenses or any "other specific uses directed" by the municipality.[73] Public school is defined to include a local school administrative unit (traditional public school); a laboratory school, authorized by G.S. Chapter 116, Article 29A; a charter school, authorized by G.S. Chapter 115C, Article 14A; and a regional school, authorized by G.S. Chapter 115C, Article 16, Part 10. Unlike a county government, a municipality may make appropriations directly to any of these public schools.

Appropriations within and Outside Municipality

A municipality's appropriation authority is further delineated by location of the public-school unit. For schools located within municipal limits, municipal appropriations may be made as a lump sum to each school or on a per-pupil basis.[74] In addition to funding general capital and operating expenses and special programs, municipal appropriations may also be used to enter into operational and financing leases for real property or mobile classroom units and to make payments on loans made to public schools for facilities, equipment, or operations.[75] Municipal appropriations may not be used, however, to obtain "any other interest in real property or mobile classroom units."[76] Thus, municipal funds may not be used to purchase land, school facilities, or mobile classrooms.

For schools located outside municipal limits, a city may allocate money to a school attended by a resident student on a per-pupil basis to fund current operating expenses or other specific uses directed by the city.[77]

There is no requirement that a municipality provide equal funding to all of the schools that serve its residents. A municipal board may choose to fund only the schools within municipal territorial boundaries, or it may choose to fund only a category of schools, such as only charter schools, or it may choose to only fund a single school unit.

This funding authority is very different from that of county governments. As discussed above, county funding for operational expenses must be proportionally apportioned, based on average daily membership (ADM), among all the traditional public-school units within the

---

72. *See* S.L. 2018-5, § 38.3, *as amended by* S.L. 2018-97, § 11.1.

73. G.S. 160A-700(b)(1), (2).

74. G.S. 160A-700(b)(1).

75. G.S. 160A-700(b)(1). Note that there is very limited authority for traditional public schools to borrow money or enter into these types of leases. *See* G.S. 115C-528 (lease-purchase and installment-purchase financing for vehicles, certain equipment, and mobile classrooms); -530 (operational leases of school buildings and school facilities); -546.13 (Needs-Based Public School Capital Fund grant-funded capital leases for school facilities). And all such leases must include a statement that they do not constitute an indebtedness or obligation of the municipality.

76. G.S. 160A-700(b)(1).

77. G.S. 160A-700(b)(2).

county. In addition, county appropriations to a traditional public school's local current expense fund must be proportionally shared, on a per-pupil basis, with other public schools attended by a student who would otherwise be served by the traditional public school.

Municipal Funding Directives

A municipality may "direct or restrict the use of funds appropriated for specific purposes, functions, projects, programs, or objects. . . . "[78] These categories correlate to the chart of accounts used by traditional public schools, whereby operating expenditures are broken down by purpose code, function code, object code, and program report code and capital expenditures are delineated by category. For the other public schools that may not follow this chart of accounts, a municipality is free to direct its funding to specific programs or expenditure items. A municipality thus has broader authority to direct school expenditures than does a county, which is limited to allocating operating expense appropriations by purpose and function and capital outlay appropriations by project of category.

Municipal appropriations to a traditional public school will not be allocated to the local current expense fund. Instead, the local school board will set up a separate fund to budget and account for these moneys. This means that, unlike county appropriations, municipal appropriations for operating expenses to public schools will not be shared with charters or other public schools.

Municipal Funding Sources

A municipality may use property tax proceeds or any unrestricted revenues from other sources to fund appropriations to public schools.[79] There is one limitation, though. Only property tax proceeds that are generated from taxes levied on or after July 1, 2018, may be used for this purpose. A municipality may not use fund balance derived from property tax collections on levies from prior fiscal years, even if those amounts are collected after July 1, 2018.

Impact on State and County Funding

G.S. 160A-700 does not, itself, alter the general state and county funding schemes. The legislature makes its school appropriations in the annual state budget and is free to change its appropriations method at any time.

With respect to counties, as detailed above, a board of county commissioners is required to provide sufficient funding, when added to all other revenues available to a traditional public-school unit, to allow the school unit to meet its constitutional minimum education requirements. Although G.S. 160A-700 appears to envision that municipal funding will supplement state and county funding ("A city may use property tax revenues authorized under G.S. 160A-209(c)(26b) and other unrestricted revenues to supplement funding for elementary and secondary public education that benefits the residents of the city."[80]), there is no explicit non-supplant provision. Thus, a board of county commissioners may reduce its appropriations to a traditional public-school unit by the amount of revenue appropriated by the municipality to that school unit, subject of course to the minimum funding formula triggered by the dispute resolution process discussed below.

---

78. G.S. 160A-700(a).
79. G.S. 160A-700(a).
80. G.S. 160A-700(a).

Note also that in a county with more than one traditional public-school unit, the county board of commissioners must apportion all appropriations for operating expenses proportionally among the school units based on ADM. So, if a municipality provided supplemental funding to one of the county's school units and not the other, any resulting reduction in county appropriations for operating expenses would affect both school units.

Other Local Funding Sources

In addition to appropriations from a county's general fund, a local school unit also may receive revenue derived from locally collected penalties and fines and a voted supplemental school tax.

Local Fines and Penalties

Under Article IX, Section 7 of the North Carolina Constitution, "the clear proceeds of all penalties and forfeitures and of all fines collected in the several counties for any breach of the penal laws of the state, shall belong to and remain in the several counties, and shall be faithfully appropriated and used exclusively for maintaining free public schools." Several locally collected fines and penalties are subject to this constitutional mandate.[81] If a county collects penalties or fines that are subject to this constitutional requirement, it must remit the clear proceeds (gross proceeds minus up to 10 percent in collection costs) to the local school unit(s) within the county within ten days after the end of the month in which the money was collected.

A county does not include these funds in its appropriations to the school unit(s), and the county board of commissioners has no control over their expenditure. The board, however, may consider the amount of fine, penalty, and forfeiture revenue received by a local school unit when determining the county's annual appropriations.

Dedicated Property Tax Revenue

There are two methods by which a county may legally dedicate property tax proceeds for public-school purposes—dedicated county general tax and voted supplemental tax.

Dedicated County General Tax

The first method is by obtaining voter approval to dedicate a portion of the general property tax for public-school purposes. If the referendum is successful, the board of county commissioners decide each year whether or not to levy the dedicated property tax rate, along with the county's general rate. If it levied the portion of the property tax dedicated to schools, it can then use the proceeds from that tax to either supplement or supplant its appropriations to the school unit(s) from other sources for capital and/or operating expenses.[82]

Voted Supplemental Tax

The second method requires a joint effort between the local board of education and the board of county commissioners. It is the closest thing to a local school board having its own taxing authority. The local board of education may petition the county commissioners to hold a voter referendum to authorize a voted supplemental school tax. If the county commissioners receive

---

81. *See* G.S. 115C-437. For a detailed discussion of the categories of locally collected penalties and fines that are subject to this constitutional provision, see Kara Millonzi, "Locally-Collected Penalties & Fines: What Monies Belong to the Public Schools?," *Coates' Canons: NC Local Government Law* blog (Nov. 17, 2011). *See also* Chapter 4, "Revenue Sources."

82. G.S. 153A-149(d).

a valid petition, the county must hold the referendum. The petition must state the maximum authorized supplemental tax rate, up to $0.50 per $100 valuation for school units having a population of less than 100,000 and $0.60 per $100 valuation for all other school units. If a supplemental tax is approved by the voters, a local board of education may request that the county levy a tax each year up to the maximum rate approved by the voters. The county decides whether or not to levy the tax and at what rate (the rate is capped at the level requested by the local board of education).

The county does not have any control over how the supplemental tax proceeds are spent by the school unit. That decision rests with the local school board, subject only to the terms of the ballot measure under which the tax was approved. The board of county commissioners, however, may consider the availability of the supplemental tax revenue when determining the county's annual appropriations.

County/School Budgeting Process

Each year, a county engages in a detailed budgetary process to estimate revenues and make appropriations for the forthcoming fiscal year. The county must include its appropriations to its local school unit(s) for capital outlay and current expenses in its annual budget ordinance. The Local Government Budget and Fiscal Control Act,[83] as supplemented by the School Budget and Fiscal Control Act,[84] prescribes the procedural and substantive requirements for adopting the county's budget ordinance and appropriating money to its local school unit(s).[85] The budgeting process is fairly straightforward and can be broken down into the following ten steps:

Step 1: County Board of Commissioners and Local School Board(s) Communicate on an Ongoing Basis.

Step 2: School Superintendent Submits Proposed Budget.

Step 3: Local School Board Considers Superintendent's Budget.

Step 4: Local School Board Submits Budget Request to County Board.

Step 5: County Board Makes Appropriations to Local School Unit(s).

Step 6: Local School Board Initiates Dispute-Resolution Process (optional).

Step 7: Local School Board Adopts School Budget Resolution.

Step 8: Local School Board Amends School Budget Resolution (optional).

Step 9: County Board Monitors Local School Unit's Expenditures of County Appropriations (optional).

Step 10: County Board Reduces Appropriations to Local School Unit(s) during Fiscal Year (very limited authority).

Each step is analyzed more thoroughly below.

---

83. G.S. Chapter 159, Article 3.

84. G.S. Chapter 115C, Article 31, Part 1.

85. See Chapter 3, "Budgeting for Operating and Capital Expenditures," for more information on adopting, enacting, and amending the annual budget ordinance.

Step 1: County Board of Commissioners and Local School Board(s) Communicate on an Ongoing Basis

A county board of commissioners and a school board must work together to ensure that each board's statutory requirements are met. The board of county commissioners and local board(s) of education should engage in ongoing communications during the fiscal year.[86] Leading up to the budget process, they should communicate about the fiscal needs of the local school administrative unit and the fiscal resources of the county. Doing so will prevent surprises to either board at budget time and will help make the budgeting process work more efficiently and effectively.

Some county boards and local school boards agree to adopt multi-year financing formulas for operational expenses, indexed to such things as enrollment growth, percentages of low-wealth or special needs students, or state funding averages. These funding agreements are not legally enforceable, but they can serve as a useful tool for financial planning.

Step 2: School Superintendent Submits Proposed Budget

By May 1, the public-school superintendent must submit a budget and budget message to the local board of education (superintendent's budget).[87] A local school board may direct the superintendent to follow certain specified guidelines and processes in preparing the proposed budget. A copy of the superintendent's budget must be filed in the superintendent's office and made available for public inspection.[88] The superintendent may, but is not required to, publish notice that the superintendent's budget has been submitted to the local board of education.

Step 3: Local School Board Considers Superintendent's Budget

The local board of education may hold a public hearing on the superintendent's budget, but it is not required to do so.[89] With or without public input or support, the school board is free to make any changes to the proposed budget before submitting it to the county for consideration.

Step 4: Local School Board Submits Budget Request to County Board

By May 15, the local board of education must submit its entire proposed budget (not just its request for county funding) to the board of county commissioners.[90] The county's budget officer must present the local board of education's requests to the county board, even if the budget officer's proposed county budget recommends different funding levels for the school unit.

The local board of education also must submit to the board of county commissioners a written summary of "the academic performance of the schools in the local school administrative unit, including the school performance grades of each school, any schools identified as low-performing or continually low-performing, and efforts by the local board of education to improve those identified schools' performance."[91] The county commissioners may require that the local board of education present this information at a public meeting.

---

86. *See* G.S. 115C-426.2.
87. G.S. 115C-427.
88. G.S. 115C-428.
89. G.S. 115C-428.
90. G.S. 115C-429.
91. G.S. 115C-429(a).

The board of county commissioners may request further information from the local school administrative unit about its proposed budget request. In fact, the county board has broad authority to obtain from the local board of education "all books, records, audit reports, and other information bearing on the financial operation of the local school administrative unit."[92] It also may specify the format in which the financial information must be presented.

In addition, a county board of commissioners can (and often does) invite the school unit's superintendent or the local school board to present the school's budget proposal at a county board meeting or during the public hearing on the county's budget. This affords the county board an opportunity to ask questions about certain expenditure items and to obtain further clarification on a local school board's policy goals and needs.

Step 5: County Board Makes Appropriations to Local School Unit(s)

The board of county commissioners makes its appropriations for capital and operating expenditures to the local school administrative unit(s) in the county's annual budget ordinance.

Budgeting Factors

In making its appropriation decisions, the county board of commissioners must carefully consider the local school board's funding request. The county is required to make appropriations for operating expenditures that, when combined with revenues to the school unit from all other sources, are sufficient to allow the school to meet its constitutional mandate to provide each student with the opportunity to receive a sound basic education.[93] (Other revenues available to a school unit for operating expenses include supplemental taxes levied by or on behalf of the school unit; state money disbursed directly to the school unit; moneys made available to the local school unit by the board of county commissioners; moneys accruing to the local school unit from fines, penalties, and forfeitures pursuant to Article IX, Section 7 of the N.C. Constitution; and any other moneys made available or accruing to the local school unit for the current operating expenses of the school system).[94] Of course a county board of commissioners also has to balance the needs of the school unit with the needs of all other county departments, particularly those that provide state-mandated services, such as public health, social services, and elections. Recognizing this, G.S. 115C-426 requires that a county board consider its fiscal resources and financial policies when making school appropriation decisions.

A county also is required to appropriate sufficient funds to meet a school unit's capital needs for the fiscal year.[95] The state makes some funds available to a county and its local school unit(s) to help with school construction, but most of this need must be met by county resources. A school unit's capital needs vary from year to year. It may be helpful for a county board of commissioners to engage its local school board(s) in the county's capital planning process or capital improvement program (CIP).

---

92. G.S. 115C-429(c).
93. *See* G.S. 115C-426.
94. *See* G.S. 115C-426(e).
95. *See* G.S. 115C-426(f).

Fund Balance

Questions often arise at budget time about the propriety of a local school unit maintaining a fund balance. Most state funds to school units revert at the end of a fiscal year if not spent. Thus, a school unit's fund balance is comprised primarily of county appropriations from previous years. There is no prohibition against a school unit maintaining a fund balance. School units, however, do not need a fund balance to meet cash flow needs to the same extent that counties and municipalities do.[96] And, unlike for counties and municipalities, the state's Local Government Commission does not prescribe a minimum fund balance level for local school units. A county board of commissioners may not force a school board to expend its fund balance for capital or operating expenditures. And a school unit is not authorized to return all or a portion of its fund balance to the county. A county board, however, will likely consider the amount of fund balance available to the school unit when making its yearly county appropriations for operating expenses.[97]

County Authority to Direct School Unit Expenditures

Allocating Local Current Expense Appropriations

Generally, appropriations for operating expenses are made to the local current expense fund. A board of county commissioners may appropriate a lump sum to the local current expense fund to support operating expenses. If a county appropriates moneys to the local current expense

---

96. The most significant revenue source for counties and municipalities is property tax proceeds. Although property taxes typically are levied at the beginning of the fiscal year (July 1), they may be paid without penalty until the following January. Thus, counties and municipalities rely heavily on fund balance to pay expenses during the first half of the fiscal year. Local school units do not have the same cash flow needs because they receive revenue disbursements from the state and county governments on a more regular basis throughout the fiscal year.

97. G.S. 115C-426 used to provide more explicit authority for a county to consider a local school unit's fund balance when making its budget appropriation to the school unit for operating expenses. That is because fund balance was considered to be part of the local current expense fund. And G.S. 115C-426(e) required that each year the local current expense fund was to include appropriations from the county that, when added to appropriations from the state and other local sources, are sufficient to provide for "the current operating expense of the public school system in conformity with the educational goals and policies of the State and the local board of education, within the financial resources and consistent with the fiscal policies of the board of county commissioners."

In 2010, in reaction to a series of cases involving apportionment of funds from the local current expense fund to charter schools, the General Assembly amended G.S. 115C-426(c) to state that "the appropriation or use of fund balance or interest income by a local school administrative unit shall not be construed as a local current expense appropriation included as a part of the local current expense fund." The impetus behind this amendment was clear. The legislature intended to shield a school unit's fund balance from being apportioned to a charter school pursuant to G.S. 115C-238.29H(b). However, in adding this language, the legislature arguably created an ambiguity as to whether or not a county board may consider a school's existing fund balance when making budget appropriations to the local current expense fund for operating expenses.

However, G.S. 115C-426(e) allows a county board to consider "other moneys available or accruing to the local school administrative unit," which provides some justification for a county board to consider a school unit's uncommitted fund balance when making its yearly appropriation decisions.

fund with no further direction, the local board of education has full discretion over the expenditure of these moneys.[98]

A county is authorized, however, to allocate part or all of its appropriation for operating expenses within the local current expense fund by purpose or function, as defined in the uniform budget format.[99] The uniform budget format (now the uniform chart of accounts)[100] defines "purpose code" to include the activities or actions that are performed to accomplish the objectives of the school unit. Function codes are first-level subdivisions of purpose codes and represent the greatest level of specificity to which a county may allocate funds for operating expenses. County appropriations may be allocated to the following purpose and function codes.

Purpose (first level) and Function (second level) Codes

- 5000—*Instructional Services*. Includes the costs of activities dealing directly with the interaction between teachers and students.
  - 5100—Regular Instructional Services
  - 5200—Special Populations Services
  - 5300—Alternative Programs and Services
  - 5400—School Leadership Services
  - 5500—Co-Curricular Services
  - 5600—School-Based Support Services
- 6000—*Supporting Services Programs*. Includes the costs of activities providing system-wide support for school-based programs, regardless of where these supporting services are based or housed.
  - 6100—Support and Development Services
  - 6200—Special Populations Support and Development Services
  - 6300—Alternative Programs and Services Support and Development Services
  - 6400—Technology Support Services
  - 6500—Operational Support Services
  - 6600—Financial and Human Resource Services
  - 6700—Accountability Services
  - 6800—System-Wide Pupil Support Services
  - 6900—Policy, Leadership, and Public Relations Services
- 7000—*Ancillary Services*. Includes activities that are not directly related to the provision of education for pupils in a local school administrative unit.
  - 7100—Community Services
  - 7200—Nutrition Services
  - 7300—Adult Services

---

98. A local school unit must distribute the per-pupil proportional share of certain local current expense appropriations (along with certain state appropriations) to each charter school (G.S. 115C-218.105(c); 115C-426(b)); UNC Lab School (G.S. 116-239.11); and/or Innovative School District (G.S. 115C-75.10) that is attended by a child who otherwise would attend school in the local school unit.

99. G.S. 115C-429. The county board of commissioners may specify that the local school board submit its budget request according to these purpose and function codes.

100. A list of the chart of accounts for FY 2022–23 can be accessed on the N.C. Department of Public Instruction's website at https://www.dpi.nc.gov/districts-schools/district-operations/financial-and-business-services/school-district-finance-operations/chart-accounts (last visited June 1, 2023).

- 8000—*Non-Programmed Charges.* Includes conduit-type payments to other local school administrative units in the state or in another state, transfers from one fund to another fund in the local school administrative unit, appropriated but unbudgeted funds, debt-service payments, scholarship payments, payments on behalf of educational foundations, and contingency funds.
  - 8100—Payments to Other Government Units
  - 8200—Unbudgeted Funds
  - 8300—Debt Services
  - 8400—Interfund Transfers
  - 8500—Contingency
  - 8600—Educational Foundations
  - 8700—Scholarships
- 9000—*Capital Outlay.* Includes expenditures for acquiring fixed assets, including land or existing buildings, improvements of grounds, initial equipment, additional equipment, and replacement of equipment.

A board of county commissioners may request that a local board of education refrain from using county appropriations for certain items of expenditure within a purpose or function code. However, it may not legally restrict these expenditures at the line-item level. Furthermore, if a county board allocates its appropriations according to a purpose or function code, the local school board may modify up to 25 percent of an allocation for operating expenses. The county board may reduce the local school board's discretion to modify allocations if it so specifies in the county budget ordinance, but not to less than 10 percent.[101]

Allocating Capital Outlay Appropriations

According to the uniform budget format (now the uniform chart of accounts), there are three categories of expenditures to which a county may appropriate capital funds to its public school(s). A county may appropriate moneys for Category I expenditures for a specific capital project or projects. Moneys appropriated for Categories II and III expenditures, however, are allocated to the entire category, not to individual expenditure items.

The following list details the authorized capital outlay expenditures in each category.

Category I

Acquisition of real property and acquisition, construction, reconstruction, enlargement, renovation, or replacement of buildings and other structures for school purposes.

Category II

Acquisition or replacement of furnishings and equipment.

Category III

Acquisition of school buses, activity buses, and other motor vehicles.

---

101. G.S. 115C-433.

If the board of county commissioners allocates part or all of its capital appropriations by project, the local school board must obtain approval from the county for any changes in the allocation for specific Category I expenditures—acquisitions of real property for school purposes and acquisitions, construction, reconstruction, enlargement, renovations, or replacement of buildings and other structures.[102] However, a local board of education has full discretion to reallocate funds within categories II and III.

Apportionment of County Funds among Multiple School Units

If a county supports more than one local school unit, county appropriations to the local current expense funds of the local school administrative units (to support operating expenses) must be apportioned according to the average daily membership (ADM) of each unit.[103] There is an exception for appropriations funded by voted supplemental taxes levied less than countywide. This occurs when a county has more than one local school administrative unit. These funds do not need to be apportioned equally among local school administrative units.

This uniform apportionment requirement does not apply to capital funds. A county may allocate unequal amounts of capital funding to different school units within a fiscal year. Furthermore, under certain circumstances a county may appropriate moneys to special funds for particular programs at one local school administrative unit without appropriating an equivalent amount to other units. The local school administrative unit must budget and account for these moneys in a fund other than the local current expense fund.

Interim Budget

The Local Government Budget and Fiscal Control Act requires that adoption of the budget ordinance take place by July 1.[104] However, sometimes county boards of commissioners are unable or unwilling to adopt a budget ordinance by this date. In such cases, a county board must adopt an interim budget that appropriates money to cover necessary expenses for county departments and the local school unit(s) until the budget ordinance is adopted.[105] In an extreme situation, the state's Local Government Commission is authorized to assume the financial duties of a county board and to adopt the budget ordinance.[106] If the county's budget is delayed beyond July 1, a local school board also must adopt an interim budget resolution to pay salaries and the "usual ordinary expenses" of the school unit.[107]

Step 6: Local School Board Initiates Dispute-Resolution Process (optional)

If the local school board "determines that the amount of money appropriated to the local current expense fund [for operating expenses], or the capital outlay fund, or both, . . . is not sufficient to support a system of free public schools," it may initiate a dispute-resolution process with the board of county commissioners to challenge the appropriation (dispute-resolution

102. G.S. 115C-433.
103. G.S. 115C-430.
104. G.S. 159-13; 115C-429.
105. G.S. 159-16.
106. G.S. 159-181.
107. G.S. 115C-434.

process).[108] For many years, the dispute-resolution process had three stages—joint meeting of the two governing boards, mediation, and litigation. As of July 1, 2018, the General Assembly replaced the litigation stage with a mandated funding formula for operating expense–funding disputes.[109] Litigation will continue as the third stage for capital funding disputes.

Stages of Dispute-Resolution Process

As stated above, there are three stages in the dispute-resolution process—joint meeting of the two governing boards, mediation, and default funding formula (for operating expense disputes) or litigation (for capital outlay disputes).

Joint Meeting of Boards

To trigger the dispute-resolution process, a local school board must so notify the county board of commissioners within seven days of the adoption of the county budget ordinance. The boards then are required to meet and make a good-faith effort to try to resolve their differences. A mediator presides over the meeting and acts as a neutral facilitator.

Mediation

If the joint meeting is not successful, the boards proceed to official mediation. Unless the two boards agree otherwise, the participants in the mediation are the chairs, attorneys, and finance officers of each board; the school superintendent; and the county manager. The compensation and expenses of the mediator are shared equally by the local school administrative unit and the county. The mediation is conducted in private, and statements and conduct are not discoverable in any subsequent litigation. The mediation must end by August 1, unless both boards agree otherwise. If the mediation continues beyond August 1, the county must appropriate to the local current expense fund a sum equal to its appropriation for the previous fiscal year.

Default Funding Formula or Litigation

If mediation ultimately fails, what happens next depends on whether operational funding levels, capital funding levels, or both are in dispute. If the dispute at least partially involves operational funding amounts, to be appropriated to the school unit's local current expense fund, then a failed mediation triggers a default funding formula. The funding formula is the final determination of the appropriation amount for operating expenses for that fiscal year. Neither the local board of education nor the board of county commissioners may file any legal action challenging the determination.

The funding formula differs depending on whether or not the funding formula had been triggered in the prior fiscal year.

Local Current Expense Funding Formula if Statutory Funding Formula Not Triggered for Prior Two Years
If the statutory funding formula was not triggered in the prior two fiscal years, the county's appropriation to a local school unit's local current expense fund derives from the following four-step formula:

1. Start with the amount of county appropriations allocated to the local current expense fund in the prior fiscal year that was actually expended by the local school unit or

---

108. G.S. 115C-431(a).
109. S.L. 2018-83.

transferred to a charter school, innovative school, regional school, or laboratory school. In other words, begin the calculation with the amount of county appropriations actually spent for the year immediately preceding the budget year. *Note that because county appropriations are comingled with other local revenue sources in the local current expense fund, it will be incumbent on the local school board to separately track the expenditure of county appropriations.*

2. Divide the amount from step 1 by the sum of the average daily membership (ADM) of the local school administrative unit from the prior year plus the share of the ADM of any innovative, charter, regional, or laboratory school whose students reside in the local school administrative unit from the prior year. This number represents the per-student allocation.

3. Multiply the amount from step 2, rounded to the nearest penny, by the sum of 1 plus the twelve-month percent change in the second quarter Employment Cost Index for elementary and secondary school workers as reported by the Federal Bureau of Labor Statistics. Unfortunately, G.S. 115C-431 does not precisely designate the data required to make this calculation. It is unclear if the reference is to the Employment Cost Index for total compensation for elementary and secondary school workers or the Employment Cost Index for wages and salaries for elementary and secondary school workers. (Note that second-quarter data are released on July 31.) G.S. 115C-431 also does not indicate whether seasonally adjusted or non-seasonally adjusted data should be used. It will be up to the local school board and board of county commissioners to determine which set of data to use in the calculation.

4. Multiply the per-student allocation in step 3, rounded to the nearest penny, by the sum of the ADM of the local school administrative unit for the budget year in dispute plus the share of the ADM of any innovative, charter, regional, or laboratory school whose students reside in the local school administrative unit for the budget year in dispute. (It is not clear what number should be used to determine the total number of students for the budget year in dispute. At the point in time that the statutory formula is likely to be triggered, a local school unit will only have its estimated ADM for the year.)

The figure resulting from step 4, rounded to the nearest penny, is the statutorily mandated local current expense appropriation for the budget year.

Local Current Expense Funding Formula if Statutory Funding Formula Triggered in Prior Two Fiscal Years or More

If the statutory funding formula is triggered a second year in a row, the formula is altered to increase the inflationary factor. The formula then becomes a five-step process.

1. Start with the amount of county appropriations allocated to the local current expense fund in the prior fiscal year that was actually expended by the local school unit or transferred to a charter school, innovative school, regional school, or laboratory school. In other words, begin the calculation with the amount of county appropriations that were actually spent for the year immediately preceding the budget year.

2. Divide the amount from step 1 by the sum of the ADM of the local school administrative unit from the prior year plus the share of the ADM of any innovative, charter,

regional, or laboratory school whose students reside in the local school administrative unit from the prior year. This number represents the per-student allocation.

3. Increase by 3 percent the twelve-month percent change in the second quarter Employment Cost Index for elementary and secondary school workers as reported by the Federal Bureau of Labor Statistics. This provision, again, leaves a great deal of ambiguity. As stated above, it is unclear if the reference is to the Employment Cost Index for total compensation for elementary and secondary school workers or the Employment Cost Index for wages and salaries for elementary and secondary school workers. (Note that second-quarter data are released on July 31.) G.S. 115C-431 also does not indicate whether seasonally adjusted or non-seasonally adjusted data should be used. It will be up to the local school board and board of county commissioners to determine which set of data to use in the calculation. Finally, it is not clear how to interpret the mandate to increase the percentage change by 3 percent. It could mean that you add 3 percent to the percent change. It could also mean that you multiply the percent change by 3 percent. I think the legislature most likely intended the former interpretation. For example, if the twelve-month percent change is 2.38 percent, you add 3 percent to that for a total of 5.38 percent or 0.05.

4. Multiply the amount from step 2, rounded to the nearest penny, by the amount in step 3, rounded to the nearest penny.

5. Multiply the per-student allocation in step 4 by the sum of the ADM of the local school administrative unit for the budget year in dispute plus the share of the ADM of any innovative, charter, regional, or laboratory school whose students reside in the local school administrative unit for the budget year in dispute.

The figure resulting from step 5, rounded to the nearest penny, is the statutorily mandated local current expense appropriation for the budget year.

Litigation for Capital Funding Dispute

If the dispute, or part of the dispute, involves capital funding amounts, the local board of education may file an action in superior court related to the capital funding only. The action must be filed within five days of the failed mediation. Either side may demand a jury trial. The judge or jury must determine the "amount of money legally necessary from the board of county commissioners to provide the local school administrative units with buildings suitably equipped, as required by G.S. 115C-521."[110] G.S. 115C-521 specifies that a local school board must provide adequate school buildings "equipped with suitable school furniture and apparatus."

In *Union County Board of Education v. Union County Board of Commissioners*,[111] the court of appeals held that the amount "legally necessary" is the amount needed to enable the local school board to fulfill its constitutional duty to provide every child with the opportunity for a sound basic education. The court also clarified that a judge or jury is limited to considering the needs of the school unit, and resources available to the school unit and the county, in the fiscal year in which the dispute arose.

---

110. G.S. 115C-431(c).
111. 771 N.C. App. 590 (2015).

In making this determination, a judge or jury must consider

> the educational goals and policies of the State and the local board of education, the budgetary request of the local board of education, the financial resources of the county and the local board of education, and the fiscal policies of the board of county commissioners and the local board of education.[112]

If the school board succeeds in the litigation, the court will order the board of county commissioners to appropriate a specific amount to the local school administrative unit and, if necessary, to levy property taxes to cover the amount of the appropriation. Any payment by the county may not be considered or used to deny or reduce appropriations to a local school administrative unit in subsequent fiscal years.

Either board may appeal the superior court's judgment in writing within ten days after the entry of the judgment. Final judgments at the conclusion of the appellate process are legally binding on both boards.

Although G.S. 115C-431 directs the trial court to take up the matter as soon as possible, it is silent as to the timing of appellate review. In practice, the appellate review process often takes a year or more to complete. Thus, even if a judge or jury determines that a local school board needs additional funds from a county to meet its constitutional and statutory educational responsibilities for a particular school year, the school unit may not receive those additional funds that school year.

Step 7: Local School Board Adopts School Budget Resolution

If the local board of education does not formally dispute the county's budget appropriations, or upon successful resolution of any dispute, the local board of education adopts a budget resolution.[113] The budget resolution reflects the county's appropriations for capital and operating expenses as well as those from the state and federal governments. It also incorporates revenues from other local sources. G.S. 115C-432 imposes several requirements and limitations on a school unit's budget. Among other things, the school unit's budget must conform to the county's budget allocations. The budget resolution must be entered into the minutes of the local board of education. Within five days of adoption of the budget, copies are to be filed with the public-school superintendent, school finance officer, and county finance officer.[114]

Step 8: Local School Board Amends School Budget Resolution (optional)

A local school board is free to amend its budget resolution any time after its adoption. The budget resolution must continue to meet the requirements specified in G.S. 115C-432, and if the county board of commissioners has allocated funds by purpose or function code, the school board must continue to honor those designations except as allowed by statute.

---

112. G.S. 115C-431(c).
113. G.S. 115C-432.
114. G.S. 115C-432.

Prohibition against Capital Outlay Fund Transfers

Occasionally during a fiscal year a local school board will want to move moneys from its capital outlay fund to its current expense fund, or vice versa, in order to cover unexpected expenditures. A local school board is prohibited, however, from transferring money between these two funds, except under limited circumstances. A transfer may occur if all of the following conditions are met: (1) the funds are needed to cover emergency expenditures that were both "unforeseen and unforeseeable" when the school budget resolution was adopted, (2) the local board of education receives approval from the county board of commissioners, and (3) the local board of education follows certain procedural requirements.[115]

A local board of education may initiate a transfer between its capital outlay and current expense funds by adopting a resolution that states (1) the amount of the proposed transfer, (2) the nature of the emergency, (3) why the emergency was unforeseen and could not have been foreseen, (4) what objects of expenditure will be added or increased, and (5) what objects of expenditure will be reduced or eliminated.

The local board of education must send copies of the resolution to the board of county commissioners and any other local school administrative units in the county. The county board must allow any other local boards of education to comment on the proposed transfer. The county board must then approve or deny the request within thirty days. The county board must notify the requesting local board of education and any other local boards of education in the county of its decision. If the county board does not act within the thirty-day period, its approval is presumed, unless the local board of education that submitted the request explicitly agrees to an extension of the deadline.[116]

Step 9: County Board Monitors Local School Unit's Expenditures of County Appropriations (optional)

The board of county commissioners has broad discretion to request information from the local school board relating to the expenditure of school funds. Pursuant to the annual budget process, the county board is authorized to inspect "all books, records, audit reports, and other information bearing on the financial operation of the local school administrative unit."[117] The county board also may request, in writing, that the school finance officer make periodic reports about the financial condition of the local school administrative unit.

In addition, the board of county commissioners automatically receives a copy of the annual audit report for the local school administrative unit.[118]

Finally, the county board and the local board of education are authorized and encouraged to "conduct periodic joint meetings during each fiscal year" to discuss the implementation of the current public-school budget and assess future capital and operating needs.[119]

---

115. G.S. 115C-433(d).

116. Note that if a board of county commissioners and a local board of education seek to use the local sales and use tax proceeds that are specifically earmarked by state statute for capital outlay expenses to fund operating expenses, the county also must seek approval from the Local Government Commission according to the procedures set forth in G.S. 105-487 and -502.

117. G.S. 115C-429(c).

118. G.S. 115C-447(a).

119. G.S. 115C-462.2.

Step 10: County Board Reduces Appropriations to Local School Unit(s) during Fiscal Year (optional)

A county may reduce its appropriations to a local school unit only under limited circumstances. The board of county commissioners may not reduce its appropriations for capital outlay or operating expenses after it adopts the county budget ordinance unless (1) the local board of education consents to the reduction or (2) it is pursuant to a general reduction in county expenditures due to prevailing economic conditions.[120] If the board of county commissioners reduces its appropriations to its school unit(s) pursuant to a general reduction in county expenditures, it must hold a public meeting and afford the local school board an opportunity to present information on the impact of the reduction and then take a public vote (that is, a vote in an open session of a public meeting) on the decision to reduce the appropriations.

Additional County Authority and Responsibilities

Although a board of county commissioners does not officially set education policy, it nonetheless influences policy through the local budgeting process. A county board also plays a role in administering public schools and shaping policy by performing a few additional statutory functions—approving certain school board contracts, conducting special school elections, approving the amount the school board proposes to spend to purchase a school site, mandating the merger of all school units in the county, setting local school board members' compensation and expense allowances, issuing bonds for school construction, and, by agreement with the local board of education, constructing school facilities.

Approving Certain Local School Board Contracts

A local school board must obtain consent from the county board of commissioners before entering into several different types of contracts. The county board's approval typically commits the county to providing sufficient funds to meet the local school board's obligations under the contracts.

Continuing Contracts for Capital Outlay

School administrative units may enter into continuing contracts for multi-year capital improvement projects or outlays, even when the school unit's budget resolution for the current year does not include an appropriation for the entire obligation incurred. Three conditions for these continuing contracts must be met: (1) the budget resolution must include an appropriation authorizing the current fiscal year's portion of the obligation, (2) an unencumbered balance of that appropriation for the current fiscal year must be sufficient to cover the unit's current fiscal year obligations under the contract, and (3) the board of county commissioners must approve the contract by a resolution binding the board to appropriate sufficient funds to pay

---

120. G.S. 159-13(b)(9).

the amounts falling due under the contract in future fiscal years.[121] The requirement for county board approval does not apply to multi-year contracts for operating expenses.

Installment Finance Contracts

Under G.S. 115C-528, local boards of education may use installment finance contracts to fund the acquisition of certain kinds of equipment: automobiles and school buses; mobile classroom units; food service equipment; photocopiers; and computers and computer hardware, software, and related support services. The contract term may not exceed the useful life of the property being acquired. A school unit seeking to acquire covered equipment must give the seller a security interest in the property being financed under the installment contract. The school board must obtain the county board of commissioners' approval of an installment finance contract if the contract term is at least three years and the total amount financed under the contract is at least $250,000 or an amount equal to three times the local school system's annual state allocation for classroom materials and equipment, whichever is less. Even if a contract does not require county board approval, a school board must submit information concerning these contracts as part of the annual budget it submits to the county board.

Guaranteed Energy-Savings Contracts

G.S. 115C-47(28a) authorizes local school boards to use guaranteed energy-savings contracts to purchase an energy conservation measure—such as a facility alteration or personnel training related to a facility's operation—that reduces energy consumption or operating costs. These contracts for the evaluation, recommendation, or implementation of energy conservation measures in school facilities are paid for over time, and energy savings are guaranteed to exceed costs. Local boards of education may finance energy conservation measures by using installment finance agreements under G.S. 160A-20. Such agreements are subject to county approval. A county board of commissioners must certify to the North Carolina Department of State Treasurer that the payments under a guaranteed energy-savings contract are not expected to require any additional appropriations to the local school board or cause an increase in taxes.[122] A county board also must indicate that it does not intend to reduce appropriations to the local school unit based on a reduction in energy costs in a manner that would inhibit the ability of the local school board to make payments under the contract. A county, however, is not legally obligated to appropriate funds to cover contract amounts due or to make payments directly under the contract.

Operational Leases

G.S. 115C-530 authorizes local boards of education to enter into operational leases of real or personal property for use as school buildings or facilities. Leases for terms of three years or longer, including optional renewal periods, must be approved by the board of county commissioners. Approval obligates the commissioners to appropriate sufficient funds to meet the payments due in each year of the lease; the school board's budget resolution must include an

---

121. G.S. 115C-441(c1).

122. *See* State of North Carolina, Department of State Treasurer, *Application for Approval of Guaranteed Energy Savings Contracts* (rev. Sept. 2015).

appropriation for the current fiscal year's portion of the obligation as well as an unencumbered balance sufficient to pay the obligation.

Also, under G.S. 115C-530, school boards may make improvements to leased property. Contracts for repair and renovation must be approved by the board of county commissioners if they (1) are subject to the competitive bidding requirement in G.S. 143-129(a) (the current threshold for which is $500,000) and (2) do not otherwise constitute continuing contracts for capital outlay.

Conducting Special School Elections

Under G.S. 115C-501, special school elections may be held to vote on proposals to

1. authorize a local supplemental tax,
2. increase the supplemental tax rate in an area that already has a supplemental tax of less than the maximum rate set by statute,
3. enlarge a city administrative unit by consolidating areas of a county unit into the city school unit,
4. supplement and equalize educational advantages by levying a special tax in an area of a county administrative unit enclosed within one common boundary line,
5. abolish a supplemental school tax,
6. authorize the county to issue school bonds,
7. provide a supplemental tax on a countywide basis pursuant to merger of all administrative units within a county,
8. annex or consolidate school areas from contiguous counties and provide a supplemental school tax in such annexed or consolidated areas, or
9. vote school bonds and taxes in certain merged school administrative units.

Involvement by the board of county commissioners begins when it receives a petition from a county or city school board requesting a special school election. The petition, which must be approved by the school board, need not originate with the school board itself. It can be submitted also by a majority of qualified voters who have resided for the preceding year in an area adjacent to a city administrative unit; these voters may petition the county board of education for an election on the question of annexing their area to the city unit. For other types of special elections, 25 percent of the qualified voters in a school area may initiate a petition and submit it to the board of education. The school board must consider the petition and decide whether or not to approve it.

If a petition is approved by the school board, it is submitted to the county commissioners; G.S. 115C-506 requires the commissioners "to call an election and fix the date for the same." In *Board of Education of Yancey County v. Board of Commissioners of Yancey County*,[123] the North Carolina Supreme Court held that, if a petition for an election on authorizing a special supplemental tax is properly presented, the duty of the board of commissioners is ministerial and not discretionary; it is obliged to call the election. This rule likely applies to the other kinds

---

123. 189 N.C. 650 (1925).

of special elections listed above.[124] The school board may withdraw a petition at any time before the election is called. All school elections, whether for county or city school administrative units, are held and conducted by the appropriate county board of elections.

If an election is held on any of these issues and the proposition is rejected, under G.S. 115C-502 another election on the same issue in the same area may not be called for at least six months. An election on whether to abolish a local tax district may not be held any sooner than one year after the election establishing the district or after an election on the issue of dismantling the local tax district.[125] If a local tax district is in debt or has unmet obligations, no election may be held on the issue of abolishing that tax district.

Approving Expenditures for School Sites

A school board may not execute a contract to purchase a site or to make any expenditure for a property without the board of county commissioners' approval "as to the amount to be spent for the site." The requirement applies whether the county has made a blanket capital outlay appropriation or has allocated moneys for this particular project. In 1975, in *Painter v. Wake County Board of Education*,[126] the state supreme court considered an earlier version of this statutory provision; its ruling indicates that this approval requirement applies only when the school board is using funds from the county.

If the two boards disagree over a site-purchase matter, they may, under G.S. 115C-426(f), settle the dispute through the judicial procedure used to resolve budgetary disputes (found in G.S. 115C-431). If they do so, the issue to be determined is the amount to be spent for the site, not its location. The school board has sole authority to choose school sites; if the court finds the amount it proposes to spend reasonable, the school board will most likely prevail.

Initiating Merger of School Units within a County

As discussed above, some counties have more than one local school administrative unit. The propriety of having multiple school administrative units within one county is the subject of much study and debate among county and school officials. The number of school administrative units has decreased substantially over time. The General Assembly merged several of the school units through local acts. Some mergers, however, came about at the behest of county governments in which the administrative units are located. The General Assembly has authorized a board of county commissioners to initiate a merger by adopting a merger plan for all school units in the county. In subsequent years, the county must provide the merged school unit local funding based on average daily membership[127] at a level at least equivalent to the highest level received by any school unit in the county during the five fiscal years preceding the merger. The boards of education do not participate in preparing the plan and need not agree to it. And a

---

124. It is not entirely clear whether or not the rule applies to petitions for school bond elections because of inconsistent provisions in the laws regulating local government debt. However, in 1975 the North Carolina attorney general issued an opinion letter stating that a county must hold a bond referendum if a proper petition is submitted to the county board of commissioners. Op. N.C. Att'y Gen. (Feb. 10, 1975) (on file with author).

125. G.S. 115C-505.

126. 288 N.C. 165 (1975).

127. Average daily membership is a calculation of a school unit's student population. For more information on that calculation, see N.C. Department of Public Instruction, note 12 above.

merger plan developed by a board of county commissioners cannot be made subject to voter approval.[128] The merger plan, however, must be approved by the State Board of Education or enacted by local act of the General Assembly.[129]

There are two other statutorily authorized ways to merge school units without legislative action. A city school board may force a merger by dissolving itself. In that case the State Board of Education must adopt a merger plan. Plans developed in this way cannot be subject to voter approval. Boards of education and boards of county commissioners do not participate in preparing such a plan and need not agree to it.[130] Alternatively, the school systems themselves may bring about the merger. The merging units adopt a written plan of merger, which becomes effective if the board of county commissioners and the State Board of Education approve it. The plan may make the merger contingent on approval of the voters in the affected areas.[131]

Setting Local School Board Members' Compensation

A county board of commissioners is authorized to fix the compensation and expense allowances paid to members of the local board of education.[132] The county board must follow the procedures set forth in G.S. 153A-92. "Funds for the per diem, subsistence, and mileage" for all local school board meetings are appropriated to the local current expense fund.[133]

Constructing School Facilities

A county board of commissioners bears primary funding responsibility for public-school infrastructure and facilities. However, state law assigns to each local school board the duty to provide adequate school facilities.[134] G.S. 115C-521(c) also directs that the "building of all new school buildings and the repairing of all old school buildings shall be under the control and direction of, and by contract with, the board of education for which the building and repairing is done." And all school buildings must be located on a site that is "owned in fee simple" by the local school board.[135]

For some capital projects, a county appropriates money to the local school unit and school personnel perform the work or contract with private entities to complete the work. A county board has no legal authority to require that a school board hire a particular contractor or otherwise proceed under a particular process (such as design-build or capital lease). A county and a school board may prefer to have the county contract for and oversee school construction and repair projects. In this case, the county and the school board must enter into a carefully crafted interlocal agreement in which the local board assigns its contracting rights to the county but retains ultimate oversight authority.[136] Furthermore, if a county issues installment finance debt to fund a school construction project, the county may need to obtain temporary ownership of

---

128. G.S. 115C-68.1.
129. G.S. 115C-67.
130. G.S. 115C-68.2.
131. G.S. 115C-67.
132. G.S. 115C-38.
133. G.S. 115C-38.
134. G.S. 115C-521(a).
135. G.S. 115C-521(d).
136. Counties and local school administrative units have broad authority to enter into interlocal agreements under G.S. Chapter 160A, Article 20.

the school property for the life of the loan.[137] Again, a carefully drafted interlocal agreement should allow the county to perform the construction or repair work while not running afoul of statutory provisions.

Funding Charter Schools

In 1996, as part of its educational reform efforts, the General Assembly authorized the establishment of charter schools, public schools that operate under a charter from the State Board of Education but are free from many of the restrictions that affect other public schools.[138]

Any child who is eligible to attend public school in North Carolina is eligible to attend a charter school.[139] A student is not limited to charter schools located within his or her school district or even his or her county. A charter school may set an enrollment cap but may not limit admission to students on the basis of intellectual ability, scholastic or athletic achievement, disability, race, creed, gender, national origin, religion, or ancestry.[140] A charter school may not charge tuition or fees, except for those also charged by the local school administrative unit in which the charter school is located. Although a statewide cap was originally set for 100 charter schools, in 2011 the legislature removed the limit.[141] In 1997–1998, 34 charter schools began operation; by 2015, 193 were in operation or approved to begin operations.[142]

State Funding

For every child who attends a charter school, the State Board of Education must allocate to that charter school an amount equal to the average per-pupil allocation for average daily membership from the local school administrative unit allotments in which the charter school is located (with the exception of allotments for children with disabilities and children with limited English proficiency).[143] This means that state funding for operational expenses follows the student to the charter school.

State funding may be used for a charter school's operational expenses. It also may be used to enter into operational and financing leases for real property or mobile units utilized as classroom facilities.[144] A charter school may not use state funds to purchase any interest in real property or mobile classroom units, however.

---

137. *See* G.S. 160A-20.

138. *See* G.S. Chapter 115C, Article 14A.

139. G.S. 115C-218.45.

140. G.S. 115C-218.45(e).

141. S.L. 2011-164, § 2(a) (June 17, 2011) (amending G.S. 115C-238.29D by repealing subsection (b)).

142. For a map of charter schools in North Carolina, as well as a list of public charter schools and a database of state charter schools and contracts, see N.C. Department of Public Instruction, *Charter Schools*, "Schools."

143. G.S. 115C-218.105(a). The state must allocate an additional amount for each child attending the charter school who is a child with disabilities or a child with limited English proficiency.

144. G.S. 115C-218.105(b).

County Funding

Under current law, a county is not required and, in fact, is not statutorily authorized, to directly fund charter schools for either capital or operating expenses.[145] A county does, however, indirectly fund some operating expenses for charter schools. For each student within a local school administrative unit who attends a charter school, the administrative unit must transfer to the charter school an amount equal to the administrative unit's per-pupil local current expense appropriation for the fiscal year. The local current expense appropriation includes direct appropriations by the county for operating expenses; revenues from local fines, penalties, and forfeitures; state moneys disbursed directly to the local school administrative unit; and the proceeds of supplemental taxes levied by or on behalf of the local school administrative unit.[146] It does not include fund balance. It also does not include moneys that are properly accounted for in funds other than the local current expense fund, such as moneys resulting from reimbursements, fees for actual costs, tuition, sales tax revenues distributed using the ad valorem method pursuant to G.S. 105-472(b)(2), sales tax refunds, gifts and grants restricted as to use, trust funds, federal appropriations made directly to local school administrative units, and funds received for pre-kindergarten programs.[147]

A county may, however, donate surplus, obsolete, or unused personal property to a charter school.[148]

Municipal Funding

As detailed above, municipalities are authorized to directly fund operational and certain capital costs of charter schools.[149]

---

145. *See* Sugar Creek Charter Sch., Inc. v. State, 214 N.C. App. 1 (2011), *review denied*, 366 N.C. 227 (2012).

146. *See* G.S. 115C-218.105(c); 115C-426(b). Note that revenue derived from supplemental taxes will be transferred only to a charter school located in the tax district for which the taxes are levied and in which the student resides.

147. G.S. 115C-426(c). If a local school administrative unit budgets or accounts for any of these moneys in the local current expense fund, however, the moneys must be distributed to the charter schools. *See* Sugar Creek Charter Sch., Inc. v. Charlotte-Mecklenburg Bd. of Educ., 195 N.C. App. 348, *appeal dismissed and discretionary review denied*, 363 N.C. 663 (2009); *see also* Thomas Jefferson Classical Acad. v. Rutherford Cnty. Bd. of Educ., 215 N.C. App. 530 (2011), *review denied*, ___ N.C. ___, 724 S.E.2d 531 (N.C. 2012).

In 2009, the Department of Public Instruction (DPI) established a separate fund, Fund 8, to which local school units may deposit moneys designated for restricted purposes. According to DPI, the fund allows local school units to "separately maintain funds that are restricted in purpose and not intended for the general K-12 population" within the school unit. *Thomas Jefferson Classical Acad.*, 215 N.C. App. at 537 (detailing Dec. 16, 2009, memo from DPI establishing Fund 8). Examples listed include state funds for a targeted non–K-12 constituency, such as More-at-Four funds; trust funds for specific schools within a school unit; federal or other funds not intended for the general K-12 instructional population; and certain reimbursement funds. Moneys budgeted and accounted for in Fund 8 are not shared with charter schools.

148. G.S. 160A-280. A county should condition such a donation on the charter school agreeing to use the property for educational purposes. *See* Frayda Bluestein, "Donating Property: Beware of Constitutional Constraints," *Coates' Canons: NC Local Government Law* blog (April 13, 2015).

149. *See* notes 73–79 and accompanying text above.

Conclusion

The North Carolina Constitution guarantees each child in this state an opportunity for a sound basic education. Responsibility for setting educational policy and standards rests largely with the state legislature, state board of education, and local board of education. The state also funds the majority of the public school system's operating expenses. Counties have traditionally been responsible for funding school facilities. Over time, however, county boards of commissioners have assumed an increasing role in funding operational expenses for school units and, thereby, in influencing educational policy. And municipalities now have a role in school funding. Time will tell what impact this new funding scheme will have on the overall funding structure.

Financing and Public-Private Partnerships for Community Economic Development

by C. Tyler Mulligan

Community Economic Development (CED) refers to efforts to stimulate markets in low-income communities in order to attract private investment in job-creating businesses, downtown revitalization, affordable housing, and other public benefits.[1] These efforts occur at the intersection of the related fields of community development and economic development. Community development programs include improving the appearance of neglected neighborhoods or commercial areas, constructing housing that is affordable to low-income workers, and alleviating problems associated with unemployment and underemployment.[2] Economic development programs often

---

1. "The premise is that the markets in low-income communities do not work well; accordingly, the remedy is to stimulate them." Roger A. Clay Jr. and Susan R. Jones, eds., *Building Healthy Communities: A Guide to Community Economic Development for Advocates, Lawyers, and Policy-Makers* (Chicago: ABA Publishing, 2009), 11. *See also* William H. Simon, *The Community Economic Development Movement: Law, Business, and the New Social Policy* (Durham, N.C.: Duke University Press, 2001).

2. *See, e.g.*, 24 C.F.R. § 570.201 (basic eligible activities for Community Development Block Grants).

include place-based development activities, such as downtown revitalization and promotion of tourism, to complement their business recruitment, retention, and entrepreneurship efforts.[3] The hope is that improving the built environment and leveraging the natural attributes, cultural heritage, and distinctive character of a place will encourage investment and growth.[4] Some CED projects are *publicly* owned and can be financed through traditional public financing mechanisms discussed in earlier chapters of this book. The focus of this chapter, however, is local government authority to use financing tools to participate directly in *private* development in furtherance of CED goals, typically through creative public-private partnerships.

This chapter proceeds in three parts. The first part articulates the rationale for local government involvement in the revitalization or redevelopment of a community's built environment—a primary focus of CED efforts. The second part describes federal and state programs that support such CED efforts. Finally, the third part explains local government legal authority to participate in public-private partnerships in order to attract private investment for CED purposes.

Revitalization and Redevelopment of the Built Environment

The built environment of a community—the buildings (houses, retail stores, manufacturing facilities) and infrastructure (roads, water and sewer, telecommunications)—is essential to attracting private investment. When built assets are dilapidated, inadequate, or lacking altogether, the implications can be far-reaching. Water and sewer infrastructure is almost always a prerequisite for economic development and job creation.[5] Access to broadband contributes to economic development and is increasingly necessary to obtain education and health care, especially in rural areas.[6] A well-maintained historic downtown—even in a rural area—confers benefits on the wider community.[7] In addition, there is evidence of a link between the built envi-

---

3. Jonathan Q. Morgan, "Economic Development," in *Budgeting in North Carolina Local Governments*, 2nd ed., ed. Whitney Afonso (Chapel Hill, N.C.: UNC School of Government, 2021), 253–75. Jonathan Q. Morgan and C. Tyler Mulligan, "Economic Development," in *County and Municipal Government in North Carolina*, 2nd ed., ed. Frayda S. Bluestein (Chapel Hill, N.C.: UNC School of Government, 2014).

4. C. Tyler Mulligan, "Community Development and Affordable Housing," in *County and Municipal Government in North Carolina*, 2nd ed., ed. Frayda S. Bluestein (Chapel Hill, N.C.: UNC School of Government, 2014), 461–69.

5. Faqir S. Bagi, "Economic Impact of Water/Sewer Facilities on Rural and Urban Communities," *Rural America* 17 (Winter 2002): 44, 45–46.

6. Peter Stenberg and Sarah A. Low, "Rural Broadband at a Glance, 2009 Edition," *Economic Information Bulletin* No. 47 (Washington, D.C.: Economic Research Service, U.S. Department of Agriculture, Feb. 2009); Peter Stenberg, Mitch Morehart, Stephen Vogel, John Cromartie, Vince Breneman, and Dennis Brown, "Broadband Internet's Value for Rural America," *Economic Research Report* No. 78 (Washington, D.C.: Economic Research Service, U.S. Department of Agriculture, Aug. 2009). The importance of broadband for access to markets, education, and tele-health was punctuated during the COVID-19 pandemic. Elizabeth A. Dobis et al., "Rural America at a Glance: 2021 Edition," *Economic Information Bulletin* No. 230 (Washington, D.C.: Economic Research Service, U.S. Department of Agriculture, Nov. 2021). North Carolina's efforts are led by the Division of Broadband and Digital Equity in the North Carolina Department of Information Technology. *See About Us,* on the Division's webpage.

7. Dagney Faulk, "The Process and Practice of Downtown Revitalization," *Review of Policy Research* 23 (March 2006): 625, 629.

ronment in a community and public health outcomes because residents who live in a thriving "walkable" neighborhood or have convenient access to full-service grocers are more likely to engage in greater physical activity and consume a healthier diet.[8] Furthermore—and of great significance to local governments—the financial health of a community is often dependent on the amount of private investment in built assets because such assets make up the bulk of the tax base on which local governments rely to finance public priorities. For these reasons, among others, local governments typically seek to preserve and revitalize existing built assets.

Local governments rarely possess sufficient financial resources on their own to accomplish all of the development and revitalization that a community needs. Private capital is required, too. Local governments therefore must leverage their limited resources to attract private investment in order to achieve their development goals. In the best-case scenario, a local government can simply establish appropriate zoning and make investments in public infrastructure, and private investment will follow on its own without any further public involvement. However, in some circumstances, especially in distressed areas, more direct public involvement in private development may be required.

The legal authority for local governments to participate in a private development project is entirely dependent on the public purpose for the government's involvement. For example, in the case of industrial recruitment, local governments possess special authority to induce an industrial facility to locate in a community only when substantial jobs and tax base might be lost to other states.[9] To create affordable housing for low-income persons, a local government may provide financial assistance to a private developer so long as the assistance flows to eligible low-income households and otherwise meets statutory requirements.[10] For all other businesses and real estate development, subsidies are not permitted, but fair market value transactions are available and adequate to achieve public goals.[11]

This chapter goes into further detail on those examples and others, and it describes the limited situations in which local government participation is permitted by North Carolina law. Before describing local government authority in this area, it is first helpful to set the context by summarizing federal and state programs that may be available to fund such efforts.

---

8. The Prevention Institute has profiled eleven examples of predominantly low-income communities that have been transformed by changes in the built environment, particularly in terms of health outcomes. *See Manal J. Aboelata, The Built Environment and Health: 11 Profiles of Neighborhood Transformation* (Oakland, Cal.: Prevention Institute, July 2004).

9. Tyler Mulligan, "When May NC Local Governments Pay an Economic Development Incentive?," *Coates' Canons: NC Local Government Law* blog (Dec. 17, 2013).

10. Tyler Mulligan, "Local Government Support for Privately Owned Affordable Housing," *Coates' Canons: NC Local Government Law* blog (May 16, 2022).

11. See, for example, Tyler Mulligan, "Legal and Business Reasons Why Downtown Development Programs Should Involve Secured Loans—Not Grants," *Coates' Canons: NC Local Government Law* blog (Sept. 19, 2017).

Federal Programs

The federal government offers multiple programs to support state and local development efforts. This section describes federal grant and tax credit programs that are commonly used to finance CED projects.[12]

Community Development Block Grants

The Community Development Block Grant (CDBG) program is the largest and most flexible source of federal community development funds. Created in 1974 as an offshoot of several different existing community development programs, the CDBG program operates in furtherance of three objectives: (1) to benefit low- and moderate-income persons,[13] (2) to prevent or eliminate slums or blight, and (3) to meet urgent needs.[14] The amount of CDBG funds distributed annually to states and populous jurisdictions is determined by a formula that comprises several measures of community need, including population, housing overcrowding, age of housing, population growth lag in relationship to other metropolitan areas, and the extent of poverty.[15]

North Carolina communities have devoted CDBG funds to a wide range of activities, including the creation of affordable housing, improvements in public infrastructure, and the enhancement of community facilities and services. The program's funds may be used to support a wide range of activities, but Congress and the U.S. Department of Housing and Urban Development have mandated that, at a minimum, no less than 70 percent of all CDBG funds must be used for activities that directly benefit low- and moderate-income persons.[16] When CDBG funds are used to provide financing for a *private* development project, a local government must conduct underwriting to determine (1) that private contributions in equity and debt are appropriate, (2) that federal funds are necessary to make the project go forward, and (3) that the project, which was infeasible without the federal financing, will attain long-term feasibility and achieve the approved public purpose after the financing is provided.[17]

The CDBG program is divided into two parts, the Entitlement Program (for large municipalities and urban counties) and the Small Cities Program (for the remainder of the state's municipalities and counties). Communities that are eligible for Entitlement Program CDBG funds are generally municipalities that have fifty thousand or more residents and urban counties. These communities receive a direct block-grant allocation from the federal government each year. In North Carolina, twenty-four municipalities and four counties participate in the

---

12. The description of federal and state programs contained in this chapter draws heavily from similar descriptions contained in Mulligan, note 4 above, and Morgan and Mulligan, note 3 above.

13. Low- and moderate-income person means a member of a family having an income equal to or less than the Section 8 low-income limit established by the U.S. Department of Housing and Urban Development (HUD). "Definitions," 24 C.F.R. § 570.3.

14. "Criteria for national objectives," 24 C.F.R. § 570.208.

15. *See* HUD, *CPD APPROPRIATIONS BUDGET/ALLOCATIONS* (current as of May 16, 2023).

16. "General policies," 24 C.F.R. § 570.200(a)(3); "Overall benefit to low and moderate income persons," 24 C.F.R. § 570.484.

17. "Guidelines and Objectives for Evaluating Project Costs and Financial Requirements," 24 C.F.R. pt. 570, app. A (Community Development Block Grant underwriting guidelines to ensure public aid is necessary).

CDBG Entitlement Program.[18] Several cities and one county have been added to the ranks of these entitlement communities since 2010. Together, all North Carolina entitlement communities received a total of approximately $31 million in fiscal year 2023 (excluding separate special allocations for disaster recovery), and that total is up from more than $28 million in fiscal year 2010, due in part to the addition of several entitlement communities since that time.

The Small Cities Program provides North Carolina (and other states) with annual block grants, which the state in turn awards to local governments that are not part of the Entitlement Program. Each state develops its own method of distributing its received funds to eligible local governments. To maximize the impact of Small Cities Program funds, most states (including North Carolina) create programs with relatively large awards and then hold annual competitions for the available funds. States may reflect statewide priorities by earmarking funds for specific activities (e.g., housing rehabilitation or economic development). States also may keep a small percentage to cover administrative costs and to provide technical assistance to local governments and nonprofit organizations. North Carolina received approximately $46 million in CDBG funds for the Small Cities Program in fiscal year 2023, down from almost $49 million in fiscal year 2010. The North Carolina Department of Commerce administers the portion of the state's CDBG funds designated by the General Assembly for economic development and revitalization projects, and the Department of Environmental Quality administers the portion designated for water and wastewater infrastructure.

The HOME Investment Partnerships Program

HOME is a federal program designed to increase the supply of housing for low-income persons. HOME provides funds to states and local governments to implement local housing strategies, which may include tenant-based rental assistance, assistance to homebuyers, property acquisition, new construction, rehabilitation, site improvements, demolition, relocation, and administrative costs. After certain mandated set-asides, the balance of HOME funds is allocated by formula between qualified municipalities, urban counties, consortia (contiguous units of local government), and states. In North Carolina, the state portion is then reallocated to remaining jurisdictions by the North Carolina Housing Finance Agency (NCHFA). In fiscal year 2023, the federal government allocated approximately $23 million in HOME funds directly to qualified local jurisdictions (up from $20 million in fiscal year 2010). Approximately $19 million went to NCHFA for use statewide (down from $21 million in fiscal year 2010). The statewide funds are allocated based on each region's housing needs and are available through both competitive and noncompetitive funding programs.

Other Federal Grant Programs

The Economic Development Administration (EDA) provides funding for local governments to engage in economic development planning and to implement projects. EDA targets its funding to economically distressed communities and regions by making grants for public works

---

18. The entitlement counties are Cumberland, Mecklenburg, Union, and Wake; the entitlement cities are Asheville, Burlington, Cary, Chapel Hill, Charlotte, Concord, Durham, Fayetteville, Gastonia, Goldsboro, Greensboro, Greenville, Hickory, High Point, Jacksonville, Kannapolis, Lenoir, Morganton, New Bern, Raleigh, Rocky Mount, Salisbury, Wilmington, and Winston-Salem.

(infrastructure), technical assistance, economic and trade adjustment assistance, and planning.[19] Other federal agencies administer and fund various types of loan guarantees for private lenders, support revolving loan programs, and provide funding for community facilities. These agencies include the Small Business Administration, the U.S. Department of Agriculture, and the U.S. Treasury Department.

Federal Tax Credit Programs

Three federal tax credit programs are designed to induce private investment for CED purposes: the New Markets Tax Credit, the Low-Income Housing Tax Credit, and the Historic Rehabilitation Tax Credit. The New Markets Tax Credit (NMTC) was enacted as part of the federal Community Renewal Tax Relief Act of 2000. Designed to stimulate billions of dollars of new investment in distressed areas, the NMTC allows taxpayers to receive a credit against their federal income taxes for investing in commercial and economic activities in low-income communities. The Low-Income Housing Tax Credit provides tax credits to private investors who develop housing with set-asides for persons earning 60 percent or less of the area median income.[20] The Historic Tax Credit provides tax credits to those who invest in the rehabilitation of historic structures. North Carolina has intermittently offered complementary state tax credits for investments in historic rehabilitation projects and affordable housing, and when combined with federal tax credits, eligible projects are even more attractive to private investors.

Most real estate developers cannot use all of those tax credits themselves, so they sell investment interests in their projects (through a tax credit intermediary or "syndicator") to persons or companies with large tax liabilities. When those entities with large tax liabilities invest in a project in order to receive tax credits—in other words, when they buy tax credits—the investment provides an infusion of capital (or equity) into the project. The amount of equity a project can receive for selling its tax credits may depend on the demand for such tax credits. When tax credits are valuable, a developer can attract more equity for a project, making the project more financially feasible. When tax credits are less valuable, which typically occurs when federal tax rates go down and therefore companies have less tax liability, developers cannot obtain as much equity for a project, thereby making it more difficult to finance a project with tax credits.

Local governments do not typically get involved with tax credit syndication, but the types of projects that take advantage of federal or state tax credits are often those that local governments wish to support. Thus, local governments must understand how tax credits work in order to evaluate the necessity of their participation in a private project that is utilizing tax credits.[21] In

---

19. Hillary Sherman, "U.S. EDA Resources Help Communities Build the Local Ecosystem for Sustainable Economic Development," *Community and Economic Development in North Carolina and Beyond* blog (Feb. 2, 2016).

20. Federal Low-Income Housing Tax Credits (LIHTC) are awarded to affordable-housing developers in North Carolina through a competitive process administered by NCHFA. Each year, NCHFA promulgates the Qualified Allocation Plan, which explains how projects will be selected to receive an award of tax credits. A 2018 change in federal law allows for "income averaging" within LIHTC properties; that is, properties may accept residents with higher average median incomes as long as the overall average of tenants in the project does not exceed 60 percent of the area median income.

21. A determination of necessity for public aid to private enterprise is legally significant. *See* C. Tyler Mulligan, "Economic Development Incentives Must Be 'Necessary': A Framework for Evaluating the Constitutionality of Public Aid for Private Development Projects," 11 *Harvard Law & Policy Review* (2017): S13.

addition, due to the fact that tax credits help make private development projects possible, local governments are usually active partners in seeking to have projects and qualified areas of their communities designated for special tax treatment.[22]

State Programs

The state's community economic development programs are centered in the Department of Commerce. Statewide economic development efforts are coordinated through the Department of Commerce and its associated nonprofit arm, the Economic Development Partnership of North Carolina.[23] These entities are often the initial points of contact for prospective businesses seeking financial incentives to locate or expand a facility in the state. The Department of Commerce also administers grants and loans for CED projects in rural or distressed communities through its Rural Economic Development Division.[24]

Approval for Industrial Revenue Bonds

Industrial Revenue Bonds (IRBs) are a potential source of financing that businesses can use for land, building, and equipment purchases as well as for facility construction. The interest paid to bondholders is exempt from federal and state income taxes, making it possible for businesses to access debt at below-market rates for the construction of industrial facilities. Only manufacturing companies are eligible to receive IRB funds, and the maximum issuance for a single company in a jurisdiction is related to job creation. IRB issues must be backed by a letter of credit from a bank, so most IRB transactions are completed in partnership with a bank that issues the letter of credit and places the bonds. Counties are authorized to create financing authorities[25] to issue the bonds after approval has been obtained from the county, the secretary of the Department of Commerce, and the Local Government Commission.[26] Although government approvals are part of the process, no government guarantees the bonds. The bonds are secured only by the credit of the company.

Discretionary Incentive Grants for Competitive Industrial Projects

At the state level, the two primary discretionary grant programs are the Job Development Investment Grant (JDIG) and the One North Carolina Fund. The JDIG program provides discretionary grants directly to new and expanding companies to induce them to increase employment in North Carolina rather than in another state. The grant amount is based on some

---

See also Mulligan, note 11 above; Andrew Trump, "How a Local Government Loan Can Make a Revitalization Project Possible," *Community and Economic Development in North Carolina and Beyond* blog (Sept. 4, 2015).

22. An example of government-designated areas receiving special tax treatment is the federal Opportunity Zones program. *See* Tyler Mulligan, "Federal Opportunity Zones: What Local Governments Need to Know," *Community and Economic Development in North Carolina and Beyond* blog (Sept. 21, 2018).

23. Chapter 143B, Section 431.01 of the North Carolina General Statutes (hereinafter G.S.).

24. G.S. 143B-472.126.

25. G.S. 159C-4.

26. G.S. 159C-7 and -8.

percentage of withholding taxes paid for each eligible position created over a period of time, with higher amounts awarded for higher levels of capital investment and job creation.[27] The terms of the grant are specified in an agreement that requires a recipient company to comply with certain standards regarding employee health insurance, workplace safety, and wages paid. The grant agreement must include a clawback provision to recapture funds in the event that the company relocates or ceases operations before a specified period of time.

The One North Carolina Fund awards grants to local governments to secure commitments from private companies to locate or expand within the local government's jurisdiction. The grants must be used to install or purchase new equipment; make structural repairs, improvements, or renovations of existing buildings in order to expand operations; construct or improve existing water, sewer, gas, or electric utility distribution lines; or equip buildings.[28] Applications for the grants are submitted according to guidelines promulgated by the state Department of Commerce, with grants being awarded on the basis of the strategic importance of the industry, the quality of jobs to be created, and the quality of the particular project. The local government must provide matching funds for any award made by the state.

Tax Credits, Benefits, and Exemptions by County Tier

The state's tax system has long been used to encourage development, and several different types of tax credits are available to companies meeting specified criteria. As noted earlier, the state has its own historic rehabilitation tax credits that are designed to complement the parallel federal tax credits.[29] The state has, at various times, also enacted other tax credits and various exemptions for companies that create jobs and invest in facilities and equipment in the state.[30] Benefits and credit amounts under state programs are often based on the relative distress of the county in which the project is located, as signified by a county tier designation assigned by the Department of Commerce. For example, the tier designation system employed in 2023 assigned the forty most-distressed counties to tier one, the next forty as tier two, and the twenty least-distressed counties as tier three.[31] The most generous benefits and tax credits are reserved for projects located in tier one counties, with lower benefit amounts offered in higher tiers.[32]

Industrial Development Fund Utility Account for Infrastructure

The Industrial Development Fund Utility Account (Utility Account) provides funds to local governments in the most economically distressed counties for infrastructure projects that are reasonably anticipated to result in job creation.[33] Utility Account funds may not be used for any retail, entertainment, or sports projects. Eligible public infrastructure projects include construction or improvement of water, sewer, gas, telecommunications, high-speed broadband, electrical utility facilities, or transportation infrastructure.

---

27. G.S. 143B-437.52.
28. G.S. 143B-437.71.
29. Articles 3H and 3L of G.S. Chapter 105.
30. See, for example, Article 3J of G.S. Chapter 105, which sunset in 2014. G.S. 105-129.82.
31. G.S. 143B-437.08.
32. See, for example, G.S. 105-129.71(a)(1)–(2) and 105-129.105(a)(1)–(2).
33. G.S. 143B-437.01.

Limited Local Government Authority to Participate in Private Development

Local governments have broad authority to engage in CED-related activities. Most of these activities involve traditional public functions. These include such economic development activities as employing agents to meet and negotiate with and assist companies interested in locating or expanding within the community, developing strategic plans for economic development, administering unsubsidized revolving loan funds, and advertising the community in industrial-development publications and elsewhere. They also include such community development endeavors as forming redevelopment commissions to purchase and improve blighted properties, offering homebuyer counseling to first-time homebuyers, developing community development plans, applying for government and charitable grants, and managing community facilities.

In addition, counties and municipalities may construct public facilities for CED purposes, such as by extending utility lines, expanding water supply and treatment facilities and sewage treatment facilities, building publicly owned affordable housing, and constructing road improvements. Publicly owned improvements can be financed by local governments through traditional public financing mechanisms discussed in earlier chapters of this book.

However, North Carolina local governments are often asked to participate directly in *private* development in furtherance of CED goals. This section describes the limited circumstances under North Carolina law when such participation is permitted.

As a threshold matter, local governments are not permitted to provide "exclusive emoluments"—in other words, gifts of public property—to private entities (Section 32 of Article I of the North Carolina Constitution).[34] This same constitutional rule, sometimes called a gift clause, appears in state constitutions across the nation.[35] Exclusive emoluments are permitted only "in consideration of public services." That is, the public must get something in return—known as "consideration" in contract law—for a payment to a private entity. North Carolina local governments are not even permitted to make donations to charitable not-for-profit entities.[36] Every government payment or transfer of property to a private enterprise must be made in exchange for adequate consideration.[37] For example, a grant may be paid to a nonprofit in

---

34. The exclusive emoluments clause of the North Carolina Constitution, which prohibits government gifts to private entities, is consistent with gift clauses found in most state constitutions across the nation. *See* Mulligan, *Economic Development Incentives Must Be "Necessary,"* note 21 above.

35. David E. Pinsky, "State Constitutional Limitations on Public Industrial Financing: An Historical and Economic Approach," 111 *University of Pennsylvania Law Review* (1963): 265, 280 ("At the turn of the century, some form of public aid limitation had been incorporated in the constitutions of a large majority of the states."). Most states have similar constitutional rules. In a recent example of gift clause enforcement, the Arizona Supreme Court, en banc in 2010, held that benefits provided to the developer of a mixed-use development were an unconstitutional gift because tax revenues alone were not valid consideration under that state's gift clause. Turken v. Gordon, 224 P.3d 158 (Ariz. 2010).

36. Frayda Bluestein, "Donating Property: Beware of Constitutional Constraints," *Coates' Canons: NC Local Government Law* blog (April 13, 2015).

37. Osborne M. Reynolds, Jr., *Local Government Law*, 4th ed. (St. Paul, Minn.: West Academic Publishing, 2015), 515 ("*Gifts* of property by local governments—at least to private individuals—are generally banned by statute or as a matter of common law; any transfer of municipal property must be supported by some reasonable compensation or benefit in return."); John Martinez, 3 Local Government Law, 2nd ed. (Eagan, Minn.: Thomson Reuters, 2017), § 21:7, at 21–25 ("Local government property cannot be conveyed

exchange for the nonprofit's promise to provide services of equivalent value managing the government's homeless shelter.

A separate set of constitutional provisions requires that expenditures by local governments and contractual payments to private entities must serve a public purpose (Section 2 of Article V of the North Carolina Constitution). As long as a payment or expenditure serves a valid public purpose, it satisfies not only the constitutional provisions regarding public purpose, but the exclusive emoluments provision as well. The courts alone—not the legislature, not statutes—decide what is a valid public purpose under the constitution.

Together, these constitutional rules indicate that direct government participation in private development is disfavored under North Carolina law, and therefore caution is required when local governments seek to partner with private entities. North Carolina courts have stated in multiple decisions that "direct state aid to a private enterprise, with only limited benefit accruing to the public, contravenes fundamental constitutional precepts."[38] In addition, government is not permitted to engage in private business.[39] These rules should be axiomatic to local government officials. If it were permissible for governments to engage in business or make grants or donations to private enterprise without requiring services in return, then legal requirements discussed in earlier chapters of this publication would become irrelevant. Laws governing property conveyance at fair market value could be worked around. Grants could be used to undermine uniformity of taxation because classes of grant recipients could receive the equivalent of tax refunds. Utility law requirements about treating similarly situated customers the same could easily be avoided. Procurement rules and the outcomes of bidding processes could be nudged up or down by offering grants to preferred vendors. State law, rooted in long-standing constitutional principles, contains a carefully constructed web of requirements and prohibitions designed to prevent direct government aid to private enterprises.[40]

An additional constitutional requirement is that North Carolina local governments are authorized to make expenditures only as specifically permitted by statute.[41] Statutes do not supersede the constitutional rules regarding exclusive emoluments and public purpose described above. All statutes must be interpreted to be consistent with the state constitution.[42] Indeed,

---

to a private party without adequate consideration, for to do so would constitute an improper gift of public property or the granting of a subsidy contrary to state constitutional constraints."). See, for example, Schires v. Carlat, 480 P.3d 639, 646 (Ariz. 2021) (holding that incentive payment violated state's gift clause because consideration was not proportional to fair market value of consideration received and fiscal impact from tax revenue calculated by expert was irrelevant).

38. Maready v. City of Winston-Salem, 342 N.C. 708, 718 (1996).

39. *See* Mitchell v. N.C. Indus. Dev. Fin. Auth., 273 N.C. 137, 156 (1968) (stating that "it is not the function of government to engage in private business"); Nash v. Town of Tarboro, 227 N.C. 283 (1947) (holding that it is not a public purpose for a town to own and operate a hotel).

40. Even when private enterprises are offered financial assistance for disaster recovery to help them handle uncompensated losses, careful attention must be paid to legal requirements. Tyler Mulligan, "American Rescue Plan Act: Aid for Small Businesses and Nonprofits with ARP/CLFRF," *Coates' Canons: NC Local Government Law* blog (Oct. 4, 2021).

41. N.C. Const. art. VII, § 1 ("The General Assembly . . . may give such powers and duties to counties, cities, and towns, and other governmental subdivisions as it may deem advisable.").

42. Comm'r of Ins. v. N.C. Fire Ins. Rating Bureau, 291 N.C. 55, 70 (1976) (citation, internal quotation marks omitted) ("When reasonably possible, a statute . . . should be construed so as to avoid serious doubt as to its constitutionality."); *In re* Arcadia Dairy Farms, Inc., 289 N.C. 456, 465 (1976) ("The cardinal principle of statutory construction is to save and not to destroy. We have repeatedly held that as between two

statutes may contain broad language with the presumption that constitutional rules control.[43] In the context of CED projects, there are several different statutes that permit a local government to participate in development in pursuit of CED goals.

The specific powers available to a local government are different depending on the purpose being pursued, whether affordable housing, historic preservation, industrial recruitment, blight remediation, or others. Each defined purpose has its own statutes and corresponding set of authorized activities. Thus, the discussion below describes the legal authority for a local government to participate in a private development project, with each allowable purpose treated separately.

First Pursue Partnership Options That Involve No Subsidy to Private Entities

As explained above, the exclusive emoluments clause of the North Carolina Constitution prohibits local governments from making gifts to private entities. There are many options for participating in a private CED project—options that improve project feasibility—without providing a subsidy (or gift) to the project. Fair market value transactions involve no subsidy, but when properly structured, they can improve the financial feasibility of a private development project. If a non-subsidy approach makes a project financially feasible, then a subsidy cannot be necessary—and any unnecessary subsidy amounts to an unconstitutional gift. Creativity is permitted so long as the local government follows procedural requirements and utilizes fair market value transactions. Some effective and legally permissible approaches include the following:

- **Educate the project developer about lawful property tax exemptions enacted by the General Assembly and made available statewide.** For example, a development project that is on a contaminated site and is made subject to a brownfield agreement with the State of North Carolina is entitled to the brownfield tax exclusion of 90 percent in the first year, decreasing to 75 percent, 50 percent, 30 percent, and 10 percent, respectively, in years two through five.[44] A property designated as a historic landmark and maintained as such is entitled to a 50 percent exclusion in perpetuity.[45] Special appraisal procedures are available to certain types of affordable housing.[46] Local governments are

---

possible interpretations of a statute, by one of which it would be unconstitutional and by the other valid, our plain duty is to adopt that which will save the act. Even to avoid a serious doubt the rule is the same.").

43. For example, the broad language of the Local Development Act of 1925, codified at G.S. Chapter 158, was enacted more than seventy years prior to the seminal economic development case, *Maready v. City of Winston-Salem*, cited in full at note 38 above. In the decades prior to *Maready*, there was no suggestion that the permissive language of G.S. 158-7.1(a) could be used to provide aid to private entities. Horner v. Chamber of Com. of City of Burlington, 235 N.C. 77, 81 (1952) (requiring the return of funds to a municipal treasury that had been appropriated to a Chamber of Commerce ostensibly for "publicity" about the municipality, pursuant to G.S. 158-7.1's predecessor statute, G.S. 158-1, because the expenditures were controlled by the chamber rather than the city). Later, the courts would strike down *loans* to businesses despite clear statutory authority. Mitchell v. N.C. Indus. Dev. Fin. Auth., cited in full at note 39 above (industrial development bonds not a public purpose), and Stanley v. Dep't of Conservation & Dev., 284 N.C. 15 (1973) (financing for pollution control not a public purpose).

44. G.S. 105-277.13.

45. G.S. 105-278.

46. Tyler Mulligan, "Taxation of Affordable Housing in Community Land Trusts," *Community and Economic Development in North Carolina and Beyond* blog (Dec. 23, 2009).

not permitted to invent their own tax exemption or abatement programs, but they can educate private businesses about the myriad lawful exemptions that are available.[47]

- **Construct** *publicly owned* **infrastructure to support private development.** Examples include lighting, public parking, and street improvements. Public parking spaces can be leased to private businesses at fair market value, subject to some limitations.
- **Enter into a public-private partnership (P3)[48] or reimbursement agreement[49] with a developer.** A P3 or reimbursement agreement involves a developer constructing *public* facilities and, following construction, a local government buying the public facilities from the developer for a reasonable price.
- **Offer loans with appropriate market-rate terms based on the risk profile of the loan** (loan forgiveness and below-market interest rates are typically impermissible gifts).[50]

Professionals with experience financing real estate development know that a loan, properly structured, will almost always make a project financially feasible. However, if a loan is not adequate, then a local government should demand a share of ownership for any equity it invests in a private project. Investing equity into a private project should be handled with care due to the prohibition against governments engaging in private business.[51] One example of an equity investment is paying the owner of a historic building a fair price for a preservation easement on the building façade.[52] An easement obtains ownership and secures important public rights such as the right to enter the property to make repairs and to charge the owner for a portion of the costs. By securing such rights for the public, the local government may possibly avoid the claim that it has made an unconstitutional gift to a private entity.

In the vast majority of development projects—even difficult projects in distressed areas— the above options are sufficient to make a project feasible. Development finance experts with a deep understanding of real estate development and finance can assist local governments with evaluating options that avoid unconstitutional subsidy.[53]

---

47. For a full list of CED-related property tax exemptions, see Chris McLaughlin, "Property Tax Exemptions and Community Economic Development," *Community and Economic Development in North Carolina and Beyond* blog (Nov. 10, 2014).

48. G.S. 143-128.1C; 160D-1315.

49. G.S. 160A-499; 153A-451. *See also* Adam Lovelady, "Reimbursement Agreements," *Coates' Canons: NC Local Government Law* blog (Jan. 19, 2016).

50. *See* Mulligan, *Legal and Business Reasons Why Downtown Development Programs Should Involve Secured Loans,* note 11 above.

51. For a discussion of equity investments by local governments, see David M. Lawrence, *Economic Development Law for North Carolina Local Governments* (Chapel Hill, N.C.: UNC School of Government, 2000), 50–51.

52. G.S. 160D-942. *See also* Tyler Mulligan, "Downtown Facade Improvement Programs," *Coates' Canons: NC Local Government Law.* blog (Jan. 16, 2020).

53. The Development Finance Initiative (DFI) at the School of Government was created for the purpose of serving local governments with public-private partnerships to accomplish public CED goals. See DFI's webpage on the School of Government's website at https://dfi.sog.unc.edu/.

Form of Subsidy: Permissible Cash Payments and Impermissible Tax Abatements

There are limited situations in which it is necessary for a local government to provide a direct subsidy to a project. The most common examples are (1) business location competitions in which significant jobs and capital investment "might otherwise be lost to other states"[54] if no incentive is awarded and (2) privately owned affordable housing for low-income persons in which deep subsidization is necessary to make the housing development feasible.[55] In these cases, provided statutory procedures are followed, case law indicates that it is permissible to provide the required subsidy.

In other states, such subsidies from local governments can come in the form of special property tax breaks or tax abatements. The tax abatements do not violate those states' constitutional gift clauses because they are available statewide and involve a reduction in taxes owed, not an expenditure of public funds.[56]

In North Carolina, local governments have almost no authority to offer such tax abatements. Under Article V, Section 2, of the state constitution, property tax exemptions and classifications may be made only by the General Assembly and then only on a statewide basis. In other words, a local government may not constitutionally offer a special tax classification to a property owner unless that classification is available statewide. Examples of such statewide property classifications were provided above.[57]

However, in the case of high-stakes interstate business recruitment, a number of municipalities and counties have developed a cash-grant incentive policy that very much resembles tax abatements. These policies follow a common pattern: a local government offers to make annual cash grants over a number of years (typically five) to businesses that make investments of certain minimum amounts in the county or municipality. The investment might be either a new industrial facility or the expansion of an existing facility. The grant payment reimburses a business for qualifying investments, but the amount of the cash grant is explicitly tied to the amount of property taxes paid by the business. For example, a company that made an investment of at least $5 million might be eligible for a cash grant in an amount up to 50 percent of the property taxes it paid on the resulting facility; larger investments would make the company eligible for a grant that represented a larger percentage of the property taxes paid.

These policies closely approach tax abatements but with two important differences: the company receiving the cash incentives pays its property taxes first, and the grant payment is contingent not solely on payment of property taxes, but also on performance of some public purpose or benefit approved in case law, namely, locating substantial jobs and tax base in North Carolina that "might otherwise be lost to other states."[58] One note of caution: no court has directly addressed whether this tax-calculated grant is an unconstitutional attempt to enact

---

54. *Maready v. City of Winston-Salem*, cited in full at note 38 above, at 727.

55. For further discussion of affordable housing, see Tyler Mulligan, "Local Government Support for Privately Owned Affordable Housing," *Coates' Canons: NC Local Government Law* blog (May 16, 2022).

56. Reynolds, note 37 above, at 129 ("Although taxes may not be levied for private (as opposed to public) benefit, *exemptions* from property taxes may validly be authorized by state law except as such exemptions are prohibited by state constitutions.").

57. See notes 42–45 and accompanying text above.

58. *Maready v. City of Winston-Salem*, cited in full at note 38 above, at 727.

a tax abatement or whether it is indeed a constitutionally permitted cash grant.[59] With that background established, the following sections describe the various statutes that permit a local government to participate in private development in pursuit of CED goals.

Economic Development

In the economic development context, statutory authority for offering incentive payments to companies is found within the remarkably broad language of Chapter 158, Section 7.1 of the North Carolina General Statutes (hereinafter G.S.), a provision in the Local Development Act of 1925.[60] Local governments are authorized to undertake economic development activities and to fund those activities by the levy of property taxes.[61] When a North Carolina local government turns funds over to a private entity for expenditure (such as through an incentive payment), the local government must give prior approval to how the funds will be expended by the private entity, and "all such expenditures shall be accounted for" at the end of the fiscal year.[62] Furthermore, the funds must be made subject to recapture in an incentive agreement in which the private entity promises to create a certain number of jobs, exceed some minimum level of capital investment, and maintain operations throughout a defined compliance period.[63] Additional procedural requirements are imposed when the expenditure involves the purchase or improvement of property, which is almost always the case for an economic development incentive that requires improvements to real property (the only way to increase the tax base).[64]

The restrictions imposed by statute, however, are not the final word. Economic development incentives involve payments of *public* funds to *private* entities in service of a mix of public and private purposes, thereby colliding with the constitutional provisions described above regarding exclusive emoluments and public purpose. This makes economic development different from other *purely public* activities of local governments and results in far more constitutional scrutiny from the courts. For this reason, it is necessary to look closely at case law to determine the extent of a local government's authority to offer economic-development incentives.

For most of the past century, North Carolina local governments were not permitted to make incentive payments to private entities. Even loans to private enterprises were prohibited.[65]

---

59. *See* Blinson v. State, 186 N.C. App. 328, 335 (2007) (dismissing the plaintiff's claim for lack of standing on the constitutional issue of uniformity of taxation).

60. G.S. Chapter 158, Article 1.

61. G.S. 158-7.1(a); 153A-149(c)(10b) (counties); 160A-209(c)(10b) (municipalities).

62. G.S. 158-7.2. *See also* Kara Millonzi, "Local Government Appropriations/Grants to Private Entities," *Coates' Canons: NC Local Government Law.* blog (June 17, 2010; updated Aug. 2013).

63. G.S. 158-7.1(h). All three recapture provisions are required. *See* C. Tyler Mulligan, "Economic Development Incentives and North Carolina Local Governments: A Framework for Analysis," 91 *North Carolina Law Review* (2013): 2021, 2040–44.

64. In *Maready v. City of Winston-Salem*, cited in full at note 38 above, at 724, the North Carolina Supreme Court approvingly noted the strict procedural requirements imposed by G.S. Chapter 158 and essentially assumed that cash payments to companies for the purchase or improvement of property were subject to the same procedural requirements as if the local government engaged in those activities directly. Mulligan, note 63 above, at 2062–67; Mulligan, note 10 above; Tyler Mulligan, "Notice and Hearing Requirements for Economic Development Appropriations," *Coates' Canons: NC Local Government Law* blog (Nov. 21, 2019).

65. *See* Mitchell v. N.C. Indus. Dev. Fin. Auth., cited in full at note 39 above, and Stanley v. Dep't of Conservation & Dev., cited in full at note 43 above.

It wasn't until 1996, following the loss of economic development projects to other states, that the North Carolina Supreme Court finally decided in the seminal case *Maready v. City of Winston-Salem*[66] that economic development incentives serve a constitutionally permitted public purpose—*under certain conditions*. Those conditions were reinforced in subsequent cases decided by the North Carolina Court of Appeals and therefore merit closer examination.[67]

In *Maready* and progeny, courts examined dozens of economic-development incentives provided by local governments to private companies pursuant to G.S. 158-7.1. In *Maready*, the court opined that economic-development incentives authorized by G.S. 158-7.1 are constitutional "so long as they primarily benefit the public and not a private party."[68] The requisite "net public benefit," according to the court, is accomplished by providing jobs, increasing the tax base, and diversifying the economy. A driving force behind the *Maready* decision was the sense that, without incentives, job-creating facilities would be "lost to other states."[69] The court openly fretted about "the actions of other states" and "inducements . . . offered . . . in other jurisdictions."[70] There was, therefore, an underlying assumption that all of the incentives in *Maready* involved interstate competition.[71]

In subsequent cases before the North Carolina Court of Appeals, the court has refused to strike down incentives that are "parallel" to those approved in *Maready*.[72] The determination of whether an incentive is "parallel" to *Maready* cannot be reduced to a simple formula, but in general, there are two basic components that should be examined.

First, the consideration (or value) that the local government receives in exchange for an incentive must result in a net public benefit, primarily from job creation and capital investment, that "might otherwise be lost to other states."[73] Every incentive approved by *Maready* involved both substantial job creation and new tax revenue that paid back the incentives within three to seven years.

Second, the *Maready* court described the typical procedures employed by a local government in approving the incentives before the court. Local governments aiming to make their incentive approval process "parallel" to *Maready* should adhere to the following procedures:

- An initial "but for" or necessity determination is made, typically in a competitive situation, that the incentive is required in order for a project to go forward in the community.
- A written guideline or policy is applied to determine the maximum amount of incentive that can be given to the receiving company.
- Expenditures take the form of reimbursements, not unrestricted cash payments.
- Final approval is made at a public meeting, properly noticed.
- A written agreement governs implementation.

---

66. 342 N.C. 708 (1996).
67. Haugh v. Cnty. of Durham, 208 N.C. App. 304 (2010); Blinson v. State, 186 N.C. App. 328 (2007).
68. *Maready*, 342 N.C. at 724.
69. *Maready*, 342 N.C. at 726.
70. *Maready*, 342 N.C. at 725, 727.
71. *Haugh*, 208 N.C. App. at 317.
72. *Haugh*, 208 N.C. App. at 319.
73. For more discussion of these forms of consideration and others, see Mulligan, note 63 above.

These criteria are not difficult to achieve in the typical economic development incentive scenario, that is, one in which a local government is engaged in competition with other jurisdictions to win a sizable facility with a significant number of permanent jobs. However, not all CED projects provide the requisite job creation and meet the other criteria listed above. That should not be surprising; "CED is *broader than economic development* because it includes community building and the improvement of community life beyond the purely economic."[74] When a project does not involve competing for job creation and capital investment, it may nonetheless be possible to participate in a development project, provided the participation does not entail a gift to private enterprise. The next section examines statutory authority for participating in private CED activities apart from economic development.

Community Development and Revitalization

Local governments have considerable statutory authority to engage in community development activities for the benefit of low-income persons and in revitalization activities to reduce or eliminate blight. Because the pertinent statutes were enacted at different times and in response to different programmatic needs, a local government's authority to undertake community development and revitalization activities is not neatly laid out in one place.

The General Assembly passed the Housing Authorities Law in 1935 to enable communities to take advantage of federal grants for public housing. This law, as amended, appears as Article 1 of G.S. Chapter 157. In 1951, responding to the broader purposes of blight eradication in the federal Housing Act of 1949, the General Assembly passed the Urban Redevelopment Law, which, as amended, appears as G.S. Chapter 160A, Article 22. Finally, in response to the Housing and Community Development Act of 1974, the General Assembly enacted G.S. 160D-1311 and -1312[75] to enable local governments to engage in Community Development Block Grant (CDBG) activities authorized by the federal act. These statutes, among others, authorize all counties and municipalities to assist persons of low and moderate incomes using either federal and state grants or local funds. Additional detail on the relevant statutes is provided below.

Urban Redevelopment

Lower-income communities, in particular, are often characterized by distressed or blighted built environments, so revitalization and redevelopment of those areas is a natural focus of CED efforts. North Carolina's Urban Redevelopment Law[76] grants authority to both municipalities and counties[77] to engage in programs of blight eradication and redevelopment through the acquisition, clearance, rehabilitation, or rebuilding of areas for residential, commercial, or other purposes. Local governments are authorized to levy taxes and issue and sell bonds for this purpose.[78]

---

74. Clay and Jones, note 1 above, at 3.

75. Formerly G.S. 153A-376 and -377 (counties) and 160A-456 and -457 (municipalities).

76. Article 22 of G.S. Chapter 160A (Urban Redevelopment Law). *See also* Tyler Mulligan, "Using a Redevelopment Area to Attract Private Investment," *Community and Economic Development in North Carolina and Beyond* blog (Nov. 20, 2012).

77. G.S. 160A-503(9) (defining "municipality" to include counties for purposes of Urban Redevelopment Law).

78. G.S. 160A-520.

A redevelopment commission must be formed to exercise the powers granted by the Urban Redevelopment Law.[79] The governing board of a local government may serve in this role.[80] Once a commission is formed, its first order of business is to create a redevelopment plan.[81] The redevelopment plan must be approved by the local governing board. Until the redevelopment plan is approved, the commission cannot exercise most of its important development powers.[82]

Once a redevelopment plan has been approved, the redevelopment commission may exercise extensive powers within its area of operation to undertake redevelopment projects directly and to enter into public-private partnerships, "including the making of loans," for the rehabilitation or construction of residential and commercial buildings in the designated area.[83] A unique and useful procedure for property conveyance is also authorized, as discussed in the section titled "Contributing Real Property in a Public-Private Partnership," below.

The exercise of statutory powers within a formally designated redevelopment area by a redevelopment commission has been upheld by the North Carolina Supreme Court as serving a public purpose.[84] This does not mean that government funds or property may be gifted to private enterprise. To the contrary, even the sale of property to charitable nonprofit entities requires payment of full consideration. The statute authorizes sale of property to a charitable entity, but the sale price must be no less than the "fair value of the property agreed upon by a committee of three professional real estate appraisers."[85]

Community Development and Affordable Housing

CED efforts typically focus on low-income communities in which markets are perceived to work poorly or inefficiently. In the American Community Survey, hundreds of thousands of households in North Carolina were reported to suffer from some kind of housing problem, whether physical inadequacy, overcrowding, or cost burden.[86] This suggests that private enterprise is unable to respond to consumer demand for safe, decent, and affordable housing. The General Assembly therefore attempted to address these problems by granting housing-development powers to cities and counties.

Local governments possess broad powers to rehabilitate or construct publicly owned affordable housing, including the use of eminent domain to take property in furtherance of that purpose.[87] These powers are derived primarily from North Carolina's sweeping Housing

---

79. G.S. 160A-504 through -507.1.

80. G.S. 160D-1311(b).

81. G.S. 160A-513.

82. G.S. 160A-513(j).

83. G.S. 160A-512; 160A-503(19).

84. Redevelopment Comm'n of Greensboro v. Sec. Nat'l Bank, 252 N.C. 595 (1960).

85. G.S. 160A-514(e)(4).

86. Data on the extent of affordable-housing problems in North Carolina as reported in the American Community Survey can be reviewed through the CHAS (Comprehensive Housing Affordability Strategy) data query tool developed by the U.S. Department of Housing and Urban Development's Office of Policy Development and Research, available at https://www.huduser.gov/portal/datasets/cp.html. The North Carolina Housing Finance Agency (NCHFA) also makes housing data available online. *See* NCHFA, *NC Housing Snapshot* (interactive map with current data), https://www.nchfa.com/about-us/policy-research/nc-housing-snapshot.

87. *In re* Hous. Auth. of City of Charlotte, 233 N.C. 649 (1951) (holding that eminent domain may be exercised for the purpose of constructing "low-rent dwellings" despite the fact that the area to be condemned may not be a "slum area").

Authorities Law.[88] Regardless of whether or not a formal housing authority has been established by a local government, its governing board may exercise the powers of a housing authority directly.[89]

In addition to constructing publicly owned housing, the Housing Authorities Law empowers a housing authority (or local government exercising the powers of a housing authority) to enter into public-private partnerships by offering grants, loans, and other programs of financial assistance to public or private developers of housing for persons of low and moderate incomes, so long as any government subsidy flows to the eligible low- and moderate-income households.[90] When financial assistance is provided to a multi-family rental housing project, at least 20 percent of the units must be set aside for low-income persons (defined as those earning no more than 60 percent of the area median income) for at least fifteen years.[91] Several local governments in North Carolina have offered financial assistance to private developers in exchange for promises to produce affordable housing as part of larger market-rate residential developments, sometimes in conjunction with land use regulations known as inclusionary zoning or inclusionary housing programs.[92]

Community development efforts are not limited to housing. Local governments are authorized to offer grants or loans for rehabilitation of private buildings as part of "community development programs and activities,"[93] which refer to programs for the benefit of low- and moderate-income persons pursuant to the federal CDBG program (described above in the "Federal Programs" section).[94] Although the statutory authority was enacted to enable local governments to participate in the CDBG program, the statute is written broadly enough that a local government can use the authority provided in the statute to undertake community-development activities outside of the CDBG program that would otherwise meet CDBG requirements.

---

88. G.S. Chapter 157, Article 1. The Housing Authorities Law was enacted in 1935 to enable the creation of "dwelling accommodations for persons of low income." Wells v. Hous. Auth. of City of Wilmington, 213 N.C. 744 (1938) (holding that the Housing Authorities Law serves a constitutional public purpose); Mallard v. E. Carolina Reg'l Hous. Auth., 221 N.C. 334 (1942) (holding that the Housing Authorities Law serves a public purpose in rural as well as urban areas).

89. G.S. 160D-1311(b).

90. G.S. 157-3(12) (defining a housing project) and 157-29 (rents for persons of low income must be set "at the lowest possible rates consistent with . . . providing decent, safe, and sanitary dwelling accommodations" and projects cannot "provide revenues for other activities of the city [or, by extension, developers or other entities])." The North Carolina Supreme Court has found that benefits offered to low-income persons can be extended to moderate-income persons when offered "with the same public purpose in mind," with the goal "to make available decent, safe and sanitary housing" to another group "who cannot otherwise obtain such housing accommodations." *In re* Denial of Approval to Issue $30,000,000.00 of Single Family Hous. Bonds & $30,000,000.00 of Multi-Family Hous. Bonds for Persons of Moderate Income, 307 N.C. 52 (1982). *See also* Mulligan, note 63 above.

91. G.S. 157-9.4.

92. A detailed examination of inclusionary housing programs and associated incentive policies applicable to any local government affordable housing program is provided in C. Tyler Mulligan and James L. Joyce, *Inclusionary Zoning: A Guide to Ordinances and the Law* (Chapel Hill, N.C.: UNC School of Government, 2010).

93. G.S. 160D-1311.

94. *North Carolina Legislation 1975*, ed. Joan G. Brannon (Chapel Hill, N.C.: UNC Institute of Government, 1975), 51–52 (explaining that the predecessor to G.S. 160D-1311 was enacted in 1975 to eliminate questions about whether North Carolina communities were authorized "to participate fully" in the CDBG program authorized by the Housing and Community Development Act of 1974).

Municipalities are permitted to use property tax revenues for such purposes;[95] counties, however, are limited in that local and state funds may be used only for enumerated housing and housing rehabilitation activities, unless pursuant to referendum.[96] The mention of "grants" in the statute does not suggest that the statute can override constitutional prohibitions against aid to private enterprise; indeed, the conveyance powers included with the statute require any conveyance of property to be made in exchange for no less than "appraised value."[97] Payments may be made to a private enterprise only as part of a contract for public services of equivalent value.

Downtown Revitalization and Business Improvement Districts (BIDs)

When the focus of CED efforts is a central business district (or other qualifying urban area in a municipality), municipalities (but not counties) may support development through a municipal service district—also known as a business improvement district or BID—in which additional property taxes are levied on property in the district for the purpose of engaging in "downtown revitalization projects" or "urban area revitalization" in certain areas outside of downtowns.[98] In addition to the service-district levy, a municipality may allocate other revenues to the service district.[99] Once the area is properly designated as a municipal service district for downtown or urban area revitalization, permissible revitalization activities in the area include making infrastructure improvements, marketing the area, sponsoring festivals, and providing supplemental cleaning and security services, among others. In particular, the proceeds from the additional tax levy may be expended for "promotion and developmental activities," such as "promoting business investment" in the district.[100] Several local governments have used this authority as the basis for creating building-façade improvement programs to induce private owners to enhance the safety and appearance of public spaces within the district.[101]

The broad statutory language quoted above does not mean that government funds or property can be gifted to private enterprise. The statute's current language was enacted prior to the *Maready* case previously described—at a time when incentives were not permissible in any form—and therefore the original language did not contemplate incentives to private entities.[102] Even if the language is interpreted broadly today, it is nevertheless subject to the constitutional limitations imposed by *Maready*.

Contributing Real Property in a Public-Private Partnership

Local governments occasionally participate in development by contributing real property to a public-private partnership. Authority for local governments to contribute property to private development projects—particularly at a subsidized price—is quite limited under North Carolina law.

---

95. G.S. 160D-1311; 160A-209(c)(9a), (15a), (31a).

96. G.S. 160D-1311; 153A-149(c)(15a), (15b); 160D-1316.

97. G.S. 160D-1312(4).

98. G.S. 160A-536.

99. G.S. 160A-542.

100. A local government is permitted to allocate other funds to the district in addition to the funds collected through the municipal service-district levy. G.S. 160A-542.

101. Mulligan, note 52 above.

102. 1973 N.C. Sess. Laws ch. 655; 1977 N.C. Sess. Laws ch. 775.

As a general rule, local governments are always required, unless an exception applies, to convey real property by following competitive bidding procedures: sealed bid, upset bid, or public auction.[103] The price reached through competitive bidding is presumed by the courts to be the fair market value of the property.[104] However, a drawback of competitive sale procedures is that they do not permit the local government to impose restrictions on the use of the property or to select the buyer for reasons other than bid amount.[105] As a result, competitive bidding procedures may not work well for CED purposes where the normal market is presumed to function poorly or inefficiently. It is often necessary for a local government to impose conditions and requirements on a buyer of real property for a CED project, and to select the buyer that is capable of meeting the requirements, in order to ensure that the property is developed in accordance with local priorities.

The statutes contemplate this necessity and offer limited exceptions to the competitive sale rule. Local governments are, in certain situations for CED purposes, authorized to place conditions on the sale of government property, either by selecting a specific buyer through "private sale" or by imposing restrictions on how the property is to be used. It should be noted that the authority to convey property by private sale does not mean that the property can be given away for less than its fair value.

The North Carolina Supreme Court expounded on the exclusive emoluments clause in the context of property conveyance in *Brumley v. Baxter*,[106] with two important conclusions. First, if a jurisdiction's conveyance of property occurs without full monetary consideration (meaning, payment is less than fair market value), then there must be consideration in the form of an enforceable promise to provide public services for the jurisdiction. Second, if the consideration is in the form of public services, the conveyance must be conditioned on the property's continued use for that purpose by the recipient, and the property must revert back to the local government in the event the recipient ceases to use it for that purpose. This rule applies even if statutes fail to impose an explicit requirement regarding sale price, such as "appraised value."

How or why a property was first acquired may constrain how it can later be conveyed to a private entity. Specified acquisition procedures must be followed for a local government to be able to take advantage of some of the more flexible conveyance statutes when the property is eventually sold.[107] A comprehensive examination of property acquisition and conveyance laws is beyond the scope of this chapter,[108] but the following discussion focuses on the key statutes which authorize a local government to deviate from competitive bidding procedures for CED purposes.

---

103. G.S. 160A-268, -269, -270. *See also* Chapter 11, "Procurement, Contracting, and Disposal of Property."

104. Redevelopment Comm'n of Greensboro v. Sec. Nat'l Bank of Greensboro, 252 N.C. 595, 612 (1960).

105. Puett v. Gaston Cnty., 19 N.C. App. 231, 235 (1973).

106. 251 N.C. 691 (1945). *See also* Bluestein, *Donating Property*, note 36 above.

107. C. Tyler Mulligan, "Follow Procedures Prior to Acquiring Property for Redevelopment," *Community and Economic Development in North Carolina and Beyond* blog (March 15, 2016).

108. Procedures for conveyance of real property by local governments are discussed in detail in David Lawrence, *Local Government Property Transactions in North Carolina*, 2nd ed. (Chapel Hill, N.C.: UNC School of Government, 2000).

Conveyance of Real Property for Economic Development

Pursuant to the Local Development Act of 1925,[109] property acquired by a local government for economic development may later be conveyed "by private negotiation [subject to] such covenants, conditions, and restrictions as the county or city deems to be in the public interest."[110] The consideration "may not be less than" the "fair market value of the interest," and the sale must be preceded by a properly noticed public hearing (G.S. 158-7.1(d)). The conveyance may be subsidized (e.g., a discount from the fair value may be offered) only if certain statutory requirements are met: the buyer must be contractually bound to construct improvements that will generate new tax revenue over ten years that will repay the subsidy, and the buyer must promise to create a substantial number of jobs paying at or above the average wage in the county.[111] A subsidized transaction (or incentive) is also subject to the *Maready* requirements discussed earlier in this chapter, such as creation of substantial jobs and tax base that "might otherwise be lost to other states."[112] These requirements apply equally to conveyances of property to nonprofit economic development organizations that work with local governments; that is, a nonprofit economic development organization must pay fair market value for any property it acquires from a local government if later it intends to sell that property to private businesses.[113]

A unit that wants to take advantage of the flexible conveyance procedures for economic development available under the Local Development Act typically *must first acquire the property pursuant to the act*. This requires strict adherence to the notice and hearing requirements of G.S. 158-7.1(c).[114] A unit that fails to adhere to these procedures has, by default, probably acquired the property for redevelopment, which is governed by a statute that imposes no acquisition procedures. However, although there are no set procedures to follow when property is acquired for redevelopment, the trade-off is that redevelopment offers less flexibility upon conveyance, as described in the next section.

Conveyance of Real Property for Redevelopment

When local governments acquire property for redevelopment, the applicable statutory authority for the acquisition is G.S. 160D-1312. No special acquisition procedures must be followed.[115] Property so acquired "shall be [disposed of] in accordance with the procedures of Article 12" of G.S. Chapter 160A.[116] In other words, competitive bidding must be employed and no conditions may be placed on the buyer, except in the case of a sale to a nonprofit organization pursuant to G.S. 160A-279 (discussed at the end of this chapter).

---

109. G.S. Chapter 158, Article 1.

110. G.S. 158-7.1(d).

111. G.S. 158-7.1(d2).

112. *Maready v. City of Winston-Salem*, cited in full at note 38 above, at 727.

113. C. Tyler Mulligan, "Conveyance of Local Government Property to Nonprofit EDC for Industrial Park," *Coates' Canons: NC Local Government Law* blog (March 17, 2015).

114. For an explanation of the acquisition procedures to follow in order to obtain greater flexibility later upon conveyance, see Mulligan, note 113 above.

115. Mulligan, note 113 above.

116. G.S. 160D-1312(3).

An exception to this general rule is provided for property "in a community development project area."[117] Such property may be conveyed "to any redeveloper at private sale" for the appraised value "in accordance with the community development plan."[118] The reference to a community development plan, as previously noted in the discussion of community development, signifies that the activity should be undertaken primarily for the benefit of low- and moderate-income persons and otherwise meet CDBG requirements.[119] Examples of a "community development project area" include a Neighborhood Revitalization Strategy Area, which is an area designated by an entitlement community for targeted CDBG programs,[120] and Community Revitalization Strategies created through the CDBG Small Cities Program.[121] In such cases, the sale may be "subject to such covenants, conditions, and restrictions as may be deemed to be in the public interest." These community development sales must be preceded by a properly noticed public hearing.

Conveyance of Real Property Pursuant to the Urban Redevelopment Law

Under G.S. 160A-514, a redevelopment commission, or a local unit's governing board exercising the powers of a redevelopment commission, may convey property owned by the commission in a designated redevelopment area. Conveyance is permitted only for purposes that accord with the unit's redevelopment plan, and the governing board must approve any sale. Competitive bidding procedures must be employed, but unlike other conveyance statutes, this one authorizes the sale to be subject to covenants and conditions to ensure that any redevelopment complies with the redevelopment plan. Typically, a competitive bidding process may not be encumbered by such restrictions on the buyer.[122] The Urban Redevelopment Law, however, uniquely combines competitive bidding procedures with the ability to place restrictions on the buyer. Only a housing authority, which is entirely exempt from typical conveyance procedures as described below, can dispose of property in a similar manner.

---

117. G.S. 160D-1312(4). For a brief discussion of the history and evolution of G.S. 160D-1312 (formerly G.S. 160A-457), see C. Tyler Mulligan, "Conveyance of Property in a Public-Private Partnership for a 'Downtown Development Project,'" *Community and Economic Development in North Carolina and Beyond* blog (June 22, 2017).

118. G.S. 160D-1312(4).

119. A CDBG grantee shall expend not less than 70 percent of its CDBG funds in the aggregate for activities that benefit low- and moderate-income (LMI) persons. This has also been referred to as the 70 percent (70%) test, LMI benefit test, or overall benefit requirement. 24 C.F.R. § 570.200(a)(3). Expenditures that count toward the benefit test include amenities that meet the "area benefit activity" test. An area benefit activity is an activity which is available to benefit all the residents of an area which is primarily residential, where at least 51 percent of the residents are LMI persons. 24 C.F.R. § 570.208. Examples of "area benefit activities" include acquisition of land to be used as a neighborhood park, construction of a health clinic, improvements to public infrastructure like the installation of gutters and sidewalks, and development of a community center.

120. For an explanation of Neighborhood Revitalization Strategy Areas, see U.S. Department of Housing and Urban Development, HUD Exchange, Notice CPD-96-01 (Jan. 16, 1996).

121. Community Revitalization Strategy areas through the Small Cities Program are described in U.S. Department of Housing and Urban Development, HUD Exchange, Notice CPD-97-1 (Feb. 4, 1997).

122. Puett v. Gaston Cnty., cited in full at note 105 above, at 235.

Conveyance of Real Property for Housing for Persons of Low and Moderate Income

A housing authority, or a unit's governing board exercising the powers of a housing authority, may convey property for purposes of constructing or preserving affordable housing for persons of low and moderate income.[123] It is important to point out that statutory disposition require-ments that apply to other public bodies are not applicable to conveyances under the Housing Authorities Law.[124] This means that a local government may impose restrictions and covenants on a conveyance of property to ensure that a buyer will use the property for affordable housing. The lack of procedural requirements in the statute does not override the state constitution's prohibition against making gifts to private entities.

In the context of affordable housing, this means that any conveyance of property to a private provider of affordable housing for less than fair market value must be subject to covenants and conditions to ensure that the property is used for housing for eligible households in perpetuity (or sold to eligible households). Although such transactions are exempt from typical conveyance procedures, as a matter of practice, many local governments exercising the powers of a housing authority voluntarily follow the statutory procedures for conveyance by private sale.[125]

Local governments may convey property outside of the Housing Authorities Law using a narrower grant of authority found in G.S. 160D-1316. The statute authorizes a local government to convey property by private sale directly to low- and moderate-income (LMI) persons or to a private entity to be "developed" into LMI housing. The entire development must be reserved for LMI persons. The statute does not authorize subsidies for developers; such authority is still found only in the Housing Authorities Law.

Although G.S. 160D-1316 does not authorize a local government to sell property at a price below fair market value, this statute can still be very helpful to a private developer of affordable housing. The statute requires the local government to impose "covenants or conditions" on the conveyance to ensure that the property will be developed for sale or lease only to LMI persons. A requirement to use the property only for LMI persons in perpetuity could reduce the revenue potential of the property, which would inherently lower the fair market value of the property under the income approach of property appraisal. The resultant (lower) fair market value, pur-suant to an appraisal that accounts for the covenants and conditions, may be used as the fair market price for conveyance to any buyer, whether for-profit or nonprofit.

There is separate statutory authority for leasing local government property for affordable housing. G.S. 160A-278 authorizes municipalities (and counties through the operation of G.S. 153A-176) to lease property by private negotiation to any entity that will use the property to construct affordable housing for LMI persons. This statutory authority may be employed without requiring the county or municipality to exercise the powers of a housing authority. The statute requires 20 percent of the housing units to be set aside for the "exclusive use" of persons of low income when the property contains housing for "persons of other than low or moderate income."

---

123. G.S. 157-9.

124. "No provisions with respect to the acquisition, operation or disposition of property by other public bodies shall be applicable to an authority unless the legislature shall specifically so state." G.S. 157-9(a).

125. Private sale procedures are found in G.S. 160A-267.

Conveyance of Real Property in Public-Private Partnership Construction Contracts

Local governments are authorized by statute to contribute property when entering into public-private partnerships for construction of downtown development projects (G.S. 160D-1315)[126] and as part of public-private partnership construction contracts (G.S. 143-128.1C).[127] The projects authorized under these statutes include joint developments with private developers in which public capital facilities are constructed as part of a larger *private* development project. Real property may be contributed by a local government to the larger development project. The statutes do not authorize the local government to subsidize the conveyance of property (and, as previously noted, the state constitution prohibits making gifts to private developers), so it is presumed that any property contributed by the local government will be valued at fair market value and that development costs paid by the local government for public facilities will be reasonable. The local government and the developer may enter into agreements governing the development project, thereby offering the local government some control over the development process and its outcomes.

Other Purposes for Conveyance of Real Property

Local governments also may convey property for other purposes, such as conveyances to historic preservation organizations or to entities carrying out a public purpose. In the case of conveyances to historic preservation organizations, the statute does not authorize any subsidy as part of such conveyance—the benefit conferred by statute is the authority to deviate from competitive bidding procedures in order to select the buyer and convey by private sale.[128] In the case of conveyances to entities carrying out a public purpose, a local government may accept non-monetary consideration (meaning the conveyance may be subsidized by accepting less than fair market value), but the "city or county shall attach to any such conveyance covenants or conditions which assure that the property will be put to a public use *by the recipient entity*."[129] Thus, the conveyance must be conditioned on the continued use for that purpose by the recipient, and the property must revert back to the local government in the event the recipient ceases to use it for that purpose.[130]

---

126. *See also* Mulligan, note 117 above.

127. *See also* Norma Houston, "New Construction Delivery Methods—Public-Private Partnerships (P3)," *Coates' Canons: NC Local Government Law* blog (March 5, 2014).

128. G.S. 160A-266(b). *See also* Tyler Mulligan, "Sale of Historic Structures by NC Local Governments for Redevelopment," *Coates' Canons: NC Local Government Law* blog (Dec. 16, 2014).

129. G.S. 160A-279 (emphasis added).

130. Brumley v. Baxter, cited in full at note 106 above.

Conclusion

Although broad statutory authority is available for public participation in private CED projects, local governments should carefully structure partnerships with private entities to comply with constitutional and statutory requirements. Furthermore, local governments should carefully evaluate whether fair market value transactions accomplish the public goals prior to considering subsidies of any kind. How to structure these transactions in order to maximize public benefit goes well beyond the scope of this chapter, but local governments should consider developing internal capacity or seek expert assistance to understand the financial and legal aspects of public-private partnerships.[131]

---

131. The UNC School of Government provides specialized finance and development expertise to local government officials regarding CED projects. More information is available on the web page for the School's *Community and Economic Development in North Carolina and Beyond* blog at https://ced.sog .unc.edu/.

Contributors

Connor H. Crews is an assistant professor of public law and government specializing in local government finance law.

Whitney B. Afonso is a School of Government faculty member who focuses on state and local public finance with an emphasis on local sales taxes.

Gregory S. Allison is a School of Government faculty member who specializes in governmental accounting and financial reporting for state and local governmental entities.

Rebecca Badgett is an assistant professor of public law and government specializing in internal control and grants management for local government.

Crista Cuccaro is an assistant professor of public law and government specializing in procurement, contracting, property disposal, and ethics and conflicts of interest related to contracting.

Christopher B. McLaughlin is a School of Government faculty member who specializes in the legal aspects of local taxation.

Kara A. Millonzi is a School of Government faculty member who specializes in local government law and local government finance.

C. Tyler Mulligan is a School of Government faculty member who specializes in development finance, community economic development, and public-private partnerships for revitalization. He launched the School's Development Finance Initiative and now serves as its faculty lead.

William C. Rivenbark is a School of Government faculty member who specializes in budget preparation and enactment.

Kristina Wilson is an assistant professor of public law and government specializing in transparency, board procedures, and general local government law.